COMPUTING SYSTEMS
RELIABILITY

COMPUTING SYSTEMS RELIABILITY

Edited by

T. ANDERSON and B. RANDELL

University of Newcastle upon Tyne

CAMBRIDGE UNIVERSITY PRESS

Cambridge

London : New York : Melbourne

Published by the Syndics of the Cambridge University Press
The Pitt Building, Trumpington Street, Cambridge CB2 1RP
Bentley House, 200 Euston Road, London NW1 2DB
32 East 57th Street, New York, NY 10022, USA
296 Beaconsfield Parade, Middle Park, Melbourne 3206, Australia

First published 1979

Printed in the United States of America
by Hamilton Printing Company, Rensselaer, New York
Bound by Payne Edition Bindery Inc., Chester, New York

ISBN 0 521 22767 4

Library of Congress Cataloging in Publication Data

Main entry under title:

Computing systems reliability.

    Bibliography: p.
    Includes index.
    1. Electronic digital computers--Reliability.
2. Computer programs--Reliability. I. Anderson, T.
II. Randell, Brian, 1936-
QA76.5.C618   001.6'4   78-75253
ISBN 0-521-22767-4

C O N T E N T S

TO: The Northern Sinfonia Appeal Fund

CONTRIBUTORS

Dr T. Anderson
Computing Laboratory
University of Newcastle upon Tyne
Claremont Road
Newcastle upon Tyne, NE1 7RU (U.K.)

Dr W. Carter
International Business Machines Corporation
Thomas J. Watson Research Center
P.O. Box 218
Yorktown Heights
New York, 10598
U.S.A.

Dr C.T. Davies
International Business Machines Corporation
555 Bailey Avenue
P.O. Box 50020
San Jose
California, 95150
U.S.A.

Professor S.L. Gerhart
USC Information Sciences Institute
4676 Admiralty Way
Marina del Rey
California, 90291
U.S.A.

Dr J.J. Horning
Xerox Corporation
Palo Alto Research Center
3333 Coyote Hill Road
Palo Alto
California, 94304
U.S.A.

Dr P.A. Lee
Computing Laboratory
University of Newcastle upon Tyne
Claremont Road
Newcastle upon Tyne, NE1 7RU (U.K.)

Mr P.M. Melliar-Smith
Stanford Research Institute
Menlo Park
California, 94025
U.S.A.

Dr R.M. Needham
Computer Laboratory
University of Cambridge
Corn Exchange Street
Cambridge, CB2 3QG (U.K.)

Professor B. Randell
Computing Laboratory
University of Newcastle upon Tyne
Claremont Road
Newcastle upon Tyne, NE1 7RU (U.K.)

Professor M.L. Shooman
Polytechnic Institute of New York
Long Island Center
Route 110
Farmingdale
New York, 11735
U.S.A.

Dr S. Shrivastava
Computing Laboratory
University of Newcastle upon Tyne
Claremont Road
Newcastle upon Tyne, NE1 7RU (U.K.)

PREFACE

There has been great growth in the complexity of the functions that computing systems are designed to provide, and in the reliance that it is wished to place on such systems, for example in environments where unreliability can lead to huge financial penalties or even loss of life. This has spurred the search for greater understanding of the pertinent reliability issues. Aspects of computing systems (such as their software) which were largely ignored in earlier discussions of reliability problems are now being addressed; in consequence, previous approaches and solutions need to be re-evaluated.

This book aims to provide a coherent account of all major aspects of computing system reliability, and also to give an up-to-date account of recent research activity. It demonstrates that although much work still remains to be done, a great deal has already been learnt about both the theory and the practice of the design of highly reliable computing systems.

Each chapter of the book was first prepared as documentation for lectures presented by the various authors at an Advanced Course on Computing Systems Reliability held at the University of Newcastle upon Tyne from 31 July to 11 August 1978. This course was sponsored by the U.K. Science Research Council under the auspices of the Information Training Group of the E.E.C. Scientific and Technical Research Committee and was directed by Professor B. Randell. The original course material has been extensively revised for publication in its present form.

1
SYSTEM RELIABILITY
AND
STRUCTURING

B. Randell

University of Newcastle upon Tyne

SYSTEM RELIABILITY

Introduction

The reliability of a computing system is of obvious importance
to all who expect to benefit from, or who are in any way dependent
on, the trustworthiness and the continuity of the service that the
system is supposed to provide. Thus, as the uses made of computers
have grown, both in number and significance, so more and more
attention has been paid to system reliability issues, and much
relevant research and development activity has been undertaken.
However, there has been some confusion as to exactly what is meant
by the "reliability" of a computing system. The concept of system
reliability is sometimes interpreted rather broadly as a measure of
the extent to which a system matches the expectations of its users
(as discussed by Naur (1977) for example). The trouble with this
view is that these expectations can be mistaken and can change
almost arbitrarily, based perhaps on experience with the system.
In this chapter a somewhat narrower interpretation of system
reliability is taken, more in line with typical formal, and often
quantitative, assessments of hardware reliability. In fact the
definition given below relates system reliability to the success
with which a system provides its specified service. By this means
the concept of the "reliability" of a system is separated from that
of the "reliance" that the users have, perhaps unjustifiably,
placed on a system.

It is, of course, to be hoped that the reliance placed on a
system will be commensurate with its reliability. When this is not
the case one or other will have to be adjusted if the system is not
to be abandoned. For example, users of a time sharing service that
has a tendency to lose the contents of current work spaces are
likely to learn to take the precaution of frequently requesting
that a copy of their work space be saved, and thereafter be
satisfied with the quality of the service that they are receiving.
Notions of reliance therefore can be as much bound up with

psychological attitudes as with formal decisions as to the requirement that a system is supposed to satisfy.

In fact the history of the development of computers has seen some fascinating interplay between reliance and reliability. The reliability of early computers was such that relatively little reliance was placed on the validity of their outputs, at least until appropriate checks had been performed, and even less reliance was placed on the continuity of their operation - lengthy and frequent periods of downtime were expected and tolerated. As reliability increased so did reliance, sometimes in fact outdistancing reliability so that additional efforts had to be made to reach previously unattained reliability levels. During this time computing systems were growing in size and functional capacity so that, although component reliability was being improved, the very complexity of systems was becoming a possible cause of unreliability, as well as of misunderstandings between users and designers about the specification of the service the system was supposed to provide.

The subject of system specifications and of how these can be arrived at and documented, validated and updated, is a large and complex topic, knowledge of which is needed by anyone seeking to understand reliability issues in systems of any significant complexity. The chapter by Melliar-Smith is therefore devoted to the subject.

The informal but, it is hoped, rigorous definitions presented below of concepts relating to system reliability presume the existence of some external specification of the requirements that the system is supposed to meet. Ideally this specification will have previously been agreed and documented; in practice, some aspects of it may exist only in the minds of persons authorised to decide upon the acceptability of the behaviour of the system. The terminology adopted here is defined in general terms, and is intended to relate to both hardware and software since in a complex computing system the reliability of both will be of great relevance to the overall reliability of the system.

Systems and their Failures

A system is defined to be a set of components together with their interrelationships, where the system has been designed to provide a specified service. The components of the system can themselves be systems and their interrelationship is termed the algorithm of the system. There is no requirement that a component provide service to a single system; it may be a component of several distinct systems. However, the algorithm of the system is specific to each individual system.

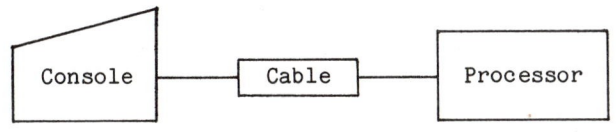

Fig. 1 A Three Component System

Example

Figure 1 is a simple schematic representation of a system
consisting of a processor, a console and an interconnecting
cable - these three components are interrelated by being
plugged together. The interconnecting lines in the diagram
represent these interrelationships, rather than any physical
component.

The <u>reliability</u> of a system is taken to be a measure of the success
with which the system conforms to some authoritative specification
of its behaviour. Without such a specification nothing can be said
about the reliability of the system. When the behaviour of a
system deviates from the specification, this is called a <u>failure</u>.
Measures of the reliability of a system, such as Mean Time Between
Failures (MTBF) and Mean Time To Repair (MTTR), can be based on the
actual or predicted incidence of failures and their consequences.
Extensive work has been done on reliability measurement,
particularly for hardware systems, and on the formulation and
analysis of stochastic models of the reliability of various types
of system and fault - these matters are discussed in the chapter by
Shooman.

Quantitative system reliability measures all concern the
success with which a system provides its specified service. The
much broader notion of reliability, which is here termed "reliance"
relates to the situation where there is a lack of understanding
and/or agreement as to the specification of a system, or where
attempts are being made to differentiate between the relative
acceptability of different kinds of system behaviour which
nevertheless falls within the strict specifications.

Errors and Faults

In contrast to the simple, albeit very broad, definition of
"failure" given above, the definitions presented below for "error"
and "fault" are not so straightforward. This is because they aim

to capture the element of subjective judgement which we believe is a necessary aspect of these concepts, particularly when an error relates to problems which could have been caused by design inadequacies in the design of a system.

The definition of "error" involves the notion of the <u>internal state</u> of a system, which is defined as the aggregation of the external states of the components of the system. The <u>external state</u> of a system is an abstraction of its internal state. During a transition from one external state to another external state, the system may pass through a number of internal states for which the abstraction, and hence the external state, are not defined. The specification prescribes only the external states of the system, the operations that can be applied to the system, the results of these operations, and the transitions between external states caused by these operations. The internal states will be inaccessible from outside the system.

An internal state of a system is said to be an <u>erroneous state</u> when that state is such that there exist circumstances in which further processing, by the normal algorithms of the system, will lead to a failure which is not attributed to a subsequent fault. The subjective judgement that is associated with the classification of a state as being an erroneous one derives from the use of the phrases "normal algorithms" and "which is not attributed" in this definition - the first of these implies the possible existence of "abnormal algorithms", which will typically be the error recovery algorithms.

The term error is used to designate that part of the state which is "incorrect". An error is thus an item of information, and the terms <u>error</u>, <u>error detection</u> and <u>error recovery</u> are used as casual equivalents for erroneous state, erroneous state detection and erroneous state recovery.

A <u>fault</u> is the adjudged cause of an error, while a <u>potential fault</u> is a construction within a system such that (under some circumstances within the specification of the use of the system) that construction will cause the system to reach an erroneous state. Such a fault may be classified as a mechanical fault or as an algorithmic fault, that is, a mistake in the algorithm of the system. Mechanical faults are those faults which are ascribed to the behaviour of a component of the system, that is, are failures of system components.

Example

A storage module which fails to store data correctly could be the fault which causes errors in the internal tables used by an operating system, errors which lead to complete system failure, perhaps by causing the system to go into an unending loop.

SYSTEM RELIABILITY AND STRUCTURING

Hopefully it will now be clear that the generality of the definitions of failure and fault has the intended effect that the notion of fault encompasses design inadequacies as well as, say, hardware component failure due to ageing. For example, it covers a mistaken choice of component, a misunderstood or inadequate representation of the specification (of either the component, or the service required from the system) or an incorrect interrelationship amongst components (such as a wrong or missing interconnection in the case of hardware systems, or a program bug in software systems).

As the definition given above implies, identification of a state as erroneous involves judgement as to which fault is the cause of a particular failure. It can, in fact, be very difficult to attribute a given failure to a specific fault. A demonstration that further processing can lead to a failure of a system indicates the presence of an error, but does not suffice to locate a specific item of information as the error. Furthermore, even precise location of an error is by no means guaranteed to identify a fault to which the failure may be attributed. Consider, for example, a system affected by an algorithmic fault. The sequence of internal states adopted by this system will diverge from that of the "correct" system at some point in time, the algorithmic fault being the cause of this transition into an erroneous state. But there need be no unique correct algorithm. It may be that any one of several changes to the algorithm of the system could have precluded the failure. A subjective judgement as to which of the resulting algorithms is the intended algorithm determines the fault, the items of information in error, and the moment at which the state becomes erroneous. Of course, some such judgements may be more useful than others.

Example

Consider a program which is supposed to set Y and X to the initial value of X and the sum-check of the ten element vector A respectively. A faulty version of this might be

Y:=X; _for_ i:=1 _step_ 1 _until_ 10 _do_ X:=X+A[i];

which could be corrected either by inserting "X:=0;" just before the _for_ statement, or "X:=X-Y;" after it. These two alternative corrections imply different judgements as to the exact fault, and as to which states of the computation evoked by the program were erroneous.

The significance of the distinction between faults and errors is most clearly seen when the repair of a system is considered. For example, in a data base system repair of a fault may consist of the replacement of a failing program (or hardware) component by a correctly functioning one. Repair of an error requires that the

information in the data base be changed from its currently
erroneous state to a state which will permit the correct operation
of the system. In most systems, recovery from errors is required,
but repair of the faults which cause these errors, although very
desirable, is not necessarily essential for continued operation.

Reliability Requirements

The reliability requirements of different environments can
differ enormously. One extreme is the case of air and space-borne
computers where only momentary cessation of service can be
tolerated, no maintenance or manual repair activity is feasible,
and incorrect results are completely unacceptable. In most other
situations, though, maintenance and manual repair is usually
possible. In some cases the reliability goals set for a system can
only be met by making it possible for such activity to be carried
out while the system is in service. Thus the repair activity is
concerned with fault situations, rather than with the situation of
the system already having failed.

In contrast, in many environments the expense of obtaining very
high reliability from a computing system is not worthwhile. This
might be because the cost of a failure is comparatively low, or
because the computer system is to be part of a system whose overall
reliability is not expected to be high, because of the low
reliability of other components such as communications lines and
mechanical peripherals. Often certain types of failure are
regarded as comparatively unimportant - for example, in
computerised telephone systems relatively infrequent isolated small
breakdowns can be tolerated, as long as the overall system remains
operational.

Yet another type of reliability requirement is that typical of
on-line data base systems, or indeed any systems which are intended
to retain valuable data. In such systems, safeguarding the data
held is usually much more important than providing continuity of
access to that data.

In fact, reliability is best viewed as a commodity - a
commodity whose provision involves costs, either direct, or arising
from performance degradation. In theory the design of any non-
trivial computing system should involve the designers in careful
calculations of trade-offs between reliability, performance and
cost. In practice, for complex systems the data and relationships
which would be needed for such calculations are quite often
unknown, particularly as far as questions of unreliability caused
by residual design faults are concerned.

SYSTEM RELIABILITY AND STRUCTURING

Types of Fault

An enumerative list of fault categories is hardly likely to be exhaustive. Such a list could include hardware component failure, communication faults, timing problems, mistakes by users and operators, design inadequacies, and the like. Faults due to hardware component failure are often classified by duration, extent and value. Duration refers to whether the fault is permanent or transient (with respect to some defined time grain), extent to whether the effect of the fault is localised or distributed, and value to whether the fault creates fixed or varying erroneous logical values. Extensions of this classification to software faults is possible, but not particularly helpful. What is significant about software faults is, of course, that these must be algorithmic faults stemming from unmastered complexity in the system design. Because hardware systems have, in the past, been much simpler than those constructed using software, algorithmic faults in hardware have been less commonly encountered, but are by no means unknown.

Incorrect interactions with a system can be regarded as a further cause of error, though here it is the encompassing environment which is at fault. Whilst the existence of such faults can often be revealed by appropriate checking, some interactions may be valid with respect to the system specification although later discovered to be incorrect. Such faults can be subtle and serious, and difficult to deal with.

Fault Avoidance and Fault Tolerance

The traditional approach to achieving reliable computing systems has been largely based on fault avoidance (termed fault intolerance by Avizienis). Quoting Avizienis (1976): "The procedures which have led to the attainment of reliable systems using this approach are: acquisition of the most reliable components within the given cost and performance constraints; use of thoroughly refined techniques for the interconnection of components and assembly of sub-systems; packaging of the hardware to screen out expected forms of interference; and carrying out of comprehensive testing to eliminate hardware and software design faults. Once the design has been completed, a quantitative prediction of system reliability is made using known or predicted failure rates for the components and interconnections. In a "purely" fault intolerant (i.e. nonredundant) design, the probability of fault-free hardware operation is equated to the probability of correct program execution. Such a design is characterised by the decision to invest all the reliability resources into high-reliability components and refinement of assembly, packaging and testing techniques. Occasional system failures are accepted as a necessary evil, and manual maintenance is provided for their correction."

There are a number of situations in which the fault avoidance approach clearly does not suffice. These include those situations where faults are likely to slip through into a system which is inaccessible to manual maintenance and repair activities, or where the frequency and duration of the periods of time when the system is under repair are unacceptable. An alternative approach to fault avoidance is that of fault tolerance, an approach at present largely confined to hardware systems, which involves the use of protective redundancy. A system can be designed to be <u>fault tolerant</u> by incorporating into it additional components and abnormal algorithms which attempt to ensure that occurrences of erroneous states do not result in later system failures. The degree of fault tolerance (or "coverage") will depend on the success with which erroneous states are identified and detected, and with which such states are repaired or replaced.

There are many different degrees of fault tolerance which can be attempted. For example, a system designer might wish to reduce the incidence of failures during periods of scheduled operation by designing the system so that it will remain operational even in the presence of, say, a single fault. Alternatively, he might wish to attain very lengthy continuous periods of failure-free operation by designing the system so that it can tolerate not just the presence of a fault, but also the activity involved in repairing the fault.

Fault tolerant systems differ with respect to their behaviour in the presence of a fault. In some cases the aim is to continue to provide the full performance and functional capabilities of the system. In other cases only degraded performance or reduced functional capabilities are provided until the fault is removed - such systems are sometimes described as having a "fail-soft" capability.

<u>Example</u>

It is now typical for the computer terminals used in banks to incorporate significant processing and storage facilities. Such terminals enable data input and possibly some limited forms of data validation to continue even when the main computer system is not operational.

Schemes for fault tolerance also differ with regard to the types of fault which are to be tolerated. The design of fault-tolerant hardware systems is based on careful enumeration of expected faults due to component ageing, electrical interference and the like, and on complete identification of their consequences. Such systems, which are surveyed in the chapter by Carter, have achieved considerable success. However, in general no attempt is made in such systems to cope with algorithmic faults in the hardware design, or in the associated software. Rather it is assumed that such faults have been successfully avoided and are not present in the system. This illustrates that fault tolerance and fault avoidance are better regarded as complementary rather than as competitive approaches to system reliability.

Design Faults

The normal (and praiseworthy) aim of a designer is the a priori elimination of design faults. Because of this many writers have equated the notion of reliability with that of correctness, particularly in the case of software. Virtually all research and development efforts relating to the practice of software design and implementation are therefore of potential relevance to software reliability, and to the overall reliability of computing systems. Two particularly relevant subjects, namely programming language design issues and program validation techniques, are dealt with in the chapters by Horning and Gerhart respectively.

However, important as these topics are, they can give no guarantee that a complex design is ever entirely fault-free or that modifications to the design will not introduce new faults. When this is conceded then the only alternative to accepting the (probably unquantifiable) reliability which results is to seek to improve matters by the use of design fault tolerance.

Most existing approaches to the design of fault tolerant systems are based on three assumptions: firstly, as mentioned earlier, that the algorithms of the system have been correctly designed; secondly, that all of the possible failure modes of the components are known; and thirdly, that all of the possible interactions between the system and its environment have been foreseen. However, in the face of increasing complexity in systems, the validity of these assumptions must be questioned. At some stage it must surely become impractical to rely on enumerating all of the types of fault which might affect a system, let alone design algorithms to detect or accommodate each possible type of fault individually.

Thus the problem which makes the use of design fault tolerance difficult is essentially that of how to tolerate faults which are unanticipated and unanticipatable, as opposed to previously enumerated and categorised. It is therefore argued that design fault tolerance requires a considerable rethinking of the techniques which have in the past proved suitable for tolerating various kinds of hardware fault. These and other issues relating to fault tolerance are dealt with in the chapters by Anderson, Lee and Shrivastava and by Davies.

B. RANDELL

SYSTEM STRUCTURE

Considerations of the reliability problems of complex computing systems, and of means for coping with them, are closely interwoven with various notions that can be collectively termed "system structuring". These concern how a system is, or is viewed as being, constructed.

Static Structure

Any system has what might be termed a _static structure_, which indicates what components it is regarded as being made out of, and how these components are interrelated.

Of course, a given system can be visualised in terms of many different structures, each implying a different identification of the components of the system.

Example

A programmer visualises a CDC 6600 as having a single sequential main processor and a set of independent peripheral processing units, but the maintenance engineer sees it as consisting of a set of parallel function units, and a single time-shared peripheral processor.

Some static structures will have a more discernible reality in the actual system than others, for example, in the case of a hardware system, by corresponding to the interrelated physical components from which the system is constructed. The important characteristic of such "actual" (as opposed to "conceptual") structuring is that the interrelationships between its components are constrained, while the system is operational, ideally to just those that the designer intended to occur. The stronger the constraints, the more the structuring is actual structuring, and the more reasonable it is to base provisions for fault tolerance on that structuring. (The "strength" of a constraint is in fact a measure of the variety of different faults that it will prevent from affecting the planned interrelationship.)

Example

When the various registers and functional units of a central processor are implemented using separate hardware components, the designer can have reasonable confidence that (presuming the absence of electrical or mechanical interference) only those registers and functional units that are meant to communicate with each other do so (along the interconnecting wires that the designer has provided).

SYSTEM RELIABILITY AND STRUCTURING

The software of a computing system serves to structure that system by expressing how some of the storage locations are to be set up with information which represents programs. These locations will then control some of the interrelationships amongst hardware components, for example, to ensure that the potential communication path between two I/O devices via working store is actually usable.

The software itself can be viewed as a system and its structure discussed in terms of the programming language that was used to construct it. Thus in a block-structured language each block can be regarded as a component, which is itself composed out of, and expresses the interrelationships amongst, smaller components such as declarations and statements (including blocks).

The operational software will have "actual" structure matching that of its source language version only to the extent that it consists of components with constrained methods of interacting.

Example

The scope rules in a block-structured language are often enforced by a compiler, which then emits unstructured code. However, the compiler could emit code in which the variables of each different block are kept, say, in different segments, and some form of protection mechanism used to impede access to those variables which are not supposed to be currently accessible.

Much work has in fact been done on protection mechanisms, which can be used to provide a very fine-grained system structure. Providing that the mechanisms are themselves reliable, they can be used to make sure that interactions take place only between designated components, and that these interactions are only of designated types. Such mechanisms therefore have a very important role in the design of reliable systems, and are discussed at length in the chapter by Needham.

Dynamic Structure

Just as a system itself can be regarded as having a static structure, so can its activity be regarded as having a dynamic structure. In fact each static structuring of a system implies a dynamic structuring of its activity. The static structure is important for understanding the sorts of faults that might exist in the system and the provisions that have been made for trying to cope with them. The dynamic structure is of equal importance for understanding the effects of these faults and how (or whether) the system tolerates them in order to continue functioning.

The activity of a given system can be visualised in terms of many different structures, depending on which aspects of this activity the designer wishes to highlight and which to ignore. One now well established concept used for describing some important aspects of the dynamic structure of the activity of a system is the "process" (Horning and Randell 1973). Depending on the viewpoint chosen, quite different processes with their interrelationships might be identified as constituting the structure of the activity of the system. Again, a dynamic structure will be "actual" rather than merely "conceptual" to the extent to which the interrelationships amongst the processes are constrained to be as the designer intended.

<u>Example</u>

Reasonably "actual" dynamic structure exists in the situation where processes correspond to the application of programs to sets of data, if the programs and data are suitably protected and processes are impeded from interacting other than via, say, an explicit message passing system.

The sequencing, or control flow, aspects of process structuring, namely the creation, existence and deletion of processes, can be shown graphically in some form such as figure 2. However, matters of information flow (intended or unintended) between processes are at least as important as control flow when it comes to considerations of reliability, and in particular the determination of the possible damage that a fault has caused. For this reason a concept such as that of <u>atomic action</u> (Lomet 1977) is needed as part of the means for expressing the dynamic structure of the activity of a system.

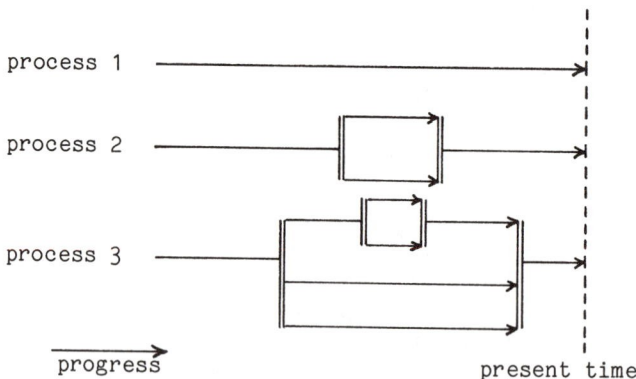

Fig. 2   Control Flow Aspect of Dynamic Structure

Atomic Actions

The activity of the system will be made up of primitive or atomic (that is, apparently instantaneous) operations which are carried out by the components of which the system is considered to consist. Atomic actions provide a means of generalising such atomic operations. In fact they are a means by which a system designer can specify what process interactions are, if possible, to be prevented in order to maintain system integrity, without having to indicate how this is achieved. They do this by enabling the designer to indicate the sections of the activity, that is, the sequences of atomic operations, of a process or a group of processes that are to be executed "atomically".

<u>Example</u>

Consider a message passing system that maintains a pool of buffers for holding messages, and uses the variable "i" as a buffer frame pointer. The action of inserting an item into the buffer might involve the sequence of operations "i:=i+1" and "buffer(i):=item". It is essential that this sequence of operations is executed as a single atomic action if the buffering scheme is to work properly.

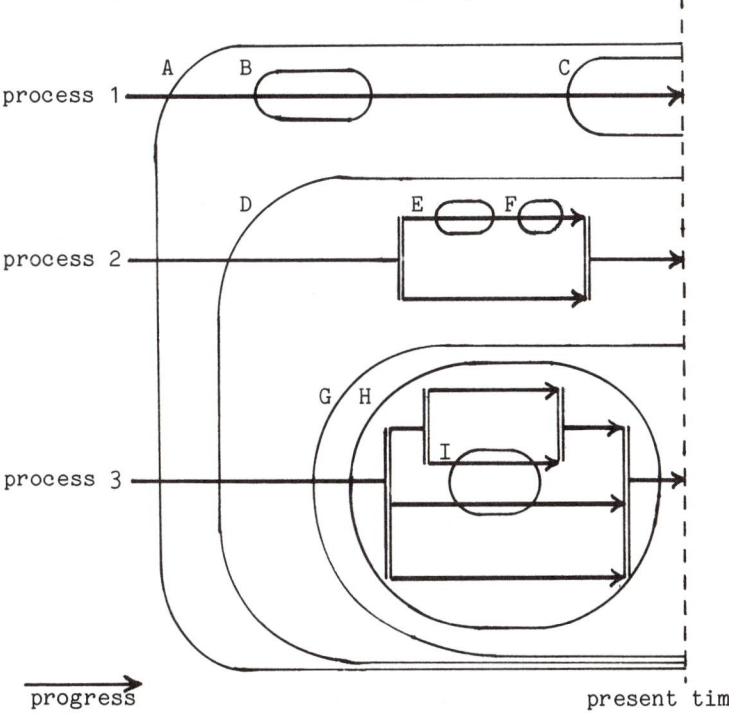

Fig. 3 Processes and their Atomic Actions

B. RANDELL

An atomic action could involve several processes, since

1. A process executing a simple atomic action could temporarily create one or more further processes to assist it.

2. Two or more processes could co-operate directly in a shared atomic action, so that their activity is atomic with respect to the remainder of the processes in the system.

These various possibilities are shown in figure 3, which is based on figure 2, but where the ovals indicate atomic actions, incomplete ovals representing atomic actions that are still in progress. The lines indicate processes, and should themselves be regarded as consisting of miniscule ovals, placed end to end, corresponding to the primitive operations out of which the processes are constructed.

Figure 3 illustrates that "atomicity" has to be regarded as relative rather than absolute, and that atomic actions can themselves involve atomic actions, as well as the basic atomic operations. It also, by implication, illustrates that atomic actions, by their very nature, cannot overlap. Methods of implementing atomic actions lie outside the scope of this chapter. However, it is worth mentioning that such methods include the use of separate processors, the disabling of interrupts on an individual (multiprogrammed) processor, and synchronisation schemes such as monitors and resource locking strategies.

So far, atomic actions have been described as merely a means for a designer to indicate what system integrity constraints should be met. However, they are also of direct relevance to techniques for achieving fault tolerance. This is due to the fact that they provide a means of error detection, and more importantly, a means of limiting and delimiting the possible consequences of a fault.

An atomic action is in fact a generalisation of the concept, introduced by data base designers, of a "transaction" (Eswaran 1976, Gray 1977, Lomet 1977). The transaction scheme allows a data base system user to arrange that a sequence of interactions with the data base will be treated as atomic, in order that desired consistency constraints on the data base can be adhered to. A transaction can thus be viewed as an atomic action involving the user and the data base system (or more exactly the process which is the user's activity, and one of the terminal support processes of the system). For reasons of performance, it is usually necessary to execute many such transactions concurrently, so atomicity is provided by file or record locking strategies (for example, see Eswaran 1976, Gray 1977).

The concept of an atomic action is itself generalised, by being made independent of the notion of a sequential process, and is

defined using occurrence graphs, by Merlin and Randell (1978).
However, the process-based concept and its informal description
introduced above suffice for the present discussion.

Levels of Abstraction

In choosing to regard a system (or its activity) as made up of
certain components and to concentrate on their interrelationships
whilst ignoring their inner details, the designer is deliberately
considering just a particular abstraction of the total system.
Thus the sorts of structuring that have been discussed so far can
be described as structuring within a single level of abstraction,
or horizontal structuring. When further details of a system (or
part of a system) need to be considered, this involves a lower
level of abstraction which shows how a set of interrelated
components are implemented and act, in terms of some more detailed
components and interrelationships (which will of course in turn
just be abstractions of yet more detailed components and
interrelationships, and so on).

The identification of a set of levels of abstraction (each of
which might relate to the whole system, or just some part of the
system) and the definition of their interrelationships again
involves imposing a structure on a system, but this is a rather
different form of structure, which is referred to here as vertical
structuring. Thus vertical structurings describe how components
are constructed, whereas horizontal structurings describe how
components interact.

The importance of levels of abstraction is that they allow the
designer to cope with the combinatorial complexity that would
otherwise be involved in a system constructed from a very large
number of very basic components. The price that is paid is the
requirement for well-documented specifications of the external
characteristics of each level - such specifications can be thought
of as the abstraction interfaces interposed between levels, much as
the specifications of the interrelationships between interacting
components within a level could be termed communication interfaces.
In each case the interface will, if well chosen, allow the designer
to ignore (at least to some extent) the workings of those parts of
the system which lie on the far side of the interface.

Example

The system shown in figure 4 has a vertical structure
comprising four levels, all but the topmost of which is
implemented by an interpreter. Each interpreter is programmed
using the set of apparently atomic facilities (objects,
operations, etc.) that are provided at one abstraction
interface and has the task of providing the more abstract set
of (again apparently atomic) facilities that the next higher

abstraction interface defines. Because of the fact that each of these abstraction interfaces is fully specified and documented, the designer of the implementation of any one level will normally need little or no knowledge of the design, or perhaps even the existence, of any other levels.

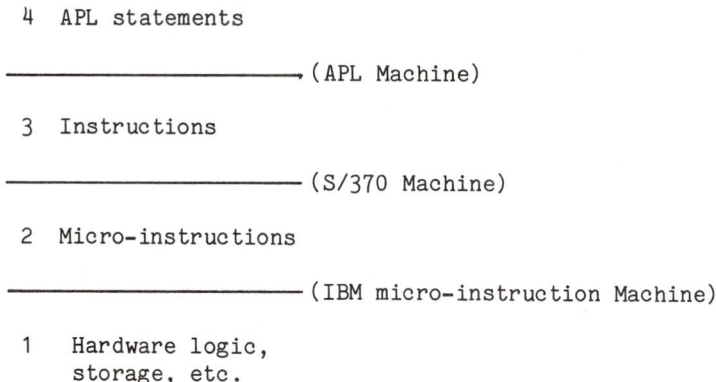

4 APL statements

————————————————→ (APL Machine)

3 Instructions

———————————————— (S/370 Machine)

2 Micro-instructions

———————————————— (IBM micro-instruction Machine)

1 Hardware logic,
storage, etc.

Fig. 4 A Fully Interpretive Multi-Level System

As with horizontal structuring, so can many different vertical structurings be used to visualise a given system. Equally, some vertical structurings will have a more readily discernible reality in the actual system than others. Once again, the important characteristic of such "actual" (as opposed to "conceptual") structuring is that, while the system is operational, the rules of usage of the abstraction interfaces are, to some degree, enforced. The greater the extent of this enforcement, the more the vertical structuring is actual. The role of the enforcement will be to try to prevent faults (or more likely, just certain of the more likely types of fault) from invalidating the abstraction that a level is designed to provide.

Example

In the THE system (Dijkstra 1968) the levels are almost entirely conceptual. They were used as a means of factoring the design effort, and of facilitating the validation of the system design. No attempt was made to incorporate mechanisms in the system which would perform run-time checks on the rules relating to the usage of the facilities provided at various levels. Thus, for example, if a memory parity error was detected there was no way of relating this to a particular level of abstraction, leave alone of directly incorporating appropriate provisions in each level for coping with such faults.

However, the more the vertical structuring is "actual", the more reasonable it is to base provisions for fault tolerance on it.

Example

Consider a multi-level interpreter system similar to that of figure 4, but where the microprogram and the program are each held in a (separate) part of the same store. Naturally, it is assumed that the microprogram has been designed to constrain the program from overwriting the part of the store holding the microprogram. Then the microprogrammed and programmed interpreters might well each have their own distinct means of recovering from a reported store parity error.

Faults and Structuring

Some examples have already been described which indicate how the provision of "actual" structure in a system makes feasible the provision of certain types of fault tolerance. Later chapters will develop these points further. The relationship between faults and structuring is really very basic, as well as subtle. Clearly the whole characterisation of faults as being mechanical faults, algorithmic faults or environmental faults which give rise to invalid interactions with (that is, misuse of) a system is based on system structure. Only after having chosen a particular perspective on a system, and having identified a vertical and horizontal structuring, can it be determined to which of these three types a given fault belongs.

Worse than this, the process of identifying a structuring seems to involve a conscious (or more likely unconscious) assumption about the sorts of fault that could occur, and should be considered. Putting this another way, just as it seems impossible to consider any object as being completely unstructured, so it seems impossible, at any one time at least, to avoid limiting the fault possibilities that can be conceived. Structurings that are useful from the point of view of considering the reliability of a system (that is, structurings which are "actual" structurings) are those which enable designers to think, and to think simply, about those faults which are likely to occur. This is not just a question of considering the relative likelihood of problems with particular pieces of hardware, or from particular types of interface, but in complex systems is also a question of the likelihood of mistakes being made by the designers themselves. Good structuring should reduce the number of such mistakes, but gives no guarantee of their absence.

B. RANDELL

REFERENCES

Avizienis, A. (1976). Fault-Tolerant Systems. IEEE Trans. on
    Computers, C-25,12, pp.1304-1312.

Dijkstra, E.W. (1968). The Structure of the "THE" Multiprogramming
    System. Comm. ACM, 11,5, pp.341-346.

Eswaran, K.P. et al. (1976). The Notions of Consistency and
    Predicate Locks in a Database System. Comm. ACM, 19,11,
    pp.624-633.

Gray, J.N. et al. (1977). Granularity of Locks and Degrees of
    Consistency in a Shared Database. In Modelling in Database
    Management Systems, ed. Nijssen, G.M., North Holland,
    Amsterdam.

Horning, J.J. and Randell, B. (1973). Process Structuring. Computer
    Surveys, 5,1, pp.5-30.

Lomet, D.B. (1977). Process Structuring, Synchronization and
    Recovery Using Atomic Actions. Proc. Conf. on Language Design
    for Reliable Software, Raleigh. Sigplan Notices, 12,3,
    pp.128-137.

Merlin, P. and Randell, B. (1978). State Restoration in Distributed
    Systems. Proc. 8th Int. Symp. on Fault-Tolerant Computing,
    Toulouse, pp.129-134.

Naur, P. (1977). Software Reliability. In State of the Art Report
    on Reliable Software, pp.243-251, Infotech, London.

2
SYSTEM SPECIFICATION

P. M. Melliar-Smith

Computer Science Laboratory
SRI International

AN APPROACH TO DESIGN

The objective of a formal specification method is the description of the external behavior of the program or program component without describing or constraining its internal implementation. The external behavior of the program or program component will include:

- what operations it can be asked to do,

- what information it must be given,

- what results are obtained, including error indications,

- the effects of prior operations on subsequent operations.

These correspond respectively to the calls on a program, the parameters of those calls, the results of the calls, and the "state" retained by the program between calls. One might also wish to include information about the resource requirements of the program, but that is still beyond the ability of existing specification methods.

The specification method should be able to define completely the external behavior of the program, since programs that have unintended or incompletely understood side effects can inflict nasty surprises. But it is very desirable that the specification of a program should not constrain the subsequent implementation of the program, provided that the external behavior is as specified.

The use of formal specification methods is becoming important for critical programming projects because:

- the presence of a precise specification provides a rugged interface between program units in a complex system. The programs that implement a specification can be designed and implemented, and subsequently modified, without consideration of the use that is to be made of them. Similarly, the programs that are to invoke the specified facilities can be designed and implemented without concern for any specific details of the implementation. The specification completely defines the interactions between the programs and hides everything else.

- the rigor of a formal specification ensures a more complete design, and a better statement and understanding of details. Important decisions cannot be overlooked or equivocated about, and the decisions are all documented unambiguously.

- the specification can serve as an interface between designer and implementer, as well as between implementer and user.

- the specification provides a reference for the documentation of the program, for the construction of tests, for the maintenance and development of the program, and for reimplementation of the program.

- (last and least) the use of a formal specification provides the opportunity for program proof and eventually perhaps even automatic programming.

Formal specification methods are still in their infancy. There are few specification languages available, and those are incomplete and inadequate in various ways. But it would be a mistake to regard formal specifications as being purely a research topic, irrelevant for the construction of real systems today. Formal specification methods are being used for real systems, and the procurement agencies are now demanding the use of formal specifications for critical systems and programs. In at least six systems, real systems, formal specifications have been demanded and are being used. If these systems are successful, we may expect to see many more such demands.

An Approach to Design

In this section we describe a possible method of designing systems that makes use of specification methods. Many other design techniques have been described, and it would be inappropriate to imply that those other techniques have no validity. Rather, we do not know what the optimal design method is, and probably we will never know. Further, many of the design techniques are complementary and can be used together, each technique being used where appropriate.

SYSTEM SPECIFICATION

The approach to design presented here is described not because it is the only approach but rather because it provides an appropriate context in which to make use of specifications. Other possible design strategies completely preclude the use of formal specifications, and it is difficult to understand the concept and utility of specifications in the context of a preconceived and incompatible design strategy. Of course we do believe that the approach has considerable merit beyond its use of specifications.

The proposed approach to design involves the following stages:

- the statement of the problem,

- the requirements on the system,

- the specification of the system,

- the design for the implementation,

- the implementation of the system,

- the operational system,

- experience of use.

A practical design process is not, of course, purely sequential but rather involves extensive iteration between stages and depends on the experience of the designers to foresee the consequences of their decisions.

It can be seen that this approach to design has been described in terms of stages that represent the description or state of the system between the various design processes. We do not know how to describe in any rigorous way the activity of design, and we do not presume to dictate how that activity should be performed. Some guidelines are becoming available, based on experience, to guide the activity of design, but the problems are great and even to assess a design as being good or bad is fraught with hazard. Rather, in these lectures, we aim to describe the product of the design activity. If the product of a stage of the design activity cannot be described, one may doubt that it is understood, and certainly there is a risk of distortion if this information cannot be precisely represented.

In current practice only the implementation and possibly the operational system are formally defined objects. It is not surprising therefore that, in the past, attention has been mainly directed towards these stages of the system development. Equally it is clear that the problem and the experience of use will not be formally defined in the near future. However, the remaining stages system requirements, system specifications, and implementation design should be capable of being precisely and formally defined.

It is noteworthy that, as systems become increasingly complex, it has been observed with concern that a decreasing proportion of the required effort is actually devoted to programming and testing the programs, whereas an increasing proportion is devoted to the "overhead" functions of management, design, specification, etc. Joel Aron of IBM has described how, for the OS system, the management and design costs were comparable to those for programming and testing, while, for the abortive FS system, only one sixth of the expenditure could be attributed to programming and testing, the remaining five sixths being absorbed in management and design. It is to be expected that other projects of a similar nature will also show similar characteristics.

Concern that so much of the effort is expended on specification and design is probably premature, for we have no evidence whatever as to the correct balance in a complex development project. More pertinent is a concern that we know so little about these evidently vital functions and that we have so little ability to represent their results.

In the absence of an understanding of what these stages entail and of an ability to test a representation of them for completeness and consistency, not only is the result of this work inadequate, but also it is not possible to decide what analyses and which decisions are required for each stage. Indeed, without the formal understanding of what we mean by a requirement, a specification, or a design, it is not obvious that we should use these terms at all. And yet, although small projects can be completed successfully without these stages, major projects cannot.

Once these stages of the development are concrete objects of the development, on a par with implementations, inadequate preparation of them will become more visible and the costs of their proper preparation an accepted and necessary cost.

Definition of the System Requirements

A requirement definition must express precisely what the user wants from the system, in contrast to a specification which states exactly what the system is to do. In general the user's requirements are very much more general. He needs a certain effect achieved, but may not need to predetermine the precise command or sequence of commands to be used, nor may he be concerned with precisely what formats are used or what the error indications will be. Occasionally a user will require exact compatibility, and then his requirement definition will have to be a specification. Otherwise, the broader the requirement definition can be made, while still requiring the function needed by the user, the more freedom is left to the designers to optimize the system and the better they will be able to make the system. Further, it is enlightening to a user to have to think about what he needs from a system, rather than to start out into the design of the system himself. Unfortunately such abstract thought may be quite difficult for many users.

SYSTEM SPECIFICATION

Periodically major projects are undertaken to develop methodologies for the definition of system requirements. Regardless of any utility such methodologies may have to their users, such projects are invariably devoid of any formal basis or justification and need not concern us here. Unfortunately the necessary mathematical basis for requirements definition is not understood and no acceptable approach to requirements exists. Only in special cases has it been possible to devise formal requirements statements. The current state of this topic and some ideas are described below.

Specification of the Program or System

The purpose of a specification is to provide a precise definition of the intended behavior of a system of programs, a program, or program component. This definition should not constrain the means by which the implementation achieves the desired results, for instance by presuming certain internal information representations or algorithms. But the specification should completely define the externally observable behavior of the program, so that the only effects that can be discovered by a user are precisely defined by the specification (resource requirements possibly excepted). In effect the specification defines a "black box" of known behavior and unknown internal construction.

We need the specification to be complete (in that for any operation we would like to know what its result is), we need it to be consistent (in that we would not like one part of the specification to mandate one result but another result to be required when some other aspect of the specification is considered). We probably also need the specification to define a function that is total throughout its domain (in that we do not want to permit completely arbitrary effects for invalid arguments), and thus we may need to be able to define that domain very precisely if the function we want is to be used only under very particular circumstances.

The specification will need to define a "syntax" for the program or program unit. This syntax must define the operations that are defined for the program, the required arguments of those operations, and the form of the results returned by those operations. In general, we shall be working in a context that requires strict type checking, and thus the syntax will define the types of each of the arguments and results.

The specification must also define the semantics of the operations -- that is, the meaning of the operations and thus the values of the results produced. This topic will be considered below.

The program or program component to be specified may be a pure procedure or function, in which every operation is strictly independent of every other, or the program may retain some "state" between operations, so that the results of an operation can depend on previous operations. Clearly the problem of specifying the pure procedure can (but not necessarily should) be regarded as a degenerate case of the more general problem. Certainly any technique found useful in the simpler case will also be applied to the more complex. For reasons that will become apparent we shall concentrate on the specification of programs whose results may depend on previous operations.

To characterize a program or program component whose operations produce results that depend on previous operations, we use the concept of a type, a concept so well understood by all who are interested in program specification that we should not need to explain it here. Thus most of the recent developments in specification techniques have been techniques for the specification of types. Not only are type specification techniques useful for describing programs that retain state, but they are essential elsewhere in the approach to design being described here.

Firstly, it is not convenient to specify a complex operation directly in any specification language. Such operations must be described in terms of simpler operations on simpler types, just as complex operations are implemented in terms of operations on simpler types. Indeed the languages take advantage of this to overcome the problems of machine arithmetic. The arithmetic types provided by the hardware are not predefined in the specification language. They must be explicitly specified using the specification language, even integer arithmetic, before they can be used to build other more complex types. Some of the languages also provide pure mathematical integers, but great care must be taken not to build them into a specification unless that specification will never be implemented.

Secondly, the implementation design technique described here makes extensive use of the concept of type.

Design of the Implementation

The objective of a design for an implementation is to determine some of the implementation decisions but not others. In principle the most important decisions should be determined first, in the design stage, while other less important decisions should be left to the actual implementation. The problem is that it is not obvious which decisions are the most important and should be determined, or how many should be determined, let alone how these decisions can be expressed so as to avoid unintentional preemption of implementation opportunities. Indeed it is not obvious that there is any single set or level of design decisions that should be separated out from the implementation. We must depend on the experience of the designer himself to decide what is most important and must be determined by him and what is less important and can be left to others.

One well-known design approach is that of top-down programming by successive refinement of abstract programs. The principal characteristic of this approach is that the most abstract decisions must be made first, a characteristic that is both its strength and its weakness. The strength is that such highly abstract programs, unencumbered by obscuring detail, are readily understood, and the design decisions implied within them are apparent and are set in an appropriate context.

SYSTEM SPECIFICATION

The weakness of a top-down approach is that the most abstract decisions, which must be made first, are not necessarily the most important decisions. There are many decisions vital to a successful implementation that involve fine detail and are not readily apparent in top-down abstract programs. Such decisions may be preempted as a consequence of an unimportant decision in the abstract program, or may be left to be determined by chance in the implementation. The top-down approach may also divert attention away from technically difficult aspects of the design, or may even conceal for too long a technically impossible project. There are many examples of top-down programs for "operations", such as growing garden vegetables or cooking a cheese souffle. The fact that the implementation on a computer of such programs is at present quite impossible does not prevent the abstract top-down design from proceeding quite a long way.

An alternative approach to implementation design is based on the specification of intermediate levels of abstraction. In this approach the implementation problem is regarded as being due to the great distance between the target specification and the specification of the supporting machine or language. To reduce this problem, intermediate levels of abstraction are devised between them. If these are chosen appropriately, the difficulty of implementing the target specification on the "machine" represented by the most abstract of the intermediate levels, and of implementing each of the intermediate levels in terms of the level below it, will be less than the difficulty of implementing the target specification directly.

Each one of these intermediate levels of abstraction may be regarded as an "abstract machine" characterized by a set of types and a control-flow mechanism. The types can be specified using the techniques described in these lectures. The specification of the control-flow is equivalent to the problem of axiomatizing (or otherwise specifying) the control flow of a programming language, and need not concern us here except to note that the control-flow axiomatization may use some of the types specified, at the very least the type Boolean.

The design process is now that of deciding on the appropriate intermediate levels of abstraction and of creating the specifications for those levels. The implementation process consists of implementing each of the types at each level in terms of the types defined at the level immediately beneath it. The decision as to how many intermediate levels are appropriate and as to what kind of "abstract machine" is appropriate for an intermediate level, must depend on the experience of the designer. Additional levels of abstraction can be introduced into the design until it is felt that the implementation of each one of these levels, in terms of the specification of the level below it, is trivial. However, this would represent a very detailed design, and it might be appropriate to regard a less detailed design as the reference design, allowing more discretion to the implementers.

One should not confuse the types specified in the implementation design, or the hierarchical ordering of them needed for their implementation, with the types that may need to be defined to facilitate the specification of a complex type. In principle each one of the levels of abstraction is specified completely in isolation, and any simpler types introduced within that specification need have no relationship to any types at any other level of abstraction. In practice, of course, the types will probably have identical or very similar definitions, both to simplify the design task and to facilitate implementation.

Examples

The PSOS Provably Secure Operating System

Level	Abstraction or Function introduced at this level
13	user request interpreter *
12	user environments and user name spaces *
11	user input-output *
10	procedure records *
9	user processes *
8	user objects *
7	directories (*)
6	extended types and extended-type objects (*)
5	segmentation (*)
4	paging
3	system processes and system input-output
2	arithmetic operations *
1	addressable storage and primitive input-output
0	capabilities *, interrupts, registers(*), and clock

Fig. 1. The levels of abstraction within PSOS.
Abstractions designated with an * are visible at the user
interface. Those designated with an (*) are partially visible.

First we consider the Provably Secure Operating System (PSOS) (Neumann,1977)
designed at SRI. Note that the design, outlined in Figure 1, does not distinguish
between hardware and software. The decision as to how to implement any one of the
levels is purely an engineering decision, hidden from the user. As hardware technology
improves one might envisage more of the levels being implemented in hardware or microprogram, particularly for the larger machines of a compatible series.

SYSTEM SPECIFICATION

The SIFT Reliable Computer System

Stages of the Design	Method of Expression
problem: the reliability of an aircraft computer	informal, MTBF
the reliability model	Markov model
requirements for the validity of the model	predicate calculus
specifications for the SIFT executive	Special specifications
implementation of the SIFT executive	Pascal programs

Fig. 2. The stages in the design of the SIFT
reliable aircraft control computer.

As a second example, Figure 2 shows the successive stages of the design of SIFT, a reliable computer, also designed at SRI (Wensley,1978). Here the problem was to design a computer system that can survive several successive hardware faults with a high degree of certainty. The reliability objective was expressed as a Markov model representing the rates of failure of processors, busses, etc.

The design had to ensure that these hardware units were implemented to the low failure rates assumed in the Markov model, and also that the error detection, reconfiguration, and recovery software of the SIFT executive could ensure that the behavior after a fault was as assumed by the Markov model, for instance that known faulty processors are discarded but good processors are not. A set of requirements has been developed, expressed in predicate calculus, and it has been proved that if the implemented system meets these requirements, then the Markov model is a fair or pessimistic model of the real system.

The next stage of the design was to specify the SIFT executive, which was done using the specification language Special. In due course, it is intended to prove that these specifications do satisfy the requirements derived above, though some further iteration and accommodation may be required. A design was prepared for the SIFT executive using three intermediate levels of abstraction, a very small number because the programs were quite simple. These specifications have now been implemented in Pascal, and are running in a simulated environment on a DECsystem-10 rather than in the aircraft computer. Here too it is the intention that the correctness of these programs will be proven, a less difficult task than you might imagine, owing to the very simple nature of the programs and the care taken in their design.

P.M.MELLIAR-SMITH

A MATHEMATICAL BASIS FOR SPECIFICATION

In this lecture, we consider the means by which one can specify the behavior of a program. Following the arguments in the first lecture as to the advantages of being able to specify a type rather than just a pure procedure, this lecture will consider only the specification of types. Much of the early work on formal program semantics originated with Floyd(1967), and Hoare(1969). However the presentation in this lecture is largely derived from the work of Guttag(1975,1977).

The specification of a type must define the syntax of the type and also its semantics. The syntax defines the set of operations of the type, the arguments to those operations with their types, the results of the operations with their types, and the form of the error indications. The semantics defines what the values of the results will be for all legal sequences of operations. The definition of the syntax presents little difficulty and will be deferred to the lectures on actual specification languages.

Specification methods fall into two general classes:

- operational specifications, in which the behavior is defined by the actions of an abstract imperative program,

- axiomatic specifications, in which the behavior is defined by logical relationships between the arguments of the operations and the results.

Specifications defined by an applicative program, such as the lambda calculus or pure Lisp, are essentially equivalent to axiomatic specifications. A useful introductory survey of some of the simpler specification methods is given by Liskov and Zilles(1975). Some more elaborate techniques are described by Marcotty (1976).

An operational specification, written in a formally defined language, is not to be despised. The language may be familiar to a large public, and the specification may be fairly readily understood. If the language definition is consistent, then it is certain that the operational specification is consistent; and if the language definition is complete and consistent, then the problem of completeness of the specification reduces to that of showing termination of the program, possibly a difficult but equally possibly an easy one.

The disadvantage of the operational specification is that it defines not only what the results of the operations are to be but also how to compute them, and it is not easy to distinguish these two aspects of the specification. Thus it is possible that the operational specification may tend to restrict the range of implementation possibilities considered by the implementors. Even assuming that the implementors are willing to consider a wider range of implementation algorithms, including algorithms not resembling the operational specification, the problem of demonstrating the equivalence of two imperative programs is one of unbounded difficulty, and such a demonstration, at least informally, is of course essential when distinctly different algorithms are employed.

SYSTEM SPECIFICATION

Thus the disadvantage of the operational specification is not that it cannot do the job, but rather that it says too much. The axiomatic specifications are preferred because they include much less extraneous detail in the definition. In their purest forms, the axiomatic specifications are probably sufficiently austere that their use by a wide public is precluded. However, forms of axiomatic specification are becoming available that retain mathematical rigor and avoid implementation biasing details, and yet are expressed in a format that is more acceptable to those who ultimately must use them. The existing languages are far from satisfactory, but their development continues.

The Concept of Type

At this stage, it is necessary to reconsider the concept of type. This concept has been of great value in improving our understanding of the programming activity and in simplifying the expression of complex programs. However, the origins of the concept in programming have encouraged a very representational view of the concept of type. It is easy to regard a type as a convenient packaging of a data structure with a restricted set of operations for access to that data structure. Even the term "data type" reflects this point of view, emphasizing the data structure aspect of the concept rather than the operations. This view of type may be useful to a programmer, though other more abstract views of type may also be appropriate for programming. But during the specification phase this mechanistic point of view is a distinct handicap. The data structures should be decided only during implementation design or even implementation itself, and yet the concept of type is very useful early in the specification of the system.

Consider for instance the type complex number. It is easy to think of the complex numbers in a way that assumes that a complex number is a pair of real numbers, the real part and the imaginary part. I would like to discourage that way of thinking, and to ask you to think of the type complex number as defining a set of values, and an associated set of operations, such that the values returned by the operations are those determined by a set of defining axioms. This set of values is quite disjoint from the set of values for any other type, and each value is atomic and without internal structure. Of course it may be possible to derive the real and imaginary parts of any value of type complex number, but only through the operations so defined by the axioms. Also it is possible to construct a model of the type complex number as a pair of real numbers, but that model is only a model, an implementation, and only one possible model out of many.

Similarly consider the type stack. Here one might think of a stack as a sequence of stacked elements, with operations push and pop that extend and access the sequence on a last-in first-out basis. Still more mechanistically one might even think of a stack in terms of an array and a pointer to the top of the stack. The more abstract view regards the stack as a set of values, and operations, such that certain axioms are satisfied. The values of the type stack are atomic and have no internal structure. There is no sequence of stacked elements, and the last-in first-out property is not determined by any ordering of, or even any recording of, the elements that have been stacked. Rather it is the axioms that require and ensure this last-in first-out property. How the values of the type stack achieve that effect is a question that we do not need to ask. Again here we can build models, for instance using sequences, arrays, lists, or any other structure we have chosen, but these models should be thought of as just that, as models or as examples of possible implementations and not as the meaning of the type stack.

The Representation of Values

It is difficult for those with a background in the implementation of programs to think about values without having available a concrete representation for those values. The notion of explicit state is deeply embedded in the background of the Von Neumann machine. Yet if we are to retain a purely abstract view of a type, we should not ascribe any concrete representation to those values. It would be possible to do so, for any arbitrary set of distinct symbols would suffice, but little use would be served, and much harm might be caused if the arbitrary symbols were to be thought to be significant.

Rather than trying to establish a specific set of symbols to represent the values of a type, it is preferable to denote a value by the expression that is the composition of operations that constructed that value. Consider the example of the type Stack, with operations:

> NEWSTACK: ( ) -> Stack
> PUSH: (Item X Stack) -> Stack
> POP: (Stack) -> Stack
> TOP: (Stack) -> Item

Here we might have a value which could be represented by the expression:

PUSH(a,PUSH(b,PUSH(c,PUSH(d,NEWSTACK( )))))

Another value might be represented by:

PUSH(a,PUSH(b,POP(PUSH(e,PUSH(c,PUSH(d,NEWSTACK( )))))))

In due course we will show how the axioms for the type Stack can be used to demonstrate that these two values are members of the same equivalence class. Similarly the value of the Item extracted from a Stack by the TOP operation might be expressed as:

TOP(POP(PUSH(a,PUSH(b,PUSH(c,NEWSTACK( ))))))

Here again the axioms can be used to demonstrate that this value of Item is in the same equivalence class as the value b.

In these examples, while denying the utility of a concrete representation for the type Stack, we have used a, b, c, etc. as values of the type Item. This is only a convenient shorthand, an example of the use of abstraction to enable us to think about the type Stack without the example's being confused by the representations of values of type Item. Formally of course the values of type Item can be represented no more easily than the values of type Stack. They too would be represented as compositions of values of the operations that were used to construct them.

Further, the values of stacks represented above are of no use to us, except as the arguments to further operations eventually yielding values of types simpler than Stack. We cannot be expected to directly comprehend a representation such as those of type Stack, and there is never any need for us to do so. However, the values of the type Item are no more to be directly comprehended than are values of type Stack, even though we chose to represent them with single letter symbols. The values of type Item, as indeed the values of type Integer, can be used only as arguments to further operations, eventually here too yielding values of yet simpler types.

Types as Abstract Algebras

An appropriate way of thinking formally about types is provided by the mathematical concept of an abstract algebra. This concept of an abstract algebra is far more general than the classical algebra with which we are all familiar. Classical algebra is only one of many possible abstract algebras. An abstract algebra is simply a nonempty set, called the carrier or phylum of the algebra, together with a finite indexed set of finitary operations defined on that carrier. A finitary operation is a mapping from the Cartesian product of a finite number of elements of the carrier to an element of the carrier (i.e. a function with a finite number of arguments). For a simple (homogeneous) abstract algebra, the domains and the ranges of the operations must be the carrier of the algebra, and thus a homogeneous algebra is not very useful for defining types.

However the concept of an algebra has been extended to heterogeneous algebras (Birkhoff and Lipson, 1970), which are algebras defined over several types rather than a single type, and which are sometimes called algebras of sorts, or many sorted algebras. A heterogeneous algebra is an indexed set of sets, the carriers or phyla, together with a finite indexed set of finitary operations defined on the carriers. For example, the set of carriers might be

{real,integer,Boolean}

and the set of operations might include

    exponentiation: (real X integer) -> real
    division: (integer X integer) -> real
    select: (Boolean X real X real) -> real.

Goguen, Thatcher, Wagner, and Wright, who refer to themselves collectively as the ADJ set, have done much interesting work on heterogeneous algebras (Goguen,1975,1977). However their work is expressed in the notation of category theory, a notation unfamiliar to most computing people. Further, they have concentrated on a rather general class of algebras for which any investigation may need powerful mathematical techniques. Possibly easier to understand is the presentation by Burstall and Goguen(1977).

More relevant to computing is the work of Guttag and Horn-
ing(1975,1977,1978,1979), which is more restricted but has the advantage that interesting properties of the algebras can be assured by very simple techniques. The
specification language developed by Guttag(1978) is the subject of the third lecture.
The thesis of Guttag(1975) is a fine introduction to the mathematical basis of
specification and is not mathematically difficult. This thesis is recommended to all who
are interested in the topic. An alternative source is the paper by Guttag and Horn-
ing(1979), which is more accessible and shorter, containing the mathematical results
but little of the explanatory material.

Unfortunately, even the mathematical techniques used by Guttag and Horning
are not fully presentable here in the time available. Thus what follows should be regarded as an introduction to facilitate and encourage the reading of Guttag's thesis. The
explanation is presented in terms of rewrite rules, a very recent concept not used explicitly in the thesis, but very helpful in understanding it.

Rewrite Rules

Rewrite rules are a systematic method for simplifying expressions in arbitrary
algebras, a part of their usefulness being that powerful techniques exist for investigating
their completeness and consistency. Unfortunately the literature on rewriting is sparse
and expressed in terms difficult for most computer scientists to understand.

Informally, a set of rewrite rules is a finite set of ordered pairs of expressions in
which, for each pair of expressions, the set of free variables of the second expression is
a subset of the set of free variables of the first expression. Each of these pairs of expressions corresponds to an identity in the algebra under consideration. Now when considering an arbitrary expression, we can find a subexpression which matches one of the
set of rewrite rules if, by an appropriate substitution of the free variables, the first expression of a rewrite rule can be made the same as that subexpression. Then we can
make the same substitutions for the free variables in the second expression of the
rewrite rule, and substitute the resulting expression for the subexpression. Thus by a
succession of such rewritings the arbitrary expression can be reduced.

For example, Knuth and Bendix give a complete set of rewrite rules for a group:

$$
\begin{array}{lll}
(1) & +(\text{ x, 0}) & \text{-> x} \\
(2) & +(\text{ 0, x}) & \text{-> x} \\
(3) & +(\text{ x, -(x)}) & \text{-> 0} \\
(4) & +(\text{ -(x), x}) & \text{-> 0} \\
(5) & +(+(x,y), z) & \text{-> } +(\text{ x, } +(y,z)) \\
(6) & -(0) & \text{-> 0} \\
(7) & -(-(x)) & \text{-> x} \\
(8) & -(+(x,y)) & \text{-> } +(-(y), -(x)) \\
(9) & +(\text{ x, } +(-(x), y)) & \text{-> y} \\
(10) & +(-(x), +(x,y)) & \text{-> y} \\
\end{array}
$$

Each of these would normally be considered to be an identity. The directional ordering
imposed on the substitutions by the -> will be considered below.

SYSTEM SPECIFICATION

Now we can use these rewrite rules to reduce, say, the expression

$$+ (\ + (\ d, \ + (\ c, \ -(c))), \ -(\ + (\ 0, \ -(a))))$$

to

$+ (\ + (\ d, \ + (\ c, \ -(c))), \ -(\ -(a)))$	using rule (2)
$+ (\ + (\ d, \ 0), \ -(\ -(a)))$	using rule (3)
$+ (\ d, \ -(\ -(a)))$	using rule (1)
$+ (\ d, \ a)$	using rule (7)

Three obvious questions arise:

- how can we know that the reduction will necessarily terminate, rather than continuing in an endless sequence of possible substitutions?

- how can we know that the result of the reduction will not depend on the order in which the subexpressions are rewritten?

- how can we know that our set of rewrite rules is sufficient to reduce any arbitrary expression?

The first of these, known as the finite termination property, is obviously important, for a rule such as

$$+ (\ x, \ y) \ -> \ + (\ y, \ x)$$

can be applied to the expression

$$+ (\ p, \ + (\ q, \ r))$$

repeatedly, generating various permutations of the free variables but never reducing the expression.

The second of these is known as the Church-Rosser property or the unique termination property, and is necessary to ensure the consistency of our rewrite system.

The third of these can only be addressed in a specific context, but fortunately is clearly defined for our concept of a type as a heterogeneous algebra.

A solution to the finite termination problem is the creation of a measure function. This measure function, which takes an expression as an argument, returns a value from a well-founded sequence of values such as the Natural Numbers. Initially each of the rules was an identity without any implied directionality and could have been used for substitutions in either direction. We chose the direction of substitution for the rule so that the value of the measure function, applied to the expression, will be reduced by that substitution. Knuth and Bendix(1969), Lankford(1976), and Guttag(1975) each offers a measure function, that of Guttag being outlined below. Since the problem of determining termination for a computation such as this is known to be, in general, undecidable, the question of whether a particular set of rewrite rules has a measure function is undecidable. For many specifications the measure functions they propose will suffice,and no existing specification system allows the user to define a measure function. However experience with recursive function definitions, which have a very similar problem, indicates that the measure function may need to be arbitrarily complex and that in the absence of an explicit measure function the set of operations may need to be augmented with additional operations of little relevance to a user of the type.

In the case of primitive recursive functions it will always be possible to find a measure function. Only two functions are likely to be encountered that are not primitive recursive. One is Ackerman's function, which was created to demonstrate the existence of functions that are not primitive recursive and will be found only in the context of such demonstrations. The other is the EVAL function of pure Lisp, or operating system primitives that convert a data structure into program.

Care must also be taken for the Theory of the Natural Numbers and for Set Theory, neither of which is a decidable. However if these theories are restricted to be finite, as they must be in a real computer, then they become decidable. Usually because of the usefulness of natural numbers and sets, and because of the inefficiencies of their reduction by simple rewriting, many systems have both natural numbers and sets built in and use special purpose algorithms for the simplification of expressions involving them.

The second question above, known as the Church-Rosser property or the unique termination property, is automatically satisfied if any operational implementation of the specification can be constructed, though demonstration that the implementation exactly matches the specification is of course program proof and may not be easy. The problem is also addressed by an algorithm due to Knuth and Bendix(1969). This comparatively simple algorithm, which regretably there is not sufficient time to describe, can be applied to a set of rewrite rules that have the finite termination property, and will generate a set of rewrite rules that have the unique termination property. This unique termination property ensures that, regardless of the order in which the rewrites are applied, the reduced form of the expression will be the same. Redundant rules will be eliminated. If the rewrite rules are inconsistent, the Knuth-Bendix algorithm will result in a degenerate set of rules, possibly even in rules that reduce every expression to the same value. If a rule is omitted, the algorithm may result in the generation of some additional rules so as to complete the set of rewrite rules, but this property of the algorithm should not be depended on. The algorithm can not be expected to deduce rules that have been omitted and the resulting set of rules may not be what was intended.

SYSTEM SPECIFICATION

Constructing a Definition for a Type

To define a type, we will construct a heterogeneous algebra defined over a set of types. One of these types is the type that we are defining, the type of interest. We require that all of the other types, the existing types, are already defined in an existing heterogeneous algebra.

We have already seen that a value of the type of interest can be represented by a composition of the operations that created that value. However such values are of little interest to us, in that they can not be used except as arguments to further operations of the type. Much more interesting are the values returned by those operations on the type that return values of other existing types, such as the operation TOP in the stack example.

We will consider that a set of rewrite rules provides a sufficient axiomatization of the type of interest if, for any expression of the heterogeneous algebra that is a value of an existing type but that involves operations of the type of interest, that expression can be reduced in a finite number of rewrites to a unique expression involving no operation of the type of interest.

Guttag's thesis provides a heuristic for the construction of a set of rewrite rules sufficient to reduce such expressions to a form excluding any operations of the type of interest. This set of rewrite rules suffices as an axiom set for the type and thus provides a very clean and elegant specification of the type. Guttag's thesis also contains a set of conditions sufficient, but not necessary, to ensure the finite termination property, a set of conditions based on a comparatively simple measure function. The existence of an implementation or the Knuth Bendix algorithm can be used to check that the set of rewrite rules has the unique termination property.

The specification method that results from Guttag's thesis is described in the third lecture, together with the heuristic and the measure function. The proofs of their properties are given in (Guttag, 1975) and (Guttag and Horning, 1979).

P.M.MELLIAR-SMITH

ALGEBRAIC SPECIFICATIONS

The Algebraic Specification method devised by Guttag(1975,1978) provides a method for specifying a type by defining an axiom set for the type. The method is largely free from any representational or operational content, thus avoiding undue bias on the subsequent implementation. A set of conditions are provided that are sufficient to ensure completeness, in that for any sequence of operations the axioms will define the end result, and an algorithm is available to ensure consistency, guaranteeing that the end result defined is unique. The method provides a heuristic that suffices to construct specifications for almost all types likely to be encountered in practice.

An Algebraic Specification contains three parts:

- the declaration of the type name,

- the declaration of the operations of the type, together with the number and type of their arguments and the type of their results,

- the axioms of the type.

The form of a specification may be seen from a very simple example, a stack. Five operations are provided for the type Stack. These are:

- NEWSTACK which returns an instance of an empty stack,

- PUSH which puts an item on the top of a stack and returns the resulting stack,

- POP which removes the top item of a stack and returns the resulting stack,

- TOP which returns a top item from the stack,

- ISNEWSTACK which tests whether a stack is empty.

The specification contains six axioms, whose form is that of the rewrite rules described above.

SYSTEM SPECIFICATION

The specification is:

```
type Stack[Item];
declare NEWSTACK( ) -> Stack;
        PUSH( Item,Stack ) -> Stack;
        POP( Stack ) -> Stack;
        TOP( Stack ) -> Item union Undefined;
        ISNEWSTACK( Stack ) -> Boolean;
for all s : Stack; i : Item let
        ISNEWSTACK( NEWSTACK( )) = true;          (1)
        ISNEWSTACK( PUSH(i,s)) = false;            (2)
        POP( NEWSTACK( )) = NEWSTACK( );           (3)
        POP( PUSH(i,s)) = s;                       (4)
        TOP( NEWSTACK( )) = undefined;             (5)
        TOP( PUSH(i,s)) = i;                       (6)
end Stack
```

It is not difficult to confirm that these axioms are satisfied for a stack. For instance the fourth axiom requires that if we PUSH an item onto a stack and then POP an item off that stack then the result is the original stack. Similarly, the sixth axiom requires that the TOP operation should retrieve an item just PUSHed onto the stack.

Further thought is required to establish that these axioms completely characterize the stack type. In particular the effect of the POP operation, and its relationship to the TOP and ISNEWSTACK operations, may be of interest. How does the sixth axiom ensure the desired result when several items have been POPped off the stack? How does the first axiom require the ISNEWSTACK operation to indicate that the stack is empty when all the items have been POPped off the stack?

Consider an expression of the form:

```
TOP( POP( POP( PUSH( a, PUSH( b, PUSH( c, NEWSTACK( )))))))
```

This reduces thus:

`TOP( POP( PUSH( b, PUSH( c, NEWSTACK( )))))`	using rule (4)
`TOP( PUSH( c, NEWSTACK( )))`	using rule (4)
`c`	using rule (6)

Similarly the expression:

```
ISNEWSTACK( POP( PUSH( a, POP( PUSH( b, NEWSTACK( )))))))
```

reduces thus:

`ISNEWSTACK( POP( PUSH( b, NEWSTACK( ))))`	using rule (4)
`ISNEWSTACK( NEWSTACK( ))`	using rule (4)
`true`	using rule (1)

The general approach of these reductions is that the expression consists of an operation yielding a value of an existing type and operating on an expression of the type of interest. The expression of the type of interest can be reduced to a canonical form, for the type above involving zero or more PUSH operations applied to a NEWSTACK. The operation yielding a value of an existing type applied to the canonical form can then be reduced to an expression involving no operations of the type of interest. Alternative sequences of reduction are often available of course.

The Heuristic

The Algebraic Specification Method contains a heuristic to assist in the development of appropriate sets of axioms. This heuristic begins by partitioning the operations of the type of interest into three classes:

- output functions, which operate on the type of interest but return a value of an existing type,

- constructor functions, which return a value of the type of interest and are used to construct expressions of the canonical form,

- extender functions, which return a value of the type of interest but which are not used to construct expressions of the canonical form. Rather they are used to convert a value of the type that reduces to one canonical form into a value that reduces to another canonical form.

Mention should be made here that it may be necessary to introduce further auxiliary functions into the specification. These auxiliary functions, typically output functions, are operations of the type that are not made available to a user of the type but rather are necessary only for the definition of the type.

There is not necessarily a unique choice for the canonical form, and thus the partitioning into constructor and extender functions is a matter of judgment as to which partitioning will yield the cleanest specifications.

In the example above of the type Stack, the partitioning was:

output functions: ISNEWSTACK, TOP
constructor functions: NEWSTACK, PUSH
extender functions: POP.

The heuristic requires two sets of axioms. One set includes axioms for the output functions, while the second set includes axioms for the extender functions. The number of axioms required depends on the arguments to the output or extender functions on the left-hand side of the axioms.

Argument positions whose type is an existing type should carry free variables, distinct for each position of any one function.

SYSTEM SPECIFICATION

If the axiom for an output or extender function is such that all argument positions whose type is the type of interest are free variables, only one axiom is required and the axiom is essentially the definition of a recursive function.

If the axioms for an output or extender function are such that all but one of the argument positions carries a free variable in every axiom, the number of axioms required is the number of constructor functions. Axioms are required in which each of the constructor functions is present in that argument position, with free variables as its arguments. The axioms above for the type Stack are all of this kind.

If the axioms are such that more than one argument position does not carry a free variable in every axiom, axioms are required for every permutation of the constructor functions in those argument positions, with free variables for the arguments of the constructor functions. Thus with N constructor functions, N*N or N*N*N axioms would be needed for that output or extender function.

The results in Guttag's thesis apply to a wider range of specifications than those constructed according to this heuristic, but most useful specifications can be expressed within this format and specifications more complex than these have an uncomfortably high error rate.

The rules for the right-hand sides of axioms are slightly different for the axioms defining output functions and the axioms defining extender functions. For axioms involving output functions, the right-hand side may be any expression of the full algebra of the correct type and including only free variables introduced on the left-hand side. It may include conditionals of the form:

if Boolean-expression
then expression-1
else expression-2.

However the measure function for the rewrite rules is the depth of nesting of operations of the type of interest, and this function must be less for the expression on the right than for the expression on the left. But the depth of nesting on the left is only two. Thus operations of the type of interest should not be nested in the expression on the right. Conditionals and operations of existing types may be nested to any depth.

For axioms involving extender functions, two additional rules are imposed. The extender functions must be ordered, and axioms defining an extender function may not involve any extender function after itself in that ordering. Further, in the right hand side of an axiom defining an extender function, the arguments of any occurrence of that function must be free variables. If the argument position of the function is one that, in the left hand expression, carried a free variable, then that argument position on the right must carry free variable from the free variable arguments to the extender function on the left. If the argument position of the function is one that, in the left hand expression, carried a constructor function, then that argument position on the right must carry a free variable from the free variable arguments to that constructor function.

Genuine difficulties in the construction of the axioms can always be overcome by the introduction of one or more auxiliary functions.

An Example

Let us now consider another specification, for the type String, adapted from (Guttag,1978). The specification defines eight operations:

- NULL, which generates a new instance of an empty string,

- ADDCHAR, which appends a character to the end of a string,

- ISNULL, which tests for an empty string,

- LENGTH, which returns the number of characters in a string,

- EQUAL, which tests two strings for equality,

- CONCAT, which joins two strings together,

- SUBSTR, selects a substring starting at the character position given by the second argument and of length given by the third,

- INDEX, which returns the starting character position of the first occurrence of a substring within a string, and a zero if there is no occurrence.

Two functions are constructors, NULL and ADDCHAR; four are output functions, ISNULL, LENGTH, EQUAL, and INDEX; and two are extender functions, CONCAT and SUBSTR. EQUAL was not present in the original version of the specification but was added during the correction of an error and thus might be regarded as an auxiliary function.

The specification is:

type String;

declare
      NULL( ) -> String;
      ADDCHAR(String,Character) -> String;

      ISNULL(String) -> Boolean;
      LENGTH(String) -> Integer;
      EQUAL(String,String) -> Boolean;

      CONCAT(String,String) -> String;
      SUBSTR(String,Integer,Integer) -> String;
      INDEX(String,String) -> Integer;

SYSTEM SPECIFICATION

for all s,t : String; c,d : Character; i,j : Integer;

```
ISNULL( NULL( )) = true;
ISNULL( ADDCHAR(s,c)) = false;

LENGTH( NULL( )) = 0;
LENGTH( ADDCHAR(s,c)) = LENGTH(s) + 1;

EQUAL( NULL( ),NULL( )) = true;
EQUAL( NULL( ),ADDCHAR(t,d)) = false;
EQUAL( ADDCHAR(s,c),NULL( )) = false;
EQUAL( ADDCHAR(s,c),ADDCHAR(t,d)) = c=d and EQUAL(s,t);

CONCAT(s,NULL( )) = s;
CONCAT(s,ADDCHAR(t,d)) = ADDCHAR( CONCAT(s,t),d);
SUBSTR( NULL( ),i,j) = NULL( );
SUBSTR( ADDCHAR(s,c),i,j) =
    if j > 0
      then if j = LENGTH(s) - i + 2
              then ADDCHAR( SUBSTR(s,i,LENGTH(s)-i+1),c)
              else SUBSTR(s,i,j)
           else NULL( );

INDEX( NULL( ),t) = if LENGTH(t) = 0 then 1 else 0;
INDEX( ADDCHAR(s,c),t) =
    if INDEX(s,t) > 0
      then INDEX(s,t)
      else if EQUAL( t,SUBSTR( ADDCHAR(s,c),
                     LENGTH(s)-LENGTH(t)+2,
                     LENGTH(t) ))
           then LENGTH(s)-LENGTH(t)+2
           else 0;
```

end String;

Most of these axioms are quite easy to understand, but a few merit attention.
Consider the axioms for CONCAT which reduce an expression such as

CONCAT(ADDCHAR(ADDCHAR(NULL(),a),b),ADDCHAR(ADDCHAR(NULL(),c),d))

through the steps

ADDCHAR(CONCAT(ADDCHAR(ADDCHAR(NULL(),a),b),ADDCHAR(NULL(),c)),d)
ADDCHAR(ADDCHAR(CONCAT(ADDCHAR(ADDCHAR(NULL(),a),b),NULL()),c),d)
ADDCHAR(ADDCHAR(ADDCHAR(ADDCHAR(NULL(),a),b),c),d)

Notice how the axioms are defined to steadily reduce one of the arguments to the function, until it is reduced to a NULL and the extender function itself can be eliminated.

An example of the sequence of reductions for a SUBSTR operation is:

```
SUBSTR( ADDCHAR(ADDCHAR(ADDCHAR(ADDCHAR(NULL(),a),b),c),d), 2,2)
SUBSTR( ADDCHAR(ADDCHAR(ADDCHAR(NULL(),a),b),c), 2,2)
ADDCHAR( SUBSTR( ADDCHAR(ADDCHAR(NULL(),a),b), 2,1), c)
ADDCHAR(ADDCHAR( SUBSTR( ADDCHAR(NULL(),a), 2,0), b),c)
ADDCHAR(ADDCHAR( NULL(), b),c)
```

The INDEX operation is left as an exercise for the reader.

In practice the kinds of full reductions demonstrated above should not be necessary to understand a specification, once one is familiar with the technique. Considerations of the local structure of the expressions, and a little practice in thinking recursively, should suffice.

Problems with Algebraic Specifications

Unfortunately Algebraic Specifications suffer from some severe disadvantages. One of the most obvious is that the technique is most appropriate for operations that return only a single value, either a value of the type of interest or a value of an existing type. But many operations found in real systems return both a modified value of the type of interest and a value of an existing type. For instance the stack example above separated the TOP and POP operations which are normally combined. Guttag has investigated approaches to this problem that involve procedures within the axioms and simultaneous evaluation and assignment. Such approaches destroy the elegance and mathematical simplicity of the technique. Alternatively one can introduce further types to represent the composite results of the operations with selector operations to extract the component results from the composite. No mathematical problems arise, but the presence of the selector functions forces the use of more complex axioms three operations deep, with a correspondingly more complex heuristic, or alternatively the definition of many auxiliary functions. Both of these seriously detract from the ease of writing and, particularly, of reading and understanding the specifications.

A second problem concerns error conditions. Guttag has extended the method to permit the statement of input assertions. However the result returned under error conditions still remains a problem. The approach of returning a result from the union of the type and a special undefined value is mathematically and implementationally unattractive. Preferable would be to make each result a composite of the result value and an error indicator, but this pushes the problem straight back to that above.

Even more serious for the widespread use of Algebraic Specifications is the very considerable difficulty experienced by average programmers in understanding them, and even experts in their use make uncomfortably many mistakes while writing algebraic specifications. Thus it is unlikely that algebraic specifications will have a major impact on computer programming at large. Their contribution lies in the understanding of the specification process and in their influence on the design of future specification methods that will be kinder to relatively unskilled users.

SYSTEM SPECIFICATION

THE SPECIAL SPECIFICATION LANGUAGE

Special is a specification language designed by Robinson and others at SRI for use in specifying real systems (Roubine and Robinson, 1977). Some examples of the real systems that have been specified in Special are:

- PSOS, a provably secure operating system (Neumann,1977),

- KSOS, a secure version of the Unix operating system (Ford,1978),

- Sift, a reliable aircraft control computer (Wensley,1978).

The language originated in the work of Parnas(1972), but has evolved significantly since. Special lacks some of the mathematical elegance of the algebraic specification, but is a more powerful language capable of expressing some specifications that cannot be expressed at all by any other specification language. If the full power of Special is used, there is no hope of showing that a specification is complete and consistent. Indeed it is a feature of Special that nondeterministic systems can be specified. However few specifications need the full power of Special, and it is possible to write specifications within the kind of restricted domain that is used for algebraic specifications and that allows straight forward derivation of the properties of the specification.

The most visible difference between a Special specification and an algebraic specification is that the Special specification encourages the user to think in terms of a state. Regardless of what view of the specification is appropriate for a computer scientist or for a designer of a specification language, it is undoubtedly true that most potential users of a specification system find it much easier to think in terms of a state than in the more abstract terms required by the Algebraic specifications.

Much of the following description of Special is adapted from (Robinson,1978).

The heart of a specification written in Special is the definition of the operations on the type. The operations are of three kinds:

- O-functions (OFUN),

- OV-functions (OVFUN),

- V-functions (VFUN).

In the absence of exceptional conditions:

- a V-function invocation (as an operation) returns a value, but causes no state change,

- an O-function invocation can cause a state change, but returns no value an OV-function invocation returns a value and can cause a state change

A V-function is denoted as visible if it is an operation of the type and as hidden if it is internal to the specification. A V-function may also be derived, meaning that its value is expressed as a function of the values of other V-functions. The "state" of the type can be thought of informally as the Cartesian product of the values of all of the V-functions other than the derived functions. Good practice in the use of Special requires that all the visible V-functions be derived, so that the state functions are all hidden.

In addition, the specification defines:

- initial values for each nonderived V-function. The specification is required to define initial values for the full domain of the V-function.

- exception conditions for each of the visible V-functions, O-functions, and OV-functions.

- the returned value for each derived V-function and OV-function.

- the values that the nonderived V-functions will acquire after an invocation of each O-and OV-function.

- assertions about relationships between the values of the parameters.

Special allows user-defined local functions. The definition of the function gives a type to the function and to each of its formal arguments, and provides a body. Any such function can be used as a sub-expression in an expression with appropriate actual arguments substituted for the formal arguments, provided the type of the actual arguments is consistent with the function definition, and the declared type of the function is consistent with its use in the expression. For example, we can define the Boolean function no-string using the following syntax

BOOLEAN no-string(INTEGER j) IS
    $j < 1$ OR $j > t\_len()$,

where the body follows the reserved word IS, and t_len() is a V-function of the module. One can use no-string(i) where a Boolean-value is expected within a scope where i has been declared as an integer.

Designators

Special uses the concept of a designator as a primitive type of the language. A designator is the name of an object or an instance of the type being defined. Designators are not manipulatable, except for being returned as the result of a function or being used as an argument to a function.

SYSTEM SPECIFICATION

Sets

In specifying a concept it is often useful to view objects as if they formed a set. The advantage of the set viewpoint is the absence of any consideration of ordering or repeated elements. The use of sets in a specification often leads to simpler specifications and averts prejudicing a specification with implementation decisions. All elements of a set are of the same type.

If s has been declared to be of type

SET_OF INTEGER

then s can be defined to be a particular integer set. The extensional constructor explicitly identifies the individual elements. The following forms are equivalent:

$$s = \{1, 3, 5, 7\}$$
$$s = SET(1, 3, 5, 7)$$

The intentional constructor can also be used:

$$s = \{INTEGER\ i \mid o < i\ AND\ i < 9\ AND\ i\ MOD\ 2 = 1\ \}$$

The general form for a integer set is

$$\{INTEGER\ i \mid p(i)\ \}$$

where $p(i)$ is a Boolean expression. The intentional form is used more often, since it permits the concise characterization of large sets.

The set of consecutive integers between two given integers can be specified using the following shorthand:

$$ss = \{7 \dots 36\ \}$$

A predefined function for sets, is CARDINALITY, which returns an integer, the number of elements in a set. Thus,

CARDINALITY(s)

would now be 4.

Another predefined function for sets is INSET, which determines that an element is in a set, returning a result of type BOOLEAN. Thus,

1 INSET s

is TRUE.

Vectors

For vectors, similar constructors are provided. If iv has been declared to be of type

VECTOR_OF INTEGER

then the extensional constructor would be used, as:

iv = VECTOR (1, 3, 5, 7)

The intentional constructor for the same vector is

iv = VECTOR(FOR i FROM 1 to 4: 2*1 - 1).

The predefined function LENGTH returns the number of elements in a vector. Thus

LENGTH(iv)

returns the integer 4.

Structures

This form is used to specify an ordered assemblage of objects, not necessarily of the same type. The elements of a structure are each identified by a unique name. The structured type employee, each value of which contains 3 elements, could be declared as follows

employee: STRUCT_OF(INTEGER id, age; VECTOR_OF CHAR title)

A particular instance, Williams, of the type employee can be expressed as

Williams = STRUCT(15024, 22, Sr_Adm_Aide).

Particular components can be referred to by using the component name as an extractor

Williams.age

has value 22.

Undefined Values

It is often useful in a specification to indicate that a particular object has no value. We use the particular symbol ? (shorthand for UNDEFINED) to represent no value. Often, the initial values of primitive V-functions are most conveniently specified to be ?, rather than some random value. In SPECIAL, ? is a member of all types unless explicitly excluded. Thus the type INTEGER consists of the values

{ ... , -2, -1, 0, ?, 1, ... }

Thus, the rules of the grammar are satisfied when a V-function is declared to be of type INTEGER, and the specification indicates that the initial value for certain of its associated V-functions is ?.

<u>Function Definitions</u>

A hidden V-function definition has the form:

VFUN v(typespec1 arg1; ...) -> typespec result;
  HIDDEN;
  INITIALLY
    expr;

The expression following INITIALLY is an expression that characterizes the initial value(s) for each possible argument. Generally, "expr" is of the form

result = expression

possibly being

result = ?,

as shorthand for: result is ? in the initial state for all possible arguments to v.

A visible V-function has the form:

VFUN v(typespec1 arg2; ...) -> typespec result;
  EXCEPTIONS
    ex1;
    ex2;

    .
    .
    .

  INITIALLY
    expr;

Each of the exception conditions is of the form

exceptionname: expression,

where exceptionname is name assigned to the exception condition, and expression is a Boolean expression of the arguments, V-functions, and parameters. The exceptionname enables a program using the operations of the type to discriminate between the possible exceptions. Generally, but not always, an abstract program invoking a visible function will test for the existence of the exceptions in the order they appear in the specification. Thus, if the expressions associated with d1, ... di-1 evaluate to FALSE for the arguments of the function invocation, and the expression associated with di evaluates to TRUE, then di will be raised; subsequent exception conditions are not tested. If "v" has no exception conditions then the "exceptions section" is omitted.

A derived V-function has the form:

VFUN v(typespec1 arg1; ...) -> typespec result
  EXCEPTIONS
    .
    .

    .
  DERIVATION
    expr;

where the expression following DERIVATION defines the result in terms of the arguments, primitive V-functions, and parameters. The type of the expression should be the type of the function.

An OV-function has the form:
OVFUN ov(typespec1 arg1; ...) -> typespec result;
  EXCEPTIONS
    .
    .

    .
  EFFECTS
    ef1;
    ef2;

    .
    efq;

Each of the effects ef1 ... efq is an assertion that relates the value of the result and/or the new (after the invocation) value of primitive V-function positions, to the values of the arguments, the prior (before the invocation) values of V-functions, and the parameters. The notation 'v(x) is used to denote the new value of a V-function. In the EFFECTS section, the results and the new values for V-functions are defined by the conjunction of all of the effects assertions. They appear as separate expressions only for ease of presentation. There is no concept of order implied here since we could have equivalently stated the EFFECTS as the single expression

ef1 AND ... AND efq.

As indicated previously, these effects occur only when an operation does not cause any of the exception predicates to be satisfied.

The schema for an O-function is identical to that of an OV-function, except that no returned result is indicated.

With this brief introduction to Special the reader should be able to follow the example specification.

SYSTEM SPECIFICATION

An Example of a Specification in Special

This example is derived from (Robinson,1978).

The module "sequences" defines a collection of word files (sequences), each of which is identified by a unique designator of type nameseg. A user of the module can request the creation of a new sequence; an existing sequence can be cleared to its initial state, but never be deleted, so that there is no recycling of nameseg designators. For reading, the words of a sequence are randomly accessed by position. A sequence is grown by appending words to the end. Two words of a sequence can be interchanged. The operations defined are:

- nameseg; a designator type, the values of which are names of sequences.

- string (nameseg n; INTEGER j) -> word w; a visible V-function that returns the word w at position j in the designated sequence n; word is a named type that is precisely defined later. As the only V-function, string captures the "state" of each sequence in the system.

- seqlen(nameseg n) -> INTEGER v; a derived visible V-function that returns the current length of sequence n. The value of seqlen(n) can be derived from the value of string(n, j).

- create_seq() -> nameseg n; an OV-function that creates a new sequence, initializes it, and assigns a designator to it.

- clear_seq(nameseg n); an O-function that clears a designated sequence.

- append(nameseg n; word w); an O-function that adds the word w to the end of the sequence.

- swap_seq(nameseg n; INTEGER i, j); an O-function that causes the words in positions i and j to be exchanged.

The specification of sequences contains three paragraphs. The FUNCTIONS paragraph contains the details of the specification for each function. The DEFINITIONS paragraph contains the definitions of local functions. The TYPES paragraph declares types that are to be referred to in the specification.

The TYPES paragraph must contain the declaration of the designated type introduced in this module. Thus we declare nameseg as the type whose values are the string sequences of interest. Other types, e.g. subtypes or aggregate types, can be declared here. In the sequences specification we declare the aggregate subtype word. Note that the definition of a word,

the set of all character vectors whose length is positive,

underscores the notion of a type as a set of values. No upper limit on the length of a word is imposed here. In the specification of the individual functions, we will confront the (inevitable) problem of handling physical storage limitations.

The next module paragraph is the DEFINITIONS paragraph. A function definition is an expression, of declared type, in terms of the V-functions, parameters, or other defined functions of the module. A definition can have arguments or not as required. Thus, the general form of a definition is

typespec defname(typespec1 arg1, ...) IS body

Now let us consider the function specifications in turn.

Stringstate

Stringstate is a hidden V-function that returns the word w at position j in the designated sequence n. As the only non-derived V-function, string captures the "state" of each sequence in the system.

The expression in the INITIALLY section,

w = ?

is shorthand for

initially, for all sequences the value of all positions is ?.

String

String is the visible derived V-function that returns the word w at position j in the designated sequence n. Its derivation is merely the hidden V-function stringstate.

A single exception corresponds to no word being present at position j. The reader might question the absence of any exception condition corresponding to the formal argument n. What if a user invokes string(nn, j) with some designator nn that is not an existing nameseg, possibly being of a different type? It would be necessary to define such an exception only in a context where such a circumstance is expected and must be guarded against. For many types, intended for use in a strictly typed context, such checks would be regarded as unnecessary, as here.

SYSTEM SPECIFICATION

Seqlen

Seqlen is a derived visible V-function that returns the current length of sequence n. The derivation (returned value) is expressed as

> consider an integer set that contains all of the
> integer positions that store a word whose value is
> not ?; the returned value is the cardinality of this
> set.

It is emphasized that this is a specification for determining the number of words in a sequence. It is not an implementation, which is simply carried out by using a memory cell to hold the current sequence length.

Create_Seq

Create_seq is an OV-function that creates a new sequence, initializes it, and assigns a designator to it. To express, as an effect, the generation of a never previously generated nameseg designator we use the notation

NEW(nameseg).

NEW is a predefined function in Special, that requires an argument of type DESIGNATOR. As part of the underlying semantics of NEW, it never returns "?".

One final note about the specification of create_seq concerns the apparent absence of any effect to express the initialization of a newly created sequence. Such an expression is not needed here since the initial value of stringstate(n, j) is ?, which is precisely what is desired of a sequence after it is created. Thus, the act of creating a sequence is to make a nameseg designator n available so that words can be appended to n, swapped and subsequently read out.

Clear_seq

Clear_seq is an O-function that clears a designated sequence. We express this effect by indicating that the value in all positions of the sequence is to be ?. This specification illustrates how a desirable concise specification can appear to be an over-specification; positions that were previously ? are re-specified to be ?. An equivalent, but less desirable specification is

FORALL INTEGER j INSET {1...seqlen(n)}: 'stringstate(n, j) = ?

indicating that all positions in the sequence that previously stored defined words, will have value ? after the invocation. The reader should note that in a specification conciseness is desirable, as contrasted with an implementation where efficiency is generally vital.

Append

Append is an O-function that adds the word w to the end of the sequence. As the effect indicates, after an invocation word w will be at position

seqlen(n) + 1

which is the newly-created end-position of the sequence. This specification illustrates the purposeful omission in the EFFECTS section of V-function positions whose values one left unchanged. The following expressions are implicit:

FORALL INTEGER j ˜= seqlen(n) + 1:
  'stringstate(n, j) = stringstate(n, j);
FORALL INTEGER j; nameseg n1 ˜= n:
  'stringstate(n1, j) = stringstate(n, j)

The first expression indicates that all positions of n except seqlen(n) + 1 are left unchanged, and the second that all positions of all other sequences are left unchanged.

Swap_seq

Swap_seq is an O-function that causes the words in positions i and j to be exchanged. Based on the above discussion the specification should be self-explanatory. Note that no order of operation is implied in the EFFECTS section. After an invocation of swap_seq both expressions will be TRUE. There is no intermediate state.

The Specification of the Module sequences

MODULE sequences
  $(maintains an unspecified number of variable length
  sequences of character strings (words) , each string of
  variable length. For reading, words can be randomly
  accessed. New words can be inserted at the end of a
  sequence. Words can be exchanged)

TYPES

nameseq: DESIGNATOR; $(names of sequences)
word: { VECTOR_OF CHAR vc | LENGTH(vc) > 0 };

DEFINITIONS

BOOLEAN no_word(nameseq n; INTEGER j)
  IS NOT j INSET { 1 .. seqlen(n) };

SYSTEM SPECIFICATION

FUNCTIONS

VFUN stringstate(nameseq n; INTEGER j) -> word w;

    HIDDEN;
    INITIALLY
      w = ?;

VFUN string(nameseq n; INTEGER j) -> word w;
      $(returns the j-th string in sequence n)
    EXCEPTIONS
      noword : no_word(n, j);
    DERIVATION
      w = stringstate(n,j);

VFUN seqlen(nameseq n) -> INTEGER v;
  $(returns the number of strings in sequence n)
    DERIVATION
      CARDINALITY({ INTEGER j | stringstate(n, j) $\bar{}= ?$ });

VFUN create_seq() -> nameseq n;
      $(creates a new sequence all words of which are
      undefined. A newly generated designator is returned)
    EXCEPTIONS
      RESOURCE_ERROR;
    EFFECTS
      n = NEW(nameseq);

OFUN clear_seq(nameseq n); $(clears sequence n)
    EFFECTS
      FORALL INTEGER j: 'stringstate(n, j) = ?;

FUN append(nameseq n; word w);
  $(appends word w to the end of the sequence n)
    EXCEPTIONS
      RESOURCE_ERROR;
    EFFECTS
      'stringstate(n, seqlen(n) + 1) = w;

FUN swap_seq(nameseq n; INTEGER i, j);
  $(exchanges words in positions i and j of sequence n)
    EXCEPTIONS
      no_word1 : no_word(n, i);
      no_word2 : no_word(n, j);
    EFFECTS
      'stringstate(n, i) = stringstate(n, j);
      'stringstate(n, j) = stringstate(n, i);

END_MODULE

The Power of Special

The domain in which Special specifications are expressed is that of Set Theory and First Order Predicate Calculus, for the language includes universal and existential quantifiers, and permits arbitrary expressions as assertions. This domain is very powerful and many specifications likely to be required in practice can be expressed in it. In particular Special can express nondeterministic functions, a property that is useful in many real systems.

Further, Special has been useful to programmers on real projects, and is not too difficult for good programmers to use. Exceptional abilities are not needed. Special has been used in several industrial laboratories, demonstrating that it can be used outside the team that created it.

Special is a very large language with many distinct features and a peculiar syntax. These characteristics are not surprising for a first language that grew in stages as inadequacies were encountered. Hopefully it will be possible to develop a cleaner version of the language in the light of experience and increased understanding.

The domain in which Special specifications are expressed is clearly undecidable. Thus Special specifications can be written whose consistency cannot be determined, and for many other specifications require powerful mathematical techniques to demonstrate consistency. Further, there exist Special specifications for which no finite amount of processing can determine the result values, and it may not be possible to determine that only one value satisfies the specifications. In practice no normal specification should encounter these problems, but they present difficulties to mechanical aids which might be useful in establishing the properties of specifications.

Consideration is being given to a set of constraints on Special specifications that would suffice to reduce the domain to one in which the specifications are more readily manipulable. Examples of such constraints are:

- replacing of all existential quantifiers by instantiating functions, which incidentally would preclude nondeterministic specifications,

- requiring that all visible V-functions be derived,

- requiring that assertions be of the form of a left-hand side containing only the new value of a hidden V-function, an equality operator, and a right-hand side restricted to prevent mutually recursive definition of two new values.

FUTURE DEVELOPMENTS AND RESEARCH AREAS

Completeness in Specifications

Above considerable emphasis has been placed on the importance of completeness in the specifications, on ensuring that the specification defines, with certainty, a unique result for any sequence of operations. A specification that defines for us a unique result is clearly valuable for it leaves little room for uncertainty in the behavior of the program. A specification that does not define a unique result allows more opportunity for ambiguity and misunderstanding. As a definition of the behavior of a system, an incomplete specification is unsatisfying, and also allows unexpected changes in the behavior of the system. As a form of communication between people, an incomplete specification permits alternative assumptions as to the behavior of the system. As a directive to the implementers, an incomplete specification delegates specification decisions to the implementers. As a form of documentation of an implementation, an incomplete specification does not document the actual implementation.

But there are circumstances where an incomplete specification might be appropriate. Two particular instances where incomplete specifications may be necessary are the specification of asynchronous systems and the definition of the user's requirements on the system. These are considered below. Incomplete specifications may also arise if the specification is not, and perhaps does not really need to be, strong enough to define a numerical result. Other instances where an incomplete specification might appear to be necessary are due to problems in the design of an appropriate abstraction. In many cases such problems can be avoided but sometimes deterministic specifications are artificial and do not express the intent of the designer.

Incomplete Specifications

As a example of an incomplete specification caused by a weak specification of a numerical result, consider a possible specification of a square root function:

$$\text{sqrt}(x{:}\text{real}) = \text{that } y{:}\text{real for which } y \geqslant 0.0$$
$$\text{and } y^2 \leqslant x$$
$$\text{and } (y + \text{delta}(y))^2 > x$$

where delta(y:real) = y * 0.00000001

ıd the specification failed to note that y should be positive, it would have been in-
ımplete by failing to distinguish between positive and negative square roots, a quite
ınecessary incompleteness. Note also that the specification leaves completely
ıdefined the value of the root for negative arguments. However even for the roots of
ısitive numbers the specification is incomplete for there are many real values for y
that satisfy the constraints, many indeed that are representable by the computer

hardware. It is possible that we do not care which value is chosen provided that these constraints are satisfied, or possibly a more precise specification could be devised. The problem with a very precise nonprocedural specification is that it may be very difficult to obtain an efficient procedural implementation of it. The problem of accepting any value satisfying the weaker specification is that such a specification may not be acceptable. For instance, one might expect the square root to satisfy:

if (x = y)   then   (sqrt(x) = sqrt(y))

and

sqrt(x * 1.000000001) $\geqslant$ sqrt(x)

At present we do not have a satisfactory method of providing nonprocedural specifications for computer oriented functions of real arguments such as square root. In practice the formal specification of such a function must currently be expressed as an algorithm leaving few implementation decisions to the implementers, an algorithm that is probably highly dependent on the precise details of the quaint number representations of the hardware.

Incompleteness can also be introduced into the specification by an inappropriate choice of abstraction. Consider a system in which a user program requests buffers from a buffer pool, and in which the buffer pool manager returns to the user program the address of the allocated buffer. About the best that can be done as a specification is:

some b:bufferaddress such that b inset bufferpooladdresses and b.free

The problem here is that the bufferaddress, which is, to the user program, quite arbitrary and dependent on the actions of other programs unknown to us, should not have been included in the abstraction made available to the user program. Much better would have been to specify a new type buffer with operations defined on it for inserting and retrieving data. Now the address of the buffer is hidden inside the buffer pool manager, where it should have been anyway, and the specification only says, informally, that you get back out of the buffer what you put into the buffer. How the buffer manager shares buffers between user programs, and how it associates buffers and users, are implementation details of no concern to the user program.

Not all such problems are so easily solved. Consider for instance some program module that maintains a sorted list, perhaps to provide a priority queue or an index of some kind. Unless all of the entries are unique, the specification of the sort must define an ordering among equal entries or the specification will be incomplete. The ordering may be of no significance to the user, and to impose a specific order may constrain the implementation. If there is no way for the user program to discover the order, the technique described above can be used. But if for instance the user program can obtain the entries one at a time in order, a common feature, then it will not be possible to hide the order inside an abstraction. Either the specification defines the order and constrains the implementation, or else the specification is incomplete.

In considering whether it matters if the specification is incomplete, it is important to distinguish between deliberate incompleteness, such as that due to the equal keys case above, and accidental incompleteness, such as that for a negative argument to the square root function. Clearly the accidental incompleteness is highly damaging and must be detected if at all possible. One of the most serious disadvantages of a deliberately incomplete specification is that it may mask further accidental incompleteness. For a specification that is intended to be complete it may be possible to use mechanical aids to detect that the specification is in fact not complete, but for a deliberately incomplete specification such aids are necessarily ineffective. Further, the verification of incompletely specified programs, and particularly the verification of programs that use an incompletely specified component, is made more difficult. Since sophisticated test data generators use very similar semantic analysis to program verification, it is to be expected that test data generation may also be complicated by incomplete specifications.

Thus if it is at all possible to derive a complete specification, that complete specification is much preferable to an incomplete one. But it is necessary to use incomplete specifications, for instance to express the effects of some asynchronous interactions or to express requirements, and therefore the resulting problems will have to be tackled. If the specifications can be made clearer or more intuitive by being left incomplete, the advantages of improved communication may well outweigh the mathematical disadvantages. However completeness should be abandoned only for the the most explicit and pressing reasons.

Specification of Asynchronous Systems

The specification of asynchronous systems is an area in which incomplete specifications are often used. This incompleteness is normally viewed as reflecting a degree of non-determinacy in the behavior of the system, the non-determinacy resulting from our lack of knowledge as to the asynchronous interactions involved. Indeed some approaches to the analysis of asynchronous interacting systems systematically convert the several interacting programs into a single non-deterministic program and then perform the analysis on that single non-deterministic program. In these approaches, non-deterministic specifications are natural and will not complicate the situation much further. However the analysis of non-deterministic programs and specifications is not easy, and these methods may be regarded as exchanging a conceptually simple but rather intractable problem for a very great quantity of complexity that can in principle be resolved.

At present these non-deterministic methods are perhaps the easiest methods for the specification of asynchronous systems, but the result is clumsy, and better approaches are being sought. It is therefore appropriate to consider what can be done to specify an asynchronous system without succumbing to non-determinism and thus to incompleteness.

Deterministic Systems

It is appropriate to note that many systems contain internal asynchrony but yet have an external behavior that is completely deterministic. The specifications of those systems can be expressed by standard specification methods and can be complete. As before an appropriate choice of abstractions can help, and possibly even slight strengthenings of the specifications may be necessary to remove those points at which the internal asynchrony might have been allowed to become visible to the user. If the system can be designed within these constraints, the design, implementation, and analysis will be much simpler, and such systems are usually regarded as having very clean designs that are easy to use. As an example of what can be done with deterministic specifications see (Flon,1977).

Serializable Systems

One stage more complex than the deterministic systems are the serializable systems (Eswaran,1976). The characteristic of a serializable system is that it serves requests from a number of sources, these requests being presented asynchronously. The system services these requests as it receives them, with presumably as much overlap as is possible. But the specifications do not reflect any of this asynchrony or overlap, but rather define the behavior of the system as though the requests were performed serially one at a time. Consequently straight forward deterministic specifications can be used.

Further the system does not have to behave as though the requests are serviced in the order in which they are received, but may produce results that would have been those to be expected had the requests been received in some other order. The order of requests from any one source must be preserved, but requests from separate sources may be reordered. Typically the system will behave as though a related group of requests from one source are serviced, followed by a related group of requests from another source, even though the serving of these requests is actually highly overlapped and the results from the second group might even be generated before those for the first group. The system is regarded as satisfying the specification if there exists some permitted ordering of the requests such that the specified results for that sequence of requests is the same as the results actually produced by the system.

The advantage of a serializable system is that the non-determinacy is all buried in the ordering of requests from independent sources, an ordering that is necessarily indeterminate. The specifications of the systems can be written as the specifications of the determinate serialized system, and any analysis of the system can be broken into two distinct stages. The first stage is to show that the system behavior is equivalent to that of a system in which the requests are actually serialized, while the second step is to show that the specification is satisfied for a serialized sequence of requests.

Most systems can be specified, with a little care, as serializable systems at the level of the user interface. However when system components are considered serialization may become unrealistic.

SYSTEM SPECIFICATION

Non-serializable Systems

Some systems cannot readily be serialized, and techniques have had to be developed to allow their specification (Owicki,1976; Owicki,1977; Lamport,1977). Much of what is now available appears clumsy and difficult to use, for as yet we have only an incomplete understanding of the appropriate techniques, though much of the difficulty is because such systems are inherently complex.

As an example of serializable and nonserializable systems, we consider an airline reservation system. Many sources of reservation requests exist and are processed concurrently, but any one passenger can only submit requests singly and cannot submit two parallel requests. Though several different passengers may be submitting concurrent requests for the same flight, the rules preclude the overbooking of flights and require that each passenger be given an irrevocable confirmation or a rejection of his request.

Consider first a system in which only single stage flights are booked. Here we can use a serialized specification which imposes on the results of each request the condition that:

```
if bookings(flight) = maximum(flight)
    then 'response = "flight fully booked"
    else 'response = "booking accepted"
        and 'bookings(flight) = bookings(flight) + 1
        and requester inset passengers(flight)
```

Note that the specification can be quite simple and need make no reference to the possibility of concurrent access to the values of, for instance, bookings(flight).

Now consider the extension of this system to one in which multiple-stage flights can be booked. Rejecting the alternative of reserving large parts of the database while all the various stages of a single request are processed, on performance grounds, tentative reservations must be made for the earlier stages until the later stages have also been reserved, and these tentative reservations must be abandoned if a later stage cannot be reserved.

Consider the situation in which one request has made a tentative reservation for a flight while subsequent stages are investigated, this tentative reservation being for the last seat on the flight. Another request is made for that flight and is rejected as the flight is full, while concurrently the first request is rejected because of some subsequent stage. It is now clear that these two requests, when processed concurrently, do not yield the result that should have been obtained by processing them serially. Had the multiple stage request been fully processed before the single stage request, the last seat on the critical flight would have been still available for the single stage request and that request would have been satisfied rather than rejected, while had the single stage request been processed first it would have obtained that seat and again would have been accepted.

(There does in fact exist an implementation of the multiple stage reservation system that is actually serializable, but that implementation is nontrivial and imposes a performance penalty that multiplies the worst case response time by a factor proportional to the number of requests being processed concurrently. The naive approach of excluding all concurrency imposes a similar performance penalty, but on all requests rather than on the rare worst case request.)

The specifications of nonserializable systems are necessarily nondeterministic. No longer is it possible to hide the nondeterminacy of asynchrony in the arbitrary ordering of requests. Thus the specifications of the flight reservation system may contain:

'response = "flight fully booked"
or ....

indicating that a request may be rejected, even though it might appear that the request could have been satisfied.

A nondeterministic specification must be designed with great care lest the specification become ambiguous and meaningless. For instance a reference to a shared value, that can be modified by some other concurrent activity, may be ill defined. At the time at which we assert that the specification is satisfied, the shared value may have been further modified by some other concurrent activity, or it may be at that moment being modified and thus be undefined.

The work of Owicki(1976,1977) has provided much of our understanding of how these specifications should be structured to avoid such problems. Owicki introduces auxiliary variables into the specification, variables that may not, and possibly could not, exist as a part of any implementation. They are therefore not dissimilar to the auxiliary functions introduced above for the standard specification methods. The purpose of the auxiliary variables is to create a private environment for each activity in which the effects of the concurrent activities is not visible. Typical auxiliary variables are history variables whose values are sequences of operations, input data, output values, etc., but other auxiliary variables may also be appropriate.

The specifications of operations are written in terms only of these auxiliary variables and not in terms of shared values. (Shared values could be used, but for any shared values cited the serialization rules would have to apply.) The specifications can therefore be written in the private context of the particular action and need not be complicated by the effects of concurrency, though they may still need to be nondeterministic.

SYSTEM SPECIFICATION

Relating the auxiliary variables of all the concurrent actions are the invariants, which ensure that the private environments of the various concurrent actions are consistent. The invariants are required to be satisfied whenever the values they relate are defined. Because these invariants do not define specific values but only relate the values of auxiliary variables,it is possible to bury the effects of asynchrony within them without introducing the complexity that might otherwise result. The design of specifications using auxiliary variables is not easy, requiring some practice to choose appropriate variables and invariants. An example is given in (Owicki,1977).

Temporal Logic

The use of nondeterministic specifications to define asynchronous systems makes no use of the concept of time, and indeed to introduce any aspect of time into the specification is quite artificial. Pnueli has investigated forms of temporal logic (Pnueli,1977) which show promise of yielding simpler specifications and proofs of asynchronous systems. These temporal logics are based on the temporal operators:

```
[]p  or  G(p)      -- henceforth p is always true,
<>p  or  F(p)      -- eventually p will be true,
q[]p               -- while q remains true, p is true,
q<>p               -- before q becomes true, p will be true.
```

The operators [] and <> are duals, so that:

```
[]p   =  ˜<>(˜p)
q[]p  =  ˜( (˜q)<>(˜p) )
```

The anticipated advantage of temporal logic for program verification is that it should be possible to retain the separation between the concurrent processes during the analysis, rather than combining them into a single nondeterministic process from which the structure must be recovered. But very little experience exists of the use of temporal logic for either specification or verification.

Requirement Definition

The approach to design described above proposes that the user's requirements of the system be defined before the system specification is created. It envisages that the user will be able to express his needs in the requirement definition, and that any system that satisfies the requirement will be acceptable, though of course some systems may be more desirable than others. The designers of the system can then proceed with the specification of the system in the knowledge that, provided they continue to meet the requirement, they can optimize their design against whatever criteria are important for the system, for instance performance, storage space, implementation feasibility, or the man-machine interface.

The distinction between the requirement and the specification of a system to meet that requirement is very important. A user seldom needs a system with a very precisely predetermined behavior, unless the need is for the system to be compatible with some previous system. In general the user's needs are very much more general. He needs a certain effect achieved, but may not need to predetermine the precise command to be used, nor may he be concerned with precisely what formats are used or what the error indications will be. Thus his requirements can be satisfied by a wide variety of systems with very different appearances. Some of these may be more desirable than others, and of course should be sought by the designers, but any of them would do. Were the user to include more in his requirement than is absolutely necessary to do the job, those extra requirements might unintentionally preclude system designs that would best meet his actual needs. Only by clearly distinguishing the requirement from the subsequent design is it possible to evaluate the full range of design choices and to confirm that the best design has indeed been chosen.

The requirement of the user may be general, but that does not imply that it will be vague or ill considered. Those aspects of the behavior of the system that are important to the user may need to be very strictly constrained by the requirement. For instance the example requirement given below for military security is very brief and says very little about the system, but that little it does say is so precise and so strict that any system meeting this requirement will be secure (and also no existing system could meet it). The precision of the requirement will be particularly important if a formal demonstration that the specification meets the requirement is to be undertaken.

Much prior work in the requirement definition area has, for lack of any techniques for the expression of requirements, consisted more of outline designs for the implementation. Lists of commands and parameters are constructed; data structures to be maintained are defined; even the processing algorithms are outlined. Such exploratory design may be appropriate to investigate the feasibility of implementation, and even implementation of a design as an experimental prototype may be used to investigate whether the requirements are understood, but as an approach to expressing the requirement such methods suffer from the same disadvantages as the use of implementations as specifications.

A requirement definition is essentially an incomplete specification, but the kinds of incompleteness required is not necessarily that obtained by simply leaving out parts of a specification written in a specification language of the kind described above. Not only is it necessary to be able to state that some result is only partially defined at the requirement definition stage, but also the set of operations themselves may not yet be determined. Typical requirements might be that there must exist some sequence of operations that would cause a certain effect, or that for any sequence of operations a certain property must be maintained.

SYSTEM SPECIFICATION

Formal requirements are difficult to construct. A part of this difficulty is because we do not yet fully understand how they should be expressed, but a part of it is due to the inherent difficulty of thinking about one's needs as distinct from a system to meet those needs. However the imposition of such thought on the user can be very valuable in clarifying the requirement and increasing the user's understanding of it, an effect equivalent to that obtained from the use of formal specifications. Very few formal requirement definitions have been constructed, and those clearly by tour de force rather than systematic application of an understanding of requirement definition.

An outline of the formal requirement for reliability in the SIFT system is given in (Wensley,1978), but we present here an example taken from (Feiertag,1977) of a requirement for security. Informally this requirement states that if two sequences of operations are each applied to a system in the same state and if these sequences differ only by operations that should not be visible at some security level, then any operation of that security level invoked immediately following the two sequences will return the same result.

FOR_ALL   s: State,   i: Operation,   p,q: Operation_Sequence

filter(p, security_level(i)) = filter(q, security_level(i))
=> result(i, effect(p, s)) = result(i, effect(q, s))

where:

- the type State represents the set of all possible states of the system,

- the type Operation represents the set of all possible operations together with their arguments, both explicit and implicit,

- the type Operation_Sequence represents the set of all possible sequences of Operations,

- the function security_level applied to an Operation yields the security level of that operation,

- the function filter applied to an Operation_Sequence and a security level yields the Operations_Sequence that results when all the operations that should not be visible from that level are removed from the given sequence,

- the function effect applied to an Operation_Sequence and a State yields the State resulting from the execution of the given sequence of operations starting at the given state,

- the function result applied to an Operation and a State yields result obtained from that operation invoked in that state.

REFERENCES

Birkhoff,G. and Lipson,J.D. (1970), "Heterogeneous Algebras," Journal of Combinatorial Theory, Vol 8 (1970), pp.115-133.

Burstall,R.M. and Goguen,J.A. (1977), "Putting Theories Together to Make Specifications," Proc.IJCAI-77, MIT, 1977, pp.1045-1058.

Eswaran,K.P. et al. (1976), "The Notions of Consistency and Predicate Locks in a Database System," Comm.ACM, Vol 19, No 11 (November 1976), pp.624-633.

Feiertag,R.J. et al. (1977), "Proving Multilevel Security of a System Design," Proc 6th ACM Symp on Operating System Principles, 1977, pp.57-65.

Flon,L. (1977), "On the Design and Verification of Operating Systems," Dept of Computer Science, Carnigie-Mellon University, May 1977.

Ford Aerospace and Communications Corporation, (1978), "Secure Minicomputer Operating System," WDL-TR7811, Ford Aerospace and Communications Corporation, Western Development Lab., Palo Alto, CA94303, March 1978.

Floyd,R.W. (1967), "Assigning Meanings to Programs," Mathematical Aspects of Computer Science 19, J.T.Schwartz,ed., pp.19-32, Amer. Math. Soc., Providence, Rhode Island, 1967.

Goguen,J.A. et al. (1975), "Abstract Data-types as Initial Algebras and the Correctness of Data Representations," Proc. Conference on Computer Graphics, Pattern Recognition, and Data Structure, 1975.

Goguen,J.A. et al. (1977), "Initial Algebra Semantics and Continuous Algebras," Jour.ACM, Vol 24, No 1 (Jan. 1977), pp.68-95.

Guttag,J.V. (1975), "The Specification and Application to Programming of Abstract Data Types," CSRG-59, Dept. of Computer Science, University of Toronto, 1975.

Guttag,J.V. (1977), "Abstract Data Types and the Development of Data Structures," Comm.ACM, Vol 20, No 6 (June 1977), pp.396-404.

Guttag,J.V. et al. (1978), "The Design of Data Type Specifications," in Current Trends in Programming Methodology, Vol IV: Data Structuring, R.T.Yeh, Ed., Prentice Hall, 1978.

Guttag,J.V. and Horning,J.J. (1979), "The Algebraic Specification of Abstract Data Types," to appear in Acta Informatica.

Harel,D. and Pratt,V.R. (1978), "Nondeterminism in Logics of Programs," Proc Symp on the Principles of Programming Languages, 1978.

Hoare,C.A.R. (1969), "An Axiomatic Basis for Computer Programming," Comm.ACM, Vol 12, No 10 (Oct. 1969), pp.576-580

Knuth,D.E. and Bendix,P.E. (1969), "Simple Word Problems in Universal Algebras," in Computational Problems in Abstract Algebra, J.Leech, Ed., pp.263-297, Pergamon, 1969.

Lamport,L. (1977), "Proving the Correctness of Multiprocess Programs," IEEE Trans on Software Engineering, Vol SE-3, No 2 (March 1977), pp.125-143.

Lankford,D.S. (1976), "Canonical Inference," ATP-25, Depts. of Mathematics and Computer Science, Univ. of Texas, Austin, 1976.

Liskov,B.H. and Zilles,S.N. (1975), "Specification Techniques for Data Abstractions," IEEE Trans. on Software Engineering, Vol SE-1, No 1 (March 1975), pp.7-18.

Marcotty,M. et al. (1976), "A Sampler of Formal Definitions," Computing Surveys, Vol 8, No 2 (June 1976), pp.191-276.

Neumann,P.G. et al. (1977), "A Provably Secure Operating System: the System, its Applications, and Proofs," SRI International, Feb. 1977.

Owicki,S. and Gries,D. (1976), "An Axiomatic Proof Technique for Parallel Programs," Acta Informatica, 6, 4, 1976, pp.319-340.

Owicki,S. (1977), "Specifications and Proofs for Abstract Data Types in Concurrent Programs," CS-77-607, Digital Systems Lab., Stanford University.

Parnas,D.L. (1972), "A Technique for Software Module Specification with Examples," CommACM, Vol 15, No 5 (May 1972), pp.330-336.

Pnueli,A. (1977), "The Temporal Logic of Programs," Proc 18th Symp on the Foundations of Computer Science, 1977.

Roubine,O.M. and Robinson,L. (1977), "The Special Reference Manual," CSL-45, Computer Science Lab., SRI International, Jan. 1977.

Robinson,L. et al. (1978), "The HDM Handbook," CSL-72, Computer Science Lab, SRI International, Apr. 1978.

Wensley,J.H. et al. (1978), "SIFT: Design and Analysis of a Fault Tolerant Computer for Aircraft Control," to appear in the Proceedings of the IEEE.

3

PROGRAM VALIDATION

Susan L. Gerhart

USC Information Sciences Institute

INTRODUCTION

Concepts and Definitions

The basic problem of program validation is to show that a program meets its specifications. Unfortunately, the technical literature uses a number of terms for this activity in a rather inconsistent and confusing manner. To clarify the task and terminology, we will first identify four concerns which play a part in the validation activity and then associate various of these terms with them.

The first concern is the purpose of the validation activity. This may be to demonstrate conclusively to a customer or to an endorsing agency that the program (perhaps together with its specifications) is suitable for distribution and use. When there is this element of authority and finality, validation is often called **certification** or **acceptance testing**. But the program may not warrant this type of activity because it is not meant to be a product or because it is not yet ready for such severe scrutiny. Or the program may be at an even more tentative stage where it is reasonably expected that the program does not meet its specifications and the purpose is to detect inconsistencies which are expected to be corrected or mediated with the requiring party. This latter type is sometimes called **debugging,** with the connotation that not only evidence of errors but the underlying faults are sought.

The second concern is the property of interest for the validation, which may be categorized as

> functional (often called **correctness**)- Does the program produce the right results when the program is subjected to

66

usage under protective assumptions?

performance- Does the program meet time and space
resource limits which will enable it to be used in its
intended environment?

robustness- Can the program continue to perform
usefully when the protective assumptions are removed and
it is subjected to stressful and abusive usage?

Of course, these properties are not mutually exclusive nor are
they always fully specifiable.

The third concern is the method of performing the validation,
currently either testing or proving. **Testing** means execution in a
suitable environment on selected data followed by some sort of
inference process (statistical or logical) about what that data
says about execution of the program on the remaining non-selected
data. **Proving** means the sole (excluding testing) use of
mathematical arguments based on given semantics of the language in
which the program is written and of the environment in which it
will execute. The term **verification** is used synonymously
(excluding testing) with proving in the literature on that
subject, while sometimes proving is called **formal verification**.

In the definitions of testing and proving, the term
"environment" means the collective hardware, software, and users
which are either co-running at the time of testing or axiomatized
at the time of proof. It is often difficult to perform validation
in exactly the environment where the program is expected to be
used, e.g. in the Viking lander on Mars, a banking system, or a
real-time system. Hence, a fourth concern is the validation
environment, and the degree to which it approximates the usage
environment. Indeed the term **validation** is sometimes confined to
execution within the actual, rather than a **simulated**, environment.

Despite all the above connotations of "quality assurance",
program validation is unlikely ever to be as conclusive as we
would like. Before we go into more depth, it is worth looking at
some of the gross possibilities for failure. The first concern is
whether the specifications really correspond to the requiring
party's notion of what the program should do. There is no formal
way of establishing this connection; it is only possible to see
that the program seems to do the "right" things. However, there
are formal properties which specifications should possess,
e.g. consistency and completeness in certain senses, without which
the whole validation process is suspect. Melliar-Smith's chapter
discusses this in detail. Assuming the specifications are
adequate, the exact effect of the program may be difficult to tie
down. Proving requires an axiomatization of the programming
language and of the parts of the environment with which the
program will interact. Testing requires that the environment be

stable, i.e., that compilers, loaders, disk managers, etc. not be changing. Proving would permit these changes as long as the axioms, if such exist, remain satisfied. Testing currently proceeds without this axiomatization, so changes in the environment can influence results from one validation time to another or from validation time to final usage.

However, assuming specification adequacy and control of the semantics of the environment, there is still a critical possibility for failure, namely, errors in the validation. As we will see, testing currently lacks the necessary inference process from tested to nontested data, while proving demands a level of rigor that currently seldom can be achieved. Even if testing had the associated inference process, errors would as likely occur as with reasoning in proving. So, any assurance provided by validation is relative to (1) the quality of the underlying theory, (2) the effectiveness of associated techniques and tools, (3) the skills of the validators, and, (4) since any validation effort will probably stop short of the ideal, any physical, temporal, or economic limitation of resources for performing it.

This concern with performability and fallibility of the validation process is central to our further discussion and will be elaborated on at length in the last section. From the overall perspective of reliability, what we are trying for is fault avoidance. We want to know that the systems we develop and use do not have design and implementation faults to the extent that these can be prevented. Validation attempts to demonstrate that such faults have been avoided, or have been found and removed, but, being fallible, still may necessitate some type of fault tolerance to achieve reliability in the final system. The activities discussed elsewhere in this course - language design, specifications, system structuring - attempt to minimize both the number and severity of faults which occur during design and implementation and to make the validation process less fallible and more cost-effective. Even with complete fault avoidance, fault tolerance would still be needed to handle hardware faults, user input errors, run-time legality checking (e.g. size of numbers), interface violations that were missed in specifications, resource allocation failures, and unverifiable conjectures. In other words, there are a range of conditions which cannot be handled other than dynamically and are best handled apart from normal validation. Validation techniques may also add to the effectiveness of fault-tolerance through identifying situations requiring it and handling it.

For the rest of this paper, we will consider validation as what goes on at a moment when development activity is frozen and we are given a formal problem: Does this program meet these specifications? Furthermore, we will concentrate primarily on validating the correctness property by the two current modes of validation. As we will discuss at greater length in the last section, both methods have their strengths and weaknesses. Testing has been by far the most practiced activity, while proving has been primarily a research activity. In this paper, we will treat them as of equal importance because conceptually they are alternative, perhaps even compatible and complementary, techniques. Our purpose here is to get some feeling for the fundamental character of each method - the theory behind it, the techniques required to perform it, the human skills involved in these techniques, the additional aids which computers can provide, and the overall strengths and weaknesses.

A Simple Example using Testing and Proving

Let us consider a very simple program as a way of seeing what thinking processes are used in each of testing and proving. Suppose we are given a sequence S and its length n and want to know whether all its elements are the same, as indicated by a Boolean variable **AllEqual**. The program we will be validating is in Figure 1a.

To test a program for this problem, we must have some precise criteria for selecting test data. Commonly used criteria are

Black Box (Criterion BB)-Systematically produce from the specifications alone some meaningful and "interesting" combinations

Elementary Iteration (Criterion EI)-Force the execution of each loop 0 times and exactly 1 time, if possible

Predicate Combinations (Criterion PC)-Force all possible logical combinations within composite predicates of loops and branches to occur during execution of test data.

The black box approach ignores program structure and concentrates on problem domain structure. Figure 1b shows some interesting combinations of up to 3 elements in the sequence S. Suppose we fix S(1) as some possible value for elements in the sequence, calling it a, and then consider its combinations with some different value b. These include no elements different from a, one element different and one the same, etc. as shown in Figure 1b. If we speculate how the program could compute, we might consider comparing each other element with one of the extreme end elements or comparing adjacent elements, while scanning either left to right or right to left. In any of these possible solutions, these eight combinations have a good chance of detecting errors; hence, their "interesting" quality. We are selecting data according to various characteristics of the problem, independent of the actual solution approach or program.

The latter two example criteria rigidly follow the program structure. Each is goaled toward forcing certain path executions for the program, which should somehow typify the overall path behavior of the program. EI focuses on the elementary (0 and 1 times) iterations of the loop. PC looks at the various combinations of truth values in the predicate AllEqual and i≤n, trying to force each one to be true at some point during the execution of the test data (multiple instances of each combination holding are permitted). Suppose, only for simplicity of comparison, that we select subsets of the combinations we would use for the black box criterion (BB) to satisfy the iterative (EI) and predicate (PC) criteria. We might come up with the test data described in Figure 1b, where expressions describe various possible test data sets. For example, EI may be satisfied by selecting either 0 or a and then selecting one of aa,ab,aba, or abb to get the loop executed exactly 0 and 1 times, respectively.

Now let's see what kind of reasoning we might use if we know that the AllEqual program executes properly for the selected data. Consider BB first. If we extend each of the sequences with an a or a b, we have either one of the old sequences or one of length 4, aaaa, aaba, abaa, abba or aaab, aabb, abab, abbb. But we can see from the program that aaaa executes exactly like aaa, only one more time. aaba, abaa, abba execute exactly like aab, aba, abb, respectively, and so on. This argument for n=4 could be repeated for any n>4. Hence, we have a kind of induction argument: the program is correct for a basis of sequences of length < 4 and, assuming the program is correct for any n, 3≤n, we can see it is correct for n+1. Of course, this argument also depends on the elements in the sequence, which could include another element c, or elements different from our a and b. But the program only uses equality between elements and S(1) is arbitrary, so there should be no different behavior for different elements in S. Thus we have backed up our feeling of meaningfulness of the 8 combinations with an induction argument based on the program.

Now consider criteria EI and PC. For EI, 0 and a are equivalent in that no comparison of elements is necessary, and AllEqual=true in both cases, so the program works properly for 0 iterations. If we have executed the loop once, AllEqual has been set to S(1)=S(2). So the loop does compare elements and set AllEqual to a value appropriate for either continuing or exiting the loop. Hence, our induction argument is that the loop works properly once, and is set up properly to continue, so it will work properly any number of times. For PC, it's a little hard to formulate any induction argument, but the combinations seem to cover starting or continuing the loop with AllEqual true and more elements to scan, AllEqual true but all elements scanned, AllEqual false while still more elements to scan, and AllEqual false at the very end of scan. Basically, these are the situations which cover

70

no mismatch or various placements of mismatches within S. Hence, we argue that the loop continues or exits in these various "states" and that the program executed on the PC data has been in each one of these states at least once. Notice that these criteria are easily satisfied with less data than for BB, where we weren't given the program and had to speculate on its possible structure.

What we have shown is that our test data selection criteria gave us some data upon which we could base various types of induction arguments. These arguments weren't formal, but seemed plausible. However, let's look at the more interesting situation where the program *isn't* correct. Figure 1c shows five versions of the AllEqual program, labelled A-E, with faults introduced by changing the initializing assignments or the loop controlling predicate. Also shown are those test data from our eight combinations which would show an error, thereby detecting the existence of the fault. Now suppose we selected data by our same criteria applied to these faulty programs, as shown in Figure 1d. What likelihood is there for detecting the fault? In the section on testing concepts, we will define more formally some terms (**validity** and **reliability**) which break this question down into (1) Does our criterion permit us to select data which would show errors? and (2) Does our criterion constrain us so that any selected data is equally likely to display an error?

As we will see from deeper analysis, only for the data selected by criterion BB and in the case of program E and the PC criterion can we answer affirmatively. In all other cases, we can either only select data for which the program works correctly or we can satisfy the criterion with some data that displays errors or with other data for which the program works correctly. Criteria EI prevents us from selecting data which could display the error for programs A and B, but, of course, trying to select data to satisfy the criteria may show anomalous behavior, such as not being able to iterate a loop 0 times, which will lead to fault detection. Moreover, if we try to base an induction argument on the few pieces of data needed to satisfy the criterion, we must inspect the program and consider other data. Failing to find an argument may reveal the fault, even if the test executed without error. This should clarify the dilemma of testing: **we cannot rely on criteria such as these for telling us whether a program is correct based on execution results alone, because the tests may not reveal errors.** We must go further and somehow argue, based on the selected data and the structure of the program, that it will work correctly for any other data. From this brief introduction, we might conjecture that black box testing could be superior because it encourages selecting a greater amount of more diverse data, while the program structural criteria are more oriented toward what the program *actually* does (in a sampling sense) than toward what it should do. We'll check this further when testing is studied in more detail.

Now consider a different type of correctness argument. We won't execute the program on any particular data, but instead investigate how it would execute on any arbitrary input data. We enter the loop with AllEqual=true and i=2. If n is less than 2, the loop terminates immediately. For n=0 or n=1, AllEqual should be true at exit, so the program is correct there. But suppose $2 \leq n$ and the loop body is executed the first time. After that i=3 and AllEqual tells whether S(1)=S(2). If AllEqual is false, the loop exits with the proper value since S(1) does not equal S(2). But if AllEqual is true, the loop will either terminate with the right result if n=2 or continue if n>2. We can extend this argument indefinitely, but let's try to reduce all these cases to one logical expression

i=2 and AllEqual=true or   ...(entry)
   $3 \leq i < n+1$ and   ...(after i-2th traversal)
      AllEqual=(S(1)=S(i-1)) and
   [S(1)=S(2) and ... and S(1)=S(i-2)] ...more formally
                              [Forall j: $2 \leq j \leq i-2$: S(1)=S(j)]

Expressions such as these have an invariant quality with respect to the loop; whenever the loop iterates (i.e. right before the condition is evaluated) this expression is true. It characterizes the state of the computation at that point in the execution. So we have made an invariant assertion about the loop. Notice that we can tell whether an arbitrary assertion has the invariant quality by an induction argument: prove it so when the loop is started, then assuming it after some arbitrary number of iterations and supposing the loop is to be executed one more time, prove it still holds after the loop body is executed. But what about when the loop exits? Then we should have that the assertion (which is still true), together with the falsity of the loop conditions, implies what we want to hold at termination of the loop. Here if n=0 or n=1, the assertion says that AllEqual = true, as it should be. But if $2 \leq n$ then the assertion says that either AllEqual = false, in which case S(1) does not equal S(i-1). Since $3 \leq i \leq n+1$, the output should be false. In the other case where AllEqual = true, i>n by the loop exit and therefore i=n+1 by the inequality in the assertion, so the assertion says that S(1)=S(2) and ... and S(1)=S(n-1) and true=(S(1)=S(n)), or altogether that Forall i: $2 \leq i \leq n$: S(1)=S(i).

This is the type of argument used in validation by proving. We create these invariant assertions for loops and then show that they hold throughout iteration of the loop. In our example, the assertion expressed everything about the state of the computation;

in fact, the assertions need only express enough to support the induction argument from time to time of iteration and also that their combination with the condition for exiting the loop guarantees what should hold after the loop. For example, the assertion can say AllEqual=[Forall j: 2≤j<i: S(1)=S(j)]. Proving also has its dilemma: It may be difficult to find these invariant assertions and the proofs of invariance may become quite difficult.

This rather trivial example should convey some of the flavor of both testing and proving. In the next sections, we will go further into the theory and techniques of each mode of validation. The critical point of each is that we need some kind of induction argument. This may seem overly mathematical, but in fact induction is the only way to argue effectively about infinite, or very large, spaces, such as we almost always have in programs. Here, the spaces may be regarded as either the domains of input data or as the computations of the program. Induction, of course, is a standard mathematical technique. One form uses a successor operation, proving the property for a basis element after which the property is proved for an arbitrary element assuming it holds for the predecessor element. Another form uses a well-ordering and proves the property for an element in the space assuming the property holds for every element lower in the ordering. As the reader may remember from mathematics courses, there are some tricks and what often looks like magic involved in induction proofs; the same phenomenon occurs here. Dijkstra (1974) discusses the inherent mathematical nature of programming.

As we will see, the forms of induction arguments differ for proving and for testing. The critical questions for validation quality are how well we can perform these arguments and maybe whether we can perform them at all. In the final section we will argue that, because the forms of induction differ and because we can err in performing either one, we should perform both!

Note: The exercises are intended to tie up loose ends and raise important questions, as well as to provide practice material for the interested reader.

Exercise: Consider another way of writing the AllEqual program:

```
i:=2;
while i≤n and S(1)=S(i) do  i:=i+1  od;
AllEqual:=i>n;
```
(1) Find the invariant assertion for this loop. (2) Consider selecting test data according to the above criteria and perform the same experiment by introducing various kinds of faults and evaluating the criteria on these faulty programs. (3) Find other ways of writing the program and repeat the exercise for these

other versions. (4) The _and_ operation must be conditional, i.e. A _and_ B must be equivalent to _if_ A _then_ B _else_ false. Otherwise, what would happen? (5) Which version seems less error prone, easier to understand, and easier to validate? What is the best language structure for expressing this solution?

THEORY AND TECHNIQUES OF PROVING

Basic Concepts and Methods

What is a proof? Loosely speaking, a proof can mean any convincing argument. There is no inherent connotation of mathematics, only that one party persuades another that a particular conclusion holds. But such informal proofs suffer from deficiencies related to human and interpersonal qualities, e.g. proof by intimidation, proof by exhaustion (of the listener), and proof by nonexistent reference. At the opposite extreme is the proof of formal logic. It requires a formal system of axioms and rules of inference; a proof is a sequence of statements, each of which is either an axiom or follows from preceding statements by the rules of inference. In fact, mathematicians' proofs usually fall closer to the informal than the formal extreme, although it is required that, at least in principle, an informal proof could be turned into a formal one. Standard mathematical proofs follow the form we have used: division into cases, e.g. $n<2$, $2 \le n$; stringing together facts, omitting reasons, e.g. AllEqual=true, but AllEqual _and_ $i \le n$ is false, so $i>n$, and furthermore $i \le n+1$, so $i=n+1$; contrapositive, to prove B from A, deny B and from that prove A is false. The effectiveness of such proofs comes from their standard and abbreviated form and from abstraction away from too much detail, while retaining the fact that someone (or perhaps a mechanical proof checker) can check each step. Proofs have additional benefits, e.g. "debugging" a claim by finding the assumptions it requires and by refining the terms it uses, that make a theorem clear and credible, even without the proof.

But what are the formal systems which underlie proofs of program correctness? And, of course, what are the theorems which express correctness? We have used the informal notion of correctness that the output specification hold for the data which satisfy the input specification. But this says nothing about whether the program aborts or runs forever. In fact, the literature distinguishes various kinds of correctness: partial correctness, which ignores proper (or clean) termination, and total correctness, which includes it. The theorems of interest say that "some given program G is (partially, totally) correct

with respect to some given input-output specifications P and Q".
Our invariant assertion method actually breaks the theorem for
partial correctness into a set of lemmas, often called
verification conditions, which express that if an assertion holds
at one point in the program and if the computation proceeds from
there to yet another assertion, then the latter assertion also
holds. These lemmas together express that the admissible program
computations always proceed from one assertion which holds to
another which holds, and therefore (by induction on the number of
assertions passed through) if the input specification holds, so
does the output specification.

The next level of consideration is the form of these
verification conditions. They must somehow incorporate the
notions of flow of control, effects of assignments to variables,
declarations, etc.; in short, the semantics of the programming
language applied to the program under consideration. The language
definition is usually packaged as **proof rules**, one rule of
inference for each programming language construct, plus various
rules for linking specific constructs together into valid
programs. A commonly used partial correctness notation is A{S}B,
also sometimes written {A}S{B}, where S is a program statement and
A and B are assertions, often called the **precondition** and
postcondition, respectively. Alternatively, a recursively defined
predicate transformer wlp(S,B) can be defined as the "weakest
precondition for the program S to produce results satisfying B, if
it terminates properly (which is not required)". Then A{S}B iff
(A _implies_ wlp(S,B)). Ultimately, these proof rules or equivalent
mechanical procedures can reduce any program to syntactic types of
constraints on the program and to logical expressions in terms of
the assertions and data expressions of the program.

For example, consider a simple language with conditional
statement _if_ B _then_ S1 _else_ S2 _fi_, loop statement augmented with
assertion _asserting_ A _while_ B _do_ S _od_, sequencing S1;S2, and, of
course, assignment V:=E. The proof rules are

P _and_ B{S1}Q, P _and_ ~B{S2}Q

P{_if_ B _then_ S1 _else_ S2 _fi_}Q

P _implies_ A, A _and_ B{S}A, A _and_ ~B _implies_ Q

P{_asserting_ A _while_ B _do_ S _od_}Q

P{S1}R, R{S2}Q

P{S1;S2}Q

P <u>implies</u> Q(V->E)

P{V:=E}Q

(where Q(V->E) denotes substituting (E) for free occurrences of V in Q)

while the predicate transformer definition is

wlp(<u>if</u> B <u>then</u> S1 <u>else</u> S2 <u>fi</u>, Q)= <u>if</u> B <u>then</u> wlp(S1,Q)
                                                <u>else</u> wlp(S2,Q)
wlp(<u>asserting</u> A <u>while</u> B <u>do</u> S <u>od</u>, Q)=A
  provided A <u>and</u> B <u>implies</u> wlp(S,A), A <u>and</u> ~B <u>implies</u> Q
wlp(S1;S2,Q)=wlp(S1,wlp(S2,Q))
wlp(V:=E,Q)=Q(V->E)

Exercise: (1) Find proof rules and predicate transformers for various common language loops: (a) <u>if</u> B <u>then</u> S <u>fi</u>; (b) <u>repeat</u> S <u>until</u> B; (c) <u>loop</u> S1 <u>while</u> B <u>do</u> S2 <u>repeat</u>; (d) <u>for</u> i:=a <u>to</u> b <u>do</u> S <u>od</u>. (2) Assignment to arrays is more complicated than for simple variables: wlp(V[I]:=E, Q)=Q(V[J]->(if I=J then E else V[J])). Alternatively, the array may be treated as a whole object with a function assign(V,I,E), defined by assign(V,I,E)[J]=if I=J then E else V[J]. Figure out what this means and how to manipulate it.

By applying the rules of inference upward, i.e. given the expression below the line generating the required conditions above the line or by evaluating the predicate transformer, we can eventually produce verification conditions. For the AllEqual example, the verification conditions are

VC1: $0 \leq n$ <u>implies</u>
        (2)=2 <u>and</u> (true)=true <u>or</u>
        $3 \leq (2) \leq n+1$ <u>and</u> [(true)] <u>and</u> (true)=(S(1)=S((2)-1))

VC2: (i=2 <u>and</u> AllEqual=true <u>or</u>
    $3 \leq i \leq n+1$ <u>and</u> [<u>Forall</u> j: $2 \leq j \leq i-2$: S(1)=S(j)]
          <u>and</u> AllEqual=(S(1)=S(i-1)))
  <u>and</u> (AllEqual <u>and</u> $i \leq n$)
<u>implies</u>
      ((i+1)=2 <u>and</u> (S(1)=S(i))=true <u>or</u>
    $3 \leq (i+1) \leq n+1$ <u>and</u> [<u>Forall</u> j: $2 \leq j \leq (i+1)-2$: S(1)=S(j)]
                <u>and</u> (S(1)=S(i))=(S(1)=S((i+1)-1)))

VC3: (i=2 and AllEqual=true or
   3$\leq$i$\leq$n+1 and [Forall j: 2$\leq$j$\leq$i-2: S(1)=S(j)]
       and AllEqual=(S(1)=S(i-1)))
  and ~(AllEqual and i$\leq$n)
  implies   AllEqual=[Forall j: 2$\leq$j$\leq$n: S(1)=S(j)]

The next task is to prove each one of these verification
conditions. Some theory of integers, with operations for addition
and inequality, is needed. Had we other data structures,
e.g. stacks or queues or heaps, we would need a set of axioms to
define the theory for them. The algebraic axiom technique
described by Melliar-Smith is a succinct and precise way of
defining the meaning of various data structures, although it is
usually necessary to prove several obvious and useful properties
of the data structure before the proofs go smoothly. Mechanical
theorem provers have been developed to assist in the proof of
verification conditions. Currently these are able to handle most
of the simple integer arithmetic and some of the other data
structure proving. Most such systems are interactive, because the
proofs require extensive searches which can get out of control.
The user may well have (and should have) a good idea of how the
proof should go by which to advise the theorem prover, or the
proof may be discovered through interactive exploration.

We also need an argument for proper termination. The assertion
guarantees that subscripts will be within range, assuming 1 origin
indexing. There are no other ways the program could abort. A
standard way of proving that the program doesn't loop forever is
to find a function which strictly decreases each time around the
loop, as well as being bounded below such that reaching the lower
bound causes loop exit. Here this function is n-i bounded at 0.
Since i gets increased by 1, the function decreases by 1. Below 0
forces the predicate i$\leq$n to be false.

To get back into perspective, the proof rules are usually used
for language definition, whereas the predicate transformer
formulation is useful for both language definition and for
verification condition generation. Proof rules for real
programming languages can become quite complex; indeed they have
been proposed as a standard measurement for complexity of various
constructs. Of course, this is not the full story since the
complexity of assertions must also be considered. For example,
the goto statement has an apparently simple proof rule, but
undisciplined control flow can severely complicate assertion
creation. To a large extent, these rules suggest restrictions on
languages that would invalidate purely logical proofs, thus
preventing the programmer from making certain types of errors,
whether a proof is performed or not. Various types of protection
mechanisms are necessary to make the results of proofs (or tests)

hold at run-time. For example, if any other user or program part can change the value of a variable in a validated part, then the run-time results will not correspond to the values assumed in the tests or proofs. In other words, the semantics assumed for validation must be enforced by protection and other mechanisms. The chapters by Horning and Needham discuss these related issues.

Methods of Program Proving

The person wanting to learn program proving should generate some verification conditions by hand and then work out most of the proof details. Once these skills are developed, it is possible to mentally check assertions without all the mechanical detail. There are perfectly good alternatives to the above form of definition and mechanization, e.g. forward from precondition to postcondition or both together. In fact, there is a calculus of useful ways of handling predicate transformers, e.g. wlp(S, A and B)=wlp(S,A) and wlp(S,B), which allows splitting a postcondition into two parts to prove separately or having proved wlp(S,A) to prove only wlp(S,B) to prove wlp(S, A and B). While current systems are not yet flexible enough to admit this calculus, there is no reason why the mechanical verification process will always be one of separately generating and then proving verification conditions. The human program prover is encouraged to follow instinct and experience and not feel bound to this mechanical approach.

In fact, there are numerous approaches to program proving, of which this rigid, a posteriori, paradigm is probably the worst. That is, it almost never is the right approach to take a given program and then find and prove invariant assertions for it. If the program was developed by some process of refinement from abstractions, then there are facts and insights gained from that process that significantly ease the proof. The data structure abstraction methodology shows how implementations of operations specified more abstractly may be proved correct and therefore any program using the operations may ignore implementation details. Factoring of the proof process is enormously beneficial because it cuts down the combinatorial complexity of the proof to reasonable size, mentally and mechanically. Of course, understandability, design assistance, and modifiability are other extremely important reasons for using abstraction.

Often a program to be proved is an instance of some more general and common construction which already has been proved or which is worth proving first, gaining the original theorem of the special case with it. For example, it is rather stupid to prove what we just did, that all elements of a sequence are equal. A more general program ignores the actual predicate being evaluated:

```
i:=k; all:=true;              i:=k;
while all and i≤n do          while i≤n and q(i) do
   all:=q(i);
   i:=i+1                        i:=i+1
od                            od
                              all:=i>n
```

Both set the variable 'all' to tell whether some predicate 'q' is true over the interval [k..n]. There is nothing of importance about the specific content of 'q', except perhaps that it be defined over the interval. In our example, q(i) is S(1)=S(i) and [k...n] is [2...n]. There are numerous instances of such program schemas, where the general control flow is described, but the details of some statements and expressions are omitted. With the specifications similarly generalized, the program schema can often be entirely proved or reduced to a few conditions which can only be proved when the details are known. It may well be that a large part of program proving can be done 'once and for all' with such schemas, then compiled into a handbook, and applied by program provers to specific programs as needed. Likewise, data structure axioms can be defined generally, and properties derived once and for all from them then used in proofs of individual programs.

Exercise: Find and prove loops for the existential quantifier,

$$\text{IsAtLeastOne= } \underline{\text{ThereExists}} \text{ i: } k{\le}i{\le}n\text{: } q(i),$$

and the unique existence operator,

$$\text{IsExactlyOne= } \underline{\text{ThereExists}} \text{ ! i: } k{\le}i{\le}n\text{: } q(i).$$

(defined as $\underline{\text{ThereExists}}$ i:$k{\le}i{\le}n$:

$$q(i) \underline{\text{ and }} [\underline{\text{Forall}} \text{ j:}k{\le}j{\le}n\text{:}i=j \underline{\text{ or }} {\sim}q(j)])$$

Even at the concrete level, there are options. For example, the invariant may be devised before the loop body, thus combining verification more with design. Other issues at either the concrete or schematic levels are functional versus iterative representation. To some extent, any preference between the two is relative to previous education and experience, since these represent styles of programming. In fact, functional representation often suppresses details in the order of evaluation of arguments and often encourages additional modularity. But iteration is often sufficient. There are proof techniques for functional versions of programs which correspond rather directly to the invariant assertion method for iterative constructs. Often the input - output specifications suffice for the induction argument, although sometimes they must be strengthened.

Whenever some generalization occurs in a data structure or program schema, there is usually some opportunity for optimization upon instantiation and combination with other program parts. For example, data structure operations are implemented independently of their combination with other operators, whereas in any program using the data structure there may be combinations of operations for which a better implementation could be found. Likewise, in program schemas it is often possible to simplify control flow or remove redundant actions in any instance of their use. Thus a companion technique to generalization is specialization. We would like this to occur without any loss of proof, in other words, correctness is preserved when the program is transformed to take advantage of specialization. Additionally, this correctness-preserving transformation approach may be used in conjunction with refinement or with program development at the concrete level. It is almost always easier to prove a simpler, less efficient version of a program than a highly optimized one. We can still have the desired degree of optimization if we stepwise transform preserving correctness. The transformations are expressed in terms of schemas and, similarly, proofs that correctness is transferred are performed at the schematic level, perhaps leaving a residue to be proved in the context of application.

A More Complex Example – Hamming Codes

We will now try to illustrate many of these ideas in a more complex example than **AllEqual**. The example is long and mathematical; the reader should not expect to master it in one gulp, but instead try to focus on the following features:

1. Axioms for sequences with operations for catenation and indexing are assumed, as are axioms for number theory. Operations peculiar to the problem, e.g. Expand, psum, and sigma2, are defined, some incompletely. From these the specifications (A), (B), and (C) which constrain the operations Encode, Decode, and Check, are proved. The Encode operation is then implemented to satisfy the axioms. Since there is a tremendous body of knowledge·about Hamming codes, it might be reasonable to accept a proof from a book or paper. However, that would not guarantee that the axioms used here meant what we thought. It is not the purpose of program proving to force known results to be reproved; it is a matter of taste and experience whether to accept prior results (math books have been known to have errors and are not always as complete as programs require). We include the proofs to show induction arguments on the lengths of sequences and some of the mathematics behind Hamming codes.

2. Program complexity is increased through several versions of the program. However, proof complexity is not significantly increased because a simple, direct program is first written,

proved, and then transformed by proving a few additional invariants and applying separately proved correctness-preserving transformations.

3. Abstract programs (like those we see in refinement examples) are used as comments along the way. These are italicized.

4. Assertions use a great deal of notation, e.g. ExpandedSoFar and UpperPowersOf2Zero, which cut down on the symbol complexity and express what each logical expression means. These may often be reasoned with separately and intuitively, thus decomposing the verification conditions into several parts. It is important for program provers not to get carried away with formalism; the principles of structuring that are advocated for programs (and others) must also be applied to assertions and proofs.

The Problem Definition and Solution Hamming codes, Hamming (1950), make it possible to communicate reliably over noisy channels by permitting error detection and correction of various degrees and kinds. For example, suppose we have an n bit message and want the ability to detect and correct single bit errors (transmissions of the wrong bit). The Hamming method in this case adds an extra k bits which "cover" certain subsequences of the transmitted message in such a way that any erroneous bit (even one of the check bits) will be shown by a certain checking process, as will the absence of an error. Occurrences of more than one error will cause the answer to be wrong. Probability considerations dictate the power of the error detection and correction method to be used. Here, we will consider only single error detection and correction.

Place the bits of the message to be encoded into the positions with nonpower of 2 indices (origin 1) of the message to be transmitted and use the remaining power of 2 indexed positions to contain bits which make certain check sums add up to 0. The addition process is modulo 2, which is equivalent to the "exclusive-or" operator which we will denote as $\neq$. For power of 2 position p, the sum includes those bits of the transmitted message for which the binary representation of the index contains a 1 as the coefficient of p. For example, let m1 m2 m3 m4 be the message to be transmitted as the sequence t1 t2 t3 t4 t5 t6 t7 where

$$t3=m1 \qquad t5=m2 \qquad t6=m3 \qquad t7=m4$$
$$t1=(t3 \neq t5 \neq t7) \qquad t2=(t3 \neq t6 \neq t7) \qquad t4=(t5 \neq t6 \neq t7)$$

The power of 2 positions are determined by the equations

$$0=(t1 \neq t3 \neq t5 \neq t7) \qquad 0=(t2 \neq t3 \neq t6 \neq t7) \qquad 0=(t4 \neq t5 \neq t6 \neq t7)$$

It can be seen that changing any single bit, say ti, causes all the sums it occurs in to add to 1, instead of 0, and since it occurs in only those sums for which there is a 1 as coefficient in the binary representation of i, the sums "tell" the position of error. A solution is obtained by thinking of first "expanding" M, the message to be transmitted, by putting in 0's in the power of 2 positions, then filling these in with the sums as shown by the equations above.

Example

```
M       1   0 1 1
      0 0 1 0 0 1 1        EXPAND
      1 2 3 4 5 6 7        INDICES(FOR REFERENCE)
T     0 1 1 0 0 1 1        FILL IN SUMS
      0 1 1 0 0 0 1        CORRUPT BIT 6 = 1 1 0
      0 1 1 0 0 1 1        CORRECT BIT 6
M       1   0 1 1
```

Axioms and Specifications for the Hamming Coding Problem

Types and Notation

    i,j:integer
    x,y:bit
    M,T,X,Y:sequence of bits
    |M| denotes the "length of M"
    M[i] denotes accessing the ith element of M
    <...> denotes sequences
    M[i..j] denotes <M[i],..,M[j]>
    & denotes catenation (of sequences)

Axioms

    (1) Inv(T,i)[j]=if i=j then ~T[j] else T[j]
    (2) Decode(<>)=<>
    (3) Decode(T&<x>)=if PowerOf2(|T&<x>|) then Decode(T)
                                        else Decode(T)&<x>
    (4) Check(T)=BinaryToInteger(Sums(T))
    (5) BinaryToInteger(x) base 10 = x base 2
    (6) PowerOf2(i)="i is a power of 2"
    (7) |Sums(T)|="maximum power of 2 < |T|"
    (8) Reverse(Sums(T))[i]=psum(T,2**i)
    (9) psum(T,p)=sigma2(i,1≤i≤|T| and Coef(p,i)=1, T[i])
    (10) Coef(,i)="Coef of p in binary representation of i"
        e.g. Coef(1,5)=1, Coef(2,5)=0, Coef(4,5)=1.
    (11) sigma2(i, q(i), f(i))=
                "sum modulo 2 of all f(i) for which q(i)"
    (12) |Encode(M)|=|Expand(M)|
    (13) Forall p:1≤p≤|T| and PowerOf2(p):
                    psum(Encode(M),p)=0
    (14) Forall i:1≤i≤|T| and ~PowerOf2(i):
                    Encode(M)[i]=Expand(M)[i]
    (15) Expand(<>)=<>

(16) Expand(<x>)=<0,0,x>
(17) |M|>0 _implies_ Expand(M&<x>)=Expand(M)&
         (_if_ PowerOf2(|Expand(M)|+1) _then_ <0,x> _else_ <x>)

Requirements

   (A) Decode(Encode(M))=M
   (B) Check(Encode(M))=0
   (C) _Forall_ i:1$\leq$i$\leq$|Encode(M)|: Check(Inv(Encode(M),i))=i

Proof that Axioms implies Requirements

(A) Decode(Encode(M))=M
Lemma 1: |X|=|Y| _and_ _Forall_ i:1$\leq$i$\leq$|X| _and_ ~Powerof2(i) :
            X[i]=Y[i] _implies_Decode(X)=Decode(Y)
Proof by induction on |X|.
  Basis: |X|=0. Obvious.
  _Induction step._Assume for |X|=|Y|, proving it for |X|+1,
        consider X&<x>, Y&<y>,
   Case 1: Powerof2(|X&<x>|)
     Decode(X&<x>)=Decode(X) by axiom 3
       =Decode(Y)   by induction
       =Decode(Y&<y>)   by axiom 3
   Case 2: ~Powerof2(|X&<x>|)   **Exercise**
Therefore Decode(Encode(M))=Decode(Expand(M)) by axioms 14 and 12
so we will prove Decode(Expand(M))=M by induction on |M|.
  Basis: Decode(Expand(<>))=Decode(<>)=<> by axioms 12 and 15
  Induction Step: Assuming the theorem for M, prove it for M&<x>
    Case 1: |M|=0.
      Decode(Expand(<x>))=Decode(<0,0,x>)=<x>
           by axioms 16 and 3
    Case 2: |M|>0
      Decode(Expand(M&<x>))
        = Decode(Expand(M)&(_if_ Powerof2(|Expand(M)|+1)
                     then <0,x> _else_ <x>))
           by axiom 17
        = _if_ Powerof2(|Expand(M)|+1)
                  then Decode(Expand(M)&<0,x>)
                  else Decode(Expand(M)&<x>)
           by conditional expression manipulation
        = _if_ Powerof2(|Expand(M)|+1)
                  then Decode(Expand(M)&<0>)&<x>
                  else Decode(Expand(M))&<x>
          because |M|<|Expand(M)| (an easy lemma)
         and because 2$\leq$i _and_ Powerof2(i)
                     implies~Powerof2(i+1)
        =Decode(Expand(M))&<x>
          by axiom 17 and
             conditional expression manipulation
        =M&<x>   by induction
(B) By axiom 13, BinaryToInteger(Sums(Encode(M))=
                        BinaryToInteger(<0,...,0>)
                        =0 by axiom 5

SUSAN L. GERHART

(C) <u>Forall</u> i: 1 $\leq$i$\leq$|Encode(M)|: Check(Inv(Encode(M),i))=0.
Lemma: <u>Forall</u> p:1$\leq$p$\leq$|Encode(M)| <u>and</u> Powerof2(p):
$$psum(Inv(Encode(M),i),p)=Coef(p,i)$$
Proof: Recall psum(Encode(M),p)=0 by axiom 13.
    Let T denote Encode(M).
Case 1: Coef(p,i)=0
psum(Inv(T,i),p)=psum(T,p)=0 since T[i] is not included
in the sum.
Case 2: Coef(p,i)=1
psum(Inv(T,i),p)
=sigma2(j,1$\leq$j$\leq$$\neq$|T| <u>and</u> Coef(p,j)=1 <u>and</u> j$\neq$i, Inv(T,i)[j])
            Inv(T,i)[i]
=sigma2(j,1$\leq$j$\leq$|T| <u>and</u> Coef(p,j)=1 <u>and</u> j$\neq$i, T[j]) $\neq$ ~T[i]
= (0$\neq$T[i])$\neq$~T[i]
= 1
Therefore, Sums(Inv(T,i),p)=<...psum(T,4),psum(T,2),psum(T,1)>
                =<....Coef(4,i),Coef(2,i),Coef(1,i)>
and BinaryToInteger(Sums(Inv(T,i)))=i.

<u>Program Construction</u>
<u>procedure</u> Encode(M)
<u>Precondition</u> True
<u>PostCondition</u> T=Encode(M) as specified by axioms 12-14
Version 1:   Writing the program in the most direct way

```
            if "M is empty"
            then "make T empty"
            else
                    "Expand M into T"
                    "Fill in psums"
            fi
            assert T=Encode(M)
        if |M|=0 then T := <>
        else
            K := 2; T := <0,0,M[1]>;
            asserting ExpandedSofar(M,T,K-1)
            while K$\leq$|M| do
                if PowerOf2(|T|+1) then T := T&<0> fi;
                T := T&<M[K]>;   K := K+1
            od;
            assert T=Expand(M);
            P := 1;
            repeat
                T[P] := psum(T,P);   P := P*2
            asserting PowerOf2(P)
               and NonPowersOf2Unchanged(T,Expand(M))
               and LowerPowersOf2SumsOK(T,P)
               and UpperPowersOf2Zero(T,P)
            until P>|T|
        fi
        assert T=Encode(M)
```

PROGRAM VALIDATION

Notation
>ExpandedSofar(T,M,K)=2$\leq$K$\leq$|M|+1 <u>and</u> T=Expand(M[1..K-1])
>NonPowersOf2Unchanged(T,M) =
>>Forall i: 1$\leq$i$\leq$|T| <u>and</u> ~PowerOf2(i):T[i]=M[i]
>LowerPowersOf2SumsOK(T,P)=
>>Forall i: 1$\leq$i<P <u>and</u> PowerOf2(i): psum(T,i)=0
>UpperPowersOf2Zero(T,P)=
>>Forall i: P$\leq$i$\leq$|T| <u>and</u> PowerOf2(i): T[i]=0

The first loop assertion is easily proved using the axioms
and the second loop assertion requires the lemmas:
(1)   T[P]=0 <u>implies</u> psum(assign(T,P,psum(T,P)),P)=0
(2) <u>Forall</u> p:1$\leq$p<P <u>and</u> PowerOf2(p):
>>psum(T,p)=psum(assign(T,P,x),p)

Version 2a: Now we will refine the statement T[P] := psum(T,P).
Note that psum(T,P)=   ((psum(T[1..P-1],P)$\neq$psum(T[P..|T|],P))
and that psum(T[1...P-1],P)=0, thus justifying the program:

```
          for K from P to |T| do
              if "Coef of P in binary K is 1"
              then "add T[K] to ps" fi
      od
```

```
      PS := 0;   K := P;
      asserting ComputingPsum(T,K,P,PS)
      while K≤|T| do
          if Coef(P,K)=1 then PS := PS≠T[K] fi;
          K := K+1
      od
      assert PS=psum(T,P)
```
Notation   ComputingPsum(T,K,P,PS)=P$\leq$K$\leq$|T|+1
>>>>and PS=psum(T[1..K-1],P)

Version 2b: The following two transformations will change the loop
structure to eventually take advantage of the alternating cycles
of 0's and 1's.
--(Absorption into <u>if</u>)
>if B <u>then</u> S1 <u>fi</u>; S2 ==>   <u>if</u> B <u>then</u> S1;S2 <u>else</u> S2 <u>fi</u>

```
---------------------------------(Inner while loop addition)
      asserting A while B1 do
         if B2 then S1 else S2 fi
      od
==>
      asserting A while B1 do
         asserting A while B1 and B2 do S1 od;
         asserting A while B1 and ~B2 do S2 od
      od
  when  A and B1 implies (B2 is defined)
-----------------------------------------------
```

to give the program

```
            while K≤|T| do
               "add in T[K] while Coef of P
                                    in K is 1"
               "don't add in T[K] while Coef of P
                                    in K is 0"
          od
      PS := 0; K := P;
      asserting ComputingPsum(T,K,P,PS)
      while K≤|T| do
           asserting ComputingPsum(T,K,P,PS)
           while K≤|T| and Coef(P,K)=1 do
               PS := PS≠T[K]; K := K+1
           od;
           asserting ComputingPsum(T,K,P,PS)
           while K≤|T| and Coef(P,K)≠1 do
               K := K+1
           od
      od
```

Version 2c: The assertions can be augmented with some information
about the parity of K when divided by P with addition of the
variable SwitchParity:

```
      PS := 0; K := P;
      asserting ComputingPsum(T,K,P,PS) and
               (K≤|T| implies DividesOddly(P,K) )
      while K≤|T| do
           SwitchParity := K+P;
           asserting ComputingPsum(T,K,P,PS)
              and DividesEvenly(P,SwitchParity)
              and BetweenDivisorsOddly(P,K,SwitchParity)
           while K≤|T| and Coef(P,K)=1 do
               PS := PS≠T[K]; K := K+1
           od;
           SwitchParity := K+P
           asserting ComputingPsum(T,K,P,PS)
               and (K≤|T| implies  DividesOddly(P,SwitchParity)
               and BetweenDivisorsEvenly(P,K,SwitchParity))
```

```
            while K≤|T| and Coef(P,K)≠1 do
                 K := K+1
            od
      od
Notation
   DividesEvenly(P,K)= (P divides K) and Coef(P,K)=0
   DividesOddly(P,K)= (P divides K) and Coef(P,K)=1
   BetweenDivisorsEvenly(P,K,SwitchParity)=
          K≤SwitchParity  and Forall i:K≤i<SwitchParity:
                                        Coef(P,i)=0
   BetweenDivisorsOddly(P,K,SwitchParity)=
          K≤SwitchParity  and Forall i: K≤i<SwitchParity:
                                        Coef(P,i)=1
```

Version 2d: The transformation

```
---------------------------------------(while predicate change)
   asserting A while B do S od  ==>  asserting A while B' do S od
   when A implies B=B'
----------------------------------------------------------------
```

now permits replacing Coef(P,K)=1 by K<SwitchParity in
the test of the first loop. The second inner loop "collapses"
by the transformation

```
---------------------------------(Iterated operation reduction)
asserting A while B(K) do K:= K+1 od ==> K:= E(K)
when A implies K≤E(K) and (Forall i:K≤i <E(K):
                                   B(i)) and ~B(E(K))
----------------------------------------------------------------
```

to K:=Minimum(SwitchParity,|T|+1)
which further simplifies to K:=K+P
if the outer loop assertion is changed to
1≤P≤Kand EitherComputingOrHavePsum(T,K,P)

Notation   EitherComputingOrHavePsum(T,K,P,PS)=
          if K≤|T| then ComputingPsum(T,K,P,PS) else PS=psum(T,P)

This gives the final version of the second loop as

```
                while K≤|T| do
                    "add in to PS the next P elements of T"
                    "jump K over the next P elements of T"
                od
           PS := 0; K := P;
           asserting 1≤P≤K and EitherComputingOrHavePsum(T,K,P,PS)
                and (K≤|T| implies DividesOddly(P,K) )
           while K ≤|T| do
                SwitchParity := K+P;
                asserting ComputingPsum(T,K,P,PS)
                   and DividesEvenly(P,SwitchParity)
                   and BetweenDivisorsOddly(P,K,SwitchParity)
                while K≤|T|  and K<SwitchParity do
                   PS := PS ≠ T[K]; K := K+1
                od;
                K := K+P
      od
```

Version 3a: Consider the first loop, which "expands" M into T.
The transformation

```
----------------------------------------(inner loop repetition)
  P{asserting A while B1 do       P{asserting Aand(B1 implies B2)
      if B2 then S1 fi;    ==>        while B1 do
      S2;                                 S1;
   od                                    repeat
  }Q                                        S2
                                         asserting A
                                         until ~B1 or B2
                                      od
                                     }Q
  when P implies (B1 implies B2)
-----------------------------------------------------------------
(because the enabling condition is satisfied with |T|=3)
gives a  program that looks like it  computes differently
             while K≤|T| do
                 "catenate a 0 onto T"
                 "catenate a run from M onto T"
             od
      T := <0,0,M[1]>; K := 2
      asserting ExpandedSofar(M,T,K-1) and (K≤|M| implies
                                      PowerOf2(|T|+1))
      while K≤|M| do
          T := T&<0>;
          repeat
              T := T&<M[K]>;    K := K+1
          asserting ExpandedSofar(M,T,K-1)
          until K > |M| or PowerOf2(|T|+1)
      od
```

Version 3b: Now we want to avoid computing PowerOf2(|T|+1)
by keeping track of the successive powers of 2

```
      T := <0,0,M[1]>; K := 2;  P := 4;
      asserting ExpandedSofar(M,T,K-1) and (K≤|M| implies
                                      Powerof2(|T|+1))
              and PowerOf2(P) and 4≤|T|+1≤P
      while K≤|M| do
          T := T&<0>;    P := 2*P;
          repeat
              T := T&<M[K]>;       K := K+1
          asserting ExpandedSofar(M,T,K-1) and
                  PowerOf2(P) and 4≤|T|<P
          until K > |M| or PowerOf2(|T|+1)
      od
```

A similar transformation allows replacing PowerOf2(|T|+1)
by |T|=P-1

```
----------------------------------------(repeat predicate change)
```

repeat S asserting A until B ==> repeat S asserting A until B'
when A implies B=B'

Completed Program
```
        if |M|=0 then T := <>
        else
            Version 3b
            P := 1;
            repeat
                Version 2d
                T[P] := PS;      P := 2*P
            asserting PowerOf2(P)
                and NonPowersOf2Unchanged(T,Expand(M))
                and LowerPowersOf2SumsOK(T,P)
                and UpperPowersOf2Zero(T,P)
            until P>|T|
        fi
```

Exercise: (1) Find transformations, if possible, which simplify
the loop controlling expressions (a) K>|M| or |T|=P-1 (b) K≤|T|
and K<KP. (2) Is the program biased by the use of sequences as
its data structure? Reimplement the program using vectors as in
normal languages. (3) Write and prove programs which precompute
as much as possible, e.g. a table of powers of 2, then use them on
the final version above. (4) This program was developed with a
vague notion of optimality. Define a precise measure of
optimality and write (and prove) programs according to it. (5)
Implement Decode and Check. How similar are the implementations
and proofs to Encode? (6) The author is all too familiar with
fallibility in proofs and proved programs, see Gerhart and
Yelowitz (1976a). Find faults in this program, its assertions,
the proofs, or the transformations.

SUSAN L. GERHART

TESTING

Basic Concepts and Definitions

What is testing? Our first view is that testing a program is like performing an experiment on it: we must be able to infer a reasonable conclusion from the results we see. Of course, if an error is detected, it is obvious that further action is required. But if no errors appear from the test, we want to achieve a high confidence that indeed there are no remaining program faults. In our introductory section, we examined some naive criteria for selecting test data and explored their ability to detect errors. In this section, we will continue this exploration, formalizing some concepts as we go.

In the AllEqual example, we used three test data selection criteria. We had a notion of test data sets T "satisfying" criteria C, which we will hereafter write as C(T). The black box criterion was very imprecise, just "interesting" combinations. Other black box criteria might be to partition the input domain into subsets, selecting one element from each subset for the test data. The intuition is that the subsets are somehow equivalence classes: any selected representative will tell us whether the program is correct for the untested members of the class. There are other reasonable structural criteria. We might consider all paths of the program, every possible sequence of statements, and then select one piece of data to drive the program through each path. Of course, this criterion is almost never satisfiable in practice - there are simply too many paths. The elementary iteration criterion is one restriction of this approach, although the limit on number of iterations can usually be lifted to at least two. A simple restriction is to require only **exercising all statements** at least once. In fact, this is popularly considered a "minimally thorough" test. It shows that at least there is no statement in the program which would always cause an error. But what about **if** B **then** S **fi** when B is false? Another criterion is **exercising every branch** in every possible direction; even though it causes no extra statements to be exercised, it generates more paths than the statement exercising criterion. These are typical of the test data selection criteria explored in the literature. We will now try to formalize desirable, but perhaps unattainable, properties of such criteria which would give us highly conclusive evidence about correctness based on successful execution of selected data.

Given program G, with its input domain D, denote ok(d), for d in D, as meaning that G executes properly for d and then OK(T), for T a subset of D, as meaning ok(d), for all d in T. An ideal test data selection criterion would tell us from OK(T) that OK(D), where T is some subset of D. Let us try to constrain C to make this possible. We can easily see that

$$(\underline{Forall}\ T: T \text{ a subset of } D: OK(T))\ \underline{implies}\ OK(D)$$

or equivalently that

$$\text{\textasciitilde}OK(D)\ \underline{implies}\ (\underline{ThereExists}\ T: T \text{ subset of } D: \text{\textasciitilde}OK(T)).$$

Since we want C to select one of the error-revealing subsets, we require the **validity** property

$$\text{\textasciitilde}OK(D)\ \underline{implies}\ (\underline{ThereExists}\ T: T \text{ subset of } D: C(T)\ \underline{and}\ \text{\textasciitilde}OK(T)).$$

But this is not sufficient, because we might select T1 and T2 such that OK(T1) but not OK(T2), so we need an associated **reliability** property

$$(\underline{Forall}\ T1, T2: T1, T2 \text{ subsets of } D:$$
$$C(T1)\ \underline{and}\ C(T2)\ \underline{implies}\ (OK(T1){=}OK(T2))).$$

That is, any set selected by C must be just as good as any other selected set at revealing the correctness of G.

Let's explore these properties by stating some facts:

1. If C(T) is (T={}), i.e. "don't select any test data", then proving validity of C is equivalent to the task of proving correctness.

2. If C(T) is (T=D), then the situation is one of **exhaustive testing**, and C is both valid and reliable. In general, if there is no freedom in selecting T, then reliability is guaranteed, but all the work goes into validity.

3. If the program is correct, i.e. OK(D), then any criterion is valid and reliable, though we don't know that without proof.

4. If C is not reliable, then it must be valid, or equivalently, an invalid criterion is reliable. This is because to be unreliable, there must be a T such that ~OK(T); hence validity follows.

5. If any d in D can be selected in some T, then the criterion is automatically valid.

These criterion properties are not expected to often be usable directly in testing, but they are very useful for evaluating criteria like those proposed above. For example, unrestricted black box criteria are valid, but reliability requires examining the program and arguing that no different selection of data would give a different result. The elementary iteration criterion is not automatically valid, because it excludes data which forces loop iterations more than the limit. The other structural criteria are valid, but tend to lose validity if some minimization of amount of data is sought. It should be clear that reliability is usually the harder property to achieve in practice. Indeed it summarizes the dilemma of testing: how do you know that selecting other data would not give different results?

Consider again the **AllEqual** example and Figure 1. For faulty program B and criterion EI the loop must go more than once to show up errors. For the other faulty programs, there is some anomaly in the way the test data group together for selection. For example, in faulty program C it seems unlikely that **aa** and **ab** can both cause loop iteration 0 times, because the program can't look at the elements. For criterion PC, in faulty program A we could miss picking an all-a string that would cause a subscript error. Notice that there is a fairly low chance (like 1 out of 8) for picking the right data for B if we only satisfy the criterion minimally. In this example, the black box criterion works well because it forces selection of many combinations.

Exercise: Examine Figure 1b carefully and figure out why each of the properties hold or do not hold for each faulty program.

From this little experiment, we might reach the following conclusions:

1. Blindly selecting data that satisfies a criterion, executing the program, and then observing its correctness on that data is obviously insufficient for concluding correctness. But how close can a criterion come if testing is performed this way?

2. The validity/reliability properties provide one measurement for quality of selected data. The tester can simply ask the questions: Is there any bias that prevents selection of some datum? If so, is there any reason to believe that an error can be revealed by the unselected datum that would not also be revealed by some datum eligible for selection. Is there any reason to believe that selecting some other data than that used for execution would produce different results? The answers can only be given informally by inspection of the program, but at least inspection is both forced and guided.

3. Just examining more data than that actually used in the test execution could reveal errors. If two pieces of data with diverse, obviously inequivalent characteristics both satisfy the criteria, there is reason to suspect the results of the test.

4. As we argued earlier, it is possible to base an induction proof on the results of test execution. While such proofs may be hard to devise, even an incomplete attempt could lead to fault detection.

5. Structural criteria are simply too weak, too easily satisfied, to justify much confidence. Of course, in larger programs they may work better, because to get the criterion satisfied in several parts of the program may invoke quite intricate combinations of conditions. The criteria get better when multiple cases satisfying the criteria are examined for plausibility.

6. Unbiased by knowledge of the program, black box criteria may force selection of more data with diverse characteristics of the problem. Of course, this is clearly insufficient alone. Suppose some datum is "shunted" along a special path. Black box criteria can't know this so can't claim anything about this datum.

7. The above arguments lead us to the overall conclusion that some mixture of black box and structural criteria are necessary, especially if no induction arguments are given.

Methods of Program Testing

We haven't yet exhausted the range of possible activities that might be considered as testing. For example, we looked at how various criteria fared on faulty programs. Suppose this idea were applied to a single program with a given set of test data. If a fault were introduced and that faulty program ran just as well, then we might conclude one of three possibilities: (1) the "fault" really wasn't one at all, but instead it simply generated an equivalent program (consider replacing i:=2 by i:=1 in the AllEqual program); (2) the test data really wasn't very good because it wasn't capable of revealing some errors and therefore another round of selection is in order; or (3) it wasn't really clear what the right answers should be or there was an error in judging whether answers were right or wrong. This **program mutation** approach might be used for serious testing although it would only be possible to sample a few of all the possible faults that could be introduced or it might be used to build intuition about selecting test data.

We have mentioned the use of **anomaly** testing previously. In fact, there are many faults which are not at all subtle, but can easily be seen to cause strange looking control and data flows. Other anomalies are variables which are set, but never can be used, or used, but never set. Sometimes, faults will make some section of code unreachable. Many of these suspicious situations may be detected by **static testing**, applying various flow analysis techniques (similar to those used in compilers) to the text of the program. Of course, many such faults are tied to weak language features, which may be designed away in new languages or avoided by conventions.

While we have been arguing by inspection that certain statements are executed by certain test data, there exist many ways of monitoring execution. Statements may be inserted by the user, by the compiler, or by a separate program preprocessor which provide trace kinds of information. Or an interpreter may accomplish the same task. An assertion language has also been developed for the programmer to express such useful information as ranges and values of variables which are then checked dynamically. Of course, such an approach changes the resource utilization characteristics of the program. It is tools such as these that have prompted our evaluation of structural criteria. It is usually possible to determine whether such criteria are met by monitoring, but the more important question is how conclusive such criteria can be.

Associated with these tools and techniques for evaluating coverage of programs by testing, i.e. the extent to which parts have been exercised, are various test data generation strategies. Suppose some statement has not been exercised by some prior test. That statement may be unreachable or it may be that the data just didn't force a path through it. It is frequently possible to derive expressions for paths leading to the statement, which may then be "solved" for new test data.

One more approach that is really quite close to proving is symbolic execution. Rather than execute the program on actual data, symbolic data is used, thus, in a sense, extending the reliability of the testing. Each path of the program is pursued in the form of an expression accumulating all the branch conditions and results of assignments along the way. For example, one path for **AllEqual** would look like

$$i.1=2 \text{ and } AllEqual.1=true \text{ and } (AllEqual.1 \text{ and } i.1 \leq n) \text{ and}$$
$$AllEqual.2=(S(1)=S(i.1)) \text{ and } i.2=i.1+1 \text{ and}$$
$$\sim(AllEqual.2 \text{ and } i.2 \leq n) \text{ which reduces to}$$
$$2 \leq n \text{ and } AllEqual=(S(1)=S(i)) \text{ and } (\sim AllEqual \text{ or } i > n).$$

Such a technique is like "desk checking", only tools are now available to do the bookkeeping and some of the expression simplification. This approach forces detailed inspection of the program by the user, but its effectiveness is somewhat dependent on a formula manipulator and theorem prover, such as those used in proving. While reliability is increased, validity is still a problem when loops must be traversed many times to expose an error. Carried to its extreme, loops may be reduced in terms of invariant assertions and the technique is equivalent to proving.

Finally, we might consider a probabilistic approach to selecting test data. Suppose there are some ranges of the input data which are expected to be executed far more frequently than others. The testing effort may be concentrated on this frequent data, thus giving a kind of probabilistic argument for correctness.

Testing the Hamming Encoder

Consider the "completed" program. We certainly would want to test with $|M|=0$ and $|M|=1$. $|M|=0$ forces while $K \leq |M|$ 0 times, repeat ... until $P > |T|$ twice, while $K \leq |T|$ 1 time (twice) and while $K \leq |T|$ and $K < SwitchParity$ 1 time (twice). We already see problems with the EI criterion, since the while loop could be a repeat loop. Going on with $|M|=2$, we see that loops are exercised in a greater variety of ways, but that predicate $|T|=P-1$ never becomes true (and so could be missing in a faulty program). Following PC requires $|T|$ to reach 7 so $|M|$ must be at least 4 to make this occur.

Exercise: Do a complete analysis of this program for criteria PC and EI. Either arbitrarily select data and see how well it exercises the program or select data specifically to exercise according to these criteria.

Considering a more black box approach, it would be appealing to see all the possible bit combinations for some $|M|$. Suppose we took $|M|=5$. We might write a **test driver** which looked like

```
for i:=0 to 31 do
    Convert i to a 5 bit string M
    Do Encode on M and print the result T
    Do Decode on T and print the result M'
    Randomly invert one bit j to give T' and do Check on T',
                    printing the result j'
```

We certainly would not want to manually enter 32 separate bit strings, if it could possibly be avoided. However, it is usually easy to write some such program in which the program to be tested is either a procedure or statement. Such extensive testing is not prohibitively expensive and serves to really exercise the program, as would be shown by some monitoring information.

What would have been tested by this data and driver? It would have been shown that M was distributed into T in the right way, i.e. subscripts were computed correctly. Notice that control flow does not vary for any message of the same length, so basically all combinations of summing have been performed, i.e. again subscripts were computed correctly. This checks both the program and the underlying mathematics. So we have a kind of induction argument: we believe from testing $|M|=0,1,2,5$ that the program will work properly with respect to message length. But, since we have tested all possible bit combinations for a single length (a "long" one such as 5), we also believe the program will work for all bit combinations for any length. Thus we have a double induction, length and content.

Exercise: (1) Try to shoot down the above testing strategy and argument. Keep the same statement structure, but vary any of the expressions and see whether the test data will fail to detect the fault. Then try omitting each of the assignment statements and see if their loss is detectable. (2) One of the difficulties of testing the above program is its complex, nested loop structure. We showed in our transformational derivation that this program is really equivalent to one with a much simpler loop structure. Try testing the simpler program. Compare the test data and induction arguments. (3) Test the psum and Expand loops separately and extensively. Combine the test results with some argument about the whole program.

COMBINED METHODS

The Testing vs. Proving Paradox

In the previous two sections we have examined both testing and proving from a rather elementary and intuitive viewpoint. In this section, we will concentrate more on the theory and practice as it appears in the literature. There's a paradox which rapidly appears. While there are hundreds of papers on testing tools, there are only a handful of papers with really interesting theoretical results and sound experiments evaluating the tools, starting only in the mid 1970's. On the other hand, there are hundreds of papers on the basic theory and techniques of proving, but only a handful of really interesting proved programs in these papers. Isn't it strange that such a widely practiced and exorbitantly expensive practice as testing has received so little scientific attention while such a scientifically grounded subject as proving has been applied so little? We'll re-examine this paradox at the end of this section.

A Survey of Proving Theory and Practice

Unlike testing, the theory behind proving dates back to the late 1960's, Floyd (1967) and King (1969). The inductive assertion method is readily accepted intuitively, once understood, although there are many variants which have developed, e.g. intermittent assertions of Manna and Waldinger (1978), originally described in Burstall (1974). The rule and axiom formulation was adapted from the ideas of Floyd by Hoare (1969), later followed by the predicate transformer notation in Dijkstra (1976). The schema and transformation ideas used in the Hamming Code example are described in Gerhart (1976) and Gerhart and Yelowitz (1976b). Bauer (1976) and Burstall and Darlington (1977) discuss various techniques for transforming recursive programs and from recursive to iterative forms. The transformation paradigm is being widely pursued; its potential effect as an implementation technique is well described in Balzer, Goldman, and Wile (1976).

The invariant assertion method is inherently independent of the actual control structures of the language (whatever these are, every loop must have an assertion) and the data structures of the language (these appear in verification conditions by substitution from assignment and from expressions controlling looping and branching). With respect to data structures, there has been considerable progress over the past few years in the use of **algebraic axioms**, e.g. see Guttag, Horowitz, and Musser (1976), and other language devices, e.g. see Wulf, London, and Shaw (1976), as instances of the more general concept of an **abstract data type**, which defines the combined effects of operations on a data structure, independent of its implementation. For example, a stack may be implemented in a vector or a linked list, but pop, push, top, etc. always mean the same thing. As discussed elsewhere in this volume, proof rules have been used as a guide in the design of new languages to control some constructs which complicate or foil proofs and algebraic axioms have emerged as a tool for specification, not just of standard data structures but also of specialized user functions.

Good surveys of the techniques and theory of proving are London (1977, 1978) and Luckham (1977). These describe again the invariant assertion method, with examples, and the structure and implementations status of mechanical verification systems. Roughly, such a system contains a parser and verification condition generator for the subject language, a simplifier to deal with the frequent expressions of the form a+0 and the propositional calculus type of logic, and more sophisticated theorem provers which contain strategies for finding proofs. Usually, at least the theorem prover component is highly interactive, expecting the user to suggest strategies, terminate exploration of unpromising paths, and transfuse knowledge about the real world, sophisticated mathematics, and programming. Another approach is that of Boyer and Moore (1975) where the theorem prover is expected to even obtain the inductive statements, but may be "trained" up to this point with lemmas for subcases or similar cases. It is not expected that there will be any system which can fully and independently prove many verification conditions within the next decade or so; mechanical theorem proving is a very hard problem. But a large amount of simple logical and algebraic reduction can be handled mechanically, and such systems can be made comfortable for users to interact with.

There has been, as yet, little direct use of proving in validation. Carter et al (1977) describes a system for verifying microprograms which is being seriously used and has revealed previously unknown faults in microprograms. The Texas GYPSY System, Good (1977), is directed toward large network systems. Likewise, its users have revealed flaws, primarily through formal specification in preparation for verification. Many papers in the literature contain (over and over again) proofs of simple programs, e.g. greatest common divisor. Dijkstra (1976) uses invariants as guides in developing some rather complex algorithms, but complete proofs are not given. Undoubtedly, proving is being used informally and tentatively, but it has not reached wide-scale usage. The difficulty seems to be analogous to opening a mathematics text, reading the definitions and axioms in the first chapter, then turning to the difficult exercises in the last chapters of the book. Any mathematical theory progresses from elementary concepts, through intermediate concepts, theorems, and techniques, to very highly structured concepts and theorems, all the while developing good definitions, notation, and techniques. In program proving, however, actual programs incorporate a mixture of complex concepts, such as those of data structures and algorithms, for which there is not yet any intermediate formalization, theorems, and techniques. It should be no surprise that program proving in practice is very difficult if the supporting theory is not yet well developed. A broad discussion of prospects, issues, and problems appears in Gerhart (1978).

Information Sciences Institute has two ongoing efforts in practical proving. One is the proof of data security properties of a kernel of an operating system, modelled after Popek and Farber (1978), carried out by UCLA graduate students using the ISI verification system. This requires a formal specification of the basic normal functions of an operating system, e.g. paging and input/output, which have never previously been formally stated in a form appropriate for proving. The kernel is being structured and re-structured to make proving easier. The other project is a module of over 1000 lines from a message system. The module's purpose is to allow several users to simultaneously update a file, which it accomplishes by outputting a list of changes the user has made to a private copy of the file and then later merging these with the system copy. The task has been specified in a few pages of algebraic axioms, from which the critical theorems will be proved and then abstracted versions of the given program will be proved to implement the functions so axiomatized (much as our Hamming code example). Both of these efforts are somewhat experimental, intended to force development of new techniques, solidify old ones, and demonstrate feasibility, along with complexity, of proving on real-world problems. At least the operating system problem is considered validation in the certification sense and the proof effort has already revealed a fault which could have led to a security breach. Both programs, when proved, will have a high carry-over of techniques and knowledge for future operating system and data base verifications.

Owicki and Gries (1976) give axioms for parallel programs which involve resource invariants and auxiliary variables for recording state and history information. This and other papers are providing a foundation for reasoning about all the problems inherent in non-sequential programming - mutual exclusion, deadlock, termination, priority, progress, scheduling, etc. The complexity of this class of problems makes testing almost impossible (there are so many combinations of possible interactions and the static structure of the program reflects so little about the computations), leaving proving as the only design and validation technique.

A Survey of Testing Theory and Practice

The theory of testing which we have been applying to various criteria originated in Goodenough and Gerhart (1975) and has been pursued independently and further by Howden (1976). Howden has analysed several testing strategies by formalizing their capabilities for detecting errors, i.e. their reliability, in the form of several theorems which look like "if the program being tested has property X compared with a correct version of the program, then selecting test data T can (will) reveal an error". Graph theory has been widely used for analyzing the sequence of data and control flow to find anomalies and paths. It is easy to show that just about any question about program flow, such as "Is this statement reachable?" is undecidable, clarifying some of the limitations of static analysis methods, e.g. see Fairley (1978).

The alternative program testing methods are discussed for example, but not only, in (program mutation) DeMillo, Lipton, and Sayward (1978), (anomaly testing) Fosdick and Osterweil (1976), (static testing) Fairley (1978), (path analysis and monitoring) Huang (1978), (monitoring and assertions) Stucki (1977), (symbolic execution) Darringer and King (1978) and Hantler and King (1976), (test data generation) Miller and Melton (1975). While there are no text books as such on testing, the tutorial Miller (1977a) contains reprints of many of the most useful testing papers, along with useful analyses and syntheses. Another comprehensive paper is Miller (1977b).

Beyond the elementary testing principles we have been discussing are various complex questions, such as system testing, and related management issues. Bottom-up testing consists of testing first very small units in a test harness of drivers, then combining these for further testing with the other units with which they interact, continuing until the entire system is linked together for testing. Top-down testing consists of testing the top-most routines using dummy modules for lower level routines, then inserting and testing these lower routines, again continuing until the entire system is linked together for testing. Of course, where these methods break down, e.g. inability to find suitable dummy modules or top-level data, a **mixed testing** approach is in order. See Fairley (1978) for a brief discussion of these issues.

There is always the question in any organization of who does the testing and how much they interact with developers. For example, does the programmer who codes also design test data or is this done by a completely separate individual or group? Personal friction is bound to occur in the case of **independent verifiers**, which can either hinder or help the validation effort. Economics is always of great importance in testing since there is currently no way of knowing when to stop testing (except when the money runs out or the due date is reached). Testing is a repetitive process - when an error is found and fixed, at least some of the testing must be repeated. This **regression testing** becomes expensive in computer time, while other design of test strategies, selection of test data, and evaluation of results is highly labor-intensive. The literature does not show a very coherent picture of how these management functions are actually performed, sometimes because the information is proprietary and other times because it is so highly linked with overall management procedures as to be difficult to explain. Suffice it to say, each organization probably has its own procedures developed over the years which operate reasonably well, even if there are no standard procedures. Many of these issues are covered in Goodenough (1977, 1978). Another management topic of recent concern is **quality assurance** based on the process, not just the product, of programming.

Although there are many tools and techniques for testing, there has been remarkably little experimentation with exactly how well these work in practice. Howden (1978) has compared several testing strategies on the faulty programs in the programming style book by Kernighan and Plauger (1974), for the purpose of both evaluation and generation of theoretical questions. The results were that 28 programs existence of errors could be caught as follows: path 18, branch 6, elementary iteration 12, symbolic execution 17, anomaly 4, assertions 7, overall 25. Thus no testing procedure worked very well, but further analysis showed different types of errors caught by different techniques, suggesting that at least more than one should be used. In another experiment, Hetzel (1976) compared (1) reading programs according to a prescribed procedure, (2) selecting test data from specifications alone, and (3) selecting test data for statement exercising coverage. The results were overall detection of 50% of the errors, with method (1) being distinctly inferior to (2) and (3) which were about equally effective. The conclusion was that the statement exercising criterion was not particularly helpful.

PROGRAM VALIDATION

The Paradox Re-visited -- Combined Methods

The only rational conclusion we can draw from our own analyses of testing and proving and from the surveys of other research are that both testing and proving must be pursued in research and practice. While it is hard to deny that testing has been effective (as the only used method) in previously validating programs, it still lacks sufficient supporting theory and experimental validation to warrant the kind of confidence we responsibly need to validate software of increasing complexity and social importance. While proving appears to have the supporting theory, it has not yet been practiced sufficiently to be experimentally validated and justify the same confidence. So what do we do when we have two insufficient methods? We try to combine the two to offset the weaknesses of one with the strengths of the other, if we know them. We might consider trying to perfect one (identify and remove its weaknesses) and then use it in practice exclusively and with extreme effort, as testing now requires and proving would certainly require. Or we might consider using both in moderation, following the principle of redundancy in fault tolerance. Or we might use, on the same job, proving in those places where it works best, and testing where it works best, again if we knew where these places were.

There is good reason to believe that testing and proving are complementary in their validation capabilities. Consider the thinking processes involved in each.

1. Testing is an increasingly affirmative process: the program can be observed correct on more and more data, but it cannot, unless accompanied by an induction argument, say more than that. Proving is a reductive process: if the verification conditions can be proved, and if the semantics associated with producing them are right, then the program is correct.

2. Testing is concrete: the actual program and actual data are used and the real behavior is observed. Proving is abstract: the general characteristics of the specifications, algorithms, data structures, etc. can be observed. Proving gives the "big picture" in rough detail; testing gives the fine detail but not necessarily the big picture.

3. Testing focuses on individual cases, showing their exact outputs and sometimes some intermediate behavior. Proving focuses on the overall formulation, independent of individual cases. Testing is likely to be accurate for what it says about individual d_i, but it really says little about the rest of D. Proving makes statements about all of D, but may fail for some d_i in D.

4. Testing tests the specifications by actual exhibition of behavior. Proving tests the specifications by consistency. Both can reveal inconsistencies and incompletenesses, but in different ways.

5. Testing is likely to miss faults which make the program nearly always correct (in a probabilistic sense), while proving is likely to miss gross faults, such as subscripts off by 1. Proving can provide guidance about how to correct faults, while testing can very precisely pinpoint problems.

6. Testing is less sensitive to unesthetic program constructions, which may throw up red flags of suspicion. Proving is likely to reject such constructions as too cumbersome for assertions.

7. Testing can reveal some language anomalies that proving, using a possibly simpler or inaccurate representation of actual semantics, could miss. Proving, having at least some semantic representation available, is likely to reveal faults associated with deep language flaws, such as aliasing, that no testing criterion can yet address.

An interesting theoretical question is whether there are precise proof techniques which might be described as either **testing-based proving** or **proving-based testing**. The former might be like our induction arguments in testing while the latter might appear like Howden's theorems.

A Possible Future for Program Validation

Overall, it may be appropriate to start raising the standards of testing and lowering the standards for proving. Testing strategies that fail too often should be revealed and ruled out. Some type of induction argument should accompany testing, whether in the form of an invariant assertion or one of reliability/validity investigations or some other method. Proving need not be a highly formal activity, complete with mechanical theorem proving. Skilled program provers can convince themselves, and others, with a mental argument that the invariant assertion method is used appropriately, i.e. that all assertions are sufficient. But, as we have argued, proving is not yet a widespread skill, nor will it ever be within the range of skills for some programmers. Testing can be practiced by almost anyone, but tools and techniques must be carefully scrutinized before lesser skilled programmers become too fluent with and trusting in them.

Proving can normally be used without undue complexity at the highest level of program development, where it works most easily, as a guide to proper development. In that way, errors can be detected earlier and some faults avoided. Testing may continue to apply much as it does today, but would be more cost-effective and convincing if there are fewer faults to contend with. For example, much of the expense of testing comes from repetition after detection and correction of faults, but that expense can be shifted to the earlier use of proving.

Proving has the important benefit, which testing completely lacks, of providing knowledge which carries over from one program development to the next. Data structure abstractions, schemas and transformations like those we have discussed can be packaged as transferable knowledge in books, papers, and handbooks, thus avoiding repetitive reprogramming which is both costly and error-prone. Carried to its extreme, this suggests the development of more software components, each of which can be carefully developed and thoroughly validated, shifting the program development process up some levels. Testing does not increase programming knowledge; proving does.

REFERENCES

Balzer, R., Goldman, N., and Wile, D. (1976). On the Transformational Implementation Approach to Programming. 2nd International Conference on Software Engineering, San Francisco, Ca, pp. 337-344.

Bauer, F.L. (1976). Programming as an Evolutionary Process. 2nd International Conference on Software Engineering, San Francisco, Ca, pp. 223-233.

Boyer, R.S. and Moore, J.S. (1975). Proving Theorems about LISP Functions. J.ACM, 22, 1, pp. 129-144.

Burstall, R.W. (1974). Program Proving as Hand Simulation with a Little Induction. Information Processing 74, pp. 208-312.

Burstall, R.W. and Darlington, J. (1977). A Transformation System for Developing Recursive Programs, J.ACM, 24, 1, pp. 44-67.

Carter, W.C., Ellozy, H.A., Joyner, W.H., Jr., and Leeman, G.B. Jr. (1977). Techniques for Microprogram Validation. IBM T.J.Watson Research Center Report RC6361.

Darringer, J.A. and King, J.C. (1978). Applications of Symbolic Execution to Program Testing. Computer, 11, no. 4, pp. 51-63.

DeMillo, R.A., Lipton, R.J. and Sayward, F.G. (1978). Hints on Test Data Selection: Help for the Practicing Programmer. Computer, 11, no. 4, pp. 34-43.

Dijkstra, E.W. (1974). Programming as a Discipline of a Mathematical Nature. American Mathematical Monthly June 1974. Also Computers and People October 1974.

Dijkstra, E.W. (1976). A Discipline of Programming. Prentice-Hall.

Fairley, R.E. (1978). Tutorial: Static Analysis and Dynamic Testing of Computer Software. Computer, 11, no. 4, pp. 14-24.

Floyd, R.W. (1967). Assigning Meanings to Programs. In Symposium in Applied Mathematics, ed. J.T. Schwartz, pp. 19-32, Volume 19, American Mathematics Society.

Fosdick, L.D. and Osterweil, L.J. (1976). Data Flow Analysis in Software Reliability. Computing Surveys, 8, no. 3, pp. 305-330.

Gerhart, S.L. (1976). Proof Theory of Partial Correctness Verification Systems. SIAM J. Computing, 5, no. 3, pp. 355-377.

Gerhart, S.L. (1978). Program Verification in the 1978's. Oregon Report on Computing. Also, ISI Research Report 78-71.

Gerhart, S.L. and Yelowitz, L. (1976a). Observations of Fallibility in Applications of Modern Programming Methodologies. IEEE Transactions on Software Engineering, 2, no. 3, pp. 195-207.

Gerhart, S.L. and Yelowitz, L. (1976b). Control Structure Abstractions of the Backtracking Programming Technique. IEEE Transactions on Software Engineering, 2, no. 4, pp. 285-292.

Good, D.I. (1977). Constructing Verifiably Reliable and Secure Communications Systems. Technical Report, Institute for Computing Science and Computer Applications, University of Texas, Austin Texas.

Goodenough, J.B. and Gerhart, S.L. (1975, 1977). Toward a Theory of Test Data Selection. IEEE Transactions on Software Engineering, 1, no. 3, pp. 156-173. Revised in Current Trends in Programming Methodology, Volume II, ed. R.T. Yeh, Prentice-Hall.

Goodenough, J.B. (1977, 1978). A Survey of Program Testing Issues. In Infotech State of the Art Report: Software Reliability. Infotech International Limited, pp. 183-216. Also to appear in Research Directions in Software Technology, ed. P. Wegner, MIT Press, 1978.

Guttag, J., Horowitz, E. and Musser, D. (1976). Abstract Data Types and Software Validation. USC Information Sciences Institute Technical Report ISI/RR-76-48,

Hamming, R.W. (1950). Error Detecting and Correcting Codes.

BTSJ, 29, pp. 147-160.

Hantler, S.L. and King, J.C. (1976). An Introduction to Proving the Correctness of Programs. Computing Surveys, 8, no. 3, pp. 331-353.

Hetzel, W.C. (1976). An Experimental Analysis of Program Verification Methods. Ph.D. Thesis, Computer Science Department, University of North Carolina at Chapel Hill.

Hoare, C.A.R. (1969). An Axiomatic Basis for Computer Programming. C.ACM, 12, no. 10, pp. 576-580 and 583.

Howden, W.E. (1976). Reliability of the Path Analysis Testing Strategy. IEEE Transactions on Software Engineering, 2, no. 3, pp. 208-214.

Howden, W.E. (1978). Theoretical and Empirical Studies of Program Testing. IEEE Transactions on Software Engineering, 4, no. 4, pp. 293-297.

Huang, J.C. (1978). Program Instrumentation and Software Testing. Computer, 11, no. 4, pp. 25-33.

Kernighan, B. and Plauger, P.J. (1974). The Elements of Programming Style. McGraw Hill.

King, J.C. (1969). A Program Verifier. Ph.D. thesis, Carnegie-Mellon University.

London, R.L. (1977). Perspectives on Program Verification. In Current Trends in Programming Methodology, Volume II, ed. R.T. Yeh, Prentice-Hall, pp. 151-172.

London, R.L. (1978). Program Verification. In Research Directions in Software Technology, ed. P. Wegner, (to appear) MIT Press.

Luckham, D.C. (1977). Program Verification and Verification Oriented Programming. IFIP Congress 77, ed. B. Gilchrist, North-Holland, pp. 783-793.

Manna, Z. and Waldinger, R.J. (1978). Is 'sometime' sometimes better than 'always'? Intermittent Assertions in Proving Program Correctness. C.ACM, 21, no. 2, pp. 159-171.

Miller, E.F., Jr. (1977a). Tutorial on Program Testing Techniques. IEEE Computer Society, Long Beach, Ca.

Miller, E.F., Jr. (1977b). Program Testing: Art Meets Theory. Computer, 10, no. 7, pp. 42-51.

Miller, E.F., Jr. and Melton, R.A. (1975). Automated Generation of Testcase Datasets. 1975 International Conference on

SUSAN L. GERHART

Reliable Software, Los Angeles, Ca., pp. 51-58.

Owicki, S. and Gries, D. (1976). Verifying Properties of Parallel Programs: An Axiomatic Approach. C.ACM, 19, no. 5, pp 279-285.

Popek, G.J. and Farber, D.A. (1978). A Model for Verification of Data Security in Operating Systems. (to appear, C.ACM), Computer Science Department, University of California at Los Angeles.

Stucki, L.G. (1977). New Directions in Automated Tools for Improving Software Quality. In Current Trends in Programming Methodology, Volume II, ed. R.T. Yeh, Prentice-Hall, pp. 80-111.

Wulf, W.A., London, R.L., and Shaw, M. (1976). An Introduction to the Construction and Verification of Alphard Programs. IEEE Transactions on Software Engineering, 2, no. 4, pp. 253-265.

PROGRAM VALIDATION

Input Domain D: Vector S of length n
Output: **AllEqual**=[forall i: 2≤i≤n: S(1)=S(i)]

<u>Program G</u>
```
      i:=2;                              (i)
      AllEqual:=true;                    (ii)
      while AllEqual and i≤n do          (iii)
              AllEqual:=S(1)=S(i);
              i:=i+1
      od
```
                     Figure 1a. Example Program

<u>Test Data Selection Criteria</u>
BB: Combinations of two elements, a and b, n≤3
EI: Cause iteration of the <u>while</u> loop 0 times and 1 times
PC: Combinations of predicates in the <u>while</u> loop: TT,TF,FT,FF

<u>Data Selected for G by these criteria</u>
Denote [] by 0, [a] by a, [a,b] by ab,[a,b,a] by aba, etc.
Let A x B mean a set with one element selected from A,
one selected from B, wherever this is possible.
For example, {a,b} x {c,d} is one of {a,c},{a,d}, {b,c}, {b,d}.

BB: {0,a,aa,ab,aaa,aab,aba,abb}
EI: {0,a} x {aa,ab,aba,abb}
PC: {aa,ab,aaa,aab,aba,abb} x {0,a,aa,aaa} x {aba,abb} x {ab,aab}
        TT   TF   FT   FF

                Figure 1b. Criteria and Selected Data

Name	Line	Old Part	New Part	Detecting Data
(A)	(iii)	AllEqual _and_ i≤n	AllEqual	0,a,aa,aaa
(B)	(iii)	AllEqual _and_ i≤n	i≤n	aba
(C)	(iii)	AllEqual _and_ i≤n	AllEqual _and_ i<n	ab,aab
(D)	(i)	i:=2	i:=3	ab,aba
(E)	(ii)	AllEqual:=true	AllEqual:=false	0,a,aa,aaa

Figure 1c. Faulty Programs and Error-revealing data

BB: Same as above, {0,...,abb}   Valid and Reliable
EI:
A {} x {ab,aba,abb}   Not Valid, but Reliable
B {0,a} x {aa,ab}   Not Valid, but Reliable
C {0,a,aa,ab} x {aaa,aab,aba,abb}   Valid, not Reliable
D {0,a,aa,ab} x {aaa,aab,aba,abb}   Valid, not Reliable
E {0,...,abb} x {}   Valid, not Reliable

PC:
A {0,...,abb} x {ab,aab,aba,abb}   Valid, not Reliable
B {ab,aaa,aab,aba,abb} x {0,...,abb}   Valid, not Reliable
C {aaa,aab,aba,abb} x {0,a,aa,ab,aaa,aab}   Valid, not Reliable
  x {} x {aba,abb}
D {aaa,aab,aba,abb} x {0,a,aa,ab,aaa,aba}   Valid, not Reliable
  x {} x {aab,abb}
E {} x {} x {aab,aba,abb} x {0,a}   Valid, Reliable

Figure 1d. Test Data Selected for Program A-E

Figure 1. AllEqual Example with Test Data

4
PROGRAMMING LANGUAGES

J. J. Horning

Xerox Palo Alto Research Center

THE RELIABILITY OF THE PROGRAMMING PROCESS

Introduction

This book is about the development of reliable computing systems that include software components. Many different approaches to obtaining reliability are being considered; they all have in common the need for (at least) nearly-correct programs. The experience of the last thirty years shows that it is generally not easy to produce such programs. This leads us to consider the programming process itself as a major source of difficulty in the development of reliable systems.

It is the goal of *reliable programming* to minimize the number of faults in completed programs. This may involve reducing the number of faults introduced during program construction and/or increasing the fraction of faults that are detected and corrected before the program is put into service. Both management tools and technical tools have been proposed for this purpose, and both can play important roles (although neither is an acceptable substitute for the use of the best available programmers).

Management tools. The structure of the team producing a system may influence the reliability of the programming process. Chief Programmer Teams [Baker 1972, 1975], in addition to various technical tools, impose a definite hierarchical structure on the programming team, with specialized functions and clearly delineated responsibilities. Egoless Programming [Weinberg 1971], while sharing many of the same technical tools, encourages a much more flexible structure and a high degree of shared responsibility. Both techniques require that all programs be read and understood by at least one person besides the author before being compiled.

Parnas [1971] has pointed out that management control of the information flow within a project can significantly affect both system structure and programming reliability. He proposes that formal policies be adopted to ensure that each programmer has access to just the information needed to produce a particular program module, and that systems be structured so that this amount of information will be small.

Finally, managers can make programmers aware that reliable programming is both practicable and desirable. Methods may range from substantial (and visible) reward structures for producing fault-free programs to simple statements in the specifications that reliability is one of the important factors [Weinberg 1973].

Technical tools. Many technical tools to support reliable programming are becoming well-known [ICRS 1975]. Each of them makes at least modest demands on the language in which programming is done: some demand the availability of particular language features (or the exclusion of others); most require facilities for modularizing a program in such a way that the consequences of particular design decisions can be isolated; some may require even more elaborate support. Excellent expositions of the aims and techniques of "structured programming" are contained in Dahl, Dijkstra, and Hoare [1972], Gries [1974], Dijkstra [1976], and Turski [1978].

This chapter is not primarily concerned with programming methodology; rather, we will be looking at the effects that the programming language can have within a fixed methodology.

The effect of programming languages on programming reliability. The programming language and system used in program development influence the probability of producing correct programs more than any other single tool. Thus it is important to use languages that assist reliable programming. However, newer programming languages are not automatically better in this respect. They are only likely to be so if language designers consciously set out to make them so, and if their customers make reliability a criterion in choosing a language.

Programming reliability was an explicit design goal of the original FORTRAN project [Backus et al. 1957]. However, it has largely dropped from sight in later language design projects (including the various revisions of FORTRAN). This neglect has had serious consequences. The cost of software is soaring past the cost of the hardware on which it runs [Boehm 1973], and dealing with software faults and their consequences (debugging, patching, system integration and test, etc.) has remained the dominant component of software costs. Furthermore, software is undoubtedly the major source of unreliability in most computer systems today.

There are many ways in which a programming language affects the reliability of the programming process, of which we will discuss five: masterability, fault-proneness, understandability, maintainability, and checkability.

If programmers are to consistently produce nearly-correct programs, they must be masters of their programming language. They must know what every construct means and how to use it effectively. The experimental approach to programming ("try it and see what happens") must be ruled out, as must the use of a language so complex that programmers do not understand it in its entirety. "Powerful" features are acceptable only if they are easy to use correctly. Simplicity of the language is a necessary, but not sufficient, condition—the language must encourage the production of simple, yet elegant, programs.

Some language constructs are easy to understand, yet are fault-prone in actual use. As will be discussed later, even such seemingly trivial things as the rules controlling the use of the semicolon as a statement separator or terminator can cause order-of-magnitude changes in the number of faults introduced by programmers. After the fault-prone constructs in a language are identified, it is often possible to redesign them to dramatically reduce the number of faults, at no cost in "power," and with little or no inconvenience to the programmer.

Ultimately, the most powerful weapon against incorrect programs is the understanding of those who write and check them. Thus, understandability must be our touchstone. The primary function of any language is communication, and programming languages should be chosen with as much concern for readability as compilability. Programmers need to understand not only the semantics of their language, but also the meanings of particular programs written in the language. It is not sufficient to be able to deduce the computation that will be invoked by a particular set of inputs; it is necessary to be able to see "what is being accomplished" at a higher level of abstraction. The communicative power of the language is largely determined by the degree to which it permits programmers to state their *intentions* along with the instructions needed to carry them out. (Experience has shown that comments and mnemonic variable names are not completely adequate for this communication, especially since they are not uniformly updated when the programmer's intentions change.)

Useful programs are continually modified. Generally, the maintenance process begins even before the program is complete, as its authors respond to changed requirements, new insights, and detected faults or inefficiencies. Maintenance itself must not introduce too many new faults. It is impractical to completely re-analyze a large program after each change, to verify its continued correctness, so we must rely on local scrutiny. A language can be of substantial assistance if it makes it possible to completely isolate the effects of a change to within a known (and preferably small) region of the source program.

Finally, languages differ widely in the amount and kind of error-checking that their implementations can perform. Such checking always relies on a certain amount of redundancy built into the language (although many kinds of redundancy are of little assistance in error-checking). On those occasions in which programs do contain faults, the promptitude and quality of diagnostics will largely control the speed and certainty of their removal. The ideal is for every likely error in the programming process to transform a correct program into one whose fault is detectable by the system as an error.

Injection, detection, diagnosis, and removal of faults

Fault injection. Faults enter programs in many different ways:

> Program specifications may be incomplete or ambiguous, or may simply fail to reflect the customer's intentions.

> Program designers may overlook interactions among various parts of the system.

> Programmers may misinterpret specifications, design algorithms or data structures incorrectly, or misunderstand some aspects of their programming language.

> Mechanical errors during coding, transcription, or entry of the program may introduce faults into the program text.

Faults from many different sources may frequently cause some of the same symptoms, but the chances of the language system providing useful diagnostics increase somewhat as we move down the list, due to the kinds of redundancy available in most languages.

Error detection. We want faults to be detected as errors. All error detection (mechanical or human) is based on redundancy. Thus, the manifestation of an error is always an inconsistency between two or more pieces of information that are supposed to agree. For example, a program's output may be compared with its specifications; if the specifications prohibit some outputs, there is a possibility of conflict, and hence of error detection. Similarly, if not all possible inputs to a compiler are acceptable, some programming faults can be detected as errors—the fraction will depend on the amount and kind of redundancy in the source language.

We frequently classify errors by the phase in the programming language system that detects them. Thus, we refer to *lexical errors, syntactic errors, semantic errors, run-time errors,* and *output errors.* Associated with each class of errors are a class of faults most likely to cause them; finally, there are faults not detected by the system at all, called *undetected faults.*

In general, the earlier an error is detected, the less persistent its associated fault will be. The difference between detecting an error at compile time or not is particularly pronounced. For example, Gannon obtained the following results for the average persistence of the faults associated with various classes of errors in the TOPPS and TOPPSII languages [Gannon 1975]:

lexical errors,	1.00 runs;
syntactic errors,	1.34 runs;
semantic errors,	1.24 runs;
run-time errors,	5.78 runs;
output errors,	8.52 runs;
undetected faults,	6.02 runs.

This general pattern was observed even when faults that caused run-time or output errors in TOPPS caused syntactic or semantic errors in TOPPSII. For example, the average persistence of faults in which = was substituted for := (or *vice versa*) was 7.13 runs in TOPPS and 1.42 runs in TOPPSII. Clearly, the amount and location of error detection has a major influence on programming reliability.

Error diagnosis. It is not sufficient to tell programmers that their programs contain one or more faults. To a very large extent, the helpfulness of the diagnostics in locating and explaining detected errors will determine their efficiency in removing faults.

Good error messages will exhibit a number of characteristics:

they will be *user-directed*, reporting problems in terms of what the user has done, not what has happened in the compiler;

they will be *source-language-oriented*, rather than containing mysterious internal representations or portions of machine code;

they will be as *specific* as possible;

they will *localize* the error, and if possible, the fault;

they will be *complete*;

they will be *readable* (in the programmer's natural language);

they will be *restrained* and *polite*.

One of the hardest things to remember in designing error diagnostics is that you don't know what fault *caused* the error. Two or more pieces of information have been found to be inconsistent, but it cannot be said with certainty where the fault lies. The safest strategy is to describe the error (the detected inconsistency) as clearly as possible before attempting to make any suggestion about the nature of the fault. Error symptoms should be described in a positive fashion wherever possible, e.g., "A right parenthesis was expected, but a semicolon was found," rather than "Missing right parenthesis."

The diagnosis of errors detected at run time should follow the same general principles as compile-time diagnosis. However, these standards can only be achieved with some forethought, and many otherwise excellent compilers abdicate all responsibility in this domain to an operating system totally unequipped to deal reasonably with run-time errors—the result is a cryptic message and a memory dump.

It is sometimes argued that efficiency considerations preclude any run-time checking or diagnosis. However, Satterthwaite [1972] has demonstrated that the cost of superb run-time checking and diagnosis can be very modest in a properly-designed system.

Fault removal. The development of systems that automatically remove faults from programs is a problem in artificial intelligence that is well beyond the present state of the art. For the foreseeable future, we must rely on humans to read programs and understand them sufficiently well to spot and correct their faults. Thus our repeated emphasis on program readability.

Empirical evidence

We cannot logically prove that particular programming language features will enhance the reliability of the programming process, much less derive the amount of improvement by analysis. However, it is possible to gather empirical evidence that tends to confirm or refute such claims by measuring the amount of improvement (or lack thereof) in actual situations. We can observe programmers at work and examine the programs they create. Experiments can be designed to investigate portions of the programming process, and to reduce the bulk of raw data the simple observation yields. However, experiments also have drawbacks [Weinberg 1971]. The behaviour of the subjects in an experiment may be so constrained that effects that are important in practice never appear.

Observations. There have been several studies of faults introduced during programming, e.g., [Moulton and Muller 1967], [Nagy and Pennebaker 1971], [Boies and Gould 1972], [Ichbiah and Rissen 1971], and [Youngs 1974]. The latter two studies yielded perhaps the most detailed results.

In the course of a language design effort, Ichbiah and Rissen identified several typical faults related to particular language constructs. These *characteristic faults* are associated with language constructs that implicitly involve the notion of ordinal position, deal with global data, or rely on information known only at run time.

Youngs studied the faults introduced while programming by observing programmers working in high-level languages. Thirty beginning programmers and twelve advanced programmers each coded one or two of nine problems. Youngs required the participants to submit both logs of all runs and all computer output from program development. He classified each fault according to a coding scheme and estimated the number of occurrences in the program of constructs of the same kind as that containing the fault. Over a quarter of the 1258 faults examined occurred in assignment statements. Although conditional branches contained fewer than five percent of the observed faults, they were five times more likely than other statements to contain faults.

Experiments. There have been a number of experimental studies of the relationship between programming languages and programming reliability, e.g., [Gould and Drongowski 1972], [Gould 1973], [Sime *et al.* 1973], [Miller 1973], [Miller 1974], [Shneidermann 1974], [Weissman 1974], [Gannon 1975], [Gannon 1977], [Love 1977]. We will discuss a few of Gannon's results.

TOPPS vs. TOPPSII. Gannon conducted a carefully controlled experiment to measure the effects on reliability of nine particular language design decisions, in the context of a complete programming language. The experiment involved observing the faults in programs written by reasonably experienced programmers (graduate and fourth-year undergraduate students in an operating systems course, including part-time students with industrial experience) using two languages to write rather small (75-200 lines), but fairly sophisticated (i.e., involving concurrency) programs. The languages had equivalent power, and differed only in ways that were expected to affect reliability. None of the subjects had prior experience in either language.

For the purposes of the study, a language was judged to enhance programming reliability if the faults introduced in the programming process were less frequent and less persistent. In addition to this overall comparison, the frequency and persistence of faults attributable to each redesigned feature were compared.

The experiment showed that in the environment studied, several language design decisions affected reliability significantly. The control language, TOPPS, had been used "satisfactorily" in that environment for several years, and each of its "bad" features is shared with other, more widely-used languages. Yet a few simple changes produced striking results.

In using the semicolon as a separator, rather than a statement terminator, TOPPS was following a long and honorable tradition (Algol 60, Pascal, BLISS, etc.). However, the TOPSII form (similar to that of PL/I) led to an order of magnitude reduction in the number of semicolon faults (from 11.4 per program to 1.3 per program). Of course, almost all semicolon faults are rather trivial (i.e., they generally do not persist more than one run). However, a small modification to the language would have eliminated faults that occurred in more than a quarter of all compilations. It is interesting to note that over 14% of the faults occurring in TOPPS programs during the second half of the experiment were still semicolon faults (compared to 1% for TOPPSII), and that missing semicolons were about as common as extra ones.

At the other end of the scale are four classes of infrequent faults with very high persistence:

	TOPPS	TOPPSII
assignment faults	7.1 runs	1.4 runs
inheritance faults	9.8 runs	1.7 runs
expression evaluation faults	8.6 runs	non-existent
relation-connector faults	11.5 runs	1.0 runs

The persistence of each of these classes of faults in TOPPS was about half the average number of runs needed to complete a program (16.1). It is reasonable to assume that these faults would be even more persistent in larger programs, adding even greater weight to the already significant improvements made by TOPPSII. Furthermore, the relative frequencies of these four classes of faults in TOPPS approximately doubled in the second half of the experiment, making it seem unlikely that they are solely due to unfamiliarity with these language features.

The fault of substituting $=$ for $:=$ or *vice versa* was statically detectable as an error in TOPPSII, but not in TOPPS. The persistence of these "assignment faults" in TOPPS calls into serious question the treatment of the assignment symbol $:=$ as "just another operator." Expression-oriented languages using this convention (e.g., Algol 68) may cause unsuspected reliability problems. Other expression-oriented languages using an assignment operator quite different from $=$ (e.g., ← in APL and BLISS) probably avoid some of these faults, but provide no better error detection.

TOPPS used Algol-style scope rules, while TOPPSII required each routine to declare the identifiers to be "imported" from the containing scope. These TOPPSII restrictions on inheritance reduced the persistence of subtle faults (i.e., those that could not be detected at compile time) at the cost of introducing a few more trivial faults. This would seem to support the claim that the unrestricted use of global variables is harmful [Wulf and Shaw 1973]. However, the TOPPSII inheritance faults that were not detected syntactically had a persistence of 6.7 runs, which demonstrates that simple restrictions are insufficient to completely eliminate unreliability due to these faults.

The expression evaluation rules of TOPPS are similar to those of APL. Only two programmers (one in each group) had previously programmed in APL, while all but one had experience using some language (not to mention mathematics) with left-to-right evaluation and traditional operator precedence. Thus, the greater *frequency* of errors in TOPPS may be at least partially explained in terms of prior experience. However, the high *persistence* of these errors seems incompatible with the claims for the benefits of "naturalness" sometimes made for the APL rules. Similarly, errors involving infix relation-connectors (logical operators) seem to be difficult to find and remove.

NT VS. ST. More recently, Gannon [1977] has conducted experiments evaluating the effect of data types on programming reliability. He studied programmer performance in relatively simple tasks using a "typeless" language, NT, in which all variables are treated simply as single words, as in BCPL or BLISS, and a statically typed language, ST, with declarations for variables of type integer, string, or integer or string array. Some of the more interesting comparisons were:

	ST	NT
runs to complete program	11.6	19.1
faults in submitted programs	0.2	0.6
faults during first program development	51.7	125.8
faults during second program development	31.4	99.6

Language design for programming reliability

This section surveys several ways in which languages can be designed to improve the reliability of programming. The language designer must make a sensible selection from a multitude of language features that have been proposed, and combine these features into a coherent whole that can be used reliably. "One thing he should not do is to include untried ideas of his own. His task is consolidation, not innovation." [Hoare 1973]

Contraction. Ironically, one of the best ways to improve the reliability of programming is to judiciously reduce the size of the programming language. "The most important decisions in language design concern what is to be left out" [Wirth 1971a]. There are two principal reasons for leaving most language features that been proposed out of any particular language: certain language features are known to have negative effects on reliability, and simplicity is itself a very considerable virtue.

There is by now an abundant literature on "harmful" language features. Generally, each article identifies a feature that detracts from program structure or readability, and argues that it should be replaced with more restricted (and more easily understood) features. A list of current candidates for removal (some more hotly contested than others) includes:

> **go to** statements [Dijkstra 1968][Knuth 1974], the first publicly proposed candidate;
>
> global variables [Wulf and Shaw 1973];
>
> pointers [Hoare 1975];
>
> selection by position [Ichbiah and Rissen 1971], long parameter lists and case statements are principal offenders;
>
> assignment statements [Strachey 1973], in their unrestricted form they are as de-structuring as **go to**s;
>
> defaults and implicit type conversions [Hoare 1973], they hide too many program faults;
>
> duplication [Clark and Horning 1973], useless redundancy at its worst.

However, great care must be taken to insure that "harmful" features are not simply replaced by something equally mischievous, and probably more complex; if one "harmful" feature is replaced by several "good" features, the language will expand, rather than contract.

An even more difficult task for the language designer is rejecting enough (separately) *good* features to keep his language as small and simple as it must be. Since languages inevitably grow, it is far better to start with a language that is too small than with one that is even slightly too big.

> "A necessary condition for the achievement of any of these objectives is the utmost simplicity in the design of the language. Without simplicity, even the language designer himself cannot evaluate the consequences of his design decisions. Without simplicity, the compiler writer cannot achieve even reliability, and certainly cannot construct compact, fast and efficient compilers. But the main beneficiary of simplicity is the user of the language. In all spheres of human intellectual and practical activity, from carpentry to golf, from sculpture to space travel, the true craftsman is the one who thoroughly understands his tools. And this applies to programmers too. A programmer who fully under-stands his language can tackle more complex tasks, and complete them quicker and more satisfactorily than if he did not. In fact, a programmer's need for an understanding of his language is so great, that it is almost impossible to persuade him to change to a new one. No matter what the deficiencies of his current language, he has learned to live with them; he has learned how to mitigate their effects by discipline and documentation, and even to take advantage of them in

ways which would be impossible in a new and cleaner language which avoided the deficiency.

"It therefore seems especially necessary in the design of a new programming language, intended to attract programmers away from their current high level language, to pursue the goal of simplicity to an extreme, so that a programmer can readily learn and remember all its features, can select the best facility for each of his purposes, can fully understand the effects and consequences of each decision, and can then concentrate the major part of his intellectual effort to understanding his problem and his programs rather than his tool." [Hoare 1973]

Redundancy and error detection. One of the major ways in which programming languages differ is in the amount of error-checking that they permit. Some languages have carried the goal of conciseness to such an extreme that almost any fault will transform a valid program into another "valid" (i.e., not detectably inconsistent program). This is false economy. Not only is a certain amount of redundancy needed for easy readability, but mechanical error detection is one of the most important contributions of high-level languages.

Not all redundancy contributes to error detection. Assembly languages are highly redundant, but since any sequence of valid instructions must be accepted as valid, there are few opportunities for effective error checking. Some forms of redundancy invite faults by requiring that duplicate information be provided. For example, the **external** attribute in PL/I (like the **common** statement in FORTRAN) permits separately compiled procedures to share variables. However, if the variables are not declared identically in each of the procedures, the fault may not be detected until run time. By contrast, the mechanisms for separate compilation in the SUE System Language [Clark and Horning 1973] and Mesa [Mitchell *et al.* 1978] require only a single identifier to be duplicated to permit sharing of variables and complete type checking.

To be effective, redundancy must cause likely faults to transform valid programs into detectably erroneous ones. We do not want a compiler to be overly "forgiving." If programmers write statements that do not conform to their stated intentions, it is better to warn them than to interpret the statements "reasonably."

Any form of redundancy will lengthen the program text, thereby increasing the opportunity for "clerical" faults. Thus, we should be careful only to introduce redundancy that leads to the detection of more faults than it causes.

Error detection by humans. To find faults, humans must read programs and spot inconsistencies; these detected errors may take the form of inconsistencies within the program itself, inconsistencies with specifications, or inconsistencies with informal expectations. Relatively little is known about the psychology of program readability [Weissman 1974], but a few general things can be said about inconsistency detection:

> First, it helps if the inconsistent items are close to each other, and the part of the program that must be checked for consistency is small; machines are better at global analysis than humans.

> Second, inconsistency between a pair of items is much easier to see than an inconsistency that is only detectable by simultaneously considering a large number of items.

Third, direct inconsistencies are more easily detected than those that are only derivable through long chains of inference.

These three considerations help to explain why mandatory declaration, including static typing of variables, contributes so much to human error detection. (It also has other merits, discussed later.) A declaration can collect and make explicit information that is otherwise distributed in implicit form throughout the program. These considerations also justify the use of modularity and explicit interfaces as tools for human understanding.

For easy readability, languages should be "well punctuated," i.e., it should be easy for the reader to directly determine statement types and major subunits, without intermediate inferences (e.g., counting blanks). This generally means the use of distinct structural words (keywords, reserved words) for distinct concepts, and avoidance of the multiple use of symbols unless they serve completely analogous functions (e.g., parentheses for grouping, commas for separating all types of lists). The meaning of a statement should be readily apparent, and unimpaired by elaborate rules for implicit conversions between types or context-dependent interpretations. An effective test of whether a language is "well punctuated" is to try to read and discuss programs over the telephone.

Lexical and spelling errors. Some faults—generally caused by mechanical errors in program preparation—can be detected purely by lexical analysis. Each token class of a language has its own formation rules, any violation of which signals an error. Many faults can be classified as *delimiter faults* involving tokens that start and end with particular symbols (e.g., comments and quoted strings). Failure to terminate such a token with the appropriate delimiter may cause much of the following program text to be inadvertently absorbed into the token. To limit the effects of such faults and speed their detection, some languages bound the length of these tokens, typically by limiting them to a single line.

Many mechanical faults in program production lead to *spelling errors*, in which tokens are well-formed, but undeclared, identifiers. Morgan [1970] claims that 80% of the spelling errors in typical programs involve insertion, replacement, or deletion of a single character, or the transposition of a pair of adjacent characters. In languages that do not require the declaration of identifiers, spelling errors must be treated as implicit declarations. However, mandatory declaration makes it possible to detect many program entry faults at compile time, particularly if programmers are encouraged to use long, dissimilar identifiers. A system such as DWIM [Teitelman 1972] can use several sorts of redundancy to suggest corrections for lexical and spelling errors.

Syntactic errors. Syntactic analysis not only plays a central role in the organization of compilers, it is also the focal point of error detection and diagnosis within compilers. Because syntactic specifications are precise, it is possible to develop parsers that accept exactly the specified languages; because they are formal, it is possible to prove that the parsers detect *any* syntactically invalid program. Typically, syntax provides the most stringent single structure within a programming language; more program entry faults and coding faults can be caught by syntactic analysis than by all other tests combined. The power of syntactic analysis as an error filter, as well as the ease of parsing, is greatly enhanced if the language is well punctuated, as previously discussed.

Static semantic errors. Much of the readability of high-level languages comes from conciseness resulting from the exploitation of context. Redundant non-local information can be used for very effective error checking. Declarations are particularly helpful, since a small amount of easily-supplied additional information can be checked in many places.

The type attribute in declarations is an effective form of redundancy, since the context of each appearance of a data item can be checked against its declared type. Both "typeless" languages (e.g., BLISS and BCPL) and languages with automatic type conversion (e.g., PL/I) defeat type checking, while languages with large numbers of incompatible types (e.g., Pascal) enhance it.

Pointers cause additional problems [Hoare 1975][Wirth 1974a]. By introducing the type **pointer** and restricting arithmetic operations on objects of this type, many high-level languages have made it possible to detect some of the faults common in the use of pointers in assembly languages. However, in PL/I, pointers may be used to access objects whose types are unknown. This problem can be eliminated by requiring that pointers be declared with the type of data they reference, as is done in Pascal and Algol 68. The further problem, of ensuring that there are no *dangling references* to explicitly freed storage, is more difficult to solve statically.

The declaration of further information about variables may permit easy detection of what would otherwise be subtle "logical" faults. Examples are the *range restrictions* of Pascal, and the provision of types and units for *dimensional analysis* [Karr and Loveman 1978]. This additional information also provides valuable documentation, and may enable the compiler to perform additional optimizations. In general, it helps to explicitly declare information that must otherwise be inferred by examining all uses of a variable.

Programmers can also supply redundant information about their programs by stating *assertions* or *invariants*. Assertions are logical expressions that are supposed to be true at a particular point in a program, while invariants are intended to hold over a region of the program, such as the body of a procedure. Type declarations may be viewed as simple invariants that involve single variables.

It is common to do most type checking at compile time. By contrast, most compilers that support the assertion feature (e.g., Algol W [Satterthwaite 1972]) generate code to evaluate and test assertions at run time. Euclid, whose design is discussed in a later section, was designed with the intent that the consistency of programs with their assertions and invariants would be checked statically, by a human or mechanical verifier. The chapter by Gerhart covers program validation in more detail.

Run-time error detection. Run-time error checking is done for a variety of reasons. Some faults have symptoms that can only be effectively detected at run time. If the cost of undetected errors may be high, or if the program must function more reliably than the compiler, hardware, and operating system that support it, it may be necessary to include redundant checking to duplicate tests made by the compiler. However, it is generally preferable to detect errors at compile time if possible, since the run-time check may be executed thousands or millions of times.

In order to perform dynamic checking, extra information associated with the program and/or data must be preserved and checked for consistency. Some kinds of checking (e.g., subscripts vs. array bounds, case selectors vs. case bounds) require modest overheads, and should almost always be performed, while others (e.g., checking for references to variables that are uninitialized) are very expensive with most current hardware, and must be very carefully justified to warrant inclusion.

Many systems allow the user to specify the amount of checking to be performed. Typically, full checking is specified during program debugging, and minimum checking during production runs. Hoare [1970] has criticised this practice on the grounds that it is only undetected errors in the production version that are harmful; he likens it to the practice of keeping a fire extinguisher in your car at all times, except when it is being driven! Another problem is that the errors caused by subtle faults may disappear or shift when checking code is added to or removed from the program. However, the economic argument is frequently compelling.

Binding time. It is frequently argued that "the advantages and disadvantages of translation-time versus execution-time bindings revolve around [the] conflict between efficiency and flexibility" [Pratt 1975]. However, this ignores the very significant effect that binding times can have on reliability. This springs from two sources: the greater facility that humans have for comprehending and checking static rather than dynamic relationships, and the reduced persistence of errors that are detected at compile time.

The language designer should make provision for binding information at the earliest feasible time. Delayed or dynamic bindings should occur only at the programmer's explicit request, never by default, so that the reliability penalty of increased flexibility will only be paid when the flexibility is considered useful. For example, the programmer should be able to bind a name to a value either statically (at compile time) or upon block entry, as well as by variable assignment. Because of the key role of static type-checking, all (or almost all) types should be bound at compile time.

"Correctness" is a static (compile-time) property of a program. Thus, it is generally unwise to allow the correctness of a program to depend on assertions that cannot be checked until run time.

Decisions. One of the principal characteristics of high-level languages is that they take many decisions out of the programmer's hands. This is one of the reasons why they are fiercely resented by so many experienced programmers. However, it is an inevitable consequence of the drive towards conciseness and checkable redundancy, and it is not undesirable.

Every decision takes time, and provides an opportunity for error. A major part of high-level languages' contributions to reliability comes from the errors they prevent (i.e., from the programs that they make it difficult or impossible to write). The language designer should try to restrict the programmer to decisions that really matter, and to get him to record those decisions within the text of the program itself.

In programming there are no decisions that *never* matter. This does not mean that all decisions should always be made by the programmer (writing in absolute hexadecimal!) and none by the compiler. Rather, it means that a programming language may need a very general (and not too frequently used) mechanism for overriding any specific decision (e.g., register or memory allocation, instruction choice) made by the compiler with one made by the programmer. This allows the programmer to be as careful as necessary in the optimization of critical decisions, but allows the compiler to make the routine decisions in a way that results in correct, and generally efficient, programs.

Programming decisions should be recorded *in the program*, independent of external documentation. A good comment convention, and freedom to choose readable, meaningful names can both assist in this process to a certain extent. However, it is better to record decisions in a form that is mechanically checkable for consistency with the rest of the program; all too often, the program is changed, but the comments and names are not.

The language designer should favor "self-documenting" features wherever possible. To cite a simple example, the declaration

> **type** Direction = (North, East, South, West)

is superior to the comment

```
/*      CONVENTION FOR DIRECTION VALUES:          */
/*          NORTH   =  1                           */
/*          EAST    =  2                           */
/*          SOUTH   =  3                           */
/*          WEST    =  4                           */
```

It is shorter. It relieves the programmer of the need to pick numerical values for each of the directions. It ensures that any change to the convention will be consistently reflected throughout the program. Furthermore, type-checking can insure that Direction and **integer** values are never confused.

<u>Structure.</u> A programming language should help the programmer structure his solutions to problems. There are several different kinds of structures that are relevant to the organization of programs. In addition to the traditional topics of *control structures* and *data structures*, we will mention *visual structures, historical structures, protection structures,* and *recovery structures*.

There seem to be only a small number of fundamental structures for control and data, which can be composed repeatedly to form more complex structures. The main ones are

concatenation: statement lists, declaration lists

selection: conditional statements, discriminated unions

fixed-length iteration: do loops, vectors

varying-length iteration: while loops, lists

encapsulation: blocks, records

abstraction: procedures, types.

Omitting any of these structures may force the programmer to awkward (and unreliable) circumlocutions; anything more elaborate can probably be built from these structures fairly easily.

Even so simple a matter as the formatting of the program text on the page can have a profound influence on the reader's ability to comprehend it readily. The visual structure of the text should correspond to the underlying control and data structures in such a way that they are easily visualized. Empirical studies of the "psychological complexity" of programs have sought to quantify the effect of good and bad styles for visual structure (paragraphing) [Weissman 1974]. It seems clear that difficulty in designing a natural and consistent paragraphing style for a programming language is a symptom of more basic flaws [Gordon 1975]. Many compilers now either automatically paragraph source listings or check for consistency between a program's indentation structure and its syntactic structure.

The historical structure of a program is the network of decisions that led to its final form. In principle, this structure includes not only the alternatives chosen, but those rejected, and the reasons for their rejection; few languages provide a reasonable mechanism for recording rejected alternatives. In most current languages, there is a strong temptation for programmers to destroy the historical structure that can be conveniently recorded in their programs. For example, much of the historical structure of a program that has been developed in a top-down fashion by stepwise refinement [Wirth 1971b, 1974b] is visible in its structure of procedures; it may be more "efficient" to eliminate those procedures by expanding out their bodies in-line at the point of call. The result of such premature optimization is often a program that can no longer be safely modified. The language designer (and compiler writer) should ensure that conceptual and historical structures can be retained in source programs with no loss in run-time efficiency, e.g., by making in-line procedure expansion a feature of the optimizer.

As systems get larger, they tend to become more vulnerable to unintended interactions, either accidental or malicious. Programming languages can reduce this vulnerability by providing protection "firewalls" against all but a specified, limited set of interactions. Many of the protection mechanisms discussed in the chapter by Needham are candidates for inclusion in programming languages [Jones and Liskov 1976].

Truly robust systems must cope with the Dynamic Corollary to Murphy's Law: "Even if it has been shown that nothing can go wrong, something will still go wrong." Recovery from hardware failures, human errors, problems in the underlying software, etc., is only feasible if advance provision has been made for dealing with exceptional conditions. It is important to clearly separate out the exception-handling portions of a program, so they do not dramatically increase our difficulty in understanding it. This will be the topic of a later section.

Modularization and interfaces. In order to build or understand large systems, it is necessary to partition them into pieces that can be dealt with almost independently. Modules are the pieces; interfaces are what separate them, and therefore make modularization useful. An interface defines *what* a module accomplishes, and should provide an opaque barrier between the users of the module, who know *why* the module is used, and the implementation of the module, which says *how* it accomplishes its ends. A useful interface is small ("narrow"), precise, and easily understood.

We want to ensure that a module accomplishes just what is specified in its interface in order to protect against errors, and against the consequences of changes elsewhere in the system. This isolation allows us to focus our attention on one module at a time, to bound the consequences of any change, and to localize the scope both of machine-dependencies and of decisions that may have to be changed. The chapter by Melliar-Smith covers the roles of modularization and specification in greater depth.

For maximum effectiveness, modularization and specification should be more than just design tools. The programming language should ensure that conceptual interfaces correspond to those in the actual program. In particular, the interface of a module must include both its explicit effects and any possible side effects, such as changes to non-local variables and error exits. The case against automatic inheritance of global variables [Wulf and Shaw 1973] is largely based on their disastrous effect on the size of interfaces.

PROGRAMMING LANGUAGES

<u>Reminders for language designers and users</u>

Simplicity is a considerable virtue.

When in doubt, leave it out.

Correctness is a compile-time property.

**The primary goal of a programming language should be
accurate communication among humans.**

Avoid "power" if it's hard to explain or understand.

If anything can go wrong, it will.

Reliability matters.

LANGUAGE FEATURES FOR FAULT TOLERANCE

<u>Introduction</u>

The previous section addressed the issue of designing a programming language to improve the reliability of the programming process. We now turn to another way in which a programming language can help to improve system reliability: by recognizing that faults are inevitable and providing means to cope with them systematically. Faults may occur in a program, or in the software or hardware of the system on which it runs—whatever the source of the difficulty, the program can contribute to system reliability by keeping faults from becoming failures.

Following the distinctions made in other chapters, we will call portions of a program that are explicitly intended to cope with errors *abnormal algorithms*—although it is not at all abnormal for a program to contain them! These can be divided into two classes based on whether they are intended to cope with particular anticipated, but unusual, situations, or are intended as a fallback when something unanticipated occurs. In the former case, *signals* and *exception handlers* provide a useful mechanism; in the latter, *acceptance tests* and *recovery blocks* are more appropriate. We will discuss both in turn, then return to the question of how to justify the complexity that these features add to programming languages.

J. J. HORNING

Signals and exception handlers

Motivation. "Why worry about exception processing? Anyone who has ever built a large software system or tried to write a 'robust' program can appreciate the problem. As programs grow in size, special cases and unusual circumstances crop up with startling rapidity. Even in moderate-sized programs that perform seemingly simple tasks, exceptional conditions abound. Consider a tape-to-tape copy program. Any reasonable programmer will handle an end-of-file condition, since it probably indicates completion of the copying operation. But what about tape errors? End-of-tape? Hung device? Record larger than expected? We could enumerate other possible exceptions, but the point is clear. Exceptions exist even in the simplest problem, and the complexity they induce in large programs can be mind-boggling. ... A look at the (dis)organization of existing large systems should easily convince us that [their] control is essential if we ever hope to make these systems robust, reliable, and understandable. ...

"Although it is obvious that any exceptional condition that arises must be handled if our programs are to be robust, we might wonder whether we need a single, general mechanism to do so. Why not simply test explicitly for an exception at all possible points in the program where it can occur? If this is prohibitively expensive or inconvenient, why not test only at a selected subset of these points? No special mechanism is required here, and the code to detect these exceptions is explicit and under the programmer's control.

"The objections to this _ad hoc_ approach should be clear. For some classes of exceptions ... the condition may occur virtually anywhere in the program. Obviously, it is impractical to include an explicit test 'at all possible points' where such exceptions can arise. Polling at 'selected' points may be feasible in principle, but in practice destroys the structural coherence of the source program. Because of timing considerations, it often becomes necessary ... to introduce tests for exceptions into pieces of the program that have nothing to do with the condition being tested. It is then impossible to read and understand such a program segment without understanding the entire structure of which it is a (perhaps very small and localized) part. Explicit polling may suffice in very limited applications but is clearly inadequate for general use. A technique must be found that preserves structural clarity." [Levin 1977]

A recent survey paper discusses exception handling features for programming languages, and identifies several uses for these features:

"Exceptions serve to _generalize_ operations, making them usable in a wider variety of contexts than would otherwise be the case. Specifically, exceptions are used:

(a) to permit dealing with an operation's impending or actual failure. Two types of failure are of interest: range failure, and domain failure;

(b) to indicate the significance of a valid result or the circumstances under which it was obtained;

(c) to permit an invoker to _monitor_ an operation, e.g., to measure computational progress or to provide additional information and guidance should certain conditions arise. ...

"*Range failure* occurs when an operation either finds it is unable to satisfy its output assertion (i.e. its criterion for determining when it has produced a valid result), or decides it may not ever be able to satisfy its output assertion. For example, a read operation does not satisfy its output assertion when it finds an end-of-file mark instead of a record to read; this is a range failure of the first kind. The second type of failure is exemplified by encountering a parity error when attempting to read a record, since in this case, it is uncertain whether repeated attempts to read will or will not eventually be successful. For a numerical algorithm, evidence of divergence is a range failure of the first kind; failure to converge after a certain amount of effort has been expended would be a failure of the second kind. ...

"Range failure requires the ability to terminate an operation prematurely (with or without production of partial results and with or without the 'undoing' of intermediate results). Range failure also requires the ability to resume the operation when further attempts at completion are deemed reasonable.

"*Domain failure* is a somewhat different type of failure. It occurs when an operation's inputs fail to pass certain tests of acceptability, e.g., the appearance of a letter in a string of digits or the inability to find enough space to satisfy a storage allocation requirement. Domain failure is distinguished from range failure in that domain failure occurs when some *input* assertion is tested and not satisfied, whereas range failure occurs when an output assertion cannot be satisfied." [Goodenough 1975]

Although Goodenough considers that "exceptions and exception handling mechanisms are not needed just to deal with errors. They are needed, in general, as a means of conveniently interleaving actions belonging to different levels of abstraction," we will be concerned here only with their use in dealing with errors.

Signals in Mesa. Mesa is a system implementation language developed at Xerox. It contains one of the more general and satisfactory exception handling mechanisms in an implemented language. The following discussion is excerpted from the Mesa Language Manual [Mitchell *et al.* 1978].

Signals are used to indicate when exceptional conditions arise in the course of execution, and they provide an orderly means of dealing with those conditions, at low cost if none are generated (and they almost never are). Signals work over many levels of procedure call, and it is possible for a signal to be generated by one procedure and be handled by another procedure much higher up in the call chain.

In its simplest form, a signal is just a name for some exceptional condition. Often, parameters are passed along with the signal to help any catch phrase which handles it in determining what went wrong. Finally, it is possible to recover from a signal and allow the routine which generated it to continue on its merry way. This is done by a catch phrase returning a result; the program which generated the signal receives this result as if it had called a normal procedure instead of a signal.

Signals may be *raised* by the detection of hardware or software errors, or explicitly within the program by using a **signal** statement. Any program which needs to *handle* signals must anticipate that need by providing *catch phrases* for the various signals that might be generated. During execution, certain of these catch phrases will be *enabled* at different times to handle signals. Loosely speaking, when a signal S is generated, the procedures in the call hierarchy at that time will be given a chance to catch the signal, in a last-in-first-out order. Each such procedure P in turn, if it has an enabled catch phrase, is given the signal S, until one of them stops the signal from propagating any further. P may still decide to reject S (in which case the next procedure in the call hierarchy will be considered), or P may decide to handle S by taking control or by attempting to recover from the signal.

Because signals can be propagated right through the call hierarchy, the programmer must consider catching not only signals generated *directly* within any procedure that is called, but also any generated indirectly as a result of calling that procedure. Indirect signals are those generated by procedures called from within a procedure which you call, unless they are stopped before reaching you.

When a catch phrase is called, it behaves like a case statement: it compares the signal code passed to it with each signal value that labels one of its alternatives. If the signal code matches, control enters the statement following the label; if not, the next enclosing catch phrase is tried. The special label **any** matches all signal codes. When a match is found, the catch phrase is said to have *accepted* the signal. The statement associated with each catch phrase has an implicit *Reject* return as its last instruction; hence if the statement completes without executing a control transfer, the signal is rejected and the search for an accepting catch phrase resumes.

Mesa guarantees that all otherwise uncaught signals will be caught at the highest level in the system and reported by the Debugger to the user. This is helpful in debugging because all the control context which existed when the signal was generated is still around and can be inspected to investigate the problem.

Having caught a signal, a catch phrase may transfer control into its containing context by means of a **goto**, an **exit**, a **retry**, or a **continue** (these are the only forms of "non-local goto" in Mesa). **Goto** explicitly indicates the next statement to be executed, **exit** leaves the enclosing iterative statement, **retry** means "go back to the beginning of the statement to which this catch phrase belongs," and **continue** means "go to the statement following the one to which this catch phrase belongs."

Another option for a catch phrase is to use the **resume** statement to return values to the routine which generated the signal. To that routine, it appears as if the signal call were a procedure call that returns some results.

A very important special signal is called *Unwind*. It is generated when a catch phrase has accepted a signal and is about to do some form of unconditional jump into the body of the routine containing it. Immediately preceding such a jump, the catch phrase will generate an *Unwind* signal for every intermediate activation record in the stack, starting from the source of the signal and terminating with the accepting catch phrase. This signal tells that activation that it is about to be destroyed and gives it a chance to clean up before dying, generally by restoring any data structures for which it is responsible to a consistent state and freeing any dynamically allocated storage.

Using Mesa signals. Properly used, Mesa signals go a long way towards meeting the objectives for exceptional condition handling discussed previously. They make it possible to clearly distinguish between normal and abnormal algorithms, and to propagate an error notification to the abnormal algorithm designed to handle it. In many cases, the handling algorithm can be placed at a level in the system where it is possible to effect a reasonable repair, report the problem in user-oriented terms, or decide to start over.

When designing a system component, it is necessary to anticipate the exceptional conditions that may arise during its operation, and to decide which of them should be reported to its users. It is necessary to document not only the names and meanings of the signals that the component may raise directly or indirectly, but also the names and meanings of any parameters supplied with the signal, whether the signal may be resumed, and if so, what repair is expected and what result is to be returned. Unless all this information is provided, it will be difficult for users to respond correctly to signals. Each programmer must decide which signals to handle via catch phrases, and which to reject (i.e., to incorporate into the interface of his own component).

The "power" and "convenience" of signals arise largely from the possibility of a signal passing through a large number of intermediate levels that need not take explicit account of it. However, the more levels through which a signal passes before being handled, the greater the conceptual distance is likely to be between the signaller and the handler, the greater the care necessary to ensure correct handling, and the greater the likelihood of some intermediate level omitting a necessary catch phrase for *Unwind*.

Jim Morris [private communication 1976] has raised the following warnings about Mesa signals: "Like any new and powerful language feature, Mesa's signal mechanism, especially the *Unwind* option, should be approached with caution. Because it is in the language, one cannot always be certain that a procedure call returns, even if he is not using signals himself. Every call on an external procedure must be regarded as an exit from your module, and you must clean things up before calling the procedure, or include a catch phrase to clean things up in the event that a signal occurs. It is hard to take this stricture seriously because it is really a hassle, especially considering the fact that the use of signals is fairly rare, and their actual exercise even rarer. Because signals are rare there is hardly any reinforcement for following the strict signal policy; i.e. you will hardly ever hear anyone say 'I'm really glad I put that catch phrase in there; otherwise my program would never work.' The point is that the program *will* work quite well for a long time without these precautions. The bug will not be found until long after the system is running in Peoria. ... It should be noted that Mesa is far superior to most languages in this area. In principle, by using enough catch phrases, one can keep control from getting away. The non-local transfers allowed by most Algol-like languages preclude such control. It has been suggested that systems programming is like mountaineering: One should not always react to surprises by jumping; it could make things worse."

It should be apparent that there are some drawbacks to Mesa signals, and users are by no means unanimous in their praise. Speaking from personal experience, there are situations where the use of signals greatly simplifies what would otherwise be a thorny programming problem. However, my own use of signals has turned out to be quite fault-prone, and I have greater difficulty locating and removing signal faults than any other kind. Each signal that is potentially raised by a procedure (directly or indirectly) is an important part of its interface. However, signals are generally the least well documented and least well tested part of the interface, and it is possible for indirect signals to be completely overlooked until they cause catastrophic crashes.

Acceptance tests and recovery blocks

Motivation. "The variety of undetected [faults] which could have been made in the design of a non-trivial software component is essentially infinite. Due to the complexity of the component, the relationship between any such [fault] and its effect at run time may be very obscure. For these reasons we believe that diagnosis of the original cause of software errors should be left to humans to do, and should be done in comparative leisure. Therefore our scheme for software fault tolerance in no way depends on automated diagnosis of the cause of the error—this would surely result only in greatly increasing the complexity and therefore the error-proneness of the system." [Randell 1975]

Although signals and related exception handling mechanisms can be very effective in dealing with the consequences of certain types of failures, there are two major limitations to their use:

Each likely kind of failure must be anticipated, and suitable handlers provided. Thus, these mechanisms are essentially useless in coping with *unanticipated* faults, such as design faults.

Recovery from failures is entirely under the programmer's control. Although this provides maximum flexibility, it carries with it the responsibility for understanding and compensating for *all* the consequences of each failure—frequently a huge task. Since failures of the underlying hardware and software should be rare, the recovery code is likely to be the least well tested (and hence most faulty) part of the system.

Thus, to provide a general mechanism for software fault tolerance, we must use language features that do *not* require the programmer to foresee all possible faults and to specify exactly how to recover from each of them. The *recovery block* is one such mechanism, which allows the programmer to supply his own error-checking, and to define units for recovery, without being concerned with either the complete set of possible faults or the means of implementing complete recovery.

Components of recovery blocks. As described in other chapters, it is useful to segment any large program into a set of *blocks* (modules, procedures, subroutines, paragraphs, clusters, etc.), each of which achieves some conceptual operation. Such a segmentation makes it possible to provide a functional description of each block. In documenting, understanding, or verifying a program that uses such a block, it is normally sufficient to use the functional description, rather than the detailed design of the block. Such blocks also provide natural units for error-checking and recovery; by adding extra information for this purpose, they become recovery blocks. This scheme is not dependent on the particular form of block structuring that is used, or the rules governing the scopes of variables, methods of parameter passing, etc. All that is required is that when the program is executed the acts of entering and leaving each block are explicit, and that blocks are properly nested in time.

A recovery block consists of an ordinary block in the programming language (the *primary alternate*), plus an *acceptance test* and a sequence of *alternate blocks*. The primary alternate is just the program that would have been written had there been no provision for error detection and recovery. The acceptance test is just a logical expression that is to be evaluated upon completion of any alternate to determine whether it has performed acceptably; it is closely analogous to the post-condition of a specification. If an alternate fails to complete (e.g., because of an internal failure or because it exceeds a time limit) or fails the acceptance test, the next alternate (if there is one) is entered. However, *before a further alternate is tried, the state is restored* to what it was just prior to entering the primary alternate. If the acceptance test is passed upon completion of an alternate, any further alternates are ignored, and control passes to the next statement following the recovery block. When no further alternates remain after a failure, the recovery block itself is considered to have failed, and recovery is attempted at the level of the next enclosing recovery block.

This mechanism has some very important characteristics:

It incorporates a general solution to the problem of when and how to switch to redundant software associated with any component, i.e., it deals with both the repair of any damage caused by the failing component and with transferring control to the appropriate spare component.

It provides a method of explicitly structuring the software system which has the effect of ensuring that the extra software involved in error detection and in the spare components does not add to the complexity of the system, and so reduce rather than increase overall system reliability.

It simplifies the task of producing alternate components. There is no need for —indeed, no possibility of—attempts at automated error diagnosis. The system state is reset after an error, deleting all effects of the faulty alternate. Thus, each alternate may be written as though *it* were the primary alternate.

It makes it possible for the system to log detected errors automatically, for off-line fault analysis and possible repair.

It provides systematic methods for testing abnormal algorithms, even in the absence of primary failures.

The recovery block scheme does have some disadvantages, as well:

The requirement that the state be restored before proceeding to a further alternate is difficult to implement efficiently on conventional hardware; various hardware aids can make this more feasible.

It is difficult to structure systems of communicating processes in such a way that state restoration is feasible without disastrous "domino effects" as each process forces others with which it has communicated to restore their states.

For systems that communicate with the external world, state restoration may be impossible, even in principle. (This is known as the "please ignore incoming rocket" problem.)

Each of these problems, and current approaches to coping with them will be discussed in the chapter on system fault tolerance. Generally, the demands placed by these approaches on the programming language are minimal.

Using recovery blocks. Although there is not yet a great deal of experience in structuring large systems for fault tolerance using recovery blocks, it is clear that two issues are critical to their effective use: the choice of acceptance tests, and the development of suitable alternate blocks.

An example that illustrates a proposed syntax for recovery blocks, and one possible style of use is given by Randell [1975]:

> **ensure** ConsistentSequence(s)
>
> **by** ExtendSWith(i)
>
> **else by** Warning("Lost item", i)
>
> **else by** Warning("Lost sequence", s);
>   s ← ConstructUnitSequence(i)
>
> **else by** Warning("Lost sequence and item, s, i);
>   s ← EmptySequence
>
> **else error**

The acceptance test follows the keyword **ensure**, and is placed at the head of the recovery block to emphasize that it defines acceptable behaviour of the block as a whole, although it will be executed *after* each alternate block that completes successfully. The primary alternate follows the keyword **by**, the remaining alternates, the keywords **else by**; the recovery block is terminated by the keywords **else error**, as a reminder that exhaustion of the available alternates is treated as an error in the execution of the dynamically enclosing recovery block.

It was mentioned that acceptance tests are closely akin to post-conditions in specifications. However, it is not generally possible just to carry these post-conditions over from the specification to the program. The minor problem is that the specification language will probably be more general (e.g., including quantifiers) than the logical expressions permitted in the programming language. The major problem is that it is usually nearly as expensive to completely check a post-condition as to achieve it, and the program to do so will probably be as complex and fault-prone as the primary block. Thus it will usually be necessary to choose an acceptance test that is somewhat less stringent than the post-condition. For example, the acceptance test for a sort routine might simply test that the elements of the array are in ascending order and that the sum of the elements in the array has not changed, rather than testing that the output array is a permutation of the input array. Choosing acceptance tests that are sufficiently stringent to ensure that a high percentage of failures are detected, yet sufficiently simple that they are themselves reliable and efficient, is an imperfectly understood art.

Ideally, alternate blocks would be written independently, directly from the functional specification. This should minimize the chance of correlated faults within separate alternates, but it could double or triple the cost of producing the program. In practice, there are a variety of reasons for using alternates that are not completely independent:

> In systems undergoing maintenance, the correction of a fault or addition of a feature often introduces a further fault; if the previous version is kept as an alternate, discovery of an error will trigger automatic fallback to the older (and perhaps more robust) version. Of course, this is only feasible if the block's interface has not changed.

> It may be more efficient to try a fast heuristic algorithm that "almost always works," and automatically fall back to a slower algorithm that *really* always works, when one of the exceptional cases is discovered.

> Among the "acceptable" behaviours for a block may be some that are more desirable than others (e.g., it is valid for a bank cash dispenser either to produce

cash for a validated customer or to refuse cash because the validation process has somehow failed, but the former is clearly preferable); a sequence of alternates encompassing the spectrum of acceptable behaviours may be designed together.

One important aspect of recovery blocks is that they provide a straightforward means for testing abnormal algorithms without relying on a sufficient number of failures in the underlying system to test all cases. Since each alternate operates on the same state—and must satisfy the same acceptance test—as the primary alternate, it can simply be substituted for the primary alternate at some stage in system testing, and tested as much as desired. More generally, a system can be "margin tested" by simply arranging for the underlying mechanism to behave as though a certain fraction of the acceptance tests failed (either by initially selecting other than the primary alternate or by rolling back after executing it and the acceptance test).

In addition to initiating recovery, failure of an acceptance test can be made to trigger logging of the error behind the scenes, for off-line analysis. This will be useful data not only for fault isolation and correction, but also for estimating failure rates within the system—and possibly for developing confidence measures in the functioning of the system as a whole.

Recovery blocks are more general than signals, and this generality inevitably exacts an efficiency toll. In circumstances where reliability has a high premium, this may be an acceptable price. However, recovery blocks and signals need not be mutually exclusive. The use of signals to deal with *anticipated* failures, and recovery blocks as a backstop for design faults and other unanticipated failures can be an attractive compromise. Signals will deal with the common cases efficiently and allow for careful programmer control where consequences can be foreseen. Recovery blocks will ensure that nothing will slip through the cracks and that the situation will never get completely out of control; this assurance may permit the signal handlers to be greatly simplified (e.g., no need to worry about what happens if we get a ParityError signal while fielding a DiskError interrupt while trying to write a page to disk to free a virtual memory page while handling a PageFault interrupt while trying to bring in the non-resident handler for the StorageFull signal while ...).

Conclusions

Relatively few programming languages contain explicit provisions for fault tolerance. In fact, PL/I is the only widely-used language with extensive exception handling facilities, and these have numerous deficiencies [MacLaren 1977][Levin 1977]. Considering our bias towards language simplicity, can we justify fault tolerant features that will necessarily increase language complexity? The answer is a qualified "yes."

By careful design, the additional complexity of these features can be minimized. For example, recovery blocks add very little syntactic or semantic complexity beyond what is already built into almost all current languages. It may be that when signals and exception handling are well understood that they can be provided by features of comparable simplicity [cf. Levin 1977].

Additional complexity is tolerable in a language if the new features remove even more complexity from typical programs. Unfortunately, fault tolerance is not the sort of feature (such as string processing or floating point arithmetic) that can be simply grafted onto a language as a *post facto* package. If it is required, there is just no simple way to program it within a language that does not provide features equivalent to those we have been discussing.

To this point we have stressed the conceptual advantages of a clear separation between normal and abnormal algorithms. However, in practice, efficiency and robustness may be even more compelling arguments. If the programming language makes it possible to separate normal and abnormal algorithms, quite different implementations may be chosen for each type. For example, in Mesa, signals are very similar to procedure variables; however, since raising a signal is expected to be a relatively infrequent event, a very different implementation technique is used that defers almost all the run-time overhead to the time when the signal is raised—if it isn't, the overhead is avoided. Similarly, it is possible to treat state-saving for recovery blocks quite differently from ordinary assignments—again, reducing average-case overhead.

It can be very important to preserve the redundancy provided by abnormal algorithms in the system at run time. If they are indistinguishably mixed with the normal algorithms, however, even a fairly simple compiler will probably detect some of the redundancies and "optimize" them out of the program entirely. Unless we are to prohibit optimization entirely, there must be some linguistic mechanism for indicating redundancy that is to be preserved.

Finally, unless the system has some way of distinguishing tests that indicate errors from ordinary program tests, it is difficult or impossible for the system to undertake automatic error logging. If the programmer is responsible for error logging, this is another burden of complexity on every program, and another source of program faults.

LANGUAGES ENCOURAGING PROOFS

Introduction

Reasoning about programs. In the development of reliable programs, it is not sufficient that a program specify a correct set of computations. The program must also make it possible to understand *why* the computations are correct. Whenever we are concerned with the correctness of computations invoked by a program, we are faced with the problem of reasoning (formally or informally) about that program [McCarthy 1962] [Floyd 1967][Dijkstra 1975]. This is not always an easy task; the complexity of many languages makes it virtually impossible to reason with confidence about even very small programs.

Our ability to compose programs reliably, and to understand them, is likely to be highly correlated with our ability to reason about them. Since many of the considerations of language design discussed earlier were motivated by concern for understandability, it is not surprising that most of them are also applicable here.

It is perhaps less obvious that the ability to reason formally about programs is closely related to the ability to reason about them informally. Formality tends to frighten many programmers; it seems to smack more of mathematical logic than "the art of computer programming." As Gerhart has pointed out, most practical proofs tend to be rather informal; however, they are more convincing if it is clear that *in principle* they could be reduced to completely formal proofs in a well-understood system. In most languages, this process is complicated by the necessity to consider many possibilities in addition to the "clear meaning" of the program (e.g., suppose that this procedure never terminates, transfers control via an error exit, or destroys the value of a global variable; suppose that this subscript expression overflows, involves division by zero, calls a function that never returns, or produces a value that is out of bounds). It is precisely the "niggling little details" that complicate the reduction to a formal proof that also provide the richest sources of pitfalls in understanding and reasoning informally about programs in these languages.

This section focusses on those aspects of programming languages that will facilitate the process of proving properties of programs using techniques similar to those discussed in the chapter by Gerhart.

Incorporation of specifications. One simple, but useful, way in which a programming language can encourage reasoning about programs is by making it easy to incorporate at least partial specifications within the program itself. Of course, comments can always be used for this purpose, but it is better both for the human reader and for the mechanical analyzer if specifications are syntactically recognizable as such. Most commonly, these specifications will take the form of input-output assertions on major program units (such as procedures) and invariant assertions on program loops. The close association of assertions with the program units provides an extremely useful form of documentation for the reader, indicating what assumptions the programmer was allowed to make about the environment, the transformations the program is supposed to effect, and the relations it is to maintain.

Most programs presented to verifiers are actually wrong; considerable time can be wasted looking for proofs of incorrect programs before discovering that debugging is still needed. This problem can be reduced (although not eliminated) by judicious testing, which is generally the most efficient way to demonstrate the presence of bugs. To assist in the testing process, some languages provide for the compilation of run-time checks for assertions in the program. This checking code provides useful redundancy for program testing. Alternatively, it could be used to initiate the abnormal algorithms previously discussed.

Of course, it is generally not feasible to incorporate complete specifications with each program unit. Global properties, such as performance, storage usage, etc., are often best specified and analyzed separately. Furthermore, even specifications that are appropriate to particular program units may need to be written in a richer language than the Boolean expressions of the programming language; for example, quantifiers and auxiliary variables are frequently needed.

Support for proof techniques. Each particular proof technique has its own strengths and limitations. By providing a set of features for which a proof method is especially suited, and avoiding those for which it is not, a language can facilitate proofs in that system. For example, the axiomatic method developed by Hoare [1969] relies on an essential "pun": no distinction is made between a variable and its value. Thus, with this method, it is difficult to simply and precisely formalize programming language constructs that rely on the notion of a variable as a location in memory rather than as merely a name for a value (e.g., reference parameters, **equivalence**, pointers). A language that avoids such features will simplify the development of axioms for the proof of programs.

An example of where a language can provide a feature needed for a proof technique is provided by Hoare's [1972] approach to the proof of correctness of data representations.

This method relies on the maintenance of a specified relationship between the "abstract" and "concrete" values of a data structure by all operations that change it. Proving that such a relationship is maintained is much more straightforward in languages that allow a data structure to be encapsulated together with all the possible operations on it, and that enforce such encapsulations.

Most proof techniques have been demonstrated in connection with "toy" languages, constructed specifically for purposes of illustration. These languages have generally not been implemented, and in any case were not designed for serious programming. The first notable exception was the programming language Pascal [Wirth 1971a], whose design was influenced by verification considerations, and whose formal definition takes the form of a set of proof rules [Hoare and Wirth 1973]. The balance of this section will be devoted to some newer languages designed with concern for both practical programming and verification.

The programming language Euclid

Euclid [Lampson *et al.* 1977] is a language for writing system programs that are to be verified. Its design proceeded in conjunction with the development of a set of proof rules [London *et al.* 1978] in the style of Hoare. It provides a good illustration of the practical consequences of attempting to design a realistic language for which proofs will be feasible. I was a member of the Euclid design team, and am hence more familiar with its successes and failures than with those of the other languages to be discussed. The following material is extracted from a paper by Popek *et al.* [1977].

Goals, history, and relation to Pascal. Euclid was evolved from Pascal by a series of changes intended to make it more suitable for verification and for system programming. We expect many of these changes to improve the reliability of the programming process, firstly by enlarging the class of errors that can be detected by the compiler, and secondly by making explicit in the program text more of the information needed for understanding and maintenance. We see Euclid as a step along one of the main lines of current programming language development: transferring more and more of the work of producing a correct program, and of verifying that it is consistent with its specification, from the programmer and the verifier (human or mechanical) to the programming language and its compiler.

The basic design of Euclid took place at four two-day meetings of a five-man committee (Horning, Lampson, London, Mitchell, Popek) in 1976, supplemented by a great deal of individual effort and uncounted Arpanet messages. Almost all of the basic changes to Pascal were agreed upon during the first meeting; most of the effort since then has been devoted to smoothing out unanticipated interactions among the changes and to developing a suitable exposition of the language.

Our changes to Pascal generally took the form of restrictions, which allow stronger statements about the properties of programs to be based on the rather superficial, but quite reliable, analysis that a compiler can perform. In some cases, we introduced new constructions whose meaning could be explained by expanding them in terms of existing Pascal constructions. These were not merely "syntactic sugaring": we had to introduce them, rather than leaving the expansion to the programmer, because the expansion would have been forbidden by our restrictions. Breaking the restrictions in these controlled ways did not violate the protection offered, because the new constructions were sufficiently restrictive in some other way.

Euclid is currently being implemented by a joint project of the Computer Systems Research Group of the University of Toronto and the Special Systems Division of I. P. Sharp Associates Limited [Sharp 1977]. Both the development of the proof rules and the implementation effort have provided useful feedback on the design of the language and the clarity of the defining report. A significant revision of the latter is currently being contemplated.

Euclid and verification. One of the fundamental assumptions in the design of Euclid is that (in principle) all Euclid programs are to be verified before use. That is, relatively formal proofs of the consistency between programs and their specifications will be done before reliance is placed on the operation of those programs; the proofs could be either manual or automatic. We used the axiomatic definition of Pascal for guidance.

Perhaps the most obvious consequence of this assumption is the provision within the language of syntactic means for including specifications and intermediate assertions. Routines are specified by pre- and post-assertions; modules by a pre-assertion, an invariant, an abstraction function, and specifications for exported routines and types. In addition, assertions may be placed at any point in the flow of control.

To assist in testing programs prior to completion of verification, any scope in Euclid can be prefixed by **checked**, which will cause the compilation of run-time checks for all *basic assertions* (Boolean expressions not enclosed in comment brackets) within the scope; this includes all *legality assertions*, which will be discussed later. If any assertion evaluates to *False* when it is reached in the program, execution will be terminated with a suitable message.

Because we expect all Euclid programs to be verified, we have made no special provisions for exceptional condition handling, as discussed in Part II. Run-time software errors should not occur in verified programs, and we know of no efficient general mechanisms by which software can recover from unanticipated failures of current hardware. Furthermore, we did not understand how to develop proof rules for exception handling mechanisms; more recent work by Levin [1977] provides some hope in this area.

We have also been led to a somewhat unorthodox position on uninitialized variables (except pointer variables). We do not forbid these syntactically (cf. [Dijkstra 1976] for a rather elaborate proposal), nor, for reasons of efficiency, do we require a default initialization. Our reasoning is as follows: verification generally places stronger constraints on variables than that they merely have values of appropriate types when they are used—they must have *suitable* values. Thus, the symptom of an uninitialized variable will generally be the inability to prove an assertion involving that variable. However, if a program can be verified without reference to the initial value of a variable, then *any* value is acceptable and initialization is superfluous.

Relying so heavily on verification has an obvious pitfall: suppose that the proof rules and the implementation don't agree? (Indeed, for Pascal, they do not.) Aside from some omissions and known technical difficulties, the major discrepancies between the Pascal definition and implementation take the form of restrictions needed by the proof rules, but not enforced by the implementation. For example, "The axioms and rules of inference ... explicitly forbid the presence of certain 'side effects' in the evaluation of functions and execution of statements. Thus programs which invoke such side-effects are, from a formal point of view, undefined. The absence of such side-effects can in principle be checked by a textual (compile-time) scan of the program. However, it is not obligatory for a Pascal implementation to make such checks" [Hoare and Wirth 1973].

In the design of Euclid, we have made a major effort to ensure that there are no gaps between what is required by the definition and what must be enforced by any implementation, and that such enforcement is a reasonable task. Gaps have been eliminated by a variety of means: removing features from the language, extending the formal definition, placing more definite requirements on the implementation, and finally, introducing *legality assertions* as messages from the compiler to the verifier about necessary checking.

Legality assertions. There are many language-imposed restrictions that must be satisfied by every legal Euclid program. In addition to syntactic constraints, many of them (e.g., declaration of identifiers before use) are easily checked by the compiler, and it would be silly to ask the verifier to duplicate this effort. Others (e.g., type constraints) can usually be checked rather easily by the compiler, but may occasionally depend on dynamically generated values. Still others (e.g., array indices within bounds, arithmetic overflow), will usually depend on dynamic information, although the compiler can often use declared ranges or flow analysis to do partial checking. (For example, $i := i + 1$ will obviously never assign a value that is too small if i was previously in range.) Our philosophy is that the verifier should rely as much as possible on the checking done by the compiler. In fact, unless the compiler indicates differently, the verifier is entitled to assume that the program has been determined by the compiler to be completely legal. The compiler is to augment the program with a *legality assertion* (which the verifier is to prove) whenever it has not fully checked that some constraint is satisfied. Any program whose legality assertions can all be proved valid is a legal program, with well-defined semantics.

The compiler may produce legality assertions only for certain conditions specifically indicated in the Euclid Report. They always take the form of Boolean expressions within the language, and are usually quite simple (e.g., $i < 10$, $i = j$, p **not**$= C.nil$). Some typical situations where legality assertions are required will be discussed in the next section. Note that legality is a more fundamental property than correctness, since:

> Legality is defined as consistency with the language specification, rather than consistency with a particular program specification. A program could be consistent with one specification and inconsistent with another.
>
> A program that is illegal has no defined meaning, and hence cannot be said to be correct or incorrect.

Also note that a particular program is not sometimes legal and sometimes illegal (e.g., depending on whether $i = j$ on some run): the verifier must prove that the legality assertions are *valid* (true for all possible executions satisfying the input assertions).

Aliasing. In most languages the rules connecting names (identifiers) to what they denote (e.g., variables) give rise to some subtle, but serious, problems for both programmers and verifiers. Probably the worst problem occurs when, at some point in the program, some variables (e.g., those passed as variable parameters to a procedure) are accessible by more than one name. Thus, assignment to x may change y. We call this *aliasing*.

The disadvantages of aliasing for programmers, readers, verifiers, and implementors have been well-documented [Hoare 1975][Fischer and LeBlanc 1977]. When assignment to *x* has the "side effect" of changing *y* it is likely to cause surprise and difficulty all around. However, programmers and language designers have been reluctant to eliminate all features that can give rise to aliasing, e.g., pointer variables and passing parameters by reference. In designing Euclid, we took a slightly different approach: we kept the language features, but banned aliasing. Essentially, we examined each feature that could give rise to aliases, and imposed the minimum restrictions necessary to prevent them. Every variable starts with a single name; if no aliases can be created, then by induction aliasing will not occur.

The case of variable parameters to procedures is typical. All of the actual **var** parameters in a call must be *nonoverlapping*. If the actual parameters are simple names ("entire variables"), this requirement merely means that they must all be distinct. However, we must also prohibit passing a structured variable and one of its components (e.g., *A* and *A(1)*). What about two components of the same variable? This is allowed if they are distinct (e.g., *A(1)* and *A(2)*), and disallowed if they are the same (e.g., *A(1)* and *A(1)*). Since subscripts may be expressions, it may be necessary to generate a legality assertion (e.g., *i* **not**= *j* in the case of *A(i)* and *A(j)*) to guarantee their distinctness.

It may appear that structured variables, such as arrays, violate our rule that assignment to one entire variable can never change another. After all, assignment to *A(i)* may sometimes change *A(j)*. We adopt the view of [Hoare and Wirth 1973, p. 345] that "assignment to an array component" is actually an assignment to the containing array. Thus *A(i) := 1* is an assignment to *A*, and can be expected to change *A(j)* if *j* = *i*.

Pointers appear to pose a more difficult problem. Assignment to *p↑* (i.e., to the variable to which *p* refers) may change the value of *x* if pointers are allowed to point at program variables, or may change the value of *q↑* if *p* and *q* happen to point to the same variable (i.e., if *p* = *q*). We avoided the former problem by retaining Pascal's restriction that pointers may only point to dynamically generated (and anonymous) variables. The usual treatment of the latter problem is to consider pointers as indices into "implicit arrays" (one for each type of dynamic variable), and to treat dereferencing of pointers as subscripting into the corresponding arrays [Luckham and Suzuki 1976] [Wegbreit and Spitzen 1976]. We adopted a variant of this solution in which each pointer is bound to a *collection*, which is an explicit program variable that plays the role of the implicit array. Thus *p↑* is just shorthand for *C(p)*, where *C* denotes *p*'s collection, and the proof rules for arrays can be carried over directly. In particular, assignment via a dereferenced pointer is considered to be an assignment to its collection. From the verifier's standpoint, the situation is slightly better than that for arrays, since the decision of whether two subscripts are equal may involve arbitrary arithmetic expressions, while the decision of whether two pointers are equal reduces to the question of whether they resulted from the same dynamic variable generation (*New* invocation).

We have not yet discussed passing dereferenced pointers as variable parameters. If *p↑* and *q↑* (really *C(p)* and *C(q)*) are both passed, the nonoverlapping requirement demands *p* **not**= *q*. Passing both *p* and *p↑* is not a problem unless the formal parameter corresponding to *p* can be dereferenced (i.e., unless *C* is also passed), but the non-overlapping requirement forbids passing both *p↑* and *C*. In fact, passing pointers themselves as parameters (like passing array indices) never creates aliasing problems, since dereferenced pointers (like subscripted arrays) are not entire variables; assignment to one of them is considered as assignment to its collection.

We allow any number of collections to have elements of the same type, with no more difficulty than arises from multiple arrays of the same type. Thus, the programmer can partition his dynamic variables and pointers into separate collections to indicate some of his knowledge about how they will be used; the verifier is assured that pointers in different collections can never point to overlapping variables. [The astute reader will have noted that we have essentially returned to the "class variables" that were in the original Pascal, but dropped in the revised version.]

One consequence of our complete elimination of aliasing is that "value-result" and "reference" are completely equivalent implementation mechanisms for **var** parameters, and a compiler is free to choose between them strictly on the basis of efficiency.

Scope of names. In traditional block-structured languages, the intimate connection between a variable's lifetime and the scope in which it is declared is a frequent source of problems. A variable whose use is intended to be narrowly confined (e.g., to a set of operations on a data structure), may have to be declared more globally, simply to ensure its continued existence. That, combined with the automatic inheritance of names into inner scopes may mean that its name is "known" over a considerable extent of the program text. Any proof that all assignments to the variable preserve a certain property may require examination of all that text.

Euclid treats routines (procedures and functions) and modules as *closed scopes*, and restricts the inheritance of names into such scopes to those *imported* by the programmer. Furthermore, names declared within a module are known outside only if they are explicitly *exported*. The basic idea is that a module should "package up" a data structure and a related set of routines for its manipulation, and should hide the internal details from the outside world. The "protection" provided by control over exported names serves as a useful first step towards abstract data types [SIGPLAN 1976]. In addition, they make it possible to separate concerns in the development and verification of data structures. Properties of the (non-exported) variables of a module can be ensured and verified solely on the basis of the inside of the module, with no concern for its use. The user of the module, on the other hand, is solely concerned with these properties (the module's interface), and not with the mechanism that ensures them.

Types. One of Pascal's principal contributions was its treatment of data types. Despite certain deficiencies [Habermann 1973], this treatment is more satisfactory than that of competitive languages. Pascal's types provide a flexible and convenient set of efficient data structuring mechanisms, and are useful conceptual tools for partitioning and organizing data within programs. It is a major undertaking to develop a new approach to data types that is both consistent and useful, and we did not attempt to do so for Euclid. Nevertheless, we felt compelled to try some small changes in the direction of safety.

Almost all type-checking in Pascal can be done at compile-time; the major exceptions are due to the incomplete specification of formal parameters that are functions and procedures and to problems with variant records [Fischer and LeBlanc 1977]. The former are not a problem in Euclid, since more serious problems of specification and verification led us to eliminate such parameters entirely, but Euclid retains variant records. The problems in Pascal arise from aliasing (which we have already dealt with), from the treatment of the *tag* (which indicates the current variant) as an ordinary, assignable field of a variant record, and from the accessibility of variant field selectors even when they do not apply to the current variant.

In Pascal, uncontrolled assignment to the tag field can change the current variant without ensuring that the corresponding fields contain values of appropriate types. We have eliminated this possibility in Euclid by making the tag a constant component of a variant record, and hence not assignable. If a variable is of a variant record type, its current variant can only be changed by assignment of a record of one of the other variant record types; this assignment supplies a complete set of fields appropriate to that variant.

Variant field selectors are only accessible within the alternatives of a *discriminating case* statement, where the alternative is selected by the current tag. In the case statement, a local name is provided for the variant record (as either a constant or a variable); within any alternative, that name has the (nonvariant) type selected by the corresponding tag value, and all field selectors of that type are accessible. If the local name is bound to a variable, the nonaliasing rule makes its more global name unusable within the scope; hence there is no danger that its type may be changed within the scope (e.g., by calling a procedure that does so surreptitiously). If the local name is a constant, the variable may still be changed, but this will not affect the (discriminated) constant in any way, so access to its fields remains safe. Thus, variant records cannot be used to circumvent Euclid's type-checking. As a minor benefit, we avoid the need for the Pascal restriction that the same field names may not be used in separate variants.

Containment of machine dependencies. Euclid contains most of the "escape hatches" (providing direct access to machine features) typical of system implementation languages [MOHLL 1975]. There is provision for machine-code routine bodies, for placing variables at fixed addresses, for specifying the internal representation of a record, and for explicitly overriding type-checking. Many of these features are difficult to define formally, and all of them pose problems for verification, yet they seem necessary in small portions of operating systems. We have not solved the verification problems; we have merely provided a mechanism for containing their effects.

Modules in a Euclid program may be explicitly declared to be machine-dependent; these are the only modules that are allowed to contain the various machine-dependencies mentioned above, or to contain machine-dependent modules. Machine-dependent modules serve to isolate these features textually, and to encapsulate their use; they may be imported into modules that are not machine-dependent (and rely only on the specifications, not the implementations, of the imported modules). This does not simplify the process of verifying that machine-dependent modules actually do meet their specifications; it merely means that the verification of all other modules can proceed in a machine-independent manner.

We expect machine-dependent modules to be used for two different purposes:

> to provide efficient machine-dependent implementations for packages whose specification is machine-independent (e.g., string manipulation, high-level input-output), and

> to provide controlled access to machine features (e.g., channels, clocks, page tables).

Programs using only the former type of machine-dependent modules should be quite portable, requiring changes to (and re-verification of) only the bodies of the machine-dependent modules. However, modules of the latter type will have machine-dependent specifications that will work against portability of either programs or proofs.

Contributions of Euclid. Even though Euclid does not represent a dramatic advance in the state of the art, we have accomplished several things:

> Firstly, we have designed a useful language (Euclid minus machine-dependent modules) all of whose features are (in principle) verifiable in their full generality by existing techniques.

> Secondly, we have demonstrated that it is possible to completely eliminate aliasing in a practical programming language.

> Thirdly, we have made variant records completely type-safe without destroying their utility.

By and large, the changes that we made to Pascal could be justified without reference to verification, and would be useful even in situations where verification is not a formal requirement. However, it is unlikely that many of them would have been made had verification not been one of our primary concerns. Furthermore, we seem to have been somewhat more successful at "getting it right the first time" when we started from a verification issue than when we worked back from an implementation concern. Perhaps this is because the construction of proof rules is a useful discipline that makes it necessary to be very explicit about the interactions of language features.

Other languages

Euclid was designed in a very short time, in order to obtain quickly a system programming language for which proofs of at least small programs would be feasible. Several contemporary language design efforts have rather less modest goals, and can be expected to make more substantial contributions to verifiability in the long term.

CLU is a programming language under development at the Massachusetts Institute of Technology. It is intended to support the use of three kinds of abstractions in program construction: procedural, control, and data.

> "CLU has been designed to support a methodology ... in which programs are developed by means of problem decomposition based on the recognition of abstractions. A program is constructed in many stages. At each stage, the problem to be solved is how to implement some abstraction (the initial problem is to implement the abstract behavior required of the entire program). The implementation is developed by envisioning a number of subsidiary abstractions (abstract objects and operations) that are useful in the problem domain. Once the behavior of the abstract objects and operations has been defined, a program can be written to solve the original problem; in this program, the abstract objects and operations are used as primitives. Now the original problem has been solved, but new problems have arisen, namely, how to implement the subsidiary abstractions. Each of these abstractions is considered in turn as a new problem; its implementation may introduce further abstractions. This process terminates when all the abstractions introduced at various stages have been implemented or are present in the programming language in use.

> "In this methodology, programs are developed incrementally, one abstraction at a time. Further, a distinction is made between an abstraction, which is a kind of behavior, and a program, or *module*, which implements that behavior. An abstraction isolates use from implementation: an abstraction can be used without

knowledge of its implementation and implemented without knowledge of its use." [Liskov *et al.* 1977]

The clear separation between abstraction and implementation made by CLU is also very helpful in partitioning the problem of program verification; each program module can be verified separately, on the basis of the specifications of the modules that it uses, without concern for their implementation. Note that this style of verification would not be safe if the language did not enforce the separation between abstraction and implementation, so that the only possible interactions are those allowed by the specification.

One of the principal features of CLU is the introduction of *clusters*, program modules that support data abstractions in a fashion analogous to the way that procedures support operational abstractions. A cluster permits a data abstraction to be implemented as a unit containing both a representation for the data object and algorithms for each operation on that object. CLU then allows only the operations within the cluster to access the representation.

A preliminary version of CLU has been implemented. Experience with its use will probably suggest further refinements. A more efficient implementation is being developed.

Alphard is a programming language under development at Carnegie-Mellon University. Its designers have set themselves even more ambitious goals than those of CLU. In addition to supporting a programming methodology based on abstraction and verification, Alphard is intended to permit both high-level programming and the convenient description of computer hardware, and is to be amenable to compilation into very efficient code (comparable to "good assembler coding") for present-day computers. Not surprisingly, its design and implementation have not proceeded as rapidly.

The Alphard *form* provides the programmer with a great deal of control over the implementation of data abstractions and of control constructs dealing with data abstractions (e.g., iteration). The primary goal of the form mechanism is to permit and encourage the localization of information about a user-defined abstraction. Specifically, it is designed to localize both verification and modification. Each form contains both a specification part and an implementation part; only the information contained in the specification part may be used outside the form.

A verification methodology is being developed concurrently with the design of Alphard; the designers say that it has provided substantial feedback to the language design itself. Particular attention has been paid to ensuring that there exists a well-understood way to verify both the implementation and use of each type of form. Several examples are contained in a series of papers on the theme of "abstraction and verification in Alphard" [London *et al.* 1976][Shaw 1976][Shaw *et al.* 1976, 1977][Wulf *et al.* 1976a,b].

One of the most radical approaches to the problem of encouraging proofs has been taken by Dijkstra [1976]. Dijkstra starts from the proposition that verification should not follow programming as a separate activity; rather, the program and its proof should be developed hand in hand. Ideally, the program should be constructed directly from its specifications, with minimum opportunity for error. Dijkstra has developed a *calculus for the derivation of programs*, based on the definition of programming language semantics in terms of the *predicate transformer* associated with each statement in the language. Basically, a predicate transformer is a rule for deriving from a predicate that is to be true "after" the statement (the *post-condition*), the weakest predicate that must be true "before" the statement (the *pre-condition*) in order that the statement defines a terminating computation that ensures the truth of the post-condition. The predicate transformer for a compound statement is generally some kind of composition of the predicate transformers for its components.

It is possible to use predicate transformers to verify the consistency of a given program with its specifications as follows:

treat the output assertion of the specification as the post-condition for the program as a whole;

apply the predicate transformer for the program to the post-condition to determine its weakest pre-condition;

prove that the weakest pre-condition is implied by the input assertion of the specification.

However, Dijkstra has proposed a much more exciting possibility: instead of taking the program and post-condition and deriving a pre-condition, take the post-condition and pre-condition and derive the program! For a variety of theoretical and practical reasons, it is not feasible to perform such derivations automatically. However, for some programming language constructs, it *is* possible to "fill in some blanks" algorithmically, so as to derive the statement that achieves a desired predicate transformation—if there is any statement of that form that will achieve it. This formalism provides a "calculus" with power similar to that of the integral calculus: there is no finite set of rules that is guaranteed to get the user from problem to solution; however, if the rules are properly followed, and indicate success, then a correct program has been derived. Thus, the programmer is still required to exercise considerable creativity, but it is primarily at the level of determining the basic *structure* of the program; the details can be generated, or at least checked, automatically. If a program has been derived in this fashion, no further proof of its correctness is needed.

Guarded commands are two forms of statements that replace the conditional and iterative statements of traditional languages, but are much more amenable to derivation by means of Dijkstra's calculus. Dijkstra's book presents a small programming language in which they are the *only* control constructs, and develops a discipline of programming in this language through an extensive set of examples. More recently, Hehner [1979] has argued that the discipline of *recursive refinement* admits of an even simpler language, avoiding the need for one of Dijkstra's two forms of guarded commands (**do—od**).

Although this approach has attracted much attention, and is likely to have a significant influence on future languages, it has not yet been tested in the development of large or useful systems. Thus, its effect on the reliability of programs remains a matter of conjecture and belief.

PROGRAMMING LANGUAGES

COPING WITH EXISTING LANGUAGES

Introduction

The previous sections in this chapter, by pointing out desirable properties of programming languages, constitute a catalog of inadequacies found in almost all widely-used languages. That most programs are written in languages that cause reliability problems should not be surprising—reliability is not an explicit concern in the initial phases of most projects. Even when reliability is a concern, the programming language is generally selected on some other basis: programmer familiarity, organizational standards, object-code efficiency, or availability; managers and customers do not insist on a language that will contribute to reliability. The major problem, however, is that there is no programming language available today that meets all our criteria; those that come closest tend to be least widely available.

We have already discussed the following common problems:

Most available programming languages are large, complex, hard to master in their entirety, and full of surprises. Languages that have enough features to meet our other requirements are particularly prone to elephantiasis.

All programming languages contain fault-prone features. Many of them do not contain enough checkable redundancy to allow the common faults to be detectable as errors.

Few programming languages incorporate sufficient structure for the construction and maintenance of modular systems. The conceptual structure that guides a program's construction is generally not visible in its text; intended modularity is often not enforced.

Features for fault-tolerance are primitive or non-existent in most widely-available languages. In the major exception (PL/I), the feature itself is so fault-prone that its extensive use does not necessarily contribute to system reliability.

In most languages, it is difficult to reason about programs with any confidence that they actually do what they appear to do in all circumstances. The number of possible special cases, machine limitations, side-effects, etc., is too large to cope with, so only those that happen to turn up during testing are likely to be considered.

Designing and implementing a new language is a difficult and expensive undertaking —in effect, a capital investment. It is rare that a single project has the luxury of specifying a programming language to meet its requirements; most projects must choose from among the already available languages. The key questions become: "Which of the available languages will contribute least to system unreliability?" and "How can that contribution be minimized?" This section is devoted to suggestions for coping with that situation.

Minimizing language-induced faults

Style. There are many different ways of using any given language. Some programming styles are less fault-prone than others. It is generally possible to find a style that emphasizes the strengths and avoids the weaknesses of any particular language. An excellent introduction to the general principles of programming style has been written by Kernighan and Plauger [1974]. It may be helpful to develop a more specific style manual for a language or project.

Language subsetting. Just because a language contains many features that contribute to unreliability does not mean that they must be used. Within even the largest languages it is sometimes possible to discover relatively clean, well-structured subsets; the ability to identify such subsets is not widespread, but should be treasured. A notable example of such subsets is SP/k [Holt *et al.* 1977]. SP/k is a sequence of nested subsets of PL/I (SP/1, ... , SP/8) designed primarily for teaching purposes. However, as we have previously argued, the clarity and simplicity needed for teaching are also major contributors to reliability. There is anecdotal evidence that programming in SP/6 is more reliable than programming in unrestricted PL/I [Horning and Wortman 1977].

A compiler for a subset language is generally much easier to construct than for the full language; the cost of implementing a language grows more than linearly with the language size [McKeeman *et al.* 1970]. However, the SP/k experience illustrates that many of the advantages of using a subset are available even without a special subset compiler. Legal SP/k programs will generally compile and run *with the same results* using any PL/I compiler; what is lost by not using the SP/k compiler is the additional checking made possible by the restricted nature of the subset. Thus illegal SP/k programs will generally be accepted by other compilers as "valid," but may produce different meaningless results.

Programmer self-discipline is necessary, but generally not sufficient, to ensure adherence to a chosen subset. Various other supplementary techniques may be used. Enforcement by the compiler, preprocessor, or another checking program (see below) is likely to be the most thorough, but simple management techniques may be all that is needed to achieve compliance.

Preprocessors. It may be possible to considerably improve a widely-available language, such as FORTRAN or COBOL, by adding a relatively small number of structuring features, and imposing more discipline and useful redundancy on the use of the language. Rather than building entire compilers from scratch, it is easier, faster, and more general to write a preprocessor that translates the improved language into the base language. If the preprocessor is written in its own language, the improved language becomes available on all machines where the base language is available.

An example of this approach is the RATFOR (Rational FORTRAN) language and preprocessor [Kernighan and Plauger 1976]. Among the advantages of this approach are its relatively low cost, easy portability, compatibility with existing libraries of programs, minimal programmer retraining, and quick payoff on investment. The disadvantages include the extra cost of preprocessing every time the program is changed, an extra level of language that must be understood (at least) when things go wrong and the compiler produces messages that are not in terms of the preprocessor's language, and the difficulty of accomodating really major language changes (e.g., for fault-tolerance).

Additional checking tools. Rather than checking and transforming a program as part of a preprocessing phase, it is possible to write entirely separate programs whose purpose is to exploit redundancy for error-checking. Checking may range from simple verification that a program conforms to standards that are not checked by the compiler [Culpepper 1975] [Bridge and Thompson 1976], to detection of anomalous interprocedural data flow [Fosdick and Osterweil 1976], to determination of whether dimensions and units are used consistently [Karr and Loveman 1978], to full-fledged program verification systems [London 1975].

A study by Boehm et al. [1976] indicates that the biggest potential improvements in software fault detection and correction come from "early application of automated and semiautomated Consistency, Robustness, and Self-Containedness checkers." A prototype Design Assertion Consistency Checker, for example, was given 967 assertions about the inputs and outputs of 186 modules in a large spacecraft software system. At a cost of $30 in computer time, it discovered over 200 genuine inconsistencies in the design (and another 600 inconsistencies in the assertions themselves). Many of the inconsistencies represented faults that "might not have been caught until very late in the testing and integration phase, and are typically the kind of errors which are difficult to correct, as their correction often causes ripple effects into other portions of the software." [Boehm et al. 1975]

Some of the advantages of separating the checking tools from the language processors are the additional modularity of the program production system, the relative ease of adding just a little more checking (without having to redesign either the language or the compiler), the ability to postpone checking until a program is believed to be correct (thereby saving the cost of a lot of checking during program development). The disadvantages are very closely related: because the checker is separate from the compiler, it will probably wind up duplicating many of its functions (certainly lexical analysis of the program, probably partial or complete parsing, and possibly global analysis of control and data flow); because checking may be postponed, faults will generally be detected later, after a greater investment of debugging time.

Manual transformation into implemented languages. "Availability" of a language need not be equated with availability of a compiler for the language. Many programmers who are not satisfied with the languages for which they have compilers use some language they like better for program design and initial coding. After they are confident that this well-structured program represents their intent, they manually transform it into the language that their compiler accepts. This technique is usually most helpful in early stages of program design—no generally-available programming language provides much conceptual assistance in design [cf. McKeeman 1975]. It has definite limitations in later stages of a project; to all the disadvantages of preprocessors are added the slowness, expense, and fault-proneness of the manual transformation.

Choosing a language

Selecting a language from among those that are available for use in a given situation is a discouraging process, one of attempting to minimize evils. The traditional criteria, particularly availability, place severe constraints on the choice. When there are two or more languages remaining, however, how should one choose? The following should be taken as hints, rather than firmly established rules:

Compare the languages with the criteria given in this chapter. Generally, members of the "Algol family" of languages conform more closely than those of the "FORTRAN family," which in turn tend to conform better than members of the "PL/I family," which conform better than members of the "COBOL family." Consider, but do not be overawed by, claims that a particular language or dialect is "structured."

Take the simplest available language that will do the job. Additional "power" and complexity are more likely to harm than help reliability.

Consider the available subset compilers and preprocessors very carefully. They may provide a considerable reliability advantage while retaining compatibility with existing systems and minimizing the need for retraining.

Look at the available program development and checking tools. A language with a full set is already a leg up.

"Better the evil that you know than one that you don't." Familiarity with a language may be of considerable assistance in avoiding its worst pitfalls.

ACKNOWLEDGEMENTS

My thinking in this whole area has been stimulated by numerous discussions over the years in IFIP Working Groups 2.3 (Programming Methodology) and 2.4 (System Implementation Languages) and in the ARPA Quality Software for Complex Tasks working group. I received helpful comments on earlier drafts of this chapter from Ed Satterthwaite, Gene McDaniel, Danny Bobrow, Roy Levin, and Tom Anderson. Other colleagues and students too numerous to mention have been instrumental in informing me about the important issues.

The first section of this chapter is based largely on a draft working paper prepared for IFIP Working Group 2.4 by its subcommittee on reliability, edited by John Gannon and myself. I am grateful to the members of WG 2.4 for their suggestions and criticism, and especially to John Gannon, without whose cooperation and research I could not have formulated the issues so clearly.

My awareness of the issues raised in the second section, and of the approaches discussed, very largely springs from my participation in the Highly Reliable Computing Systems project at Newcastle, and numerous—frequently heated—discussions with many other members of that project over a number of years. Mesa, and my colleagues at Xerox, introduced me to the practical use of signals in my own programming.

The design of Euclid was a team effort; one of its most valuable products for me was an enforced education about verification provided by Ralph London and the other team members. John Guttag and Jim Donahue provided both information and motivation. The ACM Conference on Language Design for Reliable Software [SIGPLAN 1977] [CACM 1977] helped to focus my thoughts on many issues.

The final section of this chapter is dedicated to the computer manufacturers of the world, whose efforts made it both possible and necessary.

REFERENCES

Backus, J. W., R. J. Beeber, S. Best, R. Goldberg, L. M. Haibt, H. L. Herrick, R. A. Nelson, D. Sayre, P. B. Sheridan, H. Stern, I. Ziller, R. A. Hughes, and R. Nutt [1957]. "The FORTRAN automatic coding system." In *Proc. Western Joint Computer Conference*, Los Angeles.

Baker, F. T. [1972]. "Chief programmer team management of production programming." *IBM Syst. J.* **11**, no. 1, pp. 56–73.

——[1975]. "Structured programming in a production programming environment." *IEEE Trans. Software Engineering* **SE–1**, no. 2, pp. 241–252.

Boehm, B. W. [1973]. "Software and its impact: A quantitative assessment." *Datamation* **19**, no. 5, pp. 48–59.

——, R. K. McClean, and D. B. Urfrig [1975]. "Some experience with automated aids to the design of large–scale reliable software." *IEEE Trans. Software Engineering* **SE–1**, no. 1, pp. 125–133.

——, J. R. Brown, and M. Lipow [1976]. "Quantitative evaluation of software quality." In *Proc. 2nd International Conference on Software Engineering*, San Francisco, pp. 592–605.

Boies, S. J., and J. D. Gould [1972]. "A behavioral analysis of programming: On the frequency of syntactical errors." Report RC 3907, IBM Watson Research Center, Yorktown Heights.

Bridge, R. F. and E. W. Thompson [1976]. "BRIDGES—A tool for increasing the reliability of references to FORTRAN variables." *SIGPLAN Notices* **11**, no. 9, pp. 2–9.

CACM [1977]. Special issue on language design for reliable software. *Comm. ACM* **20**, no. 8, pp. 539–595.

Clark, B. L. and J. J. Horning [1973]. "Reflections on a language designed to write an operating system." *SIGPLAN Notices* **8**, no. 9, pp. 52–56.

Culpepper, L. M. [1975]. "A system for reliable engineering software." *SIGPLAN Notices* **10**, no. 6, pp. 186–192.

Dahl, O.-J. , E. W. Dijkstra, and C. A. R. Hoare [1972]. *Structured Programming*. Academic Press, London and New York.

Dijkstra, E. W. [1968]. "Go to statement considered harmful." *Comm. ACM* **11**, no. 3, pp. 147–148.

——[1975]. "Correctness concerns and, among other things, why they are resented." *SIGPLAN Notices* **10**, no. 6, pp. 546–550.

——[1976]. *A Discipline of Programming*. Prentice–Hall, Englewood Cliffs.

147

Fischer, Charles N., and Richard J. LeBlanc [1977]. "Efficient implementation and Optimization of run–time checking in Pascal." *SIGPLAN Notices* 12, no. 3, pp. 19–24.

Floyd, R. W. [1967]. "Assigning meanings to programs." In *Mathematical Aspects of Computer Science*, ed. J. T. Schwartz, American Mathematical Society, Providence.

Fosdick, Loyd D., and Leon J. Osterweil [1976]. "The detection of anomalous interprocedural data flow." In *Proc. 2nd International Conference on Software Engineering*, San Francisco, pp. 624–628.

Gannon, John D. [1975]. "Language design to enhance programming reliability." Technical Report CSRG–47, University of Toronto Computer Systems Research Group. [Summarized in John D. Gannon and J. J. Horning, "Language design for programming reliability." *IEEE Trans. Software Engineering* SE-1, no. 2, pp. 179–191.]

——[1977]. "An experimental evaluation of data type conventions." *Comm. ACM* 20, no. 8, pp. 584–595.

Goodenough, J. B. [1975]. "Exception handling: Issues and a proposed notation." *Comm. ACM* 18, no. 12, pp. 683–696.

Gordon, Harvey [1975]. "Paragraphing computer programs." M. Sc. Thesis, University of Toronto Computer Science Department.

Gould, J. D. [1973]. "Some psychological evidence on how people debug computer programs." Report RC 4542, IBM Watson Research Center, Yorktown Heights.

——and P. Drongowski [1972]. "A controlled psychological study of computer program debugging." Report RC 4083, IBM Watson Research Center, Yorktown Heights.

Gries, D. [1974]. "On structured programming—A reply to Smoliar." *Comm. ACM* 17, no. 11, pp. 655–657.

Habermann, A. N. [1973]. "Critical comments on the programming language Pascal." *Acta Informatica* 3, pp. 47–57.

Hehner, E. C. R. [1979]. "**do** considered **od**: A contribution to the programming calculus." *Acta Informatica* (to appear).

Hoare, C. A. R. [1969]. "An axiomatic basis for computer programming." *Comm. ACM* 12, no. 10, pp. 576–583.

——[1970]. "The use of high level languages in large program construction." In *Efficient Production of Large Programs*, ed. B. Osuchowska, pp. 81–107, Computation Centre of the Polish Academy of Sciences, Warsawa.

——[1972]. "Proofs of correctness of data representation." *Acta Informatica* 1, pp. 271–281.

——[1973]. "Hints on programming language design." Technical Report STAN–CS–73–403, Stanford University Computer Science Department.

——[1975]. "Recursive data structures." *Int. J. Comp. Inf. Sci.* **4**, p. 105.

——and Wirth [1973]. "An axiomatic definition of the programming language Pascal." *Acta Informatica* **2**, pp. 335–355.

Holt, R. C., D. B. Wortman, D. T. Barnard, and J. R. Cordy [1977]. "SP/k: A system for teaching computer programming." *Comm. ACM* **20**, no. 5, pp. 301–309.

Horning, J. J., and D. B. Wortman [1977]. "Software Hut: A computer program engineering project in the form of a game." *IEEE Trans. Software Engineering* **SE–3**, no. 4, pp. 325–330.

Ichbiah, J. D., and J. P. Rissen [1971]. "Directions de travail pour un atelier de software." Preliminary Report, Compagnie Internationale Pour L'Informatique, Paris.

Jones, Anita K., and Barbara H. Liskov [1976]. "A language extension for controlling access to shared data." *IEEE Trans. Software Engineering* **SE–2**, no. 4, pp. 277–284.

Karr, Michael, and David B. Loveman III [1978]. "Incorporation of units into programming languages." *Comm. ACM* **21**, no. 5, pp. 385–391.

ICRS [1975]. "Proceedings—1975 International Conference on Reliable Software." *SIGPLAN Notices* **10**, no. 6.

Kernighan, Brian W., and P. J. Plauger [1974]. *The Elements of Programming Style.* McGraw–Hill, New York.

——[1976]. *Software Tools.* Addison–Wesley, Reading.

Knuth, D. E. [1974]. "Structured programming with **go to** statements." *Comp. Surveys* **6**, no. 4, pp. 261–301.

Lampson, B. W., J. J. Horning, R. L. London, J. G. Mitchell, and G. J. Popek [1977]. "Report on the programming language Euclid." *SIGPLAN Notices* **12**, no. 2.

Levin, Roy [1977]. "Program structures for exceptional condition handling." Ph. D. Thesis, Carnegie–Mellon University Department of Computer Science.

Liskov, Barbara, Alan Snyder, Russell Atkinson, and Craig Scheffert [1977]. "Abstraction mechanisms in CLU." *Comm. ACM* **20**, no. 8, pp. 564–576.

London, R. L. [1975]. "A view of program verification." *SIGPLAN Notices* **10**, no. 6, pp. 534–545.

——, Mary Shaw, and Wm. A. Wulf [1976]. "Abstraction and verification in Alphard: A symbol table example." Technical Report, Carnegie–Mellon University Department of Computer Science and University of Southern California Information Sciences Institute.

——, J. V. Guttag, J. J. Horning, B. W. Lampson, J. G. Mitchell, and G. J. Popek [1978]. "Proof rules for the programming language Euclid." *Acta Informatica* **10**, pp. 1–26.

Love, Tom [1977]. "An experimental investigation of the effect of program structure on program understanding." *SIGPLAN Notices* **12**, no. 3, pp. 105–113.

Luckham, D., and N. Suzuki [1976]. "Automatic program verification V: Verification-oriented proof rules for arrays, records, and pointers." Technical Report STAN–CS–76–549, Stanford University Computer Science Department.

McCarthy, J. [1962]. "Towards a mathematical theory of computation." In *Proc. IFIP Congress 62.* pp. 21–28, North–Holland, Amsterdam.

McKeeman, W. M. [1975]. "On preventing programming languages from interfering with programming." *IEEE Trans. Software Engineering* **SE–1**, no. 1, pp. 19–26.

——, J. J. Horning, and D. B. Wortman [1970]. *A Compiler Generator.* Prentice–Hall, Englewood Cliffs.

MacLaren, M. Donald [1977]. "Exception handling in PL/I." *SIGPLAN Notices* **12**, no. 3, pp. 101–104.

Miller, L. A. [1973]. "Normative procedure specification." In *Proc. 81st Ann. Conv. Am. Psychological Assn.*, Montreal.

——[1974]. "Programming by non–programmers." *Int. J. Man–Machine Studies* **6**, no. 2, pp. 237–260.

Mitchell, James G., William Maybury, and Richard Sweet [1978]. "Mesa language manual." Technical Report CSL–78–1, Xerox Palo Alto Research Center.

MOHLL [1975]. *Machine Oriented Higher Level Languages.* ed. W. L. van der Poel and L. A. Maarssen, North–Holland, Amsterdam.

Morgan, H. L. [1970]. "Spelling correction in system programs." *Comm. ACM* **13**, no. 2, pp. 90–94.

Moulton, P. G., and M. E. Muller [1967]. "DITRAN—A compiler emphasizing diagnostics." *Comm. ACM* **10**, no. 1, pp. 45–52.

Nagy, G., and M. C. Pennebaker [1971]. "A step toward automatic analysis of logically undetectable programming errors." Report RC 3407, IBM Watson Research Center, Yorktown Heights.

Parnas, D. L. [1971]. "Information distribution aspects of design methodology." In *Proc. IFIP Congress 71.* pp. 339–344, North–Holland, Amsterdam.

Popek, G. J., J. J. Horning, B. W. Lampson, R. L. London, J. G. Mitchell [1977]. "Notes on the design of Euclid." *SIGPLAN Notices* **12**, no. 3, pp. 11–18.

Pratt, Terrence W. [1975]. *Programming Languages: Design and Implementation.* Prentice–Hall, Englewood Cliffs.

Randell, B. [1975]. "System structure for software fault tolerance." *SIGPLAN Notices* **10**, no. 6, pp. 437–449.

Satterthwaite, E. [1972]. "Debugging tools for high–level languages." *Software—Practice and Experience* **2**, pp. 197–217.

Sharp [1977]. "Small Euclid transliterator." Technical Report, I. P. Sharp Associates Special Systems Division, Toronto.

Shaw, Mary [1976]. "Abstraction and verification in Alphard: Design and verification of a tree handler." In *Proc. Fifth Texas Conf. Computing Systems.* pp. 86–94.

——, Wm. A. Wulf, and Ralph L. London [1976]. "Abstraction and verification in Alphard: Iteration and generators." Technical Report, Carnegie–Mellon University Department of Computer Science and University of Southern California Information Sciences Institute.

——, ——, and ——[1977]. "Abstraction and verification in Alphard: Defining and specifying iteration and generators." *Comm. ACM* **20**, no. 8, pp. 553–564.

Shneidermann, B. [1974]. "Two experiments in programming behavior." Technical Report 17, Indiana University Computer Science Department.

SIGPLAN [1976]. Special issue on data: abstraction, definition, and structure. *SIGPLAN Notices* **11**.

——[1977]. Special issue on language design for reliable software. *SIGPLAN Notices* **12**, no. 3.

Sime, M. E., T. R. Green, and D. J. Guest [1973]. "Psychological evaluation of two conditional constructions used in computer languages." *Int. J. Man–Machine Studies* **5**, no. 1, pp. 105–113.

Strachey, C. [1973]. Lecture given at IBM Scientific Center, Peterlee, England.

Turski, W. M. [1978]. *Computer Programming Methodology.* Heyden, London.

Wegbreit, B., and J. Spitzen [1976]. "Proving properties of complex data structures." *J. ACM* **23**, no. 2, pp. 389–396.

Weinberg, Gerald M. [1971]. *The Psychology of Computer Programming.* Van Nostrand Reinhold, New York.

——[1973]. "The psychology of improved programming performance." *Datamation* **18**, no. 11.

Weissman, Laurence M. [1974]. "A methodology for studying the psychological complexity of computer programs." Technical Report CSRG–37, University of Toronto Computer Systems Research Group.

Wirth, N. [1971a]. "The programming language Pascal." *Acta Informatica* **1**, pp. 35–63.

——[1971b]. "Program development by stepwise refinement." *Comm. ACM* **14**, no. 4, pp. 221–227.

——[1974a]. "On the design of programming languages." In *Proc. IFIP Congress 74*. pp. 386–393, North–Holland, Amsterdam.

——[1974b]. "On the composition of well–structured programs." *Comp. Surveys* **6**, no. 4, pp. 247–259.

Wulf, W., and Mary Shaw [1973]. "Global variable considered harmful." *SIGPLAN Notices* **8**, no. 2, pp. 28–34.

Wulf, Wm. A., Ralph L. London, and Mary Shaw [1976a]. "Abstraction and verification in Alphard: Introduction to language and methodology." Technical Report, Carnegie–Mellon University Department of Computer Science and University of Southern California Information Sciences Institute.

——, ——, and ——[1976b]. "An introduction to the construction and verification of Alphard programs." *IEEE Trans. Software Engineering* **SE-2**, no. 4, pp. 253–265.

Youngs, E. A. [1974]. "Human errors in programming." *Int. J. Man–Machine Studies* **6**, no. 3, pp. 361–376.

5

SYSTEM FAULT TOLERANCE

T. Anderson
P.A. Lee
S.K. Shrivastava

University of Newcastle upon Tyne

PRINCIPLES OF FAULT TOLERANCE

Introduction

For systems that have a high reliability requirement, it is usual to utilise techniques which aim to ensure that faults are avoided or eliminated before reliance is placed on the systems. While such an approach is necessary, it has generally not proved to be sufficient to attain a high level of reliability. The reason for this is that complex systems will, it seems, always contain residual faults. Techniques which enable the system to tolerate the occurrence and consequences of faults are therefore also required. The purpose of this section is to discuss in general the strategies necessary to achieve fault tolerance in computing systems.

All fault tolerance measures depend on the effective utilisation of elements of the system which may be termed protective redundancy. The techniques which utilise this redundancy can be classified in various different ways; the general classification adopted here identifies strategies for (i) error detection; (ii) damage assessment; (iii) error recovery; and (iv) fault treatment.

The implementation of these strategies can take many different forms, as is discussed subsequently. In a given system the particular strategies used may vary in different parts of that system, and at different times during its operation. Indeed, it is not always possible to make a positive identification of the elements responsible for each of the constituent strategies used in a given fault tolerance technique, for, while the starting point is always the detection of an erroneous state, the order in which the other strategies are carried out can vary, and there can be much interaction between them. Thus any such identification will depend on a particular view of the structuring of the system.

T. ANDERSON, P.A. LEE and S.K. SHRIVASTAVA

Protective Redundancy

Protective redundancy is usually incorporated into the system as additional components and algorithms (that is, the abnormal algorithms of the system discussed in the chapter by Randell), which are redundant in the sense that they would not be required in a system which could be guaranteed to be fault free. Redundancy in time may also be utilised in a system, for example, by making repeated use of a particular component.

The methods by which redundancy has been introduced into systems have, in the past, been classified in various ways. Redundancy which has been introduced to mask or hide the effects of component failure such that that failure has no impact upon the environment of the component (masking or static redundancy) has been distinguished from redundancy within a component used to indicate that the outputs of that component are erroneous (dynamic redundancy). In fact, this distinction is not related so much to the type of strategy used but to the way in which the redundancy is incorporated into the structure of the system.

The application of redundancy to mask the effects of component failure is of course an application of a fault tolerance technique, and all four of the general strategies mentioned above have to be applied. The canonical example of the use of such redundancy is Triple Modular Redundancy (TMR). In its standard application, TMR is used to provide tolerance against hardware component failures. Thus, to tolerate the failure of component A in figure 1a, it could be replaced by the TMR system in figure 1b, consisting of three copies of component A (each of identical design) and majority voting circuits V which check the outputs from these components for equality. The system in figure 1b is therefore designed to tolerate the failure of any single A component by accepting any output on which at least two components agree.

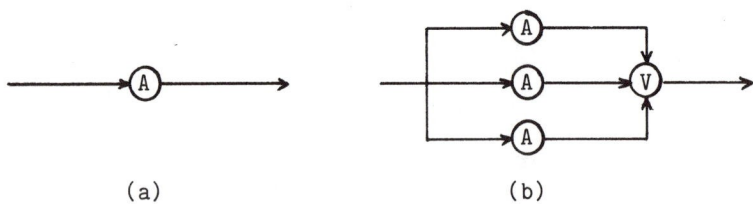

(a) (b)

Fig. 1 Triple Modular Redundancy

The way in which this TMR structure fits into the general classification of strategies will be examined in more detail in the next sections.

SYSTEM FAULT TOLERANCE

Error Detection

The starting point for all fault tolerance techniques is the detection of an erroneous state which could have led to system failure. Ideally, the checks performed by the error detection mechanisms should satisfy three criteria: firstly, they should be based solely on the specification of the service that the system is supposed to provide; secondly, they should check for absolute correctness of the behaviour of the system with respect to that specification; and thirdly, they should be independent from the system itself. If such checks could be designed and implemented, and complemented by appropriate means of recovering from the errors detected, then no single component or algorithmic fault could cause a system failure.

In practice, of course, such rigorous checking cannot be attained. The first criterion may not be satisfied because the specification of the system may be expressed in terms of information which is external to the (computational) system and which is not amenable to computational verification. If this is the case, any error detection in the computational system can only be based on a subset of the system specification.

Example

In a system consisting of a warehouse and a stock control computer, part of the specification of the system might require that the warehouse stock level was always in agreement with that held internally in the computer. However, the computer cannot guard against being given valid but incorrect data, and has no means of checking its internal state with that of the warehouse.

Even if all of the information concerning the specification is available, the complexity of attempting to check for absolute correctness is likely to detract from the usefulness of the check, as well as introducing unacceptable cost or performance constraints.

Furthermore, the independence of the system and its check cannot be absolute. The assessment of the degree of independence will be based on assumptions about what types of fault might occur and what types might not. Of course, without this independence there is the danger that a fault might affect both the system and its check and thus invalidate any error detection.

Example

The independence between the components and the error detecting voting circuits in figure 1b could be compromised by a screwdriver being dropped across the circuit - a fault which the designer had not considered.

Therefore, for all of these reasons, it is usual to attempt to enforce acceptability, a lower standard of behaviour than absolute correctness, with the hope that such checks will still enable a high percentage of errors to be detected. Acceptability checks can either be checks that the operation of the system appears to be satisfactory, or checks that specific erroneous situations have not arisen. A disadvantage of the latter approach is that only anticipated erroneous situations can be detected. However, for such situations checks can often be designed which are simpler and more specific than a general check that the operation of the system is satisfactory.

There are various criteria which can determine the place(s) in the system where the error detection mechanisms should be deployed. Clearly, the earlier an error is detected, the speedier the recovery, and useless processing can be saved. However, such early checks are not adequate for two reasons. Firstly, they will lack independence from the system as they will be dependent upon the internal algorithm of the system. Secondly, if no further checks are employed, then clearly all of the rest of the system activity is left unchecked. Thus, wherever feasible, checks should be employed at the last possible moment, just before the "results" leave the system. Ideally, such checking will be supplemented with earlier checks to gain the benefits mentioned above.

Some of the possible forms of checks in a system are:-

   (a) replication checks;
   (b) reversal checks;
   (c) coding checks;
   (d) interface checks; and
   (e) diagnostic checks.

Replication checks are a common form of error detection mechanism, involving replication of some part of the activity of the system to enable the consistency of the results to be checked. The type of replication used will depend on the type of faults that are anticipated (and of course on cost/performance constraints). Thus replication involving two or more components of independent design would be employed if design faults were expected. Alternatively, replication involving two or more components of the same design or repeated use of the same component would be used to detect permanent or transient component faults respectively.

Example

As far as hardware components are concerned, it has been observed that, because of physical degradation, permanent component faults are a (relatively) frequent occurrence.

Therefore the replication provided by the TMR system illustrated in figure 1b enables the (replication) check performed by the voting circuits to detect erroneous states arising from a failure of one of the components.

Reversal checks involve the processing of the activity or results of a system to calculate what the input to the system should have been. The calculated input is then compared with that which actually occurred. Only certain types of system, where the inverse computation is relatively straightforward, lend themselves to this type of check.

Example

The JPL-STAR computer (Avizienis 1971) employed "inverse microprogramming" which deduced what an operation should have been from the active gating signals. The deduced operation could them be compared with that actually requested.

Coding checks are also a common form of error detection, and often provide a means of reducing the cost of the error detection. Techniques such as parity, Hamming codes and cyclic redundancy codes use redundancy to enable the acceptability of a (possibly large) set of data to be checked. Checking large and complex masses of data is often infeasible without the use of coding techniques. However, it is at best a limited form of check, based on assumptions about the types and consequences of faults which might occur.

Example

Parity checks are regarded as being suitable for core stores, but not for telecommunications where the faults give rise to entirely different error characteristics.

All of the above forms of check will be founded on faith in the actual structuring of the system, based on the presumed effectiveness of the constraints that were applied to the interfaces of the system. Interface checks are one means of providing constraints, where mechanisms within components serve to check the interactions across interfaces. Checks for illegal instructions, illegal operands and protection violations are common examples of interface checks provided by hardware systems; protection mechanisms are discussed in more detail in the chapter by Needham. Clearly, interface checks can at most guarantee validity of usage, as opposed to correctness with respect to environment-level criteria.

The final form of explicit error detection to be discussed is diagnostic checking. This type of check involves using a component with a set of inputs for which the expected outputs are known and can be compared with those actually obtained from the component. Diagnostic checks are usually used periodically, interspersed with periods of time during which it is assumed that the component is working correctly. The effectiveness of such checks will depend on the frequency of their use (with respect to the frequency of the occurrence of faults) and on the amount of time and resources that can be allocated to the checks. The problem with such checks is the amount of time for which errors could go undetected and spread throughout the system. Thus diagnostic checks are not often used as a primary error detection mechanism, but are used to supplement other mechanisms - for example, diagnostic programs may be run on a computer which would otherwise be idle, to supplement any primary error detection mechanisms in that computer. However, diagnostic checking can be useful for fault location as is discussed subsequently.

The question arises as to who (or what) checks the error checking? In practice, it is to be hoped that either the checks are sufficiently simple that normal fault avoidance techniques can be used, or that fault tolerance measures can be used to ensure the reliability of the checking mechanisms. (Indeed, this is true for all aspects of the system which are relied upon to implement fault tolerance.) If, nevertheless, a fault occurs in the checking mechanism there can be two outcomes (assuming that the fault causes no damage to the system being checked): either it can detect non-existent errors, or it can fail to detect actual errors. Unless there is no recovery capability, the detection of a non-existent error cannot cause the system to fail but only to use up some of its recovery capability. However, failure to detect an actual error may be more serious and difficult to deal with.

When a component detects that its internal state is erroneous, the three further strategies discussed below will have to be invoked to achieve fault tolerance. The effects of these strategies may be kept internal to the component, masked from the environment of that component. However, in certain situations it may be necessary for the erroneous component to <u>notify</u> the error to some or all of the components with which it is interrelated. These notified components may then invoke their own fault tolerance strategies, just as if they had explicitly detected an error.

Example

The TMR system of figure 1b could be extended so that if no two components produced the same output, the voting circuits could notify the components to which it was connected of the erroneous state of the TMR system. The notified components might then wish to utilise their fault tolerance strategies to take account of this.

158

Damage Assessment

When an error is detected much more of the system state may be suspect than that actually discovered to be erroneous. Because of the likely delay between the occurrence of a fault and the detection of its erroneous consequences, invalid information may have spread within the system. Thus, before an attempt is made to recover from the error, it may be useful to try to assess the extent of the damage that has been caused to the system state.

Damage assessment is always based on a priori reasoning to a greater or lesser extent. The assessment may be based solely on a priori reasoning, or may be supplemented by the system itself adopting exploratory techniques to attempt to determine the extent of the damage. Each approach can involve reliance on the system structure to determine what system activity might have followed the occurrence of a fault. A useful concept for limiting the amount of exploration necessary, or indeed for providing a sound basis for a priori reasoning is that of an atomic action, as described in the chapter by Randell.

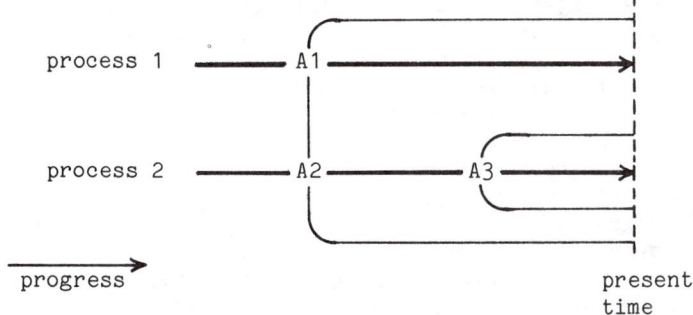

Fig. 2 Extant Atomic Actions

Figure 2 illustrates two processes with their uncompleted atomic actions. If process 2 is detected to be erroneous, then one possible strategy is to assume that all of its activity since point A3 is suspect and should be abandoned or investigated further. However, if process 1 is the one detected to be in error, then the same strategy would assume that all of its activity since point A1 was suspect, as was all of the activity of process 2 since point A2.

Example

In the TMR system of figure 1b, it is assumed that each of the A components operates atomically, that is they do not interact. The a priori damage assessment is therefore that only one component will be affected by a fault. Thus TMR is inappropriate for situations in which this is difficult to guarantee, for example, for components within a single integrated circuit package.

The relevance of atomic actions in simplifying damage assessment is that if the structure they embody in the system is actual rather than conceptual, and the fault has not damaged this structure, then the atomic action places a clear constraint on the spread of erroneous information in the system. In practice, damage assessment is often closely involved with error recovery and fault treatment, and is usually a rather uncertain and incomplete activity. Thus efforts spent in trying to limit the spread of damage by careful checking of interfaces between components are well worth while.

Error Recovery

Recovery from the consequences of a fault involves transforming an erroneous and inconsistent state into a valid state from which the system can continue to provide the specified service. Two strategies for error recovery can be identified: error recovery provided to a system and involving the restoration of a prior state of the system (or part of the system) is termed backward error recovery. In contrast, forward error recovery involves the system itself making further use of its present erroneous state to obtain another state. The aim of both strategies is to attain a state which it is hoped is free from errors. (In fact, the distinction between forward and backward error recovery is also related to the system structure, since backward error recovery can only be an abstraction provided by an underlying level. This point will be examined further in the next section of this chapter.) A reset strategy is sometimes used in systems to provide error recovery, in which the current state is discarded and replaced by some predefined state. The classification of a reset strategy as backward or forward error recovery will depend on whether the predefined state was a prior state of the system.

Backward error recovery

Backward error recovery involves the provision of recovery points, that is points in time at which the state of the system is (at least conceptually) saved for future reinstatement if required. There are various mechanisms which can be used to implement recovery points - these will be discussed in the next section. Because of the cost of maintaining a large number of recovery points, they are usually explicitly discarded when it is hoped they are no longer required. Recovery points may also become invalid, for example, due to the breach of an assumed atomic action by a flow of information. The implied reduction in recovery capability which the loss of a recovery point entails is called commitment.

SYSTEM FAULT TOLERANCE

The major importance of backward error recovery is that it is a simple technique which makes no assumptions about the nature of the fault involved (apart from assuming that the fault has not compromised the recovery mechanism), and that no effort need be expended on damage assessment. Thus, if it is available, backward error recovery is a general recovery mechanism and can provide recovery after all types of faults, even unanticipated faults in the design of the system. However, there may be situations in which it is an expensive recovery mechanism in that it involves undoing all of the activity of the system since the recovery point was established, not just those parts which were erroneous. This is of particular significance when backward error recovery in concurrent systems is considered, and this will be discussed in the final section of this chapter.

Forward error recovery

As described above, forward error recovery involves the system itself transforming its erroneous state into a valid state. However, the problem with forward error recovery techniques is that they must rely heavily on a knowledge of the nature of the fault involved and its exact consequences (influenced by knowledge of the structure of the system) and in consequence they are inseparable from the problems of damage assessment and of providing a continued service. Thus forward error recovery has, it seems, to be designed specifically for each system. Nevertheless, in situations where a fault and its full consequences can be anticipated, forward error recovery can provide efficient and simple recovery.

It is of interest to examine how forward error recovery techniques can cope with the classes of faults identified in the chapter by Randell. Forward error recovery strategies for dealing with anticipated component faults are usually termed exception handling. (The mechanistic and linguistic aspects of exception handling are discussed in the next section of this chapter and in the chapter by Horning respectively.)

Example

The voting circuits in the TMR system of figure 1b employ forward error recovery in the form of exception handlers to deal with the erroneous state when the output from one component differs from those of the other two.

A more powerful role is played when forward error recovery techniques are applied to an erroneous situation which has arisen because of interactions with another system which was itself erroneous. The basic method is known as compensation, whereby supplementary information is provided to the relevant systems with the intention of nullifying erroneous information they had received previously. (The chapter by Davies discusses this in more detail.)

T. ANDERSON, P.A. LEE and S.K. SHRIVASTAVA

Example

Consider a stock control computer which had been given the valid but incorrect information "5000 aardvarks have been issued" when the number in question should have been 500. A simple compensation message of the form "4500 aardvarks have been received" might be sufficient to restore the state of the computer. However, if the computer had re-calculated stock levels and ordered extra supplies to deal with this sudden increase in demand for aardvarks ... .

The above example also serves to illustrate the importance of the knowledge of system structure and hence of possible information flow when forward error recovery techniques are employed.

The other type of fault which can occur is a fault in the design of the system, for example, due to an incorrect algorithm. These faults are by their nature unanticipatable and it should be apparent that forward error recovery is not appropriate for dealing with them. This point serves to illustrate the fact that forward and backward error recovery should be regarded as complementary rather than competitive approaches, and both can usefully be applied in a given system. An example of such a combination is given by Melliar-Smith and Randell (1977) where forward error recovery is used to deal with simple faults, while backward error recovery is available for unanticipated faults, including those arising from faults in the forward error recovery procedures themselves.

Fault Treatment

The aspect of fault tolerance which is termed fault treatment embraces all of the (abnormal) activities of the system which are intended to ensure that the system can continue to provide its specified service despite the known presence of a fault. As such, techniques for locating, and repairing or avoiding a fault are all discussed under this heading. One approach, having the merit of simplicity, is to ignore the fault, deferring its location and treatment until manual techniques can be applied. Continued usage of a component in which there was evidence of a fault is a rational approach only when the fault is believed to be transient. For example, it may be appropriate for faults which arise from sensitivity to a very limited set of specific input patterns, or from occasional time-varying behaviour of sub-components.

Example

Continued use may be made of a magnetic tape unit even though it is occasionally necessary to make repeated attempts to successfully read the tape.

SYSTEM FAULT TOLERANCE

If it is deemed necessary that action should be taken to avoid the fault during further operation of the system, or indeed to repair the fault, it must first be located. While the detection of an erroneous state indicates the presence of a fault it does not necessarily serve to identify the fault. In simple situations the relationship between errors and faults may appear straightforward and enable a priori decisions to be made about the location of the fault. Alternatively, exploratory techniques for fault location may be required, being performed manually, or automatically by the system itself. The fault must be located to within a component whose size is acceptable as a unit of replacement. The bigger the size, the easier the location strategy, but of course the greater the redundancy overhead imposed on the system.

A fault location strategy will perforce be influenced by some preconceived ideas about the structure of the system. If the fault has caused some violation of the intended interrelationships between components, which has not been detected because of inadequate interface checks, then the fault location will be misled. Thus the task of locating a fault can be very complex, and only feasible for automation in situations which are (or are believed to be) very simple. Diagnostic checking is often used in a searching strategy. Once a failure has occurred, then diagnostic checks may be employed in an attempt to locate the fault more precisely. Such checks usually provide a fine degree of error detection, the cost of which is usually such that they cannot be used as a primary error detection mechanism.

Once a component (or algorithm) has been designated as faulty and one whose further use should be avoided during the provision of continued service, various strategies are possible. _Replacement strategies_ involve replacing the designated component by a previously idle component (usually called a standby-spare), or adjusting the interrelationships between components to achieve replacement of (part of) the algorithm of the system. Thus replacement strategies attempt to achieve the effect of repair of the fault. _Reconfiguration strategies_ have somewhat different characteristics. As their name suggests, these strategies involve reconfiguring the system to try to avoid use of the component (or algorithm) that has been designated as faulty, rather than attempting to repair the fault. In consequence, reconfiguration strategies will necessarily involve some degree of performance or functional degradation, as the rest of the system has to take over all (or at least some) of the responsibilities of the defective elements. A further categorisation of both types of strategy can also be identified which refers to whether the effects of the strategy are _permanent_ or _temporary_.

Example

The TMR system of figure 1b can be regarded as utilising a

T. ANDERSON, P.A. LEE and S.K. SHRIVASTAVA

temporary reconfiguration strategy. If a component fault occurs, the output from that component will be discarded by the voting circuit. However, such a reconfiguration is only temporary, for the next set of inputs will again cause all components to be used.

Summary

This section has provided an overview of the four fundamental strategies for fault tolerance, namely error detection, damage assessment, error recovery, and fault treatment and the provision of continued service. It has also shown how these strategies are influenced by the actual (or assumed) structure of the system.

The adoption of fault tolerance measures in a system will of necessity increase the size of the system. There is the danger, therefore, that unless these measures are introduced in a careful and coherent manner then the complexity of the system will be increased and its overall reliability reduced.

The use of some fault tolerance measures has in the past been common in hardware systems (as is considered in the chapter by Carter), and many systems have been designed and built to give reliable hardware operation, and to provide tolerance against (anticipated) hardware component failures. However, comparatively little attention has been paid to the problem of tolerating design faults - hardware systems have been sufficiently simple that faults in their design could be eliminated by standard techniques, for example, by comprehensive testing. Techniques for design fault tolerance have therefore not been required. In contrast, the major part of the complexity in computing systems has been left to the software and the software designer - consequently, design faults have been a major cause of unreliable behaviour of a computing system as a whole. Thus there is little hope that the transfer of software to hardware and the application of standard hardware fault tolerance techniques will enable the reliability problems of software to be overcome, even though such a transfer is now possible through the use of large scale integration.

Design faults are not a software problem per se, but a problem which usually occurs in complex systems. Complex systems (hardware or software) will, it seems, always contain residual design faults which are unanticipatable. It seems clear that the tolerance of design faults should be a major concern in the design of fault tolerant systems. For this reason backward error recovery is particularly important, since it provides a general approach to error recovery and makes no assumptions about the nature of the fault which gave rise to the error(s). Because of this importance, the following sections address in more detail the implementation techniques for backward error recovery and its provision in complex systems such as concurrent and multi-level systems.

SYSTEM FAULT TOLERANCE

MECHANISMS FOR FAULT TOLERANCE

Introduction

Earlier sections of this book have examined principles of fault
tolerance on which measures can be based which try to avert the
failure of a system. Such measures utilise redundant elements of
the system and are intended to ensure that any erroneous situations
which arise, due to the presence of residual faults in the system,
are detected and remedied. This section enlarges upon how these
fault tolerance measures can be employed in a computational system
and discusses various mechanisms which assist in their
implementation and provision. Corresponding linguistic notations
are described in the chapter by Horning.

Measures for fault tolerance are discussed here with reference
to the following simple framework (depicted in figure 3). A
computer system will be considered to consist of two components: an
interpreter and a program. The interpreter component actively
supports the interface between the two components and
interpretively executes the text which constitutes the passive
program component. A convenient characterisation of this interface
can be given by means of a language which provides (abstract)
objects and operations to manipulate those objects. The program
text, expressed in this language, determines a particular sequence
of operations to be performed by the interpreter. Operations are
implemented by the interpreter by making changes to "concrete"
representations of the "abstract" objects which are available to
the program.

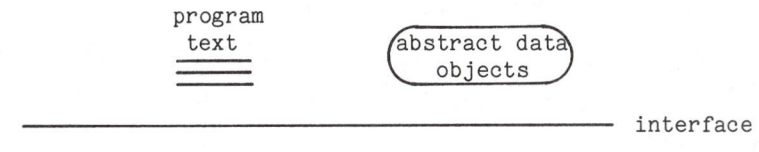

interface

interpreter

Fig. 3   Interface Between Interpreter and Program

Example

The interface between the hardware and software of a simple
computer system running a single stand-alone program has just
these characteristics. The hardware machine interprets a
machine language program which manipulates abstract entities
such as registers and words of memory.

The elementary, single program and single level system
portrayed in figure 3 is adequate for this introductory discussion

of mechanisms for fault tolerance. However, most practical computer systems are much too complicated to be modelled satisfactorily in this framework. In many systems a number of interfaces having the above characteristics can be discerned; furthermore, many systems are best modelled as systems of concurrent processes. The difficulties encountered in the provision of fault tolerance in such multi-level and concurrent systems are beyond the scope of this section and are examined in the next and final sections of this chapter.

In a discussion of the measures for fault tolerance which can be employed by the program component of figure 3 it is useful to distinguish between those measures specified in the program itself, and those which the interpreter makes available as a facility to the program. The term "mechanism" will be used to refer to any technique by which the interpreter provides facilities for the program. Measures for fault tolerance which are provided by mechanisms will have rather different characteristics to those specified at the program level.

Mechanisms for fault tolerance implemented by the interpreter will embody strategies which are intended to be of wide applicability and which are based upon simplifying, a priori, assumptions. These mechanisms may be invoked explicitly by the program, or can be initiated automatically in particular circumstances, often as a default response to erroneous situations. A further role which can be performed by the interpreter is the implementation of facilities which in themselves cannot provide fault tolerance, but which can assist or optimise the organisation of fault tolerant measures at the program level.

Measures for fault tolerance specified in the program are likely to be more specialised than those implemented by the interpreter because their design can, and often will, depend upon a knowledge of the intended functions of the normal part of the program. To enhance their effectiveness, these measures may also make use of exploratory techniques which examine the state of the abstract objects. Techniques can be implemented in the program which utilise any special facilities provided by the interpreter, and which supplement any default response of the interpreter to erroneous situations. It is advisable to ensure that fault tolerance measures specified in the program are clearly distinguished from the normal actions of the program, in order to minimise the penalties which result from any increase of complexity of the system.

Techniques for each of the four aspects of fault tolerance are now considered in the light of the above distinctions between measures specified in the program and mechanisms implemented by the interpreter.

SYSTEM FAULT TOLERANCE

Error Detection

The program can include tests to determine whether the state of the computation appears satisfactory or suspect. Clearly these tests can be as stringent or as cursory as the designer of the program chooses. Independently of these tests, the interpreter should include mechanisms for performing interface checks, and for notifying the program of any erroneous situations which are considered to relate to the program. Errors of usage of the interface constitute a major category of errors which can only be detected by the interpreter. Whenever an operation is to be performed, the validity of the operation and its operands should be checked. As well as notifying the program of any detected violations of the interface it may be necessary for the interpreter to notify the program of erroneous situations which are a consequence of faults in other parts of the system, such as any interacting programs, or even the interpreter itself.

Example

Tests can be conveniently specified in a program by means of the assert <logical expression> construct (for instance, as provided in AlgolW). Unless the <logical expression> holds the program is notified of an error.
The canonical example of an interface check performed by an interpreter is a check which detects any attempt by the program to divide by zero.

Damage Assessment

Any approach for assessing the spread of damage which is based on a priori reasoning must depend upon the existence of constraints on the flow of information in the system. These constraints can, and should, be provided at the interpreter level, for if the constraints are imposed on the program by the program itself then little confidence can be placed in their integrity in the event of a fault in the program. Attempts by the program to refine the assessment of damage (as determined by the assumed constraints) will have to examine, in some exploratory fashion, the current state of the abstract data objects. Any such exploration will adopt measures similar to those used for error detection, principally those implemented by the program itself.

The immediate purpose of constraints on information flow is usually damage confinement. In consequence, such constraints play a role in error detection (since attempts to violate them are notified to the program as errors detected by the interpreter) as well as in damage assessment. Mechanisms for damage confinement have been studied extensively and are now well established. In particular, the techniques known as protection mechanisms are sufficiently developed for a chapter of this book (that by Needham)

to be devoted to them. The concepts of an atomic action and a
sphere of control, as more general approaches to limiting the
spread of information in a system, are considered elsewhere in this
chapter and in those by Randell and Davies.

Example

An operating system capable of concurrently executing a number
of programs will often impose constraints to ensure that one
program cannot (either wilfully, or by neglect) cause any
damage to any other program.
If an error is detected, an individual program may then attempt
to determine the extent of damage by checking the consistency
of particular data structures. For this to be possible,
redundant information must have been maintained (such as a sum-
check on a vector).

Error Recovery

The aim of an error recovery technique is to transform the
current erroneous state of the system into a state which is free
from errors, since such a transformation is essential if a failure
of the system is to be averted. Any technique which can be invoked
to perform this transformation, whether a part of the program or
the interpreter, must proceed (like all other activities of the
system) by means of ordinary forward computation, since as yet it
is beyond our capabilities to reverse time. Nevertheless, the
approach employed in backward error recovery, one of the most
widely adopted recovery techniques, is to simulate the reversal of
time (as seen at the program level) by restoring some prior state
of the abstract data objects. Clearly, the restoration of an
earlier state will eliminate from the system all of the erroneous
effects which were generated by faults occurring subsequently to
that earlier state. The importance of backward error recovery, and
the ability to recover even from faults of design, both depend
crucially on this ability to repair all damage caused by any fault
whatsoever. Therefore it is essential that the technique used for
restoring a prior state should place no undue reliance on the
current state of the abstract data objects. If use is made of the
current state then there is a risk that errors already present in
that state may impair the validity of the restoration.

Backward error recovery is most conveniently and securely
provided by the interpreter. It is particularly amenable to
mechanisation by the interpreter because the state restoration
involved can be provided by a variety of relatively simple
techniques, yielding a powerful and general method of recovery.

Reset strategies, which involve replacing the current state by
some predefined state, are most conveniently supported by the
interpreter but can also be implemented by the program.

SYSTEM FAULT TOLERANCE

Any other measures for error recovery must be specified by the program, and are referred to as forward error recovery techniques. The interpreter can provide mechanisms to assist in the provision of forward error recovery but these will need to be supplemented by routines at the program level; in contrast, backward error recovery is easily implementable without recourse to such routines. Routines for recovery employed by the program will usually be more specialised due to their dependence on the particular state of the system detected as being erroneous. A prerequisite for their effectiveness in eliminating the effects of a fault is that the fault, or at least the effects that it caused, were predictable and anticipated. Only when this is the case can any confidence be placed in measures for forward error recovery.

It can certainly be argued that the most significant feature of any strategy for fault tolerance is the technique (or set of techniques) adopted for error recovery. In the majority of cases, the recovery technique has a strong bearing on what techniques are adopted for the other aspects of fault tolerance. Furthermore, mechanisms supporting error recovery are more developed than for the other aspects, with the exception of mechanisms for damage confinement. For these reasons, error recovery mechanisms are examined in more detail later in this section.

Fault Treatment

The crudest form of fault treatment is simply to ignore the fault in the hope that it will go away, or that the future operation of the system will fortuitously avoid the fault. More ambitious approaches must locate the fault so that it can either be repaired or subsequently deliberately avoided.

Since the program can have responsibility for providing tolerance to faults other than defects of the program itself, the first stage in locating a fault must be to determine whether or not the fault is in the program. Information on which to base such a decision is usually limited. If the fault is in the interpreter this may be revealed by diagnostic checking of the interpreter by the program (such testing is preferable to the interpreter checking itself because of the extra measure of independence involved). Diagnostic checking may even, to some extent, enable the program to discover where in the interpreter the fault has occurred.

Example

It has been estimated (Bowman et al. 1977) that the comprehensive use of diagnostic checking in Bell Laboratories' ESS No. 1A processor is capable of accurately locating over 95% of hardware faults.

If the fault is attributed to a defect in the program, more accurate location may proceed using error detection measures similar to those employed for exploratory damage assessment, endeavouring to isolate the cause of damage as opposed to its extent. Although this may be feasible and effective in particular anticipated situations, it is much less appropriate (and may even be impractical) when the damage is a consequence of unanticipated faults, such as faults of design.

In the event of a fault being satisfactorily located, consideration can be given to its repair or circumvention. Clearly, the repair of a faulty system can be effected by replacing the entire system, by changing some of the interconnections between components within the system, or by repairing components within the system. Alternatively, it may be possible to avoid making use of a faulty component in a system by making changes to the rest of the system; this approach is usually called reconfiguration. Both repair and reconfiguration can only be achieved by replacing components and/or changing interconnections. Techniques for these purposes have been classified by Borgerson (1973) as: _manual_, in which the system takes no part in the strategy; _dynamic_, where the system takes the necessary action in response to external stimuli; and _spontaneous_, where the actions are initiated and performed entirely by the system itself, actions sometimes referred to as "self-repair". Because of the difficulty and cost involved in providing automatic techniques for fault treatment, most systems postpone action until off-line manual intervention can take place.

Forward Error Recovery Mechanisms

All error recovery techniques are invoked in circumstances which are in some way considered abnormal. Although recovery techniques are usually applied to erroneous situations (which may or may not have been anticipated) they can also be invoked in unusual but valid situations when the designer of the system chooses to treat the (anticipated) situation as if it were erroneous. (The chapter by Randell discusses the subjective decisions involved in structuring a system into normal and abnormal subsystems.) Anticipated situations to which forward error recovery measures are applied will be termed _exceptional_, conforming to the established terminology (Noble 1968).

Example

A program reading from a magnetic tape may encounter "end of block", "logical end of tape" or "physical end of tape". All three circumstances may, if the designer of the program so chooses, be regarded as exceptional; which are considered as erroneous and which as merely unusual will depend on the viewpoint adopted.

Because the situations in which exception handling techniques
are utilised have been anticipated, the techniques can usually make
effective use of the current state, but only by relying on the
accuracy of the assessment of the extent of the damage to the
state, and often also on an appreciation of the likely fault to
which the exceptional situation should be attributed. Such
techniques will be specific to the particular program in which they
are employed and therefore cannot be provided by an interpreter;
however, an interpreter can make available facilities which
simplify the organisation of forward error recovery, in the form of
mechanisms for raising exceptional conditions and for subsequently
invoking corresponding exception handlers. These exception
handlers are forward error recovery routines supplied in the
program.

The chapter by Horning includes a review of language features
for expressing exception handling techniques. Most currently
implemented schemes operate by augmenting an operation or procedure
to make use of an extra operand. This operand can be used to
return a value indicating exceptional circumstances, or it may
indicate an abnormal return address. If the language permits the
use of variables which can refer to procedures or operations then
this feature can form the basis of an exception handling technique.

More recent proposals (Goodenough 1975, Levin 1977) have
advocated language notations especially designed for exception
handling. Basically, these notations permit the program to

(i)   declare an exceptional condition
      X: _exception_;

(ii) raise an exception
      signal X;

(iii) make available a handler for an exception
      enable <handling routine> _to_ _handle_ X;

In addition, certain exceptional conditions may be predeclared and
raised automatically by the interpreter.

Support for these facilities can be provided in a uniform
manner by the interpreter as is now briefly described. Declaration
of an exception is straightforward and merely involves inserting an
entry into a symbol table. If the raising of an exception is
expected to be a very infrequent event, then enabling a handler
need only involve recording the information that the handler is
available in the appropriate context. Then, if an exception is
signalled from a module of the program, a potentially time
consuming search of the relevant contexts must be performed to
determine which of the enabled handlers for that exception should
be invoked. Of course, by expending additional time and space when

handlers are enabled, the search needed when an exception is raised can be expedited. Parnas and Wurges (1976) and Levin (1977) have argued that the contexts which should be searched are those which can make use of the module in which the exception was raised, rather than those from which the module was invoked, that is, contexts in the "uses" rather than the "calls" hierarchy (Parnas 1974).

After an exception handler has been executed different policies can be adopted for the subsequent operation of the system, according to whether the module from which the exception was raised should or should not be terminated.

Backward Error Recovery Mechanisms

The task of a backward error recovery mechanism is to restore an earlier state of an interface, thereby undoing the effects of operations that were performed on the interface. Provision of a backward error recovery capability obviously depends upon the interpreter recording the information which is needed to enable state restoration to take place. This information is referred to as _recovery data_. Points in a computation for which the (then) current state can be restored are termed _recovery points_, in that recovery to the corresponding state is available if it is required. A fully general backward error recovery mechanism must support notations which permit the program to:

(i)   establish recovery points

(ii)   discard recovery points

(iii)   restore the prior state of a computation and ensure that any strategies for fault treatment are invoked.

These three actions may be explicitly requested by the program, or the interpreter may initiate them in response to particular situations.

Since there is no requirement that one recovery point must be discarded before another is established, it is certainly possible that more than one recovery point could be available when recovery was required. Some policy must therefore be adopted to determine which prior state should be selected for restoration. Obvious example policies are the selection of the oldest, or of the most recent, recovery point. Similarly, a policy must be adopted to determine which of a set of recovery points should be discarded when this becomes necessary (to avoid the excessive accumulation of recovery data). Because of possible interdependencies among the information recorded, discarding a recovery point may involve more than merely discarding the associated recovery data. Recovery to the remaining recovery points must not be compromised, and this may

necessitate some processing of all of the recovery data.
Discarding a recovery point entails some measure of <u>commitment</u>
since recovery is no longer available to that recovery point.

The most significant feature of a backward error recovery
mechanism is the method adopted for recording and preserving
recovery data, since this largely determines how recovery points
are discarded and restored.

The simplest and most direct method for recording recovery data
is to preserve a complete record of all aspects of the state of the
system for each established recovery point. Such records are
commonly known as checkpoints (Tonik 1975), and suffer from the
obvious drawback of requiring information to be retained about
every object in the system, despite the possibility that many of
these objects might remain unchanged. Consequently, a checkpoint
may need to be very extensive (and expensive), potentially having
to preserve a copy of all of main, disc and even tape storage.

This disadvantage can be mitigated by only recording recovery
data for those objects which are in fact updated; for example, the
COPRA system (Meraud, Browaeys and Germain 1976) attempts to assess
in advance which objects fall into this category. Alternatively,
recovery data may be recorded incrementally - that is, the state of
an object is saved just before the object is actually updated. The
recovery cache technique (Horning et al. 1974), employed in
conjunction with recovery blocks, is based on this approach and
will be described in detail subsequently. A rather different
method organises recovery data in the form of an audit trail (Bjork
1975) or log (Gray 1978), which essentially provides a historical
record of the transactions (that is, groups of operations) that
have been performed. Either each transaction must be reversible or
sufficient ancillary information maintained so that the effects of
each transaction can be nullified. An audit trail can provide a
very fine grain of backward error recovery since a recovery point
is established after every transaction.

Backward error recovery is often used to restore the contents
of data base systems and filing systems. In a comprehensive
survey, Verhofstad (1978) discusses further techniques known as
incremental dumping, differential files, backup files, and careful
replacement. Incremental dumping involves copying those files
which have been updated onto archival storage at regular intervals.
As the name suggests, backup files merely constitute a checkpoint
forming a consistent prior version of a set of files. To implement
differential files, each file must be maintained in two parts: the
main file which remains unchanged, and the differential file which
records all updates requested for the main file. The differential
file forms a type of audit trail, which is periodically combined
with the main file. Careful replacement is achieved by never
updating the original version of a file. Instead, a copy of the

file is made and the update applied to the copy. On satisfactory completion of the update, the original file can be deleted.

Each of these methods of recording recovery data represents a particular engineering solution to the many trade-offs which can be made between space and time with reference to the varying frequencies of, and costs involved in, the different aspects of supporting backward error recovery. Which method is most appropriate for a particular situation can only be determined by assessing the likely need for, and costs of, recovery in that situation. Indeed, it could be more effective to use a combination of techniques.

Example

By maintaining an audit trail between occasional checkpoints (Curtice 1977) a compromise can be made between the high storage penalty of a large number of checkpoints and the time consuming processing of a long audit trail. To restore a prior state for which no explicit checkpoint is available, the audit trail can be processed either forwards or backwards as necessary from the nearest checkpoint to the required recovery point.

In practice, for a number of reasons, backward error recovery does not usually imply that a prior state is exactly and completely restored.

Firstly, it is only necessary to ensure that the abstract state of the data objects is restored. Since there may be many concrete representations corresponding to a given abstract state this may simplify the provision of recovery.

Example

Suppose a stack is to be restored to a prior state in which it was empty. Only a pointer in the concrete representation of the stack need be restored since the values of objects representing stack elements are then irrelevant.

Secondly, it is usual to distinguish between recoverable and unrecoverable objects available on an interface. Recoverable objects are those for which backward error recovery is provided, while unrecoverable objects are those for which state restoration is not available or appropriate. As such, unrecoverable objects can also be used to model the effects of the external environment of a system, for example, a read-only clock. Since only the recoverable part of the state is restored by a backward error recovery mechanism, the program must accept responsibility for the unrecoverable objects - perhaps by applying forward error recovery techniques.

SYSTEM FAULT TOLERANCE

A third reason only applies when the states of a number of concurrent processes are to be restored. It may be preferable to restore the processes individually to prior states which did not actually co-exist at a single previous point in time.

The Recovery Cache

A detailed description is now given of a recovery cache mechanism, which was specifically designed to implement backward error recovery for recovery blocks. The particular organisation of the recovery cache described here is due to Kerr (Kerr 1978, Anderson and Kerr 1976); the description is adapted from these papers.

A recovery block is a programming construct which provides a unified, disciplined and hierarchical framework for incorporating fault tolerance measures in a single sequential program. A brief description is adequate here; for further details consult the chapter by Horning. The standard representation of a recovery block is given below:

```
        ensure   <acceptance test>
            by   <1st (primary) alternate>
        else by  <2nd alternate>
               .
               .
               .
        else by  <nth alternate>
        else error
```

All four aspects of fault tolerance provision are embodied in a recovery block. Recovery actions are invoked automatically in response to errors detected either by interface checks or by the programmer specified <acceptance test>. Backward error recovery is used so damage assessment is obviated, and protection afforded against a very wide class of faults (including software design faults). Fault treatment is achieved by means of temporary spontaneous replacement of an <alternate> which does not succeed in passing the acceptance test. Thus the alternates act as software standby spares.

A recovery point must be established whenever a recovery block is entered, and discarded when the block is successfully exited. Backward error recovery to the most recent recovery point is invoked whenever an error is detected. The basic recovery cache provides recovery for words of memory; for simplicity this is the version which is now described.

A special register records the current recovery level, that is, the current depth of dynamic nesting of recovery blocks. Initially this register has a value of zero. With each word of memory is

associated a recovery level field. This information can be held in
a separate data structure forming an adjunct to the cache itself.
The cache itself is organised as a stack, which is subdivided into
regions separated by barriers. Each region corresponds to a
recovery block which has been entered, but not yet exited, and
contains the prior values of those words of memory which have been
updated from within that recovery block. An entry in a region of
the cache contains three fields; the first contains the address of
a word in memory, while the other two preserve a copy of the value
which that word, together with its associated recovery level field,
contained when the recovery block corresponding to the region was
entered.

The next five paragraphs define the operation of the recovery
cache mechanism.

Example

It may be helpful for the reader to construct for himself the
contents of the cache at each stage in the following program:

```
a:=10;  b:=30;
ensure  test 1
   by  a:=b-a;
       ensure  test 2
          by  b:=b-a; a:=b+a;
       else by  ...  else error;
   ...
else error
```

When a recovery block is entered, the recovery level register
is incremented by one and a new barrier is placed on the cache
stack, establishing a new recovery point.

When a word of memory is first allocated, its associated
recovery level field is initialised to the current recovery level.
This provides an optimisation when memory is allocated dynamically,
in that words which are local to a recovery block are not cached
with respect to that recovery block. If all memory is allocated
initially then all words are global to the recovery blocks and no
optimisation is achieved.

When a word of memory is to be updated, its associated recovery
level field is compared with the current recovery level. If these
are equal then the word is simply updated, but if they differ this
indicates that the word in question has not yet been changed within
the current recovery block and so encachement is necessary. A new
entry is placed on the cache, consisting of the address of the
word, its current value, and the current value of the recovery
level field associated with the word. The recovery level of the
word is then set to the current recovery level and, finally, the

word can be updated. Note that the recovery level field of a word indicates at which recovery level the word acquired its value.

When a recovery block is successfully exited (by passing the acceptance test) the recovery level register is decremented by one. The most recent recovery point is then discarded, but this cannot be achieved simply by removing the top region of the cache. To maintain appropriate recovery data for any remaining recovery points the entries in the top region of the cache must be processed as· if each word recorded there were being updated at the new recovery level. For each entry, the recovery level of the corresponding memory word is set equal to the value now in the recovery level register (since the net effect of assignments in the exited recovery block is equivalent to an assignment in the enclosing recovery block). If the recovery level held in the cache entry is equal to the value in the recovery level register then the cache entry can be discarded (since the word has either already been updated or was first allocated in the enclosing recovery block). Otherwise, the cache entry must be transferred to the next to top region of the cache. When all entries from the top region have been discarded or transferred the barrier can also be discarded, and the next to top region becomes the new top region.

When backward error recovery is invoked, the memory must be restored to the state it was in on entry to the current recovery block. Preserved in the top region of the cache are the prior values of all memory words which have been updated by the defective alternate, so restoration can easily be achieved. For each entry in the top region, the value is copied back to the word designated by the address field. Also, the associated recovery level field of that word is restored from the cache entry. As each entry is processed, it is discarded from the cache.

<u>Example</u>

Returning to the program given above, after the assignment a:=b+a the recovery level is 2 and the memory and recovery cache are as shown:

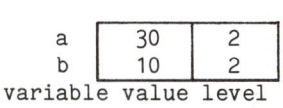

a	30	2
b	10	2

variable value level

a	20	1
b	30	0
barrier		
a	10	0
barrier		

memory   recovery cache

T. ANDERSON, P.A. LEE and S.K. SHRIVASTAVA

After passing acceptance test 2 the recovery level returns to 1 and the memory and recovery cache are as shown:

a	30	1
b	10	1

b	30	0
a	10	0
	barrier	

The recovery cache mechanism offers certain advantages over more conventional techniques for supporting recovery points. It ensures that all and only those values which might be required to be reinstated are preserved until the relevant recovery point is discarded. Furthermore, the preservation and reinstatement as necessary of such values is entirely automatic, and therefore much less susceptible to errors of omission.

Alternative recovery cache implementations are possible, each of which has different trade-offs. The original proposal (Horning et al. 1974) is likely to yield a slower implementation than that described here, but imposes a smaller storage overhead. Another suggestion is to inhibit the updating of main memory and record any new values in the cache, in a similar manner to the operation of a differential file. More powerful cache mechanisms can be devised which provide recovery for more abstract data structures than words of memory (some of the issues involved were discussed in the original proposal).

A recovery cache can furnish a program with certain extra facilities which can assist in more stringent error checking by the program. Firstly, it can allow reference to be made to the prior values of objects, enabling comparison to be made between current values and those which obtained at the most recent recovery point. Secondly, it can permit checks that all of a set of objects have indeed been updated, or conversely that only objects in a specified set have been updated (which relates to the so-called "frame problem" arising in Artificial Intelligence (Hayes 1971)). It is also possible to ally resource locking mechanisms with a recovery cache in order to implement a recoverable form of atomic action.

Ideally, a recovery cache should be implemented so as to operate at a similar speed to, and in parallel with, the memory to which it provides recovery. Alas, few memory systems are at present supplemented by such a cache, but this situation may well change in the near future, as hardware costs continue to decrease and concern for the reliability of software increases.

Summary

This section has distinguished between techniques for fault tolerance which are specified in a program, and mechanisms for fault tolerance which are implemented by an underlying interpreter. In trying to obtain a high standard of reliability from a program, despite the inevitable presence of faults, the availability of mechanisms for each of the four aspects of fault tolerance will be very beneficial. Interface checking and notification mechanisms will aid in detecting errors, while damage confinement mechanisms will assist in both error detection and damage assessment. Mechanisms can be implemented to provide backward error recovery, and to simplify the utilisation of forward error recovery by the program. Spontaneous replacement techniques are necessary for fully automatic fault treatment.

Particular emphasis has been given to backward error recovery mechanisms because of their all-important ability to provide recovery from the effects of any fault, assuming only that a state prior to the occurrence of the fault can be successfully restored.

FAULT TOLERANCE IN MULTI-LEVEL SYSTEMS

Introduction

It is now recognised that the complexity inherent in many computing systems is a major cause of their unreliable behaviour, since unmastered complexity in their design and implementation is a prime source of the residual faults that exist in such systems. In order to increase system reliability, attempts have been made to limit and master complexity. One systematic method of designing a computing system is to adopt a multi-level, hierarchical approach: starting with a given hardware machine I0, a first level of software can be added to form a new interface (or level) I1. The features available on I1 can then be used to construct the next interface I2, and so on. The advantages of such a multi-level approach are well known and not repeated here, and the approach has been adopted in the construction of some systems, for example the THE multiprogramming system (Dijkstra 1968) and the VENUS operating system (Liskov 1972).

It is clear that any approach that assists in mastering design complexity can only be beneficial to the reliability of the resulting system. However, it is widely recognised that complex systems will always contain residual faults, despite the adoption of such approaches, and any system with a high reliability requirement will also have to adopt fault tolerance techniques. The general principles and mechanisms of fault tolerance have been discussed in the previous sections of this chapter. After identifying two distinct categories of interface support for multi-level systems, this section discusses the provision of fault tolerance to independent processes in such systems. In particular, the provision of backward error recovery is examined in depth.

Multi-level Systems

In any given system, a hierarchy of abstract interfaces (or levels) can be discerned, determined by the view that is taken of the structure of the system. An abstract interface may be conveniently thought of as being characterised by a language providing objects and their associated operations. When the implementation of such interfaces is examined, two distinct classes of support can be identified: (i) _interpretation_, and (ii) _extended interpretation_. The most significant interfaces arising in a system are those supported by interpretation, as described below.

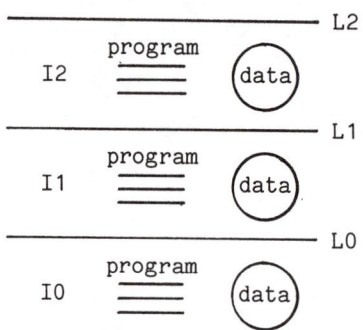

Fig. 4 Interpretive Multi-level System

Each of the interfaces Li in figure 4 is implemented by means of a program Ii which is executed on the interface Li-1. The execution of an operation in the program Ii+1 is directly supported by means of the program Ii, and any "abstract" object used by the program Ii+1 has a "concrete" representation as a set of objects in Li-1, held in a data area maintained for this purpose by Ii. Thus the interface Li is supported by interpretation, provided by the program Ii which is therefore referred to as an _interpreter_.

Example

In its normal use, the Burroughs B1700 system (Wilner 1972) employs two levels of interpretation. The lowest level, implemented in hardware, interprets the microprogram contained in the control store. The microprogram itself is an interpreter designed, say, to provide the features of an interface for supporting Cobol programs.

Interpretation is a powerful technique for constructing multi-level systems. However, the overhead that each level of interpretation entails can be significant. Moreover, each interpreter has to implement all of the features of the new interface; if the implementor of a new interface Li wishes it to have many behavioural properties in common with the underlying interface Li-1 then there is no way of optimising this structure in a fully interpretive system - the implementor will have to re-implement all of those properties for Li.

It is possible to avoid this re-implementation when an interface is supported by an extended interpreter. If the interface Li-1 provides sufficiently powerful extension facilities, it will be possible to implement Li by providing an extension to Li-1. This is illustrated in figure 5.

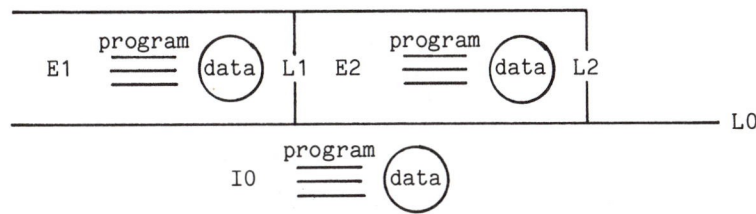

Fig. 5   Extended Interpreter Multi-level System

In figure 5, the interface L0 is supported by interpretation. Each interface Li (i=1,2) is constructed as an extension of the interface Li-1, implemented by means of the program Ei which is executed on the interface Li-1. This program is referred to here as an interpreter extension. Every interaction on the interface Li is first examined by the interpreter I0. If the interaction is not directly supported by I0, then I0 must determine which of the extensions Ej ($j \leq i$) does support the interaction, and invoke that extension. Execution of the extension Ej then proceeds (via the interface Lj-1) until the interaction originating on Li is completed, whereupon the next interaction on Li can be initiated. Any "abstract" object available on Li has a "concrete" representation which is manipulated either by the interpreter I0 or by an extension Ej ($j \leq i$). Of course, Ej manipulates the abstract objects available on Lj-1.

Example

Most operating systems are implemented as an extension to the underlying (hardware) interpreter, so as to provide a more convenient user interface than that provided by the underlying machine. The abstract objects available to users will include words of memory and file storage; words have their concrete representation in the underlying machine whereas files are represented in the data space of the operating system.

The salient features of an extended interpreter system are that firstly, it enables a new interface to have behavioural properties in common with those of the underlying interface without the need to re-implement those properties - an extension can simply add new

features and (of course) remove existing features. Secondly, the
mechanisms used to implement a multi-level extended interpreter
system are different from those used to implement an interpretive
system - in the extended interpreter system of figure 5, the
underlying interpreter I0 has responsibility for all programs
executed on interfaces Li (i=1,2), with assistance from the
extensions as required; in the interpretive system of figure 4 each
interpreter only has responsibility for the interface directly
above. The diagrammatic representation of the two systems is
intended to emphasise these distinctions. Of course, both
techniques can be used in the same multi-level system. To any
program being executed on an interface it will be completely
immaterial whether the interface was implemented by extended
interpretation or not - indeed, the distinction will only be
discernable from an examination of the implementation of the
interface, and not from the properties of the interface itself.

It should be noted that this section is only concerned with
interfaces that exist at run-time, and not those that are merely
present in a source program before being thrown away by
compilation.

Fault Tolerance in Interpretive Multi-Level Systems

As noted above, an interpreter implements, and is responsible
for, all of the features of the interface it supports. Among these
features will be any fault tolerance facilities provided for the
programs which are to be executed on that interface. The previous
section of this chapter has examined mechanisms for implementing
fault tolerance in a simple single-level interpretive system.
Since each interpreter in a multi-level interpretive system has
sole responsibility for the interface it maintains, the
implementation of fault tolerance in such a system will in general
be a straightforward repeated implementation of the necessary
mechanisms and need not be discussed further here. What does
require further examination is the possible relationships between
the various levels when faults and failures occur.

The following discussion is given with respect to a program, an
interpreter (which interprets the program), and an underlying
interpreter (which interprets the interpreter) - for instance, the
program I2, the interpreter I1, and the underlying interpreter I0
in figure 4. Of course, any program can itself be an interpreter
supporting a further program, and so on.

Failure: The first situation to be considered is if a failure of an
interpreter occurs without an error being detected. (A failure
occurs when the interpreter does not conform to its authoritative
specification, as discussed in the chapter by Randell.) In this
situation (a part of) the state of the interpreter is not well
defined, as will be the case for all higher interfaces. However,

the interpreter will continue processing until an error is
eventually detected somewhere in the system.

Example

Consider a hardware implemented interpreter, such as that
present in a computer system, which utilises core storage to
implement the abstraction "memory words" for programs. (This
example, suitably augmented, will be used throughout this
discussion to illustrate the various points raised.) If a
failure of one bit of the core storage occurred and parity
checking was not provided then the failure would not be
detected by the interpreter. Processing would therefore
continue until a possibly different error was detected by the
program or the interpreter.

Error detected: The second case to be considered is when an error
is detected by the interpreter. The fault which gave rise to this
error could be in the program, in the interpreter itself or in the
underlying interpreter. As discussed in previous sections, fault
location may be a difficult task. If the error was detected by
checks in the interpreter on the use of the interface it was
supporting then the fault must have been in the program being
interpreted. The program would then be notified of the error by
the interpreter, and the discussion would reopen at the beginning
of this paragraph, but considering the program as the interpreter.
(As described in the first section of this chapter, error
notification is equivalent to error detection at the level being
notified.)

Example

Consider the memory system discussed above, extended to provide
read-only as well as read-write memory words. An attempt by
the program to write into a read-only word would (should!) be
detected by the interpreter, resulting in error notification.

If the interpreter determines that the fault is not in the program
being interpreted, then either the interpreter itself is at fault,
or a failure of the underlying interpreter has occurred. In either
case the interpreter should make use of any fault tolerance
measures that are available to it.

Fault tolerance successful: Following the utilisation of fault
tolerance measures, the interpreter may be satisfied that all
errors have been removed from the system and that the fault has, as
necessary, been treated. If this is indeed the case then a
possible failure will have been averted and the effects of the
fault will have been masked from the program being interpreted. If
this is not the case then failure and/or further error detection in
the system are likely.

T. ANDERSON, P.A. LEE and S.K. SHRIVASTAVA

Example

If the core storage of the computing system was protected by
redundancy utilising an error-correcting code then the effects
of a fault which caused a one-bit error in a memory word could
be masked from the program accessing that word. If the error-
correction had been incorrectly implemented in the interpreter
then failure and/or further error detection are likely to
ensue.

Fault tolerance exhausted: A situation may arise in which the
interpreter is not satisfied with the state of the system after all
available fault tolerance measures have been attempted. In this
situation, the interpreter can do nothing more to avert the failure
which it has evidence is likely to occur. One possible response
would be for the interpreter to just continue in the hope that
either the failure will not actually occur, or that the effects of
failure will not be too serious.

Example

Assume that the error-correcting code of the previous example
enables one-bit errors to be corrected and multiple errors to
be detected. If a fault gives rise to multiple errors in a
word of the core storage and the interpreter has provided no
further redundancy, then tolerance for this fault has been
exhausted (since none existed) and it is likely that a failure
will occur. Of course, if the interpreter continued and
returned an arbitrary value to the program which happened
fortuitously to be the correct value then a failure would not
have occurred.

It is likely that the above response will not be considered
appropriate for applications requiring high reliability. However,
the only improvement would appear to be for the interpreter to
explicitly indicate that failure was likely so that external action
could be initiated if possible. A crude realisation of this
approach is for the interpreter to cease to provide any service at
all. As a result, the interpreter (and, no doubt, the entire
system) would presumably fail, but no further damage to the system
would ensue. This response is often used as a means of instigating
manual activities to effect a repair of the system. A more refined
technique would be for the interpreter to continue, but only after
notifying the program that a failure was likely. By analogy with
error notification, such action may be termed failure notification.

Failure notified: When the program is notified that the behaviour
of the interface on which it is being executed must be regarded as
suspect, any action taken can only be of a protective nature to try
and minimise any damage that might be caused. One likely response
of the program could be to treat this failure notification as an

error notification so as to invoke its fault tolerance measures. (Indeed, the interpreter could have produced exactly this effect directly by using the error notification mechanism instead of indicating a possible failure.) Of course, the (perhaps vain) hope is that either the presumed failure of the interpreter will not adversely affect the program, or that the fault tolerance utilised by the program will prove adequate and prevent failure of the program itself.

Example

Hardware implemented interpreters in computer systems often provide a "parity interrupt" which can be used to notify a program of a core store failure for which the erroneous consequences have not been corrected. If the program had retained a copy of the contents of the word, then the program could itself provide sufficient recovery. However, if the program was simply setting the word to zero because it had finished using that word, then the failure would not affect the program.

Failure notification would seem to be a sensible approach to adopt as a last resort measure by a fault tolerant interpreter (as has been advocated by Parnas and Wurges (1976)). It may be noted that if the specification for the interface supported by the interpreter permitted the use of the error notification mechanism for notifying failures, then by definition a failure of the interpreter would not have occurred - this action by the interpreter would have to be regarded as a part of the normal fault tolerance measures of the interpreter, and would therefore be covered by the paragraph entitled "fault tolerance successful".

Fault Tolerance in Extended Interpreter Systems

The principal aim of an interpreter extension is, as its name suggests, to extend a given interface with new kinds of abstract objects. Clearly, it is desirable for an extension to ensure that the fault tolerance provided by the underlying interpreter is extended to apply to these new objects.

Most of the strategies which this will involve will simply be applications of the fault tolerance techniques which have been discussed elsewhere. For example, the extension will provide interface checks to detect errors in the use of the new kinds of objects by higher level programs. However, some of the fault tolerance features in an extended interpreter system require closer examination, since two different viewpoints can be identified.

These two viewpoints relate to the way in which an extension is viewed as a part of the overall system. An extension can be considered to be a part of the underlying interpreter, <u>disjoint</u> from any calling program. Alternatively, a calling program may be regarded as being <u>inclusive</u> of the extension, the extension then being considered to be a nested component of the program. The two viewpoints lead to the adoption of different organisations for certain aspects of fault tolerance.

Consider a program being executed by an extended interpreter, and suppose that the extension has detected an error for which all of the fault tolerance available to the extension has proved inadequate. If the extension is to be regarded as a part of the interpreter, then the discussion in the paragraph above entitled "fault tolerance exhausted" applies: the extension could optimistically continue, pessimistically halt, or pragmatically notify the program of a likely failure and then continue. However, if the extension is regarded as a part of the calling program the obvious response is for the extension to notify the program of an error.

The remainder of this section examines in detail the salient characteristics of the provision of backward error recovery in extended interpreter systems, and discusses two different organisations of recovery arising from the disjoint and inclusive viewpoints.

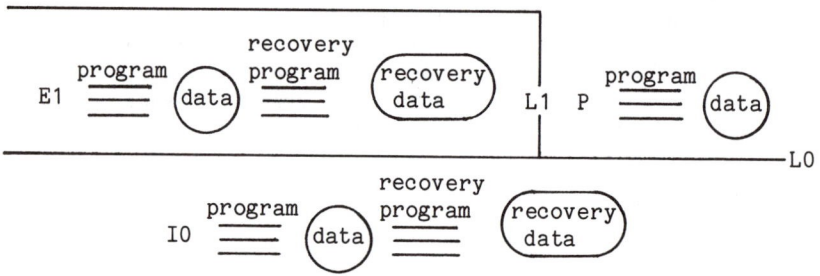

Fig. 6   Recovery Structures in an Extended Interpreter System

Consider the situation depicted in figure 6. In this system, an interpreter extension E1 and a program P are both interpreted by the underlying interpreter I0. It will be assumed that the interface L0 supports both recoverable and unrecoverable objects and permits recovery points to be established and discarded. To provide these features, I0 will include <u>recovery programs</u> for recording and maintaining recovery data, and for restoring prior states as necessary, for programs which it executes. A further useful notion is that of the <u>recovery environment</u> associated with a recovery point. The recovery environment is that set of recoverable objects which are available on the interface at the time the corresponding recovery point is established.

SYSTEM FAULT TOLERANCE

Example

In a program written in a block-structured language, a recovery
environment would consist of the set of recoverable variables
that had been declared at the time the recovery point was
established.

Suppose that the interface L1 contains recoverable objects only
and that some of these are maintained by E1 while the rest are
maintained directly by I0.

Example

In order to clarify the main points being raised an example
multilevel system with the structure illustrated in figure 6
will be used. In this system the underlying interpreter I0
provides recoverable variables held in main storage and
unrecoverable disc pages. The extension E1 implements a
rudimentary file system, giving P access to the abstraction of
a (random access) recoverable file containing lines of text.
Recoverable variables provided by I0 are also available to P.
The concrete representation maintained by E1 for the file
consists of a set of unrecoverable disc pages, a copy (called
'page_buffer') of the most recently accessed disc page, and an
array of disc page addresses (called 'file_map'). The objects
page_buffer and file_map are held in main storage. Each entry
in file_map points to one of the disc pages currently
representing the file. When P accesses the file, either to
read or write a line, the access is actually applied (by E1) to
page_buffer. If the line in question is not present in
page_buffer, because it is empty or contains the wrong disc
page, then the relevant disc page is copied into page_buffer
(if page_buffer contains an updated disc page then this must
first be copied back to the disc).

Suppose further that the program P has established a recovery
point, and that recovery for P is subsequently required. The
behaviour desired from the system is obvious; all of the objects
being used by P will need to be restored to their state at the time
the recovery point was established. Certainly I0 can restore those
objects it was directly maintaining for P. How then is the
recovery of the objects maintained by E1 to be achieved?

In general, E1 will have to provide recovery programs and
maintain recovery data in a manner similar to I0. When invoked to
manipulate objects on behalf of P, E1 can record the necessary
recovery data. Then, if recovery for P is required, the recovery
programs in E1 will need to be invoked by I0 to restore the
relevant objects used by P. For the extension to participate in
the provision of recovery in this way it will also be necessary for
I0 to invoke the recovery programs of E1 whenever P establishes or

discards a recovery point. (Conceptually this is necessary; optimisation is certainly possible.)

Example

In the example file system described above, the recovery program of E1 must be able to restore a prior version of the file if recovery for P is required. This can be achieved by ensuring that the disc pages which represent the file when P establishes a recovery point are not overwritten. When page_buffer is to be copied back to the disc, instead of overwriting the original disc page an unused disc page is acquired and page_buffer is written to this new page. (This need only be done the first time a disc page is to be overwritten after P establishes a recovery point.) Clearly, the appropriate entry in file_map must be changed to point to the new disc page, and in consequence the disc address of the old disc page must be recorded as recovery data by E1.

The question which will now be considered concerns the use of recoverable objects (on L0) by E1 to maintain abstract objects (on L1) for use by P. Are these recoverable L0 objects to be restored by I0 when recovery is provided to P?

Example

In the file system example the objects file_map and page_buffer are recoverable objects (on L0) which E1 uses to maintain the abstraction of a recoverable file for use by P. Should recovery of P cause these objects to be restored by I0?

If an extension is regarded as being a part of the underlying interpreter and independent of the calling program (the disjoint viewpoint) then, clearly, the provision of recovery to P would not imply the automatic restoration of any objects used by E1. Indeed, I0 would maintain no recovery data for E1 with respect to recovery points of P; that is, objects on the interface L0 used by E1 would not be considered to be within any recovery environment of P. In consequence, E1 would be completely responsible for the recovery of the abstract objects it was maintaining on L1. Thus, the behaviour of an extension would model that of an interpreter in an interpretive multi-level system. The scheme of recovery outlined above is, appropriately, termed the disjoint recovery scheme.

Example

If the disjoint recovery scheme is adopted for the file system example then the objects file_map and page_buffer would not be restored to their prior states by I0 when recovery is provided to P. E1 must still be able to restore the prior state of the file - but this is easily achieved. The recovery data recorded by E1 simply needs to indicate which file_map entries must be restored and the disc addresses to which they should be reset (that is, the addresses of the old disc pages discussed above). Using this information, E1 can reset file_map to its state at the time the recovery point was established and can also release the new disc pages that had been acquired. Note that page_buffer need not be restored. The recovery program of E1 merely empties page_buffer since any subsequent access of the file by P will result in a disc page being copied into page_buffer. All of these actions ensure that the file is restored to the abstract state which existed when P established the recovery point. This example also illustrates that the provision of the abstraction of recovery for an object does not imply that an exact prior state of an object must be restored; there may be many concrete states which have the same abstract state. The disjoint recovery scheme can take advantage of this, as illustrated here, when providing recovery.

One of the main aims of an interpreter extension, such as E1, is to extend an interface without incurring the inefficiency of reimplementing all of the features which are to remain unchanged in the new interface. A disadvantage of the disjoint recovery scheme is the necessity of reimplementing recoverability even in situations where the recovery which could have been provided by the underlying interpreter would have been exactly what was required.

Example

In the file system example, the recovery program of E1 had to record and restore file_map explicitly even though automatic recovery of file_map by IO could have provided that part of the overall actions required for recovery of P by E1.

The disadvantage is avoided if an extension is regarded as being a part of the calling program (the inclusive viewpoint). It then seems natural for the provision of recovery to P by IO to also involve the restoration of recoverable objects used by E1 on behalf of P. Recovery data is maintained by IO for both P and E1 in that whenever P establishes a recovery point, any recoverable objects of E1 are considered to be within the corresponding recovery environment. This recovery scheme is termed the inclusive recovery scheme.

With the inclusive recovery scheme, the extension E1 need only record recovery data relating to the use of any unrecoverable objects which it manipulates on behalf of P. Indeed, if E1 only made use of recoverable objects, then restoration of these objects by IO would automatically achieve recovery for the abstract objects supported by E1. In contrast, the disjoint recovery scheme requires E1 to record recovery data corresponding to all of the objects it manipulates.

Example

If the inclusive recovery scheme is adopted for the file system example then when recovery is invoked for P the prior states of file_map and page_buffer will be automatically restored by I0. As with the disjoint scheme, E1 must acquire new disc pages to avoid overwriting the disc pages which represented the file at the time the recovery point was established. Automatic restoration of file_map thus ensures that the file is restored to its prior state, and the recovery program of E1 merely has to release the newly acquired disc pages. It may also be noted that if recoverable disc pages were available on L0 then there would be no need for any recovery programs in E1 with the inclusive scheme. In contrast, the recoverability of the disc pages has no impact on the recovery provided by E1 with the disjoint scheme.

One disadvantage of the inclusive recovery scheme can be seen by reconsidering the data structures used within the extension E1 to hold any necessary recovery data (such as the addresses of newly acquired disc pages in the example above). If these structures are constructed using recoverable objects on L0 then it is possible that the information they contain will be lost if the objects are restored (by I0) before the recovery program of the extension is executed. A simple solution to the problem is to insist that recovery data in E1 be maintained in unrecoverable objects, but this suffers from the limitation that the recovery programs of E1 can then derive no local benefit from the recovery capabilities of I0. A more general solution is to ensure that the recovery programs of an extension behave as if they were operating under the provisions of the disjoint recovery scheme, for example, by ensuring that the recovery program of E1 is executed before recovery is provided by I0. It may be noted that the problem does not arise in the disjoint recovery scheme since all programs (including recovery programs) exhibit the necessary behaviour.

All of this discussion has been with respect to the system with one extension depicted in figure 6. Generalisation to systems containing many extensions is beyond the scope of this chapter but has been discussed by Anderson, Lee and Shrivastava (1978), who also present a detailed description of the two recovery schemes.

Summary

This section has identified two categories of interface support for multi-level systems and has discussed some of the problems of providing fault tolerance in such systems. The relationship between the various levels in a multi-level system when faults and failures occur has been examined, and led to some suggestions for last resort measures which could be incorporated into any level in an attempt to continue to provide a service.

SYSTEM FAULT TOLERANCE

The section has also examined the implementation of backward error recovery in extended interpreter systems and two organisations for the recovery (disjoint and inclusive) have been described. The behaviour of the disjoint recovery scheme models that of interpretive multi-level systems, and as such shares the main advantage and disadvantage of those systems. These are, respectively, conceptual simplicity and the inability to utilise the recoverability of lower level objects in the provision of recovery for new objects. The inclusive recovery scheme was suggested to overcome this disadvantage. However, it was shown that this scheme needs the features of the disjoint scheme at least for the recovery program parts of the extension.

Work is continuing at Newcastle to examine in more detail the ramifications of the two recovery schemes; at present it seems appropriate that an interpreter should support both of these schemes for the efficient implementation of multi-level systems using interpreter extensions.

RECOVERY IN CONCURRENT SYSTEMS

Introduction

At a suitable level of abstraction, a computer system can be viewed as consisting of a family of concurrent processes that are harmoniously exchanging and processing the information entrusted to the system. These processes may be computational activities of the computer(s), the users of the system or a combination of both. Furthermore, the information exchange may take the form of a message exchange between two or more computational activities of the computer(s); a conversation between a user (at a terminal) and the computer(s); users of the system exchanging information about the system through the postal system; or any combination of these and various other ways of exchanging information. In order to discuss the recovery actions of such processes (for example, what actions to undertake should it be decided that the information sent by a process to other processes was incorrect) some form of model is needed which suitably abstracts away the differences outlined above. A major step in this direction was taken by Davies (1973) and Bjork (1973) whose pioneering work on spheres of control and recovery has greatly influenced the ideas to be presented in this section. In what follows, the basic aspects of recovery in concurrent systems will be developed, based on the concepts such as atomic actions and commitment presented in previous sections. Emphasis will be placed upon the recovery aspects of processes supported by operating systems. The chapter by Davies contains a much broader discussion on recovery in concurrent systems involving men and machines.

T. ANDERSON, P.A. LEE and S.K. SHRIVASTAVA

On the Role of Operating Systems

An operating system can be regarded as the creator (provider) of the abstraction "virtual resource objects". A sub-system programmed to run on an operating system can then be viewed as consisting of one or more processes making appropriate use of the virtual resource objects. It is natural to assume that the operating system should also provide the abstraction of recoverability to the processes using these objects. Given appropriate hardware assistance the operating system can achieve this by providing certain recovery mechanisms which the processes can make use of. As has been seen in the previous sections, these mechanisms can include those that are needed for backward and forward error recovery. Based on the ideas presented by Melliar-Smith and Randell (1977), this section will assume that the following strategy is used for error recovery: when an error is detected, the operating system invokes any exception handlers that may have been provided for coping with that particular erroneous situation (as discussed previously, exception handling is a form of a forward error recovery). If no handler succeeds in recovering from the error, or if none is available, then use is made of some backward error recovery technique with the effect that the process is rolled back to one of its recovery points. (A process is rolled back by restoring its state to the state it was in at one of its recovery points.) If the process had communicated with other processes then backward error recovery may have to be invoked for those processes also. However, if appropriate recovery points do not exist, then the computer system is said to have exhausted its recovery capability and will go "out of control" unless some recovery actions are undertaken by the system of which the computer system forms a component. Such a system will be regarded here as the enterprise or the organisation that uses the computer system, and the recovery action may include an examination of the state of the computer system so as to decide the best course of action. It should be noted that any ensuing recovery actions (for example, the use of recovery by compensation) will be classed as forward recovery actions since any recovery is based upon a knowledge of the system state.

Many aspects of exception handling and backward error recovery can be automated by the operating system and the hardware. These include selection of appropriate exception handlers and their invocation, selection of appropriate sets of recovery points, and the subsequent roll back of the processes. The basic implementation issues for the above actions have already been covered in an earlier section, but only for a single sequential process. This section will examine how operating systems can cope with the complexity introduced by concurrency. Particular emphasis will be placed upon the provision of backward error recovery, because of the fundamental role of this technique in coping with unanticipated faults in a system. As can be appreciated, once the error recovery capability of the computer system has been exhausted, subsequent use of a forward recovery technique will usually require human intervention and the role of an operating system can only be supportive.

Backward Error Recovery

Recovery problems of interacting processes: Useful interactions between processes can be divided into competition and cooperation. Interactions for competition occur when processes need to make use of the limited resources of the system. It is then necessary for the processes to exchange certain information solely to ensure that the sharing of the resources is harmonious. Interactions for cooperation occur when processes explicitly wish to transfer information to other processes; the resources of the system are, of course, utilised in making the transfer. These two forms of interaction can be viewed hierarchically, as shown in figure 7, where it is seen that competition can be regarded as a low level activity with respect to cooperation. In figure 7(a), processes P1, ... , Pn are using the virtual resources privately. Thus, at level L1 these processes appear to be logically independent of each other. As a result, any recovery actions of these processes can also be made logically independent from each other. Figure 7(b) shows the situation where the processes are making shared use of the resources (that is, resources are being used for information exchange, as depicted by heavy arrows). As a result of the shared use of the resources, recovery actions for the processes can be interdependent.

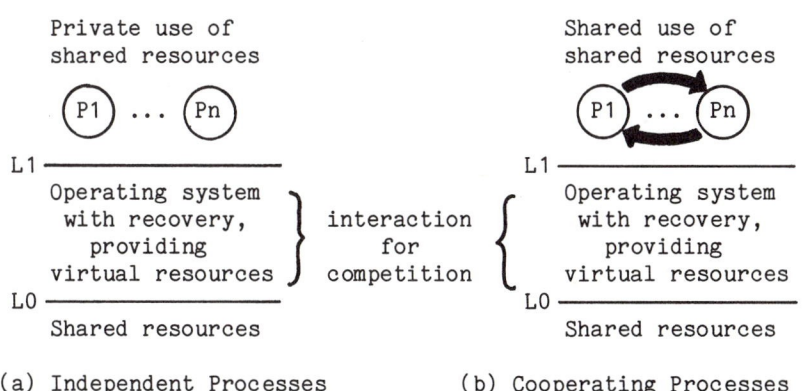

(a) Independent Processes   (b) Cooperating Processes

Fig. 7

Considering the logically independent processes first, it can be seen that if a process, after acquiring and using a resource, detects an error such that it is necessary to roll back that process to a state prior to the acquisition of the resource, then the following actions must be performed by the operating system:

(i) undo any effects arising from the use of the resource, and (ii) release the resource. These recovery actions will be studied in greater detail subsequently.

Example

In many on-line data bases, a transaction is treated as a unit of recovery in the following way: the process executing the transaction exclusively acquires all of the necessary resources and retains them until the end of the transaction. Thus, while executing a transaction, the process is independent of the other processes. If an error is detected while executing the transaction, the process is rolled back to its state at the beginning of the transaction. This is performed by undoing all of the updates resulting from the transaction to the data base and releasing the retained resources (that is, unlocking the appropriate files, records etc.).

Notice that in the above example, once a transaction has been completed, any information produced by it becomes "public" in the sense that other transactions may use the same files and records that were used by the first transaction. If it then becomes necessary to roll back the process that executed the first transaction to the state at the beginning of that transaction, then it should be appreciated that the problem is one of recovery of cooperating processes. The fundamental problem associated with the recovery of cooperating processes can be stated as follows: assume that a process sends some information to some other process(es). The receiver(s) of the information may act upon the sent information in its (their) own time. What should the first process do in the mean time? If it were allowed to proceed with its computation (during which it may send and receive further information) then there is the danger that if one of the participants of this information exchange rejects the information and takes a recovery action by rolling back, it may then be necessary to roll back the sender (and other processes) in order that information exchange may recommence. To appreciate this, consider the situation depicted in figure 8.

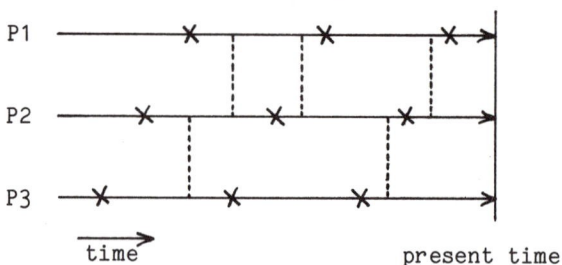

Fig. 8   The Domino Effect

In this figure, recovery points have been indicated by crosses, with dotted lines indicating information flow between the processes. If process P1 detects an error, then recovery of P1 to its most recent recovery point can be achieved without affecting the other processes, since no information has flowed from P1 to the other processes after the establishment of the most recent recovery point. However, if P3 detects an error, its recovery may initiate a series of recovery actions such that all three processes will be restored to their earliest recovery points. This effect has been termed the _domino effect_ by Randell (1975).

In order to avoid the domino effect, the progress of the sender of the information can be halted until the sent information has been accepted by the receiver(s). There is now the risk of seriously reducing the degree of asynchronism in the system. Thus the task of providing the abstraction of recoverability to cooperating processes with the property of freedom from the domino effect and with no appreciable reduction in concurrency can be difficult. As discussed later in this section, recovery requirements can impose considerable restrictions on the flow of information in a system.

Example

In many data base systems, a large number of transactions are collected together and run in a batch mode, so that if the run is not satisfactory, the batch can be re-run. Thus, in the interest of recovery, the outputs of individual transactions are not "made public" until the entire batch output is deemed satisfactory.

Logically independent processes: The recovery actions of a process that privately uses the shared resources of the system will now be considered in greater detail. Figure 9 shows a fragment of program where the operations inside the braces are assumed to be provided by the operating system. The recovery actions needed to restore the state of the process which is executing this program can now be examined by considering the detection of an error at various points during the execution of the program.

(i) _Error detected at (a)_: the state of the global variables of the process must be restored to that at the recovery point (for example by employing a recovery cache as described in a previous section) and the resource released (for example, by executing the postlude).

(ii) _Error detected at (b)_: an error detected at this point indicates that the operating system was unable to carry out some operation on the acquired resource. As has been discussed in the previous section, one way of dealing with this situation is to regard the error as if it were caused by the process, so the recovery actions are the same as at (a).

T. ANDERSON, P.A. LEE and S.K. SHRIVASTAVA

(iii) <u>Error detected at (c)</u>: the effects of the resource use must be recovered from, followed by the recovery actions described above for an error detected at (a).

(iv) <u>Error detected at (d)</u>: since the process has released the shared resource, any information contained in the resource can flow to a process which subsequently acquires this resource (if the resource is a shared file, for instance). Thus any recovery actions of the earlier process may induce corresponding actions in the subsequent process. Although the recovery of multiple processes is to be discussed in a later part of this section, two observations are worth noting at this point: a process can still preserve its logical independence if (i) the effects of the resource usage are confined to the private state space of the process, or (ii) the process can compensate by supplying corrective information to the subsequent user(s) of the resource.

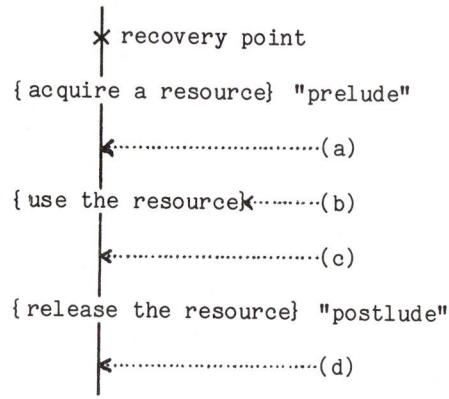

Fig. 9 Recovery Actions of a Logically Independent Process

<u>Example</u>

Assume the resource in question is a line printer and that the resource use is "print a file". In this situation, recovery from a failure at (d) (or (c)) might involve sending a compensating message to an operator indicating that the printout is to be discarded.

<u>Example</u>

In on-line data base systems which treat a transaction as a unit of recovery, the recovery point (see figure 9) is established at the start of a transaction and the execution of the postlude is treated as the end of the transaction, and also the moment of commitment (that is, the time at which the recovery point is discarded); thus no capability is maintained for backward error recovery from erroneous situations detected at points such as (d).

SYSTEM FAULT TOLERANCE

The task of programming an operating system to provide the
recovery actions for competing processes that have been described
above can be made manageable by (i) providing some primitive
recovery facilities in the operating system nucleus (and in the
hardware), and (ii) by incorporating appropriate language
constructs in the systems programming language. One such approach,
developed by Shrivastava and Banatre (1978), is briefly described
below.

An abstract data type called a <u>port</u> is used for specifying how
a resource should be acquired, used, "unused" and released.

```
portname: port (...)
...local variables...
forward entry procedure use(...);
<use of the resource>
...other procedures...
backward entry procedure unuse;
<undo the effects of the resource use>;
    <acquire the resource> "prelude"
        inner;
    <release the resource> "postlude"
end portname;
```

A process may then use a resource as follows:

```
...  using pn:portname(...) do
     begin ...  pn.use(...); ...  end; ...
```

When the above statement is executed, a local instance of the port
is created and the procedure pn.use is called. The <u>inner</u> statement
ensures that the use of the resource will be enveloped by its
acquisition and subsequent release. As the various aspects of the
resource usage have been specified, it is possible now to automate
the recovery actions discussed earlier.

<u>Cooperating processes</u>: First, the necessary terminology and notions
will be introduced so as to enable the recovery problems of
cooperating processes to be discussed unambiguously. Next, three
recovery schemes for cooperating processes will be described.
(This sub-section is an attempt to capture concisely some of the
ideas presented by Davies (1973), Bjork (1973) and Randell, Lee and
Treleaven (1978).)

As discussed in a previous section, atomic actions provide a
boundary beyond which information has not flowed. As such, atomic
actions provide a very convenient means for damage assessment and
error recovery.

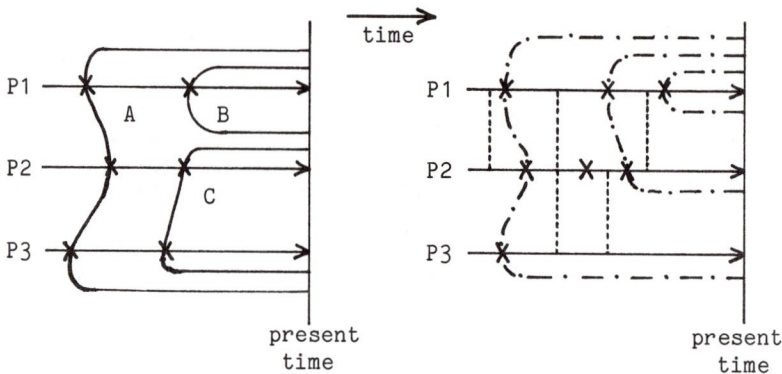

(a) Planned Recovery Lines   (b) Unplanned Recovery Lines

Fig. 10

Figure 10(a) shows three uncompleted atomic actions (A,B and C), and indicates that each process establishes a recovery point just as it enters an atomic action. Suppose process P2 detects an error such that it is to be rolled back to the recovery point at the beginning of C. The simplest and the most effective damage assessment strategy is to assume that all information flow within C is suspect and therefore the other processes in that atomic action (P3 in this case) should also be rolled back. Thus the strategy of taking recovery points when an atomic action is entered eases the task of determining the extent of roll back required for each of the processes. Such recovery points of an atomic action are said to provide a <u>recovery line</u> for the processes exchanging information (figure 10(a) shows three such recovery lines). For brevity, the activity bounded by a recovery line, that is, the atomic action with the recovery capability discussed above, will be termed a <u>restorable activity</u>.

In the situation depicted in figure 10(a), it is assumed that a means exists to enable a group of processes to enter an atomic action explicitly – that is, the atomic actions are <u>planned</u>. Hence the recovery lines and the restorable activities can also be planned. In general, this need not be the case as is exemplified by the situation depicted in figure 10(b). Assume that processes are establishing recovery points without due regard to information flow. Assume, however, that a record of information flow is being maintained by the operating system. If one of the processes detects an error, then it is necessary to examine the record of the information flow to determine whether a recovery line can be constructed; such recovery lines will be termed <u>unplanned</u> (figure 10(b) shows three such lines, giving rise to three unplanned atomic actions). The three major disadvantages of relying on the presence of unplanned recovery lines are: (i) it is necessary to maintain a record of information flow, (ii) there is the danger of the domino effect causing extensive roll back of the processes, and (iii) the

existence of a recovery line cannot always be guaranteed. It is
important to note that the end of a planned atomic action should
also be treated as the end of the resulting planned restorable
activity (by discarding the recovery points on the recovery line,
which would then cease to exist) - thus the effects produced by the
execution of the atomic action then become <u>committed</u> (recall that a
commitment occurs when a recovery point is discarded or becomes
invalid). This point can be further clarified by examining figure
11.

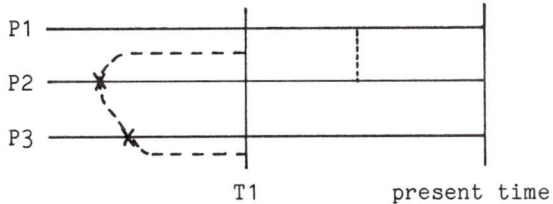

Fig. 11   Committing an Atomic Action

Assume that the atomic action involving P2 and P3 ceased at
time T1 (it has been drawn by a dotted line to indicate that it no
longer exists) but that its recovery points have not been
discarded. Because of the information flow between P2 and P1
(between T1 and the present time), the recovery points can no
longer be guaranteed to provide satisfactory roll back points for
processes P2 and P3. This guarantee can only be provided so long
as the set of recovery points form a recovery line, thus implying
that all of the recovery points of an atomic action must be
discarded at the same point in time when the action ceases. This
in turn means that the processes must be synchronised to leave a
planned atomic action simultaneously.

Recovery for cooperating processes can be divided into three
schemes, based on: (i) constraints on information flow, (ii)
information flow analysis, and (iii) information validation.

(i) <u>Recovery schemes based on constraints on information flow</u>:
these can be further classified into the following two schemes
which make use of planned restorable activities. (a) Statically
planned restorable activity: if it is known in advance which
processes are to exchange information then a restorable activity
can be pre-planned. An example of a statically planned restorable
activity is a <u>conversation</u> (Randell 1975) where processes
explicitly establish recovery points before information exchange
takes place and exit simultaneously out of such an activity
(whereupon the recovery points are discarded). (b) Dynamically
planned restorable activity: frequently, it is not possible to know
in advance which processes will exchange information. In such a
situation, planned restorable activities can be constructed
dynamically if the operating system can detect the previously

unanticipated information flow and can establish, if necessary, recovery points so as to form a recovery line for the processes exchanging information. Figures 12(a) and (b) show this diagramatically. At time T1, there are two as yet uncompleted atomic actions A and B. Assume that A and B represent two concurrently running transactions. In the interest of greater concurrency, at time T1 A releases a file which it no longer needs and then B happens to acquire that file. After time T1 therefore, A and B are no longer atomic (and hence have been drawn by dotted lines). In the interest of recovery, an operating system which permits this form of concurrency must be prepared to construct a restorable activity encompassing A and B. This can be achieved by merging the recovery lines of A and B to form a single recovery line.

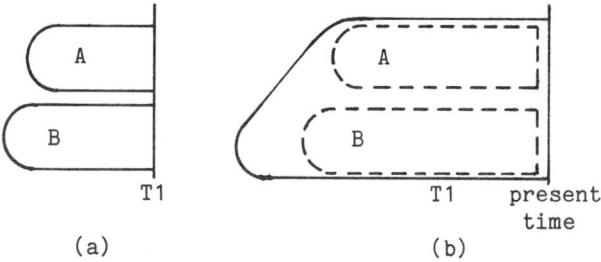

Fig. 12 Dynamic Creation of a Restorable Activity

Example

In many on-line data base systems, a user's entire session at a terminal can be made recoverable by treating the session as a transaction, implying that all of the resources acquired on behalf of the user must be retained until the end of the session. A greater degree of concurrency can be achieved if the system is capable of dynamically creating restorable activities.

(ii) Recovery schemes based on information flow analysis: if an operating system maintains a record of the information flow between processes, and processes independently establish and discard recovery points then when an error is detected, it will be necessary to examine the record of information flow to determine the possible existence of a recovery line. It has been shown above (see figure 8) that in such a situation there is the danger of the domino effect. The effectiveness of this scheme is difficult to predict and will depend upon the frequency of interactions between processes and the frequencies of establishment of recovery points for the processes.

(iii) Recovery scheme based on information validation: the recovery schemes discussed above relied on the (planned or unplanned) existence of restorable activities and as such made use of the worst possible assumption for damage assessment. This assumption is to regard all of the information flow within an activity as suspect. Quite often it is possible to be more optimistic, assuming any information received by a process to be valid, and suspecting (in the event of an error being detected) only the processing of that information. Consider the simple case of one process which is the producer of messages with another process as the consumer of the messages (see figure 13).

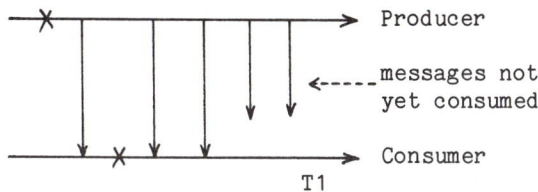

Fig. 13 Recovery Based on Information Validation

Assume that the operating system maintains copies of the messages sent by the producer. If the consumer detects an error at, say, time T1, then it is only necessary to roll back the consumer to its recovery point without causing the corresponding roll back of the producer. The copies of the messages are then made available to the consumer for reprocessing.

Example

The commonly used technique in data base systems to recover from a fault that corrupts parts of the data base can be viewed as follows: the users of the system are producers and their messages are the resulting transaction updates, information about which is kept by the system in a data structure known as an audit trail (Bjork 1975) or a log (Gray 1978); the data base system itself can be regarded as the consumer. The recovery action consists of re-running the consumer from a pre-recorded prior state with the appropriate parts of the audit trail supplying the inputs for reprocessing.

Russell (1977) has extensively studied this form of recovery for a network of producers and consumers and has established conditions for avoiding the domino effect. Clearly this is a very attractive form of recovery technique (especially as appropriate message buffering can ensure that producers can run ahead of consumers), so long as the underlying assumption is realistic. It is not surprising that recovery using an audit trail as described in the above example proves to be inadequate when the assumption of valid input information to the system no longer holds.

T. ANDERSON, P.A. LEE and S.K. SHRIVASTAVA

Forward Error Recovery

The recovery techniques to be examined in this sub-section come into play when the computer system exhausts its capability for backward error recovery. This will happen when the processes are (progressively) rolled back to the "outermost" recovery line and resumed (the operating system will make use of some fault treatment strategy, as discussed in the first section, in the hope that the resumed processes will produce acceptable results) but they fail to generate acceptable results. The only possible action left is for some external agency to perform a post-mortem of the system to determine the location of the faults and assess the damage caused by them. Typically, this external agency is the management of the organisation that uses the computer system. It can be appreciated that a detailed knowledge of the semantics of the information which the system is processing may be required to perform satisfactory recovery. Depending upon the state of the system, two recovery approaches are possible (the description that follows is a simplified account of the ideas presented by Bjork (1973)). In the subsequent discussion, it will be assumed that any recovery actions will be undertaken by the aforementioned external agency.

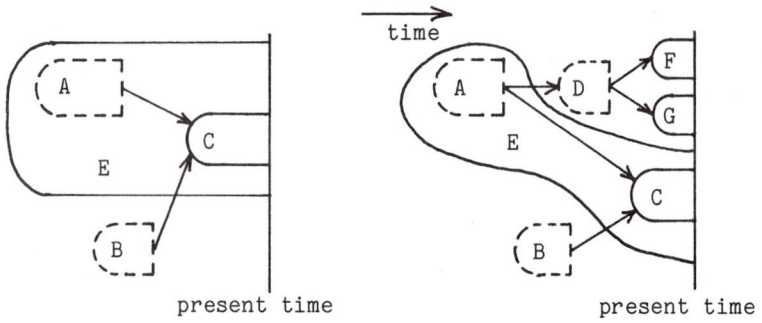

(a) Conversion to Backward   (b) Need for Compensation
        Error Recovery

Fig. 14

Figure 14(a) shows an as yet uncompleted restorable activity C that has received information from completed activities A and B. Assume that C represents the outer-most restorable activity and that an error has been detected by one of the processes in C but the recovery actions undertaken in C have not proved to be satisfactory. A post-mortem of the system reveals that C received incorrect information from A (it is assumed that the operating system maintains a record of information flow within the system for such post-mortems). An attempt is then made to construct a new restorable activity (E in figure 14(a)) in the hope that the backward error recovery of E will be satisfactory.

Example

Notices in the news media by a product manufacturer requesting
customers to return the products for modification represents an
attempt by the manufacturing organisation to create a
restorable activity involving some of its manufacturing
departments and the customers.

A slightly different and more complicated situation is depicted
in figure 14(b) where D has been committed and information from it
has passed on to further restorable activities F and G. The system
that is performing the recovery may decide to ignore, for the time
being, the information flow from A to D, and to construct the
"restorable activity" E. The inconsistent state that will result
when the recovery of E is invoked is then made consistent (possibly
at a later point in time) by explicitly supplying some corrective
information to the system. This is an example of forward error
recovery by compensation.

Example

Following on from the previous example, assume that some
customers have left the country and that no convenient means
exist for them to return their purchased products. The
manufacturer may then decide to recall the products from the
rest of the customers and to compensate the customers that have
left the country by the payment of a sum of money.

Forward error recovery as described above represents the most
global form of recovery (and typically the most complex type of
recovery) which is undertaken by an organisation. Because of the
complexities caused by information flow and commitments,
satisfactory recovery is not always possible.

Operating System Implications

The previous discussion on the recovery of logically
independent processes was sufficiently detailed to indicate how an
operating system should be constructed to provide the required
recovery facilities. If these facilities were extended to cover
the case of groups of processes, facilities for the construction of
statically planned restorable activities would be obtained. Such
activities appear to be useful mainly for enforcing certain global
constraints on a system (refer also to the discussion in the next
sub-section on recovery of a transaction in a distributed system).
As described previously, an example of such statically planned
restorable activities is the action of holding the outputs of
individual transactions that are run in a batch mode until the
output of the entire batch is deemed to be satisfactory. Such
activities are unsuitable if a finer grain of recovery is desired,
mainly because in complex systems it is rarely possible to plan all

interactions. To rely on unplanned restorable activities
represents another approach to recovery. Unplanned and statically
planned restorable activities represent two orthogonal ways of
achieving backward error recovery, while dynamically planned
activities represent a useful compromise whereby previously
unanticipated interactions are taken into account. It should be
appreciated that any attempt to implement such activities would
also require that the organisation which uses the computer system
should lay down rules for user interactions with the system for the
creation of restorable activities involving users.

The current approach taken in data base systems is to implement
operating systems to support the recovery of logically independent
processes, treating a transaction as a unit of recovery. As
discussed previously, the operating system maintains an audit trail
(log) of the ohanges made to the data base on a per transaction
basis. Should it be necessary to roll back a transaction, the
audit trail is used to "undo" the updates resulting from that
transaction. The audit trail is also useful for restoring the
system state after a "system crash" which leaves the trail intact
(a system crash occurs when the contents of the data base are
deemed to be corrupted). Starting from a pre-recorded state of the
data base (usually termed a checkpoint), the audit trail can be
used to "redo" all of the transactions performed since the
checkpoint was taken. Operating systems can play a key role in
automatically and reliably recording the data in the audit trail.
In on-line data base systems, the interval between taking
checkpoints is usually 5 to 10 minutes. The recovery process after
a system crash is briefly described below.

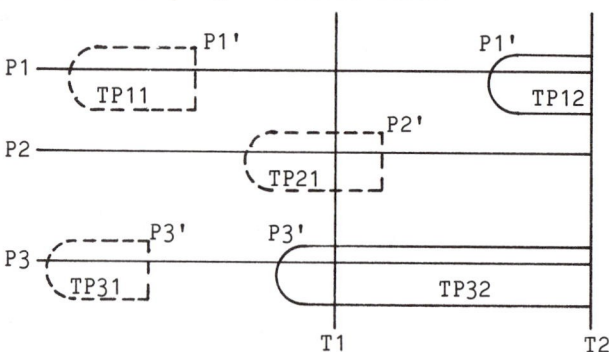

Fig. 15   Recovery After a System Crash

Suppose that there are three processes in the system (P1, P2
and P3 in figure 15) and a checkpoint was taken at time T1 when
transactions TP21 and TP32 were in progress (a transaction is shown
as a restorable activity involving a single process; completed
activities are shown by dotted lines). Thus the checkpoint will
record the state P1' (the state of P1 after TP11 has been

committed) and the then current state of P2 and P3 (this is a
simplified picture of what "taking a checkpoint" involves).
Suppose that the system crashes at time T2 but that the audit trail
and checkpoint are undamaged. The audit trail at time T2 will show
that TP21 is committed and TP12 and TP32 are uncommitted. A
consistent state consisting only of committed transactions can be
constructed by taking the checkpointed state and "redoing" TP21 and
"undoing" TP32. The following observations about this type of
recovery should be noted.

(i) A transaction is treated as the largest unit of backward
error recovery. As such, committed transactions are never
"undone".

(ii) The recovery strategy is based on information validation.

(iii) As a consequence of (ii), the recovered state is not
always satisfactory. For example, the system may again crash
after resumption because TP11 and TP31 were run with wrong
inputs, and information produced by them has been used by the
subsequent transactions. The only course which would then be
possible would be to make use of forward error recovery, such
as to run compensating transactions.

In order to reduce the need for invoking forward error recovery
as discussed here (which will, almost always, involve some form of
human intervention) it is necessary to increase the capability for
backward error recovery. This fact is, however, not yet widely
appreciated and the design of operating systems to include the
facilities for the construction of restorable activities involving
many processes remains a key area of research.

Some Concluding Remarks on Distributed Systems

Although it has not been explicitly stated, the discussion so
far has been concerned with systems with centralised control and
hence with centralised recovery control. It is thus possible (at
least in principle) for the operating system to monitor the state
of the entire computer system. The absence of any centralised
control in a system - such systems are termed distributed - poses
new recovery problems. For example, parts of a system may fail
while the remainder of the system continues processing having
received no notification of the failure; this may further
compromise the integrity of the system.

Fortunately, it is possible to impose a structure on
distributed systems so that the complexities resulting from
decentralised control become manageable. To show how this may be
done, it will be assumed that a distributed system consists of a
number of autonomous processing nodes connected together by
communication links. Execution of a user job in such a system

consists of concurrently running parts of the job at the appropriate nodes. Traditionally, a user job is executed by a single process in a centralised system. The same concept can be extended to apply to distributed systems such that there is a process at each of the appropriate nodes to execute the parts of the job.

The activities of such a group of processes (executing a given job) can be co-ordinated so that at a higher level of abstraction, the group appears as a single process. Such a group of processes has been termed a <u>cohort</u> by Gray (1978). Naturally, it is necessary for the operating systems of the various nodes to communicate with each other in order to provide the abstraction of cohorts. Figure 16 shows two cohorts, C1 and C2, on a three node distributed system; the arrows indicate the communication between the nodes. Once a distributed system has been designed to support cohorts, many of the recovery problems and concepts for interacting processes described earlier can be applied to cohorts equally well. Thus, the earlier discussion on the recovery of logically independent processes will apply to a distributed system if the term "process" is replaced by "cohort".

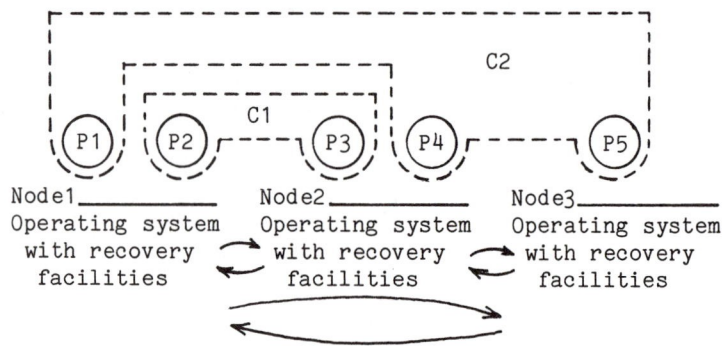

Fig. 16   A Distributed System with Cohorts

Two ingenious (and closely similar) algorithms have been suggested recently for arranging the recovery of a cohort (Lampson and Sturgis 1978, Gray 1978). As before, a transaction is treated as a unit of recovery (a transaction will be executed by a cohort), and the recovery problem is reduced to that of recovery of logically independent cohorts. This is achieved as follows: the start of a transaction is treated as the start of a planned restorable activity involving the members of the cohort, and the end of that transaction is taken as the end of the planned restorable activity. The key problem is the task of deciding when to commit the transaction. This is solved by treating one member of the cohort as a controller - the decision to commit is thus centralised. The controller first allocates the sub-tasks which each member should carry out, and waits for their completion. A

member will send a "done" message to the controller if it
successfully constructs an audit trail for the sub-task, implying
that that member has the capability for "undoing" or "redoing" that
sub-task. If the controller does not receive "done" messages from
all of the members, it decides to abort the transaction and sends
"abort" messages to the members. On the other hand, if the
controller does receive "done" messages from all of the members, it
decides to commit the transaction and sends "commit" messages to
the members (so that the members may make appropriate audit trail
entries and release any resources held); the controller makes sure
that all of the members receive the "commit" message. It is now
possible to design algorithms for recovering from node crashes.
For example, if the node of a member crashes, then the restart
procedure is to process the audit trail of the node as follows:
"redo" all of the committed sub-tasks; for all of the sub-tasks
with incomplete audit trail entries, send "abort" messages to the
appropriate controllers; and finally, for all the remaining sub-
tasks (with complete audit trail entries but with uncommitted
status) request direction from the appropriate controllers so as to
decide whether to commit or abort.

Little is known about ways of providing a larger unit of
recovery than a transaction in distributed systems. Hopefully, the
problem can be treated as the recovery of co-operating cohorts. An
indication of the recovery problems encountered can be obtained by
examining the method of constructing an unplanned recovery line
suggested by Merlin and Randell (1978). In a centralised system,
the normal activity of the system can be halted as an attempt is
made to search for a recovery line (indeed, this has been
implicitly assumed in earlier discussions). This may not be
possible in a distributed system where the state of the system may
be continually changing whilst the various recovery systems of the
nodes co-operate to find a recovery line. The essence of the
algorithm developed by Merlin and Randell is as follows: when a
process is rolled back to its most recent recovery point, "abort"
messages are sent to all of the processes with which the process
interacted. The recipient processes are rolled back in turn, and
further abort messages are sent. Eventually (assuming abort
messages travel faster than normal messages) the normal activities
of a set of processes will stop and their recovery points will
constitute the required recovery line. As noted earlier, relying
on unplanned recovery lines involves the danger of the domino
effect. However, the ideas presented by the above authors provide
a starting point for the investigation of ways of implementing
planned restorable activities.

T. ANDERSON, P.A. LEE and S.K. SHRIVASTAVA

REFERENCES

Anderson, T. and Kerr, R. (1976). Recovery Blocks in Action. Proc.
2nd Int. Conf. on Software Engineering, San Francisco,
pp.447-457.

Anderson, T., Lee, P.A. and Shrivastava, S.K. (1978). A Model of
Recoverability in Multi-Level Systems. IEEE Trans. on Software
Engineering, SE-4,6, pp. 486-494.

Avizienis, A. et al. (1971). The STAR (Self Testing and Repairing)
Computer: An Investigation of the Theory and Practice of Fault
Tolerant Computer Design. IEEE Trans. on Computers, C-20,11,
pp.1312-1321.

Bowman, P.W. et al. (1977). 1A Processor: Maintenance Software.
Bell System Technical Journal, 56,2, pp.255-287.

Bjork, L.A. (1973). Recovery Scenario for a DB/DC System. Proc. ACM
National Conf., pp.142-146.

Bjork, L.A. (1975). Generalized Audit Trail Requirements and
Concepts for Data Base Applications. IBM Systems Journal, 14,3,
pp.229-245.

Borgerson, B.R. (1973). Spontaneous Reconfiguration in a Fail-
softly Computer Utility. Datafair, Nottingham, pp.326-331.

Curtice, R.M. (1977). Integrity in Data Base Systems. Datamation,
23,5, pp.64-68.

Davies, C.T. (1973). Recovery Semantics for a DB/DC System. Proc.
ACM National Conf., pp.136-141.

Dijkstra, E.W. (1968). The Structure of the "THE" Multiprogramming
System. Comm. ACM, 11,5, pp.341-346.

Goodenough, J.B. (1975). Exception Handling: Issues and a Proposed
Notation. Comm. ACM, 18,12, pp.683-696.

Gray, J.N. (1978). Notes on Data Base Operating Systems. In
Operating Systems, an Advanced Course. Lecture Notes in
Computer Science 60, eds. Bayer, R. et al., pp.393-481,
Springer-Verlag, Berlin.

Hayes, P. (1971). A Logic of Actions. In Machine Intelligence 6,
eds. Meltzer, B. and Michie, D., pp.495-520, Edinburgh
University Press.

Horning, J.J. et al. (1974). A Program Structure for Error Detection and Recovery. In Operating Systems: Proc. Int. Symp. held at Rocquencourt. Lecture Notes in Computer Science 16, eds. Gelenbe, E. and Kaiser, C., pp.171-187, Springer-Verlag, Berlin.

Kerr, R. (1978). An Experimental Processor Architecture for Improved Reliability. In State of the Art Report on System Reliability, pp.199-212, Infotech, London.

Lampson, B.W. and Sturgis, H.E. (1978). Crash Recovery in a Distributed System. To appear in Comm. ACM.

Levin, R.A. (1977). Program Structures for Exceptional Condition Handling. Ph.D. Thesis, Carnegie-Mellon University, Pittsburgh.

Liskov, B.H. (1972). The Design of the Venus Operating System. Comm. ACM, 15,3, pp.144-149.

Melliar-Smith, P.M. and Randell, B. (1977). Software Reliability: the Role of Programmed Exception Handling. Proc. Conf. on Language Design for Reliable Software, Raleigh. Sigplan Notices, 12,3, pp.95-100.

Meraud, C., Browaeys, F. and Germain, G. (1976). Automatic Rollback Techniques of the COPRA Computer. Proc. 6th Int. Symp. on Fault-Tolerant Computing, Pittsburgh, pp.23-29.

Merlin, P. and Randell, B. (1978). State Restoration in Distributed Systems. Proc. 8th Int. Symp. on Fault-Tolerant Computing, Toulouse, pp.129-134.

Noble, J.M. (1968). The Control of Exceptional Conditions in PL/I Object Programs. Proc. IFIP Congress 68, Edinburgh, pp.C78-C83.

Parnas, D.L. (1974). On a 'Buzzword': Hierarchical Structure. IFIP Congress 74, pp.336-339, North Holland, Amsterdam.

Parnas, D.L. and Wurges, H. (1976). Response to Undesired Events in Software Systems. Proc. 2nd Int. Conf. on Software Engineering, San Francisco, pp.437-446.

Randell, B. (1975). System Structure for Software Fault Tolerance. IEEE Trans. on Software Engineering, SE-1,2, pp.220-232.

Randell, B., Lee, P.A. and Treleaven, P.C. (1978). Reliability Issues in Computing System Design. Computing Surveys, 10,2, pp.123-165.

Russell, D.L. (1977). Process Backup in Producer-Consumer Systems. Proc. 6th Symp. on Operating Systems Principles, pp.151-157.

Shrivastava, S.K. and Banatre, J-P. (1978). Reliable Resource Allocation Between Unreliable Processes. IEEE Trans. on Software Engineering, SE-4,3, pp.230-241.

Tonik, A.B. (1975). Checkpoint, Restart and Recovery: Selected Annotated Bibliography. FDT (ACM Sigmod Bulletin), 7,3-4, pp.72-76.

Verhofstad, J.S.M. (1978). Recovery Techniques for Data Base Systems. Computing Surveys, 10,2, pp.167-195.

Wilner, W.T. (1972). Design of the Burroughs B1700. Proc. FJCC, 41, Anaheim, pp.489-497, AFIPS, New Jersey.

6
HARDWARE FAULT TOLERANCE

W. C. Carter

IBM Research, Yorktown Heights, N.Y.

VERIFICATION OF HARDWARE CORRECTNESS

As defined in the chapter by Randell, correct computer hardware produces no errors during operation; an error is that part of a computer state which is incorrect; and a fault is the physical or algorithmic cause of an error. The structural theory of hardware correctness assumes that it is easier to analyze separately the occurrence and effect of physical faults and algorithmic hardware faults than the occurrence and effect of errors. This was true in the early 1950's when the Boolean algebra circuit model was widely used, and the predominate physical faults were permanent, determinate (stuck-at-1 (s-a-1) or stuck-at-0 (s-a-0)) randomly occurring independent malfunctions which affected logic gate input or output lines only. The resulting theory, now obsolescent, was published first by Eldred (1959). Avizienis (1977) showed the relative simplicity of the assumptions of structural theory by classifying physical faults as follows: by their duration - permanent, intermittent, or transient; by their value - determinate or indeterminate; and by their extent - local (independent) or distributed (correlated, multiple). A more detailed discussion of physical faults can be found in Breuer and Friedman (1976) or in Chang, Manning and Metze (1970). In the structural theory, design mistakes are postulated to be the main cause of algorithmic hardware faults.

These lectures will concentrate on algorithms and procedures suitable for computer implementation, since such aids are imperative for use with modern circuits. The structural theory is becoming inadequate in the modern world of distributed systems and designs which implement random logic using microprocessors (Sawin, 1976), Programmable Logic Arrays (PLA's) (Logue et al, 1975), or Large Scale Integration (LSI) (Correia and Petrini, 1977). This new theory is just beginning and will be considered after the structural theory has been explained.

Consider a combinational Boolean circuit C which realizes the function $g(x_1,...,x_k)$. A Boolean algebraic representation of the set of input patterns which will cause errors if an input is s-a-v can be found by using the Boolean Difference (Sellers et al, 1968a). If g is a single output function, define the Boolean Difference

$$Dx_i g(x) = g(x_1,..,x_{i-1},0,x_{i+1},..,x_k) \text{ xor } g(x_1,..,x_{i-1},1,x_{i+1},..,x_k)$$

where xor stands for exclusive or. If $Dx_i g = 1$, for a particular input pattern $a_1,...a_k$, then g depends on the value of a_i. The set of input patterns which will cause an error if x_i is s-a-1 is given by $\bar{x}_i Dx_i g$ and by $x_i Dx_i g$ if x_i is s-a-0. All other input patterns will give the correct response.

Consider the three output function G of four variables a,b,c,d with outputs $g_1 = \bar{b}(a \vee c)$, $g_2 = abcd \vee \overline{abcd}$, $g_3 = \bar{c}(b \vee d)$ (Schneider, 1967). The set of input patterns which will cause g_1 to be in error if a is s-a-v is given by $a\bar{b}\bar{c}$ and $\overline{abc}$. If a is s-a-1 then the two input patterns a=b=c=0, d either 0 or 1 will give the erroneous value 1, while the other fourteen will give the correct value. Similarly, the two input patterns a=1, b=c=0, d either 0 or 1 will give the erroneous value 0 if a is s-a-0.

It is clear from the discussion above that all errors in a computer system are intermittent. Errors occur only after the application of the input pattern which allows the fault to affect the output. Experience shows that faults are discovered at a rate proportional to the number of different input patterns encountered. To determine if faults which produce errors exist, and locate these faults, tests are used. A test is a sequence of input vectors together with the corresponding circuit output vectors. The similarity with software testing, discussed by Gerhart, should be obvious. The first test type, detection, determines if a fault exists; the second, diagnostic, determines a list of replaceable parts, one of which contains the faulty component. Detection test effectiveness is measured by the coverage, which is the percentage of possible faults detected. Diagnostic test effectiveness is measured by diagnostic resolution, which is the average number of parts in the diagnostic lists for the circuit considered. Detection will be considered first, and diagnosis in Section 3.3. An immediate concern is to find a relatively small (possibly minimal) number of test patterns. The advance first proposed by Eldred (1959) was to find test patterns by considering the logic circuit implementation. Eldred used his method to develop a very successful diagnostic program.

The classical work on devising methods to generate test patterns automatically was done by Armstrong (1966) and Roth (1966) for single stuck line faults. Let the function G of the earlier example be implemented using NOR gates connected as below, and consider finding a test for the output line of the gate h s-a-1. In the D notation of Roth, D stands for the line value which is 1 in the good machine and 0 in the bad; (not D) stands for the opposite set of values. These values are manipulated like ordinary Boolean variables.

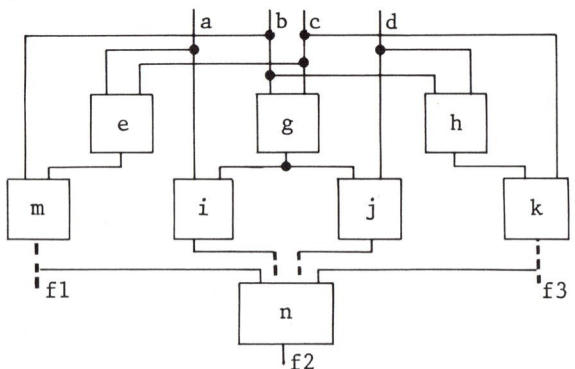

Fig. 1. Logic Diagram

Try to find a test for h s-a-1 using Armstrong's technique. Set h equal to $\overline{D}$. To make the correct value of the line h be 0, choose d=1 and leave g undetermined. The closest output line is g_3, with value $D\overline{c}$. To make the output depend on D only choose c=0; so the value of g_3 is D. The values of a and b may be chosen arbitrarily. The value of g_3 will be 1 if no fault is present and 0 if the line h is s-a-1. Clearly this test will also fail if the line d is s-a-0 , or if k is s-a-0. Armstrong's procedure is fast and efficient, but it does not always succeed. Try to test for line g s-a-0, so set g=D. To propagate the D through j set d=0, j=$\overline{Dd}$. To propagate D through n, input k must be 0. For g to be 1 (for the good circuit), both of b and c must be 0. If b, c, and d are 0, then h is 1 so k is 0. The output of i must also be 0, implying that a must be 1. But if a is 1, then the output of e is 0, and the output of m is 1, and the D does not propagate, since m=1 forces g_2 to be 0 irrespective of the value of D. An equivalent result is obtained if the D is propagated through the gate i; in this case k has output 1. Armstrong's method can not find a test for g s-a-0.

Roth's first advance was to propagate possible incorrect values down all possible lines, and provide a calculus to do so. If his technique is applied to finding a test for the fault g s-a-0 the first steps are the same; g has output D and b=c=0. Now however the D is used as input to both i and j, so to propagate the D's both a=0 and d=0. Now e=g=1, k=m=0, and n=$((0 \vee \overline{D} \vee \overline{D} \vee 0)$, so n=D, and the fault will be detected by the test a=b=c=d=0 . This test also detects the presence of eleven other faults. His second advance was to state his algorithm precisely, i.e., for the part called D-DRIVE, drive all D's forward, and determine what choices of variable values will let some D's proceed. Now in the part called CONSISTENCY make the implications from this choice. Then continue repeating the two steps, recording the choices made for variables. By proceeding through all choices he was able to prove that his algorithm is complete - that is, if a test exists for a line s-a-v, then his technique will find it. In 1975 Ibarra and Sahni proved that this problem is NP-complete, i.e., there is a polynomial time algorithm for this problem if there is a polynomial time algorithm for very hard problems such as the traveling salesman problem, knapsack problem, etc. (Karp, 1972).

Other problems remain for generating test patterns. A circuit is defined to be redundant if the function realized by the circuit without some fault(s) is the same as the function realized by the circuit with one or more of the faults. Consider the circuit of Fig. 2. The fault p s-a-1 is undetectable.

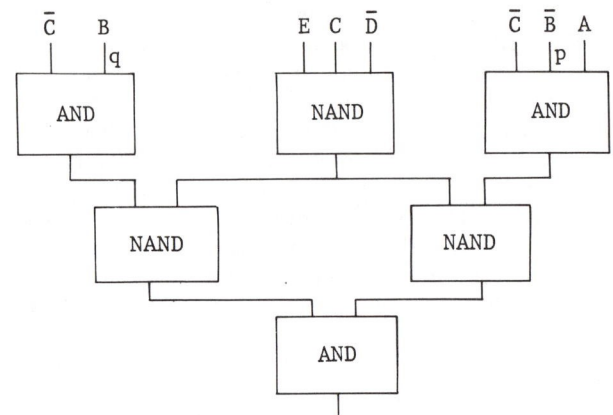

Fig. 2. Redundant Logic Diagram

The fault q s-a-0 is detectable by $B\overline{C}=1$. However, in the presence of the undetectable fault p s-a-1, the fault q s-a-0 is not detectable by $AB\overline{C}=1$. The set $T=A\overline{B}CD$, $\overline{ABC}$, $AB\overline{C}D$, $AB\overline{C}DE$, BCD detects any detectable single fault in the original circuit but does not detect q s-a-0 in the presence of the undetectable fault p s-a-1. Friedman (1967) has considered the problems associated with the generation of complete test sets for redundant circuits. For test generation, the most desirable alternative is to eliminate unnecessary redundancy. However, circuit redundancy is sometimes necessary to eliminate races and hazards (Eichelberger, 1965). Friedman (1967) showed that a set of test patterns generated using the single stuck fault assumption detected all detectable faults for Eichelberger's redundant circuits.

Since with LSI the number of circuit lines is increasing rapidly, finding equivalent algorithms which can be programmed to run rapidly is very important. Roth, Bouricius and Schneider (1967a) published an improved version of Roth's work, and included with it a new algorithm, TESTDETECT, which ascertains all faults detected by a given test pattern. TESTDETECT runs far more rapidly than the D algorithm. As is known from experience, any first test pattern tests many faults. For an efficient fault test generation system one should use randomly generated patterns and TESTDETECT until few new lines are found to be tested with each new input pattern. Then apply the D-Algorithm, beginning with the untested lines closest to the primary inputs, and after each use of the D-Algorithm use TESTDETECT to see if new lines are tested.

In his 1959 paper, Eldred reduced the number of tests for each circuit package by noticing that many faults are indistinguishable, i.e. they cause a circuit to realize the same fault function. Clearly, an n-input AND, OR, NAND or NOR gate G has $2(n+1)$ single fault patterns. The set of all single faults in G can be divided into the following indistinguishable fault classes. 1) The faults which change the output of G to the constant function 0. 2) The faults which change the output of G to the constant function 1. 3) The faults which make the output of G independent of one of the input variables. When a fault of this latter type is present, the output of the gate is determined by the values applied to the fault-free lines only. Clearly, the function G has $n+2$ single fault indistinguishability classes. Schertz and Metze (1972) and McCluskey and Clegg (1971) generalized this idea and used the results to devise methods to considerably reduce the number of faults to be considered in generating test patterns for combinational networks. The fault class structure which resulted from the application of these techniques resulted in a division of the circuit into fanout-free segments. The behavior of a circuit under fault conditions was represented using the classes of indistinguishable faults rather than the actual circuit lines as a basis for representation. This led to a two-valued Boolean expression which could be analyzed. This allowed proofs that tests which detect all single faults for certain circuits also detect all multiple faults for those circuits. The number of fault classes was reduced even more by Mei (1974). Let Ta(Tb) be the set of test patterns which detect the fault a(b). The fault a dominates the fault b if Ta contains Tb. Since only the tests for fault b need to be generated, this consequent fault reduction is called dominance fault collapsing.

Since with LSI the single fault assumption is unrealistic, call a fault involving m lines a multiple fault of multiplicity m. Every line in a circuit network N can be in one of three possible states: s-a-1, s-a-0, or fault free. Hence if N contains q lines there are (3^q) - 1 distinct multiple fault patterns. Using the previous techniques it can be shown that there are 2^n multiple fault indistinguishability classes for an n-input vertex gate. Finding tests for multiple faults is much more difficult than finding tests for single faults. Hayes (1971) showed that the single fault test set T for any AND, OR, NAND or NOR gate G detects all multiple faults in G and therefore is the minimal multiple fault detection test set for G. Furthermore, T distinguishes all faults which belong to different single or multiple fault indistinguishability classes of G. Hence T is also the unique minimal single or multiple fault location test set for G. His next step is to model a network N by an equivalent network N', with simple diagnostic properties. Define an extended gate to be an elementary gate with an inverter in any number of its input/output lines. To change a network N to a normal NAND (NOR) equivalent network, change all logic functions to NANDs (NORs) and replace all single output trees by extended gates. If N is any network and N' is its normal NAND (NOR) equivalent network, it can be shown (Hayes, 1971) that every fault in N can be modeled by a fault in N'. It should be noted that it may be necessary to model a single fault in N by a multiple fault in N'. A set of single or multiple diagnostic tests for N' can be derived more easily than for N. In addition, the multiple fault detection capability of a given single fault test set can be found.

Bossen and Hong (1971) derived similar results. They defined the checkpoints of a circuit to be (1) all the primary inputs which do not fan out (2) all the fan-out branches. In this procedure, as with Hayes, NOT gates are considered as lines. They then showed that each multiple fault in the network is indistinguishable from some set of faults on the checkpoints.

Fanout-free networks have a simple test structure. Hayes (1971) proved that if N is a fanout-free network with n inputs, there exists a minimal single fault detection test set which also detects all multiple faults in N. For such networks, Markowsky (1976) showed how to construct a test set of minimal size which will detect all possible faults. The method he gives does not require any backtracking.

Although stuck-type faults are currently the most important class of faults, other types of faults are occurring more frequently. These faults not only cause errors, but also may affect the detection of stuck-type faults. In LSI, the physical fault of two wires shorted together is becoming more common. Depending upon the circuit technology, shorts act as logical AND or logical OR, the circuit function is thus changed from f(a,b,...) to g(a,c,...). The probability of a short circuit fault occurring will depend on the circuit layout. Mei (1974) proved that if there exist shorts between inputs A and B of a vertex gate G, then any test set which detects all single input stuck faults also detects all detectable multiple input short faults. Breuer and Friedman (1976) point out if some constraints are added to the test generation program, then the generated test patterns will detect most shorts.

A fault with more complicated consequences is a shorted diode (emitter) fault in diode-resistor (or diode transistor) logic (Chang, 1968; Friedman, 1974). In the following example, assuming positive logic, (i.e. logical 1 is represented by a higher voltage than logical 0) if the diode connected to a is shorted and A=0, then F=0 and a and b are forced to 0 independent of the value of B.

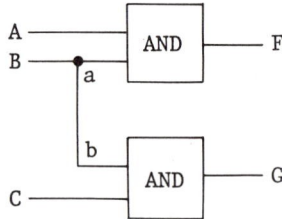

Fig. 3. Shorted Diode

If A=1, then a and b take the value assumed by B. Thus although the fault is associated with the gate F, the output F is unchanged by the fault while the output G becomes ABC. To test for shorted diodes on a line such as B that fans out, test for B s-a-0 and also choose the sensitive path so that only one AND gate has a D output (Breuer and Friedman, 1976). (Similar conditions hold for the other simple functions.) However, it is possible for a shorted diode fault to be undetectable in circuits for which all stuck faults are detectable.

Because of the difficulty and expense of regenerating test patterns when circuit modules are changed, and the problems encountered with races and hazards, some effort has been expended in deriving test patterns based upon the logical functions of a circuit rather than its implementation. The idea of the Boolean difference has been extended to partial Boolean differences and the derivation of tests for multiple faults by Chiang, Reed, and Banes (1972). Akers (1977) proposed defining a digital function in terms of "binary decision diagrams," a compact directed graph-like truth table representation of the function. A device's output values are determined by path outputs from the graph. For each path the input variables can be divided into three disjoint classes: (a) a set of fixed variables which select the path, (b) a set of sensitive variables, and (c) a set of variables which do not affect the output. If all sensitive variables but one are fixed, the value of the function output depends upon this single variable, so this pattern sensitizes a path from this input to the output (Akers, 1978).

It is more difficult to generate test patterns for sequential circuits than for combinational circuits. The most used technique involves cutting the feedback loop lines, replacing the sequential circuit by an iterative circuit, and generating tests step by step through this iterative circuit, beginning with the first copy and propagating results, replacing a time sequence by a space sequence (Putzolu and Roth, 1971). The ad hoc basic strategy for finding a test pattern for a given s-a-v fault F in circuit S is:

a) Select and cut the feedback loops so as to minimally alter the circuit behavior. The resulting circuit C has additional primary inputs and additional primary outputs (see the figure below).

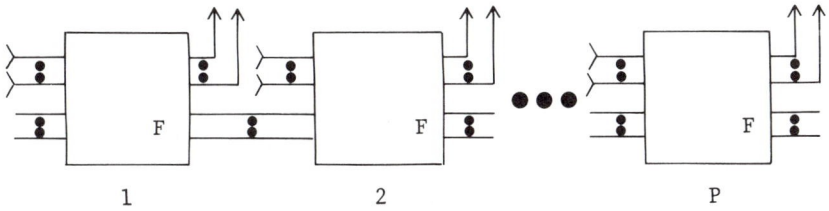

Fig. 4. Iterative Circuit of Length p

b) Compute a potential test pattern T' for the multiple failure Fp in Cp.

c) Obtain a probable test T from T' by making choices which allow T' to be simulated. After generating the potential test, eliminate all undefined variables in the inputs by arbitrary choices and merge identical patterns.

d) Finally, simulate T in S to verify whether or not T is in fact a test for F, in view of the possible inadequacies of the model. When test sequences for hardware faults are applied to sequential circuits, races and hazards often occur, so use a three valued simulator like Eichelberger's (1965). Note that before these test patterns are applied to the circuit in question, a homing sequence must be found so that the circuit is in a known state.

Unfortunately Eichelberger's theory does not always adequately treat the problems of time, delay, and input skew. Some other simulation routines go to great lengths to incorporate the concept of time, for example see Szygenda (1972). Breuer (1971) proposed using randomly generated test patterns, then evaluating them by simulation to determine if they were good tests. The book by Breuer and Friedman (1976) contains other techniques. A new technique has been developed by Chappell (1974). His circuit model treats logic circuits as interconnections of unit- and zero-time delay gates. A series of time-dependent Boolean equations are derived from the logic network (starting from the network inputs) in terms of sequences of signals on the circuit input leads. These equations account for the effect of specific circuit faults. Tests are generated from the time dependent equations using two different strategies: (i) a maximum-cover approach to detect a large number of faults quickly by generating tests for the faults on the input lines. The fault-detection level achieved by these tests is then evaluated using fault simulation. (ii) tests for individual faults not detected by the maximum-cover approach. This test generator has been used for at least 5 years at Bell Labs.

Once test patterns have been generated, they must be applied to the appropriate circuits. Subunits are tested using automatic test equipment (ATE) before final assembly, as well as being tested and diagnosed during use. There are two major categories of ATE, stored program ATE and comparison ATE (Knowles, 1976). Stored programmed testers usually contain a micro- or minicomputer and back-up storage. If a 100 IC board, or about 3000 NAND circuits are to be tested, the storage usually consists of 150K bytes of test pattern data, 600K bytes for the fault isolation dictionary and 150K bytes for the probe data. The test sequence is stored vector by vector and applied using the computer facilities following these steps.

1. Initialize circuits external to the circuit being tested so their interaction on the testing circuit will be consistent.
2. Apply inputs to the circuit under test.
3. Observe the outputs.
4. When necessary, deactivate or reinitialize the tested circuit.
5. Compare outputs with expected outputs, or the active results, and
6. Record results indicating whether the test passed or failed, and if it failed, record results about how it failed.

Comparison ATE's use pseudo random patterns as test vectors, and compare the results given by the subunit under test with the results given by a 'good' unit. They became popular because of the expense of test pattern generation by computer. Rault (1971) proposed and analyzed this testing procedure and established an heuristic relationship between the test length and some measure of test quality. The pattern recognition techniques of Pau (1974) may be used to improve the coverage of pseudo-random test patterns. These approaches discard the usual structural theory because of its cost. If the structural theory is used to determine accurate measures of test quality it is as expensive as test pattern generation (Shedletsky, 1977).

As mentioned earlier, PLA's are being increasingly used as a cost-effective way to utilize LSI (Logue et al, 1975). Converting a PLA to an equivalent logic model and then applying standard test pattern generation techniques is inadequate since the model does not represent the PLA's defects. A typical PLA structure has three kinds of fault behavior: the usual s-a-v; shorts between neighboring lines; or cross-point defects (missing or excess devices on the cross points of a search or read array). Cha (1978) and Smith (1978a), by converting a PLA to a two level logical circuit, have proposed algorithms which consider the faults likely to occur in PLA's when generating test patterns. Because of the regularity of the circuits, the number of faults classes which must be considered is greatly reduced using fault dominance. Smith shows that by using his reductions, a bound of 1920 tests is sufficient for the Signetics 825100 PLA with 16 inputs, 48 product terms, and 8 outputs. Ostapko and Hong (1978) consider the effect of errors from PLA outputs and use an abstract array representation of the AND-OR logic of a PLA. Instead of the usual structural representation, groups of cross point defects are sensitized simultaneously. For each such fault group, the totality of test patterns is generated for the faults under consideration. A covering set of tests is then selected from the total set. As an example, an 8-bit PLA adder has 16 primary inputs, 9 primary outputs, and the array has 58 words of 41 bits each. Ostapko and Hong's APL program generated 172 tests for the 2378 cross points in 10 minutes of S/370/145 CPU time; 165 cross points (about 7%) were marked untestable.

Efficient algorithms are necessary for testing semiconductor random-access memories and the usual structural theory has been shown to be inadequate. A memory can be defined to be functional if it is possible to change every cell from a 0 to a 1 and conversely, and to read every cell correctly, independently of the state of the remaining cells. Breuer and Friedman (1976) list the tests usually used, 'Walking Ones' and 'GALPAT', which are quite comprehensive but of complexity $O(n^2)$. Nair, Thatte & Abraham, (1978) have devised a new test of complexity $O(n)$. The errors considered are produced by the combinations of the following faults; one or more cells s-a-v, incorrect decoder logic, read or write logic s-a-v, or one or more pairs of cells coupled. A cell is coupled to another when a transition of values in that cell causes a transition of values in the other. They show that these faults are dominated by the usually tested memory faults. There are three test requirements. The first condition is that each cell must undergo a 0 - 1 and a 1 - 0 transition, and must be read after each transition before undergoing any subsequent forced transitions. A forced transition of a cell is initiated by the testing algorithm writing into the cell. The second condition is that for every pair of cells (i,j), cell i must be read after cell j makes a forced transition and before cells i and j make any further forced transitions, in all four possible cases. Finally, for every cell triple (i,j,k) if the test makes a transition in cell j from y to (not y) after cell i makes a transition from x to (not x) and before cell k in state z is read, then the test must possess another sequence where either (a) cell k in state z is read after an x to (not x) transition in cell i and before a y to (not y) transition in cell j, or (b) cell k in state (not z) is read after a y to (not y) transition in cell j and before an x to (not x) transition in cell i. They prove that this set of conditions is necessary and sufficient for a test to detect all faults in their fault model, and give an algorithm which can be implemented by a program of complexity $O(n)$.

Microprocessors are tested for physical faults just as larger computers are, and these techniques will be discussed in the third section of this chapter. However, since the introduction of the first general purpose microprocessors in the early 1970's, microprocessor systems have steadily replaced more and more hardwired TTL logic in dedicated control applications, their largest application (Sawin, 1976). At this time the programs involved in the applications are much smaller than those for general purpose computers (typically under 4K bytes) and they are ROM, rather than RAM, based. However, experience has shown that, because of algorithmic hardware (ROM) faults, it is no longer practical to conduct separate hardware and microprogram design efforts. An integrated software/hardware design effort is necessary from the initial stages of the design onward to provide feedback as to the efficiency and logical soundness of the proposed implementation. In addition, the required specialized I/O and other application oriented features make the development of microprocessor application programs complicated even though they are short. The most efficient tool for creating and debugging microprocessor and microcomputer designs presently in use is a microcomputer development system such as those described by Kline (1977) and Santoni (1976). Such systems typically contain a microprocessor, a sizable random access system memory, an assembly processor, a sizable random access program memory, a debug and front panel I/O board, a dual flexible disk drive and a system communication board, much like the testing ATE's. After compiling or assembling a software program, the designer can test it with the prototype hardware using an in-circuit emulation module. The in-circuit emulator typically plugs into the processor socket of a prototype system and executes that system as though the processor were present. At the same time, it provides a "window" into the user system, so the designer can receive information on the interplay of the hardware and software.

New design methods including such special testing systems have been introduced and are widely used (and sold) for testing simple microprocessor applications. This makes it clear that new design, testing, and verification methods must be introduced if the new generation of distributed fault tolerant systems are to meet their stringent reliability and availability requirements. Akers' diagrams (1978) provide a step in this direction. Thatte and Abraham (1978) have applied their functional level testing techniques to microprocessors.

Formal methods have been developed for removing algorithmic faults from larger hardware designs. Akers' diagrams (1978) can be used to test for algorithmic faults. The values given by the logic functions at the end of each path in the graph provide a complete logical description of the operation of the device involved, and may be checked against the specifications. More formal methods have been implemented by Roth (1977), Carter et al (1977), and Brand and Joyner (1978). Both techniques use a formal language to describe the specifications as abstract machines, which are represented by programs.

Roth's technique handles combinational circuits and sequential circuits by the device of loop cutting and transforming the sequential problem to one of limited iteration. Beginning with a set of specifications, Roth uses a subset of PL/1 to describe hardware satisfying these specifications. A compiler RTRAN transforms this definition into a program simulating the hardware design. A logic designer produces a design to the same specifications. These designs are used as input to a program VERIFY which seeks a counterexample to their equivalence. VERIFY assumes a one-to-one correspondence between inputs, outputs, and specified hardware registers. Two designs are said to be inequivalent if there is an input or a state such that the output or next state are different. The program runs rapidly, far faster than simulation, and has proven practically useful.

In Carter's symbolic simulation approach, the specifications are modeled as an abstract machine schema having as control a list of trees which operate upon a facility vector and whose actions are determined by a library of macro routines. The state vector components and the macros are described in a formal APL-like language *Language* for *S*ymbolic *S*imulation (LSS) described in Carter et al (1977). LSS is also used to describe the hardware attributes of the computer on which the specified architecture or program is to be implemented by code. When the assembled code to be verified is inserted in memory, and a set of symbolic inputs is given, symbolic execution can determine the outputs. These methods are similar to those described in the chapter by <Melliar-Smith>. Because the two facility vectors (specification and implementation) may have different components, to carry out the verification it is first necessary to specify a set of relations between them. These simulation relation components specify, for selected pairs of specification and implementation control points, relations between the state vector quantities which must hold at these points.

To carry out the verification, a proof tree (Birman and Joyner, 1976) must be constructed. An automated, interactive system has been designed and implemented to aid in this verification. The following process is used to build the proof tree. First, the simulation relation nodes are generated. In these nodes the most general symbolic values such that the conditions of the corresponding simulation relation component hold are given to the variables of the state vector. Any conditions which cannot be asserted in this way are placed on the predicate list. The next step is to run each abstract machine, performing symbolic computation until another corresponding pair of control points in the simulation relation is reached. One machine is arbitrarily chosen to be run first. Control proceeds as in normal execution. When symbolic constants are encountered in expressions being computed in assignment statements, the value assigned is a simplified combination involving operators and symbolic constants. When symbolic constants occur in predicates evaluated to determine possible branches, a single flow of control may not be able to be determined. In such a case all possible logically independent results of evaluating the predicate must be considered, and a node (subgoal) will be generated for each independent result. The user then chooses the path he wishes to follow (the program is interactive) and begins again. The remaining paths will be traversed later. If the predicate involving symbolic constants evaluates to true or false, no path branching occurs. After generating a series of nodes and branches, the control point corresponding to a simulation relation component is reached. Then the other abstract machine is run until a simulation control point for that level is reached.

Now the system verifies that the pair of control points reached defines the control component of a simulation relation node. The values of the two facility vectors are substituted into the simulation conditions of this component, and, using the predicate list, a proof is attempted for every one of the simulation conditions for this node. The process is repeated for each node of the tree which is not a final node. In the process a complete goal tree is formed. It may occur that a theorem can not be proved, or that a pair of stopping points not corresponding to a simulation relation component is reached, or that a stopping point is not reached. Then an error must be sought in the code or in one of the descriptions. In addition the occurrence of an unexplained branch will signal the presence of an error. This system has been used to verify both microcode and communication protocols.

The availability of LSI, PLA's and cheap storage means that more complicated systems are being designed and built. Thus system verification is more necessary - and more difficult. The basic components are more difficult to test causing the structural theory to lead to a mass of detail which must be simplified. However, a basis exists for the advances in abstraction which are necessary to solve these pressing problems.

DESIGN TO OVERCOME PREDICTABLE FAULTS

As discussed in chapters 1 and 5, the two basic traditional complementary approaches for achieving reliable systems are fault avoidance and fault tolerance. Fault avoidance attempts to assure reliability by a priori elimination of the causes of faults. Fault tolerance attempts to overcome the effects of faults. In this section we will consider methods for designing systems so that their fault avoidance and fault tolerance properties and thus their reliability are improved. To do this we make the following basic design assumptions: after error detection the system is made fault free; errors are caused by predictable faults; checkers and tests can be designed to detect errors; and in the interval between error detection, faults are predictable. Predictable faults belong to well defined finite sets called fault classes and their effects can be determined. The time of their occurrence satisfies a statistical distribution function. Such fault distribution functions depend upon the components in a system and upon the system environment. Based upon this distribution, assumptions may be made about the number of simultaneously active faults.

The principal fault avoidance technique is to develop reliable components, then ensure by extensive (and costly) testing that the system components are fault free. Since generating test patterns is a NP complete problem for the simple case of combinational circuits, and is much more complicated for sequential circuits, methods have been devised for designing systems whose test patterns can be easily generated. Better test patterns means that pre-assembly ATE testing will be improved and higher quality circuits and components will be delivered.

Designing systems so that test patterns need be generated only for combinational circuits is a useful simplification. In the IBM System/360, additional control circuits were added so that data could be read into and out of each latch in the CPU (Carter et al, 1964). The combinational circuits were checked by scanning the generated test patterns into the latches, stepping the clock, then comparing the results with the generated answers. The latches were tested separately. This technique was extended by Williams and Angell (1973) for LSI. All the latches on a chip are connected as a shift register as well as with their natural connections. The shift registers can be easily tested, and only two extra inputs per chip are needed (in general). The IBM system, Level Sensitive System Design, LSSD (Correia et al, 1977) aids in converting latches to shift registers, and in designing the sequential logic structures so that correct operation is not dependent on signal rise and fall time or on circuit or wire delay. As Eichelberger and Williams (1977) explain, the polarity-hold latches are 2 to 3 times as complicated as simple latches, 4 I/O pins are needed for shift register and timing control, and input signals must change only once per clock cycle. If the circuit size is reduced, test generation and error detection are improved. Ramamoorthy (1967) applied graph theoretical methods to the partitioning of systems to aid in their testing and diagnosis. Ramamoorthy and Mayeda (1971), Hayes and Friedman (1974), and Fox (1977) devised good methods to divide circuits still further by adding test points or extra outputs. The optimum placement of test points and outputs is determined by graph theoretic techniques. All these techniques are used and automated in the Controllability, Observability, and Maintenance Engineering Technique (COMET) system (Chang and Heimbigner, 1974). This system systematically applies COMET to a proposed or an existing digital system to determine the placement of control, access, and monitor points for diagnostic testing. The Logic Analyzer for Maintenance Planning (LAMP) system (Chang et al, 1974) provides the digital-logic simulation and analysis system necessary for logic-design verification, for generation and evaluation of fault-detection and diagnostic tests, and for the generation of fault dictionary data. LAMP has been used for 10 years at Bell Labs.

Schertz and Metze (1971) showed how to design logic circuits so that any set of tests which detect all single stuck faults in the circuit will also detect all multiple stuck faults. They then gave heuristic techniques for subdividing any network into such circuits.

In the fault tolerance approaches faults are expected to occur during the computing process, but their effects are automatically counteracted by the additional components or programs which provide alternative independent methods for valid computation. The key to successful application of protective redundancy is the systematic and balanced selection of fault tolerance techniques which complement and reinforce the best selection of fault avoidance techniques. Hardware redundancy is divided into two types, static and dynamic, based upon the terminal activity of the redundant modules. Each type must explicitly or implicitly use coding to construct valid signals, so coding will be discussed first.

In order to perform error detection or correction for the data in a module, the state space defined in the chapter by Randell must be divided into the error space and the code space for that module. The code used for the data defines this division. The following linear block codes (Peterson and Weldon, 1972) are easily used in storage or data transmission, and so are frequently used in computers. These codes use digits from a finite field of characteristic two, and consist of sets of n digit words, with k information and r check digits. The Hamming distance between two words is defined to be the number of positions in which the words differ (Hamming, 1950). Thus, a single error results in a Hamming distance 1 between a transmitted and a received word. If a code is used only for error detection and must detect all patterns of d-1 or fewer errors, it is necessary and sufficient for the minimum Hamming distance between code words to be d. If the minimum distance is d, no pattern of d-1 errors can change one code word into another. If the minimum distance is d-1 or less, there exists some pair of words at distance less than d apart, and a pattern of fewer than d errors which will carry one into the other. It is possible to decode in such a way as to correct all patterns of t or fewer errors if and only if the minimum distance is at least $2t + 1$, since after t errors the closest code word is the original word. Finally, if it is desired to correct t errors and detect d errors (d>t) then the minimum distance between code words is $t + d + 1$.

Following Peterson and Weldon (1972), any set of basis vectors for a linear block code V can be considered as the rows of a matrix G, called a generator matrix of V. A vector is a code vector if and only if it is a linear combination of the rows of G. If code vectors v have k information digits and r check digits, then $G = (I_k \ P_{kr})$, where I is a k by k identity matrix and P is a k by r matrix. If a vector u has k information digits $a_1,...,a_k$, then $v = uG = u(I_k P_{kr}) = (u,c_1,...,c_r)$, written (u,c). The r digits cj are called the check digits. A vector $v = (u,c)$ is a code vector if and only if (u,c) $(P'_{kr}I_r)' = 0$, where P'_{kr} is the transpose of P_{kr}; I_r is the r by r identity matrix, and 0 stands for the r dimensional 0 vector. The matrix $H = (P'_{kr}I_r)$ is called the parity check matrix.

If there are w erroneous digits in a word ve, then the digits in these positions can be represented by $v_j + e_j$, where j ranges over the indices of the w erroneous digits. The e_j may independently assume any digit value. Writing the erroneous word ve as $v + e$, where e stands for the vector with e_j in the erroneous positions and 0 elsewhere, $v_e H = vH + eH = eH = s$ where s is the r dimensional vector called the syndrome vector. It is clear that the code has Hamming distance d if and only if all r by d submatrices of H have rank d. For correction, let y represent the vector with t digits $x_1,...,x_t$ in any t positions, and 0's elsewhere. Correction can occur if and only if there is a vector y such that the equation $yH' = s$ has a solution, or $(v_e + y)H' = 0$. This equation has a solution if and only if the submatrix A of H' determined by the indices of y has the same rank as (A,s). For t error correction and d error detection, it must be shown that if d errors occur, then the resulting syndrome is such that any t columned submatrix will have rank less than that submatrix augmented by the syndrome.

The simplest error detection code is parity. The parity check matrix is (1,...,1). Clearly any submatrix has rank 1, so any single error is detected. Over the base field of characteristic two, errors affecting an odd number of bits are detected, and all errors affecting an even number are missed. Over any other field of characteristic two, there are 2^k digits in the field, so the probability of detecting any multiple error is nonzero, since the last erroneous digit must be the same as the sum of the previous erroneous digits for the errors to be missed.

The original Single Error Correcting (SEC) code was devised by Hamming (1950) for a field of characteristic 2. If a code of length n greater than or equal to $2^{(j-1)}$ and less than 2^j is desired, the code will have j check bits and (n-j) information bits. Each column in the parity check matrix must be chosen to have at least two nonzero bits and to represent a distinct number between 2 and $2^j - 1$. Clearly the syndrome for any single error will be one of the columns, so the submatrix represented by this column has the property that the rank of this submatrix is equal to the rank of the augmented submatrix. This submatrix is unique because any other column will be different from the syndrome, so the augmented matrix will have rank 2. A double error will be detected if the sum of the two columns is different from any column in the original matrix, otherwise a miscorrection will occur. Hamming also devised a Single Error Correcting/Double Error Detecting (SEC/DED)code by adding another bit to every column of the parity check matrix and adding one more check bit. Hsiao (1970) devised an improved parity check matrix by using a selection of columns with each column having an odd number of bits. A double error results in an even number of bits in the syndrome, and so is detected. Implementations of codes using such parity check matrices use the least decoding and encoding circuitry. If the digits represent elements in a finite field of characteristic 2, it is well known that they can be represented by powers of the companion matrix of the primitive polynomial defining the field. Bossen (1970) used this to devise a good SEC implementation for storage which is built with basic storage arrays of width b, i.e. b bits are returned for each storage access to the basic array, called b-adjacent error correction (SbEC).

The other class of codes which has been used in computers delivered to customers (Block et al, 1948) are called arithmetic error codes. These codes are preserved during arithmetic operations, as Hamming and other block codes defined over fields of characteristic two are not. Avizienis (1971) has analyzed such codes extensively. They all rest upon the well known remainder theorems for residue arithmetic. To use this idea as a check, append the residue mod t to each computer word. Now when addition or subtraction is performed, compute the residue of the sum (or difference) and compare it with the sum (or difference) of the original modulus. This check can clearly be used for a storage check. Checking Boolean logic operations requires sequential manipulations or duplication (Wakerly, 1974); (Peterson and Weldon, 1972). Avizienis et al (1971) in STAR used duplication and comparison to check the logic operations. If processors are constructed from modules which have a standard width b, then arithmetic codes are very useful for all checking (Wakerly, 1975b); (Neumann and Rao 1975).

In static hardware redundancy the effect of a fault is masked instantaneously by permanently connected and concurrently operating circuits, and codes are used implicitly. The level at which replication occurs has ranged from individual circuit components to entire microprocessors. von Neumann (1956) developed and analyzed a scheme employing triplication of logic units with majority voting at selected interfaces to perform correction, called Triple Modular Redundancy, TMR (a 1 bit Hamming SEC). He proved that if the voters are sufficiently more reliable than the logic elements, and are properly placed, then arbitrarily high reliability can be obtained from 'unreliable' components. Replication of relays, introduced by Moore and Shannon (1956) was improved to quadded logic by Tryon (1962), then to interwoven logic by Pierce (1965). Quadded logic was used in a computer (Lewis, 1963), but as the schemes got more complicated they became difficult to analyze (Abraham, 1975), so that the increase in reliability for the extra components was problematical.

Another code, Hamming 1 bit SED, called two rail logic has been used. A logic one is encoded as the twin signals 1 0, a logic 0 becomes 0 1, and the signals 0 0 and 1 1 represent errors. Each line in the original design is replaced by two lines and the original logic by new logic. AND gates are replaced by an AND gate and an OR gate, dually for OR's, and NOT becomes line interchange (the main advantage of this method). For some applications this is preferable to ordinary duplication and the S/360 Model 40 ALU was built using this code. Similarly, the signal pairs may be represented sequentially on a single line (Bark and Kinne, 1953), (Yamamoto et al, 1970), (Reynolds and Metze, 1976), and is then called alternating logic. Some hardware is saved, but every pulse must be replaced with two. For both these cases, efficient determination that an element is in the code space is still difficult.

Klaschka (1969) introduced a probabilistic redundancy technique by duplicating NOR gates then using the replicated inputs on the next level. Since studies indicated that the predominant failure mode of the circuits she used was an open connection, an error occurred only after two s-a-0 faults for the same logic variable, or a s-a-1 fault.

The most frequent application of coding in computers is in storage and in data transmission. Parity checks are used generally for storage and transmission. Recently SEC/DED codes have been used for storage in the IBM S/370 larger models and in spacecraft (Black et al, 1971).

Using codes adds to the cost of the computer. The word length is increased so the cost of storage is higher. The checking circuits themselves add circuitry, and decrease the cost/performance ratio. In addition more circuits are necessary to report and control the results of checking so they can be used in the recovery strategy. Choosing a useful set of codes is difficult, since in addition to the properties of each code, there must be translation circuits to change one to the other. For example, if storage has a SEC/DED check and transmission has a parity check bit for each b width byte, then translation circuits must be provided to do this. Larson and Reed (1972) studied and compared redundancy by coding versus redundancy by replication for fault-tolerant sequential circuits. They found that in this case replication by redundancy was generally preferable, but special cases exist in which codes proved better.

Current applications of static redundancy have frequently been at the module or processor level. Consider the two usual implementations of TMR, defined in the chapter by Anderson, Lee and Shrivastava.

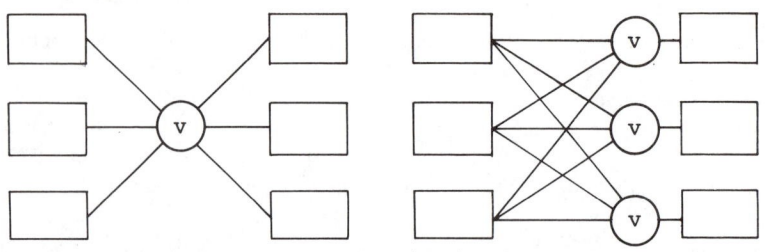

In one case the masking circuits are replicated and made part of each module, and in the other the voters stand alone (one voter for each line). The modules give the correct answer as long as all three or any two of the three are operating correctly. Assuming an exponential reliability distribution for a single module, the two TMR reliabilities may be written as $R1 = RvR^2(3-2R)$ and $R2 = (Rv)^2R^2(3-2RRv)$. Frequently a rapid analysis is done assuming perfect voters, or $Rv=1$. In this case clearly the first configuration is preferable because it uses fewer components. If $Rv \neq 1$, R2 will be greater than R1 if the inequality $2RRv \geq 3-2R$ is satisfied. If the system reliability desired is greater than $27/32$, then R2 must be used. For a reasonable use of equipment, R1 (or R2) must be greater than R, so Rv is bounded by $1 \geq Rv \geq 1/(R(3-2R)) \geq R$.

When TMR was actually used in the Saturn V Launch Vehicle, the configuration used was called TMR/Simplex (Dickinson et al, 1964). In this case, in addition to voting, each pair of lines used as inputs to the voters is compared. This allowed testing each module, so it could be shown that before launch all modules were working. If one module is consistently in error, it and another module are disconnected and the remaining module is used as long as possible. The reliability for TMR/Simplex is $3/2R - 1/2R^3$, without voters. For perfect voters, TMR/Simplex is always more reliable than TMR (Bouricius et al, 1971). However, if the reliability of voters is considered, and various values of the reliability distribution are used, a straightforward calculation shows that sometimes it is and sometimes it isn't. When any new voting scheme is proposed a similar analysis should be carried out, and the effect of the voters, the specific configuration and the types of faults expected. Perfect voters do not exist, and assuming them for quick reliability estimates will usually give wrong results. (The launch vehicle case was carefully analyzed down to the component level.) Dennis (1974b) has been considering designing static redundancy techniques using complicated masking algorithms. By using a LSI Read Only Memory as a cheap, simple, and reliable switch he obtains high reliability.

Wakerly (1976) has been applying TMR to increase the reliability of microcomputer systems. A transient fault may have an arbitrary effect upon the state of a microprocessor, and after the transient disappears, the affected processor may continue to have an incorrect state. If a second fault (permanent or transient) affects a corresponding line in another processor before the correct state of the first is restored, then the TMR system will fail (Wakerly, 1975a). Since a major reason for using TMR is to overcome short transients, the system must be structured so that each replicated processor frequently receives a synchronizing sequence during normal operation. Wakerly shows that the synchronizing sequence has length one if a design very similar to LSSD is used. Other techniques, using more complicated voting systems, will be discussed in the fourth section of this chapter.

HARDWARE FAULT TOLERANCE

The use of static hardware redundancy is based upon the assumption that failures of the redundant components are independent. This is no longer true with LSI. Other difficulties are the cost, the difficulty of ascertaining that the components are initially operating correctly, and the absence of warning when the redundant module finally fails. The advantages of static redundancy are its conceptual simplicity and its instant action, entirely transparent to the user. It also needs no diagnosis during operation, and converting a non-redundant design to such a design is relatively straightforward.

In the dynamic redundancy approach, redundant operations and algorithms are carried out by several modules, and the set of modules in use varies depending upon the number of detected faults. Since fault tolerance procedures begin after error detection, the detection function is the most important function for dynamic redundancy implementations. Fault tolerance procedures are implemented by recovery. Recovery has been defined in chapters 1 and 5 as the continuation of system operation with data integrity after an error occurs, and various types of recovery have been discussed. Fundamental to the way hardware aids to recovery are implemented is the design of the individual modules, and the operational set of programs and procedures which use them. The basic hardware design specification for dynamic recovery requires the following: all hardware errors should be detected, their existence signaled, and their contamination of data restricted; critical status information must be constructed from damage assessments; hardware functions must be rescheduled and operation restarted. There must be a centralized recovery control with the combination of hardware and software decided as an important part of the system design (Avizienis et al, (1971); Carter et al, (1971)).

The first plans for dynamic redundancy concentrated on the replacement of the faulty element or module by a standby spare (often called self-repair) or reorganization of the system into a different configuration. The classical standby configuration is shown below.

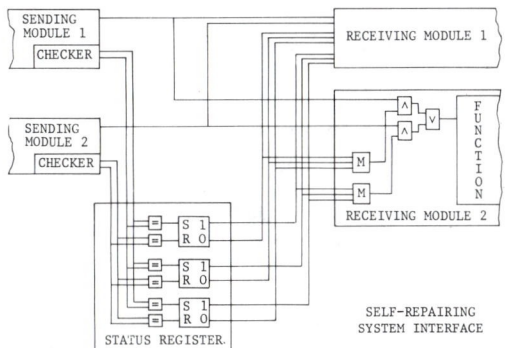

Connections go from each sending module (SMi) to each receiving module (RMi). The status register (SR) connections determine which sending module inputs are used by the receiving modules. The basic switch for a single connection line is shown on the right. Reducing the complexity of switching module interfaces by reducing the number of interface lines can be done by choosing 'natural' interfaces. The simplicity of the switch can be improved by using ripple switching (Roth et al, 1967b); (J. J. Stiffler, 1976). Fan-in/fan-out requirements are reduced by connecting the jth interface line to module input lines j, j+1,...,j+s (s is the number of spares). Since usually s is much less than the number of interface lines the fan-in is reduced to manageable proportions and the power requirements are slightly increased. The status register must work correctly. A particularly vexing system problem is the granting of reconfiguration authority (status register setting) in such a way as to prevent faulty modules from commanding undesirable reconfigurations. Each module must contain the circuitry needed for its part in computer system operation, and the checking circuitry needed to determine if a faulty component has caused an error.

Many reliability models have been proposed for such systems. A currently popular one depends on the number of modules needed for system operation (q), the number of spares (s), and the coverage (c). The coverage is defined as the conditional probability that, given that an error occurs, the system recovers. In addition the physical parameters of circuit failure rate when active λ and when passive μ are used (Bouricius et al, 1969). This paper compared TMR and standby sparing, and concluded that TMR is unbeatable for short missions, but spares with a good coverage are needed for long missions.

$$_c R_s^q(T) = e^{-q\lambda T} \sum_{k=0}^{s} \binom{q\ \lambda/\mu\ +\ k-1}{k} c^k (1-e^{-\mu T})^k$$

Reliability of Module with Stand-by Spares

If the number of modules necessary is one, an easy calculation shows that the switching circuits should always be replicated and put in each module of the redundant system. The reliability of each segment is thus the product of the status register reliability and the reliability of the modules augmented by the switching and checking circuitry. For other cases, direct calculations to determine the position of the switches must be made. For a simple approximation, if $\lambda=\mu$, and q=1, then the reliability is clearly bounded by $\exp(-\lambda T)/(1-c(1-\exp(-\lambda T)))$ which is less than 1.

It is empirically known that dividing a computer into parts and making each part redundant may increase the reliability above that attained by a similar redundancy applied to the whole computer. The usual argument (Roth et al, 1967) goes that if a computer is divided into two parts, of size a and b, then the failure rates of the parts are proportional to a/(a+b) and b/(a+b). For duplex systems, disregarding coverage and increases in switching and checking circuits,
$R \approx (1-(a\lambda T/(a+b))^2)(1-(b\lambda T/(a+b))^2)$, so $R \approx 1-(\lambda T)^2((a^2+b^2)/(a+b)^2)$ with an improvement ratio of $(a+b)^2/(a^2+b^2)$, with a maximum of 2 if a=b. However if coverage is considered, $R \approx 1-(1-c)\lambda T-(3c-1)(\lambda T)^2/2$, and after partitioning the linear term is increased by the effect of the new circuitry, and the coefficient of the quadratic term is slightly decreased. Better reliability is achieved only if the partitioning is 'natural', allows better coverage and needs little additional circuitry for switching and checking.

The importance of independent segments and coverage in reliability calculations were shown by Arnold (1973). He used a Markov process to show that the reliability of a system composed of an operating module and a spare (with off-line repair) was much less than the usual simple reliability formula would show. The circuitry which affected both the operating module and the spare defined c, which had an important and deleterious effect. Stiffler (1978) has derived an expression for the reliability of a standby spare configuration for s spares supporting q operating units where the coverage probability is a function of the number of spares which have to be tested before an operational unit is found. Dennis (1974a) and (1976) and Losq (1975) did other extensive designs and analyses of standby sparing. Dennis assumed that only open faults would occur in his switches, and had one checking 'monitor' for each segment.

Because of the importance of coverage, the most sophisticated recovery methods are only as good as the fault detection procedures which initiate their action. Checks are of two types, either interface checks at boundaries of atomic actions or functional or algorithmic, i.e. based on knowledge of specific applications. Software checks will be discussed in the third section of this chapter. Hardware checks detect approximately concurrently that data is in the code space or the error space. An important advantage of concurrent detection is that the same signals can be used to limit the spread of contamination by errors. Most of the more recent and sophisticated techniques of using hardware for dynamic redundancy have evolved because of the necessity to design adequate detection procedures.

An old error detection technique that continues to appear is duplication and comparison, implemented in either hardware or software, for example, see Ramamoorthy and Han (1975). One difficulty keeps appearing, what about undetected faults in the comparison circuitry or procedures? Some problems of detection and checking may be bypassed by using the TMR operation of three units with n standby spares called hybrid redundancy. The TMR voting unit has disagreement detectors on each pair of lines, and when a unit is in disagreement with the others it is switched out. Mathur and Avizienis (1970) did a detailed analysis of the reliability of such systems with switches, voters, and status registers of perfect reliability. Such a unit was built for the NASA Self Testing and Repair processor (STAR) (Avizienis et al, 1971) and extensively tested (Avizienis and Rennels, 1972). Clearly it is possible to use k+1 out of 2k+1 instead of 2 out of 3. This has been called NMR. NMR has been extensively analyzed by Ingle and Siewiorek (1976), who included the reliability of various switching and status register designs. Several other designs have been proposed for hybrid redundant systems. Chandy et al (1972) noted that if two units in a hybrid system happened to be in error at the same time, then the system would produce erroneous results in spite of presumably having good spares remaining. They proposed running all n units simultaneously, selecting the output with a threshold circuit with a threshold of two, and disconnecting a unit when it becomes erroneous. They called this technique self-purging redundancy, and it, too, has been extensively studied (Losq, 1976).

Connecting similar processors as multiprocessors and continuing processing in a degraded mode while faulty processors are being repaired is another old idea. However, the reliability depends very heavily upon the reliability of the interconnections. Levitt et al (1968) first carefully studied this problem for computers and devised some ingenious fault-tolerant switches. Smith (1975) considered the problem as one of determining one of many paths through a graph, with switching at the graph nodes. Since using LSI very reliable switching nodes can be designed, his solution has practical applications discussed in the fourth section of this chapter.

Since dynamic redundancy implementations can easily use complicated procedures for expected faults, intermittent faults are usually handled by a system timeout followed by a retry as in single systems, e.g. IBM S/360. If this does not work, the unit may be disconnected and subsequently tested and revalidated. Finally Miller (1966) proposed continuing running using an alternate algorithm.

As always there is one more problem, how will it be determined that the error checking or the error reporting circuits have failed? Clearly they will fail, and to attain high values for the coverage their failure must be detected. A circuit G is fault secure for a fault set F, if, for every fault from F, the circuit never produces an incorrect code output from code inputs (i.e. all faults are detected). A circuit G with code input domain A is self-testing for a fault set F if for every fault in F there is at least one input pattern in A such that the circuit G produces a noncode output for that pattern. A circuit is self-checking if it is both fault secure and self-testing. Carter and Schneider (1968) introduced these concepts, and showed that such a circuit must have at least two outputs, and no output may take on a constant value for code inputs. Two check outputs are sufficient and usually check circuits are chosen which map code outputs to (0, 1) or (1, 0). Noncode inputs must be mapped to either (0,0) or (1,1). For example, an odd parity checking circuit G can be made self-checking by dividing the q input lines into two disjoint subsets q1 and q2 (q1+q2=q), and checking each set q1 and q2 by disjoint parity check circuits. It is clear that this two output circuit is self-checking, that it maps code words into (1,0) or (0,1), and noncode words into (0,0) or (1,1). In Carter and Schneider examples of self-checking comparison and self-checking shift register circuitry were also given, so that a complete self-checking computer could theoretically be designed. The comparison circuit is derived from the important self-checking circuit which allows the combination of two (or more) of such error line pairs into a single error line pair . Further papers (Carter, 1974), gave an example of self-checking decoders and methods for designing check circuits for m out of n codes, for the fault class of all lines, including input lines, s-a-v.

These ideas were formalized by Anderson and Metze (1973). In addition to clear definitions of fault secure and self-testing, they defined a circuit G to be a code disjoint circuit if it maps noncode inputs into noncode outputs. Requiring a circuit to be code disjoint imposes severe restrictions on its implementation, but they showed that if all faults from a particular class are to be detected, then a code disjoint implementation of the checking circuit must be used. Anderson and Metze and Smith and Metze (1978) also designed self-checking check circuits for m out of n codes except for the case of m=1,n=3 and m=1,n=7, using a more inclusive fault set, all gate inputs and all gate outputs s-a-v. This fault class is larger than the previous class, with the only difference occurring during input line fan-out. The checking circuits are the same only for the circuits checking m out of 2m codes, otherwise the new circuits are much larger. The untested faults in the first implementation are some input fanout lines s-a-0. If a NAND gate implementation is used, and these lines are duplicated (using the idea for adding circuit redundancy discussed earlier) then the fault securedness properties for the two circuits are the same, but the self-testing properties will always be different.

This is a currently active research area. If F contains only part of the faults in some well defined fault set, then Wakerly (1974) called the module partially fault secure or partially self-testing. Wadia (1970) designed totally self-checking arithmetic units; Reddy (1974) designed a self-checking check circuit for the 1 out of 7 case, and

Ashjaee and Reddy (1977) have designed totally self-checking checkers for many codes. Techniques for designing self-checking circuits are also being actively studied. Smith and Metze (1978) gave some general design rules and generalized these ideas to 'strongly fault secure logic networks'; Marauf and Friedman (1977) gave more economical designs for the class of m out of n codes which can be made self-checking under the gate input and output s-a-v assumption.

In the modules considered previously, all lines were considered to be active, i.e. they change from 0 to 1 or conversely frequently while the computer is running, or were coded so that they did, i.e. the checker outputs. However, lines which in normal operation have a single value (called semipassive lines in Carter et al (1971)) occur frequently in the error and exception handling portions of a computer. Examples are syndrome lines in memory-protection circuitry, ALU or I/O exceptional condition lines, or inter-unit error control signal lines. A set of semipassive lines have little useful application as individual lines but are normally interconnected by logic operators to result in semipassive Boolean functions; e.g., the OR function that takes the outputs of several checkers and produces one output as an error signal or the function which detects and signals a double error in a Hamming SEC/DED code. In these logic functions, all input, internal and output lines are semipassive and thus susceptible to undetected failure. Such failures can mask errors, allowing them to go undetected with resulting data contamination and lack of fault-tolerance for the computer system. Carter, Wadia and Jessep (1971) showed that each semipassive line can be replaced by a pair of lines testable in normal operation, like the checking circuit outputs. Semipassive logic functions can be designed to be self-testing. Begin with a Boolean function defined conventionally. Use an algebraic morphism to relate the original variables to self-testing variables, combine these variables by use of a universal set of self-testing operators (AND, NOT, XOR), and interconnect these operators according to an algorithm. The resulting circuit will be a self-testing, checkable, acyclic automata. Using these techniques, an experimental self-checking SEC/DED to parity translator for a memory with spare planes was built (Carter and McCarthy, 1976).

This section has shown that modules can be designed so that they will detect predictable faults, and that all necessary logic for computer hardware can be modified so that it can be made totally self-checking. The problems of cost still remain. The next step is to consider the interconnection of modules to form a system, and the problems of diagnosis.

HARDWARE DESIGN TECHNIQUES FOR DIAGNOSIS, RECOVERY, AND MAINTENANCE

If correct recovery is to be achieved, then successful recovery must be an initial system specification. Design of a recovery process must begin with the careful definition of an overall strategy. The components of the system state vector must be determined, and priorities among them established. Next the hardware and software procedures to operate on the recovery variables must be specified. The basic recovery functions may be summarized as detection, diagnosis, and continuation.

In considering recovery and diagnosis, we are passing from considering a static machine structure to considering the dynamic structure of a running computer: we

231

must understand the effect of faults and how (or whether) the system tolerates the associated errors. This is the basic problem of redundancy management, probably the most important aspect of fault tolerance, and the area in which the amateur tends to become victimized. There is the urgency of detection, the necessity for accurate diagnosis and the required speed of beginning continuation. Delayed detection can pollute the system. Inaccurate diagnosis can eliminate the protection of redundancy too rapidly. Slow continuation can produce catastrophic instability in a real time system. Implicit in many designs is the assumption that only n faults or m errors will occur at a given time, not that this is the most likely situation. Planning only for the most likely situation is known as the n fault trap, and has embarrassing (catastrophic) consequences (Hopkins, 1975). The possibilities of correlated faults, undetected latent faults, the inadequacy of the fault model because of environment or fidelity of modeling, have all been discussed before. Detection uses the techniques discussed in the previous sections.

In evaluating the speed of detection, the efficiency of fault detection by checking circuits must be considered. The delay between the occurrence of a fault f' and the first error in the output was defined by Shedletsky and McCluskey (1975) as the error latency of the fault. They measured this delay EL by counting the number of input vectors applied to a digital circuit while f' is active, until the first incorrect output due to f' is observed. A more useful measure of error latency is the latency interval $n(c)$ of a fault f' which is the minimum number of applied inputs necessary to achieve a probability c of observing an error due to f'. Let the error probability q' of an active fault f' be defined to be the conditional probability of an incorrect output upon application of a randomly chosen input vector, given that the fault f' is active. The latency interval is the integral value of $(\log(1-c)/\log(1-q'))$. To find a bound for the latency interval, assume all input vectors are equally likely. Then for a combinational circuit whose output is a function of m input lines, no stuck-at fault may have an error probability less than $1/2^m$. This assumes that one or more faults are tested by a single input vector out of the 2^m possible. The corresponding maximum value of the latency interval is $(\log(1-c)/\log(1-2^{-m}))$. Assuming an input rate of 10^7 input vectors per second, the mean upper-bound error latency and upper-bound latency interval can be easily calculated. They are exponential functions, so if m, the number of inputs, is 40, the mean is 1.27 days and the latency interval for .90 probability of error occurrence is 2.92 days. If there are 50 inputs, the mean is 3.58 years and the latency interval for c=.90 is 8.24 years. If circuits with observable outputs have less than 40 inputs, then the expected error latency is small compared to a reasonable MTBF. Only when the input vectors are not equally likely can the error latency be significant. Circuits that are functions of 50 or more variables, however, have significant upper-bound error latencies. Error detection circuitry and fault diagnosis test sets designed for such circuits under a single fault assumption may well not be valid. A second fault could easily occur before the first fault ever caused an error. Shedletsky and McCluskey (1976) also show that, as usual, the error latency is even more significant for sequential circuits. These results indicate that for a high probability of error detection by hardware, periodic tests are necessary to uncover lurking faults.

After an error has been detected, diagnostic tests are used to locate faults and determine a list of replaceable parts, one of which contains the faulty component. Diagnostic effectiveness is measured by diagnostic resolution, which is the average number of parts in the diagnostic lists for the unit under consideration.

An early method of locating the fault or faults is the "combinational testing" method (Downing, 1964). Let the fault class F have n members. Define a set M of n+1 machines consisting of the good machine and all modifications of it by the n members of F (Chang et al, 1970). Simulation of the first test pattern from a fixed test T divides M into two groups, M1 and M0, depending upon whether the test pattern output is correct or not. Simulating the second test pattern results in a division into four parts, in general, with failure indices 11,10,01, and 00. Use simulation to apply all the test patterns in T to obtain a set of k possible final test groups, each with a unique index. The average number of machines in the final test groups gives the diagnostic resolution, and indicates the average number of indistinguishable faults after the test is applied. When the test is applied to an actual machine, the test equipment computes the failure index, and supplies it as an entry to the 'maintenance dictionary' so a list of parts containing the indistinguishable faults may be obtained (Downing et al, 1964). Chang (1965) gave a procedure for decreasing the test pattern redundancy.

In a second technique, called sequential testing (Carter et al. 1964), the primary sequence of patterns will be followed by an error-free machine. Let an error be detected by a primary test pattern. If this failure gives sufficient diagnostic resolution, the test is over. If it does not, then further test patterns, depending upon the test pattern which gave the error, are applied to the faulty machine until the desired diagnostic resolution is achieved. Chang (1968) derived a method which allowed the selection of efficient sequential diagnostic testing procedures.

After a system has been partitioned into diagnosable subunits following these models, efficient procedures for detection, diagnosis and continuation must be devised. For good detection, Chang and Scanlon (1969) stated that the functions of each subunit should be carefully specified, and the subunit interfaces should be simple. Then define a code for each subunit interface that will detect the expected faults. Sellers et al. (1968b) gave very general guidelines for checker placement: the error should be detectable before it corrupts other information; errors should be locatable to a replaceable unit; and the cost should be minimized. Carter and Schneider (1968) pointed out that checkers should be placed on the inputs of non-code-disjoint units, and if code-disjoint units are used, the placement of checkers can be deferred. Wakerly (1975b) added the rule that there should be a checker in every data path loop. The independent interval timer is a frequently used code-independent method of avoiding the n-fault trap (Hopkins, 1975). The timer interval is application dependent. For good diagnostic resolution the computer system must be partitioned into subunits. In this way subunit testing is easier and diagnostic resolution is improved. Contamination of data and control is restricted. Damage assessment is simplified. Partitioning and its analysis was initially done heuristically. The subunits must also be designed to provide control and information for diagnosis after error detection. This gives rise to two basic problems. The first is diagnostic analysis: given a set of diagnostic tests and a set of interconnected subunits, determine the system diagnosability. The second is the converse, diagnostic synthesis: given a specified system diagnosability, design the partitioning into subunits and the diagnostic tests.

To attack the diagnostic analysis and synthesis problem, the first formal model for the self-diagnosis of a system with multiple subunits was proposed and studied by Forbes et al. (1965) and Preparata, Metze and Chien (1967). They assumed that each subunit could be tested by some other subunit, and when one subunit tests another the result is reliable only if the testing unit is fault free. The system is modeled by a weighted directed graph, the nodes, ui, represent units, the directed arcs bij between nodes i and j represent testing links (and physical connections and control), and the weights wij associated with the arcs are 0 if the test shows no fault, 1 if it does. The cyclic set of test outcomes wij represents the syndrome of the system; obviously wij can be assigned if and only if the corresponding testing link bij exists.

Example: Consider a system which consists of five units u1, u2...u5 with testing links b12, b23, b34, b45 and b51 as shown in Fig. 5.

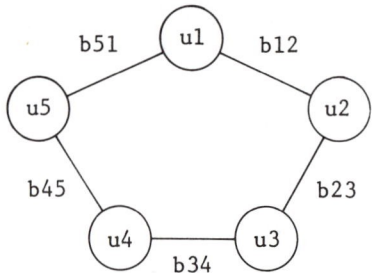

Fig. 5. A system consisting of five units

If exactly one of the five units is faulty the syndrome is

$$x \quad 0 \quad 0 \quad 0 \quad 1$$

or one of its cyclic permutations. The sequence 0 0 1 points to the faulty unit, the link whose weight is 1 tests and correctly indicates the faulty unit; thus the unique diagnosis of any single fault is possible.

The next question is whether this system is capable of diagnosing two faults. Does this mean the capability of locating (a) up to two faults instantly, or (b) at least one faulty unit if the number of faulty units present does not exceed two? These two situations will be carefully distinguished by the following definitions. A system of n units is one-step t-fault diagnosable if all faulty units within the system can be identified without replacement provided the number of faulty units present does not exceed t. A system of n units is sequentially t-fault diagnosable, or t-fault diagnosable with repair, if at least one faulty unit can be identified without replacement provided the number of faulty units present does not exceed t.

Every system that is one-step t-fault diagnosable is also sequentially t-fault diagnosable. To demonstrate the existence of systems that are sequentially t-fault diagnosable, but not one-step t-fault diagnosable we shall refer again to the example in Fig. 5. All syndromes for two faulty units form one of the following patterns: XX001 when u1 and u2 are faulty, or X1X01 when u1 and u3 are faulty. Assume that units u1 and u2 are faulty. Since X may be 0 or 1, this case can have the same syndrome as the situation in which u1 alone is faulty.

This system is sequentially two-fault diagnosable. If the syndrome contains the sequence 001 then the unit to which this sequence points is faulty. If the sequence 001 is not present then the sequence must be of the form X1101. In this case the unit to which the sequence 1101 points is faulty. After repair, further tests are necessary to determine if another unit is faulty and to identify it.

HARDWARE FAULT TOLERANCE

Preparata, Metze and Chien (1967) prove that if a system S with n units is to be one step t-fault diagnosable, then $n \geq 2t+1$ and each unit is tested by at least t other units. They also give methods of designing n unit one step t-diagnosable systems in which $n=2t+1$ and each unit is tested by exactly t units. Hakimi (1977) proves the more complicated necessary and sufficient conditions for one step t-fault diagnosability. However, if no two units test each other, then the necessary and sufficient condition is that each unit is tested by at least t other units. If the cost cij for unit i to test unit j is considered, there is a graph theoretic polynomially bounded algorithm to determine the connections for t-diagnosability if no pairs of units test each other. Sequential t-fault diagnosis requires fewer tests. Hakimi (1977) proves that for n units if $n > 2t$ there exists a sequentially t-diagnosable system with $n+t+1$ tests.

Russell and Kime (1975a,b) have devised a more abstract model which applies to both hardware and software (if levels of invisibility (Parnas, 1972) are enforced). Rather than speaking of certain subsystems testing others, the model is formulated in terms of faults, tests, and the relationships between them. A broad interpretation is given to "fault" and "test." For example, a fault may be defined as any condition that causes the malfunction of a particular part of the system such as a computer in a multicomputer complex or the arithmetic unit of a computer. A test can be any combination of hardware and software procedures used to determine if a fault has occurred. In particular each test has an associated set of invalidating units, generally a subset of the set of units cooperating for the test. When at least one unit of the invalidating set is faulty, the test outcome is unreliable.

Associated with a system S there is assumed to be a set $F=f_1,f_2,...,f_n$ of n possible faults that can occur and a set $T=t_1,t_2,...,t_2$ of p pass-fail tests that can be applied to S. The simultaneous presence of faults is allowed. A test t_j is a complete test for fault f_i if t_j always fails when f_i alone is present in S and always passes for all faults in F absent. The diagnostic graph D of a system S is a labeled directed graph that has a vertex for each fault in F and a directed edge from the vertex associated with fault f_i to the vertex associated with fault f_j if and only if f_i invalidates at least one test that is complete for f_j. The vertices and edges of D are labeled as follows: 1) each vertex is internally labeled by the fault associated with it, 2) a directed edge from vertex f_i to vertex f_j is labeled by the complete tests for f_j that are invalidated by fault f_i, and 3) each vertex f_i is externally labeled by the complete tests for f_i that are not invalidated by any fault in F. The last labeling provision is included so that the diagnostic graph can adequately represent a system in which some element can be manually tested or can be tested by the fault-free system hardware.

The following example is based on the description of the diagnosis of the IBM System/360 Model 50 (Hackl and Shirk, 1965). The system is assumed to consist of the following components: 1) main storage, 2) read-only memory (ROM) control, 3) arithmetic processor, 4) local storage, and 5) channel. The respective failed components are denoted by f_1, f_2, f_3, f_4, and f_5. In addition, a certain amount of manually checked hardcore is distributed throughout the system. The diagnostic graph in Fig. 6 is developed by considering the bootstrap diagnostic scheme employed.

235

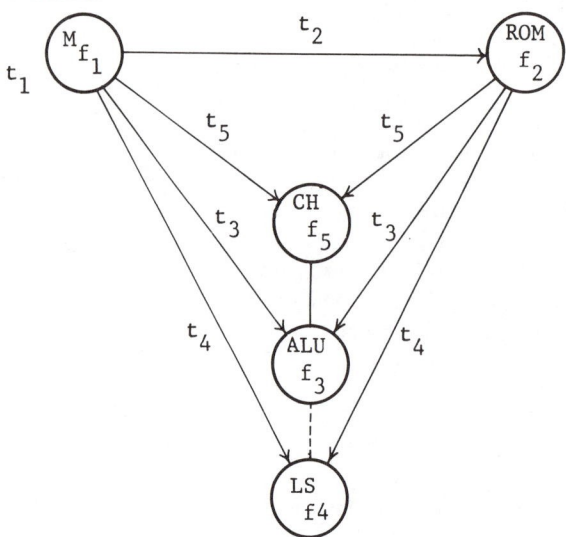

Fig. 6. Diagnostic graph for S/360 Model 50.

In the diagnostic mode, special hardcore controls are used to load tests into main storage in such a way that a storage malfunction during the load operation will cause the load control to hang up. Thus, the test t_1 on the main storage is not dependent for its validity on the absence of other faulty elements and has no edges of the diagnostic graph associated with it. After successful loading of the tests, main storage, is used as a source for both data and control to test the ROM control. Thus, if main storage is faulty, the test t_2 of the ROM control could be invalid. Hence, there is an edge from f_1 to f_2 labeled with t_2. The ROM in conjunction with the main storage tests the arithmetic processor. This test is represented by two edges labeled with t_3, one from f_1 to f_3 and one from f_2 to f_3. The remaining tests are performed using main storage, the ROM control, and the processor to test the local storage and the channel. The remainder of the graph can be developed accordingly. Russell and Kime (1975b) show that this system is five-fault detectable and five-fault diagnosable with repair. This result is heavily dependent on the completeness of the tests and the validity of the model. These papers also contain results which solve the analysis problem for one-step diagnosis for this extended model. In addition, upper and lower bounds are given for the case of diagnosis with repair.

Barsi et al. (1976) considered the diagnosability of systems partitioned into complex units in which any unit has the potential to test any other. The diagnostic routines are complete for a given class of faults in each unit, and at least one mismatch occurs between actual and expected reaction to the test stimuli even if the testing unit itself is faulty. This hypothesis assumes that a self-checking design (Carter and Schneider, 1968) is adopted for the critical parts of the testing unit. As a result of these hypotheses they are able to prove the one step diagnosability of a system with n units now becomes bounded by $t \le (n-2)$, not $2t \le n-1$.

Friedman (1975) makes the assumption that sometimes good as well as faulty modules may be replaced, depending upon the diagnostic strategy used. A system is k step t/s diagnosable without repair if by k applications of the diagnostic test any multiple fault consisting of at most t single faults can be diagnosed to within s faults. The concept of k-step t/s diagnosability can also be applied to system diagnosability with repair. Apply the test, replace s_1 modules. After the replacement apply the test again, assuming that the s_1 modules are good, and replace s_2 modules. Repeat until $\sum_1^n s_i \geq t > s$ so all faulty modules have been replaced and the tests all are passed. A repair strategy may be defined for each value of k, determined by the testing facilities available, by the maximum number of faults which are assumed to exist, and by the number of incorrect responses received in a particular test. Karunanithi and Friedman (1977) derive necessary and sufficient conditions for units connected in a single loop to be one step t/s diagnosable. Maheshwari and Hakimi (1976) have assumed that some faults are more easily diagnosed than others, and used this as a basis for replacing units. Nair (1978) considered the problem of finding at least one good unit from n units. This turns out to be as difficult as finding the faulty module in the single loop case. He proposed a system of roving diagnosis so that the k fault unit assumption could start with one and developed techniques for specifying links between units. Smith (1978b) analyzed some diagnosis algorithms which only rely on test results and are independent of system structure. The algorithms are guaranteed to terminate with a correct system, if a detectable set of faulty units is initially present.

To simplify detection and diagnostic testing, Ramamoorthy (1967) first proposed a structural theory of machine diagnosis, using a directed graph as his basic model. In addition to being a natural way to represent a system as a hierarchy of interconnected levels, the well known methods of graph theory may be used for analysis and synthesis. To improve diagnosis, Ramamoorthy and Mayeda (1971), using a directed graph to represent a system, defined a blocking gate on an edge as a gate (or set of gates) which can, upon command, block or unblock the flow of signals along the edge. Although the concept is simple, not only is detection improved, but the more expensive diagnostic process is simplified. Blocking gates control the extent to which a network's internal conditions can be controlled by input signals. Determining good positions for blocking gates is necessary. To use the concept well, after blocking part of the circuit, a sensitizing path (Roth, 1966) must be determined. Because feedback loops can not be entirely eliminated, Chang (1973) introduced the idea of a check register in his design of a microprogrammed self-checking processor. This check register is used to verify the transfer of information and the sequencing of microprogram steps. Hayes (1974) showed that by adding output points to a network, more information could be obtained about its internal states. He also showed that by systematic procedures any combinational or sequential network can be modified so the the resulting network requires only five test patterns. As usual, such results require a great deal of control logic. Chang (1974) used his Controllability, Observability, and Maintenance Engineering Technique (COMET) to properly place blocking gates and test observation points and construct a trouble location manual. If the processor is composed of more that one repairable module, disable half the processor. Run a diagnostic test on the enabled portion and determine if the fault(s) is in the enabled or disabled portion. Repeating this process recursively on the section which contains the fault(s) results in further diagnostic location improvement. The basic difference between this approach and the conventional one is that in the latter, for isolation purposes, fault responses must be determined not only from the good machine but also from every faulty machine. In this approach only the difference between the good machine and the faulty machine indications are important. Diagnostic resolution is obtained by successively reducing the circuitry under test. Another good feature of this procedure is that multiple faults in a module are locatable as long as they are detectable by the applied tests.

No matter how carefully the circuit, module, and unit hardware error analysis is performed, unforeseen circumstances will arise. For diagnostic analysis in this circumstance, the detailed state of the unit at the time of error is required. Architectures which automatically provide isolation (Fischler 1973) may have this information, if the inter-unit protocols are properly designed. Providing circuitry to record the unit state in a protected area is another solution (Carter et al, 1964). Higgins (1968) and Droulette (1971) discuss methods for using this information for diagnostic analysis and recovery. This technique is comparable to HEALS (Honeywell Error Analysis and Logging System), see (Scola, 1972).

Partitioning systems and devising good procedures for detection, diagnosis and continuation must be done iteratively, and with automatic aid. Aids like the COMET program have been implemented to provide interactive help in partitioning systems, and in inserting lines for observing internal states. After system modification, programs like LAMP (Chang et al, 1974) are used to evaluate the resulting system for diagnosability.

Software testing and diagnostic routines, used since ENIAC days, can be used to replace or supplement hardware detection and diagnosis. If all detection is done by program, it is assumed that if the test routines find no faults the computation between tests is error free. Supplemental software testing is frequently used to test maintenance logic, noncritical functions, or redundant hardware present for fault tolerance. Reconfigurable units can be tested for latent faults to ensure the protection of hardware checking or error masking is not diminished (Murray et al, 1977). If a spare is found to be faulty it can be removed from the list of available spares, avoiding many complications in the recovery process. Chang et al (1973) supplemented hardware checking by software testing for a telephone switching central. Hardware error detection techniques, using a reasonable number of centralized checking circuits, detected the great majority of processor faults concurrently. Maintenance logic, and faults not checked by logic, (as determined by simulation) were tested by frequent testing programs. Since telephone users will endure minor interruptions, costs were minimized.

Software tests apply test patterns and analyze the results. To do this effectively, the number of circuit elements that are accessible to direct program control and interrogation must be as large as possible. The interval between points at which the system state status can be determined must contain as few intermediate system states as possible. In a micro-programmed unit, design the control store so that part of it can be used for diagnostic routines called from the architectural level (Carter et al, 1964), and add circuitry for better control of such routines (Hackl and Shirk, 1965). These micro-diagnostics can be designed to have control of all or most of the unit latches. Since one unit cycle corresponds to a micro-instruction execution, the state status resolution problem is solved. Access to data stored in main storage is possible, so sufficient test patterns may be obtained. The control store words can be parity checked, and the number of circuits necessary to execute a micro-instruction is small, so building the controls in self-testing morphic circuitry is feasible.

Micro-diagnostic program design is influenced by the end use. Software testing routines assume there are no faults and test as much logic as possible with each test pattern. If an error is detected, a diagnostic routine is called. If a diagnostic routine assumes only a single error exists, it follows the ESS-1 idea of combinational testing. All tests are run, failure information is stored, and the fault is located by analysis of the failure data. Such routines run rapidly. If multiple errors are likely, the diagnostic routines use the sequential testing method. The first test starts with the smallest amount of circuitry possible. Each additional test adds a small increment to the circuitry tested. The sophistication of this approach is in the design and sequencing of the individual tests. The first failure found in the test sequence is repaired by reconfiguration, graceful degradation or physical repair before proceeding past that point. After a catastrophic failure, use bring-up tests which expect multiple component faults. Bring-up tests first verify that part of the system operates as described in its functional description, so that other routines may be applied. Functional tests generated from design specifications are not generally sensitive to obscure faults and are usually used. After confidence has been established that the necessary basic machine property has been restored, the search for complete integrity can begin. These techniques used extensively for military, resemble the recovery block method discussed in the chapter by Anderson, Lee and Shrivastava.

Gay (1977) studied how frequently test routines should be run. He used a Markov model, and showed that the optimum routine exercise frequency for a simplex unit is a function of the execution time of the test programs. The optimum frequency for redundant units is more a function of the unit switching time from standby to active. If faults affecting operation can be identified, the techniques of interleaved testing and operational testing can be used to reduce downtime to close to the theoretical minimum for a totally self-checked simplex unit.

Autonomous control is necessary for diagnosis. Maintenance control units can collect internal states, run audit programs to check execution, check information validity, and monitor the error detection signals from units. In the design of the STAR, Avizienis et al (1971) included a Test And Repair Processor (TARP) to serve as a monitor and diagnosis unit. Since for valid recovery these circuits had to work, the unit was small and protected by TMR with two spares. STAR used standby sparing for the other units, and replacement of a faulty unit was implemented by power switching. The information lines of all units were permanently connected to the buses through isolating circuits. The power switches and bus isolating circuits were made fault-tolerant by the use of redundant components (Mine and Koga, 1967). TARP initiated all recovery and replacement actions on the basis of the unit status signals. Carter et al (1971) proposed a Recovery Control Unit with standby sparing. The RCU passive circuitry was designed using morphic logic so it was self-testing, and switching to a standby unit was automatic. A self-checking array reduction analysis circuit provided the detection and diagnostic information. More recent systems (Wensley et al, 1976; Hopkins and Smith, 1977) used distributed computers as a basis for their fault-tolerant systems. Recovery is handled by partitioned and floating executive routines. These systems will be discussed in detail in the next section.

Maintenance processors have been used in less critical circumstances. Evensen and Troy (1973), and Chang et al (1973) describe the maintenance units which assist in performing initial system debugging and integration, system hardware maintenance, failure diagnosis, firmware initialization, and real-time status observation.

W. C. CARTER

In ESS-1, after an error indication, the good stand-by unit is used to test the other unit. Prell (1967) describes the circuits necessary for this testing. The two central controls are forced into step, the units synchronously execute the same test, and the matching circuits provide programmatic access to the microsteps within the unit operations. A judicious choice of the requirements for system diagnosis capability must be made if the matchers are not to be overly complex. Prell shows that the matching circuits must be able to perform both a directed match and a sampled match. In a directed match, the matchers are directed to look at match sources at specified time segments on a continuous basis. In the sampled match, the matchers are directed to look at specified sources at a specified time segment a given number of machine cycles from the point of initialization.

A similar technique is used for maintenance for the Amdahl 470 and for the IBM S/370 using RETAIN/370 (Fitzsimons, 1972). The faulty computer is connected to a communications network. Then the faulty computer and a good computer at the network central run the same diagnostic test. The good computer receives the results of the faulty computer and analyzes them against its own. The analysis results are used as an entry to a diagnostic dictionary to locate the failing part.

After error detection and diagnosis have been performed, the final step in recovery is repair - either by reconfiguration, graceful degradation or physical repair.

The greatest difficulty in hardware recovery is a proper reconstruction of control signals for external devices. The status of external devices must be determined, since frequently such signals must not be repeated, i.e., rocket firing (Avizienis et al 1969). After the control signals have been reconstituted - and this clearly depends upon the application - hardware reconstitution can begin.

For internal errors, the first standard technique used is retry, the one step backward error recovery method of chapter 5. Retry may be implemented at small cost at either the micro-instruction or instruction level (Carter et al 1977; Maestri, 1972). During the operation of an instruction (microinstruction) the state of the beginning of the previous instruction is saved until the propagation of error signals from the checking circuits indicates no error. If an error is detected the computer saves the appropriate state information for later analysis, then attempts to re-execute the previous instruction. If successful, the computer operation proceeds; if unsuccessful the above process is usually repeated N times before diagnosis begins.

After diagnosis, if standby redundancy is being used, the faulty unit must be replaced by a spare. The maintenance control unit changes the system status register and gives a reconfiguration signal. The newly connected spare is rapidly tested. Supplemental periodic testing of spares makes it likely that the spare is good. If the test fails, another spare is tried, or more complicated application-dependent recovery routines are called. If the redundancy is unit removal with degraded performance, then the unit is disconnected and checkpoint/restart procedures are begun. If the reconfiguration is to bypass the fault by replacing the faulty function by an alternate function, then this reconfiguration is made and the new function is tested. If the redundancy is continuation with decreased static protection, i.e. instead of TMR, the system will now run two units with comparison for error detection, the faulty unit is disconnected, the interfaces are correctly reconfigured, and processing can continue.

HARDWARE FAULT TOLERANCE

Recovery after detection and diagnosis has been treated very much more as a software process that is problem dependent than as a process which depends upon hardware design. Chandy (1975) and Gelenbe (1977) use the hardware failure rate to determine an optimum checkpoint interval but do not concern themselves with the probability of error detection. Shedletsky (1976) pointed out that the rollback interval depended upon the checking coverage and the component failure rate. Successful data restoration will occur only if the rollback is at least to the point of the first error occurrence. If the error detection is poor so the error latency is large, the rollback interval must be very long.

This section shows that careful design to produce a high checking coverage and efficient diagnostic procedures is necessary for the hardware upon which reliable recovery is based. All recovery procedures, hardware and software, must be specified at each design step. Careful modeling will allow the necessary evaluation to monitor the progress of the design, and ensure immediacy of detection, freedom from contamination, accuracy of diagnosis and speed of beginning continuation. The ideas discussed in the chapters by Melliar-Smith and Gerhart form a pertinent basis for such work, as will be discussed in the next section.

ADVANCED DESIGN DEVELOPMENTS

Since it is well known that those who do not read history are doomed to repeat it, let's begin advanced design developments by examining historical background. The early fault tolerant systems were designed to have the proper throughput, then the fault tolerant features were added in such a way as to cause least hardware costs. The resulting systems had some resounding successes. The IBM Launch Vehicle Digital Computer for Saturn V and Saturn IB (Dickinson et al, 1964) was a TMR error masking system, operating without backup. A computer system malfunction would have wasted a mission. The Bell Telephone ESS-1 system (Downing et al, 1964) used duplex computers with selective redundancy and used codes, reasonableness tests, and detection tests for error detection. Its success led to ESS-1A, ESS-2, and ESS-4. The major difficulties that were overcome were programming the necessary routines and the associated costs of thorough check-out. These first generation fault tolerant computer designs emphasized centralized computer systems. The advantages of such a design are the possibilities of resource sharing and peak load absorption. The growing disadvantages are the operating system, queuing problems, interference, diagnosis and testing, and obsolescence. Making changes to update the system involves revalidation and is difficult.

The second generation of fault tolerant computer designs used multi-processors, and considered the operating system design as an integral part of the system architecture. The FTSC (Fault Tolerant Spaceborne Computer), sponsored by the USAF, has a centralized design. D'Angelis et al (1976) carefully considered the operating system and recovery routines. Error detection depends upon ALU duplication and a shortened cyclic code for high error protection in data transfers and in storage (Stiffler, 1976). The Plessey System 250 is a modular multiprocessor designed for real time communications applications (England, 1972; Halton, 1972; Repton, 1972; and Hamer Hodges, 1973). Their capability mechanism defines the permitted bounds of a store block and is a secure store protection facility. A processor which detects an internal error disables all current capabilities and remains detached unless it recovers. This is an early example of non-obvious hardware/software interactive design for reliability. The Tandem 16 Nonstop Computer System (Katzman, 1977), makes excellent use of currently available inexpensive hardware. All units are duplicated to provide simplicity of recovery at some hardware expense: dual ported dual (or more) processors; dual bus structures; dual high speed buses to dual ported intelligent controllers for channels. This design has some attributes of distributed systems. In addition to this very short list, more information may be obtained from McCluskey and Ogus (1977) and Randell et al. (1978) and current computer publications.

The next step in fault tolerant design is to connect microprocessors in a distributed processing system. Distributed systems have the advantage of direct application of each unit to a limited part of the problem. Changes are isolated and easy to make, growth is simple, and the system is flexible. Independent power supplies naturally exist, and shielding from adverse environments and damage tolerance is also easier (Hopkins, 1975). With LSI the threshold cost of such systems is relatively less, but communication problems still remain. If communications are improved, these systems could use hardware and software pooling efficiently. Recently, self checking units have been designed for use in distributed processing systems. Williamson (1977) describes the realization of a self-checking and fail-safe programmable controller which uses a new control memory organization to give a simple and elegant implementation. He chose k out of n codes for checking because such circuits are self-checking for both single and unidirectional s-a-v faults, which, from his data, fits LSI fault modes well. The controller achieves fault detection for some 99% of LSI chip failures with only a 40% increase in circuitry. Carter et al (1977) designed a complete S/360 processor. Their conclusions are that complete checking is inexpensive (6.5% more components than the same design with the usual S/360 checking, and 35% more than the unchecked processor); and microinstruction and simple 360 instruction retry can be achieved with one additional LSI chip and with no apparent speed degradation.

Many system problems remain to be solved. Do you remember the flashing lights meaning processing capacity overflow and rerun during a moon landing? SKYLAB is reported to have used a dual computer system and had no hardware faults in either computer, but needed one program patch per day, on the average. New system and design techniques are imperative to meet the guaranteed reliability goals necessary in the near future. The system specification and design techniques discussed in the chapter by Melliar-Smith must be used for hardware design, as proposed by Neumann (1972). Three familiar hardware examples of "levels of invisibility" are the invisibility of pages in a virtual memory, or of a cache memory to a program, or of a transistor to a NAND gate. When a hierarchical framework is used for computer system architecture, the first design step is to establish explicitly various levels of design structure as levels of invisibility.

A second reasonable guideline is to try to have the unusual features introduced at a given virtual level made invisible at the earliest possible higher level. For example, it is desirable to have all error detection, diagnosis, reconfiguration, and recovery invisible to applications programmers, e.g., rollback is more visible than fault masking. Special machine instructions should not impact higher level languages or operating system protocol. Microcode features for executing instruction retry should not impact machine code. Error checking should minimally impact the microcode.

Associated with each level are possible configurations of fault-tolerant and fault avoidance techniques. In making the choice of such features, the most critical mechanisms must be carefully identified and separated from similar but less critical mechanisms. Criticality depends on system specification and environment, and these concepts must be used to integrate the various views of criticality. As a general rule, the processes of greatest criticality themselves must be well structured and small enough to verify and control. The most important criticality constraint is recovery. The techniques of detection, diagnosis and continuation discussed in the previous section must be specified as processes and considered as part of the system design.

Complex designs of this type must be validated, and their resulting reliability, which rests upon the criticality of processes, must be determined as the design proceeds from initial specification to detailed specification to engineering implementation. In the first section of this chapter formal techniques currently used for hardware verification were described. Their extension to a hierarchical structure is similar to that described in chapter 2 and published by Robinson and Levitt, (1977).

Next the fault avoidance techniques, discussed earlier, must be considered. Reliable components are selected, acceptable testing techniques and design techniques to allow the benefits of reliable components to be realized are devised, the best interconnection methods are analyzed, packaging and shielding of the hardware to screen out expected forms of external interference are examined, and methods of validation of the logical structure are planned.

The classes of faults that are to be tolerated by the design are identified, and for each the extent of fault tolerance is specified. Cost-effective methods of protective redundancy are then chosen to cover every identified class of faults, using the techniques described by the second section of this chapter. As each technique is chosen, the processes already in the hierarchical system model must be modified to represent the change. The necessary paths for error control and analysis must be added. Remember that multiple faults can defeat replicated redundancy, but in the absence of correlation are not likely to. Induced faults, on the other hand, are apt to be multiple and correlated. Intermittent faults are hazardous because, if latent, they may not be detected, and if non-latent, they may not be isolated and repaired. In either case their effect may cause the system to fail. As an important part of the design, system bringup and checkout methods must be devised. If possible, all redundancy features should be tested. These methods may have to be used in case of unexpected errors - the n-fault trap - so the prospect of automatically applying a subset of them in an emergency must be possible.

The next step is to evaluate and analyze the system reliability. The evaluations will show the changes needed for the next iteration, and the design proceeds until the specifications are proven to be satisfactorily implemented.

A hardware implementation which aids the type of system design just proposed is a hierarchical distributed structured system. This has a master processor controlling other dedicated processes. This has flexibility, is a short step from a digital bus structure, and lends itself to fault tolerance, especially if all processors are not of the same type, as happens in many applications.

NASA, in the past few years, has considered the application of sophisticated avionic and control systems employing computers to some of the applications having safety-critical requirements (Murray et al, 1977). From NASA's initial study, two candidate architectures were identified as having the potential of satisfying safety-critical requirements for commercial transport aircraft: Software Implemented Fault Tolerance (SIFT) (Wensley, 1972), and a Parallel-Hybrid Redundant Multiprocessor (Hopkins and Smith, 1975). These systems are typical of the modern trend of taking advantage of the potential for distribution; employing specialized electronics for each subsystem and using local and/or dedicated digital computer processing for such subsystems. These system architectures employ a fault-tolerant central computer for the primary function of simply surviving, with secondary functions of system redundancy management, contingency management, system coordination and command.

The Onboard Survivable Integrated Redundant Information System (OSIRIS) (Hopkins et al, 1977) is called a symmetric configuration because, as indicated in Fig. 7, it consists of an arbitrary number of simplex processing units and memory modules each connected to a redundant bus system in an identical way. These elements can interact with one another to form a fault-tolerant multiprocessor, in which detection, recovery, and reconfiguration are accomplished without requiring the inclusion of rerun programming in applications programs. The problem of configuration control subject to full single-fault protection is solved by the inclusion of other redundant modules called bus guardian units (BG) and bus isolation gates (BIGS).

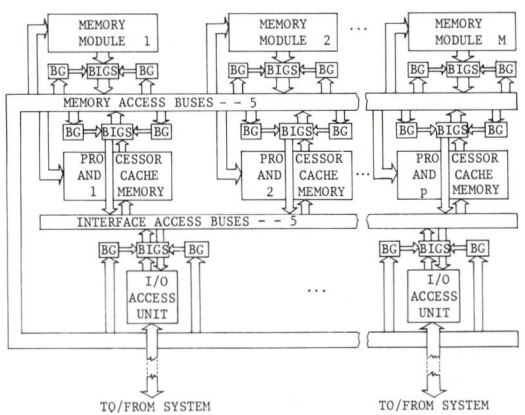

Fig. 7. Symmetric Configuration.

Processing units (i.e., processor-cache memory units) are assigned to groups of three, called processor triads. The three members of a triad operate in tight synchronism TMR with disagreement detectors. After an error, the two valid units continue to the end of the current job step, at which time all essential data will have been sent to memory. Before these two processing units embark on another job step, the unit in disagreement will be replaced by a spare. Several triads are envisioned to be multiprocessing.

Memory modules are likewise assigned to groups of three, called memory triads. The three members of a memory triad store identical data. A single error in a memory fetch is manifested as a disagreement visible to all three processing units of the processor triad that is communicating with the given memory triad. It will be necessary for error detection purposes to ensure that all data of consequence is read at least once during every test cycle of the system. The test cycle is a period, probably several seconds in duration, during which every hardware element needed for error detection and recovery is exercised to prove its capability. At the earliest opportunity following the detection of a memory unit error, the offending memory unit will be replaced by a spare. The new memory unit must then be "educated" by bringing its content into agreement with its partners.

Each high speed serial channel, time shared among all active units, communicates between processor triads and memory triads. Three buses operate as a triad in tight synchronism. Only one bus triad is operational until a fault necessitates a change. One processor triad at a time controls the bus triad, with control being granted on a demand basis. All other buses, if any, are spares. In those cases where more than one processor requests use of the bus, bus access is granted to the processor with the highest priority. Each slower serial channel (Smith, 1975) communicates between external data sources and destinations and a single processor triad designated as the triad responsible for input and output. Each slower channel is accessible by all processing units, but is used only by the I/O processor triad. These buses, too, operate as triads.

The output of each unit is routed to its own set of bus isolation gates. Each bus isolation gate acts as a crosspoint between the given unit and one of the buses. The unit itself is not empowered to enable these gates. Rather, these gates are enabled by special circuits designed for configuration control, denoted Bus Guardian Units (BGs). The function of a BG is to receive configuration control commands sent over the active bus triad from a processor triad, and accordingly to enable a selected bus isolation gate, and to control power to the associated unit. Each BG contains a voter to mask erroneous bus data. Isolation gates are non-redundant. The failure of any isolation gate in an active mode, where unwanted data is allowed to enter the bus, can make that bus useless. Therefore a bus wire with all of its isolation gates (one for each processing unit and memory module), comprises the replaceable bus unit for the purposes of fault isolation.

Since the BG is a common source of enabling signals for several bus isolation gates, the BGs are replicated, and unanimity among all BGs servicing a single unit is required to enable a processor's or memory's access to a bus. Each BG has a wired-in identity and can be addressed just as any other unit can. Messages to BGs carry configuration control data, which is stored in the BG until it is superseded by another message. In the event of power interruption, this data must be preserved in a non-volatile store, which is part of the BG. The unit's power is switched on and off by the BGs in the same manner in which the bus isolation gates are enabled. BGs themselves are always powered.

Each processing unit, memory module, and BG contains a voter. In the processor, the voter has an associated error latch that staticizes error occurrences for diagnosis and replacement. In the memory modules and BGs, no disagreement signals are derived or stored.

The primary advantage of hybrid redundancy over TMR is that injured triads are reconfigured back to a state where they can once again mask malfunctions. This is a process of tolerance renewal. In principle, the system failure rate is restored to its design value by the reconfiguration process. If reconfiguration were to fail, the system failure rate would increase, possibly by many orders of magnitude.

The fault latency problem poses an interesting design dilemma. Redundancy is employed to mask the effects of faults upon the system as a whole. But continued redundancy reliability requires testing of all logic so that all faults result in status changes and restoration of full masking protection. The resolution of this dilemma requires reconfiguration and testing of all independent system elements plus the selective generation of faulty symptoms to verify detection mechanisms. Voter testing is accomplished remotely from a processor triad by verifying the ability of the voter to interpret correctly messages containing errors. Any fault tolerant technique used must be composed of units which can be reconfigured and tested on line.

The multiprocessor's design approach to system reliability consists of a combination of shielding, environmental control, redundancy, reconfiguration, test algorithms, voting, and high reliability design and manufacture of all hardware elements. In addition, the system software must be virtually perfect.

The major system software elements are the executive, test, diagnostic, and system configuration programs; and the macro interpretation facilities. These elements are all closely related to the computer's architecture and are responsible for expediting job steps and for tolerance renewal. The executive program embraces several sub-functions which are the time queue, the event queue, job dispatch, and the cache memory functions of invocation and retirement. Cache memory management consists of the invocation and retirement of job steps and of the procedures and sub-procedures that constitute the job step activity. The reconfiguration program for the multiprocessor controls module and bus activity by sending messages to the guardian units. It maintains records of the status of each element and algorithmically responds to contingency situations. Reconfiguration programs also exist for the external parts of the system, primarily the input-output bus or network. When a malfunction is detected, a diagnostic program is invoked. This program attempts to locate the malfunction source by using any diagnostic data available from the processor triad that detected the malfunction and by reconfiguring the computer so as to cause the malfunction source to move. Macro interpretation facilities, like test programs, are quite specific to the logical design of the processors. They will exist as a combined machine language and microcode facility.

In June 1976, an experimental multiprocessor at the Draper Laboratory, employing parallel-hybrid redundancy and closely resembling the multiprocessor described here, was used as a digital autopilot in a simulated Boeing 707 aircraft. The autopilot functions performed were minimal but totally critical to flight. During the simulation exercises, malfunctions were injected in a variety of ways into the multiprocessor, which successfully recovered in every case. Although still far from a

246

highly fault-tolerant computer, this equipment has demonstrated the validity of the basic concept described here in many hundreds of hours of operation.

The SIFT (Software-Implemented Fault-Tolerance) computer (Wensley et al, 1976) is founded on a new approach to fault-tolerant computing that puts strong emphasis on software techniques for achieving reliability with corresponding de-emphasis on special hardware. The SIFT hardware consists of a set of independent general-purpose computing units (CUs), each with its own processor and memory. The CUs are interconnected by a system of independent buses in such a way that any CU may read (but not write) from the memory of any other CU over any of the buses. SIFT is described from a more abstract viewpoint in chapter 2.

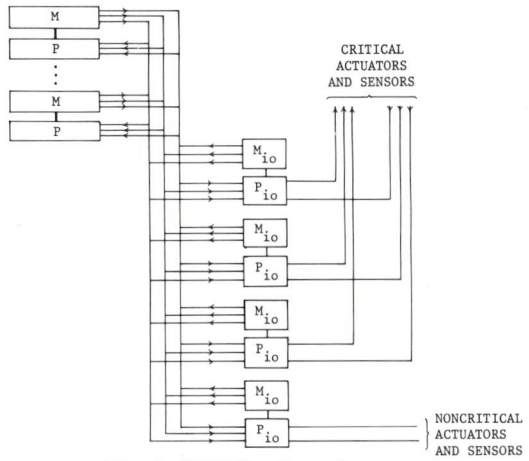

Fig. 8. SIFT Configuration.

Computational tasks are placed in modules with tasks of high criticality being replicated in several modules while less critical tasks are placed in a lesser number of modules. Each CU is multiprogrammed over a subset of the tasks, and each task is executed independently and in loose synchronism on a subset of the CUs. Within each module there is a local executive that controls all the operations with that module. The local executive includes scheduling, dispatching, error detection, error correction and error reporting.

Periodically, the intermediate results of computations of the same task are compared. Each CU working on a given task gathers (through read operations over the buses) the intermediate results computed by the other CUs working on the task, and votes on these results (including its own). It accepts the majority opinion as correct and continues. In addition, if the vote is not unanimous, it logs the disagreements for the global executive program. A different bus is chosen for each version of the data. One faulty bus will therefore not produce erroneous results in the system.

The global executive task (which is itself replicated) acts as a monitor, watching for reports of voting disagreement. When it finds that one of the CUs has logged such a disagreement, it carries out a diagnostic procedure to discover which processor or bus is at fault. If a bus is at fault, the global executive indicates (by setting a flag in a prearranged location of memory) that the bus is no longer to be used. If a CU is faulty, the system must be reconfigured (under the collective guidance of the instances of the global executive) to a new distribution of task assignments that excludes the faulty CU. So that normal task execution is not interrupted, the reconfiguration process is carried out gradually as a sequence of reallocation operations. If another fault is detected, a second reconfiguration occurs, and so on. If too many faults occur, it becomes impossible to reconfigure so as to carry out proper execution of all critical tasks, and the system fails. The voting circuits for TMR described in the second section of this chapter have been distributed among intelligent processors, with a corresponding potential increase in reliability.

Many fault-tolerant computer designs that use replication demand that the various versions of a computation of a task be carried out at identically the same time. This implies that a clock of high reliability be available for the simultaneous operations. In SIFT, this is avoided by only demanding a loose form of synchronization. The basic synchronization rule is that no task may commence an iteration of its computation before all the other replications of that task have completed the previous iteration. Thus each computation uses two buffers for the results. While one buffer contains the complete results of one iteration, the other buffer is being filled with the results of the next. The synchronization rule quoted above ensures that the first buffer will not be overwritten until the next iteration is completed. The use of this loose form of synchronization has benefits in that a system-wide transient of short duration will be unlikely to affect all of the processing modules in the same way thereby preventing the occurrence of multiple correlated errors which cannot be detected by simple replication and voting.

The input/output subsystem is connected to the bus system as shown in Fig. 8. The fault-tolerance techniques that are used are as follows. Critical sensors are replicated. Critical actuators are replicated. Non-critical sensors and actuators are not replicated. For critical input and output units, the data to and from the SIFT system flows on a multiple bus system which is connected to the main bus system of SIFT via logic that is realized by a set of microprocessors (P_{io} in Fig. 8). Each microprocessor operates according to the same rules as the central processors.

The SIFT design has been specified in accordance with a formal design methodology discussed in Chapter 2 and developed by Robinson (1976). This was used to assure a clearly-structured, easily modified design; to simplify verification of the correctness of that design; and to facilitate the analysis of certain reliability properties. The SIFT effort is the first instance of its use in connection with reliability modeling (Shostak et al, 1977). The logical structure of SIFT is depicted in Fig. 9. It consists of a hierarchical layering of system modules, application tasks, and global and local executives that utilize the facilities of the external interface of the system modules. The structure shown in Fig. 9, with a few exceptions, appears in each of the processors. Each task, including the global executive, executes in some subset of the processors. Thus the fault status and fault scheduler modules, which are accessed only by the global executive, appear only in processors executing the global executive. Fig. 9 depicts some additional inputs -- clock-tick, timer and faults. These are operations of particular modules that can be viewed as being "called" by processes that are external to the system and operate synchronously with the processing of tasks.

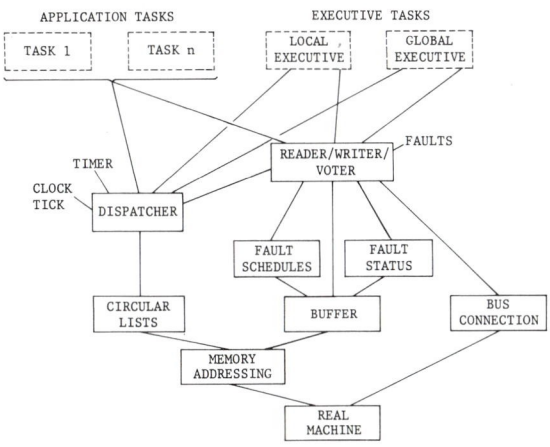

Fig. 9. Hierarchical Structure of SIFT.

In our discussion of the design methodology, it was noted that the top-level modules provide a complete external description of the capabilities of the system. Properties asserting the correctness of the system are stated and proved relative to the specification of these modules alone. The proof of correctness of the implementation is important only in that it guarantees that the specifications of the top-level modules are satisfied. Clearly, the meaningfulness of the reliability model depends heavily on the proof that the sequences of events that lead to the Fail State in the reliability model exactly correspond to the sequences of events that lead to failure in some top-level module of the system.

The first step is to express the reliability model in the form of an abstract module, i.e., as a set of abstract data structures and a set of operations that change the values of these structures. Next, the new module is implemented by the external interface modules of the design. In particular, for each state necessary for the reliability module, a representation in terms of the states of the interface modules is chosen, and a mapping function taking values of the representing states to values of the represented states is defined. Then, a sequence of operations in the interface modules is designed for each operation of the reliability module. The implementation is shown to be correct in the following sense: a transition from a state s_1 to s_2 in the reliability module must be implemented by a sequence of transitions in the interface modules that takes each state that maps to s_1 to a state that maps to s_2. Finally, a set of 'safe' states of the reliability module is identified. These states are implemented only by states of the interface modules in which proper operation of the system can be proved.

Four fault types can be shown to cover all possible single processor and bus fault occurrences that could lead to erroneous results. First, a processor produces erroneous values in computing results for tasks and/or in performing a vote and deciding which input(s) to the vote are in disagreement with the majority. Second, a bus changes the value of a word as it is transmitted between processors. Third, a processor is incapable of initiating a read operation via a particular bus. Fourth, a processor is incapable of depositing data onto a particular bus.

For evaluation, the probability of remaining within the set of safe states of the reliability module is computed as a function of time. To perform these computations, a modification of the continuous-time Markov process model has been developed. This paradigm models the functioning of the system as a finite set of distinct states with transitions between states corresponding to the occurrence of particular events. A given instance of the reliability model is represented as a directed graph whose nodes are associated with the states of the abstract reliability module and whose arcs are associated with those state transitions. Most of the events that cause transitions between states of the model exhibit random behavior having a Poisson time distribution. Almost all hardware faults in well-designed systems fall into this category. The arcs associated with such transitions are labelled with constant transition rates. The rates associated with SIFT processor failures have been approximated from chip counts and from well-established component failure data. Some transition events, however, do not occur with a random time distribution, but with fixed times and probabilities. If it is known, for example, that reconfiguration after a failure requires a given amount of time, one can compute a fixed probability that the reconfiguration is completed before a second failure occurs. In cases of this type, the arc associated with the transition is labelled with the fixed probability rather than with a rate. Now standard techniques (Cox, 1962) may be used to evaluate the model. It can be shown that this value of the probability constitutes a lower bound on the system reliability.

In summary, in the SIFT design, the major parameters are derived from the requirements and from the opportunities that are presented by recent technological advances. The use of software for error detection and correction is possible because the loose connection between tasks implies that the amount of data that must be moved from task to task is small. Software reconfiguration is also possible because the time to accomplish it is acceptable when viewed from the time constraints on the tasks and the fact that the fastest tasks tend to be small. This allows for the movement of complete tasks from one module to another. The low data transfer rate that is necessary between tasks allows a slow bus structure, using mechanisms that achieve fault isolation between units. The low cost of modern electronics allows the policy of reconfiguring on the basis of complete computing modules or buses. There are many other advantages that stem from the use of software as the principal techniques for achieving fault tolerance. These include: the degree of fault tolerance can be different for different tasks within the task set; the degree of fault tolerance can be different for the same task at different times; the total computational power available to the tasks can be varied by changing the number of computing modules; there are no special fault-tolerance restrictions on the processing modules.

The use of a formal design medium for purposes of specification, validation, and reliability modeling can be expected to play an important role in future designs of fault-tolerant computers. While a system might make extensive use of redundancy, unless the software or hardware mechanisms that manage the redundancy are correct, the system will still be unreliable. Similarly, the formulation and use of elaborate reliability models is to little avail if it can not be assured that these models actually reflect the behavior of the system.

As has been seen, a network of communicating processors forming a distributed processing architecture has many potential fault tolerance advantages over a monolithic structure (Goldberg, 1977). Distributed-processing architectures offer as well the obvious benefits of modular expandability, non-homogenous units, and highly parallel computation. However, more fault tolerant design techniques for communication between distributed units must be developed. Only Levitt (1968) and Smith (1975) have explicitly considered fault tolerant design techniques. Anderson and Jensen (1975) and Thurber (1974) have written surveys of the usual methods. This subject, which concerns both communication networks and computer buses, has been considered prosaic and has not attracted the research which is needed.

In addition, many issues need to be clarified to create a strong basis for systematic design, in particular the cost and complexity of mixed hardware/software design. In France (Costes et al, 1978) there is an ambitious nationwide plan for fault-tolerant system research which will integrate research in architecture and software engineering. New techniques for reliability evaluation and design verification are needed. In modern designs both hardware and software must have their probability of correct performance evaluated (Landrault and Laprie, 1977) and their design verified. Since fault tolerant designs must be accurately modeled and evaluated at each step to determine their effectiveness, this is a pressing need.

Module testing is still a major cost in producing microprocessors (Kline et al, 1976). More analysis of testing methods is badly needed (Shedletsky, 1977). The difficult problem of effective determination and treatment of fault modes is far from complete. There is currently inadequate knowledge about the fault modes of present and future technologies, the techniques of physical testing for manufacturing, the methods of unit diagnosis and the design of existing modules with respect to diagnosis and testing. The difficult problem of intermittent faults has hardly been touched (Ball and Hardie, 1969; Kamal and Page, 1974; Mallela and Masson, 1978).

Diagnosis has been treated either very empirically or very abstractly in determining conditions for unit interconnection to allow possible diagnosis. Recovery is beginning to be treated in a unified hardware/software manner (Randell et al, 1978).

It is hoped that recognition of these problems will stimulate the gathering of much needed experimental data, the development of new design approaches, and the continuation of theoretical studies. Such scientific endeavors are needed to meet the challenges presented by the necessary reliability and availability needs of modern computer systems.

REFERENCES

Abraham, J.A. (1975). A combinatorial solution to the reliability of interwoven redundant logic networks. IEEE TC, C-24, pp. 578-584.

Akers, S.B. (1977). On the specification and analysis of large digital functions. FTCS-7, Los Angeles, p. 88.

Akers, S.B. (1978). Functional testing with binary decision diagrams. FTCS-8, Toulouse, pp. 75-82.

W. C. CARTER

Anderson, D.A. and Metze, G. (1973). Design of totally self-checking check circuits for m-out-of-n codes. IEEE TC, C-22, no. 3, pp. 263-269.

Anderson, G.A. and Jensen, E.D. (1975). Computer interconnection structures: taxonomy, characteristics, and examples. ACM Computing Surveys, Vol. 7, no. 4, p. 197.

Armstrong, D.B. (1966). On finding a nearly minimal set of fault detection tests for combinational logic nets. IEEE TC, C-15, p. 66.

Arnold, T. F. (1973). The concept of coverage and its effect on the reliability model of a repairable system, IEEE TC, C-22, p. 251.

Ashjaee, M.J. and Reddy, S.M. (1977). On totally self-checking checkers for separable codes. IEEE TC, C-26, no. 8, pp.737-745.

Avizienis, A. (1971). Arithmetic error codes: cost and effectiveness studies for application in digital system design. IEEE TC, C-20, no.11, pp. 1322-1331.

Avizienis, A. (1977). Fault-tolerant computing - progress, problems and prospects. IFIP Congress Proceedings, Toronto, 1977 pp. 405-418.

Avizienis A., et al. (1971). The STAR (Self Testing and Repair) Computer: an investigation of the theory and practice of fault-tolerant computer design, IEEE TC, C-20, p.1312.

Avizienis, A., Mathur, F.P. , Rennels, D.A. and Rohr, J.A. (1969). Automatic maintenance of aerospace computers and spacecraft information and control systems. AIAA Aerospace Computer Sys. Conf. paper no. 69-966, Los Angeles.

Avizienis, A. and Rennels, D.A. (1972). Fault-tolerance experiments with the JPL STAR Computer. Dig. COMPCON '72, San Francisco, p. 321.

Ball, M. and Hardie, F. (1969). Effect and detection of intermittent failures in digital systems. Proc. FJCC, Vol. 35, Las Vegas, p. 329.

Bark, A. and Kinne, C.B. (1953). The application of pulse position modulation to digital computers. Proc. Nat. Elec. Conf., pp. 656-664.

Barsi, F., Grandoni, F. and Maestrini, P. (1976). Diagnosability of systems partitioned into complex units. IEEE TC, C-25, No. 6, pp. 585-593.

Birman, A. and Joyner, W.H. (1976). A problem-reduction approach to proving simulation between programs. IEEE Trans. on Software Engineering SE-2, 2, p. 87.

Black, C.J., Sundberg, C.E. and Walker, W.K.S. (1977). Development of a spaceborne memory with a single error and erasure correction scheme. FTCS-7, Los Angeles, p. 50.

HARDWARE FAULT TOLERANCE

Block, R.M., Campbell, R.D.V., and Ellis, M. (1948). The logical design of the Raytheon Computer, MTAC.

Bossen, D.C. (1970). b-adjacent error correction. IBM J R & D, Vol 14, p. 402.

Bossen, D.C. and Hong, S.J. (1971). Cause effect analysis for multiple fault detection in combinational networks. IEEE TC, C-20, p. 1252.

Bouricius, W.G., Carter, W.C. and Schneider, P.R. (1969). Reliability modeling techniques for self-repairing computer systems. Proc. ACM 1969 Ann. Conf., Las Vegas, pp.295-309.

Bouricius, W.G., Carter, W.C. et al. (1971). Reliability modeling for fault tolerant computers. IEEE TC, C-20, No. 11, pp. 1306-1311.

Brand, D. and Joyner, W. H. Jr. (1978). Verification of protocols using symbolic execution. Proc. Symp. Computer Network Protocols, Liege, P. F2-1.

Breuer, M.A. (1971). A random and an algorithmic technique for fault detection test generation of sequential circuits. IEEE TC, C-20, p. 1364.

Breuer, M.A. and Friedman, A.D. (1976). Diagnosis and Reliable Design of Digital Systems. Computer Science Press, Inc., Woodland Hills, California.

Breuer, M. A. and Harrison, T. L. (1974). Procedures for eliminating static and dynamic hazards in test generation, IEEE TC, C-23, p. 1069.

Carter, W.C. (1974). Theory and use of checking circuits. State of the Art Report, 20, ed. Bunyon, C.J., p. 413. Infotech Information, Ltd., Maidenhead.

Carter, W.C., Ellozy, H.A., Joyner, W.H. and Leeman, G.B. (1977). Techniques for microprogram validation. Agardograph No. 224, "Integrity in Electronic Flight Control Systems".

Carter, W.C., Jessep, D.C., Wadia, A.B., Schneider, P.R., and Bouricius, W.G. (1971). Logic design for dynamic and interactive recovery. IEEE TC, C-20, No.11, pp. 1300-1305.

Carter, W.C. and McCarthy, C.E. (1976). Implementation of an experimental fault-tolerant memory system. IEEE TC, C-25, p. 557.

Carter, W.C., Montgomery, H.C., Preiss, R.J. and Reinheimer, H.J. (1964). Design of serviceability features for the IBM System /360. IBM J R & D, Vol. 8, No. 2, pp. 115-126.

Carter, W.C., Putzolu, G.R., Wadia, A.B., Bouricius, W.G., Jessep, D.C., Hsieh, E.P., and Tan, C.J. (1977). Cost effectiveness of self-checking computer design. Proc. FTCS-7, Los Angeles, p. 117.

Carter, W.C. and Schneider, P.R. (1968). Design of dynamically checked computers. Information Proc. 68, IFIPS, pp. 878-883.

W. C. CARTER

Carter, W.C., Wadia, A.B., and Jessep, D.C.Jr. (1971). Implementation of checkable acyclic automata by morphic Boolean functions. Proc. Symp. Computer and Automata, Polytechnic Inst. of Brooklyn, pp. 465-482.

Cha, C. W. (1978). A testing strategy for PLA's. Proc. 15th DA Conf., Las Vegas.

Chandy, K.M., Ramamoorthy, C.V., and Cowan, A. (1972). A framework for hardware-software tradeoffs in the design of fault tolerant computers. Proc. FJCC, Vol. 14, Anaheim, pp.55-63.

Chandy, K.M. (1975). A survey of analytic models of roll-back and recovery strategies. Computer, Vol. 8, No. 5, pp.40-47.

Chang, H.Y. (1965). An algorithm for selecting an optimum set of diagnostic tests. IEEE TC, C-14, No.5, pp.706-711.

Chang, H.Y. (1968). A distinguishability criterion for selecting efficient diagnostic tests. Proc. SJCC, Vol. 2, Atlantic City, pp. 529-534.

Chang, H.Y. (1969). A method for digitally simulating shorting input diode failures. BSTJ, 48, pp. 1957-1967.

Chang, H.Y., Door, R.C., and Senese, D.J. (1973). The design of a microprogrammed self-checking processor of an electronic switching system. IEEE TC, C-22, no. 5, pp. 489-499.

Chang, H. Y., and Heimbigner, G. W. (1974). Controllability, Observability, and Maintenance Engineering Technique(COMET). BSTJ, 53, p.1505.

Chang, H.Y., Heimbigner, G.W., Senese, D.J., and Smith, T.L. (1973). Maintenance techniques of a microprogrammed self-checking control complex of an electronic switching system. IEEE TC, C-22, no.5, pp. 501-512.

Chang, H.Y., Manning, E., and Metze, G. (1970). Fault Diagnosis of Digital Systems. Wiley-Interscience, New York.

Chang, H.Y. and Scanlon, J.M. (1969). Design principles for processor maintainability in real-time systems. Proc. FJCC, Vol. 35, Las Vegas, pp. 319-328.

Chang, H. Y., Smith, G. W., and Walford, R. B. (1974). LAMP System Description. BSTJ, 53, p. 1431.

Chappell, S.G., Elmendorf, C.H., and Schmidt, L.D. (1974). Logic-circuit simulators. BSTJ, 53, pp.1451.

Chiang, A.C., Reed, I.S. and Banes, A.V. (1972). Path sensitization, partial boolean difference and automated fault diagnosis. IEEE TC, C-21, pp. 189-195.

Correia, M. and Petrini, F.B. (1977). Introduction to an LSI test system. Proc. 1977 Workshop on Design Automation, New Orleans, p. 460.

Costes, A., Landrault, C., Laprie, J.C., and Troy, R. (1978). An approach toward a unified design methodology for gracefully degradable periodically maintained computers. FTCS-8, Toulouse, pp. 200-203.

Cox, D.R. (1962). Renewal Theory. John Wiley, N.Y.

D'Angelis, D., and Lauro, J.A. (1976). Software recovery in the fault-tolerant spacebourne computer. FTCS-6, Pittsburgh, p. 143.

Dennis, N.G. (1974a) Ultra-reliable voter switches, with a bibliography of mechanization. Microelectronics and Reliability, Vol. 13, pp.299-308, Pergamon Press.

Dennis, N.G. (1974b). Reliability analyses of combined voting and standby redundancies. IEEE Tran. Rel., Vol. R-23, no.2, pp.66-75.

Dennis, N.G. (1976). Probabilistic reliability of a canonical fault-tolerant standby redundancy. Proc. IEEE, Vol. 123, No. 2., pp. 135-139.

Dent, J.J. (1968). Diagnostic engineering requirements. Proc. SJCC, Vol. 32, Atlantic City, pp. 503-507.

Diaz, M. (1974). Design of totally self-checking and failsafe sequential machines. Proc. FTCS-4, Urbana, pp. 3-19.

Dickinson, M. M. et al. (1964). Saturn V launch vehicle digital computer and adapter. Proc. FJCC, Vol. 26, San Francisco, pp. 501-516.

Diephius, R.J. (1969). Fault analysis for combinatorial logic networks. Ph.D. Dissertation, M.I.T.

Downing, R.W. et al (1964). No. 1 ESS Maintenance Plan. BSTJ, 43, pp. 1961-2020.

Droulette, D.L. (1971). Recovery through programming System/360-System/370. SJCC, pp. 467-476.

Eichelberger, E.B. (1965). Hazard detection in combinational and sequential switching circuits. IBM JR&D, vol. 9, p. 90.

Eichelberger, E.B., and Williams, T.W. (1977). A logic design structure for LSI testability. Proc. 1977 Workshop on Design Automation, New Orleans, p. 462.

Eldred, R.D. (1959). Test routines based on symbolic logic statements. JACM 6,no. 1, p. 33.

England, D.M., (1972). Operating system of System 250. Proc. IEEE 1972 Int. Switching Symp. MIT, pp. 525-530.

Evensen, A.J. and Troy, J.L. (1973). Intro. to the architecture of a 288-element parallel element processing ensemble (PEPE). Sagamore Comp. Conf. on Parallel Processing, pp. 162-170.

Fischler, M.A. and Firschein, O. (1973). A fault tolerant multiprocessor architecture for real-time control applications. Proc. 1st Conf. Computer Architecture, Gainesville, p. 151.

Fitzsimons, R. M. (1972). TRIDENT - A new maintenance weapon. Proc. FJCC, Vol. 41, p. 255.

Forbes R.E., Rutherford, D.H., Stieglitz, C.B., and Tung, L.H. (1965). A self-diagnosable computer. FJCC, Vol. 27, San Francisco, pp. 1073-1087.

Fox, J.R. (1977). Test-point condensation in the diagnosis of digital circuits. Proc. IEE, Vol.124, no. 2, pp. 89-94.

Friedman, A.D. (1967). Fault detection in redundant circuits. IEEE TC, C-16, no. 2, p. 99.

Friedman, A. D. (1974). Diagnosis of short circuit faults in combinational circuits. IEEE TC, C-23, p. 746.

Friedman, A.D. (1975). A new measure of digital system diagnosis. FTCS-5, Paris, pp. 167-170.

Gay, F.A. (1977). Reliability of partially self-checking circuits. FTCS-7, Pittsburgh, p. 135.

Gelenbe, E. (1977). On the optimum checkpoint interval, IRIA, Rapport de Recherche no. 232.

Goldberg, J. (1977). Workshop on distributed fault-tolerant computers. Computer, Vol. 10 no. 3, p. 51.

Hackl, F.J. and Shirk, R.W. (1965). An integrated approach to automated computer maintenance. IEEE Conf. Rec. on Switch. Theory & Log. Des., pp. 289-302.

Hakimi, S.L. (1977). Fault analysis in digital systems - A graph theoretic approach. In Rational Fault Analysis, Saeks, R., and Liberty, S.R., eds., Marcel Dekker, Inc., New York, p. 1.

Halton, D. (1972). Hardware of the System 250 for communication control. Proc. IEEE 1972 Int. Switching Symp., MIT, pp. 530-537.

Hamer Hodges, K.J. (1973). A fault-tolerant multiprocessor design for real-time control. Computer Design, Vol. 12, p. 75.

Hamming, R.W. (1950). Error detecting and error correcting codes. BSTJ, 29, pp. 147-160.

Hayes, J.P. (1971). A NAND Model for fault diagnosis in combinational logic networks. IEEE TC, C-20, no. 12, pp. 1496-1506.

Hayes, J.P. (1974). On modifying logic networks to improve their diagnosability. IEEE TC, C-23, No.1, pp. 56-62.

Hayes, J.P. and Friedman, A.D. (1974). Test point placement to simplify fault detection. IEEE TC C-23, no. 7, pp. 727-736.

Higgins, A.N. (1968). Error recovery through programming. Proc. FJCC, Vol. 33, San Francisco, pp. 39-43.

Hopkins, A.L. (1975). Notes for a course in reliability at CNET/Lannion, private communication.

Hopkins, A.L. and Smith, T.B. (1975). The architectural elements of a symmetric fault-tolerant multiprocessor, IEEE TC, C-24, p. 498.

Hopkins, A.L.,and Smith, T.B. (1977). OSIRIS-A distributed fault-tolerant control system. Proc. COMPCON Spring, p. 279.

Hsiao, M.Y. (1970). A class of optimal minimum odd-weight-column SEC/DED codes, IBM J. R.&D., Vol. 14, p. 395.

Ibarra, O.H. and Sahni, S.J. (1975). Polynomially complete fault detection problems. IEEE TC, C-24, p. 242.

Ingle, A.D. and Siewiorek, D.P. (1976). A reliability model for various switch designs in hybrid redundancy. IEEE TC, C-25, no. 2, pp.115-133.

Kamal, S. and Page, C.V. (1974). Intermittent faults: a model and detection procedure. IEEE TC, C-23, p. 713.

Karp, R.M. (1972). Reducibility among combinatorial problems. Complexity of Computer Computations, Miller, R.E. and Thatcher, J.W., eds. Plenum Press, New York, pp. 85-104.

Karunanithi, S. and Friedman, A.D. (1977). System diagnosis with t/s diagnosability. FTCS-7, Los Angeles, p. 65.

Katzman, J.A. (1977). System architecture for nonstop computing. Proc. COMPCON Spring, p. 77.

Klaschka, T.F. (1969). Reliability improvement by redundancy in electronics systems, II. An efficient new redundance scheme - radial logic. Royal Aircraft Estb., Farnborough, Eng. Tech Rpt. 69045.

Kline, B. (1977). The microcomputer development system, an answer to microcomputer design needs. Proc. COMPCON Spring, p. 152.

Kline, B., Maerz,M., and Rosenfeld, P. (1976). The in-circuit approach to the development of microcomputer-bases products. Proc. IEEE, 64, p. 937.

Knowles, R. (1976). Automatic Testing. Systems and Applications. McGraw-Hill, N.Y.

Landrault, C. and Laprie, J.C. (1977). Reliability and availability modeling of systems featuring hardware and software faults. FTCS-7, Los Angeles, p. 10.

Larson, R.W. and Reed, I.S. (1972). Redundancy by coding versus redundancy by replication for failure-tolerant sequential circuits. IEEE TC, C-21, no.2, pp. 130-137.

Levitt, K.N., Green, M.W., and Goldberg, J. (1968). A study of the data commutation problems in a self-repairable multiprocessor. Proc. SJCC, Vol. 32, Atlantic City, pp. 515-527.

Lewis, T.B. (1963). Primary processor and data storage equipment for the orbiting astronomical observatory. IEEE TC, C-12, No. 6, pp. 677-686.

Logue, J. L., et al, (1975). Hardware implementation of a small system in programmable logic arrays, IBM J R & D, Vol. 19, no. 2, p. 110.

Losq, J. (1976). A highly efficient redundancy scheme: self-purging redundancy. IEEE TC, C-25, p. 569.

Losq, J. (1975). Influence of fault-detection and switching mechanisms on the reliability of standby systems. FTCS-5, Paris, p. 81.

Lyons, R.E. and Vanderkulk, W. (1962). The use of triple modular redundancy to improve computer reliability. IBM J R & D, Vol. 6, no. 2, pp. 200-209.

Maestri, G. H. (1972). The retryable computer. Proc. FJCC, Vol. 41, Anaheim, p. 273.

Maheshwari, S.N. and Hakimi, S.L. (1976). On models for diagnosable systems and probabilistic fault diagnosis. IEEE TC, C-25, no.3, pp. 228-237.

Mallela, S. and Masson, G. M. (1978). Diagnosable systems for intermittent faults. IEEE TC, C-27, pp. 560-567.

Marauf, M.A. and Friedman, A.D. (1977). Efficient design of self-checking checkers for m out of n codes, FTCS-7, Los Angeles, p. 143.

Markowsky, G. (1976). A straightforward technique for producing minimal multiple fault test sets for fanout-free combinational circuits. IBM RC6222.

Mathur, F. and Avizienis, A. (1970). Reliability analysis and architecture of a hybrid-redundant digital system: Generalized triple modular redundancy with self-repair. Proc. SJCC, Vol. 36, Atlantic City, pp. 375-383.

McCluskey, E.J. and Clegg, F.W. (1971). Fault equivalence in combinational logic networks. IEEE TC C-20, p. 1286.

HARDWARE FAULT TOLERANCE

McCluskey, E.J. and Ogus, R.C. (1977). Comparative architecture of high-availability computer systems. Proc. COMPCON Spring, pp. 288-293.

Mei, K.C.Y. (1974). Bridging and stuck-at faults. IEEE TC C-23, p. 720.

Miller, E. H. (1966). Reliability aspects of the RCS/USAF Variable Instruction Computer, 1966 Aerospace Computer Symposium, Santa Monica, pp. 12-19.

Mine, H. and Koga, Y. (1967). Basic properties and a construction method for fail-safe logical systems. IEEE TC, C-16, p. 282.

Moore, E.F. and Shannon, C.E. (1956). Reliable circuits using less reliable relays. J. Franklin Inst. Vol 262, pp. 191-208 and 281-297.

Murray, N.D., Hopkins, A.L., and Wensley, J.H., (1977). Highly reliable multiprocessors. AGARDograph no.224, Integrity in Electronic Flight Control Systems, NATO.

Nair, R. (1978). Diagnosis, self-diagnosis, and roving diagnosis in distributed digital systems. Ph.D. Thesis, Univ. Illinois. Also to appear as CSL Report.

Nair, R., Thatte, S.M., and Abraham, J.A. (1978). Efficient algorithms for testing semiconductor random-access memories. IEEE TC, C-27, pp. 572-576.

Neumann, P.G. (1972). A hierarchical framework for fault-tolerant computing systems. Proc. COMPCON Fall, p.337.

Neumann, P.G. and Rao, T.R.N. (1975). Error-correcting codes for byte-organized arithmetic processors. IEEE TC, C-24, no.3, pp. 226-233.

Ostapko, D. L. and Hong, S. J. (1978). Fault analysis and test generation for programmable logic arrays (PLA). FTCS-8, Toulouse, pp. 83-90.

Parnas, D.L. (1972). A technique for module specification with examples. Comm. ACM 15, 5, p. 330.

Pau, L. F. (1974). Diagnosis of equipment failures by pattern recognition. IEEE Trans. Rel., R-23, pp. 202-208.

Peterson, W.W. and Weldon, E.J., Jr. (1972). Error-detecting codes. MIT Press.

Pierce, W.H. (1965). Failure tolerant computer design. Academic Press, New York.

Prell, E.M. (1967). Automatic trouble isolation in duplex central controls employing matching. Proc. SJCC, Vol. 30, Atlantic City. pp. 765-770.

Preparata, F.P., Metze, G. and Chien, R.T. (1967). On the connection assignment problem of diagnosable systems. IEEE TC, C-16, no. 6, pp. 848-854.

Putzolu, G.R., and Roth, J.P. (1971). An heuristic algorithm for the testing of asynchronous circuits. IEEE TC, C-20, no. 6, p. 639.

Ramamoorthy, C.V. (1967). A structural theory of machine diagnosis. AFIPS Proc. SJCC, Vol. 30, Atlantic City, pp.743-756.

Ramamoorthy, C.V. and Han, Y.W. (1975). Reliability analysis of systems with concurrent error detection. IEEE TC, C-24, no.9, pp. 868-878.

Ramamoorthy, C.V. and Mayeda, W. (1971). Computer diagnosis using the blocking gate approach. IEEE TC, C-20, pp. 1294-1299.

Randell, B., Lee, P.A., and Treleaven, P.C. (1978). Reliability issues in computing system design. ACM Computing Surveys 10, 2, pp. 123-167.

Rault, J.C. (1971). A graph theoretic and probabilistic approach to the fault detection of digital circuits. FTCS-1, Los Angeles, p. 26.

Reddy, S.M. (1974). A note on self-checking checkers. IEEE TC, C-23, pp. 1100-1102.

Rennels, D.A., Avizienis, A., and Ercegovac, M.(1978). A study of standard building blocks for the design of fault-tolerant distributed computer systems. FTCS-8, Toulouse, pp. 144-149.

Repton, C.S. (1972). Reliability assurance for System 250, a reliable real time control system. Int. Conf. on Comp. Comm., Washington, D.C., p. 297.

Reynolds, D., and Metze, G. (1976). Fault detection capabilities of alternating logic. FTCS-6, Pittsburgh, pp. 157-163.

Robinson, L. (1976). Specification techniques. Proc. 13th DA Conf., San Francisco, p. 470.

Robinson, L., and Levitt, K.N. (1977). Proof techniques for hierarchically structured programs. Comm. ACM, 20, 4, p. 271.

Roth, J.P. (1966). Diagnosis of automatic failures; a calculus and a method. IBM J R&D, Vol. 10, pp. 278-291.

Roth, J. P. (1977). Hardware Verification. IEEE TC, C-26, p. 1292.

Roth, J.P. (1978). Structured computer-design system. FTCS-8, Toulouse, p. 208.

Roth, J.P., Bouricius, W.G. and Schneider, P.R. (1967a). Programmed algorithms to compute tests to detect and distinguish between failures in logic circuits. IEEE TC, C-16, p. 567.

Roth, J.P., Bouricius, W.G., Carter, W.C., and Schneider, P.R. (1967b). Phase II of an architectural study for a self-repairing computer. SAMSO, TR-67-106.

Russell, J.D. and Kime, C.R. (1975a). System fault diagnosis: closure and diagnosability with repair. IEEE TC, C-24, No. 11, pp. 1078-1088.

Russell, J.D. and Kime, C.R. (1975b). System fault diagnosis: masking, exposure and diagnosability without repair. IEEE TC, C-24, No. 12, pp. 1155-1161.

Santoni, A. (1976). Testers are getting better at finding microprocessor flaws. Electronics, 23, p. 57.

Sawin, D.H. (1976). Microprocessors and microcomputer systems. Lexington Books, Lexington, Mass.

Schertz, D.R. and Metze, G. (1971). On the design of multiple fault diagnosable networks. IEEE TC C-20, pp. 1361-1364.

Schertz, D.R. and Metze, G. (1972). A new representation for faults in combinational digital circuits, IEEE TC, C-21, pp. 858-866.

Schneider, P.R. (1967). On the necessity to examine D-chains in diagnostic test generation - an example. IBM J R&D, Vol. 11, no. 1, p. 114.

Scola, P. (1972). An annotated bibliography of test and diagnostics. The Honeywell Computer Journal, 6, 2, pp. 97-104.

Sedmak, R.M. and Liebergot, H.L. (1978). Fault-tolerance of a general purpose computer implemented by very large scale integration. FTCS-8, Toulouse, pp. 137-143.

Sellers, F. F., Hsiao, M.Y., and Bearnson, L.W. (1968a). Analyzing errors with the Boolean difference. IEEE TC, C-17, p. 676.

Sellers, F.F., Hsiao, M.Y., and Bearnson, L.W. (1968b). Error detecting logic for digital computers. McGraw-Hill, New York.

Shedletsky, J.J. (1976). A rollback interval for networks with an imperfect self-checking property. FTCS-6, Pittsburgh, p. 163.

Shedletsky, J.J. (1977). Random testing; verified effectiveness vs. practicality. FTCS-7, Los Angeles, p. 175.

Shedletsky, J.J. and McCluskey, E.J. (1975). The error latency of a fault in a combinational digital circuit. FTCS-5, Paris, pp. 210-214.

Shedletsky, J.J. and McCluskey, E.J. (1976). The error latency of a fault in a sequential digital circuit. IEEE TC, C-25, no.6, pp. 655-659.

Shostak, R.E., Green, M.W., Levitt, K.N. and Wensley, J.N. (1977). Proving the reliability of a fault-tolerant computer design. Proc. COMPCON Spring, p. 283.

Smith, J. E. (1978a). Detection of faults in programmable logic arrays. To appear in IEEE TC.

Smith, J.E. (1978b). Universal system diagnosis algorithms. To appear in IEEE TC.

Smith, J.E. and Metze, G. (1975). General design rules for the construction of m-out-of-n totally self-checking checkers. Coord. Sci. Lab Report, R-693, Univ. of Illinois.

Smith, J.E. and Metze, G. (1978). Strongly fault secure logic networks. IEEE TC, C-27, pp. 491-500.

Smith, T.B. (1975). A damage- and fault-tolerant Input/Output network. IEEE TC, C-24, 5, p. 505.

Stieglitz, C.B. (1978). An LSI test overview. Digest of papers, Compcon '78, San Francisco.

Stiffler, J.J. (1976). Architectural design for near-100% fault coverage. FTCS-6, Pittsburgh, p. 134.

Stiffler, J.J. (1978). Fault coverage and the point of diminishing returns. To appear in J. Des. Automation & FT Comp.

Szygenda, S. A. (1972). TEGSA2 - Anatomy of a general purpose test generation and simulation system for digital logic. Proc. DA Workshop, Dallas, p.116.

Thatte, S.M. and Abraham, J.A. (1978). A methodology for functional level testing of microprocessors. FTCS-8, Toulouse, pp. 90-95.

Thurber, K.J. (1974). Interconnection networks - a survey and assessment. Proc. NCC, Vol. 43, p. 909.

Tryon, J.G. (1962). Quadded Logic. In Redundancy Techniques for Computing Systems, Wilcox, R.H., and Mann, W.C. eds., Spartan, Washington, D.C., pp. 205-228.

Usas, A.M. (1978). Checksum versus residue codes for multiple error detection. FTCS-8, Toulouse, p. 224.

von Neumann, J. (1956). Probabilistic logics and the synthesis of reliable organisms from unreliable components. In Automata Studies, Shannon, C.E., and McCarthy, J., eds., Princeton Univ. Press, pp. 43-98.

Wadia, A.B. (1970). Investigation into the design of dynamically checked arithmetic units. Ph. D. Thesis, Harvard.

Wakerly, J.F. (1974). Partially self-checking circuits and their use in performing logical operations. IEEE TC, C-23, p. 658.

Wakerly, J.F. (1975a). Transient failures in triple modular redundant systems with sequential modules. IEEE TC, C-24, no.5, p. 570.

Wakerly, J.F. (1975b). Principles of self-checking processor design and an example. Tech. Rpt. 115, Digital Systems Lab, Stanford Univ.

HARDWARE FAULT TOLERANCE

Wakerly, J.F. (1976). Microcomputer reliability improvement using triple-modular redundancy. Proc. IEEE, Vol. 64, no. 6, pp. 889-895.

Wensley, J.H. (1972). SIFT - Software Implemented Fault Tolerance, Proc. FJCC, Anaheim, Vol. 41, p. 243.

Wensley, J.A., Green, M.W., Levitt, K.N. and Shostak, R.E. (1976). The design, analysis, and verification of the SIFT fault tolerant system. Proc. 2nd Int. Conf. on Software Eng., San Francisco, p. 458.

Williams, M.J.Y. and Angell, J.B. (1973). Enhancing testability of large scale integrated circuits via test points and additional logic. IEEE TC, C-22, pp.46-60.

Williamson, I. (1977). Design of a self-checking and fault tolerant microprogrammed controller. IERE Conf. Proc. no.30, Conf. on Comp. Sys. Tech, Univ. Sussex.

Wadsack, R.L. (1978). Technology dependent logic faults. Digest of papers, Compcon '78, San Francisco.

Yamamoto, H., Watanabe, T. and Urano, Y. (1970). Alternating logic and its application to fault detection. Proc. of IEEE Comp. Grp. Conf., Washington, D.C., pp. 220-227.

7

PROTECTION

R.M. Needham

University of Cambridge

INTRODUCTION

There has been much interest in the past dozen years in the
protection of information in computer systems. An excellent
survey (Saltzer and Schroeder, 1975) gives a general account of
issues and techniques. Efforts in information protection are
related in varying degrees to reliability issues; at the most
general level there is a universal connection, since the aim of
protection is to ensure that the desired things happen in a
computer system and that undesired things do not. This goal
evidently has something to do with reliability.

This chapter first discusses the relations between protection
and reliability in more concrete terms, and then gives an overview
of a particular approach to protection in terms of capability
mechanisms at various levels.

THE RELATIONSHIP BETWEEN PROTECTION AND RELIABILITY

Protection and Redundancy

All protection mechanisms, whether compile-time or run-time,
involve the use of redundant information about what is permitted
and what is not. If all programs written were correct, it would
not be necessary to specify the types of abstract objects in a
programming language or to give explicit lists of memory regions
to which access is permitted. The purpose of the protection
features is to permit a compiler to reject wrong programs as being
out of agreement with stated intentions, or to permit run-time
protection hardware to reject execution of certain programs on
similar grounds. The emphasis in much protection work is on the
use of this redundancy to forestall the consequences of malicious
actions by programmers and others. However, in an unreliable
system accident is almost as powerful a source of events outside
the rules as is malice, and mechanisms which are provided to
protect against malice are equally effective against accident.

The converse is not true: effective protection against accident could be quite ineffective against malice, because a means of protection against accident does not have to take account of the possibility that an innocuous program might by chance turn into a very subtly malicious one. The chances of this are just too low. The relevance of protection studies to reliability arises to a considerable extent from the fact that defence against accident as opposed to defence against malice has not been very extensively studied except in particular contexts. Defence against malice has been extensively studied, and the conclusions of such studies are clearly relevant to what is, in principle, a weaker requirement.

The locus classicus of redundancy is in connection with communication, and there redundancy may be used either to detect the presence of error or to correct it. Protection in computer systems is present for error detection mainly; the furthest it goes towards correction is to give assistance in localising as far as possible the consequences of an error. There is a definite distinction between the two, even in a computer context. It would be possible to have a protection mechanism which raised a fault because some illegitimate address had just been written to, and this would be a perfectly satisfactory use of redundant information for error checking. In practice any mechanism which would be capable of doing this would also be capable of raising a fault because an illegitimate address was about to be written to, which is clearly a far more useful action. All practical protection systems accordingly do this.

Encapsulation and Reliability

It has been argued that the main influence of protection development upon reliability problems has been in relation to detection of error and prevention of its immediate effects. In general we may describe the results of protection as the encapsulation of various pieces of program, so that they are constrained to satisfy various interface requirements. This is most easily illustrated by an example related to reliability issues.

Consider an operating system module which is concerned with managing a disc channel. In some traditional operating systems this program, or parts of it, runs in a quite unprotected way and has unfettered access to the whole of memory. Accordingly, malfunctions in it have potentially corrupted anything in memory, and the only coherent action to take as a result of such a malfunction is to assume that the whole content of memory is corrupt and accordingly to restart the system. In almost no case will anything serious have been corrupted, but we cannot know. Yet channel drivers of the type mentioned can be very hard to debug; error conditions from the hardware they control are unpredictable both in nature and timing, and the indications of error may violate all reasonable assumptions. For example, the conjunction of error signals 'wrong checksum in data' and 'cylinder not found' should never happen and may confuse the software if it does. What we would like to do is to encapsulate the channel driver as much as possible, so that malfunctions in it such as wild addressing or looping, are detected before anything severe has happened. Imagine that the impossible condition just mentioned has arisen, and the channel driver has been caused by it to do something forbidden. The correct reply to the user would be 'channel driver software error' as a reason why the requested transfer had not been done - a reply on a par with 'seek error' or 'parity error'. Of course a particular transfer has not been done - but this is a great deal better than a system crash.

A primary requirement for achieving this kind of resilience is a strict adherence to a 'minimum privilege' principle in systems programs. No program should have access to any material which is not strictly necessary for the performance of its task. Furthermore, as far as possible, this limitation should apply to the particular task requested in a specific invocation of a program, rather than to the general class of tasks which the program undertakes. In the particular case in point, the channel driver should have read-only access to its own code, access to state information about the particular transaction, and nothing else. If this be achieved, one may have a reasonable degree of confidence that malfunction of the program in question cannot have had any wider effects on the state of the memory. It is now necessary to consider the action which a system should take when a program, of the general nature we have been considering, does in fact fail. In some way it is necessary that the caller of the program be informed. There are essentially two ways in which to achieve this. One is for an external agency, implicitly relied upon by all concerned, to notice that something has happened and to generate an appropriate report which is given to the caller as if it had been a genuine return from a broken program. The other way is to arrange internal mechanism inside the offending program which will attempt to recover control at any rate to the point of being able to give a genuine, rather than a simulated, error return. Both approaches have their advantages. The former is more reliable in the sense that in the design of a complete system it only has to be got right once. However, it is not so good as the latter approach in interpreting the offending occurrence in the light of the particular actions which are being at the time attempted. The weakness of the latter approach is that it depends upon the correct action of one part of a program which is, by hypothesis, known to be faulty. In practice, a combination of the two methods seems to be desirable. For example, in the Cambridge CAP computer, which implements very tight encapsulation, the fault occurring in an encapsulated program gives rise initially to interior action within the offending program. The external mechanism at this point simply notes the existence of a fault, and awaits the indication by the program that the fault is being coped with. If another fault occurs before this indication has been given the program is considered to be irretrievably broken, and a forced return to its caller is made. In the nature of the case, the information given to the caller in the circumstance is likely to be less helpful. This approach is not perfect, because error reporting could fail immediately after the indication that it has been satisfactorily proceeded with is given. In practice this approach has been found to give a consistently very high level of successful error reporting.

So far in this discussion of encapsulation it has been implicitly assumed that the purpose of the encapsulation is to prevent the encapsulated program from disturbing material outside its boundaries by erroneous actions. It is also very desirable to have the boundary fence, as it were, work the other way too. It then serves to prevent the caller of a program from misusing the called program in such a way that some disaster will ensue. A common cause of difficulty is the passage as argument of unprotected references or addresses which might have been invalid if used directly by the caller but have formally valid though undesirable effects when used by the called program. It may be noted that the requirement for great care in the validation of arguments is increased if the principle of minimum privilege has not been fully observed. If it is really the case that the called program only has access to its own code and the state information of the current transaction, then there cannot be any wider effects from bizarre failures of the current transaction. In real life this possibility cannot usually be excluded. For example, the channel driver program might be provoked into writing to the wrong part of the disc. Alternatively, the whole purpose of the encapsulated program may be to guard a data structure which is, by its very nature, common to a variety of uses of the program, so that in some sense the very complete encapsulation mentioned above is impossible. It is accordingly necessary in general to validate arguments very thoroughly, and it is well known that a fertile source of system errors is failure to do so sufficiently. It is very desirable to arrange that as much of this protection as possible should be done by standard and preferably automatic methods, so that the scope for oversight by programmers is restricted. Protection of addresses is a topic which arises naturally under the discussion of capabilities later; a different source of encapsulation failure altogether can arise, which will now be indicated.

Whenever arguments are passed in memory, it is necessary to guard against the possibility that the data area in question is being accessed simultaneously by some asynchronous activity. This may be a separate process running in the machine, or it may be autonomous hardware such as a channel. Unless great care is taken, it may be possible for disorders to arise as a result of making a validation pass over the data and then using it. The data could have changed after validation and before use. The only foolproof protection against this breach of encapsulation is to copy all of the material into known safe space before doing anything to it at all or, which is equivalent, to devise an ingenious algorithm which does the required validation and subsequent work while only touching each argument word once. The latter may not be practicable, and copying is an operation which computer software designers detest. It is interesting to note that in some kinds of distributed computer system or network this latter kind of difficulty is much easier to protect against, since the transmission of information around the network is itself a copying operation.

The general purpose of encapsulation may be informally stated as making it easier for the system to fail for one user rather than for all. Care has to be taken that the mechanisms provided do not obscure the evidence which would enable the fault to be diagnosed. This slightly alters the communication paths which have to be provided; not only does a system module have to be able to recover sufficiently to give a coherent account to its caller but it also has to be able to leave more detailed information for its maintainer. This in itself is an apparent conflict with the encapsulation goal, and its consequences appear in apparently strange pieces of system design. A computer may, for example, appear to stop for its users and then continue. What is actually happening is that diagnostic information is being recorded at a very low level by dedicated non-sharable software - and the reason is to avoid breaching encapsulation as far as possible by simply having the most basic form of information drain to the outside.

Protection and Inspectability

There is a very valuable side effect from the application of redundant constraints upon what programs may do. If the constraints are specified in a suitable way, it is possible to make quite strong assertions about the behaviour of programs without actually inspecting them. Suppose that a certain system data structure has been found to be corrupted, and we are trying to find out what is wrong. If the access constraints on the data structure are expressed in a clear manner independently of any other aspects of the program structure, then it is easy to find out which program modules could have been at fault. It is clearly possible to provide part of this power by good annotation, but it is not possible to provide all of it. Knowing that the list under examination is an enforced list of all material available for access gives a very much stronger assurance than any annotation, since annotations are notoriously hard to keep up to date. The relation of this point to reliability is somewhat indirect, since it is more concerned with the rectification of errors rather than

their toleration or avoidance. However, the practical value of it
is great.

STATIC AND DYNAMIC PROTECTION

A standard source of debate whenever protection is discussed
is as to whether the protection should be applied at compile-time
or run-time. Opinions on this matter tend to be strongly held
beyond the bounds of reasonableness, and the entire argument
seems to have some theological aspects. In these notes we attempt
to review the issues.

Static Protection

If a program is correctly written to perform a certain task,
for example to update a particular field of a record supplied as
an argument to it, the only reasonable cause of its failure is
giving a bad argument. It could be a record of the wrong sort,
or one of the right sort which is ill-formed. The problems may be
avoided by preventing misuse of programs, and this can be achieved
statically at the time that the assemblage of programs is put
together. This, in barest essentials, is the argument for
compile-time protection, since the programs are put together by a
compiler or, at any rate, a compiling system. Provided that the
nature of the correct arguments to any procedure, module, or
similar piece of code is sufficiently specified when the code is
written, then the compiling system can check whether the code is
being abused and refuse to produce an executable, but in that
sense, defective program. This line of argument leads to the
development of languages in which extra apparatus is provided to
specify the nature of objects; the terminology used is that of
types. A programmer may define a type of object, which involves
giving a list of its properties and of the operations available
on it. The language system supports the declaration and
generation of instances of objects of particular types, and can
check that the argument to a procedure is of the correct type.
The type definitions form a schedule of what is possible, and
these constitute an external, enforced, and inspectable protection
constraint of the variety mentioned earlier.

It has usually been the case that the availability of a
particular type has meant complete access to objects of that type.
Proposals for refinements on this are found in Jones and Liskov
(1976). Development in this line is not complete, and as yet
little account has been taken of the problems of integrating
filing systems into a language structure. There seems little doubt
that eventually very powerful and flexible protection mechanisms
will be provided via programming languages, though it is not clear
at what cost in complication of the languages and the computers.

Run-time protection

If arrangements are made to encapsulate programs by hardware, then the protection mechanism has some chance of catching errors made by the regular part of the computer. Addressing errors or address calculation errors produced by faulty equipment are highly likely to produce protection violations leading to early discovery of the fault. This point is clearly related to questions of reliability. All compile-time protection does is to assure one that the program used to be satisfactory; run-time protection gives some confidence that it still is.

A much more fundamental point about run-time protection concerns the environment in which programs are going to run. Compile-time protection relies upon the whole assemblage of code for execution being in some sense one program - at any rate on its being known to an appropriate language system as a unit. This is a quite inappropriate assumption in a general purpose machine, where users are entitled to produce their own programs by whatever means they wish from writing hexadecimal to writing Algo168. In such a circumstance no assertions whatever can be made about the nature of the programs, so there has to be complete reliance on run-time checking. Different attitudes at this point determine one's attitude on the whole question of when checking is done. Someone who is concerned with rather simple machines which should be cheap to produce and which are going to be used in predetermined or relatively fixed ways will see compile-time checking as the answer, whereas someone designing a shared utility (whether in one machine or not) will see run-time checking as the answer. A striking example of the contrast is afforded by the difficulties mentioned earlier, under the heading of encapsulation, to do with asynchronous access to pieces of memory containing arguments to an encapsulated program. The complete detailed survey of a set of programs done by a language system can, in principle, make sure that the difficulty is avoided either by knowing that there are no alternative references to the same material or by enforcing the correct use of some kind of lock. It is precisely the lack of this global view which may lead to the need for rather extensive run-time copying. Purely run-time protection depends on taking a worm's eye view of the immediate environment and making sure that the constraints are not violated without any helpful knowledge as to the rest of the system.

Run-time protection almost inevitably makes a machine slower. A major aspect of the design of such systems has been to minimise this effect by integrating the protection features with address translation as far as possible. It is, however, necessary to balance the speed-up against complication, lest one loses a significant advantage of run-time protection, namely the relative ease of satisfying oneself that it is correctly implemented. Unless one puts in a run-time protection system of vast elaboration, it is a more reasonable task to check that it is right than to do the same thing for a complete language system. In neither case, of course, is there any guarantee that the protection facilities will be used properly. In a run-time protection system a programmer may omit protection boundaries which ought to be included, and in a compile-time protection system he may omit to make distinctions of type or access when he should. Some work by D.J. Cook (1978) on the evaluation of the run-time protection system as actually used in the construction of operating systems for the Cambridge CAP computer gives some notable examples of what can happen even in a case where the programmers thought that they were adhering to minimum privilege principles with very great devotion. A particular feature of his observations was that various facilities of a non-destructive sort were made available, so to speak, to the general public without it being realised that they should strictly have been inaccessible to various programs which in other respects were highly privileged. Also there were cases where a program which was deliberately present as a gate-keeper and argument validator to certain facilities also had access to others which it could never validly use. These were not the result of deficiencies in the underlying protection mechanism, but rather the result of simple oversight. Cook's analysis was possible because of the strict separation of the externally enforced protection environment from the programs themselves. He was able to read all the programs and compare what they would have been entitled to do with what they actually did.

The remainder of this chapter is concerned with run-time protection (in part because this reflects the writer's experience). Current thinking about this subject seems mainly to be concerned with the use of capabilities, to which we now turn.

PROTECTION AND CAPABILITIES

This section explores a number of distinct instances of the use of the notion of <u>capability</u>.

A generic definition of a capability can only be an informal one, because of the detailed differences in behaviour of capabilities in different applications. We assume, therefore, that capabilities have the following properties.

1. Unforgeability. Capabilities may only be manufactured or altered with suitable authorisation.

2. Validity on presentation. The presentation of a capability for a desired action is sufficient evidence of authority to request the action.

3. Transferability. Capabilities may be transferred from one user or program to another; in most instances they may not merely be moved but copied.

4. Self-identification. Capabilities contain the name, or something which leads to the name, of an object. The capability will authorise the performance of some action upon or using the object.

The use of capabilities is convenient when the decision to permit some action is taken at a different time or place from the performance of the action, when the same authorisation is to serve for numerous instances of an action, when there is no suitable means of recording permission for example by principal name (since the principal requesting action is not known) and when permission to do something is unlikely to be revoked.

The idea of using transferable unforgeable tickets of permission may be exploited at various levels of generality or scale, and confusion may easily be caused by comparing protection mechanisms using capabilities with others which function at a different level. We illustrate below the use of capability ideas in three different ways: firstly in relation to protection of a filing system for a computer, and finally in relation to networks of computers. The principles involved will be recognisably similar, but the mechanisations differ noticeably.

It is conventional to have in the representation of a capability two parts which will be called the name part and the control part. The control part indicates which of the possible actions upon the object named are permitted by the capability. It is not logically necessary to do this; we could arrange that the same object had different names according to different actions upon it. No implementations are known which do this. An example would be a computer in which are used a different virtual address to read from a word from that used to write to it, and in which protection was achieved by giving capabilities for pieces of the address space. The name part either is the name of an object, or it leads to the name by some algorithm. The property required of a name is that it should lead by some algorithm to the address and boundary of the object named, so that permitted actions may be performed. The translation from name part to address may sometimes be optimised so that the name itself need not be used each time.

Protection in Main Memory

We now consider the first application of capabilities, namely the protection of information in the main memory of a computer. The original motivation for this application was the observation that the protection mechanisms available did not have enough power

or flexibility to implement a principle of least privilege in
relation to main memory. That is to say, that a program when
being executed should have access to those, and only those, words
of memory which were necessary to its correct functioning. The
mechanisms available were defective in one or both of two ways.

1. Their grain was too coarse. For example, one might have
   a protection system in which the unit of protection was
   4K bytes, whereas the units of data to which access was
   to be controlled were frequently much smaller, perhaps
   only a few bytes.

2. Their structure was inappropriate in that access by
   program A to a piece of memory might imply that program B
   had such access, necessary or not, or in that access by
   program P to memory segment Q required that it had also
   access to segment R though this was not strictly necessary
   to the application for which P was intended. This sort of
   limitation is characteristic of computers with rings or
   other hierarchical protection mechanisms.

It is of interest to note that the reason for worry about
point 1 above was mainly in connection with reliability or rugged-
ness rather than security or privacy. The purpose in fine-grained
protection is to confine the effect of error or malfunction as
much as possible, and to make it easier to replace or enhance
system components without disturbing their neighbours. There is
no necessary connection or even any very strong practical one
between fine-grainedness and privacy.

Accordingly the first computer proposed with capability-
based protection for main memory (Fabry, 1968) and the first two
actually built, the Plessey System 250 (England 1974) and the
Cambridge CAP machine (Needham and Walker, 1977) had capabilities
which were able to delineate areas of main memory in units as
small as a single word. At any time the protection environment,
as we shall call it, was represented by a collection of
capabilities, no access to memory being possible without the
presentation of a suitable capability. The control parts of the
capabilities in all three designs indicate the type of access
permitted to the memory area concerned (henceforth referred to as
a segment). In addition to the conventional possibilities of
'Read', 'Write', and 'Execute' there are two extra possibilities
'Read Capability' and 'Write Capability'. Segments with either
of the capability access statuses may only be accessed by special
instructions or special microprogram; in neither case will the
contents of the capability segment be passed into one of the
machine's general registers or the content of a general register
be copied into a capability segment. These extra access controls
may be used to enforce the unforgeability required of
capabilities; they have the additional effect that capabilities

are kept together in capability segments rather than scattered through memory. In a suitable tagged architecture capabilities could, in principle, be anywhere. We shall see later that there are distinct disadvantages to this anyway, so that it is unsurprising that there are no tagged-capability computers.

Again in all three designs the basic way of delineating a segment is by base and limit in real memory. There are, however, a variety of choices in relating the name part of the capability to the base and limit. Fabry's design simply put them in the capability as the name part. The Plessey 250 puts them in a master list, to which the name part of a capability is an index. The Cambridge CAP does not store them explicitly anywhere; they are computed from a data structure to which the name part of a capability contains an entry. These differences are of importance in relation to swapping – that is, to the operation of a virtual memory of segments. It is of the nature of a virtual memory system that an attempt to touch a word fails because the appropriate segment is swapped out, and that the process of swapping a segment in may require segments previously in main memory to be swapped out. Furthermore, a segment need not always be swapped in to the same physical place. The reaction of these facts upon capability structures is as follows. Multiple instances of capabilities for particular segments in general exist, and it is necessary to arrange that when a segment is swapped out all attempts to access it are trapped. Because of the relation of the capability to the right of access, it is either necessary to find and alter all capabilities for the swapped-out segment, or to alter something which is reliably on the evaluation path from the name part of the capability to the base and limit. The master list entry on the Plessey 250 and an analogous entry in the CAP provide this function, and indeed this is a principal reason for their existence. There is one entry per existing segment, and when swapping a segment out all accesses to that segment may be trapped as a result of overwriting it with a suitable pattern recognisable to the mechanism which computes the base and limit from the name part of a capability.

Capabilities and Addressing. This discussion implicitly involves the relationship of capabilities to addressing and the manner of presentation of a capability when making access to a word of memory. In all practical capability designs this relationship is very close. In an instruction which requires an operand from memory there is an indication of which capability should be used, and the address (or the residue of the address after specifying a capability) consists of an offset in the segment delineated by the capability. Access will, of course, not be allowed if the offset exceeds the limit of the specified segment, or if the use which is to be made of the word conflicts with the control part of the capability. There is no way in which an attempt to access memory may be made without mentioning a capability (though an

inappropriate or perhaps non-existent one might be mentioned) <u>and</u>
<u>the</u> <u>mentioning</u> <u>itself</u> <u>performs</u> <u>a</u> <u>substantial</u> <u>part</u> <u>of</u> <u>the</u> <u>address-</u>
<u>ing</u> <u>function.</u> Since, in the completed capability machines, some
computation is necessary to get from the capability to the base
and limit, steps are taken to retain the result of the computation
in an (implicitly or explicitly named) register, where it is
intended to service numerous accesses. In consequence of this,
the structure of addressing is inevitably bound up with the
structure of access to capabilities. In the CAP, for example
capabilities are specified by offset in a current capability
segment, this specification being part of the address issued by
the program. Thus an address would have a different interpretation if the current capability segment were replaced or rearranged.
This is a pointof some importance, because when moving from one
program to another with different protection needs the current
capability segment is replaced - this being the definition of the
transition. Accordingly it is necessary to be very careful when
passing addresses as arguments between programs.

This close relationship between capability structures and
addressing structures is not a necessary consequence of the use of
capabilities. It would be possible to proceed in the following
manner, although no one ever has. First arrange that an addressing structure supports segments which will be the unit of protection. Any such address structure would do - for example that of
Multics. Associate with each segment a name, which will appear in
the name part of any capabilities for the segment. It is now only
necessary to arrange that any instruction requiring an access
should offer a capability as well as the address. The addressing
hardware compares the name part of the capability, presumably
handed over in a register, with the name associated with the
segment and rejects the access if they are not the same. The
name would naturally have to go into any associative store used
to optimise segment look-up. Such a system would undoubtedly
provide capability-based protection and would not influence the
addressing structure at all in that segments must be supported
to be the units of protection. There are two reasons for not
proposing this scheme for implementation. Firstly, it is a little
uneconomical to have to use part of an instruction or address to
specify a capability in addition to everything else. This may
be regarded as a minor point. More interesting is that it throws
on to the programmer the burden of maintaining a correspondence
between segments and the capabilities which support access to
them, which would appear to require similar data-structures to
those found in present capability systems but belonging to the
user rather than the system. There is also doubt about the
practicability of managing this correspondence satisfactorily in
high-level language programs, especially when handling chains of
references which run through several segments.

We now return to the use of capabilities to express the set of segments of memory currently accessible. This set will be described as the <u>protection environment</u> in which a program runs; the notion will shortly be extended without change of name to include other varieties of capabilities as well.

<u>Protection Environments.</u> If the minimum privilege principle is taken seriously, programs will be divided into numerous parts or modules which have distinct protection requirements. Not doing such subdivision would cause capabilities to be available during the execution of regions of program to which they were unnecessary. It is thus necessary to consider the mechanism by which control may be transferred from one protection environment to another; this action itself is a controlled privilege and should be represented by a capability. Such capabilities are known as ENTER capabilities, and they specify a new capability segment (or bundle of capability segments) to become current, that is to say to constitute the current protection environment. Some mechanism needs to be provided to pass capabilities as <u>arguments</u> to the new environment; various mechanisms have been proposed and the details are not germane here. To fix ideas, consider a simple example. Suppose there is an output program whose task it is to take strings of characters from its caller and put them in a buffer in some fixed format. The caller cannot be permitted direct access to the buffer because it is not trusted to get the format right. Other special actions take place when the buffer is full. The calling program is provided with an ENTER capability to a protection environment with a fixed stock of capabilities thus:

a) for its own code

b) for the buffer

c) for some workspace, e.g. buffer pointers
    (all these are capabilities for segments)

d) for the special actions to be taken when the buffer
    is full - an ENTER capability.

In addition, wherever the output program is executed it will have access to

e) a capability permitting it to read the character string
    to be output - this will be passed as an argument.

We may envisage a rather complicated program such as an operating system being divided into a considerable number of protection environments as indicated. This rather bald remark is in some sense a description of the operating systems of the existing capability machines; it is, however, interesting to consider these programs from a rather higher-level viewpoint.

PROTECTION

Take first an example, this time from the CAP operating
system. A particular class of protection environment is used for
the management of file directories. A user program may be able
to make use of several file directories, these directories being
structures which maintain correspondences between text names of
files and internal names for them, and which also record access
control information. For each directory available to a user
there is an ENTER capability for a protection environment. This
environment contains, _inter alia_, capabilities for the code of a
standard directory manager program, for some local workspace, and
for the segment in which the representation of the particular
directory is kept. The only use which may be made of a directory
is to call the appropriate instance of the directory manager,
specifying as arguments the service requested – for example to
delete a given named file. The nature of the representation of
the directory is completely inaccessible to the caller. This is
all extremely reminiscent of the properties of typed objects in
programming languages which support the feature of abstract data
types of which some attributes only – typically procedures for
doing manipulations on the objects – are accessible from outside.
Protection environments, especially of the variety in which
numerous instances can exist differing only in their representation parts – as in our example of directory management – perform
almost exactly the same function as abstract data types in
programming languages. They perform it quite differently, though.
The encapsulation provided by programming languages derives from
the actions of a compiler in rejecting disallowed program texts.
This depends upon everything being produced by a common compiler
or, at any rate, a common language system at perhaps a lower level.
The capability mechanism performs the encapsulation by run-time
access control, and presupposes nothing about the origin of the
programs being executed. It is thus particularly attractive in
general-purpose environments, where detailed use of facilities may
not be predicted or legislated in advance. A great many operating
system facilities may usefully be regarded in this light – for
example directories, input/output streams, open files, device
handlers. When designing a system it is helpful to start off by
considering the object types and the operations to be available
on them; this has, of course, been observed to be true of
programming in general, and the developments in protection systems
and programming languages have been an interesting instance of
parallel and mainly independent activity. We shall from now on
use a terminology of mixed origin and refer to _protected objects_
as being of certain _types_, the objects being represented by
particular protection environments where code or procedural parts
implement the permitted operations.

The natural topic to consider next is the way in which
protected procedures' objects come into existence and how long
they last. A protected procedure is simply an encapsulation of a
number of capabilities in order to restrict the manner in which

they are used. Accordingly the manufacture of a protected
procedure is in no way a privileged operation. Any program may
take a collection of capabilities which it possesses and request
that they be bundled together, as it were, to make a new protected
procedure. It is clear that some privileged operation is involved
in doing this, because, at the lowest level, an enter capability
has got to be manufactured. However the operation which does
this, which is naturally itself a protected procedure, may be
publicly available. It is simply a matter of handing over as
arguments a number of capabilities already available to the caller
together with information which indicates what the shape of the
bundle is to be. For example, it has to be indicated which
capabilities are to be treated as the capabilities for a code
segment in the protected procedure being made, and in what order
they should appear. It follows that there is little immediate
advantage to a caller in causing a new protected procedure to be
made. It merely constrains the use the caller may make of
material to which it had free access already. The purpose in
doing so, of course, is to make the encapsulated procedure
available for calling by other users or programs. Sometimes the
action of the constructor of a new protected procedure is to
return an enter capability for it as a result, and sometimes it is
to preserve a new protected procedure in a filing system for
subsequent use. An example of the former is provided by compiling
systems in the Cambridge computer which, if used in what would
ordinarily be called a "compile and go" mode, return as the result
an enter capability for a protected procedure which embodies the
results of their efforts. Also, certain protected objects may be
made in a like manner. In the CAP the result of opening a file
for reading as a character stream is a new protected procedure
created for the occasion which performs the indicated functions
of reading characters, sequences of characters, or records, on
demand. The caller of such a procedure need not and indeed
cannot know what buffering arrangements the protected procedure
makes. In the majority of cases, however, a protected procedure,
and, in particular, one which is designed to implement a protected
object, is intended to be preserved for a considerable period.
This matter takes us back to some of the basic ideas of
capabilities of which its implementation consists. We therefore
have to address the question of the validity in time of the name
part of the capability.

If capabilities are conceived of as only being used for the
protection of information in main memory (which will be taken as
main memory as extended by a swapping regime if need be) then the
lifetime of the name part need only be the life time of a
particular segment in main memory. The name part in such cases
may very well be an index into some table concerned with memory
management, or perhaps an actual entry in such a table. The
evaluation route from a capability to the physical information
about a segment would be very simple in principle, and there

would be no implications or even suggestions about the structure
of any filing system or longer term storage mechanism. This
simple view is made less satisfactory if we consider a system as
essentially consisting of protected objects which have some sort
of continual existence - as witness the file directories which
certainly do. Furthermore, if the protection facilities are to
be made available to application programmers it is certainly
desirable to be able to preserve protected objects for a long
time.

In consequence, attention has been directed to the preservation in filing systems of protected objects in the sense outlined.
This has far reaching consequences for the structure of
capabilities and for the filing systems themselves.

Capabilities and Filing

Since a protected object is represented by a collection of
capabilities arranged in a certain manner, it follows that to
preserve a protected object in a filing system requires that the
component parts themselves be preserved. This essentially means
that a bundle of capabilities must be preserved, and this
preservation must imply that the object to which the capabilities
refer are preserved also. From the point of view of the designer
of a filing system, any object must be physically retained as long
as any capabilities for it are retained anywhere and, it may be
added, no longer. If no capabilities exist for something it is
intrinsically impossible for the object in question to be used
ever again, and the space occupied by the object can and should be
recovered. If it is desired that a capability system should be
extended to cope with the management of protected objects over a
long term, then ideas about the interpretation of the name part
of the capability must be revised. In addition to its previous
function of finding segments in main memory, it must also be a
key to finding them in a filing system. This dual requirement
leads to a certain tension in design; that which is most efficient
for location in main memory may be extremely inconvenient when
some filing system operation is called for, and vice versa. This
tension is made manifest when we consider the operation of
preserving a protected object for future reference. The representation of a protected object in terms of capabilities is by means
of a capability segment, or a bundle of capability segments.
Efficient use of the object in the main memory may require that
the contents of the capabilities themselves are such as to lead
to efficient access. If this be done, the operation of preservation or filing may require a reasonably complex computation, the
purpose of which is to recover the long term forms of the name
parts. To get this right is a matter of good engineering design,
and once the requirements are realised this is not intrinsically
difficult. There are, however, considerable implications for the
structure of the filing system itself.

There is an implicit structure among capabilities which is based on their occurrence in the preserved representation of protected objects. If a capability for segment A is part of the preserved form of object B, and a capability for object B is itself part of the preserved form of object C, then the existence of C implies the existence of A. Furthermore, there is no reason why a capability for C should not be found in B. This becomes particularly natural when we remember that file directories are a typical example of protected objects. If a filing system is conceived of as a systematic arrangement for maintaining objects in existence and providing access paths to them, then the natural filing system to accompany a capability-based protection scheme is a directed graph of capability lists, the direction being determined by the inclusion of a particular capability in one of the retained lists.

Such a filing system has been regarded as undesirable, because the rules for disposing of unwanted material are less simple than those for more straightforward ones. Not only may capabilities be preserved in more than one retained capability list or index, as they will be called, but the graph described may contain cycles. The former property means that the deletion of a capability from a preserved list does not imply the deletion of the object - as it does in a purely hierarchical filing system. The latter property means that the reference counts which could control deletion will not work properly. A reference count system would retain for each object a count of the number of times its capability had been preserved, so that the object itself could be disposed of when the count fell to zero. The possibility of cycles in the reference graph means that although a zero reference count is a sufficient condition for disposing of an object, it is not a necessary condition. Various methods have been proposed for dealing with this difficulty, the most usual being that of having a distinguished entry. A rule is made that every preserved object has a distinguished entry (one and only one) in one of the indexes in which an appropriate capability exists. If the distinguished entry is deleted, then so is the object - other preserved capabilities for it becoming obsolete. This system presupposes that the name parts of capabilities are unique for all time, so that an attempt to use a capability which is obsolete in the sense mentioned will lead to an error. Name parts can thus not be directly related to, for example, disc addresses, since these are almost certain to be re-used. While it is probably desirable to have system-wide unique names, they do impose an overhead which should not be incurred unless absolutely necessary, and not for this reason only.

The alternative to the use of a distinguished entry is to rely upon garbage collection, in which an object is discarded if there are found, by experiment, to be no references to it. This approach has been regarded as unsuitable, since it has usually been proposed as part of a filing system start-up sequence - which suggests that the practical viability of a filing system depends upon its being stopped and restarted at regular intervals. The interval must be short enough to make it reasonably unlikely that the disc will run out of space while a substantial amount of uncollected garbage exists. Since the exhaustion of disc space is likely to cause a system crash and consequent restart, a garbage collection accompanying the restart, the general system integrity is satisfactorily assured but any requirement for continuity of service is not very well met.

It is fortunately possible to avoid these difficulties by the use of asynchronous garbage collection, which is a reasonably economic proposition in use of resources provided that the basic filing system retains knowledge of which retained objects are indexes. The crucial observation is that for objects other than indexes a reference count system will work properly, and that therefore the garbage collector need only be concerned with indexes. Since in any ordinary machine there will be many fewer indexes than other files, the material to be scanned will be moderate, and a slowly-running garbage collector will not take too many machine resources while still completing its task in a reasonable time. The reader is referred to Birrell and Needham (1978) for an account of a practical system working on these principles.

To sum up this section: capabilities whose name parts are of longer term validity than those for segments of main memory may be used to manage the storage of protected objects: it is necessary to set up a satisfactory relationship between the two varieties of capability for the joint system to be satisfactory.

It was remarked earlier that capabilities could be protected in memory by the use of a tagged architecture, that is to say by having extra bits attached to each memory word which indicate the type of the contents. This would be just as efficient in protecting the capabilities as is the use of capability segments. The tagging idea does however have considerable disadvantages in relation to integrated filing systems of the variety outlined. The essential feature of such systems is the preservation of protected objects whose representation includes various capabilities. The great merit of the use of capability segments is that it brings the capabilities together in a known place, so that if anything needs to be done to put them into a longer-term form it can be done, and so that their presence may be noted for space management purposes. This is a practical rather than a logical point; if it is desired to maintain an object in existence as long as there are capabilities for it, it is <u>much</u> easier to be able to find them readily. If the designer settles for a distinguished entry filing system, in which the possession of a capability does not imply the existence of anything but only

a permission to use something if it exists, the point does not
arise. The SRI design (Neumann et. al 1977) for a machine to
support a provably secure operating system is like this.

Capabilities in Networks

There is a considerable amount of current interest in the
systems aspects of collections of computers connected together by
some kind of network. The model in mind here is that of a
comparatively high performance local communication network which
interconnects a number of machines some of which perform specialized services for the benefit of all or many of the others. For
example, some computers may provide filing services, others may
provide printing services, and others again may provide sheer
processing capacity. In the environment being considered it is
reasonable to think of the whole collection of computers as
constituting a system, though one of a much more loose and variable
structure than is usually considered in a single machine. Protection requirements in such a system are a little different from those
in a single machine. There is much less emphasis on needs for
protection of material in the main memory, since it is much less
common for any individual main memory to be shared in an
unpredictable manner between programs with different purposes. A
machine which is dedicated to the performance of filing services
may be expected to contain nothing but the program which does just
that. If, through reasons of economy, different services are
provided in the same main memory, then this is to be regarded
simply as a mechanical optimisation, and not as introducing any
new communication route. The consequence of this is that the only
protection requirements within such a machine will be those for
complete encapsulation of non-communicating sub-systems. To say
this may be a slight oversimplification, and perhaps it should be
replaced by saying that the only communication required between
such sub-systems is of the same nature as takes place between
different machines. Since inter-machine communication is all based
upon the use of physical communication lines, many of the more
subtle issues of protection within the main memory of a single
machine simply cannot arise. This does not, however, mean that all
protection issues have gone away. It is still necessary to control
and manage the rights of access to particular services from server
machines, so we shall now look to see whether the ideas of
capabilities have any application in this context.

Since in all known cases information passes over a network in
a neutral form simply as a collection of bits, and is indeed
handled in this way also in the lower levels of software in the
various machines, there seems little future in protecting
capabilities by collecting them into capability segments or by
tagging them as capabilities in memory. These ideas seem to be
fundamentally associated with single machine architectures or at
least with architectures in which there is a single main memory

accessed perhaps by a number of processors. It is fortunately the case that another technique is possible for ensuring the unforgeability which is the most basic characteristic of capabilities. Consider first the name part of a capability. If this is drawn from an extremely sparse and unstructured space, then it may be said that it is extraordinarily unlikely that an invalid capability will succeed in getting through whatever algorithm leads from the name part to the physical object or service without error. Various approaches may be used to implement this basic idea. One is to say that whenever a new object is created (using the term object in a general sense to refer to anything to which control access is desired - including particular instances of services) then by a suitable algorithm a completely unique name is constructed for it. It could, for example, consist of two parts one of which contains a non-repeating count of a suitable number of bits, and the other of which contains a number drawn by random or pseudo random process from a sufficiently large space. The resulting bit pattern may be passed around and used in most respects as a capability. That is to say, it may be presented to the machine responsible for managing the object in question and used as part of a look-up process. One may think of various types of tree look-up or hash table as obvious techniques. Another way of achieving the same result is to take a more conventional name for the object in question and to encrypt it using a key known only to the relevant object's manager. Provided that there is sufficient redundancy in the name for it to be clear to the manager after decrypting a proffered capability whether or not the resulting name is valid, then the encrypted name has the required properties. It should be noticed that this application of encryption does not suffer from the difficulties to do with key distribution commonly associated with the use of encryption in networks. The keys involved never pass out of the custody of the various objects' managers. This excellent idea was first put forward by Schroeder (1977). When looking at capabilities as made by either of the above techniques, we have to be careful to see how many of the features we have previously associated with capabilities are still present. One which is certainly not present is the property that capabilities are not misleading. The only way in which the validity of an alleged capability can be verified is by attempting to use it. This is similar to the situation with capabilities in a distinguished entry filing system, and need not be further discussed. A rather more subtle point concerns the control parts of capabilities; the above discussion having been only concerned with the name parts. It is clearly not possible to separate the two parts in the way in which they are separated in capabilities for main memory. A user could simply amend the control part to his taste. It is possible in the encryption model to deal with this by having the object manager take the name part and the control part and encrypt both; the result is regarded as the capability. This unfortunately removes two facilities which are

present in more ordinary capability schemes. One is that it is
no longer possible for the possessor of two capabilities to
determine readily whether they are capabilities for the same thing
or not. The other is that it is no longer possible for a user in
possession of a capability with powerful access, for example, a
capability for reading and writing an object, to manufacture
himself a capability with reduced access to pass on elsewhere.
To achieve both of the functions mentioned it would be necessary
to go back to the object manager with a request for a suitable
operation. It remains to be seen whether the increased
complication of these two operations, one of which is rare, the
other of which is very usual, will have an adverse effect on the
use of capabilities in the sense outlined. There is as yet little
practical experience with the use of capabilities in networks.
As an example of techniques which have been proposed for such use,
set forth in a little more detail, a design for a file server
working on capability principles will now be outlined.

The file server is a machine which is well-endowed with disc
storage whose task it is to maintain files on behalf of its client
machines, delivering them or parts of them over the network on
demand. In the proposed design references to files by other
machines are made by transmitting requests of the form (file,
capability, action). The physical position of the file or part
file is found by looking the capability up in a suitable structure
which reflects the disc allocation. There is no way in which the
file server program can control the existence of copies of
capabilities in other machines, so the existence of a file is made
contigent on the retention of a capability for it in one or more
special files known as <u>indexes</u>. The type distinction between an
index and a regular file is known at the most basic level of the
file server, and direct manipulation of indexes is not permitted
to outside machines. The indexes are the property of the server,
and stand in the same relation to it as the representation part
of a protected object. The requests which may be made from
outside about an index are as follows:

1) Add this capability to that index
   (specified by capability)

2) Delete capability i from that index

3) Give me capability i from that index.

These operations are done in the file server in order that it may
maintain reference counts to objects and carry out other actions
connected with disc management. The crucial decision is to make
the continued existence of an object in the file server dependent
on the presence of a capability for it in some index.

What is happening here is that client systems are given
complete freedom to handle capabilities for files, including
freedom to impose whatever restraints they wish on accessibility

of files to their own clients. The price that is paid for this freedom is the obligation to make sure that a file is properly indexed in order to maintain it in existence. Further details of these proposals belong to the study of file servers.

The possibility of maintaining indexes to control the existence of material could also be exploited as an alternative to the distinguished entry method in a one-machine system with tagged capabilities. Just as in the distinguished entry method it would be recognised that it is impossible to keep track of all capabilities; instead of making one directory entry special, one would require at least one special action of insertion into an index. Indeed, the index approach, in which a capability may be put in more than one index, may be considered a generalisation of the distinguished entry technique.

Capabilities and Revocation

At the outset of this discussion it was mentioned that capability approaches to protection are most suitable when the permission implicit in the possession of a capability does not have to be revoked. Since it is of the nature of capabilities that they may be passed from hand to hand, and in most implement-ations they may easily be copied, it is most inexpedient to base revocation on any operation which involves tracing all instances of a certain capability and disabling them. In devising schemes for dealing with revocation, it is necessary to think carefully about what exactly is meant by this action. An extreme view would be that the access conferred by a capability can be instantly removed. It is possible to devise mechanisms for this; the ramifications are explored by Redell and Fabry (1974). Essentially it is necessary to proceed by the insertion of extra indirections in the interpretation of the name part of a capability. Suppose that it is desired to issue to a particular process or user a capability for some object x which can be revoked without destroying x or, necessarily, revoking other capabilities for x. This can be achieved by creating an entry of a special character which is looked up in the chain of reference from the name part of the new capability to the physical representation, and by also creating a special capability called a 'revoker' which gives the permission to destroy the intermediate entry. The revoker remains in the possession of the agency which issued the revocable capability, and my be used to cancel it at any time. Given a capability for an object, anyone may generate a revocable copy of it, the action of doing so being completely unprivileged. Evidently the chain from the name part of a capability to physical representation may contain more than one revoker, corresponding to the number of occasions on which revocable copies have been made. In a practical implementation it would be necessary to be very careful to make sure that any lookaside memories used to optimise the interpretation of capabilities were suitably cleared out; this might add significantly to the complexity of the revocation operation, and certainly requires it to be supported at a very low level.

Although it certainly appears possible to implement immediate revocation along the lines indicated, it is not obviously desirable to do so. Earlier in this chapter reference was made to the problems which ensued from the possibility of asynchronous access to segments used by a particular program. For a capability to be revocable is a particularly drastic form of asynchronous interference, especially since it has been proposed as a design principle that a program should not be able to discover whether a specific capability given to it is revocable or not. It is possible to take an alternative view that the issuance of a capability for something should involve a commitment not to behave capriciously about its use or meaningfulness. The consequence of this view is that revocation is an altogether higher level operation, taking place in the context of a file directory system implementing more conventional access controls. Consider again the mechanism for representing in a filing system a protected procedure or object. The component parts will be referred to in the prescription for making a specific instance of the procedure either by giving the name parts of the capabilities to be constructed or by giving their filing system names (text names, for example). In the former case, which may be called 'early binding', only the immediate form of revocation is feasible, with the consequence that there is no guarantee that, when the protected procedure has been instantiated and is in course of execution, it will in fact finish correctly. In the latter case, which may be called 'late binding', the consequence of revocation of a constituent part would be that an attempt to instantiate the procedure might fail - but once the procedure had been instantiated it could by no means be interfered with by revocation of capabilities. A side effect would be that instantaneous revocation was no longer possible, since current business would have to be respected. Another consequence of relying on late binding to handle revocation is that the preservation of a capability for a protected procedure or object must be taken to mean the preservation of a capability for its unbound form, not for its current state - since otherwise future revocation could be inhibited.

There is no general agreement as to the level at which revocation should be provided. The opinion of the present writer is that revocation by interfering with the binding of texual file names is all that is necessary or desirable, instantaneous revocation of fully-bound capabilities creating more problems than it solves.

PROTECTION

General Remarks

This chapter has given an outline of protection methods and problems with an emphasis on the areas where there is a close connection with reliability. Saltzer and Schroeder (1975) give an excellent account of some neighbouring issues, and contain pointers to work on questions of security and privacy which are not relevant here.

REFERENCES

Birrell, A.D. and Needham, R.M. (1978). An asynchronous garbage collector for the CAP filing system. Operating Systems Review, 12,2, pp.31-33.

Cook, D.J. (1978). Measuring memory protection in the CAP computer. Proc. 2nd International Symposium on Operating Systems, IRIA, Rocquencourt, provisional edition.

England, D. (1974). Capability concept mechanism and structure. IRIA Int. Workshop on protection in operating systems. Rocquencourt, pp.63-82.

Fabry, R. (1968). Preliminary Description of a Supervisor for a Machine oriented around Capabilities. ICR Quarterly Report, 18,1B, University of Chicago.

Jones, A.K. and Liskov, B.H. (1976). A language extension for controlling access to shared data. IEEE Trans. in Software Engineering, SE-2,4, pp.277-285.

Needham, R.M. and Walker, R.D.H. (1977). The Cambridge CAP Computer and its Protection System. Proc. 6th ACM Symposium on Operating System Principles, pp.1-10.

Neumann, P.G. et al. (1977). A provable secure operating system: the system, its applications, and proofs. Final report on SRI project 4332, Stanford Research Institute.

Redell, D.D. and Fabry, D.S. (1974). Selective revocation of Capabilities. IRIA Int. Workshop on protection in operating systems, Rocquencourt, pp.197-209.

Saltzer, J.H. and Schroeder, M.D. (1975). The Protection of Information in Computer Systems. Proc. IEEE, 63,9, pp.1278-1308.

Schroeder, M.D. (1977). This point was made orally during a panel discussion at the 6th ACM Symposium on Operating System Principles.

8
DATA PROCESSING INTEGRITY

C. T. Davies Jr.

IBM GPD, San Jose, California

INTRODUCTION

This chapter is designed primarily to describe the protocols required and/or used in systems that have been designed to satisfy a highly reliable computing requirement, whether machine or human. The emphasis is from the point of view of application reliability, and therefore does not cover all aspects of applications and the supporting hardware and software. The entire environment is considered; man, machines, and communications. The description is abstracted up a level so as to be true for the greatest number of applications.

Data Processing

The phrase "Data Processing" is often heard. By data we mean state, and by processing we mean change of state.

Integrity

The word "integrity" is also often heard. By integrity we generally mean many things, such as: maintenance of control, acceptable results, no alarming surprises, and reliable. It is best paraphrased in the saying, "Give the job to Sam, good old reliable Sam, a man of integrity who has never let us down."

In the commercial data processing world it is not unusual to hear the various systems and application analysts describe what is going on as "Input, process, output". This is no coincidence that it sounds a lot like the hardware terms, fetch, execute, store or register (latch) the result.

One often hears the words, transaction, action, process, function, etc. What follows is an attempt to remove some of the esoteric mystique and provide a base upon which to build a discipline for the world of data processing application integrity.

DATA PROCESSING INTEGRITY

TRANSACTIONS, ACTIONS

What is a Transaction?

Your guess is probably as good as anyone else's guess. There are so many different definitions for the word that a definition has been chosen for the purpose of eliminating the ambiguity.

Data processing for the most part consists of processing or executing what one could think of as an action or actions. These actions each have a stimulus and information associated with the stimulus. These stimulii are represented in the form of data, and are output of one process or action, and become input to (perhaps the cause of) another process or action.

The actual processing by a single active element is defined as a process. It is the name for the ongoing execution (interpretation) by a processor (active element).

The amount of processing one wishes to consider as a unit is called an action. An action may consist of more than one process in the case of more than one processor. In the case of multiprogramming that could have been executed asynchronously by more than one processor it is considered more than one process. That is, multiprocessing with a common goal may be a single action for the purposes of control of recovery, commitment, etc.

A function is an amount of processing which appears to be atomic from the viewpoint of someone looking at this level of processing. However, a function is not an instance of execution. But rather, an action is an instance of execution of a function. A given function may be invoked many times, in many contexts. Each invocation is potentially an action if one wants to control at the level of detail of the function. The essential difference is that one usually perceives a function as an algorithm, whereas an action begins when one says it begins and encompasses all of the processing until one says it is the end of the action. Functions are often thought of as pre-defined prior to execution whereas actions may be defined in real time, once for each use of the function. Examples of actions are jobs, jobsteps, subroutines, the processing of individual transactions, etc.

Having defined actions as the act of changing state allows the information (status) going between actions to be defined as a transaction. Otherwise, there is no simple acceptable word that can be used as the generic name of the information output of one action and input to another action. Examples of this between action information are deposit slips, checks, parts orders, shipping orders, etc.

C. T. DAVIES Jr.

It must be noted that actions can be nested for the purposes of recovery, such as the inclusion of an already written function (action) as part of a larger function (action).

The definition chosen for a transaction may be in opposition to one of the long established uses of the word "transaction" in the phrase, "Let us complete this business transaction". Unfortunately the word transaction is used as both a noun and a verb, offtimes in the same sentence, and the context of use sometimes removes the ambiguity; but only sometimes.

It is important to note that the historical requirements of an application frequently require the recording of which transaction was input to which action (process) and what transactions did this cause to be generated; which, of course, are then input to some other action(s), etc., ad infinitum.

Action, the Verb

An action is equivalent to transaction for those people who think of transaction as a verb. An action is the act of processing from one discernable state to another discernable state. That is, it is a unit of processing which is (appears to be) atomic. This atomicity is necessary for many reasons; for example, privacy while arriving at an acceptable result, the unit of process about which one records information for later determination of the results of an action, the unit of processing one wishes to backout and perhaps redo, the units of processing (actions) between which information flowed. It is the time varying relations naming problem as applied to instances of processing, its causes and effects, rather than just objects themselves.

State to State Transitions

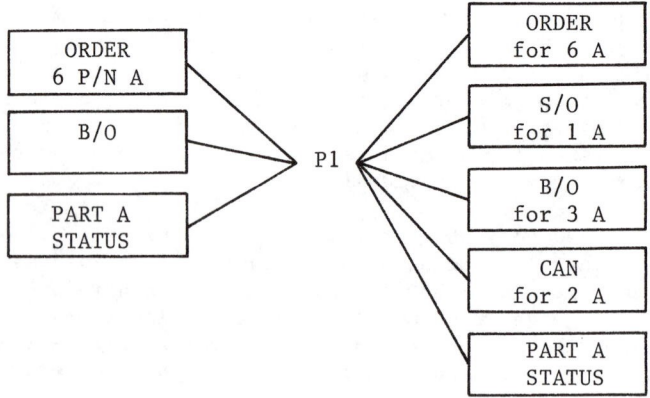

Fig. 1 Input and Output State of an Action

DATA PROCESSING INTEGRITY

Figure 1 portrays a simplified view of an action and is a
state oriented view of data processing in that it shows a
parts-order and information about that part being changed into a
new state which consists of shipping orders, back orders, cancel-
lations and a new state for the parts information. The fact that
a mapping must exist is not considered relevant enough to portray
it. This view is the typical application and systems analyst way
of thinking of a system, wherein the allowable inputs and outputs
will define the transformation or mapping. This view allows a
clearer picture of the connections between actions at the expense
of the means or mechanism of the action.

Mapping Input to Output

Illustrated in Figure 2 is a more balanced representation of
an action. The name of the transformation or procedure is specified and the actual transformation has as much importance as the
input and output of what will become an action at the time of
processing.

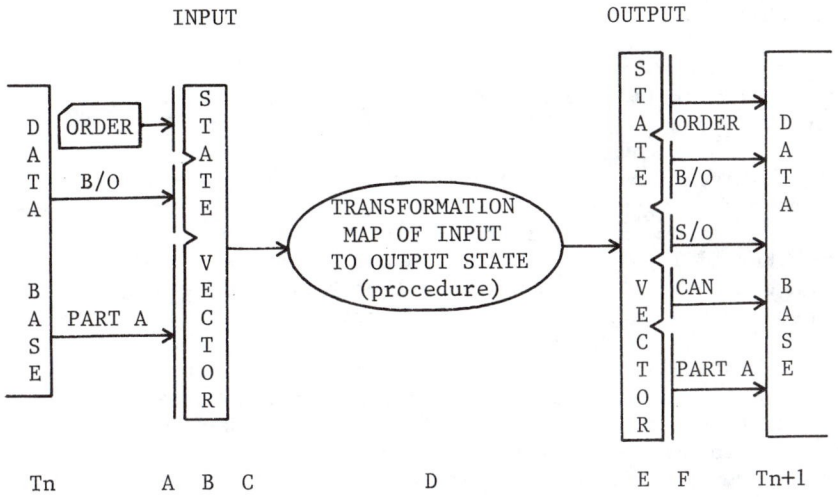

Fig. 2 An Action

Here the transformation mapping is given equal billing, but it
is still considered to be atomic. A simplistic view of this
mapping is to think of it as the set of all possible input states
mapped to the set of all possible output states. Invalid states
would also be mapped, each having the appropriate output state
that is desired for each invalid input state. Figure 3 shows this
mapping.

```
                    MAPPING
          INPUT      |    OUTPUT

        000....001   |  110111...0
        000....010   |  110111...0
        000....011   |  110111...0
             .       |       .
             .       |       .
             .       |       .
        111....110   |  100011...1
        111....111   |  110011...1
```

EXHAUSTIVE LIST OF ALL POSSIBLE INPUT STATES
(VALUES) TO THE CORRESPONDING OUTPUT STATE (VALUES)

Fig. 3 Single Step Mapping Transformation

The processor need only know to do a table lookup and select the matching output state.

This is a very inefficient way of doing things since there are usually more invalid states that there are valid states in the map unless this is a very small process control application.

A two step transformation overcomes many of the deficiencies of the single step mapping. In the two step transformation one first maps input states into an intermediate state where all the input states that will produce the same output are transformed into the same intermediate state. There are therefore only as many intermediate states as there are different valid output states.

A second map is used to transform the smaller set of intermediate states to each member's corresponding output state. The intermediate state needs a range of values (and therefore bits) only large enough to allow for the number of different output states, even though many more bits are needed to represent the actual physical state. The physical state being a sparse array (vector). Figure 4 is an illustration of this two step transformation and it is often used in small control applications.

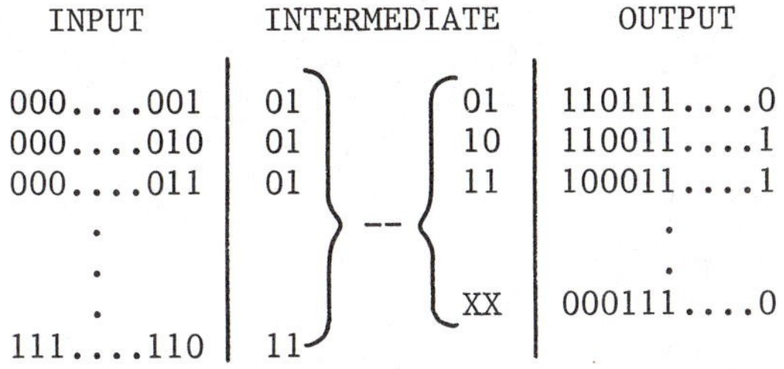

```
        INPUT          INTERMEDIATE         OUTPUT

    000....001 │ 01⎞            ⎛ 01 │ 110111....0
    000....010 │ 01 │          │  10 │ 110011....1
    000....011 │ 01 │          │  11 │ 100011....1
         .     │    ⎬  --  ⎨        │     .
         .     │    │          │     │     .
         .     │    │          │     │     .
    111....110 │ 11⎠            ⎝ XX │ 000111....0
```

ENCODE INPUT STATES (VALUES) TO ONE VALUE PER
OUTPUT STATE AND THEN DECODE INTO FINAL OUTPUT STATE.
IF INPUT STATE NOT VALID THEN USE XX FOR DECODE

Fig. 4 Two Step Mapping Transformation

In essence, the state to state map has been factored to reduce
space requirements. Note that there must always exist an output
state to represent the state to be established when an invalid or
perhaps unknown input state is given.

This is still a lot of individual states, more than one would
like to specify one by one in a typical, medium or large, application.

A procedure in pidgin English might go as follows:

IF ORDER QTY LESS THAN ON-HAND QTY (of PART A), THEN SUBTRACT
ORDER QTY FROM ON-HAND QTY AND PLACE ORDER QTY IN SHIPPING
ORDER QTY......Etc.

The decision table or procedure enters the picture at this
point. Decision tables and procedures are supposed to, and
frequently do, take less writing to specify than the state to
state map. The purpose of these is to allow wholesale replacement
of many states with a range of states and the rules or procedure
to transform to the new state.

It is the factoring of many states into one or more ranges.
It may also be thought of as the procedural specification of the
mapping that reduces the map size by more than the space taken by
the procedure. However, in this highly factored and fragmented
representation it is often more difficult to add minor pathologi-
cal deviations.

While on this subject, it is worth noting that in most procedures it is more difficult to change it to react to a different
mapping caused by what, to a decision table, is a minor rule or
action-stub statement change.

C. T. DAVIES Jr.

Sequence of Events in a Transformation

Illustrated in Figure 5 is a hardware view of an action. A, B, C, D, E, and F refer to labels in Figure 2.

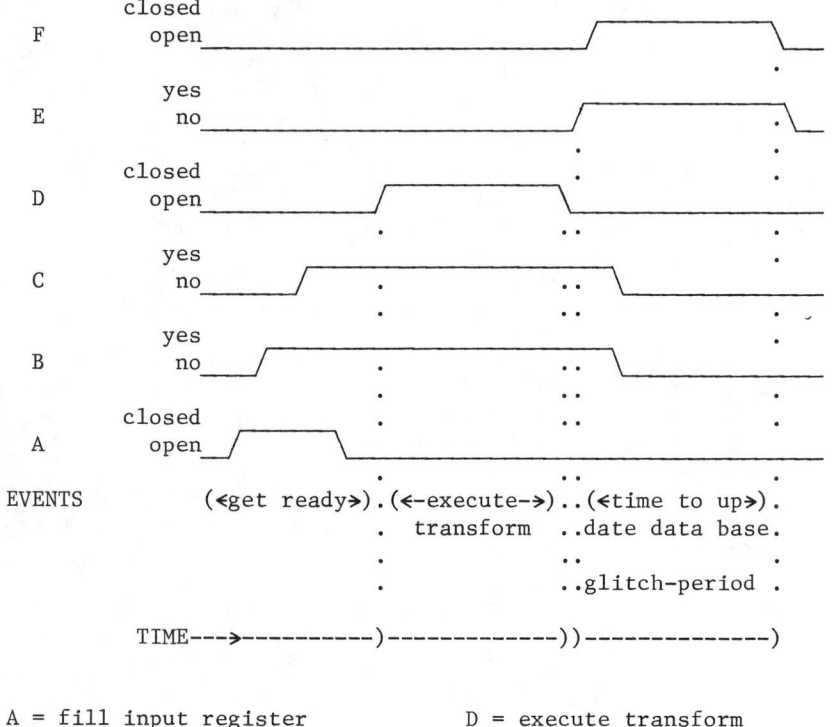

A = fill input register   D = execute transform
B = input register valid   E = output register valid
C = transform available   F = gate output to data base

Fig. 5 Timewise Logic Level View of an Action

The "what has to happen when" is clearly discernable. It is portrayed in the classical hardware manner. Well, surprise -- Figure 5 also illustrates the software view. The difference is only one of terminology.

The glitch period shown in Figure 5 is that period of time during which a failure in the creating new state function would leave inconsistency. If no storage were modified and all new states occupied new storage then integrity would not be lost by a failure during the glitch period. To overcome this deficiency it is common practice to create a log consisting of ones new state intent before beginning the state change.

DATA PROCESSING INTEGRITY

Thus if a failure should occur during the writing of the log, an action backout is performed. If a failure occurs during the real state change, then the log is used to re-do the state change.

This problem is peculiar to the technology of re-useable storage. The emerging write-once-only technology will make re-using space unnecessary and even difficult. At that time technology will have come a full 360 degrees to the manner of data processing that existed prior to re-writeable and therefore re-useable storage. For example, punched cards, paper invoices, ledgers, etc. This will permit audit trails having even greater integrity than prior to the use of Electronic Data Processing.

At the hardware level we speak of operations or instructions. Beneath this we speak of micro-instructions. Above this we speak of commands, macro-instructions or application actions. Each of these is an action but known by a different name (synonym). Actions are therefore nested, each thinking of itself as a potential top of the nest of actions. If such is not the case, then one could not permit the use of defined actions inside an action. An action never (hardly ever) knows that it is being used in another application or action.

Action in these cases probably should have been called function but it is the actual execution that does not know the hierarchy of actions.

In summary, software on top of hardware has the same gating, latching, and synchronizing requirements as does any action at any level in the nest of actions, above or below the traditional operation code or machine instruction level. This view of data processing permits the same concepts and similar designs at each level and therefore raises the degree of reliability attainable.

Transaction - The Noun

While defining a transaction to be a noun may cause some disagreement, it should be less offensive than qualifying the use of the word each and every time it is used. In the punched card days of data processing the card was frequently referred to as a transaction and a set of them input to an action (process) was called a transaction file. The transaction (card) and the recording of what it caused was known as transaction history and was frequently used for recovery and audit trail purposes. The names and function are still the same even though the transaction may never appear in any other form than bits inside a computer system.

C. T. DAVIES Jr.

Degree of Control

There exists a spectrum of degrees of control. At one end anything goes. At the other end everything is preordained, totally automatic and nothing is allowed to happen that has not been previously specified as to time (situation) and place. The less the degree of control, the less the reliability (integrity) the system will have. This is simply saying the less one constrains the greater the probability of an inappropriate action occurring. The more interactive a process is, the greater the difficulty in describing the set of allowable actions and sequences of actions.

For reliability to exist there must be a notion of right versus wrong. In most data processing systems right is what you expected or are willing to tolerate, and wrong is what you are not willing to tolerate -- expected or otherwise.

This ties in very closely with fault versus error. Fault being the creation of other than what was supposed to happen, and error being a fault which is (detected as being) outside the limits of acceptability. It is the undetected and often unthought of (faults) errors which bring a system to its knees and/or causes intolerable effects. One frequently spot checks actions either during or shortly after processing to minimize this problem. To perform checks for validity, particularly after processing has terminated, requires that the transaction, action, and output transactions be determinable from some recording which could only have been made at the time of original processing.

In effect, one has to be able to identify both transactions and actions. Since actions are a moving target they are identified by the transaction which gave rise to their existence; if it were not for the transaction there would have been no action. The result of all this is that it is necessary to establish identity for each transaction so that one might talk about their causes and effects.

Even if one has a "do anything without restriction system", it is still necessary to record who did what to whom if one ever has a question about how things got to be as they are. This is typified by such questions as, I wonder where that came from? Where did that value get to be what it is? I thought there was a part 255-7869, where did it go?

The major difference between a loosely controlled and a tightly controlled system is the size and number of the objects being controlled. Files versus fields or records, jobs rather than individual transactions; in this case the job is the transaction. The (action) audit trail history, however, is necessary to the preservation of a civilized system.

The audit trail is required even if one does not intend to audit. How often have we heard - "Lets get the record straight."? How often in the middle of text editing do you find youself in a worse position than you were before your last command? Or three commands ago. Reference in-process recovery under spheres of control. For convenience the action history (records) is often called the audit trail even though one of its major uses is recovery - both in and post action.

Transaction/Action Identity

Independent of the application, environment, or interpreter, there are certain attributes of a transaction and action that are required -- even if only for the purpose of recording "who did what to whom and when" for later verification or use. An example of use is the attempt to correct or compensate for a previous action now determined to be in error.

The identity generator function, whether distributed or not, is constrained to not generate equal values, regardless of how many places the identity generator function has been distributed.

There are many methods used to ensure transaction identity. They all must create a unique name (number) for each transaction, regardless of time and place. That is, each transaction is unique amongst the set of all transactions of all applications. The same is true for all resulting actions. Some of the identity information may be implicit. However, there is always a greater potential for error due to changes to what is implicit and therefore unseen by, and unknown to, the creator and interpreter of the transaction. A frequent cause of loss of integrity is the merging of companies, one or more of which has not allowed for more than their own transactions and/or actions.

There are many examples of distributed identity generation. Two immediately come to mind. The first example is that of naming radio stations throughout the world. This is accomplished by assigning a prefix identifier unique to a country. To this identifier each country appends any value that will be unique within that country. This is observable in England where "G" is one prefix, and in the United States where "W" and "K" are two of the prefixes used. The second example of distributed identity generation is that of a Social Security number in the United States. The States are (conceptually) divided up into many districts. Each district is assigned one or more blocks of numbers. When a person applies for a social security number they receive the next number in sequence within the block currently in use. Some blocks may be held back so that they may be assigned where most needed.

C. T. DAVIES Jr.

The following information is required for the proper identification of a transaction.

Context Identification

This is the version of the interpreter to be used to understand the rest of the identity attributes (values).

Without this, one has to carefully synchronize all identity changes in meaning, format, and representation between the creator and all interpreters. No other activity related to the changes may occur anywhere in the network during the synchronizing process. This is a real problem for multi-location companies.

With this, one can have multiple versions of all interpreters -- thus allowing for graceful migration, growth, and change. It is normally à single character, allowing for at least thirty six (36) versions, assuming the use of the normal holorith alpha-numeric set of values. Of course, as one approaches the end of the set of available values, one chooses a value which implies that the version identifier is located in another field, allowing for almost infinite expansion to the point where space is the constraint.

Source Identification

This is the unique instance of a transaction and contains:

Source Address -- which is the creating entity that generated the transaction. Examples are "store number" in an application involving more than one store. Or, perhaps "country" in an application involving many countries. This is usually represented by a key to save space or it may be implicit if only one value is possible. Watch out for the first time there can be more than one value. The entire identity scheme changes with a resulting discontinuity in the transaction history as seen by the search mechanism used later to retrieve the information for recovery or audit.

Source Serial -- may be a simple serial number or, more likely, the Julian date followed by a monotonically increasing number, starting at one (1) each midnight when the date changes. It is not unusual to use GMT time rather than have all parties worry about time zones and daylight savings times, etc. If time is not used as the serial number then time is (usually) carried along as a unit of information associated with the Source Identity.

The war stories about the wrong interpretation of time are many, not the least of which is that of air support arriving one hour later than the beach assault troops, resulting in the massacre of the latter.

This was brought about solely because each used their own time zone and they departed from different time zones. Each party can best translate GMT to their own local time and vice-versa. If the time is not in one consistent zone, then a time prefix must be used to define the particular zone in use for this transaction source, to say nothing of whether it is daylight savings time, etc.

Source <u>Authority</u> -- is the equivalent of the signature of the issuing manager or supervisor of the functional area initiating this transaction. The identity key associated with the functional entity (department) is usually used. In some cases a genuine signature is also used. In other cases a varying, day by day, coded word is used. This reduces, to almost unmeasurable proportions, the likelihood that a phoney alias will be thought to be a genuine transaction.

Predecessor Identity

This is the identification of the transaction whose action gave rise to this transaction. This is a reference back to the cause of this transaction and is used for audit and recovery purposes. The transaction history file shows effects and this identity establishes causes.

Not all transactions result in single actions. If an action is unable to fully satisfy the request of a transaction, the unsatisfied portion must be represented. The representation is in the form of another transaction(s) that will process at a later time. These secondary transactions are treated no differently than any other transaction. They do, however, have a field of information that references the (trans) action on whose behalf they were created.

An example would be a parts order for three items that resulted in two items shipped and one back-ordered. The back-order is a transaction that exists on behalf of the original order and whose processing stimulus will be the receipt of material. The audit trail requirements dictate some means of tying together all actions on behalf of an original transaction.

Frequently, when the application is small and not distributed all over the place, a shortcut method of predecessor identity is used. It consists of placing a suffix on the end of the transaction identity information, where there just happens to be space available. The suffix represents each highest-level action on behalf of an original transaction. However, watch-out for the problem of duplicate identities (ugh!) when the application goes distributed and there is no co-ordinated distributed identity generator already in existence.

C. T. DAVIES Jr.

For the case of the back-order above it is likely to have the suffix "A". Another transaction if generated would use "B", and so on. Anything that produces traceable transactions via identity of cause is acceptable. How often on a shipping list have you seen the phrases; Your purchase-order number "x"; Our customer order number "y"; Our shipping order number "z". All of these are transaction (action) identities being referenced.

Destination Identity

This is usually the (key representing the) name of the functional entity to whom this transaction is directed. This at first may be thought to be equivalent to the version of the interpreter required. However, this information merely identifies the application and the functional entity which is to interpret the transaction. The version of the interpreter is above this and understands what Destination Identity is to conote -- the function to call, (schedule or execute). Examples are "I" for Inventory Control System, "P" for Payroll System. The lack of this information has produced some interesting results; such as checks for one million Dollars or Pounds Sterling in response to a parts order accidently dropped into the accounts payable application.

Clearly, this is a failure to program what a human does without thinking. This particular point cannot be over-emphasized. The failure to program the associative checks and limits is by far the greatest reason for the errors made by any application. It is for this reason that decision tables are very useful, since they define the rules and actions which are appropriate. And it is the rules and actions which change over time. The change in procedure is a consequence, not a cause.

Transaction Code

Defines the action requested within the functional entity (application) and is therefore specifying the algorithm, or state to state transition map, or name of procedure, etc. to be used.

The transaction code is specifying the function (procedure/interpreter pair) thus allowing different procedures using different interpreters to produce the same action. One could think of this as a form of machine independence but extended to (application) language independence. The point here is that the means of implementing the transformations is not relevent - except to the implementer who uses a specific language.

The action requested also defines the data structure required -- assuming one has a catalog of such transaction code to data structure mappings. One always does. It is just a question of whether it is automated and machine readable or in someone's head or desk drawer, or lost.

DATA PROCESSING INTEGRITY

Transaction Parameters

At last we get to the data peculiar to an application. All of the preceding information is required regardless of the application. Interestingly enough this information frequently takes more space than the application dependent data below.

The transaction parameters are those that specify such things as part numbers, student numbers, etc. These parameters depend upon the specific application.

Distributed Systems and Status

Transactions in distributed systems should be no different than in non-distributed systems. If such is not the case then one experiences a great impact of change when one does go distributed. The best rule of thumb, known to work from experience, is to design as though one had a distributed system in the first place.

Actually, if one tried to prove the existence of non-distributed processing it usually gets very difficult. All humans are processors, so that it would have to be a system with only one human and no machine, or one machine (instruction stream) and no humans that have data in common or between which a dependence exists. A processor in this case is autonomous. This is indeed a rare case, since the simple task of playing chess with a machine requires that each remembers and depends upon the past actions of both.

Regardless of whether a processor is human or not does not change a fundamental requirement. For each action, on behalf of a transaction, status should be sent to the originator informing he, she, or it of the outcome of the action. This is the mechanism by which a peripheral audit is done. It allows catching discrepancies earlier than they would otherwise be caught by the large random audit, which may never catch a fault due to it never being the action which gets audited.

Returning status reduces the number of enquiries that would otherwise have to be made, clogging the system with other than vital traffic. Examples of this status are; shipping notices usually sent slightly ahead of the actual shipment(s), notices that ones request for a part has been back-ordered -- to be shipped later when in stock.

Status gives that warm feeling that someone or something cares, thus reducing the general apprehension all around. Not unlike the laws that Newton discovered -- for each action there is a reaction and it is this that an originator has a need to know, and is the basis for much of the error detection capability in a system - if one takes the trouble to design it in.

C. T. DAVIES Jr.

Too often it is not designed in and the application will suffer, with the computer system taking the blame.

DATA ACQUISITION AND TRANSMISSION

While Hamming codes spanning the unit of transmission are useful for correcting transmission errors, they fall short of catching errors involving the wrong data in the first place. If one is to reduce the incidence of this kind of error it requires semantic redundancy rather than just physical bit redundancy. Consider a parts order wherein the wrong part number was accidentally specified. How can one guard against that? Suppose someone (or something) changed the unit of issue and you ordered one (dozen). Your one (dozen) may turn into one (carload). There exist many examples of this phenomenon, usually seen as piles of surplus something or other in back lots.

Both of the above situations have a common solution. Be redundant in specifying facts which you believe to be true and are depending on as fact. That way there is a greater likelihood of catching misunderstandings before any damage is done. For example, when you order a part, give the part number, quantity, unit of issue, unit cost, color, size, composition, used in, etc. It is true that something may change that you do not care about, but it stops an awful lot of wrongly identified parts from being shipped.

Coding, Hamming or otherwise, is more useful when it spans information having a semantic relationship (additional redundancy), since it is frequently possible to take a college educated guess at what the value should be. For example, a unit of issue in error could have been either "EA" or "EC". The set of possibilities is deliberately small (sparse) to allow this form of error detection and correction. In this case, "EA" is valid, because there was no other "Ex" or "xC" in the list of valid units of issue. A carefully designed set of values, units of issue in this case, takes sparseness and other human factors into careful consideration.

A wrongly specified part number is much more likely to be detected by semantic redundancy, somewhat in proportion to the number of its other attributes that are also specified (and checked). This sort of thing is particularly useful when interfacing with an application with which you are not thoroughly knowledgeable, and as a consequence you do not know what information is able to detect potential errors in identity.

A stored record is not necessarily the unit of information having a semantic relationship to an application and is therefore not as good a choice as a logical record.

However, the complexity of multiple intersecting Hamming codes may cause one to stay with the stored record as the unit of span for coding purposes.

Transactions disappearing into oblivion is not an uncommon ailment that can beset one's system. However, this is a phenomenon that can be readily discovered by appropriate application design. The design consists of tightening the control over what is going on. For example, status back to originator, all transactions held in addressable queues, (even if they are sequential) and once per some unit of time each member (transaction) is examined for its legitimacy. One should not, and therefore can not, just put a transaction someplace. All rejected or partly processed transactions should follow the same rules. A typical implementation would place all rejected transactions into one logical queue for examination purposes.

After a certain amount of time, any transaction that has been a member of the set of rejected transactions, causes a status transaction to be sent to the functional area of the business having control over the portion of the application involved. No transaction should ever be allowed to just rest (disappear). The very least that should be done is to cancel the transaction, and show this fact in a history file together with the cancelled transaction and its attributes and status back to originator, if known. Sometimes the originator is not known because the data is not even a real transaction. For example, it is a program source or object card that accidently (?) was placed in the system as though it were a transaction.

Note that this return of status requirement is true at all levels in the nest of actions. Sometimes it is at the transaction/action level, othertimes it is at the processor/channel or channel/control-unit level, etc. Maintainance of identity is necessary regardless of the nested level of action or the system component in question.

While touching on the subject of queues it is worth noting that in a chained queue it is worthwhile doing both forward and backward chaining -- specifically because there is redundancy at all times, particularly during the chain modification. This assumes of course that only one entry is being chained in or out at a time and that the one pointer is not modified until the other has been modified. This problem of update in place is further discussed in the sphere of control topic. The reason for picking on queues is that they tend to have their members stored in random space, whereas one tends to group data records about parts or employees into areas or extents that are organised in some key sequence having significance to the application, usually the application record identity attribute, for example part number.

C. T. DAVIES Jr.

TRANSACTION/ACTION RELATIONSHIPS

Transaction Creation

During the processing of a transaction it is frequently
desirable, and sometimes necessary, to create another transaction. There are many reasons for this requirement but the transactions created fall into two classes.

The first class of created transactions are formal and represent requests for action that are to be traceable, for audit
purposes if nothing else. This class of transaction is visible to
someone looking at the application from the outside. For example,
it is a back-order, a request for payment, status returning to the
originator. Each of these transactions is a part of the external
specification of the application.

The second class of created transactions are informal and are
totally transparent from outside the application. A queued
request for the use of a procedure that takes a while to stage-in
to main storage is an example. This class of transaction is not
(usually) required to be auditable although they have all (most)
of the attributes of a formal transaction, such as; who created
it, the action required, who to report back to, etc. This information is often highly encoded. For example, it is likely to be a
pointer to the work controller's data about the action that
created the informal transaction.

This class does not need to be auditable in an application
sense. However, for debugging the system hardware/software it may
be necessary to record this informal class of transaction as
though it were a formal transaction. The difference is that the
audit trail for informal transactions may be purged at the discretion of the system management rather than application management.

There are transactions that are created to be processed
synchronously and others processed asynchronously relative to the
creator of the transaction. The various kinds are illustrated
below as Figures 6A, B, C, and D. They all have the horizontal
scale from left to right represent the passage of time.

Fig. 6A An Action

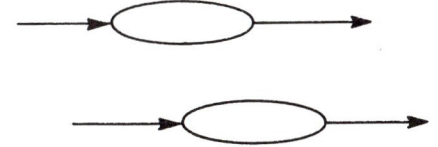

Fig. 6B Two Unrelated (Asynchronous) Actions

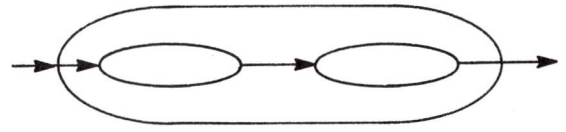

Fig. 6C Two Synchronous Nested Actions

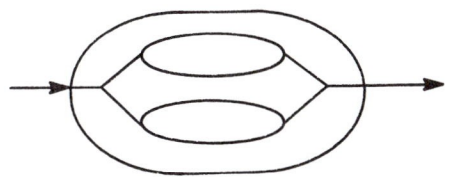

Fig. 6D Two Asynchronous Nested Actions

Asynchronous (trans)action processing allows for parallel processing if resources permit, but they can be processed sequentially.

FAULTS AND ERRORS

Detection

Faults are mistakes that may or may not make a difference to the action in which the fault occurred. It is unrealistic to assume that all faults can be detected and, in particular, that each fault should have its own correction scheme. It would result in the amount of recovery procedure being an exponent of the amount of original procedure.

Quite frequently the fault will make no difference to the
action. Other times the action in which the fault occurred will
create an entirely inappropiate and intolerable result. Duplication and triplication of all hardware will reduce the probability
of undetected hardware faults, but it will do absolutely nothing
to reduce the probability of a fault (now error) caused by incorrect command sequences, procedure, or human data-entry mistakes.

Hardware and software redundancy may catch some failures but
they will be within small execution units. Error detection
schemes that encompass reasonably large units of execution must
understand the semantics intended, at least to the point of
recognizing an unacceptable state.

You could run an entire day in triplicate producing the same
three wrong outputs, certain you are correct because the answer
was the same three times out of three. This topic is further
discussed later under consistency and spheres of control. However, the important point is that each (trans)action knows best what
results are satisfactory and therefore actions are best able to
check for faults (errors) by checking the result against the rules
and assertions for the action and/or the affected data.

An action has no semantics that the hardware understands,
except perhaps the current state and therefore can never discover
improper procedures, except to the extent that assertions have
been provided and checked.

Correction

The places in an action when an error (fault) may be detected
are so numerous that no-one can afford a separate recovery procedure for each place an error could occur. That is, different
recovery procedures for each instruction in a procedure that might
fail.

Examples of errors are; an addressing exception, an overflow,
an underflow, an invalid branch, invalid operation, wrong data
type, and on and on. The list is practically endless.

The concept of an action is designed to mitigate the over
abundance of error situations by bounding the units of physical
processing that are to be considered an atomic operation.

The atomic operation (action) has only one beginning state to
which one can always return, assuming the state was saved. If the
state was not saved at the beginning of the action in error, then
the state must have been saved in some prior or hierarchicaly
superior action. If the highest level action did not save state
(or be able to reconstruct), then there will be loss of integrity
and therefore loss of reliability. Caveat Emptor.

DATA PROCESSING INTEGRITY

Prevention

It is much easier to solve a potential problem by prevention
rather than by correction. Correction may not always be possible,
therefore prevention reduces the probability of arriving at an
unacceptable state. There are many possible mechanisms involved
in the prevention of an error. It is not unlike a medical
doctor's bag of tricks. Some of the practical mechanisms known to
help are listed below and suggest other means.

Run diagnostics from time to time. This is not just at the
machine instruction level but also at the application action
level. This is accomplished by processing a dummy transaction
that goes all the way to the end, at which time the output is
set aside for audit and state is restored if required. This
is also an excellent de-bugging tool since there can never be
an error that propagates, because of the backout capability
used.

The processing of dummy transactions designed to result in an
error is also a useful way of testing the error detection
mechanisms. In the punched card days it was usual to throw an
out of sequence transaction into the hopper of a merge operation, for the sole purpose of testing the out of sequence
detector.

List and check valid transaction types that can be generated
at each level in the nest. This works extremely good in well
organized and pre-planned types of systems, in contrast to the
do anything anytime system. In the latter system there would
be no errors, by definition.

List and check the valid operation codes that are acceptable.
Just because a machine has a square root instruction does not
make the use of it correct. This is similar to the preceding
but at a different level in the nest of actions. The implementation is not as difficult as one might imagine. For
example, create a bit vector, one bit per instuction, and at I
fetch time check to see if the instructions corresponding bit
is on. In this case the value of the instruction operator is
the offset in the table. This sort of checking frequently
occurs in applications at a higher level of action. It is
amazing how many errors can be caught in this manner, particularly wrong branches.

Use instructions (operation codes) that are data type dependent. This is the checking for a decimal number when executing a decimal add. This may at first appear to be a slap in
the face of data independence. However, this does not mean
that a compiler cannot recompile or even run interpretively.

C. T. DAVIES Jr.

The point is that an addressing failure may have occurred, and the odds are in favor of the data type being wrong, either because the data is the wrong type or the beginning of a data item was not at the target address.

List of valid entry points. Many branch errors result from a wrong calculation that causes a branch to either the wrong instruction or a non-instruction. In this regard, machines that mark the physical beginning of an instruction fair very well at catching branch errors, being proportional to the average length of an instruction. Of course, in a structured program there should be little need for branching into an instruction. However, the hardware may accidently do so.

Addressability only to the data one may address. This requires one indirect address operation for each data reference. The indirect address can either be through a vector of addresses which in turn is addressed through an unmodifiable register, or all the data one can legally address can be moved into addressable space. The finer the resolution of checking, the greater the probability of catching a missaddressing problem, no matter what the cause.

ERROR RECOVERY

In-Action Recovery (forward and backward)

Since the unit of processing is the action, one need only be able to return to a state that existed at the beginning of a non-committed action. That is, someplace in the hierarchy of nested actions where the action has not yet completed. This could be any of the labelled points in Figure 7 below.

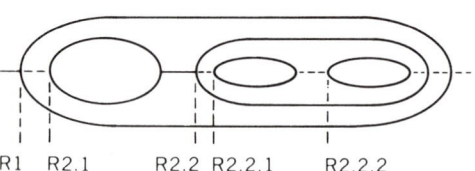

R1   R2.1   R2.2 R2.2.1   R2.2.2

Fig. 7 Backward Error Recovery Backout Points

It is not necessary that all actions be separately recoverable (backoutable) except for the highest level action (the top of the nest.) The more places one can recover back to, the faster the response time to recover when it becomes necessary.

DATA PROCESSING INTEGRITY

The cost however, may not be justified - particularly if it is a batch process that consists of multiple actions treated as one for recovery and allocation purposes. In on-line and in-line systems the actions quite frequently involve multiple interactions with a human who rebels at the thought of re-doing earlier actions not in error. Especially if it was an arbitrary decision to not have many nested actions that are each separately recoverable. Forward error recovery is compensation discussed under spheres of control. Backward error recovery is returning to a previous state.

Post-process Recovery (forward and backward)

Reference post process recovery under spheres of control.

AUDIT

Why Audit?

Auditing is necessary to the preservation of a controlled system - as opposed to a runaway out of control non-system. The act of auditing is the validation of the results of processing. There are many reasons for this validation. Some of them are:- detection of fraud, detection of errors (faults that are signifi- cant), prevention of situations whose cost of recovery or correc- tion is too great, prevention of situations whose time to correct is too long, etc.

One might assume that a proven and certified program (func- tion, procedure, etc.) needed no further verification or valida- tion. However, each instance of use of a transformation mechanism has a probability greater than zero that the actual transformation will result in other than that which was intended. That is, a fault that may also be an error.

Who Audits?

There are two classes of auditors, internal and external, relative to a legal entity, usually a company.

Internal auditors report to upper management and are responsi- ble for the verification of employees and departments adherence to company policies - particularly in the fiscal, accounting and procedural areas, etc. The internal auditor frequently places checks (procedures) at the end of processing of a transaction to check for discrepencies. These checks are performed in-line. With somewhat less frequency, many actions are audited post-ac- tion. That is, a transaction is picked for audit and its causes, processing, and effects are examined for validity.

C. T. DAVIES Jr.

The external auditor is an independent accountant who has
nothing to gain or lose and who audits actions after the fact -
that is, post action (process) and acts as an auditor of the
auditors as it were.

Selection Criteria

Actions are selected for audit based on the history of errors,
or lack thereof, legal or fiscal exposure, safety and similar
reasons. Not all actions are selected for a complete audit. It
would require more resources to audit each action than the original action used.

If all actions are not to be selected, then those that are to
be selected must be picked without the processor being able to
identify the actions. Otherwise the actions selected for audit
could be made to come out right, and all others wrong, for whatever purpose. The actions audited are picked at random by an
algorithm and key known only to the auditors and their staff. The
algorithm is biased to pick actions having a greater potential for
exposure more often than small exposure actions.

Frequently, the auditor will enter a totally dummy transaction
for the sole purpose of determining what the output is for a given
input. In such a case it is usual to merely write the audit
trail, do a backout when the action is complete and look at the
audit trail for the results. Reference in-action recovery under
spheres of control.

Another technique is that of creating a commitment boundary
that allows multiple actions to be audit trailed and backed-out.

Traceability

The purpose of an audit trail is many fold. However it can
best be expressed as the need to verify the correctness of an
action or sequence of actions by doing a logical re-run of those
actions. This requires the input to the actions (causes), the
transformation (procedure), and the output of those actions
(effects) all be retrievable after the fact!

Audit depends upon the establishment of a basis for the action
to be audited. A basis can only be proven if it is possible to
re-run (at least logically) from the beginning and obtain the same
results as the original action. Frequently it is necessary to go
backwards through process (action) time and show the input to the
actions whose outputs are the input to the action being audited.
If this sounds confusing, it is. It is a very complex necessary
capability, without which one has an unknown, unauditable, and
therefore uncontrollable system.

DATA PROCESSING INTEGRITY

Journal and Trail Generation

The journal is a logical object since the trail of actions may be kept in many files in many sequences. However, what is important is that there are various needs for an audit trail of activity. Examples are monthly audit, income tax justification, recovery from an error discovered after the fact. Each of these uses for a written record of what happened more often than not cover differing periods of time. This may be implemented in many ways. A file may be created for the trail of activity for each user of such information, producing the most space consuming implementation. Or a single file may be created for the trail of activity with each user represented by a "bit" in a vector of such bits concatenated to the journal record. Each bit describes the need or not of a particular journal record by a particular user. All ones means every user needs the journal record and all zeros (noughts) means no user needs it and it may be purged (deleted) at will. Obviously, a one anywhere in the bit vector means keep the journal record.

Under no circumstances may a journal of actions be modified. It is a write-once-only activity.

Time Domain Addressing

We normally think of addressing a file by record identifier and retrieving the one and only record having that identifier. For example, requesting the record for part number 123-4567. However, such a request has an implicit version identifier. It must have otherwise all records back through time with part number identity 123-4567 would be retrieved. Unless otherwise stated the latest version is usually implied. This is the case when you want to know how many items of part number 123-4567 are currently in stock.

Sometimes one needs to know what the on-hand quantity was as of a certain time and date. Othertimes one wants to know what the on-hand quantity was prior to a particular action and what it was after that action. In this latter case the parts file logically exists as a set of records, each member a push down stack for a particular part number. Each pushed down record is the previous version. The file is then said to be in time domain sequence for each record and may also be for the set of records. Time domain addressing is the ability to ask for previous and next version based on time or actions that modified each record in question. If one asks for the version of the file as of a particular action or time, the file would appear exactly as it existed at the stated time. An action implicitly has a time associated with it even if not physically thought of that way. That is another reason for actions being atomic operators.

C. T. DAVIES Jr.

Journal Purge Criteria

Journal entries are not always of the permanent indelible variety, in fact few are. However, for the period of time they exist they are read only - or more correctly, write-once-only. It is taboo to make modifications. The question is one of, when may we erase, delete, or destroy a particular journal record (entry). The answer is simple. When no one needs it anymore. The criteria determining need is, unfortunately, not so simple. For tax purposes it is 3 or 7 years, depending on whether you believe Uncle Sam will claim fraud is involved. For legal reasons it may be after the actions with a company are ten years old. To reduce this complexity to manageable proportions as far as the log is concerned, each type of log record has a prefix, each portion of the prefix representing a particular need for this log record. The bit vector described below is often the implementation.

Journal Purge Status

Each potential user, or group of users, who have a different purge criteria for the journal entry will have a flag to signify the purge status. Each differing criterion must be represented by at least one bit. A logical implementation would be to assign one bit per differing need for the journal entry and have the corresponding bit be 0 if not needed. If the need changes one can always change the status, assuming it has not already been deleted. There are companies who have warehouses full of history records dating back centuries. As previously stated, when all need status is null, the entry may be deleted.

Journal Implementation

There are many ways to implement the journal(s) or audit trail. It is almost always an optimization trade-off among many criteria. For example, the recovery procedures need fast access, the managers of the data may demand a journal for their own data. It is usual that the journal starts out time ordered although it may subsequently be sorted to other sequences.

Audit will retain its credibility and control only when a copy of the journal is sorted and the original left intact, in a deep vault. The emerging write-once-only technology will not only favor this but will bring back the unmodifiable storage space that existed before the electronic computer allowed update in place on a physical medium.

Prior to electronic data processing all records were kept on write-once-only media and hence created their own audit trail naturally and believably. Somehow, when something is modifiable without evidence of such, one always has that niggling feeling that all may not be what it seems to be.

DATA PROCESSING INTEGRITY

DATA PROCESSING SPHERES OF CONTROL

Introduction

Spheres of control define process bounding for such purposes as recovery, audit, commitment and algorithm (procedure) replacement, etc.

A technique for controlling processing in a multinode, multiprocessing system must first delineate, via operators and descriptors, the boundaries of the spheres of control for each active and passive element of the system. The kinds of control considered here, for which there are potentially many instances, are process atomicity (action), process (action) commitment, controlled dependency, resource allocation, in-process recovery, post-process recovery, system recovery, intra-process auditing, inter-process auditing, and consistency. Examples of other types of spheres of control are privacy control, transaction control, and information version control for both data and procedure (instruction data).

PROCESS CONTROL

Process control ensures that the scope of processing at each level of operation in a hierarchy is defined by the set of operation codes implemented at the next lower level. Even though operation codes of one level are implemented as a sequence of operation codes at the next lower level, _ad infinitum_, only the operation codes of the next lower level are defined (made acessible).

Each level in the hierarchy of operation codes is merely an implementation of the operation codes which invoked it. That is, each operation code may require many other apparently primitive operation codes in its implementation. Each of the primitive codes is in turn implemented in one or more potentially different operation codes. The languages used may differ considerably from level to level.

Each call to a subroutine is an example of a primitive at one level of implementation invoking a set of primitives at a lower level of control. The level (operation code) which is or was processing at a given instance is called an atomic process. It may be a payroll application to some people, the square root subroutine to others and the ADD operation of a computer to others. The classical passing the buck down a chain of command is an instance of nested processes (actions).

C. T. DAVIES Jr.

Process control also ensures that the information that is required by this atomic process is not modified by others, and constrains the dependency that another process may place on the updates made by this process, as described below.

Process Atomicity (Action)

Process atomicity is the amount of processing which one wishes to consider as having identity for one or more reasons. It recognizes that data processing involves discrete units of process which we call digital. Therefore, regardless of the implementation of a function, it is either performed in its entirety or not at all. Examples are machine instructions like add, subtract and move.

Atomic processes provide the greatest possible implementation independence. If a function is rewritten, only the changed function and the lower (nested) layers are affected.

Frequently it is also desirable to have one process terminate and another start, perhaps at the interface between two active elements. This is the typical way in which one allows for the humans of today to transfer their workload to the machines of tomorrow and vice-versa without acquiring grey or null hair. Process subdividing allows for a defined interface which provides compatibility independent of the specific implementation of either atomic process, assuming that the data at the interface is capable of being represented in the structure required by the subsequent process.

The atomic process, often called action in the commercial data processing, bounds the unit of function to be executed and the interpreter to be used. For example, one atomic process may be described in COBOL, and another in PL/1. One may even have written the function in one language which calls a subroutine written in an entirely different language.

In a system of many nodes, each having a potentially different interpreter (instruction set), it is mandatory to know the interpreters needed, availability and their location. This is because some nodes and/or levels may have their procedures written in Cobol, others in PL/1 and yet others in APL or one of many possible assembly languages, etc. It is not necessary that the interface between them know the implementation of the other nodes or levels other than in a semantic sense as viewed through a common defined interface.

In human terms this is equivalent to procedure manuals written in various human languages that then require humans who understand those languages. I remember well a procedures manual written in six languages, any one portion in not more than two languages.

314

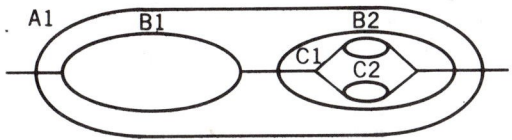

Each sphere of control is an atomic process (single
operation) when viewed from the next higher level
of control.

Fig. 8 Nested Actions

Figure 8 illustrates some nested atomic processes (actions)
where A1 is the function someone outside A1 is viewing; B1 and B2
are what A1 sees and C1 and C2 are parallel processes visible to
B2.

In summary, process atomicity is the control over processing
which permits an operator to be atomic at one level of control,
while the implementation of that operator may consist of many
parallel and/or serial atomic operators at the next lower level of
control. A fully nested structure exists which yields implementation independence of each level relative to the upper level
(Davies 1972). Every defined atomic operator can be given a name.
Only an atomic operator has the potential to have versions. Only
defined atomic operators may be moved to and executed in other
nodes.

Process (Action) Commitment

While a function is in process, changes of state are being
made only by that function or are expressly known to that function. An example is a payroll application in which the first job
accepts time cards and writes paychecks, a transaction history,
and deductions, certain of which provide input to the employee
stock purchase program (job). From a logical point of view one
could run only the portion for time card input and paycheck
output. However, to reduce the potential error correction time,
it is desirable to hold the paychecks in suspense until after the
transaction history has been audited and the stock purchase
program run.

C. T. DAVIES Jr.

Holding the paychecks in suspense allows the establishment of a single point to return to for rerun purposes independent of the error detected or the number of functions since that point. In particular, holding the pay checks in suspense prevented other functions from depending upon them for the purposes of commitment. This in turn permits the writer of the paychecks to revoke them, without having to be concerned about the consequences. This allows the establishment of a single point to which one can return for rerun purposes independent of the error detected or the number of functions since that point.

Preventing process (action) commitment by holding (controlling) the use of its results permits the system to perform a unilateral backout (process undo) over much larger units of process. Unilateral here means without having to request permission from each participant in a process. This allows for correction of mistakes not detected (detectable) until quite late in the processing, at the expense of response time. It is often used as a method of reducing stress that management and operators would otherwise have to endure.

So far, we have discussed the containment of process commitment as though it were always pre-planned. However, such is not the case.

When an error is detected and its source is not yet fully determined or the action to correct not fully known, it is necessary to contain the effects of processing until it can be determined if releasing the effects will adversely affect subsequent processing. Constraining a potentially erroneous process in such a way that outputs or updates are not released until it is no longer required to be able to be unilaterally backed out, and the processing rerun to a potentially different conclusion, is dynamic control over commitment. This boundary of control preventing commitment may extend to as much processing as it is economical to control.

The sphere of dynamic control is extended over process commitment and permits processing to continue rather than requiring it to end abruptly. The initiation of a dynamic commitment control boundary is usually done by a very worried looking individual responsible for the output and is first perceived as a blur of frantic arm waving.

Often, when the error is better understood or discovered to be non-existent, the boundary is simply removed, resulting in the controlled resources being released from commitment control, often referred to as unlocking, unallocating, or releasing a local variable to become a global variable with respect to this level in the nest of actions.

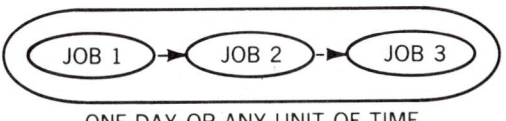

ONE DAY OR ANY UNIT OF TIME

Boundary around the effects of a process, even after processing is complete, allows for independent
audit and back-out and for rerunning to a different
conclusion.
Preplanned for audit: static shape.
Suspected error: dynamic shape.

Fig. 9 Sphere of Control Over Commitment

Figure 9 is an illustration of the notion of control over
process commitment. Any data depended upon or created (modified)
by any of the contained functions Jobs 1, 2, 3 is assigned to the
control sphere of all three until the termination of the sphere.
The effect is the creation of larger domains of process.

In summary, process commitment control is the containment of
the effects of a process, even beyond the end of the process.
This mechanism is sometimes used as a less expensive recovery
scheme at the expense of response time. As an example, an entire
day's processing may be contained within a sphere of control over
commitment with the result that the entire day may be rerun to a
different conclusion at the expense of not being able to commit to
any of the results until the end of the day.

Multinode process atomicity and commitment

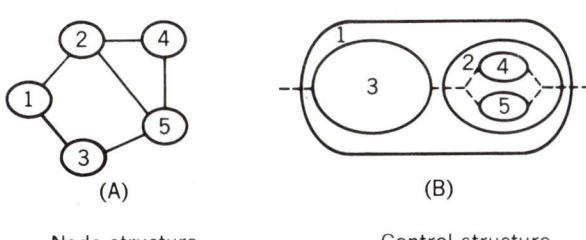

| (A) | (B) |

Node structure   Control structure
(communication)   (processing)

A node is a processing resource, man or machine.
A sphere of control over process commitment encompasses all work, man or machine, on behalf of
the initiating man or machine.

Fig. 10A, and B Network Structure Versus Control Structure

317

C. T. DAVIES Jr.

Figure 10A shows a typical multi-node network of active
elements with their associated data connected via communication
lines. The nodes may contain human or machine active elements.

Figure 10B represents one possible calling sequence for doing
some work. Portrayed is the initiation of work in node 1 which
calls upon node 3. When control is returned from 3 to 1, node 1
calls upon node 2. Unknown to node 1, node 2 calls nodes 4 and 5
to perform some work, and upon their completion node 2 returns
control to node 1.

The key point here is that completing work in any particular
node does not necessarily mean that the results may be depended
upon by (committed to) a disjoint process in the same node.
Disjoint here means not the immediately superior level of actions
in the nest of actions. One can think of this as similar to a job
having one of its jobsteps executed in another geographical
location. The completion of the remote jobstep (job) must be
considered as not complete until the original job is complete.

In particular, no output of any process may be depended upon
by other than the next higher level in the processing nest. The
highest level is the universe of discourse represented by the
collection of man and machines under discussion. If such is not
the case, then it is possible to arrive at a point where one can
neither continue nor return to a prior point of acceptability.
Such a state of affairs implies loss of control and therefore of
integrity.

Controlled Dependency

From time to time, the output of one process which is input to
a subsequent process is available prior to the completion of the
creating process. In such cases, it is logically required that
the output of the creating process be held (contained, not depended upon) until after the point of commitment. Such a point is at
least no earlier than the end of the highest level atomic process
in the nest, although it may be much later for management reasons.
This situation is a poor performer for the simple reason that
minimum parallelism exists. The best performance is achievable
when a process begins as soon as its resources are available or
will be available without deadlock.

To begin a process physically earlier than is logically
correct (from a commitment point of view) requires that the
controlling element extend its influence to include dependencies
not yet commitable. Consider the payroll application mentioned
earlier where paychecks, transaction history and stock purchase
deductions are the output of a process. Some subsequent process
(usually next) inputs the stock purchase deductions and generates
a stock purchase transaction if required.

While these processes may be logically sequential, that is, not in parallel at all, it is clear that considerable parallelism is possible and frequently desirable to meet a deadline. This form of logically sequential although physically parallel processing is typical of many applications in the commercial data processing world. An example of the parallelism possible is illustrated in Figure 11. The dotted line represents the containment of dependencies on a result of process A2.1. An alternative way to think of it is that a boundary of control over commitment is dynamically grown to include dependent processes started earlier in process time so as to maximize parallelism.

Humans frequently operate in this mode. How often has a friend or colleague given you a copy of a new paper to review, with the constraint that it is not to be passed on until after it has been published, or at least finalised?

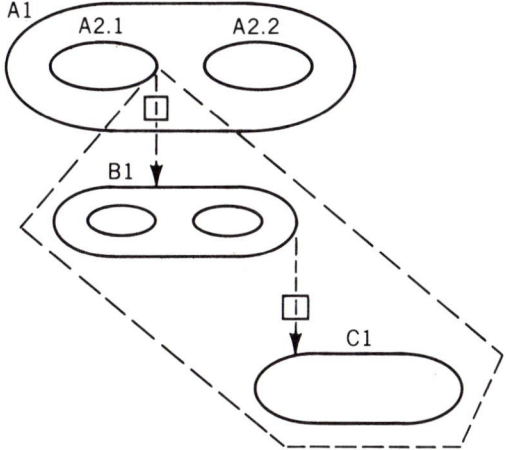

Allowing parallelism while preserving back-out rights results in controlled dependencies. A dependent is allowed whenever the depender guarantees the ability to back-out and the creator of resources guarantees probability of resource stability equal to or greater than that required.

Fig. 11 Sphere of Controlled Dependencies

Atomic process A1 creates (by the end of A2.1) the data which represents the stock purchase deductions. The disjoint atomic process B1 accepts as input a named version of these deductions and creates stock purchase transactions as appropriate.

C. T. DAVIES Jr.

This latter process can run with the following constraints. It does not lock onto a resource (value) that the process started earlier in time wishes to update (create new version), and this process does not update (create new version) a value which the process started earlier in time is depending on or will depend upon. This property has been given the name bi-phase (Gray 1973). Simply stated, no process may be allowed to commit its results with any greater degree of certainty than that of the process' inputs. It is usual that the results of multi-processing or multi-programming must be no different than each transaction processing alone. Naturally, a different result may occur depending on the sequence of processing of each process separately.

In summary, controlled dependency is the control over the use of results of a process that cannot yet be committed. From a wholly logical point of view, such a concept is usually not necessary. However, without such a concept, there would be strict sequentialization of all processes where one depends upon the output of another, resulting in the longest possible (non-stop) processing time which may be longer than time permits.

RESOURCE ALLOCATION

The sphere of control over resource (e.g., data) allocation is generally the same as the sphere of control over process commitment. However, there are environments where this would produce excessive de-allocation and re-allocation of the resource and performance of that processing would degrade.

To alleviate process performance degradation, it is usual to establish a boundary of control not unlike that of commitment but encompassing many commitments.

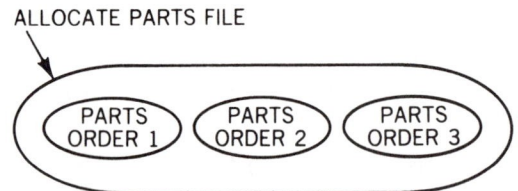

ALLOCATE PARTS FILE

Boundary is around many disjoint actions, which, for purposes of performance, are considered a single unit of work (e.g., a batch job).

Fig. 12 Sphere of Resource Allocation Control

Figure 12 illustrates the point. The three units of processing labelled parts order are boundaries of control over an atomic process (action), commitment and in-process recovery all at the same time for each of the three units of process.

Since all three require the same file, the sequential and otherwise unrelated processes are allocated the resource as though they were related. However, the processing may terminate at the end of any boundary of commitment which occurs after each parts order processed. The boundary of commitment in this case is sometimes referred to as a synch point.

In summary, the resource allocation sphere of control is the assignment (locking) of resources for a potentially greater period of time than is strictly required for correct processing. In particular, it is the grouping together of unrelated processes for the purpose of saving the resource un-bind and re-bind time which would otherwise have to occur. Mechanical machines like cranes, bulldozers, and so forth are often scheduled in this manner, as are data processing machine resources.

RECOVERY CONTROL

Over and above the containment of the results of an operation being required to preserve integrity, there exists the probability that a user will decide that a previously taken course of action is inappropriate. If the course of action were prior to a point of commitment, the resulting operation to recover is called in-process recovery. If the course of action has already been committed, then it is post-process recovery. Both in-process and post-process recovery spheres of control are application related, and both require occurrence graphs (Randell 1977) which are similar to occurrence or causal nets (Petri 1976, 1977). These references are of particular importance in distributed data processing.

If one has not yet committed the results of processing, and has allowed only for (machine) errors for which a rerun from a checkpoint would suffice as a solution, then we call it system recovery (non-application related).

In-process (In-action) Recovery

To preserve integrity it is necessary that an atomic process either not start or start and finish in an acceptable manner. However, since atomic processes may, and frequently are, made up of other nested atomic processes, there are as many potential places to return to as there are atomic processes in the nest.

This does not mean that one must return to the beginning of an atomic process which cannot be completed satisfactorily. In fact, it is only minimally necessary to be able to back out to a point at or prior to the atomic process involved. However, should a change of nodes involving long response time or high communication cost be involved, it is usual to have a backup point upon entry into the node for this process. This is particularly true if more than one human is involved and the second human makes an error, causing the first human to re-do work already completed.

The foregoing speaks of procedures as though they were always pre-defined, as is the case in classical batch processing. In the realm of interactive, on-line or in-line processing, the procedure may very well be dynamic by virtue of a human invoking functions in real time. In this latter environment, the boundaries constituting an atomic process and a recoverable (backoutable) process must be specified by the human (invoker) in the form of operators (commands) in-line in the ongoing processing. Function keys on terminals are most often used for this purpose.

An example of the need for nested recoverable (backoutable) units of process follows, and is illustrated in Figure 13.

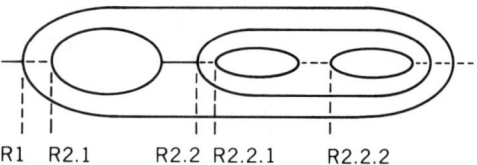

R1   R2.1   R2.2 R2.2.1   R2.2.2

Application may be backed out to points having semantic significance to the application. Subsequent processing may take a different path.

Each sphere of control must save information necessary to back out, since each is potentially transparent to the next higher level.

Fig. 13 Sphere of In-process Recovery

Some work bounded by AR1 is initiated by a human. The work involves the entry of a parts order which may be in error and have to be re-entered. This is the function of AR2.1 which allows backout of the erring data entry portion of the parts order.

Subsequently, in the processing bounded by AR2.2 the parts file is searched and a set of choices evolves via the processing bounded by AR2.2.1. The item is discovered to be under special management control (short supply) and management approval is required to ship. The work done by the approving manager is bounded by AR2.2.2. Should the manager discover in the middle of processing (decision making) that an error has been made, he requests backout of the process to the beginning of AR2.2.2. (The callouts in Figure 13 indicate points where a command is given to initiate each sphere of control.)

This nested backout is essential for the following reasons. Without it, the entire process would have to be backed out and the parts order re-entered. If the solution were to have many disjointed sequential processes, then a parts order discovered to be in error during processing could not be corrected. This is because the user would already have entered and received confirmation of the entry, thus committing the user to a potentially erroneous action on his behalf. A formal (complete with audit trail) cancellation transaction followed by re-submission of a new (corrected) parts order becomes the only realistic and sometimes legal default.

In summary, in-process recovery is the control of the recording and subsequent use of whatever data is required to return to a previous point in the process, namely, the beginning of this recovery sphere of control (Randell 1977). These control spheres can be, and frequently are, nested. The processing bounded by the spheres of control over process atomicity and in-process recovery are often one and the same. The boundary of recovery must coincide with the boundary of an atomic operator at some level in the nest to allow for procedure replacement.

Post-process (Post-action) Recovery

The purpose of post-process recovery is to determine the source of, and correct for, an error discovered during processing but whose cause is no longer contained within an in-process recovery sphere of control.

There are four basic activities necessary to recover from an error discovered after process completion. Each will be discussed using Figure 14 as a basis.

C. T. DAVIES Jr.

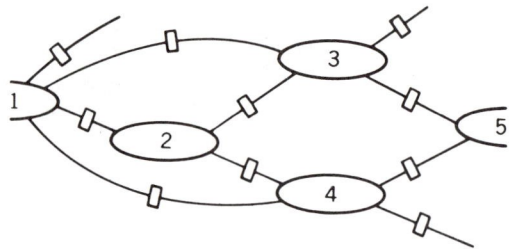

Numbers represent processes. Search backward to
determine error source. Search forward to bound
scope of dependencies.

Fig. 14 Data (by Version) Dependency Graph

First, the symptom of the error is detected, say in process 5.
This may be done via a check on the relation between two or more
data items which yields a result of invalid relation. For example, the quantity of parts received minus the quantity shipped
does not equal the quantity currently on hand. Note that this is
not the original error which has been found, but only a symptom or
consequence of the error.

Second, the data elements believed to be involved in the error
are brought into the sphere of control over processing established
for the purposes of post-process recovery. The source (last)
process to create or modify the data elements in question is
determined from a journal(s). The (past) processes involved (3 &
4) have their outputs and inputs brought into the post-process
recovery sphere of control, which is nothing more than a dynamic
atomic action sphere of control.

Third, it is necessary to determine the extent and exposure as
a consequence of the original error. This is partially accomplished by searching forward along the paths of dependency to
ascertain those which depended upon the error directly (2 and 3 of
Figure 14), that is, those which depended upon a value which was
wrong and is now right. There may be many such elements of data.
For example, the wrong element may have been updated, resulting in
two errors.

Fourth, for each process which would have had a different
input, it must be decided whether it makes any difference to the
outcome of that process. If yes, then it must further be decided
whether one is going to back out the old process (its effects) and
rerun to generate differences or whether one is merely going to
compensate via another action (transaction).

DATA PROCESSING INTEGRITY

The effects of the above are examined to see which outputs
would have been different, and the third and fourth recovery
activity is repeated until no more processes are affected. As
each process history is no longer needed, it is released from the
(post) process recovery sphere of control to permit other (potential recovery) procedures to use it, providing one is willing to
commit to the recovery actions taken to date.

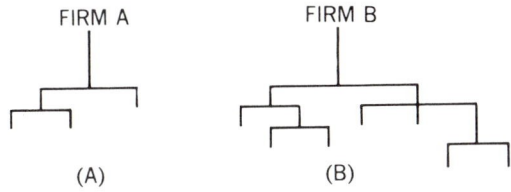

Fig. 15A, and B Control Structure

Post processing recovery sphere of control can be explained
using an analogy of management. Figures 15A and B illustrates the
management hierarchy which exists at two different companies.

INTERNAL ACTIONS   EXTERNAL ACTIONS

- decommit   - decommit
- compensate   - compensate
- escalate   - escalate
                                  - negotiate
                                  - adjudicate

Fig. 15C, and D Recovery Options

Figure 15C lists the choices for action to recover from an
error where the cause and effect process (action) have a single
manager somewhere in the chain of command. One manager first
tries to decommit the action. If this is not possible, the
manager tries to compensate for the error. If compensation is
refused by the manager affected by the past process (action), then
the problem is escalated. Escalation always results in decommit-
ment or compensation, since at some level in the chain of command
there exists a single manager common to the cause and effect. It
is always possible to solve the problem by edict, since there
exists a manager responsible for both the error-creating and the
error-using process (action) who will decommit or compensate.

C. T. DAVIES Jr.

Figure 15D lists the choices for action to recover from an error where the cause and effect process (action) do not have a single manager anywhere up the line. An attempt is first made to decommit (withdraw) or compensate (negate the effects of) the action, represented as data, which is in error. If this is not bilaterally agreeable, negotiations are initiated to find a compromise. Should this not be successful, both parties submit to adjudication via the establishment of temporary common control. It should be well noted that if only one company has kept records they will be considered to be the facts. Therefore, the only defense is a good (offense) set of records which have the dual property of being useful for recovery and necessary for audit.

In summary, post-process recovery is the control over the processing which is searching backwards to ascertain the error source and subsequently forward to bound the propagated effects of the error (Bjork and Davies 1972). It is necessary that the recovery process be a normal process and contain all the relevant resources within its sphere of control over processing. Otherwise the network of resources would have to be locked as a unit, with the result that the recovery process could be the only active process over the entire network of humans and machines.

System (State) Recovery

System recovery is the restoring of a system state which existed at some prior point in time. It is characterized by taking checkpoints which represent the state of things as they were at some point in time. These checkpoints are often taken transparently to the process being checkpointed. As a result of the mechanism, the checkpoint philosophy is useful in two cases.

Case 1 is an application error where no commitments or dependencies have been made since the checkpoint. This allows the subsequent reprocessing to take a different path from the original processing. This is nothing more than a transparent in-process recovery sphere of control. It is useful in a batch environment where the operator controls commitment.

Case 2 is a system failure, such as a machine check, where the checkpoint is used as a means of returning to a prior point from which the processing will be repeated. The original outputs or the rerun outputs have to be discarded or duplicates will exist. This is useful for failures whose recovery does not involve producing different results.

Unfortunately, the checkpoint philosophy does not graciously allow for the replacement of an erring procedure, since the checkpoint may be taken anywhere relative to the boundaries of a procedure. If the checkpoint is taken at the boundary of a procedure and atomic process (action), it is really an in-process recovery sphere of control. However, all concurrent disjoint actions would have to have been at an in-process (action) recovery boundary at the same time for it to be viable - a practical impossibility.

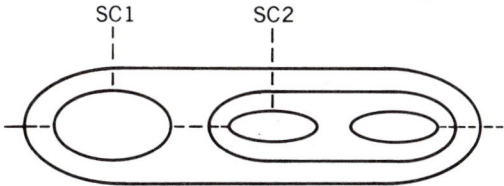

Controls unilateral back-out and (potential) rerun of uncommitted processing. Checkpoints (SC1, SC2) are applied to process, not machine.

Valid only for regenerating lost bits that have not been used to take a wrong path (wrong direction). Undoing of uncommitted processing does not require semantic knowledge.

Fig. 16 System Checkpoints

Figure 16 illustrates two system checkpoints (SC1 and SC2) at arbitrary points within an atomic process (batch run).

In summary, system recovery is the control over the recording and subsequent use, for recovery or restart purposes, of global data which is modified (created). Since the system does not understand what the application did or meant, it can only roll back processing when no commitments have been made. Since no dependencies are maintained, any application committing its results commits all applications. If not, then in-process recovery spheres of control are being used.

C. T. DAVIES Jr.

AUDIT CONTROL

In any system where there exists accountability for one's actions, there must exist a mechanism for remembering each action and such a mechanism should be transparent to the process being audited. The kinds of audit required are in-process immediately prior to process termination and post-process as soon after process termination as possible. To audit a process (action) means that one has defined the unit of process which is to constitute the action from an auditing point of view and has recorded all the data necessary for reconstruction of the action.

Intra-process Audit (Single Action)

The auditing of a process (action) is the mechanism by which the validity of the processing is determined. Intra-process audit validates the processing of single actions; for example, translating a parts order into a shipping order or back order or a combination of these. Single actions are those for which no point of commitment occurs except at the end of the highest level atomic process (action).

There are two mechanisms of single action audit.

First, there is the in-process audit which is a procedure specified by the auditor and designed to catch undesirable process consequences. For example, a parts order for two items results in a shipping order for twenty items and the unit of issue is the same. However, if instead of two items shipped, one item is shipped and the other back-ordered, this is not an error in which the external auditor is necessarily interested. The (company) internal auditor may be interested in it, if it represents a deviation from policy.

Second, there is the post-process audit of an action which requires the complete reconstruction of the information necessary to determine what input was used, who initiated the action, when, and what the result of the action was. This applies to the data and procedure, since both change over time.

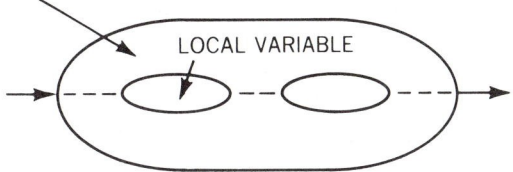

Who entered what data? When? What was the result
of the action? Why (how)? That is, which version of
what data and procedure was the basis for and
consequence of what action?
Implicit is that auditable actions have identity.

Fig. 17 Sphere of Intra-Action Audit

Figure 17 illustrates two auditable actions (sub-actions)
within an action. Note that it is only necessary to save (or
reconstruct) global variables relative to the auditable action,
since local variables would be recalculated.

However, if there are auditable sub-actions, then the global
variables with respect to the sub-action must be saved even though
they are local to the larger action. Otherwise, they must be
reconstructable by an auditor-approved mechanism. This latter
point of requiring auditor approval of reconstruct mechanisms is
true for all reconstructs. Otherwise, one could simply claim a
certain thing was true.

To the extent that an in-process recovery sphere of control
has one and the same boundary as an intra-process audit sphere of
control, the data which need be recorded (saved) is the same. It
will then be used by the post-process recovery function and the
auditor.

In summary, intra-process audit is the control over the
recording of the inputs to, and outputs from, a process, together
with the subsequent reconstruction of the information for the
specific purpose of verifying and validating the original processing (Bjork 1975). Intra-process audit validates the outcome of
each transaction independent of the source or recipient of the
transaction. Depending on the nature of the system, the nested
atomic processes may be required to be independently auditable, in
which case their inputs and outputs must be reconstructable
(either stored or the process is repeatable from what is stored).

C. T. DAVIES Jr.

Inter-process Audit (Many Actions)

Inter-process audit validates an actions processing which is disjointed as a function of time. It is the checking, tracing and reconstruction of the various causes and effects of actions which are on behalf of a particular action.

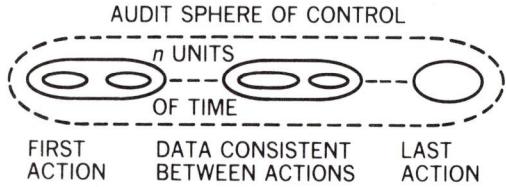

AUDIT SPHERE OF CONTROL

FIRST ACTION   DATA CONSISTENT BETWEEN ACTIONS   LAST ACTION

Trace of the disjoint actions performed on behalf of an original transaction.

Fig. 18 Sphere of Inter-Action Audit

Figure 18 illustrates three timewise-disjointed but related actions. Inter-process audit, like intra-process audit, has both in-process and post-process components.

The in-process components are procedures specified by the auditor and are designed to catch undesirable outcomes relative to the original action which may not be an error as a stand-alone action.

The post-process components are those procedures (and random samplings) used later in time which look back at the collection of actions and verify the original processing. This audit also requires the same knowledge as intra-process audit along with the ability to tie related actions together even though they may be disjointed as a function of time and of process and have other (non-related) actions ocurring in between them.

To audit properly, within standards set up for the purpose (AIC 1975, SAC 1977), requires that all actions be audited or that a random (later in time) selection of actions be audited. Otherwise, the audit could be invalidated by performing properly only the processes (actions) that will be audited.

As a consequence, all information necessary to post-process audit any action must be saved at the time of the original processing. In the case of interactive specification of procedure, the procedure must be recorded rather than referenced as in the case of a canned procedure.

DATA PROCESSING INTEGRITY

The point here is that the actual procedure must be reconstructable by some means. It may be recorded each time as executed or it may be recorded only once and referred to by name upon each subsequent use. If the latter method is chosen, the name must include the version, implicitly or explicitly.

In summary, inter-process audit is the control over the recording and subsequent retrieval of the data necessary to verify the set of disjointed processes on behalf of an original transaction. Inter-process audit validates the sequence and outcome of a set of related processes which are disjointed on the basis of time.

RELATIONAL INTEGRITY CONTROL

Relational integrity is the maintenance of the set of relations in such a manner that a procedure (process) receives the valid and correct version of information (collection of data) it requires. This does not necessarily mean that the relations are correct at all times. It does mean that at the time a process needs them to be correct the necessary actions to update to correctness have occurred. In addition, any process which attempts to create an invalid relation is prevented from doing so. The sphere of control over consistency is one of many required mechanisms to effect relational integrity.

Consistency

The sphere of control over consistency includes the set of rules and assertions about a collection of related information. As pointed out by Eswaran, et al. (Eswaran 1974). The assertions describe the facts regarding truths which must be held true. The rules describe the conditions under which a procedure may acquire and/or create information or a subset. Consider the example illustrated in Figure 19.

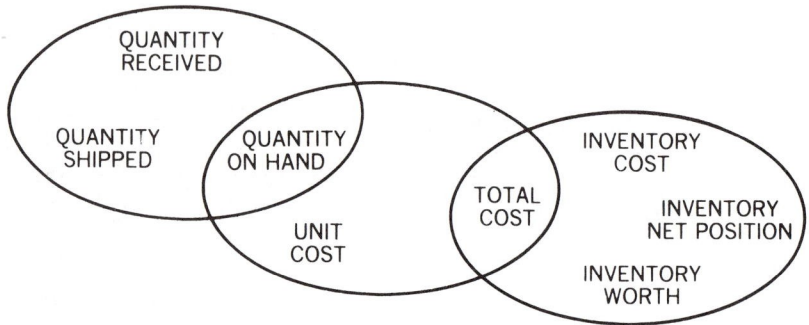

An update to an element of a sphere of consistency implies that no other update is possible by a disjoint action.

Spheres of consistency have versions.

Binding causes the enlargement of a sphere of consistency, or creation of another.

Fig. 19 Spheres of Consistency

Shown are three spheres of consistency. Sphere 1 asserts that the receipt quantity minus the ship quantity equals the on-hand (OH) quantity. Sphere 2 asserts that the on-hand quantity times the unit cost equals the total cost. Sphere 3 makes similar assertions that cause the field(s) of information called total cost to lie in two spheres simultaneously.

The rules associated with a sphere of consistency describe, as a result of the assertions, the fields of information which are involved and the relationships which must be maintained for each procedure. Locking in all its forms are various implementations of these relationship preserving rules. The important point is that it is necessary for information to be consistent only at the time it is needed.

In summary, consistency is the control over the permissible uses of subsets of a collection of related resources. For example, the unit of issue, quantity on hand and unit cost are related in such a way that if the unit of issue is to change, so must the unit cost. But if the unit cost is to change, the unit of issue does not have to change; in fact, it should not.

DATA PROCESSING INTEGRITY

PROCESSING ENVIRONMENTS

The implementation of spheres of control depends on processing environments. For example; if a process is running in the batch mode, the spheres of control can be implemented sharing much the same information and control structures. However, as applications go on-line and/or in-line, the various spheres of control usually must be implemented separately. In any event, they should be described separately to allow a choice. For a description of the spheres of control inter relationships in various environments (batch, on-line, and in-line) reference (Davies 1978).

OBSERVATIONS

The designers of the semantics of applications are mainly concerned with the spheres of control described, with a concern for performance a strong second. It is not unusual to eliminate automation of an application if adequate performance can be achieved only by failure to properly use the spheres of control presented.

Computer scientists are striving for performance, sometimes at the expense of function. This lack of function frequently takes the form of not providing as much support for the various spheres of control as applications often require.

This apparent dichotomy leads to small disjointed portions of applications being implemented with the required spheres of control accomplished manually.

The processing environment is migrating towards on-line and in-line environments where the data exists in the machine or does not exist at all. Consequently, the humans who used to perform the functions required to live within the rules described are no longer able to perform that function. As a consequence the rules and their enforcement must also be automated.

Much of the procedure written for an application is involved in providing the required audit and control capability. A standardized set of protocols which these concepts permit could alleviate each application from having to provide (program) their own unique solutions.

Automated digital data processing will not be successful in integrated or geographically distributed data base applications unless the concepts and rules of the described spheres of control are adhered to in the implementation. This is particularly true when one examines the increasingly heavy demand the auditors are placing on traceability and accountability in modern data processing systems, aggravated by the real-time on-line and in-line

terminal oriented systems the business community finds more and
more useful.

The capability to describe the boundaries of the various
spheres of control should be added to the languages used to
describe applications and direct (command) computers.

CONSISTENCY IN GENERAL

Introduction

Consistency is the name given to a broad range of things.
Fundamentally, it can best be described as the existence of what
one expects when one expects it. Or, the relations perceived are
within tolerable limits. This allows for inconsistencies between
perceptions of the relations. Of course, inconsistencies between
perceptions are not really inconsistencies because they will not
be visible to anyone who needs consistency. This is something
like; "If a tree fell in the forest and no one heard it, did it
make a noise?" I hasten to point out that those algorithms that
correct for inconsistency do not consider their input to be out of
range or inconsistent.

The fact that relations are involved, as opposed to single
facts, is what makes consistency a difficult subject, especially
when the relations are a moving target as a consequence of the
on-going activity (actions).

Procedural Dependence

Each procedure, especially if written ahead of time as is
usual, expects a specific range of input values. So much so is
this true that the presentation of data not within the value set
expected, and therefore not programmed for, will almost always
cause a fault. And if left undetected and uncorrected it is quite
likely to result in an error. Fault and error here have the same
meaning as for hardware discussed in earlier lectures, and for the
same reasons.

The reason a procedure has this problem is because it is a
procedure - as opposed to a table that maps each possible input
state to its corresponding output state. Specifically, a procedure considers ranges of input states and applies an algorithm for
creating the appropriate output state. This works well providing
no input data values lie outside the range for which the particular procedure was written.

DATA PROCESSING INTEGRITY

The most sucessful systems, so far as solving this sort of problem is concerned, are those that precede each (portion of) procedure with an edit (audit) to detect the various fields whose values are outside the procedures capability. This may be accomplished by a data management extention, or by writing audit procedures that get executed for each data unit passed to the program, or imbedded in the procedure and having tight control over the programming effort. This is often not as simple as it sounds. For example, a time field is allowed to have any value between 0800 and 1700, except if it is Wednesday, in which case the value cannot be larger than 1200, except if it is the third Wednesday of any odd numbered month, in which case the time value can range only between 0900 and 1500 (hours). If this sounds like decision table language it is fortuitous.

A classic example of what not to do is illustrated below. It is a quasi English language representation of a (bad) coding sequence (procedure). "x" is supposed to have the value 1, 2, or 3.

```
      IF x=1, DO A; It's a 1
ELSE IF x=2, DO B; It's a 2
ELSE ....... DO C; It's a 3 - right?
```

WRONG!! It's not a 1 and not a 2.

This example may be considered too trivial. However, choose any example you wish where there is room for ambiguity. Consider the fact that most errors in a system are caused by subsequent change to what exists, due to implicit rather than explicit specification. It is called the impact of change problem and is as devastating today as it was years ago (Davies 1967). It has been given the name the "data-independence problem" to the extent the changes are to the representation or format of the data.

Not only has the procedure been written so that wrong values will produce wrong results, but it has also been written so that future expansion to other valid values of "x" will be processed as though they had the value 3, which may or may not be a correct assumption.

Worse yet, the places in the procedures where wrong assumptions would be made are well hidden. A well behaved (reliable) system would note each place in a procedure where a particular value or set of values was expected. Then, when an enlargement of the expected set occurred, the procedure itself would help in the re-write of the procedure to allow for the extra valid values. Also, should any place in the procedure not get modified to allow for the greater range it would be automatically detected when executed as shown below.

C. T. DAVIES Jr.

```
        IF x=1, DO A; It's a 1
ELSE IF x=2, DO B; It's a 2
ELSE IF x=3, DO C; It's a 3
ELSE output an error message and backout action.
```

If we assume, and we should to be safe, that input data values might not be within the range expected, and/or the execution of a procedure may err, then we can look at an action as containing multiple phases. In the hardware world we would probably call them clock sub-cycles. And they would be divided into two cycles, I time and E time.

Edit (audit) stimulus

Call procedure

Input data, (lock)

Validate data for acceptability, (audit)

Execute procedure, (change state and latch new state)

Validate result, (audit output (trans)actions and data)

Output result, (propagate new state and unlock)

Units of Consistency

Each of us has a feeling or rigorous definition for which inventory part can have which colour and which size, etc. However we are each looking at it from our own viewpoint. For example, a retailer is interested in the stock on hand and the stock due-in from a wholesaler. A wholesaler on the other hand is interested in knowing how many parts are on hand and how many are promised to the retailer. In addition the wholesaler is interested in how many parts are due-in from the manufacturer.

It is clear that the retailer has one domain for consistency while the wholesaler has another domain for consistency. A subset of each domain forms an intersection (quantity due retailer). It is possible that from the viewpoint of each, everything is consistent, but from the viewpoint of a larger domain there may be inconsistency. This is because there are relations that must be adhered to even if one of them does not necessarily know about them. For example, range of colours, size, and texture; which may depend on the specific wholesaler/retailer combination and whether it is an imported item or not, etc.

DATA PROCESSING INTEGRITY

Obviously someone (thing) has to know, and it is frequently the relation descriptors associated with the data that carry the information. A dictionary is most often used for this purpose. Too often, however, the relation descriptors are in someone's head or desk drawer. Or worse yet have long since been forgotten. This latter case is typical of a lot of applications and usually results in not being able to change the procedure without destroying the application.

The problem is one of rendering unto Caesar that which is Caesar's. Many have ascribed the consistency attributes to the data, regardless of the procedure. Others argue that it is the procedure which demands the consistency. After all, if it were not for the procedure there would be no need for consistency – since there would be no (planned) use of the data.

It seems clear that both kinds of consistency specification are required. A procedure should state the range over which it will operate correctly, and the data should have any relational constraints associated with the data, independent of the procedures. After all, the writer of the procedure that created the data had a set of semantics in mind, although the user of the data may not require the full set of semantics. This allows for the necessary temporary difference between old and new relational constraints during migration to the next version of a function or application. It also allows each pre-defined procedure to state it's dependencies and at the same time it allows real time function invocation to be constrained to the results permitted by the consistency specification associated with the data.

This latter point is significant in that in a real-time do-your-own-function type of system, the data is the only place one could describe the relational constraints on the results of a process (action). One could constrain the function names and sequences. However, it is hard to say that a particular function should never be used in combination with some other function. The hierarchy of all permissable function calls would be a very large body of data and still permit unacceptable results.

Locking

Because of the necessity to maintain relational consistency, all of the data involved must be protected against update by other than the one action currently updating. Just because an action will not modify a field of information does not mean that the action does not require stability of the field.
A field whose value is depended upon by an action must not be allowed to be assigned to other actions for any other use than read only. Locking protocols shall not be dwelt upon here inasmuch as they are described and referenced by Jim Gray in his lecture notes on operating systems for data base (Gray 1977).

C. T. DAVIES Jr.

Prevention of Inappropriate Action

Semantic redundancy is often used to catch, and therefore prevent, faults (errors) by detecting potentially incorrect actions prior to the completion of an action. Let us assume that you want to order a part but it has been several years since the last time you ordered that particular item. By now it is possible the item is no longer manufactured, or worse the part number has been re-assigned.

The re-use of identity names is loss of identity and should be given a great deal of thought as to the consequences before going ahead and doing it.

This usually results in such things as ordering an egg holder and receiving an elephant cage. To lower the probability of this sort of thing happening, one should be redundant with as many facts as possible. This is even true when there is a copy of the master parts list at each node in a network. It is always possible that something happened that caused the update to the copy of the master parts list not to occur. Perhaps a scheduling error, a communication line failure, etc.

Rule of Reciprocity

For every action a system can do there must exist a way of logically (or physically) undoing that action. Sounds a bit like Newton again. This requirement is perhaps more readily apparent by example. A wholesaler must be able to receive material back from, as well as ship to, a retailer. If not, then how do you correct for a too large a quantity that accidently got shipped.

If a payroll program was not able to accept money back, there would be no way of correcting for an overpayment. It is necessary that any action be able to be undone by compensation. Compensation subsumes action backout (backward recovery) as well as true compensation (forward error recovery) by a different action. A system that cannot do this will constantly create surprises whose response time to fix is frequently longer than the time available. It is then called an out of control system, and gets worse as a function of time and process. One wonders if the word system would still be appropriate.

Correction of Inconsistency

While most actions are constrained to begin with a consistent input state, it is quite obvious that an action designed to correct for inconsistency should not be prevented from processing just because the input data is inconsistent. The actions testing for inconsistency and correcting for it must still obtain entire units of consistency.

This gives rise to the requirement to define actions that require, and other actions that do not require, consistency. Each transaction, while processing as an action, may require a different subset of the total available consistency specification. If a given transaction does not define the consistency/inconsistency requirement then the test for consistency must be located in the application code rather than factored into a system function on the data access path associated with the relational descriptors.

It should be noted here that if an application does not consist of preprogrammed functions and is not designed to correct for inconsistencies, then the consistency required must be stated as part of the relational descriptors. A failure to do so and a failure to check for consistency in the application program will frequently produce wrong (unacceptable) results. It will also frequently take longer to correct that there is time to correct prior to the use of the incorrect data. This is a suicidal situation since an ever expanding sphere of incorrectness is being created.

Also, while checking for inconsistency, the usual propagating transactions that get built whenever field "x" is changed may have to be suppressed. For example, it is found that one of many quantity fields has a wrong value. The summary of these quantity fields is also a field and has the correct value for the case when all the component quantity fields are correct. It is usual to increment to or decrement from the summary field to keep it up to date to allow for (maximum) parallelism. That is, each component field may be used by different actions at the same time. Any need to replace rather than algebraically correct a summary must in essence lock the entire set of quantities, since they all are part of a unit of consistency.

In this particular case of correcting an inconsistency all the quantity fields including the summary have to be considered as one unit (sphere) of consistency and locked as a unit. Then, following the correction of the quantity field in error, the sum of the quantity fields is placed (re-placed) in the summary field and the entire unit of consistency is unlocked (unallocated). If the entire unit of consistency is allocated to an action, then any method of update is allowable. This is because there are no updates or use by others that will interfere with the action. This allows absolute rather than incremental change. This is a generality that is true for all local variables. In fact it is the difference between a global and a local variable.

C. T. DAVIES Jr.

Consistency Versus Correctness

There is a notion of relative correctness versus absolute correctness and yet maintaining consistency. An analogy would be a chocolate cake made by using exactly two times each of the ingredients. The cake has the same consistency but is relatively larger. Only the absolute values have changed, not the ratios.

For example, an order for some parts results in shipping one part and backordering the other part. A backorder is a note that promises to ship a part later when supplies come in. It is possible, and frequently done on purpose, to have an item backordered even though there were items enough to ship all that was requested. In this case it may be company policy to do one or the other, or it may be a mistake (fault). However, even though some incorrectness may have occurred it is not necessarily an error from either companies point of view.

The consistency check executed just before action termination will frequently be a simple - 'parts ordered = parts shipped + parts backordered'. This allows the degree of freedom necessary when changing versions of algorithms or procedures. It saves having to precisely synchronise algorithm and consistency specification over the entire network of systems. In this particular case any algorithm would be acceptable that maintains the relation specified.

Actions Related But Disjoint In Time

Many transactions are only partially processed by the first action to occur on their behalf. However, under no circumstance may this partial processing result in inconsistency - assuming you are interested in a viable application/system.

The unprocessed portion of the transaction must be held as a transaction in its own right and is in a relation with the original transaction and any partial products (transactions) of any actions on behalf of the original transaction. For example, you order 6 pairs of nuts and bolts. Unfortunately the party from whom you ordered the items has only four pairs in stock. There are at least three choices to solve this dilemma while maintaining consistency.

The first choice may be to ship four pairs and remember that there are two more pairs to be shipped when they come in. This is usually referred to as a backorder for two pairs and is in itself a formal transaction in a queue related to the field that is keeping track of material that is due-in from the source.

DATA PROCESSING INTEGRITY

The second choice may be to hold the entire request for six
pairs until six pairs are available at the same time. This is
also a formal transaction that is placed in a queue associated
with the field keeping track of incoming material for this item.
In this case no apparent processing has taken place other than
to remove a transaction from one queue and place it on another
queue. Status should never-the-less be sent to the originator
because it is a change of state that may not be satisfactory to
the originator.

The third choice may be to reject the entire transaction with
an explanation (status). The audit trail must still show the
arrival and disposition of the transaction even though no real
processing has occurred.

As to which of the above three choices is used is either
company policy or an arrangement between the two companies. The
point here is that at the end of one action, while waiting for
another action disjoint in time, all of the relations must be held
consistent and reflect the status of what from the outside appears
to be a partially processed transaction. The unprocessed portion
of a transaction is always represented as another transaction and
has its own identity and stimulus, and references back to the
(identity of the) transaction whose action created this transaction. Thus a full audit trail is available by pulling on the
thread connecting the transactions and actions.

DISTRIBUTED SYSTEMS

Distributed Data, Process, and Control

The systems here referred to are logically as well as physically distributed systems. Two systems may be sitting side by
side in a small room, but if they have a relationship that
involves shared data, duplicate data, or do work on behalf of the
other, they must coexist within a larger, albeit conceptual,
system. Any processing done by one system on behalf of another
system must consider the processing to be incomplete until the
originator states it is complete. Control for a process belongs
to the creator which in this example is not in the same system.

Without this there may be processing that can never be undone
when the next higher level of control does a backout. The result
is loss of control and integrity that then results in general
chaos.

With this, one maintains control over processing on one's
behalf and insanity is avoided. This topic is covered in greater
detail in the notes on sphere of control over commitment.

C. T. DAVIES Jr.

It is noteworthy, however, that processes on behalf of someone else can never release their results to anyone but the initiating party (higher level of control) - even if it is half way around the world. The initiator of that work may pass the results of the action to its higher level of control over commitment, which may be on yet another node (part) of the system, or even the same node as any arbitrary level within a hierarchy of actions.

TRANSACTION SCHEDULING

Time Dependent Transactions

Time dependent transaction scheduling is the name given to the requirement for a transaction to process at a specified time (and date). Time here is unique in all history regardless of day of year or year. An example of a time dependent transaction is one that causes the transfer of an employee from one department to another - effective 2400 hours on a certain day and year. Any query on the department of the employee should yield the old department up until 2400 hours of the correct day. Thereafter it should yield the new department. Mail (post) distribution is an example of a user need to know and get the right answer. There are a raft of items that fall into this category; promotions, payraises, changes in the law, purchase prices, etc, and in particular, identity changes (oh no!) are examples.

There are two ways of performing or handling time dependent transaction process scheduling.

The first way is to queue the transaction on a time queue and wait until the correct time and day, and then process. Of course, while the many potential transactions are processing it is necessary to prevent any other transactions which require any of the same spheres of consistency with update intentions. This latter statement is true in general, but due to the potentially large number of transactions to process at the appointed time there is a greater problem in allocating spheres of consistency and avoiding clashes. This method of processing time-dependent transactions also has great difficulty if the processors are not working at the appointed time, whether because the processors are down or on scheduled non-use. In this case the time dependent transactions must process first and in time (dependent) sequence until the next transaction is for a later time than now.

DATA PROCESSING INTEGRITY

The second way to do time dependent process scheduling is to
process the transaction ahead of time and hold the updates until
the appointed time. This is accomplished by allocating the sphere
of consistency that will change content and not de-allocate until
the appointed time when the saved updated data is released as the
new version. However the actual work of updating has already
taken place. The updates are sitting on the path to the data and
the accessor of the data asks if there are updates whose time has
arrived. If yes, the new values are used.

This method of time dependent scheduling has one overwhelming-
ly desirable reason for using it. By processing ahead of time any
reasons for not concluding the action in an acceptable manner are
discerned prior to the appointed time. It is like processing to
see what the result would be. If it is all right, then use the
results at the appointed time. If it is not all right there is
still time to backout the action, make some changes (corrections)
and reprocess. This is a much preferred method by those who like
to work during the day rather than at the appointed hour that may
be midnight. Most changes of this sort usually are effective at
midnight.

This second method, just as for the first method of processing
time dependent transactions, has a disadvantage. The disadvantage
of this method is that no updates are allowed that are supposed to
logically occur before the already processed time dependent
action; unless one is willing to backout the previous time dependent action which should have been processed later, process the
earlier transaction and reprocess the original transaction that
was backed out.

The second method has an advantage if the updates caused by
the transaction must be accessed soon after the effective time.
In a large network of related and duplicate data this method is
often the only way of achieving correct and synchronised updates.

The cost of this advantage is the constant overhead of the
data accessor asking the question "Is there a time dependent
update whose time has arrived?" on each and every access to the
data that could have updates held in abeyance. However, if there
are relations between two or more distributed (portions of)
systems such that if any one (portion) system rejects the transaction then all should, preprocessing is a very desireable and
necessary alternative. As the probability of one or more rejec-
tions goes up, so does the desirability of attempting pre-process-
ing.

Given a system with a built-in commitment control mechanism,
no harm could ever occur by doing a trial process of the
(trans)action, since backout of the action is by definition always
possible prior to commitment.

C. T. DAVIES Jr.

This assumes one has had the sense to establish a backout capability. To not do so is asking for whatever trouble results and is the antithesis of (commitment) control.

Automatic Update

One is frequently faced with the problem of updating some related data when a specified data field is modified. For example, to reduce response time to the question "How many lorries (trucks) do we have in total?" it is expedient to carry the total as a field of information. Then when a change is made to a field that is a component part of total lorries the same quantity is incremented or decremented from the field called total lorries. However, it is not always possible for the total lorries field to be accessable by all functions all the time. Perhaps it is sometimes held exclusive for long periods of time. In this and similar circumstances the update yet to occur is represented by another transaction in a queue on the availability of the total lorries quantity. This permits processing when the total field is not available. It is assumed here that the individual fields the sum of which are the total lorries field were not held at the same time as the total field.

The only requirement is that for actions that require the correct value of the total lorries quantity must request allocation of the entire sphere of consistency and this would cause the processing of any queued up transactions that were waiting to process.

The main point is that one can make a choice about scheduling of updates only if they are not bound into the application program. A system function associated with the data and on the path to the data will decide based on specifications from the data manager.

Versions of Data

Contrary to popular belief there is no such thing as global data update-in-place and at the same time have integrity without the use of an audit trail (journal). The question is, when should one and when should one not update in place?

An update in place destroys the value of a specific but probably unknown version of a field and replaces it with another value, whose version is equally unknown, except that it is one later.

When can one destroy the value of a field and not be able to recreate the value for a specific version desired? For example, the value that existed at 0800 hours this morning.

DATA PROCESSING INTEGRITY

When a field is a global variable, a function does not know the precise version because the variable was passed to it. So, if an update in place is to occur, the old value needs to be journalled before the new value re-uses the same space as the old value used to use. Note that this now is not update in place, but rather the re-use of old space.

When a field is a local variable (created by and under one's total control) it may be updated in place because the original value is trivially determinable by doing an action backout and re-process. After all, the variable did not even exist before the start of the action, and has not been committed or it would be a global variable or of no further interest.

If it becomes necessary to know the value of a particular local variable within an action already terminated, and the variable was not passed to become a global variable, then a trial re-process (holding and then discarding the output) will re-create the variable. This assumes that all updates and creates of global variables are journalled. In this context any input from external sources (terminals, etc.) are by definition global variables and are assumed to have been journalled, as necessary for audit or backout/recovery.

A variable that is local to one action becomes a global variable to any nested actions for the purpose of audit. This being so the global variable must be saved before the update. An exception may exist if your auditor is willing to go through the processing manually to perform the audit. Few auditors are, for the simple reason the system has all the data and the complexity of the queries necessary to reconstruct the action and it's nested sub-actions is frequently more expensive than saving the nested actions local variables in the first place. Some actions, that may have been nested, are sometimes required by law to be auditable separately from the action within which they are (were) nested.

A new version of a field(s) or file(s) is said to exist whenever one or more, that are locked at the same time, change value or create another later value.

Synchronising the Real and Represented Worlds

One of the most aggravating things about data processing (paper work or machine) is the frequent lack of synchronisation between the real world (parts) and the represented world (part number and quantity). For example, a part falls off the shelf and is not reported for various reasons. Usually it is a case of no-one wanting to take the blame. Or perhaps an action error in a different node left a wrong value for what was supposed to be the same value in all nodes of the (distributed) network.

C. T. DAVIES Jr.

The solution to this problem is to have as frequent as necessary reconciliation where adjustments are made for any discrepancies found. It is necessary that all such reconciliations alter fields of data in an incremental rather than replacement manner where quantities are involved. An example here is worth a thousand words and a parts/inventory example is probably the most easily understood.

First one establishes a cycle for when one is going to check for correctness independent of knowing whether an error has occurred. For most business' this is the annual inventory that is usually required to compute the inventory tax due the various authorities. After the inventory count it remains only to compare this with the recorded value inside the parts inventory system. The counting process takes quite some time and one cannot afford to close down the business while the count is ongoing.

The solution used is to name a time, date and year when the inventory will be taken. At that time all material arriving or leaving is made note of in a special file. The same is done inside the system. To compare the two counts it is only necessary to take the count, subtract the arrivals and add the shipments since the appointed time. The result is exactly how many were on the shelf at the appointed time. The same is done for the actions within the (computer) system controlling the inventory system.

Since the real world is right (by definition in this case) the algebraic difference if any is added to the represented quantity inside the inventory control system. This brings the real and represented worlds into aggreement. Needless to say it takes a formal transaction to accomplish this correction because real parts worth real money are involved, and someone (not something) has to sign as accepting responsibility and be held accountable for the action.

Did the computer goof? Most likely not. The major cause of differences are the humans who either break, beg, borrow or steal a part and forget to notify the inventory control system. Over a period of time a considerable discrepancy may exist and the first inkling occurs when a warehouse clerk refuses to ship because there are not enough parts in stock. The inventory (computer) system still thinks there is enough stock. An occurrence of this kind usually automatically triggers a reconciliation for the specific part in question.

If all related systems, the real and represented worlds, could be made to stand still long enough, the problem could be solved more easily by just counting and replacing the correct value. Unfortunately items are being received and shipped all the time and some parts are stored in so many places it takes weeks to count them all.

DATA PROCESSING INTEGRITY

Time Synchronisation

For any scheme such as the above reconciliation it is necessary that all parties agree on what time it is. If the accuracy of the time is such that no node is more than a minute out from correct real time, then there will be at most a two minute potential error period. Therefore all actions relative to the error are suspended for two minutes at each node. In this context, the real parts on the shelf are also a node, since they are a part of a unit of consistency.

If the right (fortuitous or planned) method for creating identity of all actions has been used, then one can count actions that occurred since the last action prior to the appointed time.

OBSERVATION

The associative process of humans, together with their data base, makes an extremely powerful consistency checker. When automating an application it is necessary to program consistency checking in all those places a human used to do it. In many cases it does not get completely programmed in, and the application will often have less integrity when automated than it had when humans were the processors and hard copy was the storage medium.

CITED REFERENCES

AIC (1975). Advanced Electronic Data Processing Systems and the Auditor's Concerns, Journal of Accountancy 139, No. 1, 66-72 (January 1975). This is a preliminary report of the Auditing Advanced EDP Systems Task Force, Computer Services Division, American Institute of Certified Public Accountants.

Bjork Jr., L. A. and Davies Jr., C. T. (1972). The Semantics of the Preservation and Recovery of Integrity in a Data System, Technical Report TR 02.540, IBM General Products Division, 5600 Cottle Road, San Jose, California 95153

Bjork Jr., L. A. (1975). Generalized Audit Trail Requirements and Concepts for Data-Base Applications, IBM Systems Journal 14, No. 3, 229-245

Davies Jr., C. T. (1967). A Logical Concept For The Control And Management Of Data, Report AR-0803, IBM Systems Development Division, Poughkeepsie, N.Y.

Davies Jr., C. T. (1972). A Recovery/Integrity Architecture for a Data System, Technical Report TR 02.528, IBM General Products Division, 5600 Cottle Road, San Jose, California 95153

C. T. DAVIES Jr.

Davies Jr., C. T. (1978). Data processing spheres of control, IBM Systems Journal 17, No 2, 179-198.

Eswaran, K. P., Gray, J. N., Lorie, R. A., and Traiger, I. L. (1974). On the Notions of Consistency and Predicate Locks in a Data Base System, Research Report RJ 1487, IBM Thomas J. Watson Research Center, P. O. Box 218, Yorktown Heights, New York 10598

Gray, J. N., Traiger, I. L. and others of the IBM Research Division, San Jose, California. (1973). Personal communication.

Gray, J. N. (1977). Notes on Data Base Operating Systems. In Operating Systems, an Advanced Course. Lecture Notes in Computer Science 60, eds. Bayer, R. et al., pp. 393-481, Springer-Verlag, Berlin.

Petri, C. A. (1976). Nichtsequentielle Prozesse; Internal Report 76-6, GMD-ISF, Bonn, W. Germany (1976).

Petri, C. A. (1977). General Net Theory; Proc. of the Joint IBM/University of Newcastle upon Tyne Seminar on Computing System Design (edited by B. Shaw); Computing Laboratory, University of Newcastle upon Tyne, England (1977) pp. 131-169.

Randell, B., Lee, P. A., and Treleaven, P. C. (1977). Reliable Computing Systems, Technical Report Series 102 (May 1977); also P. M. Merlin and B. Randell, Consistent State Restoration in Distributed Systems, Technical Report Series 113 (October 1977), Computing Laboratory, University of Newcastle-upon-Tyne NE1 7RU, England.

SAC (1977). Systems Auditability and Control Study, Executive Report (order number G320-5791), Data Processing Control Practices Report (order number G320-5792), and Data Processing Audit Practices Report (order number G320-5790), prepared for The Institute of Internal Auditors, Inc., Altamonte Springs, Florida, by Stanford Research Institute under a grant from the IBM Corporation (1977).

DATA PROCESSING INTEGRITY

GENERAL REFERENCES

The author is deeply indebted to Michael J. Miller of IBM for much of the research that produced this list of general references on the overall topic of control and audit, a subject whose implementation is a prerequisite to reliability.

Control and Audit

"Auditability," Data Processor (June, 1975) pp. 13-14.

"Auditing the Advanced Computer Systems," Management Accounting, R. E. Bates, (June, 1970), pp. 34-37.

Auditing Automatic Data Processing (A Survey of Papers on the Subject), A. B. Frielink, member of Netherlands Institute of Accountants, 1972.

"Auditing Control and Electronics," The Journal of Accountancy, A. B. Toan, Jr., (May, 1955), pp. 40-45.

Auditing and EDP, G. Davis (New York: American Institute of Certified Public Accounts, 1968).

Business Information and Accounting Systems, W. Carrithers and E. H. Weinwurn, (Columbus, Ohio: Charles E. Merrill Books, Inc., 1967).

"Computer Auditing, A Broader Perspective," The Chartered Accountant in Australia, (February, 1975), pp. 15-18.

Computer Control Guidelines, (The Canadian Institute of Chartered Accountants, 1970).

Computer Audit Guidelines, (The Canadian Institute of Chartered Accountants, 1975).

"Computer Auditing for Profit," The Internal Auditor, O. E. Raffensperger, (January/February, 1974), pp. 49-55.

The Computerized Society, J. Martin and A. R. Norman, (Prentice-Hall, Series in Automatic Computation, 1970).

"Data Control: A Vital Link of Information Processing," The Internal Auditor, (July/August, 1975), pp. 39-44.

Data Control Guidelines, J. R. Sharrott, (National Computing Centre Limited, Guay House, Manchester, England, 1974), (Book review in EDPACS, October, 1975, pp. 12-14).

C. T. DAVIES Jr.

"General Audit Techniques in Data Processing," Data Management, C. D. Hurtado, (October, 1970), pp. 28-31.

First Annual EDP Auditors Conference Proceedings, (1973), (EDP Auditors Association, P. O. Box 15562, L. A., Calif. 90015.)

Modern Concepts of Internal Auditing, Auditing Computer Centers, (Orlando: The Institute of Internal Auditors. 1974).

"Official Release - Statement on Auditing Procedure No. 54: The Auditor's Study and Evaluation of Internal Control," The Journal of Accountancy, (March, 1973), pp. 56-71.

Operational Auditing Handbook B. Cadmus, (New York, N. Y.: The Institute of Internal Auditor's, Inc., 1964).

Security, Accuracy, and Privacy in Computer Systems, J. Martin, (Prentice-Hall, Series in Automatic Computation).

Theory of Knowledge, R. Chisholm, (Englewood Cliffs: Prentice-Hall, Inc., 1966).

Computer Abuse and Fraud

Computer Abuse D. Parker, S. Nycum, and S. Oura, (Stanford Research Institute, 1973).

"Computer Fraud - A Management Trap," Business Horizons, R. N. Freed, (Graduate School of Business, Indiana University, Blooming-ton, Ind. 47401), (June, 1969), pp. 25-29.

"Auditing Control and System Design," Journal of Systems Management, F. Brown (April, 1975), pp. 24-31.

"Audit Review of System Development: Audit for the Future," The Internal Auditors, (March, 1975), pp. 61-67.

"EDP Controls to Check Fraud," Management Accounting, J. M. Horne, (October, 1974), pp. 43-46.

"Embezzler's Guide to the Computer," Harvard Business Review, B. Allen, (July/August, 1975), pp. 79-89. (Review in EDPACS, Oct. 1975, pp. 14-16).

"Fraud: Conning by Computer," Newsweek, (April 23, 1973), pp. 90-93.

"How the Computer Can Be Used to Commit Fraud," The Practical Accountant, J. W. Varis, (March/April, 1975), pp. 63-64.

DATA PROCESSING INTEGRITY

"How Jerry Schneider Took On Ma Bell, Won For a While, Then Lost and Wound Up Rich Anyhow," PEOPLE, B. Wilkins, (July 28, 1975), pp. 62-63.

"Relationship of Auditing Standards to Detection of Fraud," The CPA Journal, G. R. Catlett, (April, 1975), pp. 13-21.

"SEC Halts Trading in Equity Funding Corp. As It Begins Study of Firm," Insurance Unit, The Wall Street Journal, W. E. Blundell, (March 29, 1973), p. 5.

"Using the Computer to Steal," Journal Systems Management, H. S. Gellman, (October, 1974), pp. 28-32.

Auditing and Systems Design

"The Auditor's Role in System Design," EDPACS, (Sept., 1975, Vol. III, No. 3), pp. 1-8.

"The Auditor's Role in New Systems Development," The Internal Auditor, E. G. Keyes, (January/February, 1972), pp. 32-30.

Auditor's Role

Auditing EDP Systems, (Long Range Planning Service, Stanford Research Institute, 1974).

"Concepts of Internal Auditing, Establishing the Internal Audit Functions in EDP--Job Descriptions," The Internal Auditor, (The Institute of Internal Auditor), (October, 1974).

"Management Information Systems--The Auditor's Role," The Internal Auditor (September/October, 1975), pp. 40-48.

"Should the Internal Auditor Help Develop EDP Programs," The Internal Auditor, (published by the Institute of Internal Auditors, Inc.), (January/February 1975), pp. 51-59.

The Internal Auditor and the Computer, EDP Analyzer, (March, 1975, Vol. 13, No. 3).

Computer Aided Auditing

"An Approach to Auditing EDP System Testing," The Internal Auditor, (September/October, 1975), pp. 65-68. "Audit Control Over Computer-Assisted Audit Techniques," EDPACS, (September, 1975, Vol. III, No. 3), pp. 9-11.

C. T. DAVIES Jr.

"An Audit Management System," The Internal Auditor, (January/February, 1975), pp. 68-72.

"Audit Software Requirements," EDPACS, D. L. Adams, (November, 1973), pp. 14-16.

"Computer Audit Software," EDPACS, P. Pomeranz, (January, 1974), pp. 15-16.

"Auditing Using the Computer in a Decentralized Large Corporation," EDPACS, (June, 1975), pp. 13-15.

Auditing With the Computer, W. Boutell, (Berkely, California: University of California Press, 1965).

"The Computer as an Auditing Tool," The Internal Auditor, O. Leishman, (January/February, 1971), pp. 22-27.

"Computer-Based Auditing," Canadian Chartered Accountant, H. J. Will, (November, 1972), pp. 11-12.

"Computerized Auditing Methods: an Evaluation," The Internal Auditor, S. Tyrnauer, (January/February, 1971), pp. 55-61.

"Demise of Generalized Audit Software Packages," Journal of Accountancy, R. Litecky and R. Wilber, (November, 1974), pp. 45-46.

"Interactive Auditing with ACL," EDPACS, H. J. Will, (March, 1974), pp. 12-14.

"A Survey of Audit Retrieval Packages," EDPACS, G. F. Clark, (October, 1973), pp. 8-10.

"IBM Program Products for Systems Audits and Lists," EDPACS, D. L. Adams, (June, 1975), pp. 1-9.

"Interpreting and Evaluating Attribute Sampling," The Internal Auditor, (July/August, 1975), pp. 45-56.

"A Look At Base-Case Testing," The Internal Auditor, (July/August, 1975), pp. 64-68.

"Software to Audit Computer Records," Journal of System Management, G. F. Clark, (December, 1974), pp. 26-31.

"A Survey of Audit Software," The Journal of Accountancy, D. Adams and J. F. Mullarkey, (September, 1972), pp. 39-66.

"Symposium on Computer Audit Packages-Proceeding," (British Computer Society, 29 Portland Place, London, WIN4AP, England,

1970).

"Systems Auditing With Test Decks," Management Accounting, G. H. Kiefer, (June, 1972), pp. 14-18.

"Using the Computer in Audit Work," Management Accounting, C. O. Smith, (October, 1972), pp. 34-38, 42.

Data Base/Data Communications Auditing

"Auditing and On-Line Computer Systems," The Arthur Young Journal, W. F. Lewis, (Winter/Spring, 1971), pp. 2-15.

"Cost-Performance Trade Offs in Real-Time Systems Design," EDPACS, B. E. Cushing and D. H. Dial, (April, 1974), pp. 16-18.

"The 'Data Administrator' Function," EDP Analyzer, (November, 1972, Vol. 19, No. 11).

Principles of Data-Base Management, J. Martin, (Prentice-Hall, Series in Automatic Computation, 1976).

Auditability Information Catalog, (IBM publication - GB21-9893, 1975).

"Audit Review of Program Code," EDPACS, (August, 1975, Vol. III, No. 2), pp. 1-7.

"Control of Super-zap," EDPACS, (July, 1975, Vol. III, No. 1).

"IRS Audit of EDP Systems," Management Accounting, (April, 1975), pp. 13-15.

"Parallel Simulation - A Technique For Effective Verification of Computer Programs," EDPACS, W. C. Mair, (April, 1975), pp. 1-4.

"Software Security, An Unresolved Problem," Data Management, D. A. Vervois, (October, 1974), pp. 16-19.

"Systems Documentation, Internal Control, and the Auditor's Responsibilities," The CPA Journal, J. D. Green, (July, 1974), pp. 25-29.

Bibliographies

A Bibliography of Selected Rand Publications: Privacy in the Computer Age, (Santa Monica: Rand Corporation, February 1974).

C. T. DAVIES Jr.

An Annotated and Cross-Referenced Bibliography on Computer Security and Access Control in Computer Systems, G. Bergart, M. Denicoff and D. K. Hsiao, (Technical Report Series OSU-CISRC-TR-72-12).

Annotated Bibliography of Electronic Data Processing, (Accounting Series No. 2, Gainesville, Florida: Accounting Department, College of Business Administration, University of Florida, 1968).

Computer Yearbook and Directory, Vol. 2, 2nd ed. (Detroit: American Data Processing, Inc., 1969, bibliographical index to periodical articles from 1962 through 1968 and bibliography of books from 1957 through 1968 in the data processing field.)

"Data Processing Security: A Selected Bibliography," Management Adviser, G.H. Rittersbach, (September-October, 1973).

EDP Auditing: Concepts and Techniques, (New York: Management Information Service, American Management Associations, September 1973.)

"EDPACS Subject Index - Volumes 1 and 2," EDPACS, (April 1973 - June 1975).

Internal Auditing of Electronic Data Processing Systems, (Orlando: The Institute of Internal Auditors, 1967.)

Law and the Computer: A KWIC Bibliography, M. A. Duggan, (New York: Macmillan Information, a division of Macmillan Publishing Co., Inc., 1973).

Managing the Security of Data Processing. (New York: Management Information Service, American Management Associations, February, 1974.)

Modern Internal Auditing: An Operational Approach, V. Z. Brink, J. A. Cashin, and H. Witt, (New York: The Ronald Press Company, 1973).

Privacy and Security Research At Rand, R. Turn, (March, 1972).

"Public Accountability and Public Auditing," The Internal Auditor, (March/April, 1975), pp. 50-60.

Quarterly Bibliography of Computers and Data Processing, 1970-71 Culmination, (Phoenix, Arizona: Applied Computer Research, 1972).

Quarterly Bibliography of Computers and Data Processing, 1972 Culmination, (Phoenix, Arizona: Applied Computer Research, 1973).

9

SOFTWARE RELIABILITY

Martin L. Shooman

Polytechnic Institute of New York

INTRODUCTION

The Concept of Software Reliability

The term reliability has a dual meaning in modern technical usage. In the broad sense, it refers to a wide range of issues which pertain to the design of a product which will operate well for a substantial time period. In a narrower sense, reliability is a metric which is the probability of operational success of the software. Since this metric can be predicted, measured during program development, and demonstrated upon program completion; reliability analysis and testing serves as one of the most important means of quantifying the management of software.

Those who are unfamiliar with probabilistic models often question the validity and basis of the concept. For example, in the case of hardware reliability, failures of equipment are concrete events which occur due to particular, definite reasons. If the winding of a motor burns out, the copper wire has been heated to a temperature above its melting point and held there long enough for some particular spot to melt and interrupt the circuit. The cause of the high temperature would most likely be a local hot spot in the winding, or a large current transient with a long enough duration to cause significant temperature rise. These are certainly deterministic events; however, we are unable to predict when they will occur. Thus, the model of failures becomes a probabilistic one and the random element (the random variable) is the time to failure.

Intuition tells us that the number of errors and also the rate of code writing, test, and debugging (productivity) is proportional to the complexity of the problem and the program which solves the problem. We will shortly show that most of the software reliability models which are in use relate reliability to number of errors. Thus, problem and program complexity measures are directly related to reliability prediction and conveniently also to productivity computations. This chapter is adapted from portions of Chapter

3 and Chapter 5 of a forthcoming book, Shooman (1978, 1980).

Definition of Software Reliability

A formal definition of program reliability includes: (1) an appropriate definition of system success, (2) the operational conditions of the software, and (3) specification of the random variable in question. One definition which has been proposed in the literature (Dickson, Hesse, Kientz, and Shooman (1972); Shooman (1973)) and is accepted by many is:

Software Reliability

Software reliability is the probability that the program performs successfully, according to specifications, for a given time period.

The specifications must include precise statements of the host machine(s), the operating system and support software, the operating environment, the definition of success, details of any hardware interfaces with the host machine, complete details of the ranges and rates of input and output data, and the operational procedures. Although not a necessity, it would be helpful if the specification also included a definition of hardware failure and operator errors.

A careful definition of software errors will be needed for the measurement and demonstration phases of reliability. Theoretically, we can define software failures in the abstract; however, in practice our raw data is in terms of system failures. When a system failure occurs, we record all available data and subsequently analyze and divide our errors into hardware, software, operator, and unknown errors. If our unknown category is not smaller than 10% or 20%, the situation becomes too muddled and uncertain to proceed until the definitions and diagnostic techniques are improved. Thus, the utility of our software reliability definition is improved by not only saying what software reliability is, but also by delineating what it isn't.

The random variable included in the definition is operating time, t . We must carefully define t since there are many time variables of interest during software development. There is operating time; calendar time during operation; calendar time during development; working times (man hours) during coding, development testing, and debugging; and the computer test times throughout the various stages of the program. Operating time is the cumulative time the computer is up and working once the system has become operational. Clearly, there is also the downtime of the computer during operation. If the development phase is defined in terms of subphases, other time variables appear. One must also add the category of unknown errors to that of hardware, software, and operation errors. Not all recognized errors can be diagnosed even into these broad classes.

The choice of time as the random variable assumes that failures occur due to random traversing of paths in the program which contain bugs for some value(s) of the input parameters. These bugs are residual because they were undetected during development. The prime reason they remained undetected is that the path was tested for other parameter values and the program worked well. The program size did not allow exhaustive testing so these bugs remained hidden. This means that as operating time increases, the probability of encountering at least one bug increases.

Other models of software failure may require a different random variable. For example, in a time shared system it is well known that failures generally occur when the system is heavily loaded, i.e. servicing many users. If such is the case, perhaps we should use user hours. Thus, if n is the number of users and t is operating hours as previously defined, our random variable might be cumulative values of nt. Similarly, we could visualize a program which primarily operates in an idle condition waiting for input data to arrive either periodically or aperiodically. If failures only occurred when the data arrived and processing began and failed, then a different choice of random variable would be in order, i.e. the number of input cycles. If the input arrival rate were periodic, then operating time and cycles would be linearly related; however, in the aperiodic case they would not, and cycles would have to be used. There are many analogous hardware examples. In the case of a transistor, time is the best choice; however, for a relay, cycles may be better, and in an automobile, miles traveled is generally used. A detailed experimental and conceptual study of the type of problem is necessary in general to choose the appropriate random variable.

Consider an idealized situation in which we have 100 identical computers all with the same operating system (same release, configuration, patches, etc.), and similar and equivalent input streams (as regards variety, load, features used, etc.). If at the same instant some morning we inspect all the installations and find 97 are up and 3 are down, then the availability of the system is estimated to be 97/100. If we repeated this calculation many times over, say a month, then the average of the estimates should approach the true availability. Similarly, if all the systems are being operated in a normal manner (no new releases, personnel changes, major job stream changes, etc.), then they should all exhibit the same steady state availability. If we obtain careful records for one system of the system down times $(t_{d_1}, t_{d_2}, \ldots)$ and the system up times $(t_{u_1}, t_{u_2}, \ldots)$ then the steady state availability is given by

M. SHOOMAN

$$A_{ss} = \frac{T_{up}}{T_{up} + T_{down}}$$

where

$$T_{up} = \sum t_{u_i}$$

$$T_{down} = \sum t_{d_i}$$

If we calculate A_{ss} for each of the 100 systems, then the average of the results should approach the true availability.

Definition of Software Errors

We now focus on the definition of a software bug. The differences between a software error and a software bug, and the meaning of a multiple or single occurrence of an error is discussed. A somewhat more specific definition of software reliability is given in terms of the definition of software errors.

We begin the discussion by defining a software bug.

Software Bug

One or more software bugs exist in a system if a software change is required to correct a single major error or minor error so as to meet specified or implied system performance requirements.

Thus, a bug is simply the colloquial and highly descriptive term for a software error.

The above definition of a software bug contains several terms which are defined below:

Code Change

Change - Any alteration (addition, deletion, correction) of the program code whether it be a single character or thousands of lines of code.

Major Errors

Major Error - A catastrophic event which interrupts (or could interrupt) most or all major system functions. e.g., an infinite loop, system crash, a major memory overflow, data base corruption, etc.

Minor Error

Minor Error - A marginal event which allows (or could allow) some portions of the system to operate properly while interrupting others, e.g., some missing output, some wrong output, an inaccurate computation, a recoverable transient error, etc.

Performance Specification

Specified performance requirements - A written requirement, figure of merit, or parameter which qualitatively or quantitatively defines system performance.

Implied Specification

Implied system performance - An unwritten requirement which is understood by the majority of the project team to be essentially equivalent to a written requirement.

The definition of change includes all changes regardless of their reason. We are primarily interested in changes which are made to correct bugs; however, changes to correct or add documentation as well as changes to implement new or changed requirements (specifications) impact the work schedule and are also of interest. Since all changes are generally mixed together in recording data, it is necessary to indicate in recording change data the reason for the change and to segregate the changes into at least three categories: documentation, changes in specifications, and changes to correct bugs.

The meaning of implied system performance is best given by an example. When Bell Laboratories develops a switching computer system for a telephone network, they do specify number of lines to be served, call rates, types of phone equipment, etc., in a precise quantitative fashion. They do not specify that the caller will be an American who is accustomed to the use of our telephone system and not a European who is strange to the ways of our telephone system. The latter is an implied specification.

Inherent in the above definitions and discussion is the assumption that errors can be and are detected and recorded. Furthermore, it is assumed that each error is sufficiently well investigated so that it can be classified as hardware, software, operator, or unknown, and that the unknown category is small, say less than 20%. The detection of errors can be effected by monitoring the system (or simulated system) performance or by reading the code.

M. SHOOMAN

We must amplify on the previous definition in order to cover the cases of repetitious errors, multiple errors corrected by one change, and multiple changes to correct one error. We now introduce the concept of internal and external errors.

External Error

An external error is a performance error of the system which is generally detected by executing the code.

Internal Error

An internal error is a coding error which is always found by reading the code (either man or machine reading).

We may think of internal errors as causes and external errors as effects. Thus, if a single internal error results in an associated single external error, we call it a single bug. If an internal error results in a minor or no detectable external error, then no bug exists (e. g. , error recovery). If an external error exists and we are sure it is a software problem, then a bug exists regardless of whether or not we can find the corresponding internal error.

ERROR DATA

Introduction

One of the major problems in software development is that there have been too few quantities which one could measure as the project progressed. This has made very difficult the estimation of the state of the project and time needed to complete it. Traditionally, software managers keep track of the number of lines of code written, the estimated total number of lines of code in the final program, and the number of lines of code debugged. Most managers also keep track of the number of errors removed from a program (Fig. 1). The obvious inference is that once the cumulative number of errors removed curve begins to approach a horizontal asymptote, the debugging is nearing completion. The author, being an engineer and a student of probability, does not believe in perfection, thus he feels that the achievement of such an asymptote does not represent the removal of all bugs. It only represents the removal of most bugs, or more specifically, all the bugs which can be ferreted out using the test methods and sets of test data which were employed. A few managers and software analysts feel it is too difficult to define and count bugs; therefore, such efforts are useless. As a rebuttal, I cite the hypothetical case where the manager of a computer controlled chemical plant schedules the installation of a new release of an operating system over a weekend. During mid-morning there is computer trouble, and the process is shut down for two hours. All the hardware diagnostics are run and check perfectly. The old version of the operating system is reloaded, everything works fine and production is restarted. Try and convince this manager that the concept of a software bug is too nebulous to define! The remainder of this section discusses various models and methods for estimating and measuring the number of bugs in a program.

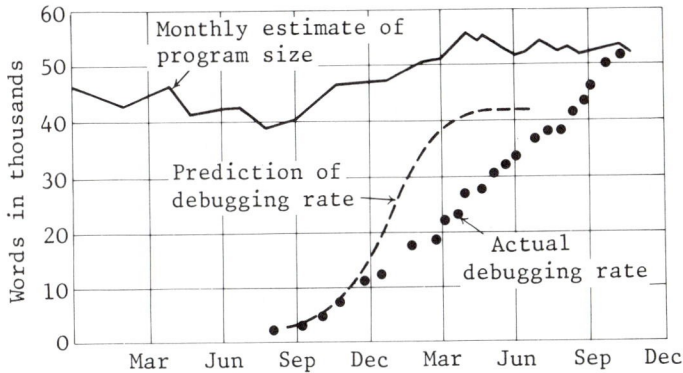

Fig. 1 Cumulative number instructions debugged actual and predicted, Brooks (1975).

Historical Data

The first thought which comes to mind when we are investigating how to judge the number of bugs left in a program is to compare this program with previous ones. Inherent in such a suggestion is the assumption that the total number of bugs in similar programs are similar. To phrase things more succinctly, we postulate:

Constant Number of Bugs

The total number of bugs in similar programs is approximately constant.

We now have to define what is meant by similar programs and approximately constant. We begin with a discussion of the term approximately constant. First of all, we are discussing a macroscopic model of a complex stochastic process, the debugging of a large piece of software by a team of programmers. Thus, the constant we will attempt to estimate is not a fundamental physical constant such as the speed of light, but merely a parameter in a probabilistic model. Secondly, we will only use such a constant for initial planning purposes and rough initial predictions, thus if our constant varies within a range of 2:1 or 3:1, we are still justified in calling the hypothesis valid. The definition of similarity is more complex. First of all, we must assume an equivalent skill mix in each of the programming teams. Secondly, we must assume that similar techniques were used to test the software. We might expect the same constant for all bottom-up unstructured programs; however, a different constant would be valid for the class of top-down structured programming. Also, we must define "similar" in terms of the phase of the development. If we focus on a conventional bottom-up development process, there are three phases: module coding and test, system integration and test, and lastly field operation. Some variation in these divisions exist. For convenience in very large systems, the task is divided into several processes, thus system integration is a two-phase task divided into a process integration phase followed by system integration of the processes. Also, in many large systems it is recognized that the best test is actual operation. Thus, often the first several months of test operation is actually the last part of final integration and test. In such cases, the release date (when ownership of the software is transferred from developer to user) occurs several months after rather than at the beginning of field deployment.

Some of the first data which was published in the open literature (Dickson, Hesse, Kientz, and Shooman (1972)) represented a set of data which was collected from three manufacturers on their operating systems and from a government agency on four versions of an operating system (see Table 1). The size (measured in machine language instructions) of most of these programs was between 210K and 240K, where the abbreviation K as used here is not in the engineering sense where K=1000, but in the computer science sense where $K=2^{10}=1024$. All those in the supervisory category were similar types as were all those in the applications program category.

From Table 1 we see that among the application programs the total number of changes (we assume each change is an error and denote the total by E_T, also called E_O in some research papers) varies between 3,270 and 1,725, a ratio of 1.9:1. In the case of the supervisory programs, $1,325 \leq E_T \leq 1,890$, and the ratio is about 1.4:1. Lumping all the programs together, the ratio for E_T from smallest to largest is about 2.5:1.

Similarly we can examine the rate at which errors are removed as a function of debugging time τ. Denoting this error rate, $\rho(\tau)$, we can compute the average value of $\rho(\tau)$ over the interval 0 to τ which is also given in Table 1. Note that the average rates vary by about 2.9:1 for the whole set of data. Thus we may formulate a new hypothesis which is substantiated so far by the data.

SOFTWARE RELIABILITY

Table 1 Number of Bugs Removed Per Month for Seven
Different Large Programs (from Hesse (1972)
and Shooman (1972)). (Note: Hesse's raw data
was in terms of program changes, and the
data in this table and the Hesse paper were
adjusted by dividing by an estimated 17 changes
(bug).)

Month	Application A 240,000 Inst. Bugs	Application B 240,000 Inst. Bugs	Application C 240,000 Inst. Bugs	Application D 240,000 Inst. Bugs
1	514	905	235	331
2	926	376	398	397
3	754	362	297	269
4	662	192	506	296
5	308	70	174	314
6	108	---	55	183
7	---	---	60	158
8	---	---	---	368
9	---	---	---	337
10	---	---	---	249
11	---	---	---	166
12	---	---	---	108
13	---	---	---	31
Total Changes	3,270	1,905	1,725	3,207
AVG/Month	545	381	246	247

Month	Supervisory A 210,000 Inst. Bugs	Supervisory B 240,000 Inst. Bugs	Supervisory C 230,000 Inst. Bugs
1	110	250	225
2	238	520	287
3	185	430	497
4	425	300	400
5	325	170	180
6	37	120	50
7	5	60	--
8	--	40	--
Total Changes	325	1,890	1,639
AVG/Month	189	236	273

Constant Removal Rate

The average rate per month at which bugs are removed from similar programs is approximately constant.

Now in order to compare bug content for large and small programs, we must normalize E_T and $\rho(\tau)$ by the total number of instructions I_T . (The normalization of E_T through division by I_T was conceived prior to the research on token length as a measure of complexity which is developed in the section on Zipf's law. It now appears that it might be better to normalize with respect to token length. If this is true, then future software data gathering efforts should record not only I_T but token length.) This gives rise to two new hypotheses:

Constant Normalized Number of Bugs

The normalized number of bugs in similar programs is approximately constant. (The normalization is performed by dividing the total number of bugs by the number of machine language instructions.)

Constant Normalized Removal Rate

The normalized rate at which bugs are removed from similar programs is approximately constant. (The normalization is performed by dividing the rate of bug removal per month by the number of machine language instructions.)

The normalized data for the total number of instructions and average removal rate, ρ_A , is compared in Table 2.   The variation in E_T/I_T is 2.1:1, thus normalization has reduced the variation from 2.5:1.   Similarly the range in ρ_A becomes 2.5:1 which again represents a reduction from the 2.9:1 range for the unnormalized values.   Of course the real test of the utility of normalization will be to try it on smaller (and larger) programs than those given in Tables 1 and 2.

Table 2   Computation of Normalized Total Errors and Error Rates (from the Data of Table 1)

Program	Size	E_T/I_T	ρ_A
Supervisory A	210 K	6.14×10^{-3}	0.875×10^{-3}
Supervisory B	240	7.97	0.996
Supervisory C	230	7.48	1.25
Application A	240	13.20	2.20
Application B	240	7.70	1.54
Application C	240	7.00	1.00
Application D	240	12.90	0.995
Average		8.92	1.26

SOFTWARE RELIABILITY

One program we have already discussed is the STUDY program, Shooman and Bolsky (1975), which contained approximately 4000 machine words and had 63 bugs removed. The ratio $E_T/I_T = 15.8 \times 10^{-3}$, and compares well with the data in Table 2. In the paper by Itoh and Izutani (1973), two similar programs were debugged with and without a test tool. The results were $E_{T_1}=335$, $I_{T_1}=14,302$, and $E_{T_1}/I_{T_1}=23.4 \times 10^{-3}$ and $E_{T_2}=345$, $I_{T_2}=16,037$, and $E_{T_2}/I_{T_2}=21.5 \times 10^{-3}$, again reasonable agreement is obtained.

Another set of data for small programs appears in Table 3.

Table 3   Computation of Normalized Total Errors and Debugging Rates(Akiyama (1971)).

Program	Size	E_T/I_T	ρ_A
MA	4.03 K	25.4×10^{-3}	2.54×10^{-3}
MB	1.32	13.7	1.37
MC	5.45	17.1	1.71
MD	1.67	15.6	1.56
ME	2.05	34.6	3.46
MF	2.51	14.7	1.47
MT	2.10	12.4	1.24
MG	0.70	22.9	2.29
MH	3.79	13.2	1.32
MX	3.41	23.4	2.34
Average		19.3	1.93

Note that the values given in Table 3 (and by Itoh) are somewhat higher than those in Table 2. One explanation for this is that Akiyama's and Itoh's data covers three phases of program development: module debugging, (M), integration testing, (I), and field deployment, (F).

Time Variation of Debugging Rate

We now look in more detail into the rate of removal of bugs from computer programs. We are looking for error behavior during debugging which will possess some generality for both large and small programs. Thus, rather than plotting the error rate, we will plot a normalized error rate

$$\rho(\tau) = \text{errors/total number of instructions/month of debugging time} \qquad (9.1)$$

where

$$\tau \equiv \text{months of debugging time}$$

M. SHOOMAN

In Table 1 we see that the average number of bugs removed per month is approximately constant for the 7 systems, varying between 545 and 189. In Table 2 we see that the normalized average rate, ρ_a, varies between 2.20 x 10^{-3} and 0.875 x 10^{-3}. If we calculate $\rho(\tau)$ for the data of Table 1, we obtain the graphs shown in Fig. 2 and 3. Although several curve shapes might be fitted to these data (Hesse (1972) and Shooman (1972)), one characteristic is common for all curves. The normalized error rate decreases over the entire curve, or at least over the latter two-thirds or half of the curve. Initial behavior of $\rho(\tau)$ differs from example to example in Fig. 2 and 3.

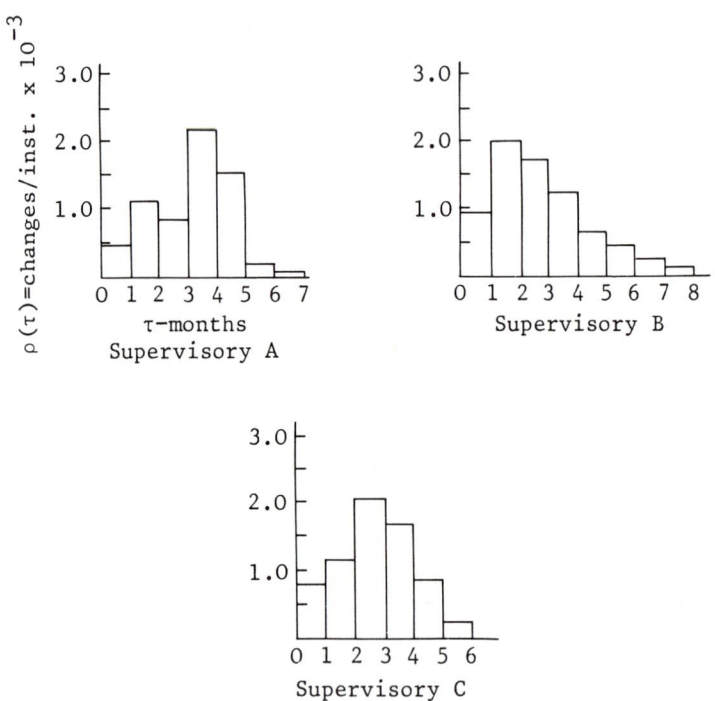

Fig. 2   Normalized Error Rate Versus Debugging Time for Three Supervisory Programs.

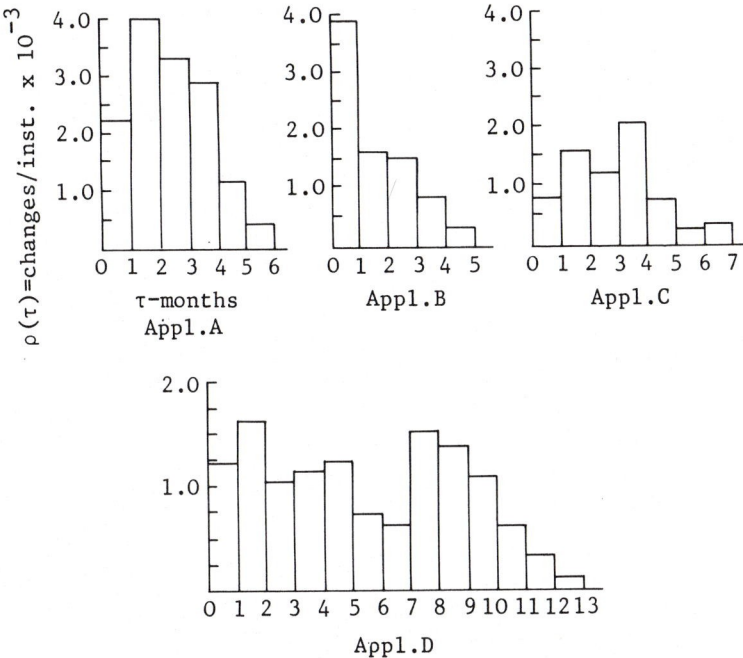

Fig. 3   Normalized Error Rate Versus Debugging Time for
Four Applications Programs.

Since we are interested in the normalized total number of
errors removed, we will define a cumulative error curve, $\epsilon(\tau)$,
which is the area under the $\rho(\tau)$ curve:

$$\epsilon(\tau) = \int_0^\tau \rho(x)dx = \text{cumulative errors/total number of instructions} \qquad (9.2)$$

and $\rho(\tau)$ is, of course, the slope of the $\epsilon(\tau)$ curve:

$$\rho(\tau) = d\epsilon(\tau)/d\tau \qquad (9.3)$$

A curve of the cumulative error data for the supervisory
system A of Fig. 2   is shown in Fig. 4.   If similar curves for
$\epsilon(\tau)$ were drawn for the other six examples of Fig. 2 and 3,
all would build up initially with a constant or increasing slope
and then decreasing curvature, appearing to become asymptotic.
Similarly, in the paper by Miyamoto (1975), he presents cumulative curves of $\epsilon(\tau)$ which have a shape similar to Fig. 4.

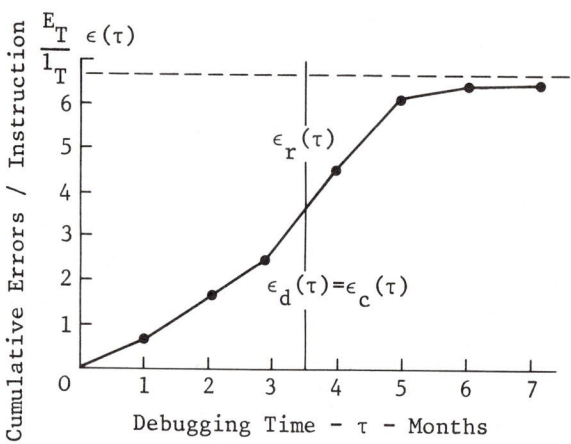

Fig. 4   Cumulative Error Curve for Supervisory System A
Given in Fig. 2.

AN ERROR PROPORTIONAL (MACRO) MODEL

Introduction

The basic philosophy behind this macro model is that software errors are caused by discovery of residual bugs in a program. Furthermore, if we consider all bugs to be alike, the
program to be large and essentially nonrepetitive in nature, then
the failure rate should be proportional to the number of remaining bugs. We use the previous notation to describe the number of remaining errors, relate this to the failure rate, and then
use classical reliability theory to complete the model. In order
to compute the constants of the resulting models, we use historical data, tagging techniques, or use the results of simulated operation as if it were test data and apply statistical estimation
theory.

Basic Assumptions

We assume that operational software errors occur due to the
occasional traversing of a portion of the program in which a hidden software bug is lurking. We begin by writing an expression
for the probability that a bug is encountered in the time interval
Δt after t successful hours of operation. This must be proportional to the probability that any randomly chosen instruction contains a bug, i.e. the fractional number of remaining bugs $\epsilon_r(\tau)$
(See Eq. 9.9). We must derive an expression for the number of

remaining bugs in a program. If we denote the initial number of bugs in the program by E_T, the program contains I_T instructions, and it is assumed that there are no new bugs created in debugging, then the asymptote which the $\epsilon(\tau)$ curves approach is E_T/I_T. If we also assume that all detected errors ϵ_d are corrected errors ϵ_c, then by inspection of Fig. 4, we can write an expression for the number of residual errors, ϵ_r

$$\epsilon_r(\tau) = (E_T/I_T) - \epsilon_c(\tau) \tag{9.4}$$

If in any sizeable program, it is impossible to remove all errors, then even as τ becomes large

$$\epsilon_c(\tau) < E_T/I_T \tag{9.5}$$

$$\epsilon_r(\tau) > 0 \tag{9.6}$$

From a study of basic probability and reliability theory, we learn that the probability of failure in time interval t to $t + \Delta t$, given that no failures have occurred up till time t, is proportional to the failure rate (hazard function) $z(t)$ (See Appendix).

$$P(t < t_f \leq t + \Delta t \mid t_f > t) = z(t) \Delta t = K \epsilon_r(\tau)\Delta t \tag{9.7}$$

$$z(t) = K \epsilon_r(\tau) \tag{9.8}$$

where $t_f \equiv$ operating time to failure (occurrence of a software error)

$$P(t < t_f \leq t + \Delta t \mid t_f > t) \equiv \text{probability of failure in interval } \Delta t, \text{ given no previous failure.} \tag{9.9}$$

K = an arbitrary constant

Note in Eq. 9.8 two time variables appear: first, there is t, the operating time in hours of the system, and second, there is τ, the debugging time in months (or more generally, the debugging resource variable). Once the assumptions in Eq. 9.8 have been made, the reliability and mean time to failure functions follow directly.

Reliability Model

Using Eq. 9.8 and the Appendix developments, and assuming that K and $\epsilon_r(\tau)$ are independent of operating time t, we obtain for the reliability function

M. SHOOMAN

$$R(t) = \exp\left(-\int_o^t z(x)\,dx\right) \tag{9.10}$$

$$R(t) = e^{-\left[Ke_r(\tau)\,t\right]} = e^{-\gamma t} \tag{9.11}$$

where γ is a constant dependent on τ but not t.

Basically, the above equation states that the probability of successful operation without software bugs is an exponential function of operating time. When the system is first turned on, t=0 and R(0) = 1. As operating time increases, the reliability monotonically decreases as shown in Fig. 5 . We depict the reliability function for three values of debugging time, $\tau_0 < \tau_1 < \tau_2$. From this curve we may make various predictions about the system reliability. For example, looking along the vertical line $t = 1/\gamma$ we may state:

1. If we spend τ_0 hours of debugging, then $R(1/\gamma) = 0.35$

2. If we spend τ_1 hours of debugging, then $R(1/\gamma) = 0.50$

3. If we spend τ_2 hours of debugging, then $R(1/\gamma) = 0.75$

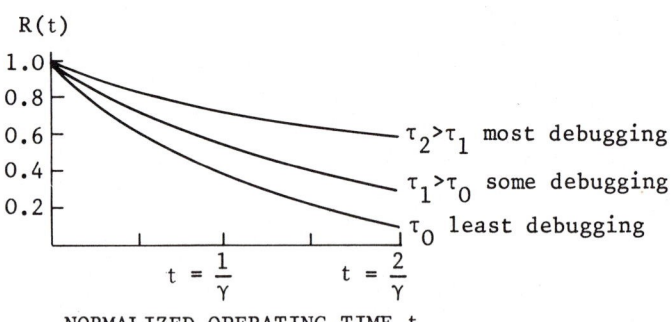

Fig. 5   Variation of Reliability Function R(t) With Debugging Time τ.

SOFTWARE RELIABILITY

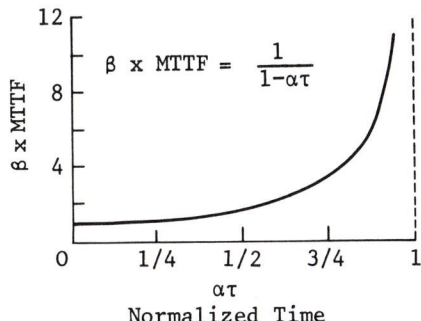

Normalized Time

Fig. 6   Comparison of MTTF Vs. Debug Time for
the Constant Error Debug Rate Model.

MTTF Model

A simple way to summarize the results of the reliability
model is to compute the mean time to (software) failure, MTTF,
by substituting Eq. 9.11 into the MTTF expression of the Appendix.

$$MTTF = \int_o^\infty R(t)dt \qquad (9.12)$$

$$MTTF = \frac{1}{K\, e_r(\tau)} \qquad (9.13)$$

If we let $\rho(\tau)$ be modeled by a constant rate of error correction ρ_o (See Hesse (1972) for other models), then solution of
Eqs. 9.13, and 9.4 yields

$$MTTF = \frac{1}{\left[K\,\frac{E_T}{I_T} - \rho_o\,\tau\right]} = \frac{1}{\beta(1 - \alpha\,\tau)} \qquad (9.14)$$

where $\beta = \frac{E_T}{I_T} K$ and $\alpha = \frac{\rho_o I_T}{E_T}$

In Fig. 6, $\beta \times$ MTTF is plotted vs. $\alpha\tau$. We see that the
most improvement in MTTF occurs during the last 1/4 of the debugging.

371

Experimental Verification

The macro model developed above has been verified by two investigators in the literature. Isao Miyamoto (1975) analyzed the software errors accumulated on a 500 line (communication) real time message switching system developed between 1968 and 1970. He categorized the errors into 5 categories and observed 96 errors of the severest level during the integration and test stages. The final system exhibited a software MTBF of 396.5 hours and a hardware MTBF of 480 hours. The growth curve of mean time between software errors which he calculated is given in Fig. 7 and compares very well with the behavior predicted by the model in Fig. 6..

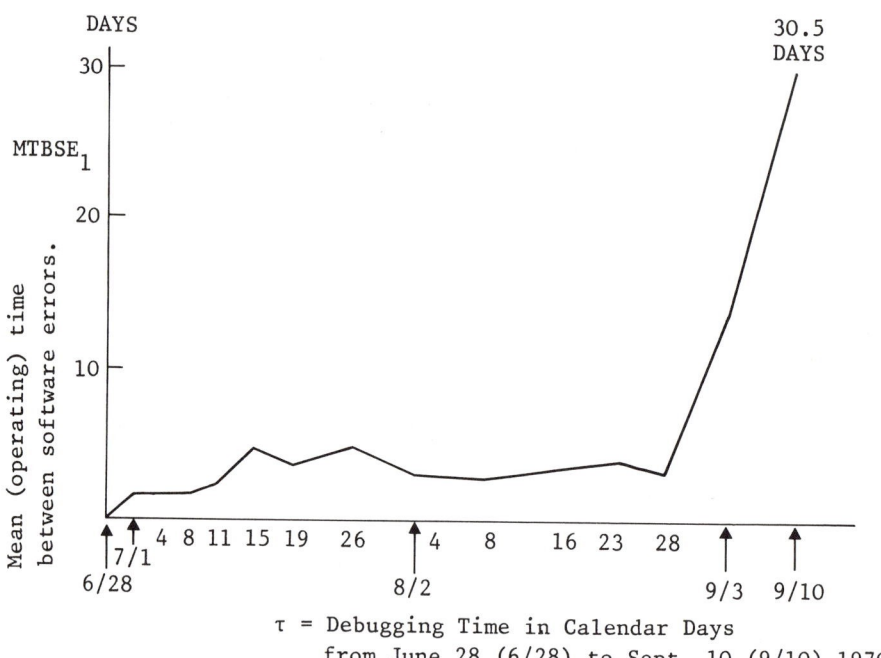

Fig. 7   Growth Curve of Software Reliability Mean Time Between Software Errors. (Miyamoto, 1975.)

372

SOFTWARE RELIABILITY

J. D. Musa (1975) develops a model very similar to the macro model just developed and has applied it to 4 programming projects. Musa used the models to predict the progress of the projects before the development began, to manage the software as it was developed, and compared the operational performance with the predictions. A plot of the mean time to failure vs. test time is given in Fig. 8 for Musa's Project 1. Again, the overall behavior of Fig. 6 is verified; however, if we look more closely at Fig. 8, the plateau between 10 and 18 test hours is apparent. Also, Musa's ordinate is test hours rather than development days.

First of all, we can readily appreciate that test time and development days will be roughly proportional to each other. The plateau in the figure is open to two interpretations. One might observe that the plateau might have represented a period during which essentially the same tests which were performed during the interval 0-10 hours are rerun (as is done in regression testing). Note that if we eliminate the 10-18 hour time segment, the curve increases monotonically. The alternative interpretation is that there are two types of tests which were run. The first type was successful in eliminating errors over the 0-10 hour period, and was continued for another 8 hours without improvement until it was clear that no further progress could be made, and then at 18 hours a new type of test was begun. Note that neither of these two interpretations conflict with the macro model developed. Since the derivation of Eq. 9.14 depended on the assumption of a constant rate of error correction, so did the particular shape of Fig. 6. Clearly, in the case of an actual development, the error correction rate would vary. The main features which all three curves (Figs. 6 - 8) have in common is a monotonically nondecreasing behavior (except for minor ripples) and a sharp rise near the end of the test or development time.

Musa's results strongly support the utility of such models and the final predictions of the software MTBF correspond closely to the observed times (cf. Table 4). The differences between the measured and predicted MTBF are +31%, +12%, -20%, and +34%. Thus, a wise working rule might be to overdesign a bit for safety and not release the software until we predict a reliability which exceeds our goals by perhaps 20-30%.

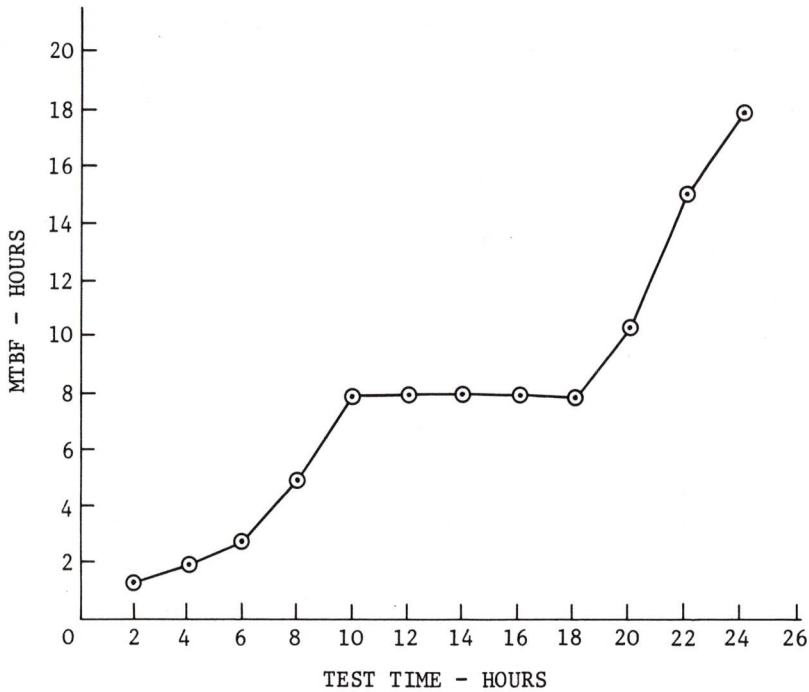

Fig. 8   MTBF Vs. Test Time for Project 1. (Replotted From the Data of Fig. 3, J. Musa (1975).)

Table 4   Comparison of Measured and Predicted MTBF
(hours)(Musa (1975))

	Project 1	Project 2	Project 3	Project 4
Measured (during use period)	14.6	31.4	30.3	9.2
Predicted (at end of test period)				
Max. Likelihood point estimate	19.1	35.2	24.4	12.3
50% confidence range	13.5-28.8	>19.8	>12.9	6.4-23.6
Program size in assembly-machine inst.	19,500	6,600	11,600	9,000
Number of programmers	9	5	6	7
Project length in months	12	11	12	10

(The reader is referred to Musa's paper for further details of his model and how he computed the results.)

M. SHOOMAN

Other Models

Other similar models have been proposed in the literature. Jelinski and Moranda (1972) propose a hazard function of the form

$$z(t) = \varphi[N - (i - 1)] \tag{9.15}$$

where:

φ = Constant of proportionality.
N = Total number of errors present.
i = Number of errors found by debugging time τ_i.

Comparison of Eq. 9.15 with Eqs. 9.4 and 9.8 shows them to be identical if

$$E_T = N \tag{9.16}$$

$$\frac{K}{I_T} = \varphi \tag{9.17}$$

$$\varepsilon_c(\tau) = \frac{i-1}{I_T} \tag{9.18}$$

Equations 9.16 and 9.17 are merely notational differences and Eq. 9.18 is nearly the same (i.e. would be identical if $\varepsilon_c(\tau) = i/I_T$) .

In another paper, Schick and Wolverton (1972) modify Jelinski and Moranda's model and assume that the failure rate is proportional to the number of remaining errors and increases with operating time t

$$z(t) = \varphi[N - (i-1)]t \quad . \tag{9.19}$$

One rationale for postulating an increase in z(t) would be if operation were viewed as a succession of different trials which gradually closes in on the remaining errors (sampling without replacement). However, one could argue to the contrary that z(t) should decrease with t, since the latter errors are the subtle ones which take a long while to encounter in operation. The author believes that in most cases of large, intricate, well tested, real-time systems, the hazard will remain constant once the initial field debugging of a new release is finished. The small number of subsequent patches generated should not be significant. Failure should be caused by rare combinations of input data and path traversals, with the time between failures governed by an exponential distribution, yielding a constant hazard. Experimental data is necessary to choose among these hypotheses.

Other related reliability and error models are discussed in the literature. We now turn in the next section to a discussion of how we can experimentally measure reliability and use these measurements in conjunction with the models of this section to determine the unknown model parameters K and E_T.

MEASUREMENT OF MODEL PARAMETERS

Experimental Reliability Data

If we had just deployed a large hardware-software system for field use, we could monitor its reliability by carefully recording the operating time and documenting each failure in detail. Thus, we could obtain the times between failure. Investigation of each failure should allow one to classify all failures as hardware, software, operator, or unknown. If we segregate the software times between failure and plot their average week by week, we will have a quantitative measure of operational software reliability. We would expect the operational MTTF to increase for the first month (year, in some cases) or so as software bugs detected in service are removed, then gradually to level off to a relatively constant value. This is, of course, an after-the-fact evaluation of the software design and does not allow one to measure progress and/or need for improvement of the software design while it is under development.

The earliest stage at which an entire system can be functionally tested is during system integration using the system exerciser (functional test) program. If this test is performed at the beginning of system integration, the result will be a succession of very short runs and immediate crashes. Most software test personnel would instinctively comment that this is as expected since the system is still in "poor shape", and such a test should be delayed until the end when the system is in "good shape". A bit of reflection leads one to the conclusion that it is just this frequent crashing which leads to a quantitative assessment of the poor initial reliability.

We now focus on the test data and how it should be analyzed. The necessary information which must be recorded for each run of the system test program is how long the test ran, whether an error occurred, and if the error is a software error. Sufficient dumps and other documentation must be recorded for subsequent analysis in order to segregate errors into hardware, software, operator, etc., errors. Each of the r successful runs represent $T_1, T_2, \ldots, T_r$ hours of success. (In many programs the running time will not vary and all $T_i = T$.) If there are n total runs, then each (n-r) unsuccessful run represents $t_1, t_2, \ldots t_{n-r}$ successful run hours before failure. (We are, of course, assuming that the times t_i at which the program "bombs" are carefully recorded or estimated in all cases.) The total number of successful run hours H is given by

$$H = \sum_{i=1}^{r} T_i + \sum_{i=1}^{n-r} t_i \tag{9.20}$$

Assuming that the failure rate is constant, we denote it by λ and compute it as the number of failures per hour

$$\text{Failure Rate} = \lambda = \frac{n-r}{H} \tag{9.21}$$

The MTTF for a constant failure rate is the reciprocal (see Sec. 1.2) of the failure rate

$$\text{MTTF} = \frac{1}{\lambda} = \frac{H}{(n-r)} \tag{9.22}$$

Now Eqs. 9.21 and 9.22 represent the total system failure rate and MTTF. Since we are mainly interested in software failures, we assume that the outputs as well as dumps are carefully investigated for the $(n-r) = x$ failures. Based on the above analysis, the failures are divided into x_h hardware failures, x_s software failures, x_o operator failures, and x_u unknown failures. Hopefully, the unknown ratio x_u/x will be 25% or smaller so that most of the data is classifiable.

Then the software failure rate and MTBF are defined by

$$\lambda_s = \frac{x_s}{H} \tag{9.23}$$

$$\text{MTTF}_s = \frac{H}{x_s} \tag{9.24}$$

Based on the results of this occasional test, we can plot λ_s and MTTF_s vs. τ the debugging time. Such charts should allow a quantitative measure of the progress in improving software quality. After τ_a hours of debugging, we would have a measure of MTTF and R(t), and by extrapolation of the curves, we could predict MTTF and R(t) after $\tau_b > \tau_a$ months of debugging. Unless we knew the functional form of the variations in R(t) and MTTF with τ and could determine an appropriate extrapolation scheme, accurate predictions would be limited to small excursions into the future.

Estimation of Macro Model Constants

Rather than use the raw experimental data and extrapolation for prediction, we can assume an underlying model for λ_s and MTTF_s and use the data to estimate the model parameters. If the hypothesized model is correct, then predictions using this technique should be superior to the extrapolation technique of the previous section.

For the software reliability model defined in Eqs. 9.4 and 9.10-9.13, assuming the data collection and analysis of the previous section

$$R(t, \tau) = \exp\left[-K\left(\frac{E_T}{I_T} - \epsilon_c(\tau)\right)t\right]$$ (9.25)

$$MTTF(\tau) = \frac{1}{K\left[\frac{E_T}{I_T} - \epsilon_c(\tau)\right]}$$ (9.26)

Note that if we assume a known program size and careful collection of error data, then I_T and $\epsilon_c(\tau)$ are known values and only the constants K and E_T remain to be determined. These two unknowns K and E_T can be evaluated by running a functional test after two different debugging times, $\tau_1 < \tau_2$ chosen so that $\epsilon_c(\tau_1) < \epsilon_c(\tau_2)$. We then equate Eqs. 9.24 and 9.26 at times τ_1 and τ_2

$$\frac{H_1}{x_{s_1}} = \frac{1}{K\left[\frac{E_T}{I_T} - \epsilon_c(\tau_1)\right]}$$ (9.27)

$$\frac{H_2}{x_{s_2}} = \frac{1}{K\left[\frac{E_T}{I_T} - \epsilon_c(\tau_2)\right]}$$ (9.28)

Taking the ratio of Eq. 9.27 to 9.28 and using Eqs. 9.23 and 9.24 yields

$$\hat{E}_T = \frac{I_T\left[\left(\lambda_{s_2}/\lambda_{s_1}\right)\epsilon_c(\tau_1) - \epsilon_c(\tau_2)\right]}{\left(\lambda_{s_2}/\lambda_{s_1}\right) - 1}$$ (9.29)

Once $\hat{E}_T$ has been computed from Eq. 9.29, we obtain $\hat{K}$ by substituting Eq. 9.29 into 9.27 which yields

$$\hat{K} = \lambda_{s_1} / \left[(\hat{E}_T/I_T) - \epsilon_c(\tau_1)\right] \quad .$$ (9.30)

The "hats" above E_T and K in Eqs. 9.29 and 9.30 denote estimates of the parameter. Note that if there was no debugging between τ_1 and τ_2 so that $\epsilon_c(\tau_1) = \epsilon_c(\tau_2)$, $\lambda_{s1} = \lambda_{s2}$, the numerator and denominator of Eq. 9.29 becomes zero, i.e., Eqs. 9.27 and 9.28 are no longer independent and the estimate fails. One can also use the powerful technique of Maximum Likelihood Estimation to obtain slightly better parameter estimates (in a statistical sense) and confidence bounds (c.f. Shooman, 1980).

Another technique for estimating the number of bugs in the computer program E_T is the so-called bug seeding technique discussed in the following section.

Seeding Models

The so-called bug seeding method is an outgrowth of a technique used to estimate the number of animals in a wildlife population or fish in a pond (Bailey (1951) and Feller (1957)). The technique is best illustrated by discussing the estimation of the number N of a specific species of fish, say bass, in a small pond which contains no other type of fish. We begin by procuring a suitable number of bass, N_t, from a fish hatchery and tag each one with a means of identification which will remain reliably attached for the length of the measurement period. The N_t tagged fish are then added to the N original fish and allowed to mix and disperse. After an appropriate number of days a sample is fished from the lake (by hook or net) and separated into n_t tagged bass and n untagged bass. If we assume that there was no difference in the dispersion or ease of catching of the tagged and untagged fish, then we can set up the following equation which equates the proportions of tagged fish in the fished sample to the original fraction seeded (for derivation, see Appendix A, M. Shooman (1978)).

$$\frac{N_t}{N + N_t} = \frac{n_t}{n + n_t} \qquad (9.31)$$

We may solve the above equation for N in terms of the known quantities N_t, n, and n_t, yielding

$$\hat{N} = \frac{n}{n_t} \times N_t \quad . \qquad (9.32)$$

By direct analogy we may consider N to be the unknown number of bugs in the program at the start of debugging, and $N_s = N_t$ is the number of seeded bugs (unknown to the debugger). After τ months of debugging, the bugs which have been removed are examined by someone other than the debugger who has a list of the seeded bugs. He classifies them as n_s which come from the seeded group and n which were not seeded. Direct substitution in Eq. 9.32 yields

$$\hat{N} = \frac{n}{n_s} \times N_s \qquad\qquad (9.33)$$

(Note: N is the same as E_T, defined previously.)

The possibility of seeding bugs in a program and using this to measure the initial bug content was first realized by Mills et al. (1970). The results of the early experiments in this area were inconclusive because it was difficult to make up realistic bugs.

A different approach was suggested by Hymann (1973) which circumvented the problem of seeding bugs. He proposed that one employ two (or more) independent debuggers to work on the same program initially. Suppose that it is estimated that debugging will take four months and that debugger No. 1 is assigned to the program for four months (or the duration of the job). Debugger No. 2 is only assigned to the job for one or two months at the beginning of the project. The two debuggers work independently, and after a few weeks the results of their efforts are evaluated by a third analyst who estimates the number of program bugs N by a formula similar to Eq. 9.32 (to be derived below). (For pedagogical clarity we speak of a third analyst, who could in fact be debugger No. 1 or No. 2 or both working together if only a single estimate is planned. For multiple estimates over a time period, a third person is needed to avoid destruction of independence.) The estimates are repeated every few weeks, and when the third analyst is satisfied that the value N is sufficiently well estimated, the results of debugger No. 2's work is given to debugger No. 1, and debugger No. 2 is reassigned. Now, after one quarter to one half of the project has been debugged, we have a reasonable estimate of the total number of bugs in the program, and knowing the number of bugs already removed, by subtraction we obtain the number of remaining bugs. In addition, only a portion of debugger No. 2's findings duplicate debugger No. 1. Thus, debugger No. 1 is able to rapidly incorporate much of debugger No. 2's work, thereby producing almost a step change in the number of bugs found. In most cases the benefits should far outweigh the costs - one or two extra man months of debugging time (the cost may be minor, zero, or negative if debugger No. 2 really finds many independent errors which shorten debugger No. 1's efforts). A detailed development of the estimation formulas appears in Shooman (1980), and Rudner (1976), and yields

$$\hat{B}_o = \frac{B_2}{b_c} \times B_1 \qquad\qquad (9.34)$$

T ≡ Development time in months

M. SHOOMAN

$B_o \equiv$ Number of bugs in program at $\tau = 0$ (same as N and E_T)

$B_1 \equiv$ Number of bugs found in program by debugger No. 1 up to time τ_1

$b_c \equiv$ Number of bugs which debugger No. 2 finds up to time τ_2 which are common, i. e. in set B_1

$b_I \equiv$ Number of bugs which programmer No. 2 finds up to time τ_2, which are independent, i. e. not in set B_1

$B_2 = b_c + b_I \equiv$ Number of bugs found in the program by debugger No. 2 up to time τ_2

OTHER MODELS

Bug Generation Models

The error models developed previously were all based upon the fundamental assumption that errors were corrected in the debugging process, but no new ones introduced. Thus, the number of errors must start at some initial value which we called E_T, and be monotonically non-increasing (i. e. decreasing or constant). The concept was that after sufficient debugging, the number of errors removed would approach the total number of errors originally present, thus the notation E_T was adopted. In practice, the debugging process is an imperfect one. Thus, a certain amount of generation of errors is associated with any debugging procedure. Therefore, the total number of errors does not remain a constant. Some of the ways in which errors may be generated are:

(1) A typographical error may arise invalidating the result of bug correction.

(2) The correction is based upon faulty analysis, thus complete bug removal is not accomplished.

(3) The correction is accomplished; however, it is accompanied by the creation of a new error.

(4) Errors which are detected but not corrected act in many ways like generated errors.

Depending upon the efficiency of debugging, the error generation rate could be greater than, equal to, or less than the error correction rate. The resulting error behavior in the three cases is shown qualitatively in Fig. 9. (Fig. 9 is a particular case where there is no generation) c.f. Fig. 4 . The time T_1 is when debugging stops. Note that the number of errors remaining is always positive, in each case.

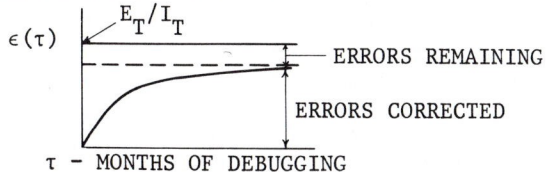

(a) APPROACHING EQUILIBRIUM, HORIZONTAL ASYMPTOTE, NO GENERATION OF NEW ERRORS

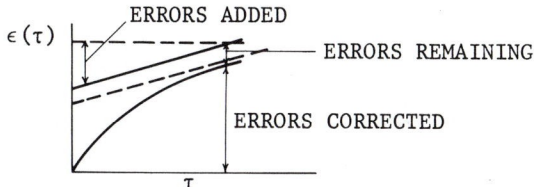

(b) APPROACHING EQUILIBRIUM, GENERATION RATE OF NEW ERRORS EQUALS ERROR

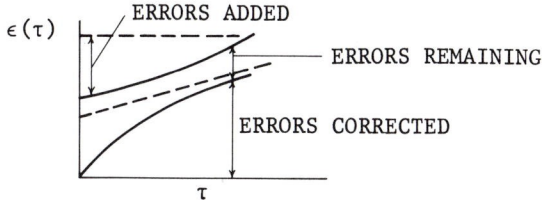

(c) DIVERGING PROCESS, GENERATION RATE OF NEW ERRORS EXCEEDS ERROR REMOVAL RATE

Fig. 9   Cumulative Errors Debugged Versus Months of Debugging.

A detailed development of this model appears in Shooman (1978) and Shooman and Natarajan (1976a).

M. SHOOMAN

Decomposition Model

We now introduce a micro model which concentrates more on the structure of the program than the previous macro model.

The decomposition model which will be proposed in this section is based upon several assumptions. We first assume that the program has been designed using a structured or modular philosophy, and as a result, there emerges a natural structure of the program which can be described as consisting of a number of paths, cases, parts, modules, or subprograms. The decomposition focuses upon this natural structure. In general,we will primarily use the term paths from now on to designate the paths, cases, parts, modules, subprograms, or any other important substructure. We also assume that the majority of the paths are independent of each other. (One could probably tolerate some type of dependence in the model if it were limited.)

The decomposition model will be developed from the probabilistic viewpoint of relative-frequency. We will hypothesize a sequence of tests which either uncover a bug (failure) or run to completion without uncovering a bug (success). We begin our development of the model by defining the following variables and parameters:

N $\equiv$ The number of tests .

i $\equiv$ The number of software paths (cases, parts, modules, etc.) .

t_i $\equiv$ Time to run case i (if time is not deterministic,we can substitute the mean value of t_i, i. e., $\bar{t}_i$) .

q_i $\equiv$ Probability of error on each run of case i (The probability of no error $p_i = 1 - q_i$) .

f_i $\equiv$ Frequency with which case i is run.

n_f $\equiv$ Total number of failures in N tests.

H $\equiv$ Total cumulative test time in hours.

z_o $\equiv$ Software error discovery rate

Development of the model yields, Shooman (1976b)

$$z_o = \frac{\sum_{j=1}^{i} f_j q_j}{\sum_{j=1}^{i} f_j (1 - \frac{q_j}{2}) t_j} \tag{9.35}$$

SOFTWARE RELIABILITY

We now wish to examine Eq. 9.35 under special constraints. These are listed in Table 5. Note that the units of z_o are clearly seen from case 4 to be failures per hour, or just $hr.^{-1}$.

Table 5   System Probability of Failure and Failure Rule for Special Cases

Constraints	$q_o \equiv \sum_{j=1}^{i} f_j q_j$	$z_o \equiv \dfrac{q_o}{\sum_{j=1}^{i} f_j (1 - \frac{q_j}{2}) t_j}$

Case 1

$$q_j << 1$$

$$\sum_{j=1}^{i} f_j q_j$$

$$\frac{q_o}{\sum_{j=1}^{i} f_j t_j}$$

Case 2

$$q_j << 1$$

$$f_1 = f_2 = \dots f_i = f = \frac{1}{i}$$

$$\frac{1}{i} \sum_{j=1}^{i} q_j$$

$$\frac{\sum_{j=1}^{i} q_j}{\sum_{j=1}^{i} t_j}$$

Case 3

$$q_j << 1$$

$$f_1 = f_2 = \dots f_i = f = \frac{1}{i}$$

$$q_1 = q_2 = \dots q$$

$$q$$

$$\frac{i \, q}{\sum_{j=1}^{i} t_j}$$

Case 4

$$q_j << 1$$

$$f_1 = f_2 = \dots \dots f_i = f = \frac{1}{i}$$

$$q_1 = q_2 = \dots \dots q$$

$$q$$

$$t_1 = t_2 = \dots \dots t$$

$$\frac{q}{t}$$

M. SHOOMAN

Availability Models

As was previously discussed, in addition to reliability, availability is an important measure of performance for the quality of any system. Many computer systems do not have the rigid requirements that a real time system has for continuous operation. Time shared systems and batch systems can and often do go down without causing severe problems to the user. The real item of importance here is how frequently the system goes down and for how long it stays down.

The mathematical technique which is generally used to analyze system availability is the use of a Markov model. A brief summary of the theory and application of Markov models is given in the Appendix.

In this section, we will describe the assumptions and the configuration of the basic Markov model. Much of this section is based on Trivedi and Shooman (1975). We will describe only the basic structure so as to reveal the essential details of the model. Useful generalizations of the basic model will be discussed later.

We assume that the software system under consideration is fairly large, of the order of 1000 words (or more) of code, so that statistical deductions become meaningful. Software systems for which performance evaluations are relevant will usually be large. We assume that the system contains initially (at t=0) an unknown number n of unknown bugs. It is noted that t is taken to be the operating time of the system measured from initial activation. The time origin could be chosen as the beginning of the phase known as process integration and test. In such a case, the model would be useful for evaluation of the quality of the software during final simulation or field testing, and would provide a measure of the software availability which would be useful in managing this crucial stage in software development, and would provide a quantitative index of its field performance.

In most large systems, the first 6 months to 1 year of deployment is essentially a "shake down cruise", during which errors are discovered and fixed in the field or through a software support group which supports field operation from the development site. In such a case, the time origin t=0 might be the time at which field deployment starts. Also the model could be used during both stages of development.

The basic Markov model assumptions are that at most one error is discovered or fixed (debugged, tested, and a code change inserted) in any instant of time, and that the transitions between states in the model depend only on the state we are in and the state we are going to, and not on the past history of states.

SOFTWARE RELIABILITY

Let the sequence of system "up" states be $\{n, n-1, n-2, \ldots\}$. This is the set of states in which the system exists if no error has occurred, or if an error has just been repaired. Similarly, let the set of "down" states of the system be $\{m, m-1, m-2, \ldots\}$. In general, the system will be in state $(n-k)$ if the $(k-1)^{th}$ error has been corrected, and the kth error has not yet occurred, while the system will be in state $(m-k)$ after the kth error has been discovered but not yet corrected $(k = 0, 1, 2, \ldots)$. The configuration of the states of the model, together with the transition probabilities between states, is shown in Fig. 10.

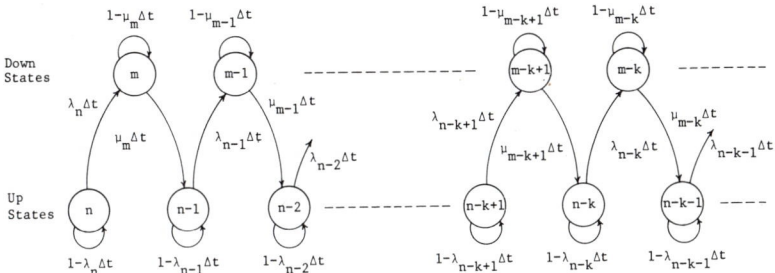

Fig. 10   A Many-State Markov Model for Software Performance Evaluation.

Fig. 10 depicts a Markov process of the discrete-state, continuous-time type. The Markov model is therefore defined by the set of transition probabilities $\{p_{ij}\}$, where p_{ij} denotes the probability of a transition from state i to state j and depends only on the states i and j, and not on any of the previous or later states. The probability of transition from state $(n-k)$ to state $(m-k)$ is $\lambda_{n-k}\Delta t$, for $k = 0, 1, 2, \ldots$. Similarly, the transition probability from state $(m-k)$ to state $(n-k-1)$ is $\mu_{m-k}\Delta t$, for $k = 0, 1, 2, \ldots$. The transition rates λ_j and μ_j depend, in general, upon the present state of the system. In the context of our software system, we note that λ_j represents the error occurrence rate, while μ_j represents the error repair rate. We see that the probability of transition from state r to state r-2 through state r-1, in the time interval Δt, contains the product term $(\Delta t)(\Delta t)$, and we therefore assume this probability to be negligible.

The mathematical details of model development above appear in Trivedi and Shooman (1975).

A typical availability solution assuming constant failure rates $(\lambda=1)$ and repair rates $(\lambda=2)$ is shown in Fig. 11.

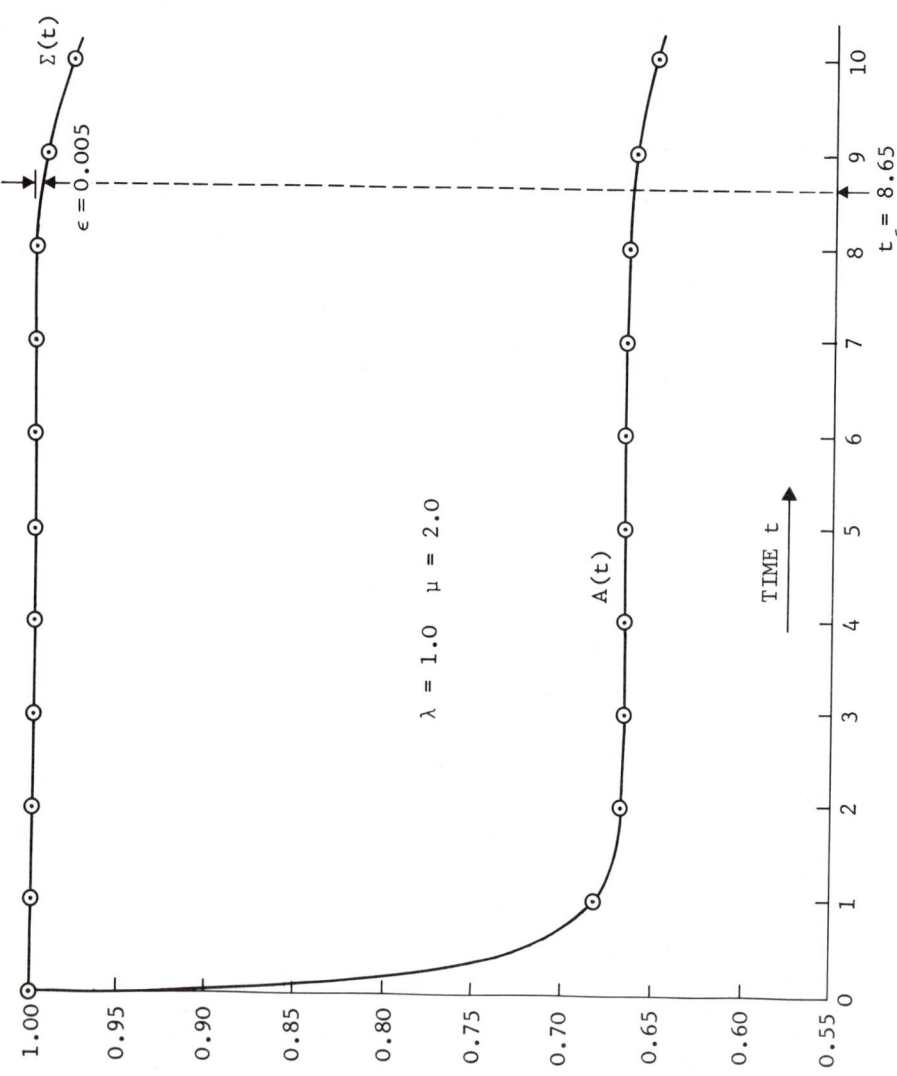

Fig. 11   Availability and Sigma Function (Constant
Parameter Case; From Numerical Solution).

SOFTWARE RELIABILITY

COMPLEXITY VS. ERRORS AND PRODUCTIVITY

Introduction

As was previously discussed, in our quest for good software we must focus on several measures of goodness. Some of these measures will be qualitative, and we will call them attributes. Other measures of goodness will be quantitative and we will call them variables.

The preceding topics of this section focused on the quantitate variables of reliability and availability. These measures, as well as the crucial variable of cost, are related to the complexity of the problem and the software. Thus, we focus in this section on complexity models and complexity estimation. Many of the key variables of interest are specified in a software contract.

The various phases of the software development cycle (Shooman (1978)) are: conceptualization, specification, design, testing, debugging, etc. This development cycle was portrayed as the typical one for a large hardware-software- (operator) system which is to be used by the buyer and produced under contract by the seller. In some cases in large military or industrial organizations, however, complexity is a somewhat different matter. We do not know, nor are we likely to, see a specification with regard to the complexity of a system. However, one of the first steps in preliminary design is to form an intuitive feeling for the complexity of the problem and how it compares with other problems for which the analyst may have some data. In most cases, we also want a quantitative measure of complexity to use in the design phase so as to compare the calculation with the initial intuitive estimate. Also, storage, processing time, testing, and reliability are all related to complexity. Thus, the models and analysis techniques for all these quantitative quantities are a function of the complexity. We can learn much about not only the problem at hand, but software in general, if we can define and analyze the complexity.

Table 6   Factors Influenced by Complexity

1. Development time
2. Number of initial and final bugs
3. Reliability and availability
4. Number of test cases
5. Cost

Table 7 Types of Complexity

Type	Literary Analogy	Software Measure
1. Type, size, bulk	number of book pages	number of instructions
2. Difficulty of text (language and concepts)	James Joyce vs. Winston Churchill relativity vs. wood-working	operators + operands
3. Structural	flashbacks and mingled subplots	graph and algo-rithmic proper-ties

Complexity is related to many factors, the four most promi-nent ones are given in Table 6. In discussing the various types of complexity which are developed in this book, the literary analogy given in Table 7 is useful. The lowest level of com-plexity relates to the length or bulk of the work. Often the total number of machine language instructions, I_T, is used for this measure (c.f. Eq. 9.4). At the next level we focus on the complexity of language and syntax which the author uses, as well as the intellectual complexity of the subject under discussion. In this section we will relate this level of program complexity to the operator plus operand count. Lastly, the highest level of complexity, the structural complexity, will be related to the graph cyclomatic complexity. (McCabe (1976))

A Statistical Approach to Program Complexity

In this section we focus on some recent work (Shooman and Laemmel (1977)) which provides a computational procedure, as well as a set of useful relations, among complexity, development time, and errors.

The approach is based on the viewpoint that the complexity of the program is related to the length of the program. The length is not to be measured in terms of numbers of executable state-ments (excluding storage, comments, declarations, etc.), but in terms of the number of operators and operands. Of course once we have a program, it is simple, but time consuming, to count the operators and operands. Thus, this technique alone will not help us in estimating complexity at the early stages. However, if we look further into the matter, we find that the number of different types of operands is simply the number of input variables + number of output variables + number of intermediate variables + number of constants. Thus, from an analysis of the problem,there is a chance that we might estimate the number of different types of operands, but how does this help us count total usage of operands? Similarly, the number of types of operators is fixed by the computer language. In PL/1, for example, the operator vocabulary is fixed by the number of comparison operators + number of built in functions + number of other KEY WORDS. Not every programmer knows or uses all of these (400-500), but we could still estimate the number of distinct types which he might use. Again, the number of types doesn't tell us how to estimate the total usage. It is a remarkable fact that there are statistical laws which relate the total number of occurrences of operators (operands) to the number of distinct types. Such laws allow us to estimate the total operator (operand) length based on an estimate of the number of distinct types. Laws of this type were first studied by Zipf in conjunction with natural languages.

Zipf's Laws of Natural Language

Introduction

Any investigator who has studied ways of describing the structure of computer languages comes to the immediate conclusion that the task is a formidable one due to the seemingly infinite variety of programs we can write with a computer language. Much can be learned in tackling this problem by studying the analogous and even more complex problem of describing the structure of a written or spoken natural language. A set of analogies between the elements of natural and computer languages is given in Table 8.

Inspection of Table 8 shows that there is overall agreement between natural and computer languages in that they are built up from elements using rules of construction.

Table 8   Analogies Between Elements of
Natural and Computer Languages

Natural Literature (or dialog)	Computer Programs (Software)
Book or Speech	Software System
Chapter, Article, Conversation	Program
Paragraph, Section	Subprogram, Module
Sentence	Statement
phrase, clause	expression, loop
subject	
predicate	
Word	Element between spaces
noun	operand
adjective, adverb	?
verb	operator
auxiliary verb	?
preposition, conjunction	?
pronoun	?
article	?

Before we discuss Zipf's law, it is convenient to introduce a few terms used in dealing with natural language. Unfortunately, the term word is ambiguous in the sense that all the words in the first chapter of this book mean something different than all the words in the dictionary. We use the term token to refer to all the words of the chapter. The term type is used to refer to the words in the dictionary. To be more precise, if we looked up the word "give" in the dictionary, within the body of the entry we would expect to find the related types: gave and given. Thus, for clarity we would define give as a lexical unit. Much of our effort will be centered on the counting of the number of times, n_r, particular types occur in a sample of n tokens. We have used the subscript r because in our comparison of word types, we will order the types in terms of their frequency and assign ranks. The most frequently occurring type will be assigned rank 1, the second most frequent type, rank 2, etc. If we assume there are t word types in our sample of n tokens, then clearly

$$\sum_{r=1}^{t} n_r = n \qquad (9.36)$$

Clearly, when we begin to collect our statistics, there will be a number of types, t_k, which occur the same number of times, k. These will essentially tie for the same rank r, so we can arbitrarily assign the ranks from r to $r + t_k - 1$ to these types which occur k times. Using the above definitions, we can write a summation equation similar to Eq. 9.36 for the types

$$\sum_{k=1}^{n} t_k = t \qquad (9.37)$$

The absolute frequency of occurrence for type r is n_r; however, the relative frequency of occurrence f_r is simply n_r/n.

Zipf studied the relationship between frequency of occurrence f_r and rank r for words from English, Chinese, and the Latin of Platus (Zipf 1965). The resulting data is given in Fig. 12, where Zipf plotted the $\log_{10}$ of n_r on the abscissa and the $\log_{10}$ of r on the ordinate. Note that the data for English is an excellent fit to a straight line, as is the data for Latin for ranks larger than 10.

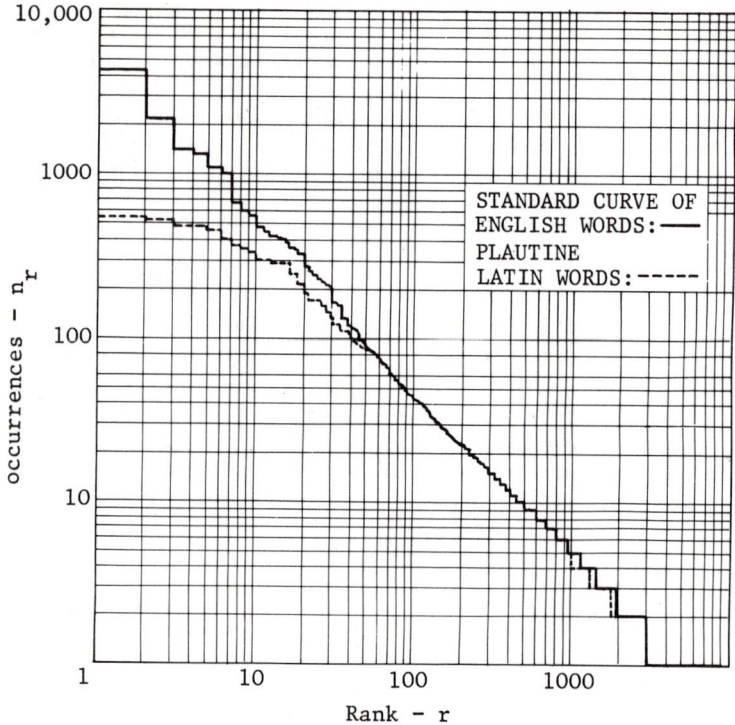

Fig. 12   Occurrence Frequency Vs. Rank for
English and Latin Words. (From Zipf
(1965), Plate IV).

If we had plotted $\log_{10} f_r$ on the abscissa, we would have obtained
the same result shifted by the scale factor n.   The straightness
of such plots on log-log paper is an empirical justification (we
will discuss later theoretical justifications) for the relationship

$$f_r \cdot r^a = \text{Constant} = c \qquad (9.38)$$

Careful study of Zipf's data and that of others shows the constant
a, (the slope on log-log paper) is approximately 1, thus we arrive at the simple relationship, generally called Zipf's first law,
given below

$$f_r \cdot r = c \qquad (9.39)$$

which can also be written in the form

$$n_r = \frac{c \cdot n}{r} \qquad (9.40)$$

SOFTWARE RELIABILITY

Inspection of Eq. 9. 39 yields the fact that the constant c can be interpreted as the relative frequency of the rank 1 word type. Also we can interpret the relative frequency ratio $f_r n_r/n$ as the probability of rank r, p_r.

We can obtain other fundamental relations via summation of Zipf's Law. If we sum both sides of Eq. 9. 40, we get a different result:

$$\sum_{r=1}^{t} n_r = cn \sum_{r=1}^{t} \frac{1}{r} \tag{9.41}$$

The summation of the series $1/r$ is given by Jolley (1961)

$$\sum_{r=1}^{t} \frac{1}{r} = 0.5772 + \ln t + \frac{1}{2t} - \frac{1}{12t(t+1)} \cdots . \tag{9.42}$$

(Note that the constant 0. 5772 is called Euler's constant.)

Substitution from Eq. 9. 36 and Eq. 9. 42 (retaining only 2 terms for modest size t) into Eq. 9. 41, and rearrangement yields an expression for the constant c in terms of t.

$$c = \frac{1}{0.5772 + \ln t} \tag{9.43}$$

If we substitute Eq. 9. 43 into Eq. 9. 40 and solve for n we obtain

$$n = n_r r(0.5772 + \ln t) \tag{9.44}$$

If we can obtain relationships for n_r and r for some value of r, we can complete our derivation.

We consider the smallest rank which is where $r_{max} = t$ (eg. if there are 100 types, then the largest rank is obviously 100). In most cases the rarest type (largest rank) will occur only once, thus, $n_{r_{max}} = 1$. Substituting these values in Eq. 9. 44 yields

$$n = t(0.5772 + \ln t) \tag{9.45}$$

In many cases, the experimental fit to Zipf's first law is only close enough for the ensuing theory to be thought of as a gross approximation. In such cases, two generalized forms of Zipf's laws will yield a better fit between theory and data. In such cases, the algebraic expressions and computations become more cumbersome. However, a simple computer program solves the computational problem and parametric studies provide sensitivity information on how the results change as parameters vary. Of course the simple Zipf theory will still hold well enough to provide some insight into the results.

One generalized form of Zipf's law (suggested by several authors) is of the form

$$P_r = \frac{n_r}{n} = \frac{C}{(r + A)^B} \qquad (9.46)$$

A sketch of Eq. 9.46 on log-log paper is given in Fig. 13.

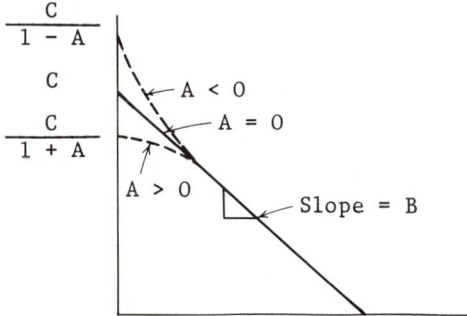

Fig. 13 Role of Coefficients A, B, C in Eq. 9.46.

The theoretical development of generalized Zipf models is treated in Shooman (1980).

In the preceding material, we introduced Zipf's law as an experimental law based upon observation and heuristics. Many authors, notably Mandelbrot, have been able to derive Zipf's laws by assuming a model of how words are built up from letters and by applying a minimum effort approach to the word lengths and frequencies. (See Mandelbrot (1954, 1961), Cherry (1970), and Good (1965).)

Another approach is to define a branching probabilistic process. The resulting linear graph model (Laemmel (1973) and Shooman and Laemmel (1977)) can be used to derive a binomial distribution with one configuration, and a Zipf law model with a different configuration.

For the details of these derivations, the reader is referred to the cited references. The important point is that the validity of Zipf's law is further strengthened by these theoretical derivations. (Actually the experimental evidence is strong enough in its own right.)

Zipf's Laws Applied to Computer Language

In Table 8 we began our discussion of the analogies between natural language and computer language. In essence, the analogy is close enough so that we suspect at the outset that computer language will obey one of the original or generalized forms of Zipf's law. Other convincing evidence would be the development of a stochastic model similar to that discussed in the preceding section which generates computer programs. Of course, in the final analysis, proof is dependent on how well experimental data plotted on log-log paper fits Zipf's laws and by the prediction accuracy of any formulas developed in the analysis.

We have examined a number of computer programs and always find that some form of Zipf's law seems to fit the data fairly well. The data are listed in Table 9 and the Zipf plots for program 1 given in Figs. 14 and 16.

Table 9   Experimental Data on Computer Programs
and Zipf's Laws (Shooman (1978))

Program	Figures	Types	Tokens
1. PL/I Fibonacci: Numbers Program - 11 Lines long	3-8 Operators 3-9 Operands 3-10 Operators and Operands	12 9 21	31 Operators 24 Operands 55 Total
2. PL/I Student Grades Program - 27 lines long,	3-11 3-12 3-13	20 31 51	117 Operators 105 Operands 222 Total
3. MIKBUG - Executive Program for M6800 microprocessor	3-14	25 62 87	190 Operators 132 Operands 322 Total
4. PDP - 11 Assembly Language Programs	3-15 Operators	39	1572 Tokens
5. Variable Names in 3 PL/I Programs	3-16 Codes	50, 24, 34	370, 238, 193
6. FORTRAN Statement Types	3-17 3-18	40	200k, and 10k

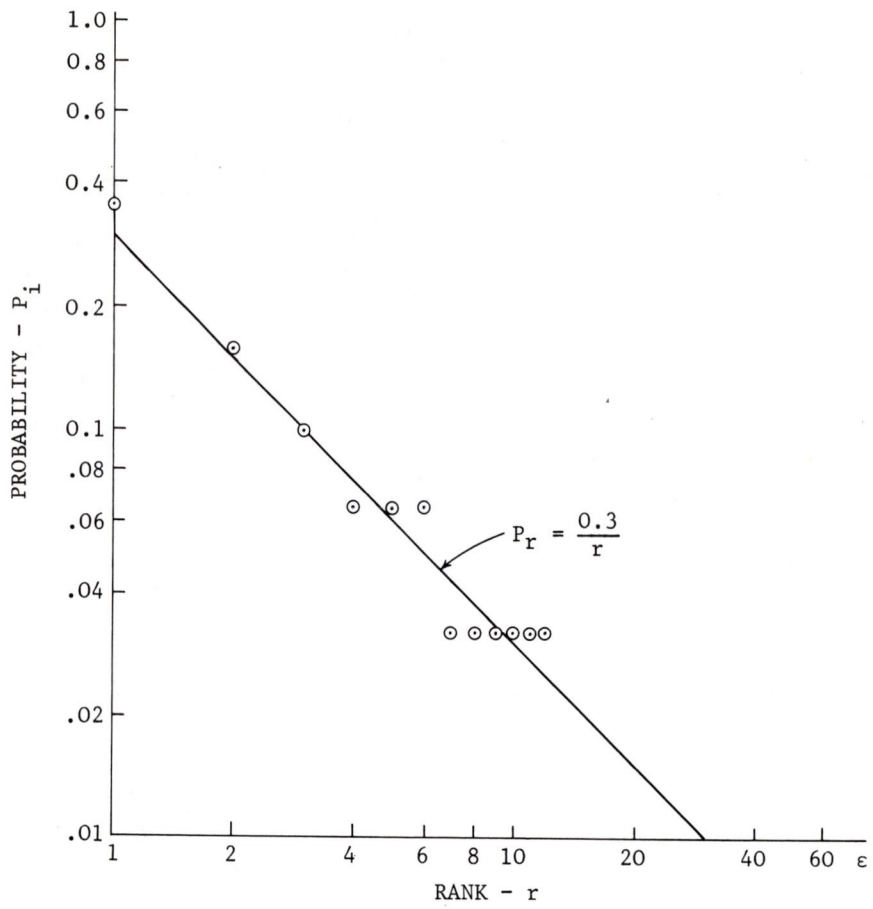

Fig. 14   Zipf Law Plot for Operators in Program No. 1.

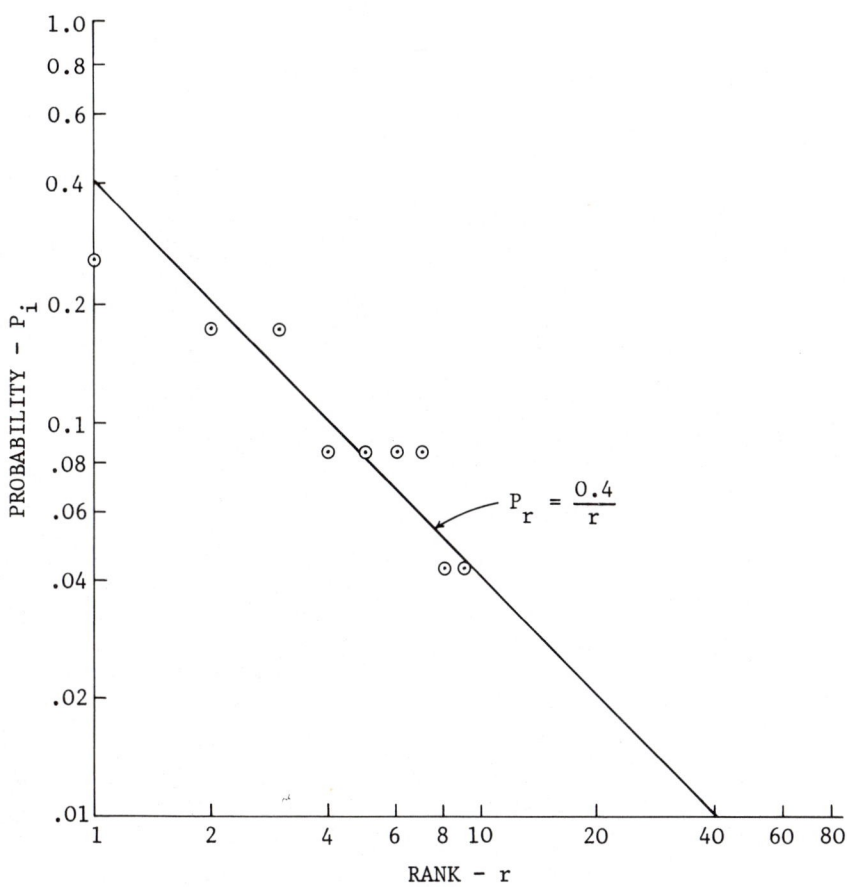

Fig. 15   Zipf Law Plot for Operands in Program No. 1.

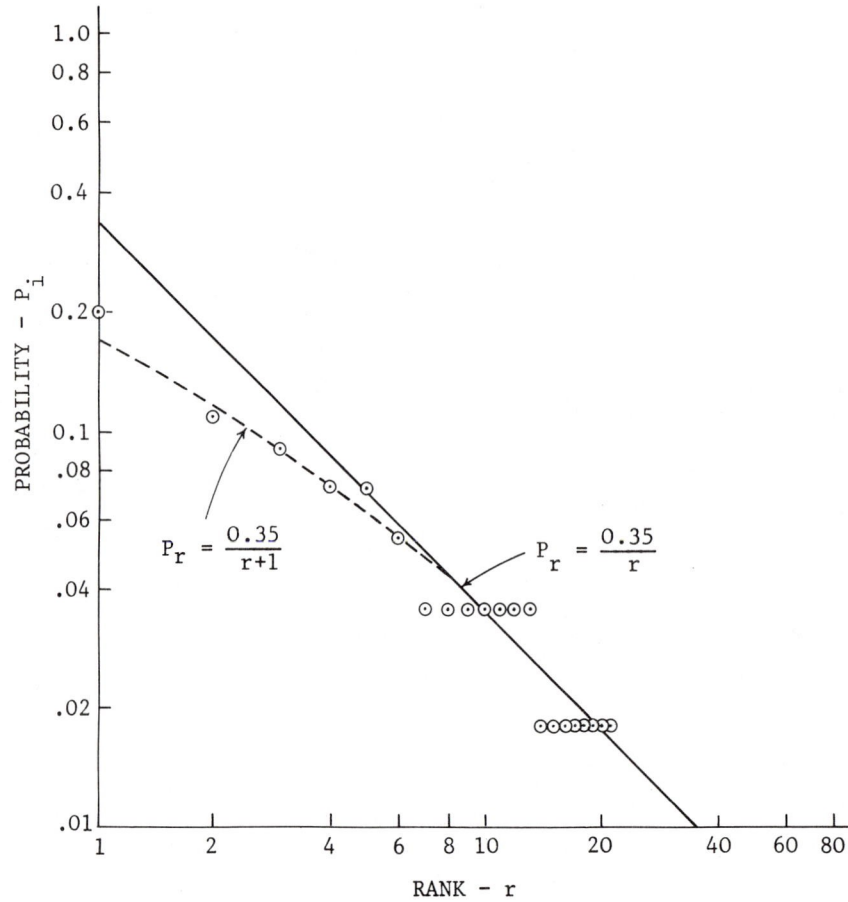

Fig. 16 Zipf Law Plot for Combined Operators
and Operands in Program No. 1.

SOFTWARE RELIABILITY

One method of initially estimating program length (number of tokens), remembering that we do not include certain nonexecutable code such as: comments, declares, assembler directives, etc., is to estimate the number of types. We assume the analyst initially has a complete description of the problem and that a partial analysis and choice of key algorithms has been made. An elementary approach might be to estimate the token size by

(1) Estimating the number of operator types which will be used in the language by the assigned programmers.

(2) Estimating the number of input variables, output variables, intermediate variables, and constants which will be needed.

(3) Summing the estimates of step (1) and (2) and substituting in Eq. 9.45.

Relationship to "Software Science"

The initial motivation for the application of Zipf's law to computer languages came from a review of Halstead's work (1975, 1977) on Software Physics. (which he now calls Software Science). Early in his work he arrives at a formula for program length.

$$L = \eta_1 \log_2 \eta_1 + \eta_2 \log_2 \eta_2 \tag{9.47}$$

where

$L \equiv$ Program length

$\eta_1 \equiv$ Number of operator types

$\eta_2 \equiv$ Number of operand types .

In terms of our notation the analogous quantities are

$$t = \eta_1 + \eta_2 \tag{9.48}$$

$$n = L \tag{9.49}$$

Note that Eq. 9.47 and Eq. 9.49 are of similar form. In fact, substitution of Eqs. 9.48 and 9.49 into Eq. 9.45 allows direct comparison.

$$L = (\eta_1 + \eta_2) \times (0.5772 + \ln(\eta_1 + \eta_2)) \tag{9.50}$$

We begin our comparison of Eqs. 9.45 and 9.50 by investigating certain limiting cases. For the case where $\eta_1 \gg \eta_2$ (or vice versa) and $\eta_1 = \eta_2$ the two formulas differ by about 30%.

A direct numerical comparison can be made between the two length formulas for the examples given in Table 9 and in Halstead's report (op. cit.). Such a comparison shows that both equations estimate the operator-operand length, knowing only t, within 15-20% of the actual count. For a theoretical derivation of the Halstead formula, see Shooman, op. cit.

Information Content of a Program

Whereas we can enter into almost endless debate on the meaning of a program, use of Shannon's information theory allows us to quantify the meaning of information. The applicable formula from Shannon's theory is that for the information content of a message. The information content is called the entropy, H, and has the units of bits. If we have a message which is selected from a set of i messages, each with a probability of occurrence, p_i, then the entropy is given by (see Pierce (1961), Shannon and Weaver (1975))

$$H = -\sum_{j=1}^{i} p_j \log_2 p_j = \sum_{j=1}^{i} p_j \log_2 (1/p_j) \qquad (9.51)$$

For computation it is convenient to remember that

$$\log_2 x = (\log_{10} x)/(\log_{10} 2) = 3.3219 \log_{10} x$$

$$\log_2 x = (\ln x)/(\ln 2) = 1.4427 \ln x$$

If all the messages are equiprobable, then $p_j = 1/i$, and Eq. 9.51 becomes

$$H = \log_2 i \qquad (9.52)$$

For illustration, suppose that our family of messages are the 16 different binary numbers we can express with a 4 digit binary number. In this case, i = 16, and if we assume $p_i = 1/16$, then Eq. 9.52 yields H = 4 bits. This example illustrates the appropriateness of the unit "bits" for H.

If the probabilities of each symbol are equal, then $p_j = 1/(\eta_1 + \eta_2)$, and the entropy is given by

$$H = N \log_2 (\eta_1 + \eta_2) \qquad (9.53)$$

In his work on "Software Physics", Halstead chooses to call this volume, V. (Also note that N = n = L in our previous notation.)

We now return to our Zipf's law model of a program and assume that the probabilities p_j are given by Zipf's law (Eq. 9.44, where $f_r = p_j$). It can be shown that (Laemmel (1973))

$$H = \frac{N}{\ln 2} \left(\frac{(\ln t)^2}{2(\ln t + 7/12)} + \ln(\ln t + 7/12) \right) \qquad (9.54)$$

This can be simplified to give for large t

$$H \approx \frac{N}{2} \log_2 t \qquad (9.55)$$

The minimum information content of a program is that taken by Halstead. He defines the minimum number of operators to be two, a function which does all the work of the program and an assignment symbol (equal sign). The minimum number of operands are the sum of the required input and output parameters. We denote these with an asterisk, and substitution in Eq. 9.53 yields the minimum information content, which Halstead calls the potential volume V^*.

$$\text{Min } \eta_1 = \eta_1^* = 2$$

$$\text{Min } \eta_2 = \eta_2^* = \Sigma \text{ input/output variables}$$

$$\text{Min } N = \eta_1^* + \eta_2^*$$

$$H_{min} = V^* = (2 + \eta_2^*) \log_2(2 + \eta_2^*) \qquad (9.56)$$

A direct extension of the concept of minimum volume is to define the level, ℓ, of a program as the ratio of minimum volume to actual volume

$$\ell = \frac{V^*}{V} \qquad (9.57)$$

Thus, the highest level program language approaches or reaches level unity, and lower level program languages rate between unity and zero on the scale which has been created.

Complexity Vs. Bugs and Development Time

The complexity measures developed in the preceding sections are useful in two ways: (1) they provide a metric which allows the comparison of the relative complexity of two different designs or algorithms, (2) when multiplied by an appropriate proportionality constant, they should provide estimates and predictions for the number of bugs and development effort of a program.

The Halstead Effort Measure, E, is directly proportional to the volume and inversely proportional to the level. This assumption yields E in mental discriminations.

$$E \sim V$$

$$E \sim \frac{1}{\ell}$$

$$E = \frac{V}{\ell} = \frac{V^2}{v^*} \tag{9.58}$$

Using Akiyama's data (1971) we plot number of bugs vs. I_T, n, E. The results are shown in Fig. 17 and Table 10.

Table 10   Comparison of Proportionality Constants

2×10^{-2} bugs per statement = 1×10^{-2} bugs/token

1×10^{-3} bugs per bit - yielding -10 bits/token

0.67×10^{-6} bugs/discrimination - yielding - 1.5×10^{4} disc/token

1.25×10^{-1} bugs/(decision + call) - yielding - 8×10^{-2} (dec. + call)/token

Further study of data is needed to choose among these hypotheses; however, use of one or more of these measures with the appropriate proportionality constant will probably yield a good rough initial estimate.

We now turn to the problem of relating programming time (man-hours) to program complexity measures.

The data previously discussed which appears in Table 1 was all based on the length hypothesis. Difficulties occur when the data from many different sources is studied if the language is not carefully specified so that all lengths can be expressed in terms of machine language instructions. For this reason, it would be preferable to state lengths in terms of tokens. This would force one to convert all the data to one well defined length metric. From Akiyama's data we find that his 25,000 step machine language program took 100 man months to produce. This time represented the entire development cycle, and extended from the initial phase of checking the specification to the final phase of field testing. Assuming that the 25,000 step program represents 50,000 tokens, we obtain a productivity rate of 500 tokens per man month. Assuming an average of 20 working days per month, this becomes 25 tokens per day. This is equivalent to 12.5 instructions per day which coincides well with the literature data. In a similar manner, we can relate the totals for the various hypotheses to the 100 man month figure as is done in Table 11.

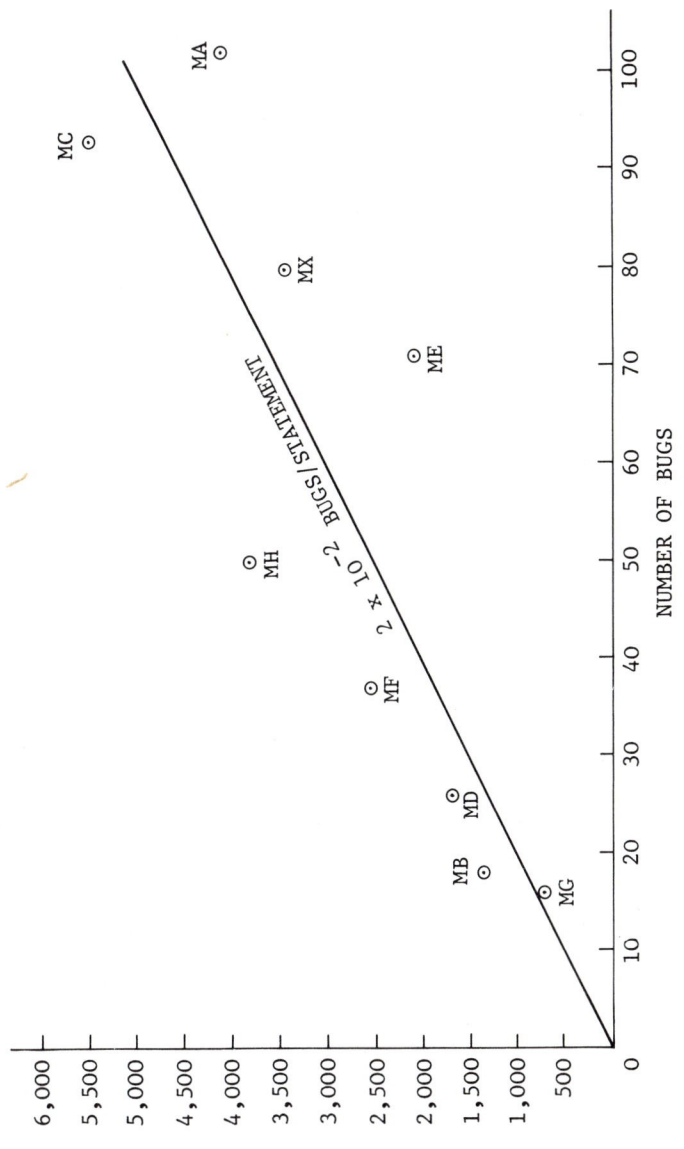

Fig. 17   Number of Bugs Vs. Number of
Machine Language Statements .

Table 11   Coefficients of Productivity.

Hypothesis	Total	Per man month	Per man day
Length	50,000 tokens	500 tokens/mm	25 tokens/md
Information	4.76×10^5 bits	4.76×10^3 bits/mm	2.38×10^2 bits/md
Effort	9.03×10^8 disc	9.03×10^6 disc/mm	4.52×10^5 disc/md
Decision/call	4.10×10^3 dec.	4.10×10^1 dec./mm	2.05 dec./md

SOFTWARE RELIABILITY

RELIABILITY THEORY

Introduction

Since its beginnings following WWII, reliability theory has
grown into an engineering science in its own right. (Also, see
Shooman (1968)). Much of the initial theory, engineering, and
management techniques centered about hardware; however, human and procedural elements of a system were often included.
Only since the late 60's has the term software reliability become popular, and sometimes people erroneously refer to reliability theory as hardware reliability to distinguish it from some
of the newer concepts and models being employed in the software
area.

The conventional approach to reliability is to decompose the
system into smaller subsystems and units, generally drawing a
reliability block diagram or graph to represent the structure.
Using combinatorial reliability, the system probability of success is expressed in terms of the probabilities of success of the
elements. Then, using failure rate models, the element probabilities of success are computed. These two concepts are combined to calculate the system reliability.

When the reliability or availability of repairable systems is
to be computed, Markov models are generally used to solve for
the needed probabilities.

Material in this Appendix has been extracted from Probabilistic Reliability, Shooman (1968), and readers desiring more
detail are referred to this text.

Cut-Set and Tie-Set Methods

A very efficient general method for computing the reliability
of any system not containing dependent failures can be developed
from the properties of the reliability graph. The reliability
graph consists of a set of branches which represent the n elements. There must be at least n branches in the graph, but
there can be more if the same branch must be repeated in more
than one path (A.1). The probability of element success is
written above each branch. The nodes of the graph tie the
branches together and form the structure. A path or tie set is
a group of branches which forms a connection between input and
output when traversed in the arrow direction. We shall primarily be concerned with minimal tie sets, which are those containing a minimum number of elements. If no node is traversed
more than once in tracing out a tie set, the tie set is minimal.

If a system has i minimal tie sets denoted by $T_1, T_2, \ldots, T_i$, then the system has a connection between input and output if at least one tie set is intact. The system reliability is thus given by the probability of the union of the events, tie set T_1 through T_i is good.

$$R = P(T_1 + T_2 + \cdots + T_i) \qquad (A.1)$$

One can define a cut set of a graph as a set of branches which interrupts all connections between input and output when removed from the graph. The minimal cut sets are a group of distinct cut sets containing a minimum number of terms. All system failures can be represented by the removal of at least one minimal cut set from the graph. The probability of system failure is, therefore, given by the probability that at least one minimal cut set fails. If we let $C_1, C_2, \ldots, C_j$ represent the j minimal cut sets and $\overline{C}_j$ the failure of the jth cut set, the system reliability is given by

$$P_j = P(\overline{C}_1 + \overline{C}_2 + \cdots + \overline{C}_j)$$
$$R = 1 - P_j = 1 - P(\overline{C}_1 + \overline{C}_2 + \cdots + \overline{C}_2) \qquad (A.2)$$

As an example of the application of cut-set and tie-set analysis, we consider the graph given in Fig. A.1. The following combinations of branches are all minimal tie sets of the system:

$$T_1 = x_1 x_2 \quad T_2 = x_3 x_4 \quad T_3 = x_1 x_6 x_4 \quad T_4 = x_3 x_5 x_2$$

From Eq. A.1

$$R = P(T_1 + T_2 + T_3 + T_4) = P(x_1 x_2 + x_3 x_4 + x_1 x_6 x_4 + x_3 x_5 x_2)$$
$$\qquad (A.3)$$

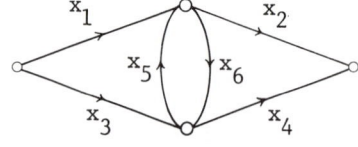

Fig. A.1 Reliability graph for a six-element system.

Similarly we may list the minimal cut sets of the structure

$$C_1 = \bar{x}_1\bar{x}_3 \quad C_2 = \bar{x}_2\bar{x}_4 \quad C_3 = \bar{x}_1\bar{x}_5\bar{x}_4 \quad C_4 = \bar{x}_3\bar{x}_6\bar{x}_2$$

Using Eq. A. 2

$$R = 1 - P(\overline{C}_1 + \overline{C}_2 + \overline{C}_3 + \overline{C}_4) = 1 - P(\bar{x}_1\bar{x}_3 + \bar{x}_2\bar{x}_4 + \bar{x}_1\bar{x}_5\bar{x}_4$$
$$+ \bar{x}_3\bar{x}_6\bar{x}_2)$$

$$(A. 4)$$

In a large problem, there will be many cut sets and tie sets, and although Eqs. (A. 1) and (A. 2) are easily formulated, the expansion of either equation is a formidable task. Several approximations which are useful in simplifying the computations can be utilized (M. Shooman and M. Messinger (1967) and Shooman (1968)).

Failure Rate Models

The previous section has shown how one constructs a combinatorial reliability model which expresses system reliability in terms of element reliability. This section introduces failure models for the system elements. These element failure models are related to life-test results and failure-rate data via probability theory.

Part failure data are generally obtained from two sources: the failure times of various items in a population placed on a life test, or repair reports listing operating hours of replaced parts in equipment already in field use. Experience has shown that a very good way to present these data is to compute and plot either the failure density function or the hazard rate as a function of time.

The data we are dealing with are a sequence of times to failure, but the failure density function and the hazard rate are continuous variables.

We begin by defining piecewise-continuous failure density and hazard-rate functions in terms of the data. It can be shown that these discrete functions approach the continuous functions in the limit as the number of data becomes large and the interval between failure times approaches zero. Assume that our data describe a set of N items placed in operation at time t=0. As time progresses, items fail, and at any time t the number of survivors is $n(t)$. The data density function (also called empirical density function) defined over the time interval $t_i < t \leq t_i + \Delta t_i$ is given by the ratio of the number of failures occurring in the interval to the size of the original population, divided by the length of the time interval.

M. SHOOMAN

$$f_d(t) = \frac{[n(t_i) - n(t_i + \Delta t_i)]/N}{\Delta t_i} \quad \text{for } t_i < t \le t_i \, \Delta t_i$$

(A. 5)

Similarly, the data hazard rate (sometimes called hazard or failure rate) over the interval $t_i < t \le t_i + \Delta t_i$ is defined as the ratio of the number of failures occurring in the time interval to the number of survivors at the beginning of the time interval, divided by the length of the time interval.

$$z_d(t) = \frac{[n(t_i) - n(t_i + \Delta t_i)]/n(t_i)}{\Delta t_i} \quad \text{for } t_i < t \le t_i + \Delta t_i$$

(A. 6)

Since the numerators of both Eqs. (A. 5) and (A. 6) are dimensionless, both $f_d(t)$ and $z_d(t)$ have the dimensions of inverse time (generally the time unit is hours).

The failure data for a life test run on a group of 10 hypothetical electronic components are given in Table A. 1. The functions $f_d(t)$ and $z_d(t)$ computed from the data appear in Fig. A. 2a, b.

Since $f_d(t)$ is a density function, we can define a data failure distribution function and a data success distribution function by

$$F_d(t) = \int_0^t f_d(\zeta)d\zeta$$

(A. 7)

$$R_d(t) = 1 - F_d(t) = 1 - \int_0^t f_d(\zeta)d\zeta$$

(A. 8)

where ζ is just a dummy variable of integration.

The functions $F_d(t)$ and $R_d(t)$ are computed for the preceding example by appropriate integration of Fig. A. 2 and are given in Fig. A. 2. From Eqs. A.5-A.8 $R_d(t_i) = n(t_i)/N$.

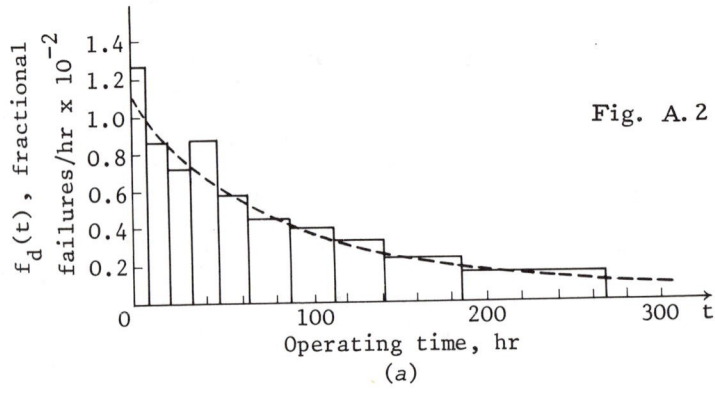

Fig. A. 2

$f_d(t)$, fractional failures/hr x 10^{-2}

Operating time, hr

(a)

410

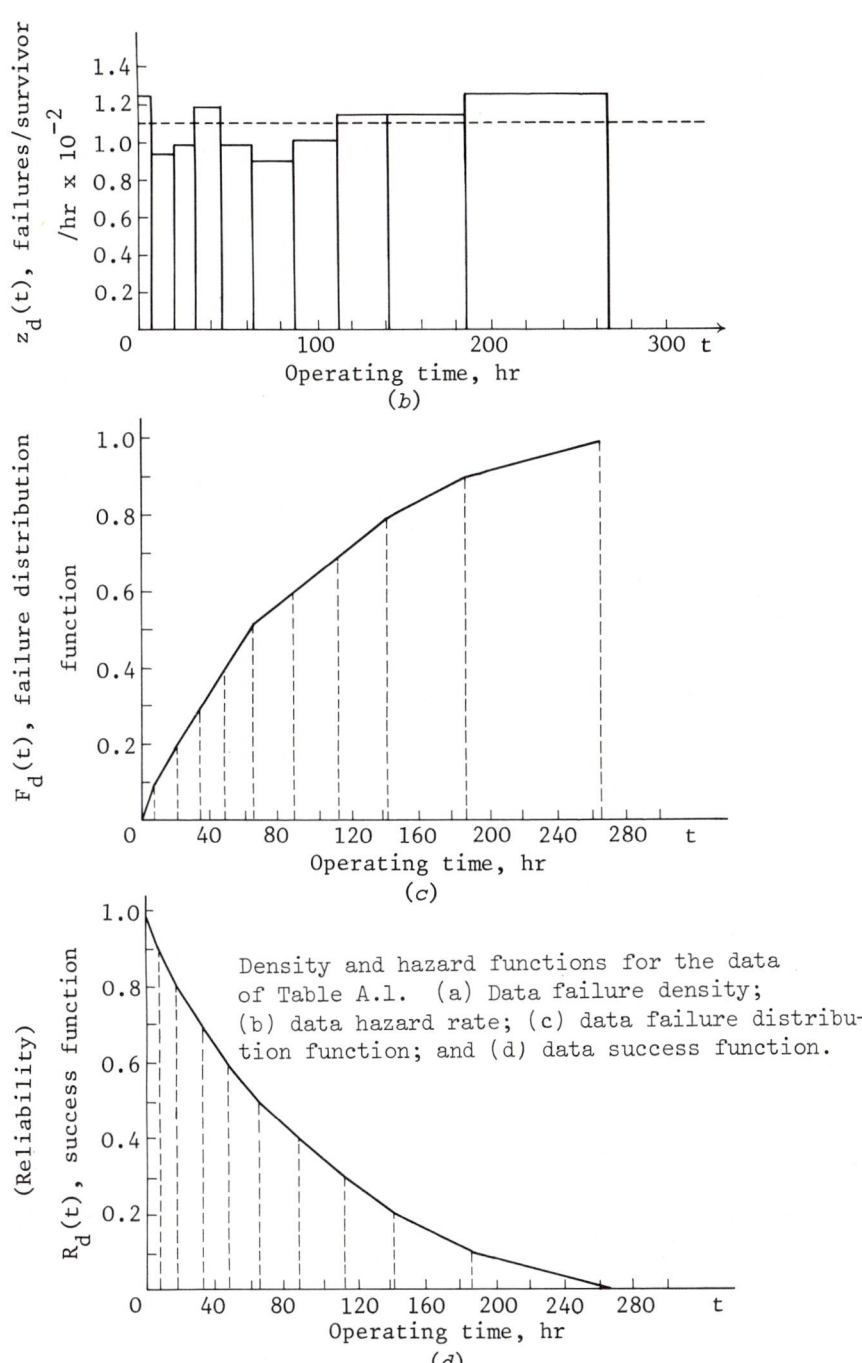

Density and hazard functions for the data of Table A.1. (a) Data failure density; (b) data hazard rate; (c) data failure distribution function; and (d) data success function.

M. SHOOMAN

Combining Eqs. (A. 5) through (A. 9) and letting $\Delta t \to 0$ yields

$$z(t) = \frac{f(t)}{R(t)} = -\frac{1}{R(t)} \frac{dR(t)}{dt} \qquad (A.9)$$

Solving differential equation (A. 10), along with initial condition, $R(0) = 1$ yields

$$R(t) = \exp\left[-\int_0^t z(\zeta)d\zeta\right] \qquad (A.10)$$

Hazard Model and Handbook Failure Data

After plotting and examining failure data for several years, people began to recognize several modes of failure. Early in the lifetime of equipment or a part, there are a large number of failures due to initial weakness or defects: poor insulation, weak parts, bad assembly, poor fits, etc. During the middle period of equipment operation fewer failures take place, but it is difficult to determine their cause. In general they seem to occur when the environmental stresses exceed the design strengths of the part or equipment. It is difficult to predict the environmental-stress amplitudes or the part strengths as deterministic functions of time; thus the middle-life failures are often called random failures. As the item reaches old age, things begin to deteriorate, and many failures occur. This failure region is quite naturally called the wearout region. Typical $f(t)$ and $z(t)$ curves which illustrate these three modes of behavior are shown in Fig. A. 3, often such a $z(t)$ is called a bathtub curve. (Carhart (1953)).

Table A.1 Failure data for ten hypothetical electronic components

Failure number	Operating time, hr
1	8
2	20
3	34
4	46
5	63
6	86
7	111
8	141
9	186
10	266

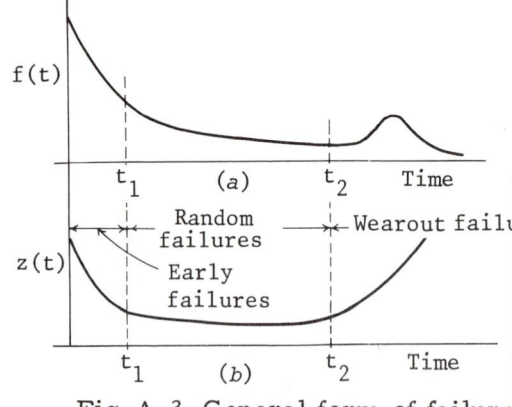

Fig. A. 3 General form of failure curves. (a) Failure density; (b) hazard rate.

412

The early failures, also called initial failures or infant mortality, appear as decreasing $z(t)$ and $f(t)$ functions. The random failure, or constant-hazard-rate mode, is characterized by an approximately constant $z(t)$ and a companion $f(t)$ which is approximately exponential. In the wearout, or rising-failure-rate region, the $z(t)$ function increases $f(t)$ has a humped appearance.

On first consideration it might appear that if failure data and graphs such as Fig. A.2 are available, there is no need for a mathematical model. However, in drawing conclusions from test data on the behavior of other similar components, it is necessary to fit the failure data with a mathematical model.

Constant Hazard

If a constant hazard rate $z(t) = \lambda$ is assumed,

$$z(t) = \lambda \tag{A.11}$$

$$f(t) = \lambda e^{-\lambda t} \tag{A.12}$$

$$R(t) = e^{-\lambda t} = 1 - F(t) \tag{A.13}$$

Linearly Increasing Hazard

When wear or deterioration is present, the hazard will increase as time passes. The simplest increasing-hazard model that can be postulated is one in which the hazard increases linearly with time. Assuming that $z(t) = Kt$ for $t \geq 0$ yields

$$z(t) = Kt \tag{A.14}$$

$$f(t) = Kt e^{-Kt^2/2} \tag{A.15}$$

$$R(t) = e^{-Kt^2/2} \tag{A.16}$$

Mean Time to Failure

It is often convenient to characterize a failure model or set of failure data by a single parameter. One generally uses the mean time to failure or the mean time between failures for this purpose. If we have life-test information on a population of n items with failure times $t_1, t_2, \ldots, t_n$, then the MTTF is defined by

$$\text{MTTF} = \frac{1}{n} \sum_{i=1}^{n} t_i \tag{A.17}$$

M. SHOOMAN

Often the term meantime between failures, MTBF is used inter-
changeably with the term MTTF; however, strictly speaking the
MTBF term is more appropriate when one is discussing a renewal situation.

If one is discussing a hazard model, the MTTF for the probability distribution defined by the model is given by

$$MTTF = E(t) = \int_0^\infty tf(t)dt \tag{A.18}$$

One can express Eq. (A.18) by a simpler computational expression involving the reliability function. (For the derivation, see
M. Shooman (1968), p. 197.)

$$MTTF = \int_0^\infty R(t)dt \tag{A.19}$$

As an example of the use of Eq. (A.19), the MTTF for several different hazards will be computed. For a single component with a constant hazard,

$$MTTF = \int_0^\infty e^{-\lambda t} = \frac{e^{-\lambda t}}{-\lambda}\bigg|_0^\infty = \frac{1}{\lambda} \tag{A.20}$$

For a linearly increasing hazard,

$$MTTF = \int_0^\infty e^{-Kt^2}dt = \frac{\Gamma(\frac{1}{2})}{2\sqrt{K/2}} = \sqrt{\frac{\pi}{2K}} \tag{A.21}$$

Markov Models

The basic properties of Markov models are discussed in
Shooman (1968). In this section, we shall briefly review some of
the assumptions necessary for formulation of a Markov model and
show how it can be used to make reliability computations.

In order to formulate a Markov model, we must first define
all the mutually exclusive states of the system.

For example, in a system composed of a single, nonreparable
element x_1 there are two possible states: $s_0 = x_1$, the element is
good, and $s_1 = \bar{x}_1$, the element is bad. The states of the system at
$t = 0$ are called the initial states, and those representing a final or
equilibrium state are called final states. The set of Markov state

equations describes the probabilistic transitions from the initial to the final states.

The transition probabilities must obey the following two rules:

1. The probability of transition in time Δt from one state to another is given by $z(t)\,\Delta t$, where $z(t)$ is the hazard associated with the two states in question. If all the $z_i(t)$'s are constant, $z_i(t) = \lambda_i$, and the model is called homogeneous. If any hazards are time functions, the model is called non-homogeneous.

2. The probabilities of more than one transition in time Δt are infinitesimals of a higher order and can be neglected.

For the example under discussion the state-transition equations can be formulated using the above rules. The probability of being in state s_o at time $t + \Delta t$ is written $P_{s_o}(t + \Delta t)$. This is given by the probability that the system is in state s_o at time t, $P_{s_o}(t)$, times the probability of no failure in time Δt, $1 - z(t)\Delta t$, plus the probability of being in state s_1 at time t, $P_{s_1}(t)$, times the probability of repair in time Δt, which equals zero.

The resulting equation is

$$P_{s_o}(t + \Delta t) = [1 - z(t)\Delta t]P_{s_o}(t) + 0 P_{s_1}(t) \qquad (A.22)$$

Similarly, the probability of being in state s_1 at $t + \Delta t$ is given by

$$P_{s_1}(t + \Delta t) = [z(t)\Delta t]P_{s_o}(t) + 1 P_{s_1}(t) \qquad (A.23)$$

The transition probability, $z(t)\Delta t$, is the probability of failure (change from state s_o to s_1), and the probability of remaining in state s_1 is unity. (Conventionally, state s_1 would be called an absorbing state since transitions out of the state are not permitted.) One can summarize the transition equations (A.22) and (A.23) by writing the transition matrix given in Table A.2

Table A.2 State transition matrix for a single element

Initial states	Final states	
	s_o	s_1
s_o	$1 - z(t)\Delta t$	$z(t)\Delta t$
s_1	0	1

Note that it is a property of transition matrices that its rows must sum to unity. Rearrangement of Eqs. (A.22) and (A.23) yields

$$\frac{P_{s_o}(t + \Delta t) - P_{s_o}(t)}{\Delta t} = - z(t)P_{s_o}(t)$$

$$\frac{P_{s_1}(t + \Delta t) - P_{s_1}(t)}{\Delta t} = z(t)P_{s_o}(t)$$

Passing to a limit as Δt becomes small, we obtain

$$\frac{dP_{s_o}(t)}{dt} + z(t)P_{s_o}(t) = 0 \qquad (A.24)$$

$$\frac{dP_{s_1}(t)}{dt} = z(t)P_{s_o}(t) \qquad (A.25)$$

Equations (A.24) and (A.25) can be solved in conjunction with the appropriate initial conditions for $P_{s_o}(t)$ and $P_{s_1}(t)$, the probabilities of ending up in state s_o or state s_1, respectively. The most common initial condition is that the system is good at t = 0, that is, $P_{s_o}(t = 0) = 1$ and $P_{s_1}(t = 0) = 0$.

It is often easier to characterize Markov models by a graph composed of nodes representing system states and branches labeled with transition probabilities. Such a Markov graph for the problem described by Eqs. (A.22) and (A.23) or Table A.2 is given in Fig. A.4

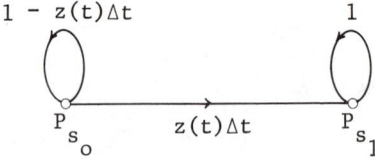

Fig. A.4 Markov graph for a single nonrepairable element.

Repairable Systems

In general, whenever the average repair cost in time and money of a piece of equipment is a fraction of the initial equipment cost, one considers system repair. If such a system can be rapidly returned to service, the effect of the failure is minimized. Obvious examples are such equipment as a television set, an automobile, or a radar installation.

In order to describe the beneficial features of repair in a system that tolerates shutdown times, a new system function called availability is introduced. The availability function, $A(t)$, is defined as the probability that the system is operating at time t. By contrast, the reliability function $R(t)$ is the probability that the system has operated over the interval 0 to t. Thus, if $A(250)$ = 0.95, then if 100 such systems are operated for 250 hr, on the average, 95 will be operative when 250 hr are reached and 5 will be undergoing various stages of repairs. The availability function contains no information on how many (if any) failure-repair cycles have occurred prior to 250 hr. On the other hand, if $R(250)$ = 0.95, then if 100 such systems are operated for 250 hr, on the average, 95 will have operated without failure for 250 hr and 5 will have failed at some time within this interval. It is immaterial in which stage of the first or subsequent failure-repair cycles the five failed systems are.

Reliability and Availability Functions

As long as the failure and repair density functions are exponential, i.e., constant hazard, we can structure Markov repair models, as done in the previous section. The reliability and availability models will differ.

The reliability of a single component x_1 with constant failure hazard λ and constant repair hazard μ can be derived easily using a Markov model. The Markov graph is given in Fig. A.5. Note that repair in no way influences the reliability graph. Element failure $\bar{x}_1$ is an absorbing state, and once it is reached, the system never returns to x_1.

If we wish to study the availability, we must make a different Markov graph. The Markov graph is given in Fig. A.6 and the differential equations and state probabilities in Eq. (A.26).

$$\dot{P}_{s_o} + \lambda P_{s_o} = \mu P_{s_1} \qquad \dot{P}_{s_1} + \mu P_{s_1} = \lambda P_{s_o} \qquad (A.26)$$

$$P_{s_o}(0) = 1 \qquad P_{s_1}(0) = 0$$

Solution yields the probabilities

$$P_{s_o}(t) = \frac{\mu}{\lambda + \mu} + \frac{\lambda}{\lambda + \mu} \, e^{-(\lambda + \mu)t} \qquad (A.27)$$

$$P_{s_1}(t) = \frac{\mu}{\lambda + \mu} - \frac{\lambda}{\lambda + \mu} \, e^{-(\lambda + \mu)t}$$

By definition, the availability is the probability that the system is good, $P_{s_o}(t)$.

$$A(t) = P_{s_o}(t) = \frac{\mu}{\lambda + \mu} + \frac{\lambda}{\lambda + \mu} \, e^{-(\lambda + \mu)t} \qquad (A.28)$$

The availability function given in Eq. (A.28) is plotted in Fig. A.7.

An important difference between $A(t)$ and $R(t)$ is their steady-state behavior. As t becomes large, all reliability functions approach zero, whereas availability functions reach some steady-state value.

In the normal case, the mean repair time $1/\mu$ is much smaller than the time to failure $1/\lambda$, and we can expand the steady-state part of Eq. (A.28) in a series and approximate by truncation

$$A_{ss}(t) = A(\infty) = \frac{1}{1 + \lambda/\mu} = 1 - \frac{\lambda}{\mu} + \frac{\lambda^2}{2\mu^2} + \cdots \approx 1 - \frac{\lambda}{\mu} \qquad (A.29)$$

Thus, if we use a component with an MTTF of 10^4 hr, a little over 1 year, and a mean repair time of 100 hr (about 4 days), then from Eqs. (A.20) and (A.29) we obtain a steady state availability of ≈ 0.99.

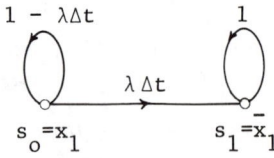

Fig. A.5 Markov graph for the reliability of a single component with repair.

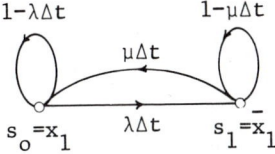

Fig. A. 6 Markov graph for the availability of a single component with repair.

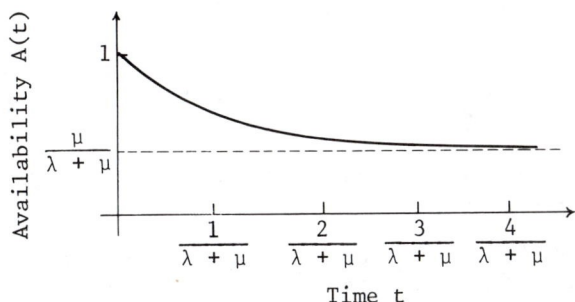

Fig. A. 7 Availability function for a single component.

REFERENCES

Akiyama, F. (1971). An Example of Software System Debugging. IFIP Congress 71, Ljubljana, Yugoslavia. pp. 353-359.

Bailey, N.T.J. (1951). On Estimating The Size of Mobile Populations from Recapture Data. Biometrika 38, pp. 293-306.

Brooks, F.P., Jr. (1975). The Mythical Man-Month. Addison-Wesley Pub. Co., Reading, Mass.

Carhart, R.R. (1953). A Survey of the Current Status of the Reliability Problem. Rand Corp. Res. Mem. RM-1131, Aug. 14, 1953.

Cherry, C. (1970). On Human Communication. M.I.T. Press, Second Edition.

Dickson, J., Hesse, J., Kientz, A., and Shooman, M. (1972). Quantitative Analysis of Software Reliability. Annual Reliability Symposium Proceedings, IEEE.

Feller, W. (1957). An Introduction to Probability Theory and Its Applications. Vol. 1, 2nd Edition, John Wiley and Sons, Inc., New York, New York.

Good, L.J. (1965). The Estimation of Probabilities. An Essay on Modern Bayesian Methods. M.I.T. Press, p. 70.

Halstead, M.H. (1975). Software Physics: Basic Principles, IBM Research Report RJ 1582, T.J. Watson Research Center, Yorktown Heights, N.Y.

Halstead, M.H. (1977). Elements of Software Sciences, Elsiver North Holland, N.Y.

Hymann, M. (1973). IBM, Morris Plains, N.J. Private communication, Summer 1973.

Itoh, D. and Izutani, T. (1973). FADEBUG-I, A New Tool for Program Debugging. 1973 IEEE Symposium on Computer Software Reliability (1973 SCSR), Cat. No. 73 CHO741-9 CSR, p. 38.

Jelinski, J. and Moranda, P.B. (1972). Software Reliability Research. In Probabilistic Models for Software, Ed. Freiberger, W., pp. 485-502, Academic Press, New York.

Jolley, L. (1961). Summation of Series. Dover Publications, N.Y. p. 35, n. 200 and p. 14, n.70.

Laemmel, A. (1973). Study of General Digital Codes with Emphasis on Signal Compression. Report No. PIBEP-73-125, Polytechnic Institute of Brooklyn, Farmingdale, N.Y.

Mandelbrot, B. (1954). On Recurrent Noise Limiting Coding. In Proceedings of the Symposium on Information Networks, p. 205, Polytechnic Press, Brooklyn, N.Y.

Mandelbrot, B. (1961). On the Theory of Word Frequencies and on Related Markovian Models of Discourse. In Proceedings of Symposia in Applied Mathematics, Vol. XI, p. 190, American Mathematical Society, Providence, R.I.

McCabe, T.J. (1976). A Complexity Measure. IEEE Trans. on Software Engineering, Dec. 1976, p. 308.

Mills, H.D., Ditto, F.H., Hurley, J.S., Kessler, M.M. (1970). SAFEGUARD Code Certificate Memo. IBM/FSD Report for BTL, Sept. 18, 1970.

Miyamoto, S. (1975). Software Reliability in Online Real Time Environment. Proceedings 1975 Intl. Conf. on Reliable Software, IEEE Cat. No. 75CMO940-7CSR, p. 194.

Musa, J.D. (1975). A Theory of Software Reliability and Its Application. IEEE Trans. on Software Engineering, Vol.SE-1, No. 3, Sept. 1975, p. 312.

Pierce, J.R. (1961). Symbols, Signals, and Noise. Harper and Row, N.Y.

Rudner, B. (1976). Seeding/Tagging Estimation of Software Errors: Models and Estimates. Research Report, Polytechnic Institute of New York, Spring 1976.

Schick, G.J. and Wolverton, R.W. (1972). Assessment of Software Reliability. 11th Annual Meeting, German Operations Research Society, Hamberg, Germany.

Shannon, C. and Weaver, W. (1975). The Mathematical Theory of Communication. Un. of Illinois Press, Urbana, Ill.

Shooman, M. and Messinger, M. (1976). Reliability Approximations for Complex Structures. Proceedings of the 1967 Annual Symposium on Reliability, Jan. 10-12, 1967, Washington, D.C. pp. 292-301.

Shooman, M.L. (1968). Probabilistic Reliability: An Engineering Approach. McGraw-Hill Book Co., 1968.

M. SHOOMAN

Shooman, M.L. (1972). Probabilistic Models for Software Reliability Prediction in Statistical Computer Performance Evaluation, Ed. Frieberger, W., pp. 485-502. Academic Press, N.Y.

Shooman, M.L. (1973). Software Reliability: Analysis and
Prediction. NATO Conference on System Reliability, Un. of
Liverpool. (Proceedings to be published by American Elsiver
Pub. Co. in 1974.)

Shooman, M.L. and Bolsky, B.I. (1975). Types, Distributions,
and Test and Correction Times for Programming Errors. 1975
ICRS, p. 347.

Shooman, M.L. and Natarajan, S. (1976a). Effect of Manpower
Deployment and Bug Generation on Software Error Models In
Proceedings 1976 MRI Symposium on Computer Software Engineer-
ing, pp. 155-170. Polytechnic Press, Brooklyn, N.Y.

Shooman, M.L. (1976b). Structural Models for Software Reliability Prediction. Second Intl. Conf. on Software Engineering,
13-15 October, 1976, IEEE Cat. No. 76CM1125-4C, pp. 268-280.

Shooman, M. and Laemmel (1977). Communication Theory, Information Theory, Statistical Theory of Computer Programs. Digest
of Papers, Fall COMPCON, Sept. 6-9, 1977.

Shooman, M.L. (1978). Software Engineering: Reliability,
Design, Management. Polytechnic Institute of New York, Class
Notes for CS606.

Shooman, M.L. (1980). Software Engineering: Reliability,
Design, Management. McGraw-Hill Book Co., N.Y.

Trivedi, A.K. and Shooman, M.L. (1975) Computer Software Reliability: Many State Markov Modeling Techniques. Polytechnic
Institute of New York, Report No. POLY-EE/EP-75-005-EER 116.

Zipf, G.K. (1965). The Psycho-biology of Language: An Introduction to Dynamic Philology. First Edition 1935 by Houghton
Miffin Co., First M.I.T. Press paperback edition, 1965.

ANNOTATED BIBLIOGRAPHY

S.K. Shrivastava

University of Newcastle upon Tyne

INTRODUCTION

This bibliography is divided into eight sections. The first section contains a list of journals and conferences relevant to the topics discussed in this book; also included are references to some text books and papers which present an overall picture of reliability and integrity. The second section covers reliable computer system architecture while the third section deals with hardware reliability modelling, test generation and diagnosis. The fourth section covers the subject of information protection. The fifth section covers the topic of system specification and validation. The sixth section contains references to a selection of papers that deal with the structure of reliable software systems. Papers which concentrate on system structuring have been selected. The seventh section deals with the modelling of software reliability, and finally, the last section contains references to papers on the reliability, integrity, recovery and auditing of operating systems, real time systems and data bases.

1 GENERAL REFERENCES

Listed here are the journals and conferences that are noted for high quality research papers and review articles on the subject of computer system reliability and integrity. Also included are some papers and text books which provide an overall view of this subject.

1.1 Journals

(i) IEEE Transactions on Computers - a prime source of references for hardware reliability and computer architecture.
(ii) IEEE Transactions on Reliability - occasionally contains articles on reliability modelling and analysis of computer systems.
(iii) IEEE Transactions on Software Engineering - a source of references for all aspects of software reliability.
(iv) Communications of the ACM - same as above.

(v) The Computer Journal - same as above.
(vi) Software: Practice and Experience - same as above.
(vii) ACM Transactions on Database Systems - the best source for papers on data bases.
(viii) ACM Computing Surveys - contains survey and tutorial articles.

1.2 Conferences

(i) IEEE Int. Symposium on Fault-Tolerant Computing - held annually, this is the main source for the latest research ideas on hardware aspects of computer system reliability; occasionally contains papers on the software aspects.
(ii) IEEE Symposium on Computer Architecture - held annually, contains papers on reliable system architectures.
(iii) Int. Conf. on Software Engineering - held every other year, for all aspects of software reliability. Selected papers from the conference are usually published in the IEEE Transactions on Software Engineering.
(iv) AFIPS National Computer Conf. - held annually, usually contains papers on computer system reliability and integrity.
(v) IFIP Congress - held every third year, noted for the state of the art papers.
(vi) ACM SIGMOD Conf. (SIGMOD stands for Special Interest Group on the Management of Data) - held annually, contains papers on the recovery, integrity and reliability modelling of data bases.
(vii) Int. VLDB Conf. (VLDB stands for Very Large Data Bases) - held annually, contains papers on all aspects of data bases.

1.3 Gibbons, T.K. Integrity and recovery in computer systems. NCC Publications (UK) and Hayden Book Company (USA), 1976.

This book gives a concise and easy to read account of current practices for integrity and recovery in commercial installations. There are not many books available on this subject; at £4.50, this book is value for money.

1.4 Randell, B., Lee, P.A. and Treleaven, P.C. Reliability issues in computing system design. ACM Computing Surveys, 10,2, pp. 123-165, June 1978.

This paper presents an analysis of the various problems involved in the design of highly reliable computing systems. Highlights of the paper are: (i) a discussion on the fundamental role of system structuring in understanding and mastering complex systems, (ii) use of an information flow model (based on the work of Davies and Bjork, see entries 6.1 and 6.2) to describe recovery strategies and (iii) a unified and concise description of several reliable computing systems.

ANNOTATED BIBLIOGRAPHY

1.5 Verhofstad, J.S.M. Recovery techniques for data base systems. ACM Computing Surveys, 10,2, pp. 167-195, June 1978.

This paper contains a comprehensive survey of recovery techniques used in data base systems. The techniques reviewed include: (i) salvation programs, (ii) incremental dumping, (iii) audit trails, (iv) differential files, (v) backup and current version, (vi) multiple copies, and (vii) careful replacement.

1.6 Nielsen, N.R. and Ruder, B. Computer system integrity safeguards. Information Processing 77, North Holland (Proc. of IFIP Congress, Toronto, Aug. 1977), pp. 337-342.

In this interesting paper, the components of 'computer system integrity' are classified as security (protecting system integrity from compromise), audit (verification of integrity and monitoring the correct application of proper processing), and recovery (restoring system integrity). Two hitherto unexplored aspects of integrity are considered: to identify safeguard measures that would have been effective in preventing actual reported computer system integrity violations, and to evaluate the effectiveness of the identified safeguards. A total of 294 reported system integrity violation cases were analysed by the authors and their colleagues and the main results of the work are reported in this paper. The authors have classified the integrity safeguards into four categories: (i) management safeguards, (ii) system safeguards, (iii) industrial security safeguards, and (iv) educational and legal safeguards. Included is a discussion on the effectiveness of these safeguards (assuming they were employed) in preventing the reported integrity violations. The work reported here deserves careful reading.

1.7 Avizienis, A. Fault-tolerant computing - progress, problems, and prospects. Information Processing 77, North Holland (Proc. of IFIP Congress, Toronto, Aug. 1977), pp. 405-420.

Information processing systems that continue to provide the expected service despite faults in the system are termed fault-tolerant. This paper presents an excellent review of the methodology of fault-tolerant system design. The topics covered include: fault classification, fault masking, fault detection, hardware controlled recovery systems, software controlled recovery systems, and modelling and analysis of fault-tolerant systems. In the author's view the current 'roadblocks' to fault-tolerant computing are (i) lack of continuity - many of the techniques are never disclosed (trade secrecy) thus resulting in the repetition of many mistakes of the past, (ii) lack of cost/benefit measures, (iii) lack of specifications and acceptance tests, (iv) fragmentation of efforts, (v) inertia in the design process, and (vi) resistance to potential impact - successful introduction of fault-tolerance may cause some de-emphasis of several currently flourishing activities. The paper contains a valuable list of 56 references.

1.8 Dahl, O.J., Dijkstra, E.W. and Hoare, C.A.R. Structured programming. Academic Press, 1972.

This book needs no introduction. The importance of well structured software can not be overstressed.

1.9 Myers, G.J. Software reliability: principles and practices. John Wiley, 1976.

This book is divided into 4 parts: (i) concepts of software reliability - contains a general introduction to the subject, (ii) designing reliable software - contains a discussion on user requirements and their specification, and on systematic programming methods, (iii) software testing, and (iv) additional topics in software reliability - topics include management techniques, reliability modelling and software support systems. This book collects together, for the first time, much of the material that is dispersed in journals and proceedings, and as such is recommended.

1.10 Text books on reliability theory.
(i) Shooman, M.L. Probabilistic reliability: an engineering approach. McGraw-Hill, 1968.
(ii) Amstadler, B. Reliability mathematics. McGraw-Hill, 1971.

A good understanding of the basics of reliability theory is essential for appreciating the papers on hardware reliability modelling (section 3) and software reliability modelling (section 7). The first book is justly regarded as the standard text book on reliability theory. However, less mathematically inclined readers may prefer the second book.

2 RELIABLE HARDWARE SYSTEM ARCHITECTURE

The first two papers in this section present overall views on the design of reliable hardware systems. The second paper is particularly recommended as it presents design guidelines for achieving a given degree of system reliability. The remaining eight papers describe particular computer system architectures that have been developed to support a high degree of reliability. It should be noted that quite often the software needed for controlling recovery and reconfiguration of the system forms an integral part of the system; as such, it is not always possible to describe the hardware of a system without mentioning the associated software. Nevertheless, the papers chosen here are notable for their innovations in hardware architecture. Certain systems referenced here are also well known for their software (e.g. PRIME). For this reason, papers describing the software for such systems have been

included in section 8 (dealing with the overall reliability of
computer systems).

2.1 Avizienis, A. Architecture of fault-tolerant computing systems.
    Proc. of 5th IEEE Int. Symp. on Fault-Tolerant Computing,
    Paris, pp. 3-16, June 1975.

    The paper presents a systematic methodology for the
incorporation of fault-tolerance into the architecture of computing
systems. Two approaches to reliable system design are presented:
fault-tolerance and fault-intolerance. In the first approach,
reliability is obtained by the use of protective redundancy for
error detection and recovery, while in the second approach,
reliability must be obtained by the a priori elimination of the
causes of unreliability. The paper contains a discussion on the
types of faults and on various redundancy techniques. Included is a
valuable list of 97 references in the field of hardware
reliability.

2.2 Wensley, J.H., Levitt, K.N. and Neumann, P.G. A comparative
    study of architectures for fault-tolerance. Proc. of 4th IEEE
    Int. Symp. on Fault-Tolerant Computing, Urbana, Illinois,
    pp. 4-16 - 4-21, June 1974.

    The paper examines the reliability, availability, recovery
time, data protection and maintainability requirements for five
classes of computer applications: (i) general purpose time-shared,
(ii) general purpose batch, (iii) communication, (iv) superfast,
and (v) aerospace. Next, the many ways of introducing redundancy in
a typical computer system are studied and the corresponding
improvements in system availability are analysed. Twelve possible
ways of introducing redundancy are given - starting from a system
containing only byte-error detection in memory through to a system
containing 'uniform redundancy' (i.e. where programs are run
simultaneously on two computer units). From this study the paper
concludes "Techniques exist to provide adequate fault tolerance for
all application fields. In most cases, these techniques are
economical ..." Highly recommended.

2.3 Avizienis, A. et al. The STAR (Self Testing And Repairing
    Computer): An investigation of the theory and practice of
    fault-tolerant computer design. IEEE Trans. on Computers,
    C-20,11, pp. 1312-1321, Nov. 1971.

    The STAR is a fault-tolerant computer primarily intended for
use in spacecraft guidance, control and data acquisition systems on
long unmanned space missions. Notable features of this computer
are: (i) use of a special processor (TARP - Test And Repair
Processor) to monitor the performance of the computer and to
arrange recovery when it detected an error, (ii) use of hybrid
redundancy - STAR employed masking redundancy (triple modular

redundancy) for the implementation of TARP and standby sparing redundancy for the other modules of the computer (e.g. arithmetic unit, input-output processor), and (iii) use of arithmetic codes in the arithmetic unit. This is one of the best known fault-tolerant computers.

2.4 Hopkins, A.L. and Smith, T.B. The architectural elements of a symmetric fault-tolerant multiprocessor. IEEE Trans. on Computers, C-24,5, pp. 498-505, May 1975.

The paper describes a hybrid-redundant multiprocessor organisation for space applications. Each processing unit and each memory unit is triplicated and there are a number of spare units available to replace failed units. It is interesting to note that the approach adopted in the STAR computer (developed in the late sixties) was to use redundancy in the computer itself (e.g. spare arithmetic units, spare I/O control modules). However, the emergence of LSI technology has made it possible for the designers of the Symmetric Multiprocessor to use redundancy at a higher level (e.g. spare processors, spare memory modules) in an economic fashion.

2.5 Meraud, C., Browaeys, F. and Germain, G. Automatic roll back techniques of the COPRA computer. Proc. of 6th IEEE Int. Symp. on Fault-Tolerant Computing, Pittsburg, pp. 23-29, June 1976.

A multiprocessor system for aerospace application is described. The system uses standby sparing redundancy for processors and memory units. The notable features of this system are (i) it is reconfigurable - processors and memory units can be removed or added dynamically, (ii) the provision of an automatic rollback facility whereby the state of a computation can be restored to an earlier state, (iii) implementation of this rollback facility by hardware, and (iv) automatic generation of rollback points so that a programmer is not concerned with their specification. A breadboard version of the system has been built and is currently undergoing tests. This is an interesting paper.

2.6 Hamer-Hodges, K.J. Fault resistance and recovery within system 250. Proc. of Int. Conf. on Computer Communications, Washington D.C., pp. 290-296, Oct. 1972.

System 250 is a multiprocessor system designed by the Plessey Co. Ltd. (UK) for real time communication applications. Applications such as stored program control of telephone exchanges require a mean time between failures (unavailability exceeding 10 minutes) of 50 years. The system therefore has extensive provisions for hardware and software fault-tolerance; this paper concentrates on the former (for software see entry 8.3). The system consists of functionally equivalent processors connected to store and input-output modules. An important aspect of these processors is their use of a capability mechanism for the protection of information stored in memory modules (the subject of protection is covered in section 4). When a processor detects an error (because of capability checks, parity checks or microprogram checks) it generates a 'fault interrupt' so that programmed error recovery may be initiated. The pioneering work on protection described in this paper has had significant influence on the designers of secure computer systems.

2.7 Budlong, A.H. et al. 1A processor: control system. The Bell System Technical Journal, 56,2, pp. 135-179, Feb. 1976.

No. 1A processor is a special purpose processor developed for use in Bell Laboratory's Electronic Switching Systems (ESS). The processor consists of a fully duplicated 'central control' unit with both units generally working in synchronism (one unit as active and the other as standby). The storage in the system consists of 'program stores' and 'call stores' (call stores contain the information regarding telephone calls). The system employs both hardware and software error detection techniques (for a paper describing the software of the 1A system see entry 8.8). The hardware techniques include (i) replication checks (e.g. two central control units working synchronously), and (ii) coding checks - the system uses various types of error detecting codes. When an error is detected the recovery actions are software controlled. Under this control it is possible for the system to be reconfigured such that faulty units can be removed or serviced units can be added to the system.

2.8 Baskin, H.G., Borgerson, B.R. and Roberts, R. PRIME - a modular architecture for terminal-oriented systems. Proc. of AFIPS Spring Joint Computer Conf., 40, Atlantic City, pp. 431-437, May 1972.

The design aim for PRIME was to construct a system providing a continuous service as a general purpose multi-access interactive system. The interesting thing about PRIME is its attempt to achieve the above aim without introducing any significant redundancy in the system; all working units are available for use (there are no standby spares) and when a unit fails, the system is spontaneously reconfigured to run without that unit (albeit, providing a possibly degraded service). This paper makes interesting reading, particularly because the system architecture proposed is well suited for microprocessor based systems. See also entry 8.4 for a paper describing the philosophy of an operating system for PRIME.

2.9 Ornstein, S.M. et al. PLURIBUS - a reliable multiprocessor. Proc. of AFIPS Nat. Computer Conf., 44, Anaheim, pp. 551-559, June 1975.

The paper describes a multiprocessor system designed for use as a switching node in the ARPA network. The reliability goal was to construct a system that would survive not only transient failures but also solid failures of any single component. Also, "...to operate correctly most of the time so long as outages are infrequent, kept brief, and fixed without human intervention". The hardware consists of buses joined together by special bus couplers allowing units on one bus to access those on another. The buses are of the three kinds: (i) processor bus, each bus can contain two processors with local memory, (ii) memory bus, to house the segments of large shared memory, and (iii) I/O bus for device controllers. Hardware reliability is achieved by keeping sufficient 'extra copies' of hardware resources and by ensuring that these hardware copies are isolated as much as possible (so that a failure of one unit should not affect others). The paper also describes the software strategies used for error detection and recovery.

2.10 Fischler, M.A. and Firschein, O. A fault-tolerant multiprocessor architecture for real-time control applications. Proc. of IEEE Symp. on Computer Architecture, Florida, pp. 151-157, Dec. 1973.

A design philosophy for multiprocessor systems intended for ultra reliable real time applications is described. The design conditions are: (i) use of 'off-the-shelf' components and subsystems, (ii) realistic cost constraints (i.e. only a limited use of hardware redundancy), and (iii) dedicated application usage. The authors make two observations: (i) the increasing use of LSI circuits would make exhaustive testing of complex units infeasible, and (ii) in the case of software, "it is common knowledge that the complexity of such programs also makes their exhaustive testing impractical". Thus, both the hardware and software might contain undetected design faults. The design presented in this paper is tolerant to both classes of undetected faults. The basic idea is to run three or more versions of the application software on a suitably designed multiprocessor system that is capable of checking for any discrepancy in the results (see also entry 6.10).

3 HARDWARE RELIABILITY: MODELLING, TEST GENERATION AND DIAGNOSIS

There are many ways of introducing redundancy into computer systems. Mathematical modelling plays an important role in the selection of appropriate techniques for meeting the given reliability goal. The reliability of a system can be quite sensitive to even small variations in certain design parameters; mathematical models provide the understanding and insight into the nature of this sensitivity. The first four papers present models of well known redundancy techniques (e.g. TMR, NMR, hybrid) while the latter two papers make use of these models for the analysis of reliable computer systems. There is a large body of literature on the subjects of test generation and diagnosis. The state of the art is discussed in the book by Breuer and Friedman.

3.1 Lyons, R.E. and Vanderkulk, W. The use of triple-modular redundancy to improve computer reliability. IBM Journal of Res. and Dev., 6,2, pp. 200-209, April 1962.

A thorough mathematical analysis of the triple-modular redundancy (TMR) technique is presented. A TMR configuration with perfect voting circuits is first analysed and then the effect of imperfect voters on the reliability is considered. From this analysis the authors conclude that "...for maximum reliability the modules into which the computer is subdivided must have the same size as the voting circuitry..." Further topics covered include (i) analysis of module interconnection techniques, and (ii) the use of the Monte Carlo simulation technique.

3.2 Mathur, F.P. and Avizienis, A. Reliability analysis and architecture of a hybrid-redundant digital system: generalised triple modular redundancy with self-repair. Proc. of AFIPS Spring Joint Computer Conf., 36, Atlantic City, pp. 375-383, May 1970.

The standby sparing redundancy technique has gained widespread usage in the implementation of fault-tolerant computers since it offers several advantages over static redundancy techniques. Computers employing the standby spare redundancy technique often need a 'hard core' module for error detection and recovery. This module must be ultra reliable since its failure would leave the system fault intolerant. The authors propose a 'hybrid redundancy' technique for the design of hard core modules. It consists of a TMR (or its generalised version - NMR) system with standby spares. A detailed mathematical analysis of such a 'hybrid redundant' system is presented to show that a significant improvement over NMR systems can be obtained.

3.3 Bouricius, W.G. et al. Reliability modelling for fault-tolerant computers. IEEE Trans. on Computers, C-20,11, pp. 1306-1311, Nov. 1971.

In this widely referenced paper, the authors present reliability equations for most of the well known redundancy techniques. These techniques include: (i) TMR, (ii) TMR with sparing (hybrid redundancy), (iii) NMR with sparing (hybrid redundancy), and (iv) standby sparing. The last technique needs the facility of error detection and automatic reconfiguration (replacement of the failed component by one of the spares). Hence the authors introduce the important notion of coverage, defined to be the conditional probability that, given the existence of a failure in the operational system, the system is able to recover. A comparison of TMR and standby sparing is performed which indicates that "TMR is almost unbeatable for short missions but that, even with relatively poor coverage, sparing will be superior for longer missions". Recommended reading for anyone interested in reliability modelling and analysis.

3.4 Mathur, F.P. and De Sousa, P.T. Reliability modelling and analysis of general modular redundant systems. IEEE Trans. on Reliability, R-24,12, pp. 296-299, Dec. 1975.

The authors have developed a generalised reliability model (named GMR: general modular redundancy) such that the different redundancy techniques become particular cases of the model. It is therefore possible to present a unified treatment of reliability modelling. The advantage of this approach is that several different redundancy techniques can be compared with relative ease.

3.5 Borgerson, B.R. and Freitas, R.F. An analysis of 'PRIME' using a new reliability model. Proc. of 4th IEEE Int. Symp. on Fault-Tolerant Computing, Urbana, pp. 2-26 - 2-31, June 1974.

A reliability model of PRIME (see entry 2.8) is developed. A 'crash' is defined as an interruption in the availability of a predefined minimum amount of computing power for a period of time exceeding the system's automatic recovery time. Four distinct causes of crashes are assumed: (i) time domain multiple faults - crash due to a fault while recovering from an earlier fault, (ii) resource exhaustion - not enough resource units left to provide an acceptable service, (iii) space domain multiple faults - a crash due to the inadequacy of fault detection and recovery mechanisms, and (iv) solitary faults - the inability of the system to recover from a single fault. Many of the parameters cannot be estimated in advance (e.g. probability of solitary faults, coverage), so graphs showing the inter-relationships between such parameters and their influence on the reliability of PRIME are given.

3.6 Breuer, M.A. and Friedman, A.D. Diagnosis and reliable design of digital systems. Computer Science Press, 1976.

The topics covered in this book include test generation for combinational and sequential circuits (with a choice of fault models), logic level simulation for fault diagnosis, and a short chapter on design techniques. The book is introductory in nature.

ANNOTATED BIBLIOGRAPHY

3.7 Sacks, R. and Liberty, S.R. (editors). Rational fault analysis. Marcel Dekker, 1977.

The papers in this collection were presented in a symposium at Texas Technical University in 1974. The purpose of the symposium was to determine the state of the art in rational procedures for the detection, location and prediction of faults in a wide variety of systems, and to consider directions for future research in these areas. The topics covered include fault analysis of digital and analogue circuits, fault analysis in analogue and digital systems, fault modelling techniques for digital circuits and hardware/software systems, fault prediction, and bibliographies for fault detection and location in both analogue and digital circuits. The treatment is rigorous and at a research level, and provides guidelines and many references for more detailed investigations.

4 PROTECTION OF INFORMATION

One of the essential properties a reliable system must possess is that of error confinement: the property of preventing an erroneous or corrupted software module from damaging other modules. Of equal importance is the requirement that the information stored in the system be secure from unauthorised access. The first seven papers discuss information protection issues and mechanisms, mainly within the context of operating systems. The next paper addresses itself to the as yet little understood problem of guaranteeing secure information flow and the last two papers deal with the complex problem of protecting shared information in data bases.

4.1 Wilkes, M.V. Time sharing computing systems. American Elsevier/Macdonald (2nd edition), 1972.

Contains a concise and very readable account of protection in computer systems. The chapter on memory management describes the two well known protection schemes: access list based and capability based; included is a discussion on hardware features necessary to support these schemes. Later chapters describe user authentication mechanisms and file protection techniques. An additional advantage is that the book also contains details of file recovery techniques and methods of system restart after a failure. Highly recommended.

4.2 Saltzer, J.H. and Schroeder, M.L. The protection of information in computer systems. Proceedings of the IEEE, 63,9, pp. 1278-1308, Sept. 1975.

A very comprehensive survey of techniques for protecting computer-stored information from unauthorised use or modification. Eight design principles for designing a protection system are given: (i) economy of mechanism, (ii) failsafe defaults, (iii) complete mediation, (iv) open design, (v) separation of privilege, (vi) least privilege, (vii) least common mechanism, and (viii) psychological acceptability. Next, a capability based protection system is developed and its main advantages are discussed. The disadvantages of such a protection scheme (e.g. revocation of access is not easy) are also discussed. Another protection scheme - based on access control lists - is then developed and its advantages and disadvantages are also described. The paper concludes by pointing out areas for further research. The paper contains a valuable list of references to papers on protection and related topics.

4.3 Lampson, B.W. Protection. Fifth Princeton Conf. on Information Sciences and Systems, Princeton University, pp. 437-443, March 1971. Reprinted in ACM Operating Systems Review, 8,1, pp. 18-24, Jan. 1974.

In this influential paper Lampson introduced the idea of an 'access matrix'. If A is an access matrix, then element A[i,j] specifies the access (e.g. read, write) which domain i has to object j. Rules are specified for adding/deleting entries from A. For example, a domain d1 can remove access attributes from domain d2 if it has 'control' access over d2 . An access matrix together with these rules represents an abstract model of protection which exhibits the properties of most protection mechanisms. Lampson then describes how the model can be implemented; if the access information is attached to domains then one has capability based protection system. On the other hand, if the access information is attached to objects, one gets the access list based protection system. A hybrid approach is also described.

4.4 Saltzer, J.H. Protection and the control of information sharing in Multics. Communications of the ACM, 17,7, pp. 338-402, July 1974.

This paper contains a critical account of the protection techniques used in the Multics system, which is a good example of an access list based protection system. With each segment ('segment' is synonymous with 'file' in Multics) is associated an open-ended list of names of users who are permitted to access this segment, together with the kind of access permitted. This list is called the access control list of a segment and a user is allowed to access a segment only if he is mentioned in the corresponding list. Such a check is carried out for every access, and hardware support is provided for speeding up this process. This hardware mechanism essentially consists of copying the access information from the access control list to the user's segment descriptor. Multics also contains a hierarchical protection scheme (called the rings of protection) for the creation of protected subsystems. The paper contains a valuable discussion on weaknesses of the Multics protection mechanisms.

ANNOTATED BIBLIOGRAPHY

4.5 Popek, G.J. and Kline, C.S. A verifiable protection system.
Proc. of Int. Conf. on Reliable Software, Los Angeles,
pp. 294-304, April 1975.

This paper describes the work currently being undertaken at the
University of California at Los Angeles with the aim of building a
kernel for multi-user operating systems. The special feature of the
kernel is that it is intended to provide a <u>provably secure</u>
environment for information exchange (the term 'security kernel' is
often used to refer to such kernels). The basic security is
achieved by the creation of isolated virtual machines - the
isolation guaranteeing the error confinement property. Great care
has been taken to keep the security kernel as small and simple as
possible so as to make the task of proving its correctness
manageable. The paper contains a good discussion on the design and
implementation of the kernel.

4.6 Jones, A.K. The narrowing gap between language systems and
operating systems. Information Processing 77, North Holland
(Proc. of IFIP Congress, Toronto, Aug. 1977), pp. 869-873.

This paper is tutorial in nature and contains a discussion on a
programming language approach to access control in operating
systems. In current programming languages, access to data is
provided on an all-or-nothing basis; if an object is accessible,
then every component of it is accessible. The paper describes an
approach whereby a user of an object can be restricted to perform
only a subset of the accesses defined for that object. The
advantage of the programming language oriented approach to
protection is that it not only enhances the readability and
understandability of programs but also a great deal of access
checking can be performed at compile time rather than at run time;
thus security can be achieved without excessive run time overheads.

4.7 Denning, D.E. A lattice model of secure information flow.
Communications of the ACM, 19,5, pp. 236-243, May 1976.

The protection mechanisms considered so far have been concerned
with guaranteeing the protection of information and not with the
<u>flow</u> of information. It has proved very difficult to guarantee that
a process will not, intentionally or unintentionally, leak
information to other processes. This paper develops an 'information
flow' model which can be used to specify secure information flow
requirements. Some existing security systems are described using
this model. It is shown that practical systems will need both
access control (characterised by Lampson's access matrix model) and
flow control to satisfy all security requirements.

4.8 Hsio, D.K. and Baum, R.I. Information secure systems. Advances in Computers, 14, Academic Press, pp. 231-272, 1976.

This very good review paper discusses information protection in data bases. Protection problems in data bases are a great deal more complicated than the corresponding problems in operating systems. In the access matrix model of Lampson, it is assumed that if 'i' wants to access an object 'j', then it is only necessary to check the access rights associated with the entry A[i,j] and not any other entry, say A[i,k]. However, in the context of data bases, this form of checking is rather primitive. This is because the information present in a data base system must be considered as a collection of semantically inter-connected data items. This means that by accessing a given item, a user can implicitly gain some knowledge of other semantically connected items. The protection mechanism, however, must protect the data despite these connections. The paper discusses various protection techniques with this property. The highlight of the paper is its use of simple examples to explain the difficult protection problems. Highly recommended.

4.9 Stonebraker, M. and Rubinstein, P. The INGRES protection system. Proc. of Annual ACM Conf., Houston, pp. 80-84, Oct. 1976.

This interesting paper describes the protection scheme used in the 'INGRES' relational data base system, implemented on a PDP11 computer with the UNIX operating system. INGRES supports a relational data language (called QUEL) which allows a user to manipulate relations; the protection is provided for the shared relations in the data base. Pertinent details of the implementation are given. Included is a discussion on the reasons for adopting a particular approach to protection (e.g. why only physical relations are protected and not virtual relations). The paper contains references to some publications describing work on related topics (the reader may also find the paper 'Views, authorisation and locking in a relational data base system' by Chamberlin, D. et al. in Proc. of AFIPS Nat. Conf., 1975, of interest).

5 SYSTEM SPECIFICATION AND VALIDATION

Almost always, the users of a proposed system have only imprecise notions of what they need from a system. The first three papers in this section describe techniques for obtaining precise functional specifications of a system. The next two papers deal with the problem of specifying software modules. References 6 to 10 address program proving. References 11 to 13 survey the theory and practice of testing, attempting to link the two.

ANNOTATED BIBLIOGRAPHY

5.1 Boehm, B.W. Some steps towards formal and automated aids to
    software requirements and design. Information Processing 74,
    North Holland (Proc. of IFIP Congress, Stockholm, Aug. 1974),
    pp. 192-197.

In this paper Boehm states: "Often, the difference between
success and failure on a large software project lies in the
consistency and completeness with which the system requirements
have been specified and translated into design specifications.
Yet...relatively little has been done to develop formal methods for
requirements analysis". A case study is described where system
requirements were first determined by discussions with users. A set
of questions were used to discover implied operational
requirements. A formalism which uses a requirements/properties
matrix is described to help check the consistency and completeness
of the requirements.

5.2 Ross, D.T. and Schoman, K.E. Structured analysis for
    requirements definition. IEEE Trans. on Software Engineering,
    SE-3,1, pp. 6-15, Jan. 1977.

All too often, design and implementation begin before the real
needs and system functions are fully known. Requirements definition
includes, but is not limited to, the problem analysis that yields a
functional specification - it yields a careful assessment of the
needs that a system is to fulfil. The authors describe their
approach to requirements definition using the SADT (Structured
Analysis and Design Technique) approach they have developed. SADT
provides methods for (i) thinking about large complex problems,
(ii) communication of ideas in clear precise notations, (iii)
documentation of current results, and (iv) planning, managing and
assessing the progress of team efforts. The authors state that the
SADT approach has been successfully applied to a "wide range of
planning, analysis and design problems involving men, machines,
software, hardware, databases, communications, procedures and
finances".

5.3 Belford, P.C., Bond, A.F., Henderson, D.G. and Sellers, S.L.
    Specification: a key to effective software development. Proc.
    of 2nd Int. Conf. on Software Engineering, San Francisco,
    pp. 71-79, Oct. 1976.

The authors describe their efforts to "devise an advanced
engineering methodology that supports the design, development,
validation and unambiguous communication of complete and consistent
data processing subsystem performance requirements". A method of
decomposing the system into 'decomposition elements' is given and
software aids are provided for consistency checking. The major part
of the paper is concerned with automating verification techniques
for specifications. The software developer need then only be
concerned with the validation of the generated code.

5.4 Parnas, D.L. A technique for software module specification with examples. Communications of the ACM, 15,5, pp. 330-336, May 1972.

Two principles for the specification of a software module are stated in this widely referenced and influential paper. First, to provide a user of the module with all the information needed to use the module - and nothing more. Second, to provide the implementor of the module with full information about the intended use of the module - and nothing more; in particular, no information about the structure of calling programs should be conveyed. A specification technique based on these principles is presented, and illustrated with the help of many simple but realistic examples. The specification of error handling in modules is also discussed.

5.5 Liskov, B.H. and Zilles, S.N. Specification techniques for data abstractions. IEEE Trans. on Software Engineering, SE-1,1, pp. 7-19, March 1975.

A critical review is presented of current approaches to formally specifying program modules. Six criteria are presented for evaluating specification methods: (i) formality, (ii) constructability, (iii) comprehensibility, (iv) minimality, (v) applicability, and (vi) extensibility. A program module is taken to mean a "program unit supporting a data abstraction". Specification techniques are classified as those using (i) some well established mathematical discipline (for instance, graph theory), (ii) state machine models, (iii) axiomatic descriptions, and (iv) algebraic definitions. These specification techniques are explained with the help of a simple stack example. It is pointed out that no one technique is superior to all the others. This paper forms a useful introduction to the specification of data abstractions, a topic on which there is much current research.

5.6 Dijkstra, E.W., Programming as a discipline of a mathematical nature. American Mathematical Monthly, 81,6, pp. 608-612, June 1974. (Also in Computers and People, Oct. 1974.)

This little paper discusses a wide range of fundamental topics: accuracy in algorithm design, generality of an algorithm with respect to the computations it invokes, confidence levels in testing and proving situations, concurrent development of programs and their proofs, natural and formal languages, hierarchical decomposition, and mathematical curricula. The unifying theme is that the competent programmer must use mathematical precision, generality, and discipline to develop programs which warrant high confidence levels. Dijkstra also discusses the reasons why mathematical methods are difficult to use.

5.7 London, R.L., Perspectives on program verification. In Current
Trends in Programming Methodology, Vol. 2, Program Validation,
R.T. Yeh (ed.), Prentice-Hall, 1977, pp. 151-172.

The range of reasons for considering verification (proving) are
discussed, along with the basic assumptions, caveats, and
limitations. Examples show the basic principles of the widely used
inductive assertion method, supplemented by a discussion of the
creation of the necessary assertions. The task of mechanising the
proving process is described and evaluated. An extensive
bibliography (muddled by combination with those of other authors in
the volume) gives a broad view of verification activity.

5.8 Luckham, D.C., Program verification and verification oriented
programming. Information Processing 77, North Holland (Proc. of
IFIP Congress, Toronto, Aug. 1977), pp. 783-793.

This paper covers much of the same ground as that of London,
but shows more details of mechanical verification. Several kinds of
properties, including fairness of a queueing system, and related
programs are described with respect to verification. The
possibility of debugging by studying unprovable verification
conjectures is introduced. A range of issues about verifying real
programs and confidence in the verification process is discussed
relative to the research problems which underlie them.

5.9 Dijkstra, E.W., A Discipline of Programming, Prentice-Hall,
1976.

Chapters 3 to 7 describe the basic theory of program proving -
transforming predicates according to the semantics of a programming
language into a collection of theorems which express that the
program behaves in ways that satisfy its specification and
termination requirements. The main difficulty is the formulation of
loop invariants in such a way that the theorems can be proved. The
developments of several examples are driven by concerns for the
loop invariant and termination requirements. However, this method
is not used consistently throughout the book, nor are general
principles or known algorithms which underlie the examples used
where they might be helpful.

5.10 Owicki, S. and Gries, D. Verifying properties of parallel
programs: an axiomatic approach. Communications of the ACM,
19,5, pp. 279-285, May 1976.

Hoare's axiomatic proof technique as applied to parallel
programs is extended, principally to allow the use of auxiliary
variables in a program. Axioms are presented, and proof techniques
described, which enable various properties of parallel programs to
be established. Proofs are given for freedom from deadlock, mutual
exclusion and termination of a solution to the ubiquitous dining

philosophers problem. The basic method requires an invariant for a resource, which is true initially and remains true outside critical sections, and thus reduces to proofs about sequential statements inside critical sections.

5.11 Goodenough, J.B. and Gerhart, S.L. Toward a theory of testing: data selection criteria. In Current Trends in Programming Methodology, Vol. 2, Program Validation, R.T. Yeh (ed.), Prentice-Hall, 1977, pp. 44-79.

Very little is understood about program testing, even though it is far more often practised than program proving. This paper defines some basic properties of criteria for test data selection and shows that satisfaction of these properties is equivalent to program proving. Although commonly used criteria, such as exercising every statement, seldom have these properties they may be studied as to how well they approximate the ideal of a proof. The paper defines types of errors and discusses how well various criteria perform in selecting test data which reveals the errors. A text formatting program which appeared in the literature on programming methodology is used as a case study for errors and testing.

5.12 Howden, W.E., Reliability of the path analysis testing strategy. IEEE Trans. on Software Engineering, SE-2,3, pp. 208-215, Sept. 1976.

This paper is one of several by the author in a long-term research project to find a theoretical basis for, and to evaluate, various testing strategies widely used in practice. A testing strategy is said to be 'reliable' for a given program P if either P is correct or the test strategy can select test data which shows that P is incorrect. The path analysis testing strategy generates test data which causes selected paths to be executed. Several examples of published incorrect programs are studied as to how well path testing can detect their errors. Papers such as this are extremely valuable for their insight, terminology, and initial evaluation mechanisms for the poorly understood area of program testing.

5.13 Miller, E.F. Program testing: art meets theory. Computer, 10,7, pp. 42-51, July 1977.

This paper attempts to build a bridge linking the theory and practice of program testing. The characteristics of a testing methodology, for both modules and systems, are described and a hierarchy of testing measures is identified. Some of the emerging theory described by Howden and Goodenough and Gerhart (see entries 5.12 and 5.11) is applied to the measures. Practical experience, particularly analysing strategies and measures succeed or fail, is reviewed and more such work is called for.

ANNOTATED BIBLIOGRAPHY

6 RELIABLE SOFTWARE SYSTEM STRUCTURE

All of the ten papers chosen in this section address themselves to the problems of designing and implementing reliable software. The first two papers are unique in that the ideas contained in them can be applied to any man-machine organisation. The remaining papers deal with the topics of software fault-tolerance, system structuring and language design criteria.

6.1 Davies, C.T. Recovery semantics for a DB/DC system. Proc. of ACM Annual Conf., Atlanta, pp. 136-141, Aug. 1973.

In this important paper, Davies introduces the concept of 'spheres of control' as a bound around a process for describing and solving, among other things, error recovery problems between processes exchanging information. When a process is inside a sphere of control, any effects produced by the process are not regarded as committed and the process can back out without affecting processes not in that sphere. On the other hand, once a process exits from a sphere of control, the effects produced by it are regarded as committed, so any recovery actions must be taken by an enclosing sphere. How a sphere may be 'activated' and 'deactivated' is described. This paper contains ideas of major significance and requires careful reading.

6.2 Bjork, L.A. Recovery scenario for a DB/DC system. Proc. of ACM Annual Conf., Atlanta, pp. 142-146, Aug. 1973.

This is a companion paper to that of Davies referenced above. The paper discusses in detail how spheres of control are dynamically created and completed, and how, when an error is detected, a backward search is made to decide the extent of the back out needed to return to a consistent state. Like the companion paper by Davies (entry 6.1), this paper contains important ideas on recovery.

6.3 Randell, B. System structure for software fault-tolerance. IEEE Trans. on Software Engineering, SE-1,2, pp. 220-232, June 1975.

The paper presents a convincing case for incorporating fault-tolerance in software. It states "...all software faults result from design errors. The relative frequency of such errors reflects the much greater logical complexity of the typical software design compared to that of a typical hardware design". A method is proposed for dealing with software faults which consist of a program structure (known as a recovery block) for error detection and recovery. The essence of this scheme is that it provides a facility for a computation to backtrack to an earlier state if an error is detected, and then proceed again using a possibly different algorithm. The paper also discusses error recovery problems between interacting processes, and presents a methodology for reliably constructing complex systems. Recommended reading for everyone interested in software fault-tolerance.

6.4 Parnas, D.L. The influence of software structure on reliability. Proc. of Int. Conf. on Reliable Software, Los Angeles, pp. 358-362, April 1975.

A strong distinction is made between reliability and correctness, in that correct software can be quite unreliable. This happens when the specification for the software is not a complete description of what is expected from the software specifications. The paper presents three guidelines for reliable system design: (i) when specifying system modules, take into account the behaviour which is desired when perfect behaviour is not obtainable, (ii) when specifying interfaces between modules, specify not only what the interfacing elements should do in the normal case, but also which assumptions should be verified at run time, and (iii) include in the interfaces conventions for informing affected modules about things which have gone wrong elsewhere in the system. Some examples are given to support the author's proposals. This is a thought provoking paper.

6.5 Wulf, W.A. Reliable hardware-software architecture. IEEE Trans. on Software Engineering, SE-1,2, pp. 233-240, June 1975.

The paper describes the lessons learned from the design of a reliable hardware-software system (the system in question is HYDRA, built at Carnegie-Mellon University). The paper states that "...since hardware malfunction must be assumed to have a non-zero probability, software correctness is not a sufficient condition for a reasonable degree of reliability". The approach adopted in the design of HYDRA is then described - the goal was to recover from hardware errors. Each module is designed such that it is responsible for maintaining the integrity of the abstraction it implements. In conclusion the paper rightly states "software reliability involves a great deal more than correctness..."

6.6 DeRemer, F.L. and Kron, H. Programming-in-the-large versus programming-in-the-small. IEEE Trans. on Software Engineering, SE-2,2, pp. 80-86, June 1976.

The authors distinguish the activity of writing large programs from that of writing small ones. It is argued that structuring a large collection of modules to form a system (this activity is referred to as programming in the large) is an essentially distinct and different intellectual activity from that of constructing the individual modules. The authors then discuss the characteristics of a 'module interconnection language' (MIL) - the language for supporting programming in the large. MIL should serve as (i) a project management tool, (ii) a means of communication between members of a programming team, (iii) a means of establishing overall program structure, and (iv) a means of documenting that structure in a clear, concise, formal and checkable way. The authors conclude that a proper use of MIL can be a significant contributing factor in the design of reliable software.

6.7 Wirth, N. Towards a discipline of real-time programming. Communications of the ACM, 20,8, pp. 577-583, Aug. 1977.

The author classifies programming into three categories with increasing complexity of reasoning in program validation: (i) sequential programming, (ii) multi-programming (programming for concurrent processes), and (iii) real-time programming (programming for concurrent processes with real-time constraints). The philosophy that led to the design of the author's language MODULA (a language intended for multi-programming and real-time programming) is then described. The author in conclusion states "...the use of a suitable high-level language together with adherence to a strict programming discipline ... may be the only viable way towards genuine reliability in real-time systems".

6.8 Liskov, B.H. A design methodology for reliable software systems. Proc. of AFIPS Fall Joint Computer Conf., 41, Anaheim, pp. 191-199, Dec. 1972.

The paper first discusses a method of 'modularising' by partitioning a system into hierarchically organised levels of abstractions. Guidelines are presented for selecting 'useful' abstractions. A design is regarded as finished when the following three criteria are satisfied: (i) all major levels of abstractions have been identified, (ii) the system exists as a structured program showing how flow of control passes among the levels, and (iii) sufficient information is available so that the skeleton of a users' guide to the system could be written. The author illustrates her ideas using an example from the VENUS operating system.

6.9 Kopetz, H. Software robustness and system reliability. Proc. of the European Computing Conf. on Software Systems Engineering, London, pp. 249-261, Sept. 1976.

The author defines a software system to be robust if the effect of an error on the level of system performance in a given application is inversely proportional to the probability of occurrence of this error in the given application. This means that failures which are expected to occur frequently should only have a minor effect on the given application. The paper reviews some error detection and recovery mechanisms.

6.10 Fischler, M.A., Firschein, O. and Drew, D.L. Distinct
software: an approach to reliable computing. Proc. of Second
USA-JAPAN Computer Conf., Tokyo, pp. 573-579, Aug. 1975.

The authors discuss the various stages involved in the design
of an information processing system, from system requirement
definition through to system operation. They point out that because
of the complexity of the design process, an information system can
contain undetected design faults. They therefore suggest the
concept of 'distinctness' - alternative ways of performing a
specific task using separate hardware and different software - as a
means of coping with such faults (the approach presented here is,
in many ways, similar to that proposed in entry 6.3). Some
techniques for producing distinct software are then discussed,
followed by an analysis of a few experiments in this area performed
by the authors. In conclusion, the paper states that "...distinct
software can play an important role in all aspects of system
design, and is a viable economic alternative to conventional
methods for attaining reliability".

7 SOFTWARE RELIABILITY MODELLING

There is an increasing trend at present to apply reliability
modelling techniques (based on the approaches developed for
hardware discussed in section 3) to software. It has been observed
that if during the test and integration phase of software
development (when individually tested modules are combined to form
a system and then tests are made) sufficient data is collected
about detected errors, time to correct errors, mean time between
software errors etc. then predictions about reliability and project
schedules can be made. The first five papers in this section
describe current efforts to predict software reliability, while the
following three papers present such error data (and its analysis)
collected during tests. The last two papers are slightly different
- they develop models intended to characterise the run-time
behaviour of a system.

7.1 Jelinski, A., and Moranda, P. Software reliability research. In
Statistical Computer Performance Evaluation, W. Freiberger
(ed.), Academic Press, 1972, pp. 465-484.

This is one of the earliest (and quite influential) papers
describing an effort to predict software reliability using
traditional reliability theory. The authors state that a 'constant
failure rate' assumption can be applied to software error detection
and hence software reliability at time t can be stated as: $R(t) = \exp(-St)$ where S is the failure rate. The failure rate can be
assumed to be proportional to the residual errors in the software;
the authors present a technique whereby error detection data
collected during tests can be used to estimate the failure rate.

7.2 Shooman, M.L. Operational testing and software reliability
   estimation during program development. Proc. of IEEE Symp. on
   Computer Software Reliability, New York, pp. 51-57, April 1973.

A very similar model to that of Jelinski and Moranda has been
independently developed by Shooman. The model can be used to
predict software reliability given the debugging effort involved in
removing errors. The model is applicable to the last phase of
software development: test and integration. The failure rate is
assumed to be equal to $CEr(t)$ where C is a constant (indicating
'instruction processing rate') and $Er(t)$ is the number of residual
errors after t months of debugging time. Shooman presents a
technique for estimating C and $Er(t)$ so that the reliability at
time T for software that has undergone t months of debugging can be
stated as: $R(T,t) = \exp(-CEr(t)T)$.

7.3 Schneidewind, N.F. An approach to software reliability
   prediction and quality control. Proc. of AFIPS Fall Joint
   Computer Conf., 41, Anaheim, pp. 837-847, Dec. 1972.

In contrast to the previous two approaches, Schneidewind has
taken an empirical approach and suggests a reliability prediction
scheme based on fitting failure intervals with an appropriate
reliability function. First, data is collected in the form of 'time
between software troubles'. The nature of this distribution
contains clues as to what distribution function (e.g. exponential,
normal, Weibull) can be fitted to it. Schneidewind then describes
how goodness of fit tests (such as Kolmogorov-Smirnov or Chi
Square) can be used to check that the chosen distribution function
appropriately represents the test data. Once the distribution is
determined, a prediction of the reliability can be obtained by
using standard results from reliability theory. The feasibility of
this approach was demonstrated by applying it to Naval Tactical
Data system data; the details of this experiment are, however, not
given.

7.4 Musa, J.D. A theory of software reliability and its
   application. IEEE Trans. on Software Engineering, SE-1,3,
   pp. 312-327, Sept. 1975.

This is one of the best papers on this subject. The author
develops a model (called the execution time model) incorporating
many of the features described in the previous three papers; this
model is then validated by applying it to four medium-sized
software development projects. The model can be used, in advance of
a project, to estimate the amount of testing (stated in terms of
execution time) needed to achieve a specified reliability goal. The
required execution time can be related to calendar time thus
allowing project schedules to be developed. The author also
presents a method (employing the maximum likelihood estimation
technique) for estimating model parameters.

7.5 Trivedi, A.K. and Shooman, M.L. A many state Markov model for the estimation and prediction of computer software performance parameters. Proc. of Int. Conf. on Reliable Software, Los Angeles, pp. 208-220, April 1975.

A model is developed to predict reliability and availability of large software systems (100K words of code or more) given the error occurrence rate and the error repair rate. A discrete-state, continous-time Markov model is developed under the assumption that the system contains an unknown number of bugs, and that error detection and correction occur alternately and sequentially. Some extensions to the model are also suggested - e.g. inclusion of several categories of errors (critical, non-critical) - which are currently under investigation by the authors.

7.6 Endres, A. An analysis of errors and their causes in system programs. IEEE Trans. on Software Engineering, SE-1,2, pp. 140-149, June 1975.

The paper presents interesting data on errors in a system program (DOS/VS release 28). The data was collected when the modules of the system were ready for test and integration. A somewhat surprising observation was that 85.1% of the errors could be corrected by changing only one module per error (in an operating system where modules are interdependent, one would have expected changes to many modules to correct an error). It was also found that 46% of the errors were due to incorrect understanding of problems to be solved and 38% of the errors were due to incorrect implementation of a given algorithm. It is thus seen that systematic programming can only avoid at most half of the mistakes - the other half must be attacked by employing better tools for problem specification (such as specification languages).

7.7 Isao Miyamoto. Software reliability in online real time environment. Proc. of Int. Conf. on Reliable Software, Los Angeles, pp. 194-203, April 1975.

The paper gives actual error and reliability data collected from a large telephone switching system. In effect, this data validates the Shooman model referenced earlier. The data was collected during the test and integration period of the system and included cumulative number of errors detected, time to correct each error and MTBF of the system. The form of reliability improvement (as the errors were corrected) closely resembles that predicted by Shooman. The author describes in detail the selection of a testing environment to simulate the actual working conditions. The main conclusion of this work, as the author points out, is that if sufficient data is collected during system testing, realistic software reliability estimation can be performed.

7.8 Fumio Akiyama. An example of software system debugging.
Information Processing 71, North Holland (Proc. of IFIP
Congress, Ljubljana, Aug. 1971), 1, pp. 353-359.

This paper demonstrates that if error data is collected during
software module tests, estimations about the number of errors in
similar modules and the time needed to correct them can be made.
This data is thus useful in project planning and scheduling. The
author observed a strong correlation between the number of errors
detected and the nature of the program.

7.9 Chandy, K.M., Ramamoorthy, C.V. and Cowan, A. A framework for
analysing hardware-software trade-offs in fault tolerant
computing systems. Proc. of AFIPS Fall Joint Computer Conf.,
41, Anaheim, pp. 55-63, Dec. 1972.

The paper defines four indices for evaluating reliability: (i)
hardware reliability efficiency index (HRE), (ii) software
reliability efficiency index (SRE), (iii) real-time criticality
index (RTC), and (iv) inclusion factor. For a given method of
achieving reliability, HRE and SRE are measures of the increase in
reliability of the system per unit of expenditure. RTC is a measure
of the penalty incurred for a late completion of the system
mission. HRE, SRE and RTC, together with the penalty incurred if
the mission fails, are related by the inclusion factor:

software inclusion factor = (SRE/RTC) x penalty of mission failure

The inclusion factor is the ratio of the decrease in expected cost
of mission outcome and the cost incurred in achieving this
decrease. A design guideline for choosing a particular software
method for achieving reliability is that its inclusion factor
should be greater than one. The paper then presents a method for
calculating SRE for rollback and recovery techniques of achieving
reliability. Methods for calculating HRE for some hardware
techniques are also presented.

7.10 Chandy, K.M., Browne, J.C., Dissly, C.W. and Uhrig, W.R.
Analytic models for rollback and recovery strategies in data
base systems. IEEE Trans. on Software Engineering, SE-1,1,
pp. 100-110, March 1975.

Rollback and recovery strategies consist of taking periodic
copies of the data whose integrity is to be preserved (such copies
are called checkpoints) and keeping a record of all the
transactions (after taking a checkpoint) performed by the system.
When an error is detected, the previous version of the data is
restored (making use of the checkpoint) and the recorded
transactions are reprocessed. While this technique is widely used
in practice, little mathematical analysis has been performed
regarding the cost effectiveness of checkpoint procedures. A model

is developed in this paper where the effects of the following four
parameters are analysed (i) cost of recovery, (ii) demand for
system services, (iii) rate of error detection (including the rate
during recovery), and (iv) the reduction of reprocessing time with
respect to normal processing. An optimal checkpoint interval is
then calculated.

8 SYSTEMS RELIABILITY, INTEGRITY, RECOVERY AND AUDITING

This last section contains a collection of papers describing
mechanisms, procedures and techniques used to ensure high
reliability and integrity in computer systems. In particular,
papers on real-time systems, operating systems and online data
bases have been chosen.

8.1 Connet, J.R., Pasternak, E.J. and Wagner, B.D. Software
defenses in real-time systems. Proc. of 2nd IEEE Int. Symp. on
Fault-Tolerant Computing, Newton, pp. 94-99, June 1972.

This is a good example of a real-time system (Bell System's
Traffic Service Position System) incorporating software fault-
tolerance. The designers realised that a complex system will
contain residual design errors, so extensive checks were
incorporated for protecting data from corruption. Independent check
programs (audits) were employed to monitor the system and undertake
corrective actions whenever data corruption was suspected. The
paper contains many illustrative examples to describe the audit
techniques used. It was observed that from 10 to 100 errors per day
were detected and corrected by audits in a typical operational
system. When audits fail to provide recovery from errors, system
restart is used: this was happening at the rate of about once every
two months. This paper provides interesting reading.

8.2 Taylor, J.M. Redundancy and recovery in the HIVE virtual
machine. Proc. of European Conf. on Software Systems
Engineering, London, pp. 263-293, Sept. 1976.

An experimental, high integrity transaction oriented system is
described. It consists of a set of asynchronous parallel processes
whose job is to cyclically process transactions. Capability based
protection is used for ensuring error confinement. Four versions of
every file are kept; two read only versions (on secondary storage)
for global, cold start recovery and two read-write versions for
run-time recovery. If a process is unable to process a transaction
its state is reset to that just before the beginning of the cycle,
for reprocessing; if the system crashes, then all the processes are
reset to their states at the beginning of their respective cycles.
These recovery actions are described in detail in the paper.

ANNOTATED BIBLIOGRAPHY

8.3 Repton, C.S. Reliability assurance for system 250 - a reliable, real-time control system. Proc. of Int. Conf. on Computer Communications, Washington D.C., pp. 297-305, Oct. 1972.

The paper describes the philosophy behind the recovery strategies employed in the Plessey System 250 multi-processor system. A recovery action involves three phases: (i) error detection, (ii) fault location (this is not always possible - e.g. the error may be due to a design inadequacy in the hardware or software), and (iii) selection of the appropriate restart procedures, which include process restart, area restart and area reload. Initially the procedure causing the least disruption is used (process restart). If this fails to clear the error then increasingly powerful (and hence more disruptive) procedures are employed (area restart, then area reload). The paper discusses the structure of the recovery system in detail.

8.4 Fabry, R.S. Dynamic verification of operating system decisions. Communications of the ACM, 16,11, pp. 659-668, Nov. 1973.

The operating system for the PRIME system is described. One of the goals of this operating system was to considerably reduce the possibility of one user's information becoming available to another user even when a fault occurs. This goal has been achieved by ensuring that every operating system decision in the system concerned with the flow of information from one user to another is dynamically verified. Each user is allocated a virtual subsystem consisting of a virtual processor, some virtual memory and a virtual disc unit, none of which are shared with other subsystems. The subsystems can cooperate by making use of a virtual communications system which allows messages to be exchanged. The strong isolation between the subsystems is one of the key factors that facilitate the implementation of data privacy despite faults in the system. One important aspect of the PRIME system is that consistency checks which are performed on a decision are executed by a unit independent from the one that executed the decision algorithm. For example, the decision algorithm for address mapping can be executed by any processor, but the consistency checking is performed by the appropriate memory block unit. A recommended paper.

8.5 Rowe, L.A., Hopwood, M.D. and Farber, D.J. Software methods for achieving fail-soft behaviour in the distributed computing system. IEEE Symp. on Computer Software Reliability, New York, pp. 7-11, April 1973.

The Distributed Computing System (DCS) is a network architecture developed at the University of California, Irvine, with the aim of providing a reliable, fail-soft service at low cost. The hardware consists of a number of mini-computers connected to a digital communication ring. The system software consists of a resident nucleus for each processor and a collection of processes. Software failures in the DCS are classified into two classes - nucleus failure and process failure. Error detection mechanisms are concerned with the message passing system (e.g. a check is included to ensure that the process name in a message is actually the name of the sender). Any inconsistency in a message is regarded as the failure of the appropriate nucleus. The nucleus recovery action consists of loading a new copy of the nucleus. Detection mechanisms are also employed for detecting process failures. Many stages of recovery actions are provided, all of which are discussed briefly in the paper.

8.6 Johnson, J.S. and Shaw, J.L. Fault-tolerant software for a dual processor with monitor. Proc. of Symp. on Computer Software Engineering, New York, pp. 395-407, April 1976.

This paper describes the software developed to run on a dual-processor with a synchronised execution system, intended for avionics applications. The execution of the two processors is monitored by a 'monitor box' module. If the monitor module detects any discrepancy between the outputs of the processors (both of the processors execute the same programs) then the execution of both programs is halted and the computation is rolled back to a previously saved state; the processors are resynchronised and the execution of the program is restarted. The above mentioned recovery actions are performed by the system executive. The components of this executive - resynchronisation routine, rollback routine, fault isolation routine etc. are described in detail in the paper.

8.7 Wensley, J.H., Green, M.W., Levitt, K.N. and Shostak, R.E. The design, analysis and verification of the SIFT fault tolerant system. Proc. of 2nd Int. Conf. on Software Engineering, San Francisco, pp. 458-469, Oct. 1976.

The paper describes work currently in progress at the Stanford Research Institute for the development of the SIFT (Software Implemented Fault Tolerance) system. The system consists of a set of hardware modules, each with its own processor and memory. The computations of the system are divided into a number of task programs. Each processor is multi-programmed over a subset of the tasks, and each task is simultaneously executed on a subset of the processors. The results of the same task are periodically compared to detect any disagreements. The paper describes how the faulty processor(s) or bus(es) are determined when a disagreement is detected, and how the system is reconfigured to run without the faulty units. As with the previous paper, only the tolerance of hardware faults is considered; no mention is made of tolerance for software faults.

8.8 Bowman, P.W. et al. 1A processor : maintenance software. The
Bell System Technical Journal, 56,2, pp. 255-287, Feb. 1977.

Comprehensive maintenance software is required to meet the
system reliability objective of less than 2 minutes per year of
outage from all causes. The system in question is any telephone
switching system based on the 1A processor. The probable causes of
system outages have been classified into 4 categories and allocated
a reasonable portion of the total system down time of 2 minutes:
(i) software deficiencies - 15%, (ii) hardware deficiencies - 20%,
(iii) procedural errors (imperfect repair) - 30%, and (iv) recovery
deficiencies - 35%. The last category is expected to be the largest
source of outages; this is because it can never be guaranteed that
all impending troubles will be identified and isolated before they
can jeopardise system operation. The paper describes the fault
recognition and recovery techniques used in detail.

8.9 Lynch, W.C., Langner, J.W. and Schwartz, M.S. Reliability
experience with CHI/OS. IEEE Trans. on Software Engineering,
SE-1,2, pp. 253-257, June 1975.

The CHI/OS is a full scale operating system developed to run on
a UNIVAC 1108 computer. It went into operation in November 1973 and
has proved to be a very reliable system. In this paper the authors
examine in retrospect the environmental factors that have
contributed to the reliability of the software of the system. The
major factor has been the project organisation. According to the
authors "the key points of this organisation are the employment of
skilled personnel,..., the involvement of the development group in
the design process, and the judicious application of large
quantities of machine time". Another factor that contributed to the
reliability of the operating system is the fact that large portions
of CHI/OS have been programmed in a high level language. The
authors discuss how the high level language helped in the
production of a well structured system. An interesting paper.

8.10 Burk, J.M. and Schoonover, J.E. Computer system
maintainability at the Lawrence Livermore Laboratory. Proc. of
AFIPS Fall Joint Computer Conf., 41, Anaheim, pp. 263-272,
Dec. 1972.

System maintenance policies used at the Lawrence Livermore
Laboratory's giant computer network complex (three CDC 7600, a CDC-
STAR, a CDC 6600, two PDP-10, several minicomputers) are presented.
The system is in operation 24 hours a day, 7 days a week, so
maintenance procedures that do not seriously degrade the available
services must be employed. The paper describes how and what
diagnostic software (manufacturer's and developed in-house) is used
on-line and off-line and what fail-safe procedures and techniques
are available. As a result of the maintenance policies used, the
total availability of the system (with all devices on-line) has

been observed to be 75 percent and the partial availability of the system (at least one computer capable of doing work) has been 100 percent.

8.11 Linde, R.R. Operating system penetration. Proc. of AFIPS National Computer Conf., 44, Anaheim, pp. 361-368, May 1975.

Preserving the integrity of any data entrusted to a computer system requires that the system be capable of preventing unauthorised access to the data. This means that a high integrity computer system must be based on a secure operating system. However, how can the secure-worthiness of an operating system be assessed? This important paper presents an approach (developed at the System Development Corporation) which consists of systematically trying to 'beat the system' - and thus infer possible weaknesses in the system. Such an effort has been termed 'penetration' and the penetration strategy developed has been called the 'flaw hypothesis methodology'. This methodology consists of (i) knowledge of the system's control structure, (ii) flaw hypothesis generation, (iii) flaw hypothesis confirmation, and (iv) flaw generalisation. These aspects are discussed in detail in the paper.

8.12 Attanasio, C.R., Markstein, P.W. and Phillips, R.J. Penetrating an operating system: a study of VM/370 integrity. IBM Systems Journal, 15,1, pp. 102-116, Jan. 1976.

This interesting paper presents a case study on penetration using the methodology described in the previous paper. A team of 'penetrator-analysts' (the authors) was formed to attempt to penetrate the IBM Virtual Machine Facility/370 (VM/370). A total of 880 'flaw hypotheses' were generated out of which 76 warranted detailed study. Of these, 35 flaw hypotheses were confirmed. It was found that almost every flaw in the system involved input/output in some manner. Other elements that contributed to flaws were those concerned with concurrent operations, resource allocation, and the human interface. The authors conclude that the penetration methodology "...provided a systematic and a reasonably comprehensive approach to testing VM/370 security strengths and weaknesses".

8.13 Giordano, N.J. and Schwartz, M.S. Data base recovery at CMIC. Proc. of the SIGMOD Conf., Washington D.C., pp. 33-42, June 1976.

This paper describes the recovery techniques employed at CMIC (Commonwealth of Pennsylvania's Central Management Information Center) computer system consisting of a Univac 1110 with the FMS-8 data base management system. Failures are classified into two categories: 'hard crash' (happens infrequently) which results in the corruption of the information held in the mass storage and 'soft crash' which leaves the mass storage contents intact. The authors describe the modifications made to the recovery facility of FMS-8 so that recovery from a soft failure is fast - within 15 minutes of the failure. In essence, the scheme consists of maintaining an audit trail which records the 'after images' of the modified records; this trail is then used to update the database when a soft crash occurs.

8.14 Severance, D.G. and Lohman, G.M. Differential files: their application to the maintenance of large databases. ACM Trans. on Database Systems, 1,3, pp. 256-267, Sept. 1976.

The differential file approach works as follows: changes performed to the records of a data base over a period of time are accumulated in a 'differential file' which contains the modified records. Periodically, the data base is updated from the file. The advantage is that it is no longer necessary to modify the data base at each update transaction. This greatly eases the task of data base maintenance and recovery - mainly because the changed part of the data base is clearly separated from the unchanged part. The authors describe ten advantages of this approach, the first six of which relate to integrity and recovery: (i) reduces data base dumping cost, (ii) facilitates incremental dumping, (iii) permits both real-time dumping and re-organisation with concurrent updates, (iv) speeds recovery from a 'soft' data loss, (v) speeds recovery from a 'hard' data loss, (vi) reduces the risk of a serious data loss, (vii) supports 'memo' files efficiently, (viii) simplifies software development, (ix) simplifies main file software, and (x) reduces future data base storage costs. Highly recommended.

8.15 Curtice, R.M. Integrity in data base systems. Datamation, 23,5, pp. 64-68, May 1977.

This is a nice tutorial on the subject. It classifies integrity mechanisms into two classes: those invoked in a normal mode of processing and those which come into play during abnormal modes of processing. Mechanisms in the former class include those that are concerned with concurrent updates and deadlock detection and resolution. Mechanisms in the latter class include those that are concerned with recovering the data base after, say, a head crash (loss of physical data base), abnormal termination of a program and a complete loss of the system (say, due to a power failure). Currently used mechanisms are described with examples drawn from commercially available data base systems.

8.16 Fraser, A.G. File integrity in a disc-based multi-access system. Operating Systems Techniques, Academic Press, 1972, pp. 227-254.

This paper describes the integrity techniques used in the filing system of the TITAN computer system which was in use at Cambridge University. First of all there are programs that are concerned with the integrity of files on the disc store itself. These programs will check for any inconsistency in the filing system and remove any corrupted data. Secondly, an incremental dumper is used to guard against the failure of the disc store. The dumping technique used is described in detail. The paper also describes the file protection scheme used.

8.17 Astrahan, M.M. et al. System R: relational approach to data base management. ACM Trans. on Database Systems, 1,2, pp. 97-137, June 1976.

The paper describes an experimental relational data base system and contains an interesting account of the recovery techniques used. A transaction is treated as a unit of consistency and recovery. Integrity assertions about data are checked and enforced at the end of a transaction. If some assertion is not satisfied, the transaction is backed out to the nearest 'save' point. The recovery information for a transaction is maintained in a time ordered list which contains information about each change to recoverable data. During transaction recovery, special routines are used to undo all of the listed modifications back to the most recently recorded save point. Two system recovery mechanisms are also employed: one to deal with main memory corruption and the other to deal with disc storage corruption (see the following paper).

8.18 Lorie, R.A. Physical integrity in a large segmented database. ACM Trans. on Database Systems, 2,1, pp. 91-104, March 1977.

The storage management system used in System R (see the previous entry) is described in detail. Recovery from a system failure is ensured by maintaining two versions of any page which has been modified - the current page and its 'shadow' page (the previous version); an elaborate mechanism is used such that a consistent version of the segments containing the pages can always be constructed, no matter when a system failure occurs. Recovery from an auxiliary storage failure is ensured by copying onto tape only those pages modified since the last checkpoint. Possible overheads due to these recovery mechanisms are considered.

ANNOTATED BIBLIOGRAPHY

8.19 Gray, J.N. Notes on data base operating systems. Lecture Notes in Computer Science, 60, Springer Verlag, pp. 393-481, 1978.

A highly readable account of operating system needs and requirements to support transaction oriented data base systems. Topics covered include data management, data communications and transaction management. Under transaction management, the author discusses scheduling, locking and recovery. Recovery problems in distributed systems are also discussed; a 'two phase' recovery protocol is presented for such systems (the protocol is similar to that developed by Lampson and Sturgis, see entry 8.20). Truly an outstanding paper.

8.20 Lampson, W. and Sturgis, H. Crash recovery in a distributed data storage system. Communications of the ACM (to appear).

A problem peculiar to decentralised systems is that a part of the system may crash but other parts of the system may continue to operate without knowledge of this event - the overall system may therefore produce incorrect results. This paper describes a method of structuring a transaction oriented distributed system such that it is capable of recovering from crashes in one or more of the constituent computers. The authors first describe certain essential properties that each computer must possess (one such property is that the secondary storage must be 'stable', i.e. possess the atomic property that updates are either carried out or not). An algorithm is then developed for recovering from crashes such that a user's transaction is either carried out or not performed at all. Reasoning about the correctness of the algorithm is also presented.

8.21 Shrivastava, S.K. and Banatre, J-P. Reliable resource allocation between unreliable processes. IEEE Trans. on Software Engineering, SE-4,3, pp. 230-241, May 1978.

Consider a process that establishes a checkpoint (a rollback point), after which it acquires certain resources and uses them. If this process now detects an error so that it is to be rolled back to the checkpoint established earlier, then the following two actions must be performed as the process is rolled back: (i) any effects resulting from the use of the acquired resources must be undone, and (ii) the acquired resources must be released. For example, if the process had acquired a file and performed some updates on it, then the effects of the updates must be undone and the file released as the rollback is performed. This paper describes some programming language features that can be incorporated in systems programming languages to ease the task of programming the above mentioned recovery actions.

8.22 Martin, J. Security, accuracy and privacy in computer systems. Prentice-Hall, 1973.

A very readable text, with material for both the auditing and data processing communities. The following chapters relate directly to auditing computer systems - 2. Security Exposure; 3. Computer Errors; 5. Design Procedures; 6. Accuracy Control on Batch Processing; 7. Accuracy Controls on Real-Time Systems; 37. Auditors.

8.23 Computer control guidelines. The Canadian Institute of Chartered Accountants, 1970.

The most definitive work in this field to date for the auditor. This text classifies control techniques from pre-installation through to system operation in terms useful to management, users, data processing personnel, internal and external auditors.

8.24 Davies, C.T. Data processing spheres of control. IBM Systems Journal, 17,2, pp. 179-198, 1978.

In this paper Davies applies the ideas on spheres of control developed earlier (see entry 6.1) to the audit and control aspects of data processing applications. A strong case is presented for designing systems that adhere to the concepts and rules of spheres of control, particularly because of "...the increasing emphasis that auditors are placing on traceability and accountability in modern data processing systems..." Highly recommended.

8.25 Bjork, L.A. Generalised audit trail requirements and concepts for data base applications. IBM Systems Journal, 14,3, pp. 229-245, 1975.

In this influential paper, Bjork defines auditing an application as "certifying the integrity of the system by verifying that rules and policies dictated by laws, business agreements, etc. are being followed by the application". Concepts of a data base audit trail are presented; an audit trail records "who did what to whom, when and in what sequence".

ACKNOWLEDGEMENTS

The material presented here is a much extended and revised version of a bibliography prepared for the Infotech State of the Art Report on Systems Reliability and Integrity, 1978. For this extension and revision, I received many helpful comments and suggestions from my fellow contributors. I would specifically like to thank W.C. Carter, C.T. Davies and S.L. Gerhart for providing me with a number of annotated entries.

ON SYSTEMS AND RELIABILITY
(an after dinner talk)

F.J.M. Laver

Sidmouth, Devon

Let me begin by confessing that I am an adult convert to computing; I was not born in the faith. My formative years were, in fact, spent in tele-communications, in which sheltered environment I was most carefully brought up to believe that:

-- 24 hour operation was normal, and quite unremarkable;
-- total system breakdown was inconceivable;
-- economic lives of less than 40 years were a profligate waste of resources.

Imagine, then, my initial shock on encountering the erratic, expensive and ephemeral computers of the mid 1950s.

I had approached computing through steam O and M with its heavy emphasis on a complete and thorough analysis of the user's requirements _before_ system design, and on the merit of deep thought throughout the design process. However, as Bertrand Russell once commented:
"Most people would die rather than think;
in fact they do."
Not too many system designers are dead yet! Early computer systems seemed to me to have been designed bottom-up, starting from the order code, and to have finished like inverted pyramids perched on a single central processor whose reliability was undoubted - but low. This was asking for trouble from bottlenecks and breakdowns; a request that the Gods often granted.

Office work, on the other hand, had for centuries used flexible, resilient and (on the whole) reliable groups of communicating and cooperating clerks. Hence, around 1961, I proposed to do away with large computers for office work, replacing them with communicating and cooperating groups of small machines which would be linked together for big jobs and split up for small ones, or for tasks suited to parallel processing - as most office work is. An extra machine for every four workers could quickly take over from a faulty unit, which could be disconnected, for I saw no point in living dangerously when I could R.I.P. - repair in

peace. However, no suitable small computer was then available, and
so it is with particular interest that I watch today's moves
towards multi-computer systems in which total system failure will
be a rare, but no doubt awe-inspiring, event.

As microcomputers grow ever smaller and cheaper, and reach the
asymptotic 'Zero-cost Information Processor', or ZIP, so -
connected together by data-links acting as ZIP fasteners - they
will be used in vast numbers until eventually the U.K. will be
covered with a thin layer of rather pure silicon in which dispersed
processors and stores will constitute a kind of two-dimensional gas
whose randomly distributed particles are bound by data exchange
forces. Only in a weak sense will this be a 'system', and we may
have to analyse its behaviour by thermodynamics - entropy, after
all, is negative information to a communications engineer.

Of course, communications engineers have quite a different idea
of information from other folk; their interest is in bulk only, not
value - like a removal man's artless approach to works of art (for
example, 200 pounds of Picassos), and for exactly the same reason.
Here was another conceptual shock, for computing professed the
heresy that an electronic system could increase the information in
a set of data. Shannon, I felt, would have turned in his grave -
had he been dead - for he was preaching that in a fallen world all
that we did must corrupt or destroy information. Indeed, under the
iron hand of the great Second Law, the universe was moving bit by
bit towards its information death. Clearly information theory was
valueless when designing computer-based information systems: it was
valueless precisely because it was value-free, for it took no
account of meaning, relevance, correlation, timeliness, or anything
else of actual importance to users. Unfortunately, no other body
of theory did either. But we must always appraise and seek to
measure our systems not in terms of their elegance, efficiency or
ineffable cleverness, but in terms of how far they meet the crude
everyday needs of their users; it is too easy to bask in the
educated approval of the few we acknowledge as our peers.

Jargon is, of course, the trip wire that every expert erects to
detect the approach of the ignorant, and to induce the proper
attitude of bemused respect. We use it also as an electric fence
to mark off separate specialist grazing grounds within the broad
field of computing. In reliability, for instance:

-- A Recovery Block is not something erected to impede recovery,
although I gather that it has occasionally retarded the completion
of a program.
-- Database Integrity has nothing to do with ethics, or has it?
-- Automatic Diagnosis does not mark a disturbing step down the
path to the full industrialisation of medicine, but it is not
without its own risks, and I implore you to walk delicately,
although I am bound to warn you that when Agag did just that he was

hewn in pieces before the altar - Samuel 15, 32 for those who have
forgotten the reference. However, there are rather few altars in
computer science departments and the risk I fear is that of giving
our systems too Slavonic a temperament by making them overly
introspective so that they fret neurotically: "I feel alright, but
am I really? I bet my test routines are up the creek again". This
distressing condition of 'analysis paralysis' can be avoided by
collecting only diagnostic data that can be interpreted
unambiguously (the rest is clutter), and by making only those tests
that indicate some remedial action that is actually possible and
not too alarming. There is a risk of being too clever and over-
complicating the system, on which allow me to remind you that
St. Thomas Aquinas was once moved to comment (in a somewhat
different context) that:
> "Not everything that is more difficult
> is more meritorious".

Solid-state electronics is pretty reliable stuff, but
peripherals are unavoidable. In hot pursuit of reliability you
will, no doubt, seek to reduce the number of mechanisms in your
systems - or, of course, to increase them, should you favour
redundancy. Infinite reliability seems to require that the number
of mechanisms be either zero or infinite - mathematics can give
invaluable guidance in such matters. Again, to err is human, so
will you decide to multiply the number of operators, in the hope
that their aberrations are asynchronous? If so, then they had
better not belong to the same union. Probably the tele-
communications approach is better, namely to make every user his
own operator, for we are unsurprisingly tolerant of our own
failures.

Reliability is not to be won without cost - or everyone would
want it - hence, as ever-higher reliability is achieved, the
problems of its economic evaluation will arise and clamour ever
more loudly for solution as diminishing returns set in. Absolute
perfection is strictly for billionaires - and governments. There
is a related marketing problem, for I doubt whether many customers
will be crystal clear about the exact cash-value to them of each
successive increment in reliability; certainly it will vary widely
with the customer and the application. How to express the measure
of reliability also deserves some thought. Perhaps we want
something like the chemists' pH scale, so that pR6 corresponds to
failure for not more than 10^{-6} of the in-service time. At least
equal increments of pR would be roughly equally difficult to
achieve, and pR values would get bigger as the system improved; it
is psychologically easier to charge more for more, rather than for
less.

Doctors agree that prevention is better than cure - if somewhat
less profitable - so it was good to see a reference to fault-
tolerant architecture. That topic hasn't been much discussed in

these parts since the 12th Century when the Normans decided to build Durham's cathedral about 10 times thicker than theory suggests. Of course, in those days ecclesiastical architects were expected to get an O-level in Old Testament as well as in Art and Arithmetic. No doubt Judges, 16, 29-30 was constantly on their lips, and - with another Samson in mind - they provided more than two roof pillars, more than 2 metres apart. Obvious as it is that no single fault should be able to crash the system, ignoring the obvious is what many have succeeded in doing. Yet auditors, firemen and others have long known about limiting the propagation of disaster by defining sub-system interfaces (or fire breaks), and spheres of control (or fiddle limits).

Cathedral builders had only hardware to worry about, and that is honest straightforward stuff; when it goes wrong you can kick it, software you can only curse. Speaking of software, as now and then we must though we needn't dwell on it, there appear to be optimists abroad in the land who believe that it will be possible to _prove_ that a given program is free from error. More timid souls speak only of verifying or validating, and we seem to have an irregular English verb whose future tense goes:

> 'I shall verify;
> Thou wilt validate;
> He proposes to prove.'

I suspect that its past tense may have only the 3rd person impersonal:

> 'Alas, it did not work.'

My own view is that programs are much more like hypotheses in science than theorems in axiomatics, and as an unashamed Popperian I do not believe they can be proved, but only corroborated. The highest praise that a hypothesis or a program can win is that it has not, so far, been shown to be wrong. This could be the place for a casual reference to Hilbert and Proof Theory, with knowing nods in the directions of Tarski and Godel, but that would seem like name-dropping, which I never do - or the equivalent of kicking for touch, which I have rarely done successfully.

Again, reference has been made to designing a programming language which will encourage proofs, and in this I am an obstinate Orwellian - notice how well read we are in Devon, in fiction as well as mathematics if you will pardon so nice a distinction. More people talk about 1984 than have ever read the book, and fewer still have read its splendid appendix on "The Principles of Newspeak". I commend it to you. Newspeak was a language specifically designed to serve the ideological purposes of Big Brother by making it impossible to formulate any valid sentence critical of his regime. Like Cobol, by cutting down the choice of acceptable words it succeeded in diminishing the range of original thought that could be expressed. A related ploy is to seek to design a programming language which will minimise errors, but will it also restrict what useful statements can be made? Obviously it must exclude certain classes of statements - declared to be erroneous - what else might it not unintentionally exclude?

Similarly, easier-to-verify programs would be marvellous things, and no reliable system should be without one, but not if this were to mean that they had to be, for instance, too brief or too trivial to be of much practical use. The programs used in commercial data processing are extraordinary constructions, sickeningly rich in rococo detail and as long and as arbitrary as the history and mythology of the business requires. It would be a pity if least help were to be available where most is needed. Not that lack of practical application would worry every computer scientist; some of us are lost in a love affair with technique, and are more concerned to fashion elegant tools than to dirty them on the work of the real and mucky world. This failing is not confined to computer people; it is a common human trait, as can be illustrated from one of the other ancillary arts - photography. Some amateur photographers collect exotic lenses rather than take pictures; some are so absorbed in apertures and exposures that they never actually <u>see</u> the places they visit; real enthusiasts only recognise their wives when they see them through a viewfinder.

It is time to attempt to herd together these vagrant ruminations. I can best sum up in the earthy pragmatism of the 80:20 rule. Almost always and everywhere in life you can get 80% of the benefits for 20% of the cost, time, trouble or constraints; similarly for the residual 20% and so on. Samuel Butler put it rather well when he said:
> "Aim at imperfection,
> there is some chance of getting it".

But, of course, you must do so with serious intent, and not merely achieve imperfection by neglect, or by that casualness which produces one of those systems that look as if they had been designed in the lift - on the way down to lunch.

user's requirements for
systems, 22,55,61-3

validation of programs, 66-108
values
  representation of, 30-1,35
  undefined, 46-7
variant records, and Euclid,
  138-9,140
VENUS system, 179,443
verification, 67
  see also proving
verification conditions, 75,76-7
vertical structuring, 15-17
V-functions (VFUN), 43-4
  derived, 48,49,50,51,54
  hidden, 47,50,54
  visible, 47,49,50,51,54
virtual memory, of segments, 274
virtual resource objects, 192,
  193-4
visual structure of programs,
  121
VM/370, 452
volume, potential, of a
  program, 403

voting units, 154,157,224,226
  forward error recovery by,
    161
  in hybrid redundancy system,
    229
  notification of erroneous
    state by, 158
  in OSIRIS, 246
  reliability of, 226
  in SIFT, 247-8
  temporary reconfiguration
    by, 164

'walking ones' test, 219
wearout failure region, 415-16
words, and Zipf's laws, 392-401

Zipf's laws of natural languages,
  391-7
  applied to computer languages,
    397-407
  derivation of, 396
  first law, 394-5
  generalized forms of, 395-6